The Coalition Effect, 2010-2015

The British general election of May 2010 ...st coalition government since the Second World War. David Cameron and Nick Clegg pledged a 'new politics' with the government taking office in the midst of the worst economic crisis since the 1930s. Five years on, a team of leading experts drawn from academia, the media, Parliament, Whitehall and think tanks assesses this 'coalition effect' across a broad range of policy areas. Adopting the contemporary history approach, this pioneering book addresses academic and policy debates across this whole range of issues. Did the coalition represent the natural 'next step' in party dealignment and the evolution of multi-party politics? Was coalition in practice a historic innovation in itself, or did the essential principles of Britain's uncodified constitution remain untroubled? Fundamentally, was the coalition able to deliver on its promises made in the Coalition Agreement, and what were the consequences – for the country and the parties – of this union?

Anthony Seldon is a leading contemporary historian and political commentator, and the 13th Master of Wellington College. A Fellow of King's College London, he has authored or edited over thirty-five books on contemporary history and politics. With Peter Hennessy, he co-founded the Institute of Contemporary British History, now part of King's College London.

The is the eighth 'Effect' book he has edited.

Mike Finn is Director of the Centre for Education Policy Analysis and Lecturer in the History of Education at Liverpool Hope University. He has taught history and politics at a number of institutions, including as a Research Fellow of Lady Margaret Hall, Oxford, and as a Bye-Fellow of Magdalene College, Cambridge. In 2006 he was Head of Research and political speechwriter to the Leader of the Liberal Democrats during the transition from Charles Kennedy to Ming Campbell.

In 2001 he won the Palgrave/Times Higher Education Humanities and Social Sciences writing prize. A former Kennedy Scholar at Harvard University, he is the editor of *The Gove Legacy: Education in Britain after the Coalition* (2015).

The Coalition Effect, 2010–2015

Edited by
Anthony Seldon and Mike Finn

Assistant editor
Illias Thoms

CAMBRIDGE
UNIVERSITY PRESS

CAMBRIDGE
UNIVERSITY PRESS

University Printing House, Cambridge CB2 8BS, United Kingdom

Cambridge University Press is part of the University of Cambridge.

It furthers the University's mission by disseminating knowledge in the pursuit of
education, learning and research at the highest international levels of excellence.

www.cambridge.org
Information on this title: www.cambridge.org/9781107440180

First published 2015

Printed in the United Kingdom by TJ International Ltd. Padstow Cornwell

A catalogue record for this publication is available from the British Library

ISBN 978-1-107-08061-4 Hardback
ISBN 978-1-107-44018-0 Paperback

CONTENTS

Contributors *page* viii
Acknowledgements xv

David Cameron as Prime Minister, 2010–2015: The verdict of history 1
Anthony Seldon

Part I The coalition and the government of Britain

1 The coming of the coalition and the Coalition Agreement 31
Mike Finn

2 The coalition and the constitution 59
Martin Loughlin and Cal Viney

3 The coalition beyond Westminster 87
Neil McGarvey

4 The coalition and the executive 113
Peter Riddell

5 The coalition and Parliament 136
Philip Cowley

Part II The coalition and policy

6   The coalition and the economy   159
Paul Johnson and Daniel Chandler

7   The coalition and energy policy   194
Dieter Helm

8   The coalition and infrastructure   209
Julian Glover

9   The coalition and society (I): Home affairs and local
government   228
Tony Travers

10   The coalition and society (II): Education   257
Alan Smithers

11   The coalition and society (III): Health and long-term care   290
Howard Glennerster

12   The coalition and society (IV): Welfare   317
Nicholas Timmins

13   The coalition and foreign affairs   345
Michael Clarke

14   Europe: The coalition's poisoned chalice   370
Julie Smith

15   'What the coalition did for women': A new gender consensus,
coalition division and gendered austerity   397
Rosie Campbell and Sarah Childs

16   The coalition and culture: 'Bread, circuses and
Britishness'   430
Rory Coonan

Part III **The coalition and political culture**

17   The coalition and the Conservatives   467
Philip Norton

18   The coalition and the Liberal Democrats   492
Mike Finn

19   The coalition and the Labour Party   520
Guy Lodge and Illias Thoms

20   The coalition and the media   553
Peter Preston

21   The coalition, elections and referendums   577
John Curtice

Part IV **Conclusion**

22   Conclusion: The net coalition effect   601
Mike Finn

Index   608

CONTRIBUTORS

Rosie Campbell is Reader in Politics at Birkbeck, University of London. She has research interests in voting behaviour, political participation, representation, political careers, and gender and politics. Rosie is Vice Chair of the Political Studies Association's (PSA) Executive Committee. She teaches modern British politics and research methods. Her book *Gender and the Vote in Britain* was published in 2006 and she has recently published in the *British Journal of Political Science*, *British Politics*, *Political Quarterly*, *Political Studies* and the *British Journal of Politics and International Relations*.

Daniel Chandler is an economist at the Institute for Fiscal Studies. Previously, he worked in the Prime Minister's Strategy Unit and in the Deputy Prime Minister's office, where he led projects on welfare policy and social mobility, and at the Resolution Foundation think tank, where he co-wrote the *Commission on Living Standards*. He has a BA in History from Cambridge and an MSc in Economics and Philosophy from LSE, and pursued graduate study in economics and politics at Harvard, where he was the Henry Fellow. His current research interests include housing, labour markets, living standards and inequality.

Sarah Childs is Professor of Politics and Gender at the University of Bristol. Her research centres on the relationships between sex, gender and politics. It is concerned, both theoretically and empirically, with questions of women's descriptive, symbolic and substantive representation. She has published extensively on women's political representation in the UK since 1997, especially regarding the feminization of British political parties and the recruitment of women to the UK Parliament, with monographs on *New Labour's Women MPs* (2004), *Women and British Party Politics* (2008), and *Sex, Gender and the Conservative Party* (2012, with Paul Webb). Her current research looks at gender and intra-party democracy; gender and party regulation; and conservatism, feminism and representation.

Michael Clarke is Director General of the Royal United Services Institute. Until July 2007 he was Deputy Vice-Principal and Director of Research Development at King's College London, where he is now also Visiting Professor of Defence Studies. He has been a Specialist Adviser to the House of Commons Defence Committee since 1997, having served previously with the House of Commons Foreign Affairs Committee 1995–6, and the Joint Parliamentary Committee on Bribery in 2009. In 2004 he was appointed the UK member of the United Nations Secretary General's Advisory Board on Disarmament Matters. In 2009 he was appointed to the Prime Minister's National Security Forum and in 2010 to the Chief of Defence Staff's new Strategic Advisory Group. He also serves on the Strategic Advisory Panel on Defence for UK Trade and Industry. His recent publications include: *The Afghan Papers: Committing Britain to War in Helmand 2005–06* (2011) and 'Does War Have a Future?', in Lindley-French and Boyar (eds.), *The Oxford Handbook of War* (2012).

Rory Coonan is Chairman, Design for Care. From 2005 to 2011 he was Director of Planning, Design and Architecture for Circle Health, pioneering the 'compact' hospital concept to designs by the architectural practices headed by Lord Foster and Lord Rogers. A former director of architecture at the Arts Council of Great Britain, he devised the design policies of the National Lottery and served as chair of the National Lottery Design panel. In 1994–7 he conceived and developed NESTA (National Endowment for Science, Technology and the Arts). He was educated at Oxford University and the Royal College of Art. He has served as architecture correspondent of the *Financial Times* and *Observer*, and as a member of the Franco-British Council. He is an honorary fellow of the Royal Institute of British Architects. The National Portrait Gallery Collection has acquired works by him as a photographer.

Philip Cowley is Professor of Parliamentary Government at the University of Nottingham. He is author of *The Rebels: How Blair Mislaid His*

Majority (2005), co-author with Dennis Kavanagh of *The British General Election of 2010* (2010), and editor with Robert Ford of *Sex, Lies and The Ballot Box: 50 Things You Need to Know about British Elections* (2014). He runs www.revolts.co.uk.

John Curtice is Professor of Politics at the University of Strathclyde and President of the British Polling Council. He has been a co-editor of NatCen's annual British Social Attitudes reports since 1994 and co-director of the Scottish Social Attitudes surveys since their inauguration in 1999. Between 1983 and 1997 he co-directed the British Election Study, the principal instrument for the survey-based study of electoral behaviour in Britain.

Mike Finn is Director of the Centre for Education Policy Analysis and Lecturer in the History of Education at Liverpool Hope University. Born in Liverpool, he was educated there and at Oxford, Cambridge and Harvard, where he was a Kennedy Scholar. He held Fellowships at Magdalene College, Cambridge and Lady Margaret Hall, Oxford before serving as Head of Research and political speechwriter to the Leader of the Liberal Democrats in 2006. He was the recipient of the 2001 Palgrave/*Times Higher Education* Humanities and Social Sciences Writing Prize. His research interests focus on contemporary politics, the British constitution, the history of the post-war British state, and the politics of education. He is the editor of *The Gove Legacy: Education in Britain after the Coalition* (2015).

Howard Glennerster is Professor Emeritus of Social Policy at the London School of Economics and Political Science and an associate of the Centre for Analysis of Social Exclusion (CASE). He is author of *British Social Policy since 1945* and numerous books and papers on the economics of social policy in general and health care in particular. He has lectured widely abroad and has spent several sessions as a visiting scholar at the Brookings Institution in Washington.

Julian Glover was a special adviser at the Department for Transport between 2012 and 2015. He was a speechwriter for the Prime Minister between 2011 and 2012 and worked as a journalist for *The Guardian* between 2001 and 2011.

ACKNOWLEDGEMENTS

Anthony Seldon would like to thank his co-editor Mike Finn for exceptional support and insight, without whom the project would not have been possible. He would also like to thank his assistant editor Illias Thoms for providing administrative and editorial assistance throughout the entire process. Huge thanks are due to the editorial team at Cambridge University Press of John Haslam, Carrie Parkinson, Jessica Ann Murphy, Malcolm Todd and William Jack as well as to Angela Reed and Hani Edwards at Wellington College for their invaluable assistance. Also at Wellington, he would like to thank his senior management team including Robin Dyer and his head of politics Dibran Zeqiri. He is also immensely grateful for the work of all the contributors, who provided pieces of exceptional quality, insight and style.

Finally, he would like to thank his wife, Joanna, and his family who continue to be a source of inspiration, support and love, and Ian MacEwen, fellow politics teacher, for introducing him to Mike.

Mike Finn is immensely grateful for the support and guidance of his co-editor, Sir Anthony Seldon. He would like to thank assistant editor Illias Thoms for first-rate editorial work and support beyond the call of duty and the editorial team at Cambridge University Press, John Haslam and Carrie Parkinson. He would also like to thank Hope Kilmurry for research support and Dr Richard Huzzey for insightful discussions of Liberal Democrat politics and values. In addition, thanks are due to friends and colleagues at Liverpool Hope University, especially Dr Gary Anderson, Dr Phil Bamber, Dr Heather Ellis and Dr Steven Shakespeare. A special thank you is reserved for Dibran Zeqiri and Ian MacEwen, exceptional teachers of politics and invaluable friends and sounding boards. He also wishes to record his great intellectual debt to Frank Ledwidge and Alexander Donnelly, and to Dr Jon Lawrence for inspiring his academic interest in politics in the first place.

He would also like to thank those (necessarily anonymous) Conservative and Liberal Democrat politicians, staff members and activists who supplied him with invaluable context for his research. Finally, he would like to dedicate his efforts in this work to his mother and father, Rita and Tom Finn, in gratitude for their enduring forbearance and love.

DAVID CAMERON AS PRIME MINISTER, 2010–2015

The verdict of history

ANTHONY SELDON

Morten Morland for The Times / News Syndication

The historic significance

Win or lose the election in 2015, this government will be remembered as one of the most historically significant and unusual since the end of the

Second World War. The first coalition government for sixty-five years, it was also the first coalition in peacetime since the 1930s. Conventional wisdom has always had it that coalition governments – rendered unlikely because of the simple majority voting system – would not survive long if ever one came into existence. The government defied the sceptics, and endured.

The fact of coalition is not the only reason why this government will be of exceptional interest to historians. The scale of the economic recession, unseen since the 1930s, makes it equally so. The economic crisis that erupted in 2008 was still being played out across the Eurozone as the coalition government was being formed in May 2010. Against the backdrop of violent protests in Portugal and Greece, the advice from Whitehall officials was that the national interest demanded stable government. Governing in association with the Liberal Democrats, as well as the economic constraints, significantly affected what David Cameron and the Conservatives were able to achieve.

Many counterfactual questions cry out to be asked. How might a Gordon Brown government have been different if he had formed a partnership with Nick Clegg in May 2010? What might the Conservatives have done had Cameron won an outright majority? What would they have done indeed had there been no recession? What might a government headed by Cameron's principal lieutenant and strategist, George Osborne, have done differently? To what extent indeed was this a joint leadership, akin to Blair–Brown in 1997–2007?

Phases of the Cameron premiership

As the noise subsides, one can see that the government went through four distinct phases, each associated with a dominant and forceful figure.

Phase one: 'Full pelt'
(May 2010–March 2012)

Gus O'Donnell, the Cabinet Secretary until December 2011, believes that Cameron's team had been avidly imbibing Blair's memoir, *A Journey*, which contains a stark message – do not squander precious time in the first term when political capital is highest, but arrive in office ready to execute a clear and activist plan. Detailed preparation was undertaken in opposition in two centres: a Treasury team overseen by George Osborne, and a policy unit team headed by Oliver Letwin with manifesto and policy unit chief James O'Shaughnessy, his principal lieutenant. Watching over it all, albeit from California until the final months, was Steve Hilton (Cameron's chief strategist, close friend and mentor). All domestic departments were to hit the ground running, each with a 'business plan' mapping out what they needed to do once in power. Michael Gove, the feisty new Education Secretary, was thus able to move quickly and introduce his first Bill before the summer recess, which became the Academies Act 2010. Governing in coalition resulted in momentum being lost because portfolios needed to be given to Lib Dems, and some Conservative shadow ministers were given posts for which they had not prepared.

The fragile parliamentary position heightened the Conservatives' sense that they might have only one term in office and that there was not a moment to lose. Frenzied activity took place in those opening months in health, welfare, public sector reform and open government. Osborne introduced his Emergency Budget on 22 June, only six weeks after becoming Chancellor. That November, his Autumn Statement spoke of the UK economy recovering from 'the biggest financial crisis in generations'. It announced significant spending reductions, albeit not in 'protected areas' – the NHS, schools and international development. The aim, Osborne said, was to eliminate the deficit within the lifetime of the Parliament. The pace of reform was frenetic. Hilton was ubiquitous, driving his 'Big Society' (comprising localism, public sector reform and social altruism), transparency and family policy agendas forward like a man possessed. In his latter phase, he became a dyspeptic warrior for liberal Thatcherite policies, as on the labour market, which challenged Cameron head on. Inevitably, he increasingly fell out with some ministers, civil servants and – fatally – key figures within the Prime Minister's inner circle, which culminated in his departure in early 2012. With him went a highly creative if disruptive force at the heart of government.

Phase two: 'Momentum lost' (March 2012–March 2013)

In March 2012, the Prime Minister and Chancellor went on a high-profile visit to Washington to see President Obama. Two years into the government, Cameron and Osborne were beginning to feel some sense of relief at the progress, and at the impression of competence that the government was projecting nationally and internationally. Osborne returned from the trip – judged a great success – to deliver his 2012 'omnishambles' Budget. It was to be the least successful of his five by a distance, upsetting many in the business community, the Conservative Party and commentariat. At a stroke, it shattered the impression that he had carefully cultivated that 'we're all in this together'. His reduction of the top rate of income tax from 50 to 45 pence at a time of recession, and a series of gauche lesser measures that had been hurriedly put together, rebounded catastrophically, unleashing criticisms long simmering below the surface. Elements in the press, notably the *Telegraph* and *Mail* Groups, had never forgiven Cameron for setting up the Leveson Inquiry in July 2011 into the culture, practices and ethics of the press, following the News International phone-hacking scandal. Here was payback time. The whole cogency of the government's strategy and aura of competence since 2010 began to unravel. The NHS reforms, initiated by Health Secretary Andrew Lansley, ran into major opposition, there appeared no end in sight to the economic woes, and the partnership with the forlorn Lib Dems appeared increasingly fragile. Furthermore, the polls had dipped sharply. Suddenly, Labour under leader Ed Miliband and Shadow Chancellor Ed Balls began to be treated with seriousness as a government in waiting.

For Osborne personally, the nadir was being booed at the Paralympic Games in London's East End in September 2012. The press attacks rained down not only on Osborne but on Cameron. The question 'what does he stand for – if anything?' came sharply to the fore. Many Conservative backbenchers, long simmering with anger towards him, now became openly critical. Some hostility dated back to his compliant response to the expenses scandal in 2009, which left them out of pocket. Many more blamed him for the Conservatives' failure to win an outright majority at the 2010 election, which they attributed to lack of clarity in the message he delivered, and its lack of resonance with core Tory voters. Coalition with the Lib Dems was further anathema to many, who were rankled by the (not wholly incorrect) suspicion that Cameron was happier in a *de jure* coalition with the Lib Dems than he would have been in a *de facto* coalition with his own right-wing backbenchers.

Jeremy Heywood, who succeeded O'Donnell as Cabinet Secretary on 1 January 2012, was a dominant figure during this period.

He was the supreme civil servant of the first fifteen years of the new century, and had been a major steadying hand and guide during the Blair and Brown premierships. For Cameron's first year and a half, he was Cameron's Permanent Secretary at Number 10, and after becoming Cabinet Secretary, he remained intensely involved in Downing Street, helping to beef up Number 10 with a larger policy unit. He helped Number 10 get a grip upon difficult policy areas including the health reforms and restored order to the centre. At a time when many in Downing Street came under fire, Cameron placed considerable trust in Heywood's intellect, legendary work rate and judgement.

Regaining clarity on policy was aided by Andrew Cooper, a long-standing strategist and modernizer in the party, who had joined Downing Street in 2011 as director of political strategy. He had become concerned by the lack of any clear strategy beyond Osborne's economic 'Plan A', a gap that the departure of Hilton highlighted still further. Cooper's beloved tool of polling led him to conclude that Cameron's and the Tory message needed to be better refined around two key positive themes, which were unveiled at the October 2012 party conference in Birmingham. They were the need for Britain to compete in the 'global race', and the building of an 'aspiration nation' which offered equality of opportunity and which celebrated honest endeavour and hard work. Cameron's advisers had been telling him throughout 2012 that he needed to make a clear statement about his own beliefs and why he had entered politics, given the cacophony of questions about him. Never comfortable speaking about himself, he nevertheless consented to deliver a personal 'credo' at the conference, notably in the passage of his leader's speech in which he talked about his father. It equalled 2014 as the most important and impressive of his five party conference speeches as Prime Minister.

The 2012 speech began to steady Conservative nerves. Together with Boris Jonson's re-election as Mayor of London in May 2012 (a loss would have been a massive blow to Cameron), the beginnings of better economic news and Cameron's Bloomberg speech in January 2013 (offering a renegotiation of British membership and an in-out referendum on Britain remaining in the EU in 2017), a new sense of purpose was in the air. The government deported itself more confidently through the mid-term waters. The impact, though, was yet to translate into more favourable polls.

Phase three: 'Initiative regained'
(February 2013–April 2014)

This transitional period was the least defined of the four and witnessed turbulence continuing on many fronts. Cameron himself suffered a series of defeats at the hands of backbenchers, most notably in August 2013 over his proposal to intervene against the Assad regime in Syria after its alleged use of chemical weapons, a historic reversal for a Prime Minister on a major foreign policy initiative abroad. The coalition's very survival had come under severe strain. Earlier, it had sustained severe damage after the Lib Dems lost the referendum to introduce the Alternative Vote (AV) and the Conservatives were defeated on all-important boundary changes. Backbenchers and members of both parties became increasingly critical of the coalition. The personal chemistry between Cameron and Clegg, and between Osborne and Chief Secretary Danny Alexander, held the coalition together at this volatile time, as did the electoral logic that it was not in the interests of either leadership to see it break up. On the Lib Dem side, the lack of a credible anti-coalition alternative to Clegg was a powerful factor. Clegg had very carefully bound his party into the coalition, and ensured that his party would support it. It was the only option in town.

This third period started with some very bleak moments, notably the loss of Britain's triple-A credit status in February 2013. Two months later, Oliver Blanchard, the IMF chief economist, famously opined that Osborne was 'playing with fire' if he continued upon the course of austerity, while the Office of National Statistics (ONS) simultaneously talked of the risk of a 'triple-dip' recession. This anxious period continued until April 2014 when the IMF went volte-face, admitted that it had underestimated the UK economy and predicted that it was likely to grow quicker than any other advanced economy. Osborne and his team had been through an utterly torrid time since the 2012 Budget and now took the credit for the new optimism.

This better economic news was the key factor reviving confidence and regaining the support of the press. Cameron's January 2013 EU referendum announcement had given Eurosceptics some of what they sought, which further tipped the press in his favour, as did the dawning realization that, with the 2015 general election rapidly approaching, an unreconstructed Ed Miliband might be the next Prime Minister. However, it was not until the spring of 2014, notably with

desperately to keep hold of Coulson as the hacking furore grew from late 2010; indeed, he held on long after it would have been wise to let him go, which is admirable loyalty or naive depending on how one views it. The only outsiders to penetrate Cameron's inner circle during these five years were Lynton Crosby and Craig Oliver, Coulson's successor, who joined Number 10 from the BBC in early 2011, an unknown to Cameron and his team.

At a less elevated level, Number 10 was full of a series of long-standing advisers whom Cameron trusted deeply and who remained throughout these years, and who all were regular attenders of his 8.30 a.m. and 4 p.m. meetings in his office in Number 10, which continued throughout his premiership. They included Oliver Dowden, promoted to be deputy chief of staff; Gabby Bertin as his trusted press secretary until her maternity leave in 2012; Liz Sugg, who masterminded his visits; and Ameet Gill, who was moved from writing speeches to running the 'grid' in October 2011. Another long-standing figure in this inner circle was Osborne's chief economic adviser, Rupert Harrison, a powerfully confident figure who wielded astonishing influence, especially considering his relative youth, just over thirty in 2010. Rohan Silva had also been in Osborne's team, but came over to join Cameron. He kept the flame of Hilton's reforming zeal alive after he left, notably on new technologies and enterprise, until he himself left Number 10 in 2013.

Cameron's reliance on this tight circle of trusted advisers aroused particular concern among his own party, not the least from those who were excluded. They saw him as cliquey and overly reliant upon those from the same narrow social background, a trait memorably summed up by backbencher Nadine Dorries in one of the most devastating quotations of the last decade, that Cameron and Osborne were 'two posh boys who don't know the price of milk'. Sexism was another criticism, a claim inflamed after he repeatedly told Labour's Angela Eagle in the House of Commons to 'calm down dear'. In successive reshuffles he sought to promote women, though never enough for his critics. The sexist charge is tempered by his liking for the advice of women in his close circle: Fall, Bertin, Sugg and above all his wife Samantha were powerful female voices.

Cameron favoured continuity too among his Cabinet ministers. He viewed previous Prime Ministers as erring in believing that reshuffles improved the standing and effectiveness of their governments (he had only two reshuffles, in September 2012 and July 2014, neither major).

He strove to keep his key ministers in place. Osborne remained Chancellor throughout, as did Theresa May as Home Secretary. William Hague only moved from Foreign Secretary in the July 2014 reshuffle – the most decisive of Cameron's premiership, but sparked by Hague's own announcement that he would cease to be an MP after the general election, and the desire to damp down speculation that Osborne might succeed as Foreign Secretary in 2015, with any implications that might have for a discontinuity in economic policy. Other senior changes were mainly forced upon him by events, such as the resignation of Liam Fox in October 2011 over an allegation of improper access being given to an aide, Adam Werritty. Gove's shift from Education to Chief Whip in July 2014 stands out as the only occasion Cameron voluntarily moved a senior and trusted Cabinet minister. Gove then became a punchy Chief Whip and a strong voice in Cameron's inner team.

Cameron was a better leader than a manager. He made it clear at the outset that he wanted his Cabinet ministers to run their own departments, following their business plans, an admirable principle but problematic when it came to ensuring strong oversight, performance management and consistency. Some ministers were given too much leeway – notably Lansley at Health. Others were left too long in post when they were showing too little drive, such as Ken Clarke as Minister Without Portfolio, while neither Energy nor Transport were areas that showered themselves in glory, with failure to give a strong lead evident over energy sources, infrastructure projects and the expansion of Heathrow airport. The regular 'stock-taking' meetings at Number 10 that Blair and Brown had held with departmental ministers to ensure that they were delivering their agendas were only resurrected in late 2012/ early 2013, when Cameron re-invented himself more as a 'chief executive' than the 'chairman' he had first set out to be. He has learnt the hard way that his trait of trusting people to be on the same side and work to a common end did not work for a Prime Minister in his relationships with his Cabinet ministers, with their own agendas.

The perceived lack of effectiveness and direction began increasingly to be blamed on the team in Number 10. The initial decision to cut back on the size of the Policy Unit, a reaction by Cameron to the expenses scandal, was blamed. A lack of capacity in Number 10, as well as a much quicker pace than in Thatcher's first term, may well have contributed to its early mistakes, including the U-turn over the selling of the national forests in 2011 and the failure to understand precisely what

Lansley was planning with his NHS reforms. Whitehall insiders comment that they received a clearer and quicker response from the Treasury than from Number 10, and that the former was much the more decisive force in exerting control from the centre. Number 10's grip improved under first Heywood, until he became Cabinet Secretary, and then Chris Martin, the PM's Principal Private Secretary from 2011. This Number 10 team was better than many.

Cameron appeared slow to learn from the frequent difficulties that he experienced in opposition from 2005. The resentments that many backbenchers possessed were exacerbated by uneven man management and diplomacy. Cameron was wont to ignore his backbenchers as he walked through the lobby in the House of Commons, leaving many feeling slighted. By late 2012, Cameron and his team, in the midst of this turbulent third period, recognized change had to come, and he made a concerted effort to reach out to the parliamentary party. By then the damage had been done; the narrative became established of a Prime Minister who was never greatly interested in the views of his backbenchers, who could be commanding when speaking to large gatherings of MPs and Tory peers, but who could be high-handed and dismissive to his party colleagues in closed meetings.

Some in the party were antagonized that Cameron was not a Prime Minister with an ideological Tory vision either at home or abroad. He did exhibit strongly conservative instincts, compared most closely to those of Harold Macmillan (1957–63), a supreme pragmatist. Many of Cameron's sternest critics were strong admirers of Margaret Thatcher, who inconveniently died halfway through the Parliament, reminding the world of her commanding, and commandingly ideological, presence. In marked contrast, Cameron's empirical approach grated with worshippers of the great lost leader. His early quest to 'detoxify' the Tory brand, heartily driven by Hilton, epitomized by the 'Big Society', never chimed with the right of the party. When Cameron started to abandon this agenda from 2011 because of the economic outlook and electoral logic, he failed to produce a fresh set of policies to take their place, fuelling the criticism that he was an insubstantial and lightweight figure who lacked deep conservative beliefs of his own.

It was not that he lacked principles. His sticking by 'Plan A' on the economy and his deep personal commitment to protecting international development spending show his steel. Cameron was at heart a social reformer, as on adoption, who genuinely wanted to extend opportunities for all and to see the economy flourish. He pressed ahead with legislation on gay marriage even when many in his party, even in his own inner circle, were telling him that it would cause far more harm than good to the Conservative cause. This example of principled leadership counters the charge that he was a pragmatist with no inner convictions; significantly, this was the very issue that powerfully inflamed the right wing, alienated cultural conservatives and boosted the UKIP vote.

The accusation of opportunism was levelled at his foreign policy. After the Arab Spring took off in 2011, Cameron initially favoured intervention, notably in Libya, a strongly personal stance praised at the time by both the right and left. But his early successes were not consolidated, and Libya slid back into instability. Number 10 blamed the Libyans themselves for their failure to build on the platform that the Anglo-French initiative had bequeathed them. After Parliament blocked his proposed intervention in Syria in August 2013, however, he became cautious at the very moment when critics believed that the time had come for Britain to take a strong stance against the Islamic State jihadists in Iraq and Syria, and against Russia over its aggression in Ukraine. His European policy critics equally felt to be overly dictated by opinion at home, difficult though it was to navigate a steady course at such a volatile time on the Continent.

He could be overly loyal and indeed stubborn in holding on to ministers for too long, e.g. Maria Miller as Culture Secretary until public opinion effectively forced her to resign over an expenses issue in April 2014. He was heavily criticized for acting impulsively without adequate homework and diplomacy behind the scenes – as in his unsuccessful bid to stop Jean-Claude Juncker from becoming European Commission president in the summer of 2014. This was a painful reminder of how isolated Cameron had become, and Britain were fortunate to emerge with a key brief for Lord Hill, financial services. His public utterances could be ill-considered and unstatesmanlike, as when he described UKIP supporters in 2006 as 'fruit cakes, loonies and closet racists', or when he was picked up by microphone in New York after the Scottish referendum claiming that the Queen had 'purred' when she learnt the result, an indiscretion he bitterly regretted. It is salutary to remember that Cameron was young (43) when he became Prime Minister. Not since Lord Liverpool 198 years earlier had there been such a youthful incumbent in Downing Street. Blair was a similar age when he

on Cameron's pre-election pledge that there would be 'no top-down NHS reorganizations'. Lansley's Bill was the government's worst domestic error.

At the Department of Work and Pensions, Iain Duncan Smith introduced significant if controversial reforms to the benefits system that went some way to ensuring that welfare was targeted at the most deserving. The amount that could be claimed in welfare was capped at average family earnings, and his success in getting people formerly dependent upon welfare back into work played a contested part in the reduction of unemployment, contributing to the proportion of out-of-work households reaching its lowest level for nearly twenty years (indeed, it was the first government ever to cut benefits in absolute terms). Some other reforms, such as to disability benefit, were more criticized, while the introduction of his flagship policy, Universal Credit – a unified and important benefit replacing six means-tested benefits and tax credits – was repeatedly delayed due to technical and ICT problems. By mid-parliament, Duncan Smith's master plan had lost any lingering confidence from Osborne and the Treasury, but he resisted attempts to move him in the mid-term reshuffle. It came into effect only in February 2015.

Further successes came with Chris Grayling, who as Justice Secretary from 2012 stood up to the entrenched legal profession. High hopes were entertained in 2010 about elected mayors in major British cities. Only Liverpool, Leicester, Bristol and Salford, however, subsequently elected mayors, the disappointment attributed in part to Cameron's failure to campaign and drive the initiative – one of Hilton's enthusiasms – from the centre. Communities Secretary Eric Pickles nevertheless introduced a steady stream of reforms, such as the Localism Act of 2011, and satisfaction with local government rose despite the cuts, whilst Home Secretary Theresa May ran a tighter operation at the Home Office than had many previous Home Secretaries. She managed to deport Abu Qatada and Abu Hamza, and oversaw a reduction in crime despite severe cuts to her budget. She fell out, however, with a Number 10 increasingly critical of her grip and her ambition.

Public sector reform, driven by Francis Maude, Minister for the Cabinet Office, had some success in achieving more open and efficient government. Cameron's early decision to accept the report on Bloody Sunday in June 2010 helped pave the way for a new era in British–Irish relations, boosted also by the final settlement of the outstanding devolution issues on policing and the judiciary, and by the long-planned state visit by the Queen to Dublin in May 2011. Britain also enjoyed peaceful years. Despite the troubled economy, cuts and high unemployment, the government managed to avoid significant disruption from trade union unrest or civil disorder, with the exception of the November 2010 student and 2011 summer riots. Cameron deserves some credit for this. He took very seriously his job to ensure peace and harmony on the streets of Britain, and read with obsessive detail intelligence reports he regularly received about terrorist threats.

Following the SNP's winning of a majority in the 2011 election for the Scottish Parliament, Cameron's decision to grasp the nettle and hold a referendum in September 2014 could be seen as brave. It was very much his own and was an example of his decisive leadership; many Prime Ministers could have tried to avoid such a potentially destructive event. But he was criticized for his handling of the campaign, making just one major speech on the subject in Edinburgh in February 2012 (written mostly by Gove), until becoming personally engaged again very late in the day. His defence is that his strong advice from the 'Better Together' campaign was that he should not be involved directly in the campaign. But his grip seemed uncertain to many, and his promises in the final week smacked of panic.

Abroad, Cameron had a bumpy ride in Europe, not helped by the Eurozone suffering prolonged economic crisis throughout the parliament. He did not lack successes in Europe. In June 2013, he achieved the most significant EU budget rebate since Thatcher and won the grudging support of Merkel for a referendum based upon a renegotiation of Britain's relations with the EU. He came to power in 2010 with the express hope that Europe would not overshadow his premiership. He failed to achieve a settled relationship for Britain with the EU in 2010–15. Whether he can achieve it if he wins in 2015 is yet to be seen.

Cameron prevailed over his service chiefs to set a date of 2014 for the return of British forces from Afghanistan, a sensible timetable, which he balanced with a plan to try to ensure that the Afghans would be able to run their own country peacefully after the troops left. This brought to an end the long British involvement in that chronically unsettled country but left Afghanistan with an uncertain future. Cameron was a stickler, after all the furore over Blair's sofa government in the run-up to the Iraq War in 2003, for correct process. This decision was thus formalized and overseen by the National Security Council – a new body Cameron set up soon after the general election, which met weekly on the same morning as Cabinet, Tuesday, and which he chaired very decisively himself. It was Cameron's most significant personal innovation to machinery as Prime Minister, receiving praise from Iain Lobban, the head of GCHQ (2008–14): 'The NSC is one of the best things this government has done . . . It galvanizes everything. Brilliant.'[2] (The three intelligence chiefs liked the new structure as it brought them centre stage in decision-making.) On defence, Cameron took great pains to support the troops and was meticulous about visiting them in Afghanistan, restoring the confidence the military lost in the Prime Minister under Brown. Despite perhaps predictable complaints about interference from David Richards in his memoirs, relations with the military improved despite the cuts. Disagreements with service chiefs came over the size and nature of the cuts, the speed of withdrawal from Afghanistan, Cameron's readiness to deploy British forces in Libya and his aspirations to become involved in Syria.

Inconsistency in foreign policy is not unusual with premierships. Two criticisms of Cameron's foreign policy were regularly voiced in 2010–15. First, he was so preoccupied with his battles at home against his own backbenchers, the Lib Dems, Labour and UKIP, that he was insufficiently focused upon foreign policy. This is not a valid criticism: his political team were often exasperated at foreign matters eating into his time. Second, was he more of a reactor than a shaper of policy? His veto at the December 2011 EU Council was received with an uproarious response by Eurosceptics at home. But was it a pyrrhic victory? Britain's standing in Europe and the rest of the world is not higher in 2015, though it would be harsh to attribute the blame to Cameron purely. For all his commitment to refocusing Britain's foreign policy in the SDSR in 2010, its aims in the world were no clearer by 2015.

Adverse factors

Cameron benefited from some good fortune as Prime Minister, including having Ed rather than David Miliband as Labour leader from the autumn of 2010, and the lack of any viable alternative leader within his own party. Nevertheless, the climate faced by Cameron was

---

[2] *Daily Telegraph* interview by Charles Moore, 11 October 2014.

overwhelmingly adverse, and was more hostile than that faced by most Prime Ministers. None since James Callaghan (1976–9) had such a difficult hand to play. The economic outlook and need for harsh cuts shocked Cameron when he first learnt in 2008 about the extent of the problem, and the continuing travails in the Eurozone provided a fraught backdrop to his premiership. From early 2011 until mid-2014, he had a critical right-wing press, especially the *Mail* and *Telegraph* titles, whereas most Conservative leaders could depend upon a supportive right-wing press.

The lack of an overall Conservative majority in Parliament and the requirement to work with the Liberal Democrats were constraints that no post-war Prime Minister of any party has had to face for any extended duration, with the exception of Callaghan. What might Cameron have done had he not been in the coalition? He would have had more freedom of manoeuvre on Europe. He would have gone further on welfare reform and on spending cuts. He would have insisted on more value for money from the green agenda, and pushed the 'Big Society' agenda harder. He would have focused less on civil liberties and more on the need for tough national security. Above all, the boundary changes would almost certainly have been implemented.

Conservative backbenchers remained a constant thorn in his side; the concessions they secured, either claimed or real, included the defeat of the proposal to intervene in Syria, the reduction in the EU Budget as opposed to a mere freeze (though it was debatable whether their actions really counted here), stopping voting rights for prisoners, and defeat of House of Lords reform. No Conservative Prime Minister since 1945 had faced such angry and independent-minded backbenchers – not even John Major (1990–7), whose entire premiership was overshadowed by turbulence.

Backbenchers saw their hold over the government significantly enhanced by the so-called Wright Reforms introduced in 2010. These resulted in the election by secret ballot of select committee chairs and members, thereby increasing their independence from the executive and powers. The reforms also created a Backbench Business Committee, which controls a portion of parliamentary debating time. This has been used for debates on topics that formerly would have been kept off the parliamentary agenda because they were embarrassing for the government, such as the first vote, in September 2010, on British involvement in Afghanistan since the beginning of the conflict there, as well as a debate and vote on an EU referendum in October 2011. In the latter vote, eighty-one Conservative MPs defied a three-line whip to vote for a referendum.

The Fixed-term Parliaments Act 2011, a mechanism devised to stop the coalition from breaking apart, further contributed to the confidence of backbenchers. By removing the power of the Prime Minister to call an election at a time of his choosing, the Act means that Prime Ministers can no longer bring their backbenchers back into line with threats of calling an early election. Cameron further found himself confronted by a House of Lords that has grown ever more assertive since the removal of most of the hereditary peers in 1999 gave it an increased sense of legitimacy, boosted by the considerable expertise of many of its members. Cameron's Leaders in the Lords, Strathclyde and Hill, and, in his final year, Tina Stowell, found they often had torrid times bringing independent-minded Tory peers into line.

Not only was Cameron constantly checked by forces in both houses of Parliament, the judiciary also wielded far greater power. The Human Rights Act, in force since 2000, empowered the courts to strike down government actions that infringed a claimant's human rights. Human rights issues have caused Cameron considerable difficulty, most notably over the delayed deportation of the cleric Abu Qatada. European Union law proved yet a further frustration, preventing Cameron from coming even close to his declared target of restricting immigration to tens of thousands rather than hundreds of thousands – a key election promise in 2010. A fundamental principle of the EU – some say its *most* fundamental principle – is the right to free movement of all EU citizens throughout the EU. A further fundamental right conferred by EU law is the right of EU migrant workers to receive equal treatment with regards to social advantages – i.e. benefits – even when they are working as little as ten hours a week. Cameron found himself – to UKIP's glee – in a Brussels straitjacket.

Cameron's freedom of manoeuvre on exacting concessions from the EU was thus severely constrained. With significant numbers of British voters favouring nothing less than restrictions on the principles of free movement and equal treatment, he found himself forced to set out increasingly explicit red lines on these issues in the 2015 election campaign. Yet any attempts to reform these areas will meet severe resistance from the EU. If he fails to secure the promised concessions (which will require the unanimous agreement of the other member states), he will be unable to maintain his authority over his party unless he delivers on his threat to advise the British public to vote to leave the European Union. This issue, along with cuts to public services, will define the next government after 2015.

It is unusual for a Prime Minister to find their freedom of manoeuvre as severely constrained in foreign policy as in domestic policy. The weakest US Administration on foreign policy since Jimmy Carter (1977–81) did not help him; the UK is always stronger when the USA walks tall in the world. The Arab Spring, the growth of militant Islam and an assertive Russia under Vladimir Putin all raised urgent questions to which there were no ready answers, any more than there was low-hanging fruit to pick on EU affairs. Britain's economic woes diminished its standing in the world in his first three years (until its recovery won grudging admiration), while the parliamentary position and the new emphasis on legalism post the Iraq war were further constraints. It is against the backdrop of all these multiple constraints, rather than the fictional 'la-la' land commentators often inhabit where they imagine all Prime Ministers operate on a level playing field, that history must judge Cameron.

The omnipresence of the 2015 general election

The approaching 2015 election was the inescapable factor in Cameron's mind from the day the coalition government was formed. The failure to achieve boundary commission changes ahead of the 2015 general election – revenge from the Lib Dems for failure to achieve the Alternative Vote and House of Lords reform – resulted in significant political damage to Cameron. He had told his backbenchers that they must support the disliked House of Lords reform as the price for achieving boundary reform, which he said was essential to secure a majority at the general election. Boundary reform would have badly damaged the Lib Dems as they would have lost the benefit of incumbency in settled constituencies; defeat over boundaries, therefore, should have come as no surprise. But it did. So Cameron had to face a party deeply concerned by the defeat and its dire implications. Failure to achieve boundary reform left the electoral logic stacked against the Conservatives, with Miliband needing as little as 34 per cent of the popular vote to win a majority, while the Tories needed close to 40 per cent.

Without the boost boundary reform would have brought, the election remained wide open to the end, complicated by the uncertainties of the UKIP vote and the need for Cameron to be fighting on three fronts at the same time – Labour, the Lib Dems and UKIP. Douglas Carswell's defection to UKIP and the party's victory in the Clacton by-election in October 2014 were wildcards in a highly volatile electoral position. The UKIP challenge dwarfed any other faced by a post-war PM, eclipsing utterly that of the Referendum Party formed by James Goldsmith to fight the general election of 1997. The failure of the electorate to respond more to the better economic news, upon which the Conservatives had counted, did not help their cause.

How history will judge Cameron

Cameron's standing in the eyes of contemporaries will depend much on whether he wins an outright majority in 2015, especially after his failure to do so in 2010. However, the judgement of *history* upon the years 2010–15 will be less dependent upon the result of the 2015 election. His place in history indeed is already secure: by holding together the coalition for five years, significantly improving the economic outlook from a weak starting point, overseeing some steady (if still unproven) domestic reform, restoring dignity to the office of PM and winning the Scottish referendum, controversial though it remains, Cameron ensured that he will be seen as a Prime Minister of enduring importance, whatever the result of the general election. No one can take away his two particular achievements as Prime Minister: sticking to 'Plan A' on the economy, to the extent it was, and holding the coalition together. The 'big, open and comprehensive offer' was his initiative and his alone. For better or worse, and I think better, the coalition was *his*, and history will judge him for it. He showed coalitions can work in Britian. He educated the country. The years 2010–15, it may be noted, were also not a time for heroes among national leaders. Obama in the US, Hollande in France, and leaders across the EU and beyond grappled often unsuccessfully with the problems they faced. Only Merkel in Germany emerged with credit from these halcyon years.

Osborne may not have succeeded in achieving expected cuts to a bloated public sector, matched by private sector expansion in exports tilting the economy away from its reliance on financial services, or indeed the southeast. The economy, however, recovered more strongly than any other advanced economy, and achieved remarkable success on job creation, if not productivity, which declined. His emphasis on a credible fiscal policy and an activist monetary policy was complemented by a major drive on structural reforms including planning, higher education, welfare, schools and labour market. His focus on financial regulation proved effective, including his abolition of the Financial Services Authority, creation of the Financial Policy Committee and the Financial Conduct Authority, setting up the Vickers committee and bringing prudential regulation onto the banks. But for the prolonged Eurozone crisis and faltering world economy, the ballooning welfare bill and the disappointing tax yield, the recovery would have been more pronounced.

Was this effectively a diarchy, with the Chancellor as powerful as the PM? Osborne was more creative on policy: there was no Cameron-ism akin to Thatcherism or even Blairism. Osborne's contribution to this government will rank as high in history as that of any post-war Chancellor (though he had less reach over the wide-ranging *substance* of domestic policy than Gordon Brown, Chancellor 1997–2007). Osborne was responsible for so much of the tactical thinking of the government. He is a more natural political operator than Cameron, and possesses the quickest mind amongst the PM's advisers about what to do and whom to promote or dismiss. They spoke to each other almost every morning and every evening. They enjoyed the most successful and closest political relationship at the top of the last 100 years. The Chancellor/PM relationship, when it goes wrong, does so for two reasons: significant differences over policy and ambition by the junior to replace the senior; neither applied in this partnership. Osborne always knew when to bite his lip, defer to Cameron, and never briefed against him. There were differences of emphasis certainly. Osborne would have wanted to have been more aggressively liberal on social issues, more of a neo-con on foreign policy, tougher on colleagues and backbenchers, and more of a tax and economic reformer, though it was the economic situation rather than Cameron that was the principal restraint. Cameron, the older figure by five years, was always more of a shire Tory, while Osborne was more an urban liberal. The two men, though never close personal friends, remained inseparable politically to the end.

Regardless of the debate amongst economists about austerity, it can be said with absolute certainty that by working together so productively, the Conservative–Liberal Democrat coalition provided the country with political stability at a time when it was so desperately needed, and that this stability made a significant contribution to the economic recovery. As polls showed, the country rated him above Miliband and Clegg.

The case for the prosecution appeared in early 2015: Polly Toynbee and David Walker's *Cameron's Coup: How the Tories took Britain to the Brink*.[3] They argue great harm was done to the public realm because of the government's 'dogma and disarray'. Ideological reform such as the NHS reform, Universal Credit and free schools exacerbated financial woes. The government, in short, was run in the interests of the rich and at the expense of the least well off. The value of such critiques is damaged by the relentless negativity. Would Labour have acted differently, or better? The experience of Brown's government might make us cautious in answering in the affirmative. The authors fail to provide balance or context of what was possible for any government to have achieved in these difficult five years. The authors who follow offer more nuanced interpretations.

From Cameron's personal perspective, his reputation might well be higher in history if he lost the 2015 election. Many Prime Ministers remain too long beyond their high-water mark: Blair would have stood much higher if he had quit in 2002, and Thatcher in 1988. Leaving aside the problems of piloting the country through a period of intense retrenchment after 2015, the biggest cloud on Cameron's horizon, should he win the general election, will be the EU referendum due in 2017. Of course, if he secures a new and popular deal for British membership in 2017, and resets Britain's membership of Europe for the next forty years, his standing would be even higher. But is such an achievement realistic given the political forces operating in the EU and the 'Brexit' fervour inside Britain? Carswell and Reckless' defections were widely seen as a harbinger of a long-awaited split on the Right over Europe. Cameron now finds himself backed into a corner from which the only escape – if the EU refuses to agree to his demands – may be to take Britain out of the EU. This is something that Cameron undoubtedly feels would be severely damaging for Britain, not the least for its unpredictable impact on the economy. That said, in his final

---

[3] Polly Toynbee and David Walker, *Cameron's Coup: How the Tories took Britain to the Brink* (London: Guardian Faber, 2015).

months in Number 10, his exasperation at the EU and his irritation at the problems membership brought, not least immigration, reached altogether new heights.

The worst-case scenario for Cameron in 2015 might be winning the general election with a very small majority, leaving him prey to the whims of his Eurosceptic and right-wing backbenchers. His skills as a leader were ideally suited to the fudges and compromises of coalition politics. A new era could call for a leader with an entirely different skill set, and a far more defined set of beliefs. 'Cometh the hour, cometh the man' might well be Cameron's epitaph. The 'hour' was 2010–15, the man, David Cameron. It is hard to imagine that Gordon Brown, David Davis, Nick Clegg or Ed Miliband would have had the stamina, equilibrium or negotiating skills to have led the country as well in these difficult years. All successful leaders in history need a degree of luck. Cameron's was to be the Prime Minister at this particularly febrile point in British history.

Part I

The coalition and the government of Britain

Morten Morland for The Times / News Syndication

1 THE COMING OF THE COALITION AND THE COALITION AGREEMENT

MIKE FINN

> I am a liberal conservative.
>
> > DAVID CAMERON, LEADER OF THE CONSERVATIVE PARTY
> > *(11 September 2006)*[1]

> Lots of people would just walk if we went in with the Tories.
>
> > NICK CLEGG, LEADER OF THE LIBERAL DEMOCRATS
> > *(10 May 2010)*[2]

> In every part of this agreement, we have gone further than
> simply adopting those policies where we previously overlapped.
> We have found that a combination of our parties' best ideas
> and attitudes has produced a programme for government
> that is more radical and comprehensive than our individual
> manifestos.
>
> > PRIME MINISTER DAVID CAMERON AND DEPUTY PRIME
> > MINISTER NICK CLEGG
> > *(20 May 2010)*[3]

---

[1] David Cameron, speech to the British-American Project, 11 September 2006 (accessed at www.theguardiapolitics/politics/2006/sep/11/conservatives.speeches, 17 August 2014).

[2] Quoted in Andrew Adonis, *5 Days in May* (London: Biteback, 2013), p. 87.

[3] David Cameron and Nick Clegg, 'Foreword', in *The Coalition: Our Programme for Government* (London: Cabinet Office, 2010), p. 8.

Changing leaders

On 6 December 2005, after a protracted contest, David Cameron was elected as Leader of the Conservative Party.[4] Cameron had been in Parliament for less than five years and was initially an outsider candidate in the Tory leadership contest, representing a 'caucus' which aimed (according to Matthew d'Ancona) to do little more than lay down a marker for the future, in turn 'establishing themselves as a powerful force within the party'.[5]

But Cameron won. That he did so is commonly held to be partly the result of his performance at the Conservative Party conference in the autumn, where he spoke passionately and without notes. His main rival, David Davis, by contrast failed to deliver.[6] This infused the Cameron campaign with momentum, not least in terms of growing support from the press.[7] The implications of Cameron's victory were clear, at least according to him. In his victory speech, he claimed a clear mandate for change:

> I said when I launched my campaign that we needed to change in order to win. Now that I've won we will change. We will change the way we look. Nine out of 10 Conservative MPs, like me, are white men. We need to change the scandalous under representation of women in the Conservative party and we'll do that. We need to change the way we feel. No more grumbling about modern Britain. I love this country as it is not as it was and I believe our best days lie ahead.[8]

Cameron's diagnosis – that the Conservative Party had failed to move with the times, had become ossified in its perennial obsessions (such as Europe) and suffered from brand 'toxicity' gave him and his allies a

---

[4] Francis Elliott and James Hanning, *Cameron: The Rise of the New Conservative* (London: HarperPerennial, 2009), p. 296.

[5] Matthew d'Ancona, *In It Together: The Inside Story of the Coalition Government* (London: Penguin, 2014 edition), p. xiii.

[6] D'Ancona, *ibid.*; Elliott and Hanning, *Cameron*, pp. 285–8; Tim Bale, *The Conservative Party from Thatcher to Cameron* (Cambridge: Polity, 2011), pp. 275–8.

[7] Bale, *The Conservative Party*, pp. 276–7.

[8] David Cameron, speech at the Royal Academy, London, 6 December 2005 (accessed at www.thegpolitics/politics/2005/dec/06/toryleadership2005.conservatives3, 1 August 2014).

clear plan for shock therapy to remake the party both in image and substance in order to secure an election victory.[9]

The ideological genesis – such as it was – of the 2010 coalition government can then, in part, be traced to a major speech by Cameron at Hereford on 16 December 2005 which spelled the end for Charles Kennedy's leadership of the Liberal Democrats. Entitled 'LibDems4-Cameron', and with an accompanying website, Cameron made a specific plea to disaffected Liberal Democrats. He argued that the 'values' of his 'modern, compassionate conservatism'

> reach far beyond the Conservative Party. Many Liberal Democrats share these values. And many Liberal Democrats share with us a clear analysis of why Labour have failed to live up to their promise. It's because this Labour Government doesn't live by the values we need to succeed in the twenty-first century. Instead of trusting people, Labour tell people what to do. Instead of sharing responsibility, Labour take responsibility away from people ... Labour's style of government shows how little they trust people, and how reluctant they are to share responsibility.[10]

It was the arrival of this 'young, dynamic leader', directly reaching out to Liberal Democrat voters, which Stuart McAnulla claims inspired Kennedy's internal critics to action.[11] The removal of the leaders of the 2005 general election campaign was, as David Laws noted, integral to the ultimate possibility of coalition between the Conservatives and the Liberal Democrats in 2010:

> All three parties had changed leaders since 2005. Each change made a Lib Dem–Conservative coalition more likely. It is difficult to imagine a Lib Dem–Conservative coalition government being formed if the Conservative Party had been led by Michael Howard, and the Liberal Democrats by either Charles Kennedy or Menzies Campbell.

Most important of all had been the arrival of David Cameron:

> The election of David Cameron as leader of the Conservative Party was clearly very significant. Ever since his election as leader,

---

[9] Elliot and Hanning, *Cameron*, pp. 296–306.

[10] David Cameron, speech at Hereford, 16 December 2005 (accessed at www.ukpolitics.org.uk/node/3733, 17 August 2014).

[11] Stuart McAnulla, 'Explaining the forced exit of Charles Kennedy: Pushing the public-private boundary', *Politics*, 29:1 (2009), p. 42.

David Cameron had been seeking to lead his party back onto the centre ground. And he had made a specific pitch for liberal votes by emphasizing issues such as the environment and civil liberties.[12]

So although in the aftermath of the 2010 general election many commentators and participants – most notably in the Labour Party[13] – feigned surprise at the apparent willingness of the Liberal Democrats to abandon the 'progressive left' and enter coalition with the Conservatives, the longer-term origins of coalition government lie in the 'orientation' of the Conservatives towards the Liberal Democrats and the Liberal Democrats' 'orientation' towards the Conservatives in the period up to 2010. To close observers of both parties, the ultimate conclusion – partnership in government – was not so surprising. Internal changes, both in terms of personnel and ideology, and the dynamics of Opposition politics, pushed the Conservatives and the Liberal Democrats closer than they had been since the formation of the latter party out of the old Liberals and the Social Democrats in 1988.

As stated by Laws, chief amongst the personnel changes were the leaders themselves. David Cameron's espousal of what he termed 'liberal conservatism' from 2005 onward was a pragmatic approach to the Conservatives' electoral fortunes.[14] The Conservatives had been comprehensively defeated by Labour in three successive general elections. During the wilderness years, previous attempts had been made to fight Labour for the centre ground and to reform party structures, notably in the early stages of William Hague's leadership.[15] Too often, however, the party had drifted back to solidly-right issues come

---

[12] David Laws, 22 *Days in May: The Birth of the Lib Dem–Conservative Coalition* (London: Biteback, 2010), p. 268.

[13] Adonis, *5 Days in May*, p. 7.

[14] For a discussion of the concept as articulated by Cameron see Stuart McAnulla, 'Liberal Conservatism: Ideological coherence?', in Timothy Heppell and David Seawright (eds.), *Cameron and the Conservatives: The Transition to Coalition Government* (London: Palgrave, 2012).

[15] Bale, *The Conservative Party*, pp. 77–86; Peter Snowdon, *Back from the Brink: The Extraordinary Fall and Rise of the Conservative Party* (London: Harper Press, 2010), pp. 52–6; Gillian Peele, 'Towards New Conservatives? Organisational reform and the Conservative Party', *Political Quarterly*, 69:2 (1999), pp. 141–7.

election time, including in Hague's one attempt at restoring the party's standing in the polls.[16] In many respects, Cameron's rise to the leadership of the Conservative Party mirrored the ascent of Blair in the 1980s and 1990s; that this was at least to some extent consciously so was reflected in Cameron's remark that he saw himself as 'the heir to Blair'.[17]

The Labour modernizers' legend was well-known to Cameron and his circle.[18] The volume chronicling it, *The Unfinished Revolution* by Labour pollster and Blair adviser Philip Gould, was, according to Danny Finkelstein writing in *The Times*, 'the big red book which saved the Tories', without which it was 'very possibly the case that ... David Cameron would not have become Prime Minister.'[19] Osborne was alleged by another source to 'keep a copy at hand'.[20] For Osborne, Cameron's true strategist-in-chief, *Unfinished Revolution* was a playbook, party modernization by numbers; as one Conservative source told Peter Snowdon, 'he frames everything we need to do in terms of "This is what Labour did"'.[21]

The key lesson the group drew from Gould was that a political party could not be hostage to its extremes if it wished to gain power in modern Britain. It was the third successive defeat in 2005 which gave Cameron the opportunity to seek the leadership; the Conservatives had, apparently, suffered enough of their own electoral trauma to modernize. Cameron's diagnosis of the party's ills was echoed in Lord Ashcroft's post-election review, where he mused ruefully that 'the Conservative Party's problem is its brand. Conservatives loathe being told this but it is an inescapable fact.'[22] Cameron's overt courting both of Liberal Democrat parliamentarians (including a direct approach by George Osborne to David Laws offering him a senior post were he to

---

[16] David Butler and Dennis Kavanagh, *The British General Election of 2001* (London: Palgrave, 2001).

[17] Elliott and Hanning, *Cameron*, p. 287.

[18] Sometimes dubbed the 'Notting Hill set' by the press; Elliott and Hanning, *Cameron*, p. 253.

[19] Daniel Finkelstein, 'The big red book which saved the Tories', *The Times*, 19 September 2011.

[20] 'Tribune of the strivers', *Economist*, 8 November 2011.

[21] Snowdon, *Back From the Brink*, p. 230.

[22] Michael A. Ashcroft, *Smell the Coffee: A Wake-up Call for the Conservative Party* (London: Michael A. Ashcroft, 2005), p. 4.

defect[23]) and Liberal Democrat voters was both a rhetorical means of driving his centrist message home, and a pragmatic recognition of the fact that were the Conservatives to form a government they would have to take a significant number of Liberal Democrat seats. The last Conservative leader to win a majority in the House of Commons, John Major, had done so in 1992 as the Liberal Democrats were reduced to a mere twenty MPs.[24]

Taking back previously Conservative seats from the Liberal Democrats was not a 'magic bullet' to solve the problems facing the party, but it was an area they could not ignore. In 2005, the party had included '34 Lib Dem held seats' in its targeting strategy.[25] Significant studies conducted in the late 1990s and early 2000s by Andrew Russell and Ed Fieldhouse profiled Liberal Democrat voters and discovered they largely originated 'from a similar social background to Conservative supporters (particularly in terms of class)'.[26] The Liberal Democrats were 'the most middle class party in terms of voter profile in 1992'[27] and their consistently 'similar social profile to ... the Conservatives' begged the question of 'why Liberal voters chose to support a third party and not their "natural" party, the Conservatives'.[28] They found that

> On four major policy dimensions – government spending, internationalism, economic choices and egalitarianism – Liberal Democrat voters occupied a position closer to Labour. Indeed, on two issues, law and order and environmentalism, the party was the most liberal of all the three major parties ... In short, Liberal Democrat voters may be more like Conservative supporters in terms of class, but politically they are more similar to Labour voters.[29]

[23] Laws, 22 Days in May, p. 268; Jasper Gerard, The Clegg Coup (London: Gibson Square, 2011), pp. 74–5; Iain Dale, 'First defection to Cameron is a change of gear', Daily Telegraph, 30 March 2007.

[24] The SDP–Liberal Alliance which had contested the 1987 general election, before the 1988 merger of the two parties, had secured twenty-two seats at that election.

[25] Ashcroft, Smell the Coffee, p. 7.

[26] Andrew Russell, Ed Fieldhouse and Iain MacAllister, 'The anatomy of Liberal support in Britain, 1974–1997', British Journal of Politics and International Relations, 4:1 (2002), p. 49; Andrew Russell and Ed Fieldhouse, Neither Left nor Right: The Liberal Democrats and the Electorate (Manchester: Manchester University Press, 2005).

[27] Russell, Fieldhouse and MacAllister, 'Anatomy', p. 53.   [28] Ibid., p. 58.

[29] Ibid.

In the build-up to the 2010 general election the Liberal Democrat problem for the Conservatives had been, as Ashcroft noted following the formation of the coalition, acute:

> Many of these [target] constituencies were once safe Conservative seats where people had abandoned the party for the Liberal Democrats in the 1990s (which also meant that Mosaic types who would be considered Solid Conservatives in Labour-held seats were not necessarily so on the Lib Dem battleground). Voting for an unchanged Conservative Party would have been no more attractive a prospect for these voters than it had been in 1997 or 2001, whatever their opinion of the Labour government.[30]

It had been such insights which had influenced Cameron's attempts to rebrand the party in Opposition, but movement towards the centre was a transition taking place in both the Conservative Party and the Liberal Democrats between 2005 and 2010, driven by the leaders – Cameron from December 2005 and Clegg from December 2007. For the Liberal Democrats, even before the 2005 general election, the publication of the subsequently mythologized *Orange Book* (edited by City hedge-fund investor Paul Marshall and former party Director of Policy David Laws) represented the emergence of a substantive internal debate about the party's ideological direction and policy platform.[31] Much of the tone of Laws' and Marshall's contributions seemed a calculated attack on the social democratic wing of the party. There were unambiguous assaults on the Attlee government and the establishment of the post-war welfare state. Marshall began by stating that 'the twentieth-century experiment with state socialism and the mixed economy now looks like just an expensive interlude'[32] before arguing that 'state socialism ... disfigured British politics in the twentieth century'.[33] He then claimed that 'social-ism has been one of the greatest enemies of a civil society, not least in our own country ... socialism introduced social class as the organizing principle of political analysis'.[34] Laws evoked the memory of Glad-stone's 'masses against the classes' remark, stating that 'liberalism

[30] Michael A. Ashcroft, *Minority Verdict: The Conservative Party, the Voters and the 2010 Election* (London: Biteback, 2010), p. 79.
[31] Paul Marshall and David Laws (eds.), *The Orange Book: Reclaiming Liberalism* (London: Profile, 2004).
[32] Paul Marshall, 'Introduction', in Marshall and Laws (eds.), *Orange Book*, p. 1.
[33] *Ibid.*, p. 2.   [34] *Ibid.*, p. 15.

has always stood against narrow class interests, sectional interests, and purely national interests, and in favour of the general interest'.[35] Such remarks were taken by critics on the left of the party to echo Margaret Thatcher's statement that 'class is a communist concept. It groups people as bundles and sets them against one another.'[36]

It was significant that the then Nick Clegg MEP wrote for the volume.[37] Clegg was a rising star with powerful patrons in the party: Paddy Ashdown encouraged him to stand for leader immediately on Charles Kennedy's resignation in January 2006, and had vacillated on his commitment to his old friend Ming Campbell until he was certain Clegg would not put himself forward.[38] Clegg was identified as an 'Orange Book' economic liberal on the right of the party, close to Laws and Danny Alexander, another newcomer in the 2005 intake who would eventually co-organize Clegg's campaign for the party leadership.[39] When the consistent barrage of press ageism took its toll on Kennedy's successor Campbell in October 2007, Clegg contested the leadership with fellow Orange Booker, Chris Huhne.[40] Though Huhne had run for the leadership before, Clegg was elected party leader in December.[41] Thus by half-way through the 2005 Parliament, both the Conservatives and Liberal Democrats found themselves led by comparatively young men, from similar social backgrounds, committed to the modernization of their parties both structurally and ideologically, striving to move to the centre ground and – in many places – fighting for the same seats.

Changing the parties: Policies and image

Cameron's attempt to 'change' the Conservative Party was initially divorced from a serious engagement with policy: 'travelling light', as

35 David Laws, 'Reclaiming liberalism: A liberal agenda for the Liberal Democrats', in Marshall and Laws (eds.), *Orange Book*, p. 21.

36 Margaret Thatcher, 'Don't undo my work', *Newsweek*, 27 April 1992.

37 Nick Clegg, 'Europe: a Liberal future', in Marshall and Laws (eds.), *Orange Book*, pp. 69–103.

38 Chris Bowers, *Nick Clegg: The Biography* (London: Biteback, 2011), pp. 163–4.

39 Bowers, *Nick Clegg*, pp. 89–90, 186.

40 Menzies Campbell, *My Autobiography* (London: Hodder & Stoughton, 2008), pp. 299–311; Bowers, *Nick Clegg*, pp. 181–8.

41 Bowers, *Nick Clegg*, p. 188.

Peter Snowdon describes it.[42] On becoming leader, he immediately focused on style over substance, placing policy development in the hands of 'policy groups', scheduled to report in eighteen months.[43] In the short term, the emphasis was on the need for 'drastic changes to the party's image'.[44] One early Cameron speech as leader was to the King's Fund in January 2006:

> The world is changing. And so is the Conservative Party. Over the next few weeks, I'm going to be setting out, in a series of speeches, the most significant social and economic challenges faced by Britain and the world and how the Conservative party is changing to meet those challenges ... I'm starting today with the issue that I think is most important: Health.[45]

For a Conservative leader, pitching his tent on the ground of the National Health Service was, to say the least, audacious. Cameron's ambition in devoting a major speech to health was not to 'seize' the NHS from Labour, but to begin the process of 'detoxification'. Cameron and his circle knew that the electorate felt the Conservatives were not trusted with public services, especially the NHS.[46] Cameron's task therefore was to state that it was safe in his hands, that a modern 'compassionate' Conservative Party sought quality health care for all. It was a case that he was uniquely well placed to make. His first son, Ivan, was born in 2002 with cerebral palsy and epilepsy. As a consequence, Cameron had first-hand experience of the NHS and spoke on the subject with genuine passion in the King's Fund speech:

> I have a child who's not too well, so I've seen a lot of the NHS from the inside. In fact, in the last three years, I've probably spent more time in NHS hospitals than any politician apart from the few doctors in the House of Commons. I've spent the night in A&E departments and slept at my child's bedside ... I know, from

[42] Snowdon, *Back from the Brink*, p. 223.
[43] Bale, *The Conservative Party*, pp. 287–90.
[44] Snowdon, *Back from the Brink*, p. 224.
[45] David Cameron, speech to the King's Fund, 4 January 2006 (accessed at www.thegpolitics/society/2006/jan/04/health.conservativeparty, 10 November 2014).
[46] Andrew Lilico, 'What went wrong with Conservative Party modernisation?', *Daily Telegraph* (blog), 1 September 2014 (accessed at http://blogs.telegraph.co.uk/finance/andrewlilico/100027989/what-went-wrong-with-conservative-party-modernisation, 1 September 2014).

personal experience just how important the NHS is to everyone in
this country.[47]

He then turned to the Conservative commitment:

> I want us to leave no one in any doubt whatsoever about how we
> feel about the NHS today. We believe in it. We want to improve it.
> We want to improve it for everyone in this country.[48]

It was difficult for Cameron's opponents to call into question his personal investment in the NHS, as they might have done with previous
Conservative leaders. It was a strong performance, which offered a clear
commitment whilst being (deliberately) light on detail. Beyond health, 'if
there was one issue that defined Cameron's first year as leader of the
Opposition, it was the environment'.[49] The environment offered a
number of possibilities for Cameron to remake the party's image – not
least the basic one of changing the party's iconography. Ahead of the
autumn party conference in 2006, he unveiled the party's new official
logo, a cartoon tree which replaced the torch emblem that Margaret
Thatcher had introduced in the 1980s.[50] The logo change was intended
to epitomize the adoption of Cameron's personal green mission by
the party as a whole. Through the whole of 2006, Cameron sought
to be portrayed as a younger leader in touch with 'green issues' – of
significance to the Liberal Democrat voters the Conservatives were
targeting.[51] As Elliott and Hanning note, 'Cameron even made the
environment the theme of his first electoral test, fighting the local council
elections under the slogan, "Vote Blue, Go Green".'[52] In a 'green
manifesto' released before the local elections, Cameron claimed that

> The Conservatives intend to lead a new green revolution in
> Britain ... Whether we're in power or in opposition, Conservatives
> will seek to build a cross-party consensus for local policies to
> safeguard and enhance the environment.[53]

---

[47] Cameron, speech to the King's Fund, 4 January 2006.   [48] *Ibid.*
[49] Francis Elliott and James Hanning, *Cameron: Practically a Conservative* (London:
4th Estate, 2012), p. 311.
[50] 'Tories show off scribbled logo', *BBC News*, 15 September 2006 (accessed at http://
news.bbc.co.uk/1/hi/5348630.stm, 27 August 2014).
[51] Bale, *The Conservative Party*, p. 299.
[52] Elliott and Hanning, *Practically a Conservative*, p. 311.
[53] David Cameron, foreword in *Vote Blue, Go Green* (London: Conservative Party,
2006), p. 1.

Writing in 2009, Neil Carter noted that Cameron had made the environmental agenda 'his signature issue.'[54] It was a question of brand, yes – but it was also a focused attempt to deal with what one Tory strategist would later describe as 'the Lib Dem phenomenon'.[55]

Both the Conservative and Liberal Democrat leaders who were to contest the 2010 general election campaign were self-conscious modernizers, striving for the centre ground. Cameron aped New Labour and its original leader Tony Blair. In Clegg's case, his one-time rival for the Liberal Democrat leadership had condemned him in stark terms as 'David Cameron's stunt double', a phrase which resonated for years beyond its original utterance.[56] This might have been unjust, but it was true that both men shared a belief in the modernization of their parties and the inspiration of New Labour was clearly present. As such, both appeared to adopt Blairite tactics. Both had 'Clause IV' moments, by which was meant moments where they faced down their parties in a manner reminiscent of Blair in the debate over nationalization in 1995.[57] Both related to education policy, in Cameron's case grammar schools[58] and in Clegg's university tuition fees.

In Clegg's case, it was a 'clause four moment that wasn't'. In the course of 2008–9, the leadership repeatedly tried to reverse the policy through the party's democratic structures, but were defeated. Clegg's attempts to face down the party activist base had failed. By the summer of 2009, using the financial crisis as a rhetorical vehicle to trim the sails of Liberal Democrat expenditure pledges, he tried again – this time with a pre-manifesto, *A Fresh Start for Britain*, which accepted the decisions of the policy apparatus within the party, but which reduced all policies the leadership deemed unachievable in the short-run to the status of 'aspirations'.[59] Given the take-it-or-leave it nature of the pre-manifesto, the party conference approved it, but not without disquiet from MPs

[54] Neil Carter, 'Vote blue, go green? Cameron's Conservatives and the environment', *Political Quarterly*, 80:2 (2009), p. 283.

[55] Bale, *The Conservative Party*, p. 258.

[56] George Parker and Alex Barker, 'Man in the news: Nick Clegg', *Financial Times*, 9 April 2010.

[57] Tim Bale, 'David Cameron, 2005–2010' in Timothy Heppell (ed.), *Leaders of the Opposition: From Churchill to Cameron* (Basingstoke: Palgrave, 2012), p. 231.

[58] *Ibid.*

[59] *A Fresh Start for Britain: Choosing a Different, Better Future*, Policy Paper 94 (London: Liberal Democrats, 2009).

such as Steve Webb, who claimed that Clegg had 'overdone the despair'.[60] More broadly, the pre-manifesto had committed the party to a cuts package which Clegg had elsewhere described as 'savage'.[61] In practice, this meant that there was little clear yellow water between the Liberal Democrat leadership's views on fiscal retrenchment and those of George Osborne.

The manifestos and the Coalition Agreement

The story of the formation of the Conservative–Liberal Democrat coalition, and specifically the coalition negotiations between those parties – and the parallel negotiations between the Liberal Democrats and Labour – has been much discussed, not least for the level of political drama involved. The 'five days to power'[62] – from Friday 7 May 2010 to Tuesday 11 May, when Gordon Brown resigned as Prime Minister and David Cameron formed a government – have been the subject of numerous insider accounts and instant academic verdicts.[63] The essential facts were that no party had secured an overall majority of 326 seats in the House of Commons: the Conservatives had gained 306 seats, Labour 258 and the Liberal Democrats 57.[64] In the minds of those

[60] 'Clegg's cuts message wins backing', *BBC News*, 22 September 2009 (accessed at http://news.bbc.co.uk/1/hi/uk_politics/8268573.stm, 8 September 2014).

[61] Patrick Wintour and Allegra Stratton, 'Britain needs "savage" cuts, says Liberal Democrat leader Nick Clegg', *The Guardian*, 19 September 2009.

[62] The title of Rob Wilson MP's account.

[63] Wilson, *5 Days to Power: The Journey to Coalition Britain* (London: Biteback, 2010); Laws, *22 Days in May*; Adonis, *5 Days in May*; Ben Yong, 'Formation of the coalition', in Robert Hazell and Ben Yong, *The Politics of Coalition: How the Conservative–Liberal Democrat Government Works* (Oxford: Hart Publishing, 2012); Peter Mandelson, *The Third Man: Life at the Heart of New Labour* (London: Harper Press, 2010), pp. 540–57; Dennis Kavanagh and Philip Cowley, 'Five days in May: The formation of the coalition', in Dennis Kavanagh and Philip Cowley, *British General Election of 2010* (London: Palgrave, 2010); Ruth Fox, 'Five days in May: A new political order emerges', in Andrew Geddes and Jonathan Tonge (eds.), *Britain Votes 2010* (Oxford: Oxford University Press, 2010).

[64] Kavanagh and Cowley, *British General Election of 2010*, p. 351. The figure of 307 cited in Kavanagh and Cowley includes both the delayed poll in Thirsk and Malton (27 May) and the Speaker, John Bercow. The result given in the text here includes Thirsk and Malton but excludes the Speaker due to his official neutrality.

seeking to defend the arrangements that ultimately came to pass, a key factor was the numbers game: a Conservative–Liberal Democrat coalition would have the clear majority necessary to provide stable government. Even amongst the Labour leadership, initially the prospect of a 'rainbow' coalition was less than appealing; Adonis notes that he and Brown had to convince senior figures such as Mandelson that (given the abstention of Sinn Fein MPs and neutrality of office holders) a coalition with the Liberal Democrats was in fact feasible.[65]

Adonis is correct that the legislative arithmetic did make a Labour–Liberal Democrat arrangement possible but this did not mean that it made it politically desirable. As has been demonstrated, there had been a process of ideological convergence between the Conservatives in the Liberal Democrats in the 2005–10 parliament which had been a self-conscious one on the part of both party leaderships, committed as they were to their respective 'modernization' agendas. When Clegg announced during the election campaign that the Liberal Democrats would choose to negotiate first with the party with the 'most votes and the most seats' – in violation of the constitutional norm that the sitting Prime Minister should have first attempt to form a government – this inevitably meant that the Liberal Democrats would talk to the Conservatives first.[66] Contrary to the shock many in the Labour Party affected to feel at this, there were cogent ideological and policy-based reasons for doing so. In places, the Conservative and Liberal Democrat manifestos – the ultimate product of their respective leaderships' modernization programmes – echoed each other almost verbatim. Taking page 27 of each manifesto as an almost surreal example, in terms of rebalancing the economy away from the public sector, the Liberal Democrats expressed their support for co-operatives, noting

> that mutuals, co-operatives and social enterprises have an important role to play in the creation of a more balanced and mixed economy. Mutuals give people a proper stake in the places they work, spreading wealth through society, and bringing innovative and imaginative business ideas to bear on meeting local needs.[67]

---

[65] Adonis, 5 Days in May, pp. 2–3, 16, 23–5.   [66] Ibid., pp. 6, 26.
[67] Liberal Democrats, Liberal Democrat Manifesto 2010 (London: Liberal Democrats, 2010), p. 27.

The Conservatives, for their part stated that

> we will support co-operatives and mutualisation as a way of transferring public assets and revenue streams to public sector workers. We will encourage them to come together to form employee-led co-operatives and bid to take over the services they run.[68]

More broadly, as Mark Pack has claimed, the 'Big Society' emphasis of the Conservative manifesto had strong echoes of the Liberal Democrats 'community politics' agenda.[69] The Big Society, in part the product of Steve Hilton's role as Cameron's policy guru, had a strong focus on localism and the devolution of power. Localism – a consistent presence in Liberal Democrat thinking – had come to be of increasing interest to the Conservatives, with the think tank Policy Exchange (then headed by future Conservative MP Nicholas Boles) publishing Simon Jenkins' book *Big Bang Localism* in 2004.[70] It was read by politicians of both parties. In the 2010 Conservative manifesto, the commitment to the devolution of power was made both implicitly (one interpretation of the manifesto's title, for instance) and explicitly:

> The Big Society runs consistently through our policy programme. Our plans to reform public services, mend our broken society, and rebuild trust in politics are all part of our Big Society agenda. These plans involve redistributing power from the state to society; from the centre to local communities, giving people the opportunity to take more control over their lives.[71]

The Liberal Democrats still claimed ownership of the agenda in their own manifesto:

> Liberal Democrats are the only party which believes in radical political reform to reinvent the way our country is run and put power back where it belongs: into the hands of people. We want to

---

[68] The Conservative Party, *Invitation to Join the Government of Britain: The Conservative Manifesto 2010* (London: Conservative Party, 2010), p. 27.

[69] Mark Pack, 'The Liberal Democrats and the coalition', seminar at the UCL Constitution Unit, 26 January 2011 (accessed at www.ucl.ac.uk/constitution-unit/events/public-seminars/201011/libdem-coalition, 10 November 2014).

[70] Simon Jenkins, *Big Bang Localism: A Rescue Plan for British Democracy* (London: Policy Exchange, 2004).

[71] Conservative Party, *Manifesto 2010*, p. 37.

see a fair and open political system, with power devolved to all the nations, communities, neighbourhoods and peoples of Britain.[72]

The two manifestos agreed with each other on significant 'big ticket items' up for discussion in any potential coalition negotiations. Critically, this centred on the issue of economic policy. The rhetorical justification for the coalition – which would outlast the initial 'honeymoon' phase – was that the two parties had come 'together in the national interest'.[73] This specifically located the motive force of coalition in dealing with the crisis in government finances bequeathed to the two parties by the preceding Labour government. Both parties had had to revise their policy commitments in the pre-election period following the near-collapse of the banking system in later 2008, with the effect that both parties entered the 2010 general election campaign urging not merely fiscal restraint but more or less severe reductions in public spending. The Conservatives early in Cameron's leadership had sought to 'share the proceeds of growth' and agreed to match Labour's spending commitments; this pledge was unambiguously abandoned by the time the manifesto was drafted.[74] Though the Liberal Democrats ostensibly disagreed with the Conservatives over the pace of retrenchment, they agreed in principle. As the pre-manifesto put it, 'the only certainty is that the next government will have to make very hard choices about spending – cuts will be necessary to deliver any priorities'.[75] The manifesto confirmed it, baldly stating that 'we will seek to eliminate the deficit through spending cuts'.[76]

Cutting the deficit and restoring sound public finances were shared objectives of the two parties, despite differences over detail. In terms of their priorities overall, the Conservative manifesto outlined several discrete areas: economy, society, political reform, the environment and the promotion of the 'national interest' – foreign policy.[77] The Liberal Democrats (in a much shorter manifesto) identified four priority

[72] Liberal Democrats, *Manifesto 2010*, p. 87.
[73] Which ultimately became the title of the coalition's mid-term review: HM Government, *The Coalition: Together in the National Interest* (London: Cabinet Office, 2012).
[74] Peter Dorey, '"Sharing the proceeds of growth": Conservative economic policy under David Cameron', *Political Quarterly*, 80:2 (2009), pp. 259–69.
[75] Liberal Democrats, *A Fresh Start for Britain*, p. 7.
[76] Liberal Democrats, *Manifesto 2010*, p. 97.
[77] Conservative Party, *Manifesto 2010*, pp. iv–v.

areas: tax reform, job creation through 'greening' the economy, schools reform (including the implementation of a 'pupil premium' for children from disadvantaged backgrounds) and the classic Liberal Democrat staple of constitutional reform.[78] Across these priority areas, there were significant overlaps and areas of agreement between the two parties. Beyond fiscal retrenchment, there was a shared onus on job creation through the 'green' economy, with the Conservatives arguing that the 'low carbon economy ... provides exciting opportunities for British businesses',[79] while the Liberal Democrats claimed they would be 'boosting support for green jobs'.[80] Banking reform – and diversifying the economy away from financial services – was another area of convergence. The Liberal Democrats had established credibility in this area through the public perception that Vince Cable had 'predicted' the financial crisis:

> [It] starts with banking reform. Banks must be made to behave responsibly. And we need to support and develop new ways of financing growing businesses, with equity rather than debt, and without relying too heavily on the financial centre of the City of London. More diverse sources of finance will provide the funding needed to develop innovative new products and reverse the decline in the UK's manufacturing base.[81]

The Conservatives for their part were anxious to throw off the impression that they were too soft on the banks (and bankers), and their manifesto claimed they would 'create a safer banking system that serves the needs of the economy'.[82] More substantively, the manifesto stated that

> the financial sector must not put the stability of the whole economy at risk. We will put in place a levy on banks. We are prepared to act unilaterally if necessary ... [we will] pursue international agreement to prevent retail banks from engaging in activities, such as large-scale proprietary trading, that put the stability of the system at risk; [we will] empower the Bank of England to crack down on risky bonus arrangements ...

[78] Liberal Democrats, *Manifesto 2010*, pp. 6–7.
[79] Conservative Party, *Manifesto 2010*, p. 31.
[80] Liberal Democrats, *Manifesto 2010*, p. 66.
[81] Liberal Democrats, *Manifesto 2010*, pp. 21–2.
[82] Conservative Party, *Manifesto 2010*, p. 29.

Even on some of the more 'niche' issues, namely civil liberties and constitutional reform, there was apparent convergence, if not always agreement. The Conservatives claimed they would 'work to build a consensus for a mainly-elected second chamber to replace the current House of Lords',[83] whilst the Liberal Democrats sought to 'replace the House of Lords with a fully-elected second chamber with considerably fewer members than the current House'.[84] Either way, Lords reform was a stated objective of both parties, with both tying 'political reform' to the objective (in the Conservatives' words) of 'clean[ing] up Westminster'.[85] This objective was further developed by a shared commitment to the introduction of 'recall' systems to remove MPs found guilty of 'serious wrongdoing'.[86] The use of exactly the same phrase in both manifestos served to obscure the difficulties that would subsequently be faced in defining just what constituted 'serious wrongdoing'. In terms of civil liberties, there was a general repudiation of New Labour's security state in keeping with the tone of Cameron's leadership and longstanding Liberal Democrat values, culminating in the shared objective of scrapping identity cards and the Contactpoint database.[87] Both parties committed themselves to further codification of rights, though apparent rhetorical convergence concealed the reality that for the Conservatives this was a means to 'replace the Human Rights Act' whilst for the Liberal Democrats it was a process to strengthen it and part of the journey to a 'written constitution'.[88]

The manifestos reflected the personalities of the two parties' leaders: much emphasis has been laid on the personal dynamic between Cameron and Clegg supposedly underlying the formation of the coalition, but it was their impact on their parties as leaders which made it possible for there to be this opportunity in the first place. In contrast to 2005, the Conservatives now had commitments to localism and the environment, in addition to a determination to scrap identity cards, introduce House of Lords reform and reform banking regulation. The Liberal Democrats now had a commitment to fiscal responsibility – shunning their perceived

[83] *Ibid.*, p. 67. [84] Liberal Democrats, *Manifesto 2010*, p. 88.
[85] Conservative Party, *Manifesto 2010*, p. 67.
[86] *Ibid.*, p. 65; Liberal Democrats, *Manifesto 2010*, p. 89.
[87] Conservative Party, *Manifesto 2010*, p. 79; Liberal Democrats, *Manifesto 2010*, p. 94.
[88] Conservative Party, *Manifesto 2010*, p. 79; Liberal Democrats, *Manifesto 2010*, pp. 88, 94.

image as 'tax and spenders' and the freedom of movement that came from the downgrading of many traditional policies to the status of 'aspirations'. The Conservatives had also adopted the idea of the 'pupil premium' which the Liberal Democrats had originally developed. The parties' policies – notwithstanding traditional differences on Europe, nuclear energy, nuclear weapons and electoral reform – were now sufficiently close to allow the possibility of co-operation in the event of a hung parliament.

It was also a possibility that both parties anticipated, albeit with differing degrees of enthusiasm. The Liberal Democrats, aware that their best chance of a place in government rested on the eventuality of a hung parliament, undertook detailed planning.[89] A team established 'secretly' in late 2009, headed by Danny Alexander, analysed areas of convergence in party manifestos and developed coalition negotiating documents.[90] On the Conservative side, the dawning realization of the electoral mountain to climb motivated Cameron and Osborne to ask Oliver Letwin to develop plans for a hung parliament.[91] The Labour leadership, by their own admission, failed to give the prospect any serious consideration.[92] When the much-vaunted hung parliament came to be, this accurately reflected the hierarchy of preparation the three parties had engaged in. The drama of the 'five days' was, in truth, merely an outworking of the policy changes and repositionings of the previous parliament, conditioned by political arithmetic. This is not to say that coalition between the Liberal Democrats and the Conservatives was inevitable, merely to note that it was a choice which had been well prepared for, despite the politics of denial which both parties – for different reasons – subscribed to after May 2010.

The pivotal event of the five days was the 'big, open and comprehensive offer' by David Cameron to the Liberal Democrats in a speech on Friday 7 May.[93] It removed any residual doubt in Liberal Democrat minds that the Conservative leader was serious about the prospect of a full coalition, and – taken together with Nick Clegg's stated ambition to negotiate with the party with the 'most votes and the most seats' – ensured that the Liberal Democrats would open negotiations with the Conservatives first. Mandelson, for his part, was

---

[89] Yong, 'Formation of the coalition', pp. 28–9.   [90] *Ibid.*, p. 28.
[91] Elliott and Hanning, *Practically a Conservative*, pp. 385–6.
[92] Adonis, *5 Days in May*, p. 29.
[93] Adonis describes it as 'a thunderbolt' (*5 Days in May*, p. 29).

impressed, considering the move 'bold'.[94] It was thus the case that the two parties' negotiating teams met formally on the morning of Saturday 8 May in the Cabinet Office, whilst the first meeting with Labour that evening was an informal one and did not – in the eyes of the Liberal Democrats at least – constitute negotiations on an equal footing. Labour's dilatory preparations for the meeting – both in terms of the consideration of policy and the composition of the team – did not impress the Liberal Democrats, though the extent to which over the course of the following days they affected to find Labour's approach offensive and unreasonable may have been self-serving.

It is a fact, however, that the negotiations between the Conservatives and the Liberal Democrats were a success and those between the Liberal Democrats and Labour resulted in failure. Why this was so has been the subject of recrimination. Adonis' account, the last of the three 'party political' books on the negotiations to appear, implicitly accuses the Liberal Democrats of acting in bad faith and using the talks with Labour as a strategic device to extort a better deal from the Conservatives.[95] There is no doubt truth in Liberal Democrat assertions, made most forcefully by David Laws, that the Liberal Democrats found the Labour approach unprofessional and offensive (members of the Labour team, apart from not knowing that they themselves were to be in the negotiations until shortly before they took place, did not even recognize the former Liberal Democrat Chief Whip).[96] However, the extent to which this – and the varying accounts of conversations between Nick Clegg and Gordon Brown – have been played up perhaps attests to the need for Liberal Democrat negotiators to justify coalition with the Conservatives to their members and constituents.

The first of the published coalition policy documents, namely the short, informal summary agreed on 11 May, had eleven sections and was seven pages long. The sections were as follows, and in this order: deficit reduction, spending review, tax measures, banking reform, immigration, political reform, pensions and welfare, education, relations with the EU, civil liberties and the environment.[97] It was

[94] Interviewed on *Five Days That Changed Britain* (BBC). Originally broadcast 29 July 2010 (BBC2).

[95] Adonis, *5 Days in May*.   [96] *Ibid.*, p. 50.

[97] 'Conservative-Liberal Democrat coalition negotiations: Agreements reached', 11 May 2010 (accessed at www.conservatives.com/~/media/Files/Downloadable%20Files/agreement.ashx?dl=true, 8 September 2014). Reproduced in Laws, *22 Days in May*, pp. 321–33.

followed on 21 May by another document, entitled the *Coalition Agreement for Stability and Reform*, which outlined the basis of how the machinery of government would operate and the political executive be constituted.[98] The focus of both was clearly on addressing the economy and the public finances, by now a shared Conservative–Liberal Democrat goal. The emphasis on 'stability' echoed Chris Huhne's push for a full coalition, on the basis that only a full coalition would be able to guarantee the stability of government action required to tackle the crisis in the public finances and soothe the nerves of the markets.[99] It reflected what those such as Laws would later argue were the exigencies of the circumstances in which the coalition was formed and which made it possible rather than the long-term convergence of the two parties' platforms. Critical to it was the agreement that there would be an Emergency Budget and a comprehensive spending review.[100]

On 20 May, the coalition published the full policy document on the basis of which it would govern, entitled *The Coalition: Our Programme for Government*.[101] This document was notably more systematic, closer in look and feel to a party manifesto, with an accompanying slogan – 'freedom, fairness, responsibility'.[102] The order of priorities was changed, with thirty-one sections and deficit reduction now featuring in ninth place. The tone of the language was also much more positive than had been the case in the two perfunctory earlier documents, which had been situated firmly in the context of economic malaise. With the coalition now finding its feet, the *Programme for Government* sought to encapsulate the atmosphere of the famed Rose Garden press conference of 12 May. The foreword – jointly authored by Cameron and Clegg in their new roles as Prime Minister and Deputy Prime Minister – made bold claims for the 'new politics':

> As our parties have worked together it has become increasingly clear to us that, although there are differences, there is also common ground ... we have found in this coalition that our visions are not compromised by working together; they are strengthened and enhanced. That is why this coalition has the potential for

---

[98] *Coalition Agreement for Stability and Reform* (London: Cabinet Office, May 2010).
[99] Laws, *22 Days in May*, p. 266.   [100] 'Agreements reached', p. 1.
[101] HM Government, *The Coalition: Our Programme for Government* (London: Cabinet Office, 2010).
[102] *Ibid.*, p. 3.

> era-changing, convention-challenging, radical reform ... We have
> found that a combination of our parties' best ideas and attitudes
> has produced a programme for government that is more radical
> and comprehensive than our individual manifestos.[103]

The *Programme for Government* shifted gear from fiscal damage control to the 'new politics' which had clear echoes of Cameron's rhetoric from long before a hung parliament made coalition possible. It was the result of a highly centralized process; as Ben Yong notes:

> Drafting of the PfG was determined by a much smaller group of
> people than the government formation process. It was negotiated in
> detail by Lib Dem Danny Alexander and Conservative Oliver
> Letwin, who were best qualified to undertake the task, having been
> in charge of their respective parties' election manifestos. They were
> supported by Polly Mackenzie (Liberal Democrat) and James
> O'Shaughnessy (Conservative); key party political staff members
> who later became special advisers ... and by a small team of civil
> servants ... departments were only shown 'their' chapters at the
> end of the process; in many cases they were given only 12 hours to
> comment.[104]

Much has been written – at the time and subsequently – on the issue of who 'won' in the coalition negotiations. Initially, the Liberal Democrats were euphoric with the deal they felt they had obtained. Simon Hughes remarked in a BBC documentary later in 2010 that at one point in the negotiations the Liberal Democrats had felt that the 'fruit was coming off the tree so readily ... [that we should] seize the moment' due to the Conservatives' apparent enthusiasm for compromise.[105] One assessment of the winners and losers in the coalition negotiations seemed to reinforce this, stating that 'the actual outcome [of the negotiations] was further left than predicted' when considering the parties' relative standing in the legislature, and that 'by these standards the Liberal Democrats appeared to have done rather "better" than the Conservatives in the agreement'.[106] However, the authors noted that this failed to encapsulate the whole of the material in the agreement

---

[103] *Ibid.*, p. 7.   [104] Yong, 'Formation of the coalition', p. 36.
[105] Interviewed on *Five Days That Changed Britain*.
[106] Thomas Quinn, Judith Bara and John Bartle, 'The UK Coalition Agreement of 2010: Who won?', *Journal of Elections, Public Opinion and Parties*, 21:2 (2011), p. 302.

(focusing as it did on the left–right axis), and others were more sceptical of the 'deal', at least in terms of what it delivered for the smaller party. Yong notes that the relationship between manifestos and the final *Programme for Government* can 'be subject to misinterpretation. The Liberal Democrat manifesto contained well over 300 pledges, while the much larger Conservative manifesto consisted of over 550. So even though a higher proportion of the Liberal Democrats' manifesto commitments made it into the PfG, in absolute terms the PfG included more Conservative pledges.'[107] Furthermore, Yong cited another study which

> Categoris[ed] PfG pledges by whether they were Conservative; Liberal Democrat; both; neither; or a compromise between Conservatives and Liberal Democrats. In this analysis, if the total contribution of the Conservatives was taken into account, this made the PfG roughly 75 per cent Conservative.[108]

The emphasis on economic policy and addressing the deficit was not as profound in the *Programme for Government*, which was ostensibly a more positive document, but it could hardly have been more prominent in the interim agreement, with the first sub-heading entitled 'Deficit reduction':

> The parties agree that deficit reduction and continuing to ensure economic recovery is the most urgent issue facing Britain ... We have therefore agreed that there will need to be:

> – a significantly accelerated reduction in the structural deficit over the course of a Parliament, with the main burden of deficit reduction borne by reduced spending rather than increased taxes;
> – arrangements that will protect those on low incomes from the effect of public sector pay constraint and other spending constraints; and
> – protection of jobs by stopping Labour's proposed jobs tax.[109]

The interim agreement also contained the commitment to the emergency budget and the comprehensive spending review. Notwithstanding Liberal Democrat posturing during the election campaign, it was far from clear that this could really be characterized simply as 'Tory cuts' given the approach the party had taken since the publication of its 2009

---

[107] Yong, 'Formation of the Coalition', p. 37.   [108] *Ibid.*
[109] 'Agreements reached', p. 1.

pre-manifesto. If economic and fiscal policy was the defining feature of the coalition, and if it was taken to be a 'win' for the Tories – then it was a win that pre-dated the election, let alone the coalition negotiations. On public services, these were obviously a second-order priority for both parties (due to the implications of deficit reduction), but the NHS was ostensibly protected. Significantly, no mention was made of the looming reorganization under Andrew Lansley, which gave both the Liberal Democrats and the Conservative leadership greater freedom of action later when the reforms ran into trouble.[110]

The critical issues for the Liberal Democrats were agreement on electoral reform, higher education funding and nuclear energy. This might appear odd given the centrality of financial concerns in the Coalition Agreement and its attendant documents, not to mention both parties' campaigns for office. However, the first issue was critical because a coalition would not have been possible without it; indeed, Cameron only convinced his parliamentary party to back an offer of a referendum on the Alternative Vote system of election for Westminster in light of what turned out to be specious rumours of a rival offer made by Labour to the Liberal Democrats. AV was not a proportional system, and was (as Nick Clegg himself had once described it) a 'grubby little compromise',[111] giving none of the supposed 'fairness' and 'equal votes' envisaged by the Liberal Democrats' previous focus on the Single Transferable Vote. However, it would conceivably benefit the party in electoral terms and thus was the red line in negotiations, and one which Cameron accepted in terms of a proposed referendum on the issue.

Higher education funding and nuclear energy were more marginal issues in the minds of both party leaderships but they are critical to understanding which party benefited most from the agreement. The Browne Review was scheduled to report on the financing of higher education later in 2010; the interim agreement, reinforced by the *Programme for Government*, made explicit provision for Liberal Democrat MPs (and Liberal Democrat ministers) to derogate from support for the government should its recommendations contain proposals for further rises in tuition fees.[112] In relation to nuclear energy, the provisions

[110] Peter Waller and Ben Yong, 'Case studies II: Tuition fees, NHS reform, and nuclear policy', in Hazell and Yong, *Politics of Coalition*, pp. 177–84.
[111] See chapter eighteen, this volume.
[112] 'Agreements reached', p. 5; *Programme for Government*, p. 32.

were even stronger, recognizing the long-standing opposition by the party to 'any new nuclear construction ... [through] allow[ing] Liberal Democrats to maintain their opposition' in government.[113] Yet despite these arrangements, the subsequent history – the overwhelming defeat of the AV proposal in the 2011 referendum, which infamously became a 'referendum on the Liberal Democrats',[114] the introduction of higher tuition fees in a debate led by the Liberal Democrat Business Secretary, Vince Cable, and the championing of nuclear power by a Liberal Democrat Energy Secretary, Chris Huhne (who had steadfastly opposed it in speeches only months earlier) – represented defeats and U-turns on policies which whilst not always central to the leadership's view of the party, were integral to the concerns of their electoral support and activist base. Through the presence of Liberal Democrat Cabinet ministers at departments introducing policies antithetical to the classic Liberal Democrat voter Russell and Fieldhouse described, the Conservatives also ensured that the Liberal Democrats would take the blame for the policies disproportionately – notwithstanding the number of Liberal Democrat MPs who would rebel. In political terms, it was masterly. The Tories had their 'fall guy'.[115]

The 'wins' the smaller party achieved – such as the raising of the tax threshold and the introduction of the pupil premium – were difficult to 'sell' against the media's blanket coverage of purported 'treachery' over tuition fees and the environment. The pupil premium was also lost to the Liberal Democrat public narrative, not least because the Conservatives had already appropriated it for their manifesto before the election. The substantive constitutional change – the introduction of fixed-term parliaments – neither fired the public imagination nor was conceived as anything other than a political fix to secure the coalition's future in the legislature. The Conservative 'wins' by contrast were numerous, and some would alienate Liberal Democrats, not least the emphasis on an immigration cap.[116]

The immigration cap was one aspect of the Tory attempt to deal with their problems on Europe; although the cap had to be aimed

---

[113] 'Agreements reached', p. 7.

[114] Mike Finn, 'AV: A referendum on the Liberal Democrats', *YouGov-Cambridge Programme*, 11 May 2011 (accessed at http://cambridge.yougov.com/news/2011/05/01/av-referendum-liberal-democrats, 8 September 2014).

[115] Yong, 'Formation of the Coalition', p. 43.

[116] *Programme for Government*, p. 21.

at non-EU migrants due to European freedom-of-movement rights, immigration had risen up the public's priority list largely due to large-scale immigration to the UK from the EU following the accession of the new 'A8' Eastern European member states in 2004.[117] Perversely the policy set out in the agreement could not address this, but Europe was an issue where there would inevitably be tensions between the two parties and the section on Europe was a mélange of ideas in stark contrast to one another including the 'referendum lock', support for further enlargement and the possibility of a 'United Kingdom Sovereignty Bill'.[118] More generally in foreign affairs there was room for agreement – international development was a symbol of Cameron's party modernization strategy and the commitment to 0.7 per cent of GDP as development aid was a genuinely shared one, at least on the part of the party leaderships and Andrew Mitchell, the incoming Conservative secretary of state.[119]

Beyond policy, the *Coalition Agreement for Stability and Reform* – the 'rules' for the formation and composition of the executive – ensured that the great offices of state remained in the hands of the Conservatives, not least because in a perhaps vainglorious move Nick Clegg accepted the title of Deputy Prime Minister without the power base of a major department. Their other posts – Business, Energy, the Scotland Office and first Laws' and then Alexander's tenures as Chief Secretary to the Treasury – were a mixture of second-order Cabinet departments in terms of status, or in Alexander's case second-order posts in departmental point of fact. As will be discussed elsewhere in this volume, the mechanisms for managing intra-executive dissent, notably the Coalition Committee, fell into disuse due to the success of the 'Quad', the four-man body made up of Cameron, Osborne, Clegg and Alexander which would, in effect, run the coalition government as a whole.[120]

According to Eimear O'Casey, the allocation of ministerial portfolios beyond cabinet-level representation represented a process known as 'ministerial twinning'.[121] In the most common example, Liberal Democrat junior ministers were expected to act as party representatives

[117] Carlos Vargas-Silva, *Migration Flows of A8 and other EU Migrants to and from the UK* (Oxford: Oxford University Migration Observatory, April 2014).
[118] *Programme for Government*, p. 13.   [119] *Ibid.*, p. 22.
[120] See chapter four, this volume.
[121] Eimear O'Casey, 'The experience of coalition: domestic and abroad', in Hazell and Yong, *Politics of Coalition*, p. 19.

in departments where there was a Conservative Cabinet minister. O'Casey further notes that:

> A further strategy is 'cross-cutting', whereby a junior partner minister holds a portfolio across several departments ... Its effectiveness is debatable ... Cross-cutting portfolios are likely to be even more demanding for junior ministers, who find it hard enough to make an impact in just one department.[122]

The portfolio allocations represented a little of both: though Clegg was not a junior minister, he was certainly cross-cutting, and when his key ally David Laws returned to the government in September 2012 his was a cross-cutting brief between the Department for Education and the Cabinet Office. Ministerial twinning and cross-cutting were examples of international experience of coalition government being brought to bear in the British context.[123] The Liberal Democrats, though not the Conservatives, had spent years poring over foreign (and particularly European) coalition models both as preparation for the reality and in order to better make the arguments for the only form of government likely to offer the Liberal Democrats a pathway to power. Yong notes that an alternative model – depth – was available to the party, but they chose breadth instead. He cites a damning comment from an anonymous Conservative early in the life of the government:

> From a governing point of view, [breadth] may be right. But from a political strategy point of view, I think if they said, 'Okay. We're going to have some slightly Lib-Demy stuff: we're going to have International Development, we're going to have Energy ... and we're going to have Education or Health. Then we'll go back to the British people and say, "Look at the things we did. Give us more". I think that's an easier way to carve out a distinctive legacy ... than it is to say, 'Oh, well. The pupil premium was us, and we stopped them doing this and we got them doing that.'[124]

It was prophetic. One Liberal Democrat minister, speaking under condition of anonymity, put it bluntly to Yong: the Coalition Agreement, in short, was 'a completely duff deal'. The fate of many of the Liberal Democrat 'wins' – on electoral reform and the House of Lords most notably – would prove the unnamed minister right.

---

[122] *Ibid.*   [123] *Ibid.*   [124] Yong, 'Formation of the coalition', p. 43.

their own terms. Cameron could not convince his party to 'modernize' in the way he initially envisaged; failing here, nor could he ultimately convince the electorate that his party had, in fact, modernized. Clegg was unable to convince his party to abandon cherished policy pledges central to the party's identity, and despite the ephemeral moment of 'Cleggmania' following the first prime ministerial debate of the election campaign, neither was he able to convince the country that it was time to embrace a new 'main' party. And yet, despite both leaders losing the election, they ended up in power together. 'A new politics', as Cameron termed it, was foisted upon an electorate who had not chosen it. The deal hatched between the two party leaderships was a programme of government which sought to build consensus, but which lacked a mandate. The extent to which it could be implemented as anything other than a legislative menu – with all the pitfalls that entailed – would have significant implications for both parties' futures and the assessment of the 'coalition effect' on British politics as a whole.

2 THE COALITION AND THE CONSTITUTION

MARTIN LOUGHLIN AND CAL VINEY

On 12 May 2010, after five days of negotiations following the general election, the Conservatives and Liberal Democrats concluded a *Coalition Agreement for Stability and Reform*.[1] Since many conventional practices of governing, especially relating to Cabinet government and collective responsibility, have evolved in the context of single-party majority governments, the formation of a coalition government, the first in peacetime since the 1930s, might itself be viewed as a constitutional innovation. But of perhaps greater significance is the fact that the Liberal Democrats were unwilling to enter into coalition without a formal agreement being struck over certain measures of constitutional reform.[2] For the first time in modern political history a government of the United Kingdom was founded on a binding commitment to introduce a programme of constitutional reform.

The ambition underpinning this joint undertaking should not be underestimated. That the British constitution presents itself as a flexible scheme of institutional arrangements that has evolved from habitual practice, with many aspects of this scheme being susceptible to change through the ordinary processes of legislation, is widely understood.

---

[1] *Coalition Agreement for Stability and Reform* (London: Cabinet Office, May 2010).

[2] David Laws, *22 Days in May: The Birth of the Lib Dem–Conservative Coalition* (London: Biteback, 2010), esp. pp. 298–9, 319–20; Rob Wilson, *5 Days to Power: The Journey to Coalition Britain* (London: Biteback, 2010), p. 160: 'the Lib Dem strategy was simple: focus on getting the constitutional package they wanted (specifically voting reform), and don't waste political capital elsewhere that might distract matters'.

But there is considerable distance between conservative and liberal philosophies of government. Conservatives believe that political values emerge from a tradition of civility, whereas liberals place greater faith in the power of reason; conservatives regard law, whether in the form of judicial precedent or enacted legislation, as codified social practice, whereas for liberals law specifies general standards of right conduct; conservatives believe that good government rests on an elite conscious of its responsibilities, whereas liberals, being suspicious of all power-holders, advocate the need for formal institutional limitations on the exercise of all aspects of governmental power. The Conservatives are a unionist party who believe in strong government formed on a simple majority principle reflected through the institution of a sovereign Parliament. The Liberal Democrats, by contrast, advocate a federal principle of sharing power across the various levels of government, legitimated by elections based on proportional representation.

There is no denying the fact that the main impetus for coalition was the need to agree an austerity programme in the face of the financial crisis, and on these matters the two parties were not so far apart.[3] But the critical issue on which the formation of the coalition rested was that of constitutional reform and on this, and notwithstanding a degree of overlap of policies, the distance between the parties was considerable. These differences were resolved and formally agreed in the coalition government's programme for constitutional reform. In this chapter, we briefly consider how their manifesto commitments were converted into a programme for government.[4] We then examine the main initiatives taken to implement that programme and finally try to draw some general conclusions about this experience.

From manifesto commitments to programme for government

Although the Liberal Democrat demand for electoral reform was the pivot on which the post-election negotiating process revolved, each of the parties included in their election manifestos a package of commitments

---

[3] This is especially so given the influence within the Liberal Democrat leadership of the so-called 'Orange Book' faction: see Paul Marshall and David Laws (eds.), *The Orange Book: Reclaiming Liberalism* (London: Profile, 2004).

[4] For more detailed background see chapter one, this volume.

on constitutional reform. Of these, not surprisingly, the Liberal Democrat policies were the more radical.

The Liberal Democrat manifesto had proposed the introduction of a proportional voting system (with a preference for a Single Transferable Vote (STV)), a consequential reduction in the number of MPs in the Commons to 500, the lowering of the voting age to 16, the establishment of fixed-term parliaments, and the replacement of the House of Lords with 'a fully-elected second chamber with considerably fewer members than the current House'.[5] They also advocated further empowerment of the Scottish Parliament and a significant extension of the powers of the Welsh National Assembly, so it could become 'a true Welsh Parliament'.[6] Most strikingly, the Liberal Democrats pledged to draft a written constitution for Britain, one that might be developed in a citizens' convention and confirmed through a referendum.[7]

The recurrent theme is a desire to strengthen the principle of popular sovereignty. This is exhibited in their policies of involving citizens in constitutional forums and specifically in their advocacy of the use of referendums to legitimate certain constitutional reforms. Consequently, they also committed themselves to 'an in/out referendum the next time a British government signs up for fundamental change in the relationship between the UK and the EU'.[8] The Liberal Democrats presented themselves as 'the only party which believes in radical political reform to reinvent the way our country is run and put power back where it belongs: into the hands of people'.[9]

Though less radical, the Conservative Party manifesto also contained proposals for constitutional change. It promised that a Conservative government would 'equalize the size of constituency electorates' so as to ensure that 'every vote will have equal value', though it remained convinced of the need to retain 'the first-past-the-post system for Westminster elections because it gives voters the chance to kick out a government they are fed up with'.[10] It pledged to 'work to build a consensus for a mainly-elected second chamber to replace the current House of Lords'.[11] And it stated that 'we will not stand in the way of the

---

[5] Liberal Democrats, *Liberal Democrat Manifesto 2010* (London: Liberal Democrats, 2010), p. 88.

[6] *Ibid.*, p. 92.   [7] *Ibid.*, p. 88.   [8] *Ibid.*, p. 66.   [9] *Ibid.*, p. 87.

[10] Conservative Party, *Invitation to Join the Government of Britain: The Conservative Manifesto 2010* (London: Conservative Party, 2010), p. 67.

[11] *Ibid.*

referendum on further legislative powers requested by the Welsh Assembly'.[12] But the manifesto also expressed the convictions of a party wedded to the union and parliamentary sovereignty. So although reference was made to possible further devolution of powers to Scotland, it reiterated the point that 'the Conservative Party is passionate about the Union and . . . will never do anything to put it at risk'.[13] Similarly, with respect to relations with the European Union, they pledged to 'introduce a United Kingdom Sovereignty Bill to make it clear that ultimate authority stays in this country, in our Parliament' and 'to amend the European Communities Act 1972 to ensure that there could be no further transfers of powers or competences to the EU without a referendum first being held'.[14]

After the electoral results yielded no overall majority, intense negotiations commenced. Superficially, there was significant overlap in their respective agendas for constitutional change, especially on further devolution, on House of Lords reform, the use of referendums to decide on the UK's position in the EU, and on a commitment to some form of electoral reform. The glaring difference was over the prospect of moving from a first-past-the-post system to a system of proportional representation. This became the main issue on which the prospect of coalition revolved. The bottom line was that the Liberal Democrats insisted that without the promise of a referendum to be held no later than June 2011 to give the British people the choice of the adoption of a 'fairer voting system' no deal would be possible.[15] The Conservatives quickly recognized that a referendum on the Alternative Vote system (the only move from a simple majority they were prepared to contemplate) 'was the deal maker or the deal breaker',[16] and on this they sought and obtained parliamentary party support. They therefore were able to offer to introduce a whipped government Bill for a referendum on AV, though it was accepted that party members would remain free to campaign for or against the AV proposal.[17]

The Coalition Agreement of 12 May laid out the general terms, but it was the policy document released on 20 May 2010, entitled *The*

---

[12] *Ibid.*, p. 83.   [13] *Ibid.*, p. 83.   [14] *Ibid.*, pp. 114, 113.

[15] Laws, 22 *Days in May*, p. 320.

[16] William Hague MP (lead negotiator on the Conservative team), Interview in BBC2 Documentary, *Five Days that Changed Britain* (BBC2; originally broadcast 29 July 2010).

[17] Wilson, *5 Days to Power*, pp. 220–2; Laws, 22 *Days in May*, p. 299.

Coalition: Our Programme for Government, that specified in more detail the package of reforms to be introduced.[18] This document superseded the party manifestos and in certain cases directly contradicted their proposals; although it became the key policy framework document of the government, it had not acquired its mandate from the electorate. The word 'constitution' is never mentioned in its thirty-one sections, with the main proposals for change coming in section 24, headed 'political reform'. This opened with a dramatic statement: 'The Government believes that our political system is broken.'

One consequence of the formation of the coalition government is that certain adjustments to standard operating procedures were required. Some of these had been contemplated in advance. In February 2010, for example, PM Gordon Brown tasked Sir Gus O'Donnell, the Cabinet Secretary, with producing a Cabinet Manual, specifying the rules and practices of Cabinet government, and this document included a section on procedures to be followed in the event of a hung parliament.[19] Further, recognizing that the principle of collective responsibility might be strained, the *Programme for Government* also identified five issues on which the parties could agree to differ: in addition to the AV proposal, these were university tuition fees, renewal of Trident, nuclear power, and provision for a tax allowance for married couples. The main implications of this modification were addressed in a third document, published on 21 May, which specified the procedures and principles on which the parties 'would jointly maintain in office Her Majesty's Government'.[20]

This third document claimed that there is 'no constitutional difference between a Coalition Government and a single party Government' and that it was mere working practices that needed adapting. It stated that government appointments would be allocated between the parties on a roughly proportionate basis, and would be agreed between David Cameron, as Prime Minister (PM), and Nick Clegg, as his Deputy (DPM). All Cabinet committees were to include representation from

---

[18] *The Coalition: Our Programme for Government* (London: Cabinet Office, May 2010).

[19] Sir Gus O'Donnell, *The Cabinet Manual – Draft: A Guide to Laws, Conventions and Rules on the Operation of Government* (London: Cabinet Office, 2010). For analysis see Vernon Bogdanor, *The Coalition and the Constitution* (Oxford: Hart, 2011), pp. 11–24.

[20] *Coalition Agreement for Stability and Reform* (London: Cabinet Office, May 2010), Introduction.

each party. It was also intended that a new Cabinet committee, the Coalition Committee, would be established to manage coalition issues but in practice this formal committee hardly ever met. Its role was taken over by an informal body that had not been contemplated in coalition negotiations. Called 'the Quad', the name given to regular meetings between the PM, DPM, Chancellor of the Exchequer and Chief Secretary to the Treasury, this body operated in effect as an inner Cabinet.[21]

It might be noted finally that as DPM Nick Clegg chose not to head a department and instead defined his role as having oversight across government. Crucially, Clegg assumed control of the constitutional reform programme and, since he was based in the Cabinet Office, eighty staff from the Constitution Directorate in the Ministry of Justice were reassigned to his office to offer official support for the delivery of that programme.[22] We now turn to consider the implementation of this programme.

Fixed-term parliaments

According to the Septennial Act 1715, as amended by the Parliament Act 1911, if a Parliament was not dissolved in the period up to five years after the day it is summoned to meet it automatically expires. Earlier dissolutions were within the Crown's prerogative power and by convention were exercised on the advice of the PM. Many felt that this power of the incumbent PM effectively to determine the date of the next election gave the governing party a strategic political and electoral advantage.[23] The Liberal Democrats, though not the Conservatives, had long opposed the maintenance of this power. But a reform proposal was agreed relatively amicably between the parties,[24] with the Coalition

---

[21] For analysis of the functioning of Cabinet government under the coalition see Robert Hazell and Ben Yong, *The Politics of Coalition: How the Conservative–Liberal Democrat Government Works* (Oxford: Hart, 2012), ch. 4 (see chapter four, this volume]

[22] Hazell and Yong, *Politics of Coalition*, p. 157.

[23] On whether it has in fact done so, see Bogdanor, *The Coalition*, pp. 114–15.

[24] Although the Conservative Party manifesto was silent on fixed-term parliaments, in 2009 David Cameron had stated that the Conservatives would 'seriously consider the option of fixed-term parliaments when there's a majority government': David Cameron, 'A new politics: Electoral reform' (*The Guardian*, 25 May 2009). The Labour

Agreement providing for the establishment of five-year fixed-term parliaments.[25] This required the repeal of the earlier legislation and modification of the prerogative power of dissolution and its replacement with powers vested in the House of Commons.

This reform was implemented in the Fixed-term Parliaments Act 2011. Introduced in the House of Commons in July 2010, the Bill was the subject of critical reports from three select committees.[26] Despite the Coalition Agreement, it faced intense opposition from some Conservative backbenchers in the Commons and also in the Lords, where Labour peers argued that the appropriate term was four rather than five years. Yet it survived unscathed and actualized several constitutional reforms.

First, it fixed the date of the next general election as 7 May 2015 (s.1(2)). It also fixed the date of each following general parliamentary election as the first Thursday in May five years from the date of the previous election (s.1(3)). This means that even if a Parliament does not reach its full five-year term (under provisions set out below), the period is reset, with each new Parliament being accorded a new fixed five-year term. Provision is made for the PM to extend the period by a further two months, but this is achieved by introducing a statutory instrument subject to the affirmative resolution procedure in both the Lords and the Commons (s.1(5)–(7)).

The Act is in a sense misnamed since it also makes provision for the holding of an early general election. This can be achieved either by the House of Commons passing such a motion with a two-thirds majority in favour of an early election (s.2(1)),[27] or passing a motion,

Party, it might be noted, also supported the establishment of fixed-term parliaments in its 2010 manifesto.

[25] *Programme For Government*, p. 26.

[26] Political and Constitutional Reform Committee, *Fixed Term Parliament Bill* (Second Report of Session 2010–11, House of Commons, 9 September 2010); Government response (Cm 7951, November 2010); House of Lords Constitution Committee, *Fixed Terms Parliament Bill* (HL 69, Eighth Report of Session 2010–11, 16 December 2010); Government response (Cm 8011, 28 February 2011); Delegated Powers and Regulatory Reform Committee, *Tenth Report of Session 2010–11* (HL 100, 10 February 2011).

[27] The Coalition Agreement had provided that dissolution could occur if 55 per cent or more of the House votes in favour. This was criticized as a political fix since a subsequent Labour/Lib Dem agreement could command the support of only 53 per cent of MPs, whereas the Conservative/Lib Dem coalition constitutes 58 per cent. The two-thirds threshold thus requires cross-party agreement.

by simple majority, that the 'House has no confidence in Her Majesty's Government' (s.2(4)). In the latter case, an early election must take place unless within fourteen days a subsequent motion of confidence in a government is passed (s.2(3)). This provides for the possibility of a new government being formed within that period. With respect to these early triggering mechanisms, the election date remains set by royal proclamation on the advice of the Prime Minister (s.2(7)). Dissolution of Parliament will then occur seventeen working days before that date (s.3(1)).

Given the provisions that make it clear that 'Parliament can not otherwise be dissolved' (s.3(2)), the 2011 Act shifts the UK's constitutional position from one in which the power of dissolution of Parliament involves the exercise of a Crown prerogative to one in which the House of Commons asserts the power to dissolve itself.[28] It is not self-evident that an arrangement that fixes in advance a five-year term of a parliament will always be beneficial; governments often run out of initiative and live on beyond their 'natural' term. But although the Liberal Democrats considered the reform a corollary of a scheme of proportional election and a Parliament with a multiplicity of parties, it might be noted that the immediate motivation was not constitutional but political: it was designed to protect the minority coalition party from the possibility of the PM using this power to dissolve Parliament at a time that might advance the dominant Conservative Party's electoral interest.[29]

From a constitutional perspective, Vernon Bogdanor has argued that the reform exhibits a tension between the principles of parliamentary government and popular government. Once we enter an era of multi-party politics, 'the fact that a government enjoys the support of parliament does not necessarily mean that it is acting in accordance with democratic principles'. That is, a coalition formed after the election (and therefore one which voters have not had the opportunity to endorse) or an adjustment in coalition partners during a parliamentary term may uphold the principle of parliamentary

---

[28] It might be noted that, although the proposal was contained in the Coalition Agreement, because the Bill was being promoted by the DPM, civil servants felt it necessary to brief the PM separately about the amount of power the PM was relinquishing: see Hazell and Yong, *Politics of Coalition*, p. 163.

[29] Laws, *22 Days in May*, p. 184.

government but not that of popular government. And a rule that makes early dissolution more difficult may promote parliamentary deal-making and be 'deleterious because it makes an appeal to the people more difficult'.[30] In the words of a former French Prime Minister, the ability to dissolve 'is not a menace to universal suffrage, but its safeguard'.[31] In short, the reform does not intrinsically support the principle of popular sovereignty.

Voting reform

Prior to the general election the Conservatives were stridently opposed to any change to the first-past-the-post voting system. The Liberal Democrats by contrast had expressed their intention to 'change politics and abolish safe seats by introducing a fair, more proportional voting system for MPs', with a preference for STV.[32] Neither party manifesto had mentioned holding a referendum on the issue. As we have indicated, this became the critical issue on which the Coalition Agreement revolved.

The deal, as stated in the Coalition Agreement, was that the government 'will bring forward a Referendum Bill on electoral reform, which includes provision for the introduction of the Alternative Vote'. Both Parliamentary parties in both Houses would be whipped to support the Bill, though 'without prejudice to the positions parties will take during such a referendum'.[33] This compromise left the parties in the position of bringing forward a major change that neither truly favoured. Indeed, the proposal to hold a referendum on the adoption of AV had first been included in the Labour government's Constitutional Reform and Governance Bill of 2010, though this had foundered owing to lack of parliamentary time. This proposal nevertheless offered the best chance for Liberal Democrats to achieve a change in a voting mechanism that bolstered the two-party system.

The Bill to authorize the referendum was introduced very swiftly on 22 July 2010, only ten weeks after the formation of the

[30] Bogdanor, *The Coalition*, p. 121.
[31] Pierre Waldeck-Rousseau (1902): cited in Bogdanor, *ibid.*
[32] Liberal Democrats, *Manifesto 2010*, pp. 87–8.
[33] *Programme For Government*, p. 27.

government and without any prior white paper or consultation period and without much Cabinet committee discussion.[34] The government had aimed to ensure maximum cross-party support by incorporating the referendum proposal together with the proposal to reduce and equalize parliamentary constituencies as two parts of the same Bill. This Bill was tightly whipped, generating considerable backbench resentment. It too was the subject of three reports from parliamentary committees, which were critical of the tight timetable and lack of consultation.[35] And it emerged unscathed as the Parliamentary Voting System and Constituencies Act 2011 (PVSC). The process offers a clear illustration of how a central plank of the coalition's programme had, for vital political reasons, to be railroaded through Parliament.

Part I of the PVSC Act provided for the 2015 general election to operate on the AV, so long as that voting system was supported at a referendum to be held on 5 May 2011 (s.8(1), (2)).[36] But the Act also linked the commencement of the AV provisions to the measures for constituency equalization in Part II (and examined below). This meant that AV would not become operational until the equalization measures had been introduced (s.8(1)(b)). By contrast, the equalization arrangements could take effect even if the AV referendum failed.

The proposed AV reform was intended to shift from the current system, in which the candidate who achieves the highest number of votes wins, to what is technically an optional preferential system. This gives electors the option to place numbers in order of preference against the names of some or all of the candidates, with the candidate with the fewest number of first preferences being eliminated and their ballots reallocated by preference and the process repeated until one

---

[34] Hazell and Yong, *Politics of Coalition*, p. 160.

[35] Political and Constitutional Reform Committee, *Parliamentary Voting Systems and Constituencies Bill* (HC 437, Third Report of Session 2010–11, 7 October 2010); Welsh Affairs Committee, *The Implications for Wales of the Government's Proposals on Constitutional Reform* (HC 495, First Report of Session 2010–11, 21 October 2010); Select Committee on the Constitution, *Parliamentary Voting Systems and Constituencies Bill: Report* (HL 58, Seventh Report of Session 2010–11, 10 November 2010).

[36] In this respect it differed from the earlier proposal in the Labour government's bill, which provided for a consultative pre-legislative referendum.

candidate has more votes than the other remaining candidates put together (s.9).

The precise question to be determined by the AV referendum had not been resolved in coalition negotiations and the question proposed on the Bill's publication was subsequently amended after referral to the Electoral Commission.[37] The question to the electorate on 5 May 2011, in the UK's first binding referendum, read: 'At present, the UK uses the "first-past-the-post" system to elect MPs to the House of Commons. Should the "alternative vote" system be used instead?' The answer given by the electorate was overwhelmingly negative. On a turnout of 42.2 per cent, 67.9 per cent voted against change, with only 32.1 per cent voting in favour.[38]

The impact of this result was profound. AV may not have been the chosen system of the Liberal Democrats but it had become the centrepiece of the Coalition Agreement and they no doubt hoped that, once adopted, it might open the way to further voting reform. In reality, the outcome has knocked back any possibility of Westminster voting reform for the foreseeable future. Since they had been warned that the referendum could not be won without an extended period of public deliberation,[39] the Liberal Democrats must take responsibility for trying to push through an important item of constitutional business so quickly. This failure also had a major impact on coalition dynamics. That the coalition partners had openly and aggressively campaigned on opposite sides created severe strains. The subsequent Liberal Democrat inquiry attached major responsibility to 'the Conservatives' desire to win at all costs' and their belief that 'the Tory leadership clearly decided their party unity was a higher priority than Coalition harmony'.[40] The episode damaged relations between the coalition partners and had a significant impact on the subsequent implementation of the constitutional reform programme.

---

[37] Electoral Commission, *Referendum on the UK Parliamentary Voting System: Report of Views of the Electoral Commission on the Proposed Referendum Question* (Electoral Commission, 2010).

[38] For details see: Electoral Commission, *Referendum on the Voting System for UK Parliamentary Elections: Report on the May 2011 Referendum* (Electoral Commission, October 2011). For analysis see chapter twenty-one, this volume.

[39] Hazell and Yong, *Politics of Coalition*, p. 162.

[40] James Gurling, *Liberal Democrats Consultative Session: Election Review* (Policy Unit, Liberal Democrats, August 2011), p. 7.

Constituency reform

The impact of damaged coalition relations was eventually to be felt with respect to the implementation of Part II of the PVSC Act. As indicated, Part II had provided for a reduction in the number of seats in the Commons from 650 to 600 (s.11). This reduction, which also required each constituency to be not less than 95 per cent and not more than 105 per cent of the UK electoral quota (s.11(2)), was to be put into effect through a boundary review. Consequently, the Welsh, Scottish, Northern Ireland and England Boundary Commissions had been required to issue their first periodic report by 1 October 2013 and thereafter to report every five years (s.10(3)). This tight initial timetable was determined by the objective of bringing about the reduction in constituencies in time for the 2015 election.

The justification for these reforms was that Commons membership had grown from 625 in 1950 to 650 by 2010, even though a number of devolved bodies had recently been established. Equalization of constituency size was touted as a democratic measure: one person, one vote of equal value. But the measure could have an impact on parliamentary business: reducing the number of MPs while retaining the number of Ministerial positions was likely to diminish the effectiveness of parliamentary scrutiny. Also, an arithmetical equality of constituency size might be achieved only at the cost of cutting across the natural boundaries of integrated local communities. What can be said with some certainty, however, is that equalization of constituencies would work to the Conservatives' political advantage.[41]

Such comments are, however, speculative, since later political events came to render this component of constitutional reform impotent, at least as concerns the coalition's first term. This is because in January 2013 Liberal Democrat peers supported a Labour amendment to the government's Electoral Registration and Administration Bill, the effect of which was to defer the timetable for boundary reviews from 2013 to (at the earliest) 2018. The Conservatives sought to reverse this controversial interference by the Lords in electoral processes to the Commons, but were defeated by 334 to 292 in a Commons vote, with Liberal Democrat Ministers voting for the first time against their

---

[41] See Bogdanor, *The Coalition*, pp. 84–9.

Conservative colleagues on a government Bill. On 31 January, the Boundary Commissions consequently announced the cancellation of their 2013 review. It remains uncertain whether, and on what basis, the 2018 review will be conducted.

The cause of this split between coalition partners was not the delayed fallout of oppositional campaigning over the AV referendum. Rather, it was the result of the failure of the Liberal Democrats to gain Conservative support for reforms to the House of Lords which were introduced in 2012 (and which are considered below). The Liberal Democrats viewed the withdrawal of Conservative support for an elected upper house as amounting to a major breach of the Coalition Agreement. Maintaining that the proposals to alter the make-up of the Commons and the Lords were part of a common package of constitutional reforms advocated in the 2010 Agreement, they argued that the withdrawal of Conservative backbench support on Lords reform violated their coalition commitments. With the Conservatives protesting that constituency and Lords reforms were separate issues,[42] this dispute exposed a major political fault line, one that was undermining the success of the coalition's constitutional reform programme.

House of Lords reform

The status of a hereditary House of Lords has been a highly contentious matter for over a century. The Preamble to the Parliament Act 1911, which removed the House of Lords' power to veto legislation and replaced it with a power only to delay, had expressed a future intention to replace that chamber with one constituted on a popular basis. Yet until the end of the twentieth century no action had been taken to deliver on that pledge; instead the House had been able to acquire a second life by virtue of the Life Peerages Act 1958, which had the effect of giving party leaders the power to make patronage appointments. The House of Lords Act 1999, which removed the right of hereditary peers

---

[42] Lord Strathclyde, Leader of the House of Lords 2010–13, went so far as to call the Liberal Democrat action to delay the boundary review 'an outrage . . . extraordinary behaviour': see Select Committee on the Constitution, *Constitutional Implications of Coalition Government* (HL 130, 5th Report of Session 2013–14, 12 February 2014), para. 71.

to sit and replaced it with an ability to elect ninety-two of their number to represent their interests in the House, was supposed to be the first step towards more comprehensive reform. But that initiative reached stalemate over questions of composition and mode of membership, and it was only with the formation of the coalition government that Lords reform was placed back on the agenda.

Both coalition parties committed themselves to bringing about reform, with the Conservatives pledging to 'work to build a consensus for a mainly-elected second chamber'[43] and the Liberal Democrats supporting the establishment of 'a fully-elected second chamber with considerably fewer members'.[44] There therefore appeared to be a clear consensus and this was reflected in the Coalition Agreement commitment to 'establish a committee to bring forward proposals for a wholly or mainly elected upper chamber on the basis of proportional representation'.[45]

Detailed proposals for reform, including a draft Bill, were published on 17 May 2011.[46] This provided for the establishment of a hybrid House of Lords with 300 members, 240 of whom would be elected and 60 appointed, with 12 Bishops sitting as ex-officio members. Elected members would serve for a fifteen-year term (i.e. three election cycles under the fixed-term parliament reforms) and would be elected by STV. Appointed members would be nominated by a Statutory Appointments Commission for recommendation by the PM for appointment by the Queen. In April 2012, the Joint Committee on House of Lords Reform reported on the proposed reforms.[47] It recommended that, although the proposed 80–20 split between elected and appointed members was appropriate, lowering the number of Lords to 300 was too drastic and a figure of 450 would be more appropriate. It also concluded that the Bill failed adequately to protect the primacy of the Commons and that 'in view of the significance of the constitutional change brought forward for an elected House of Lords, the Government should submit the decision to a referendum'.[48]

---

43 Conservative Party, *Manifesto 2010*, p. 67.

44 Liberal Democrats, *Manifesto 2010*, p. 88.

45 *Programme For Government*, p. 27.

46 *House of Lords Reform Draft Bill* (Cm 8077, May 2011).

47 Joint Committee on House of Lords Reform, *Draft House of Lords Reform Bill* (Report, Session 2010–12, Vol. 1; HL 284–I, HC 1313–I, 23 April 2012).

48 *Ibid.*, p. 108.

Following the Committee's report, a Bill was introduced in July 2012.[49] This included many of the reforms set out in the initial draft Bill. It provided for the creation of elected members, elected under a semi-open list system that would allow electors to vote either for a specific member or a party. Elected members would serve non-renewable fifteen-year terms. This reform was to be implemented through a gradual three-stage process which would move the House from an appointed to a predominantly elected chamber. In the first phase, 120 members would be elected and 30 appointed and they would serve alongside ministerial and transitional members; in the second electoral period, the total would increase to 240 elected members with 60 appointed members; and finally, in the third electoral period, there would be 360 elected members, 90 appointed members, and up to 12 Lords spiritual (combined with ministerial members, but including no further transitional members). Appointed members were to be recommended by a Statutory Appointments Commission. Reflecting concerns expressed in the Joint Committee Report on the issue of Commons' primacy, the Bill also provided that the Parliament Acts would apply to the reformed House of Lords.

The House of Lords Reform Bill had its second reading in the Commons on 9–10 July 2012. Although the government won the second reading vote, more than ninety Conservative MPs voted against. Consequently, the government did not move its programme motion, which meant that the Bill was not sent to committee. Instead, on 6 August, Nick Clegg announced that the Bill would not proceed further. On 3 September 2012 Clegg confirmed that it had been withdrawn.[50]

These developments caused understandable anger within Liberal Democrat ranks, with Clegg complaining that in the face of manifesto commitments and the Coalition Agreement, and despite 'painstaking efforts' being made to construct a reform package that could elicit widespread support, Conservative backbenchers had united with Labour to block any further progress.[51] Claiming that their actions constituted a fundamental breach of the Coalition Agreement,

---

[49] House of Lords Reform Bill (HC Bill 52, Session 2012–13).

[50] See Paul Bowers, 'House of Lords Reform Bill 2012–13: Decision not to proceed' (House of Commons Library Standard Note SN06405, 25 September 2012) (accessed at www.parliament.uk/briefing-papers/SN06405, 6 November 2014).

[51] 'House of Lords reform: Nick Clegg's statement in full', *BBC News online*, 6 August 2012 (accessed at www.bbc.co.uk/news/uk-politics-19146853, 6 November 2014).

he maintained that the Liberal Democrats would, as a consequence, withdraw their support for the equalization of constituencies legislation.[52] That pledge was made good in the following January when, as has been explained, the Liberal Democrats voted with Labour to scuttle the boundary review reporting date of 2013, thereby preventing the 2015 general election from being held according to the proposed new equalized constituencies.

After the failure of the Lords Reform Bill, the Political and Constitutional Reform Committee opened an inquiry that sought to ascertain whether a consensus might be reached on certain smaller-scale changes to the composition of the House of Lords. Its Report recommended a number of relatively minor changes, such as enacting powers to expel peers convicted of serious offences and to remove persistent non-attendees.[53] But any hope of more basic reform to the second chamber seems presently to have evaporated. Meanwhile, contrary to the coalition intention of reducing the size of the House of Lords, the PM has been very active in using his prerogative powers to appoint new peers. Having created 161 peerages overall by October 2013, Cameron has been creating new peerages at the fastest rate for at least 200 years.[54] At the same time, the Appointments Commission method of appointing 'people's peers' seems to have run out of steam;[55] from an average rate of appointment of five or six per annum up to 2010, it has since dropped off significantly to a rate of less than two per annum.[56]

---

[52] Ibid.

[53] House of Commons Political and Constitutional Reform Committee, *House of Lords Reform: What's Next?* (HC 251, Ninth Report of Session 2013–14, 17 October 2013).

[54] See: David Beamish, *United Kingdom Peerage Creations 1801 to 2014: A List Compiled by David Beamish* (accessed at www.peerages.info/admintable.htm, 6 November 2014). Since October 2013, only one new peer had been created to July 2014, but on 8 August 2014 it was announced that twenty-two new peers would be appointed, taking the size of the House of Lords to almost 800 and making it, after China's National People's Congress, the largest legislative chamber in the world: see 'Karren Brady and Sir Stuart Rose among new life peers', *BBC News*, 8 August 2014 (accessed at www.bbc.co.uk/news/uk-politics-28703150, 6 November 2014).

[55] The House of Lords Appointments Commission was established in 2000 as an advisory body to make recommendations to the PM for non-political nominations of people with a distinguished record of achievement and who would be able to make an effective contribution to the work of the House. See: House of Lords Appointments Commission (http://lordsappointments.independent.gov.uk, accessed 6 November 2014).

[56] Ibid. (http://lordsappointments.independent.gov.uk/appointments-so-far.aspx).

Notwithstanding the high hopes expressed in the Coalition Agreement of bringing about fundamental reform to the second chamber, that prospect seems as far away as ever.

Sovereignty and the European Union

The position of the UK within the EU is one on which the coalition partners fundamentally disagree. Liberal Democrats believe strongly in the value of the EU and of the UK's enhanced position within it, whereas most Conservatives harbour misgivings about UK membership.[57] Such opposed positions could be accommodated in the Coalition Agreement only because both sides believe that the UK's position within the EU should be managed through the use of referendums.

The Coalition Agreement maintained that any future treaty that transferred further competences to the EU would be subject to a referendum.[58] This was taken almost verbatim from the Conservative manifesto.[59] But the manifesto went further: it promised that 'a Conservative government would never take the UK into the Euro'[60] and proposed that since the 'steady and unaccountable intrusion of the European Union into almost every aspect of our lives has gone too far', they would 'make it clear that ultimate authority stays in this country, in our Parliament'.[61]

The Liberal Democrat manifesto, by contrast, had expressed the conviction that 'it is in Britain's long-term interest to be part of the euro', although it was recognized that 'Britain should only join when the economic conditions are right, and in the present economic situation, they are not'. It also accepted that 'Britain should join the euro only if that decision were supported by the people of Britain in a

---

[57] For details on coalition dynamics over the EU see chapter fourteen, this volume.

[58] *Programme For Government*, p. 19.

[59] This reflected the position taken by David Cameron in 2009, when he stated that the Lisbon Treaty should not have been ratified without a referendum being held in the UK and pledged that 'never again should it be possible for a British government to transfer power to the EU without the say of the British people': 'Full text: Cameron speech on EU', *BBC News*, 4 November 2009 (accessed at http://news.bbc.co.uk/1/hi/8343145.stm, 6 November 2014).

[60] Conservative Party, *Manifesto 2010*, p. 113.   [61] *Ibid.*, p. 114.

referendum'.[62] More generally, the Liberal Democrats maintained that since 'the European Union has evolved significantly since the last public vote on membership over thirty years ago', they are 'committed to an in/out referendum the next time a British government signs up for fundamental change in the relationship between the UK and the EU'.[63] The Coalition Agreement thus reflected the tone of the Conservative position, with consensus being reached only on the importance of giving the last word on any proposed change in the UK's position in Europe to a popular vote.

The government gave effect to these provisions in the European Union Act 2011. This Act determines that any further transfers of competences to the EU cannot be realized simply by a vote in Parliament: they will also require affirmation in a referendum (ss.2–3). The Act then indicates the type of change needed to trigger a referendum. These include not only the conferral of a new competence or extension of an existing competence (s.4), but extend to a broad range of other EU decisions, including the use of passerelle provisions under the Lisbon Treaty (e.g. to alter a voting arrangement from unanimity to qualified majority vote)(s.6). The Act also strengthens the parliamentary controls over approval of various EU decisions (ss.7–10), but it is the so-called 'referendum lock' provisions that have engaged most constitutional interest. Since a referendum would be required only if a government proposed supporting such treaty changes, there is a clear intention that the 2011 Act should bind the actions of future administrations.

The constitutional issues raised by the Bill were assessed in a report from the Select Committee on the Constitution.[64] Highlighting 'the complex and highly technical nature of the referendum lock provisions' and noting that the referendum requirements were 'wholly unprecedented in UK constitutional practice', the Committee questioned whether 'UK-wide referendums are a constitutionally appropriate and realistic mechanism in the case of many of the specified Treaty provisions'.[65] Recommending that if referendums are to be used they should be reserved for 'fundamental constitutional issues', the Committee concluded that, in specifying 'over 50 policy areas where a referendum

---

[62] Liberal Democrats, *Manifesto 2010*, p. 67.   [63] *Ibid.*, p. 66.
[64] Select Committee on the Constitution, *European Union Bill* (HL 121, 13th Report of Session 2010–11, 17 March 2011).
[65] *Ibid.*, paras 27, 28.

would be or might be required', the EU Bill makes 'a radical step-change in the adoption of referendum provisions'; it applies to a wider range of issues than provided for by any other Member State and extends far beyond what might sensibly be regarded as a fundamental constitutional issue.[66]

The EU Act 2011 is a strange constitutional innovation. Since it remained entirely within the authority of the coalition government to reject any extension of EU powers, the referendum lock seems redundant. Yet it raises the possibility of having to commit to a referendum over what might amount to a fairly technical extension of competence, such as a passerelle clause that alters EU voting rules. The prospect of having to hold a UK-wide referendum on a technical issue, at a cost of around £75 million and at considerable delay to the ratification process,[67] seems unlikely to endear the government to voters, taxpayers or EU partners. And if it generates, as in all probability it would, a very low turnout, it is difficult to see how the referendum could be touted as a democratic measure.

The 2011 Act falls into the category of symbolic legislation: by establishing a mechanism which was designed not to be utilized for preventing any further transfer of powers to the EU, it provided a sop to Eurosceptic Conservative backbenchers. But it also came to be overtaken by events: in January 2013 David Cameron promised to hold an in-out referendum on UK membership of the EU, though one that would only be held in 2017, after the next general election.[68]

Rights protection

The coalition parties had few difficulties in reaching agreement that 'the British state has become too authoritarian', that 'over the past decade . . . [it] has abused and eroded fundamental human freedoms'

---

[66] *Ibid.*, paras 30, 33, 37.

[67] The Electoral Commission reported that the cost of holding the AV referendum in 2010 was £75.265 million, and because it was held at the same time as several local elections across the UK, the cost represented a significant saving over that of a free-standing referendum: Electoral Commission, *Referendum on the Voting System* (2011) , at p. 8.

[68] David Cameron, 'EU speech at Bloomberg' 23 January 2013 (accessed at www.gov.uk/government/speeches/eu-speech-at-bloomberg, 6 November 2014).

and that there was a 'need to restore the rights of individuals in the face of encroaching state power'.[69] But there was considerable ambivalence over the means by which this objective might be realized. In opposition, the Conservatives had advocated repeal of the Human Rights Act 1998 and its replacement with a British Bill of Rights,[70] and this commitment was included in their 2010 manifesto.[71] The Liberal Democrats also supported the introduction of a Bill of Rights, though crucially this was to be part of a written constitution,[72] and their 2010 manifesto promised to preserve and protect the Human Rights Act.[73] The Coalition Agreement expressed a compromise between these positions. It proposed the establishment of 'a Commission to investigate the creation of a British Bill of Rights', thereby reflecting the Conservative view. But the Agreement went on to state that this Bill of Rights will incorporate and build on the UK's obligations under the European Convention on Human Rights, thereby adhering to the Liberal Democrat policy position.[74] Much would depend on the findings of the proposed Commission.

Given these differences, there was an understandable reluctance to press the issue, but in 2011 political controversy over human rights issues once again erupted. In response to a parliamentary question about rulings of the European Court of Human Right on prisoner voting[75] and a Supreme Court ruling giving offenders the possibility of coming off the sex offenders' register,[76] the Prime Minister stated that 'a commission will be established imminently to look at a British Bill of Rights, because it is about time we ensured that decisions are made in this Parliament rather than in the courts'.[77] That commission

---

[69] *Programme For Government*, p. 11.

[70] David Cameron, 'Balancing freedom and security: A modern British Bill of Rights', 26 June 2006; quoted in Alexander Horne and Lucinda Maer, *Background to Proposals for a British Bill of Rights and Duties* (House of Commons Library, SN/PC/04559, Feb. 2009), p. 5.

[71] Conservative Party, *Manifesto 2010*, p. 79.

[72] Liberal Democrat Party Policy Paper, *For the People, By the People* (September 2007), as quoted in Horne and Maer, *Background*, p. 6.

[73] Liberal Democrats, *Manifesto 2010*, p. 94.

[74] *Programme For Government*, p. 11.

[75] *Hirst* v. *UK (No.2)* (2005) ECHR 681; Commons Hansard, 10 February 2011, col. 493.

[76] *R (on the application of F) and Thompson* v. *Home Secretary* [2010] UKSC 17.

[77] Commons Hansard, 16 February 2011, col. 955.

was established on 18 March 2011, but with the coalition parties each nominating four members, and with the Liberal Democrats proposing human rights advocates and the Conservatives proposing critics of the Human Rights Act, the task of the chair (Sir Leigh Lewis) was an unenviable one.

Rumours of tensions between the two groups of commissioners plagued its work and were confirmed when in March 2012 one of the Conservative nominees resigned, claiming that fellow commissioners were 'ignoring the prime minister's desire to reassert the sovereignty of Westminster over the European court'.[78] The Commission delivered its report to the DPM and the Justice Secretary in December 2012.[79] It is necessary only to peruse the conclusions, mostly divided into majority and minority positions, together with the eight personal views of individual commissioners which were appended to the report, to get a sense of the failure of the Commission to reach any authoritative position on the key issues. The majority concluded that 'on balance, there is a strong argument in favour of a UK Bill of Rights'.[80] But this was rejected by a minority on the grounds, *inter alia*, that commissioners had been unable to come close to agreement on content and that the main object of many in the majority was to establish a Bill of Rights that would entail 'a reduction of rights' for some.[81] Even some of those in the majority complained that 'the key issue' to be addressed – activism in the European Court of Human Rights – had not been adequately considered.[82]

With such a polarization, it is clear that, other than providing a period of diversion, the Commission could never have achieved its aims. This may have suited the Conservatives, whose stance on repeal of the Human Rights Act has hardened. Since the publication of the Report, Theresa May, the Home Secretary, has stated that the

---

[78] Conal Urquhart, 'Bill of rights commissioner resigns over bypass of Commons', *The Guardian*, 11 March 2012; Michael Pinto-Duschinsky, 'Commission must not compromise by recommending bill identical to HRA', *The Guardian*, 13 March 2012.

[79] Commission on a Bill of Rights, *Report: A UK Bill of Rights? The Choice Before Us*. Vol. 1 (Commission on a Bill of Rights, 18 December 2012).

[80] *Ibid.*, p. 176 (para. 12.7).

[81] Baroness Kennedy and Philippe Sands, 'In defence of rights', *ibid.*, pp. 221–30, at 222, 227.

[82] Lord Faulks and Jonathan Fisher, 'Unfinished business', *ibid.*, pp. 182–90, at 182.

2015 Conservative manifesto would pledge to repeal the Act,[83] and Chris Grayling, the Justice Secretary, has promised to publish draft legislation on the UK's relationship with the European Court of Human Rights.[84] Such statements reflect a widespread antipathy that Conservatives are expressing, not just on human rights protection but also on the growth of judicial review of governmental action more generally. The Justice Secretary's recent proposals to curb legal aid and judicial review[85] have led to widespread criticism,[86] including the claim that he may be in breach of his statutory duties to respect the rule of law and defend the independence of the judiciary.[87] This is a constitutional issue on which there remains a wide gulf between the positions of the coalition partners.

Scotland and Wales in the United Kingdom

The coalition government pledged to effect 'a fundamental shift of power from Westminster to people'[88] by giving new powers to local councils and local communities,[89] and to continue the process of

---

[83] David Barrett, 'Tory manifesto will promise to scrap Labour's Human Rights Act, says Theresa May', *The Telegraph*, 30 September 2013.

[84] Chris Grayling, '2013 Conservative Party Conference Speech' (accessed at www.conservativepartyconference.org.uk/Speeches/2013_Chris_Grayling.aspx, 6 November 2014). This legislation had not appeared by July 2014: Owen Bowcott, 'Why are the Conservatives against the European court of human rights?', *The Guardian*, 17 July 2014. See Conservative Party, *Protecting Human Rights in the United Kingdom* (October 2014).

[85] *Judicial Review – Proposals for Further Reform: The Government Response* (Cm 8811, February 2014).

[86] Ben Jaffey and Tom Hickman, 'Loading the dice in judicial review: the Criminal Justice and Courts Bill 2014', *UK Const. Law Blog*, 6 February 2014 (accessed at http://ukconstitutionallaw.org/2014/02/06/ben-jaffey-and-tom-hickman-loading-the-dice-in-judicial-review-the-criminal-justice-and-courts-bill-2014/, 6 November 2014). See e.g. the caustic comments by Sir Stephen Sedley, 'Beware kite flyers', *LRB*, 12 September 2013: 'Since the mid-17th century, no non-lawyer has held the office of Lord Chancellor. The decision in 2012 to put a political enforcer, Chris Grayling, in charge of the legal system carried a calculated message: the rule of law was from now on, like everything else, going to be negotiable.'

[87] Joint Committee on Human Rights, *The Implications for Access to Justice of the Government's Proposals to Reform Judicial Review* (HL 174, HC 868, 13th Report of Session 2013–14), paras 18–23.

[88] *Programme for Government*, p. 11.   [89] See chapter nine, this volume.

devolving powers to Wales and Scotland.[90] With respect to Wales a referendum was held on giving greater legislative powers to the Welsh Assembly and, after a positive vote in 2011, those reforms were instituted.[91] In relation to Scotland, the Government introduced legislation to implement the Calman Commission's proposals to extend the powers of the Scottish Parliament.[92] Because of the Sewel Convention, according to which Westminster would not legislate for Scottish devolved matters without the consent of Holyrood, the legislative process stretched over eighteen months so as to permit both Parliaments concurrently to examine the Bill. This legislation, which extended the Scottish Parliament's power to raise or lower income tax by 10p, gave it borrowing powers and devolved control of stamp duty and landfill tax revenues, was enacted as the Scotland Act 2012.

The 2012 Act, the main powers of which were not due to come into force until 2016, had already been overtaken by an important political event: in the election of 5 May 2011, the Scottish National Party was returned with an overall majority (with 69 of the 129 seats) for the first time in the Scottish Parliament's short history. Given the additional member system of proportional representation that had been adopted, this was a remarkable achievement. And because the SNP came to power with a promise to legislate to give the people of Scotland a referendum on Scottish independence, it had major constitutional implications.[93]

---

[90] *Programme for Government*, p. 28. See chapter three, this volume.

[91] On 9 February 2010, Assembly Members voted in favour of a referendum on further law-making powers: the UK Government enacted legislation enabling a referendum to be held on 3 March 2011, which resulted in 63.5 per cent voting in favour. The Assembly acquired its new powers on 5 May 2011 under the Government of Wales Act 2006, Pt. IV and Schedule 7. Further proposals to strengthen financial arrangements were made in the (Silk) Commission on Devolution in Wales, *Empowerment and Responsibility: Financial Powers to Strengthen Wales* (November 2012) (accessed at http://commissionondevolutioninwales.independent.gov.uk/files/2013/01/English-WEB-main-report1.pdf, 6 November 2014).

[92] Commission on Scottish Devolution, *Serving Scotland Better: Scotland and the United Kingdom in the Twenty-First Century* (Final Report, June 2009) (accessed at www.commissiononscottishdevolution.org.uk/uploads/2009-06-12-csd-final-report-2009fbookmarked.pdf, 6 November 2014).

[93] While the proposal was hardly a consequence of the UK coalition government's programme, the SNP majority was in many respects a consequence of the unpopularity of coalition policies: whereas the Conservatives' popular vote dropped and they

Given this clear mandate for a referendum on independence, the PM accepted the need to work constructively with Alex Salmond, Scotland's First Minister. These negotiations culminated in the Edinburgh Agreement. Signed on 15 October 2012, both Governments agreed that the referendum should 'have a clear legal base; be legislated for by the Scottish Parliament; be conducted so as to command the confidence of parliaments, governments and people; and deliver a fair test and a decisive expression of the views of people in Scotland and a result that everyone will respect'.[94] Since the power to hold an independence referendum was beyond the power of the Scottish Parliament under the Scotland Act 1998,[95] it was agreed that an Order in Council would be passed under Section 30 of the 1998 Act. This authorized the Scottish Parliament to legislate on an independence referendum provided the poll would be held before the end of 2014 and that the ballot paper would give the voter a simple yes/no choice.

It was initially proposed that the referendum question should ask: 'Do you agree that Scotland should be an independent country?' But on referral to the Electoral Commission this formulation was criticized on grounds that the preface 'do you agree' made it a leading question. The Commission instead recommended: 'Should Scotland be an independent country?'[96] This formulation was adopted in the Scottish Independence Referendum Act 2013, which also set the date of the referendum for 18 September 2014.[97]

We cannot here explain the many complex issues raised by the prospect of Scottish independence. The issues were widely canvassed by the Scottish Government in its 670-page white paper, Scotland's

---

lost two seats, the Liberal Democrats found that their share of the vote had halved and their representation was reduced from seventeen MSPs to five.

[94] Edinburgh Agreement (15 October 2012) (accessed at www.scotland.gov.uk/Resource/0040/00404789.pdf, 19 November 2013).

[95] The Scotland Act limits the legislative competence of the Scottish Parliament and sets out 'reserved matters' in relation to which the Parliament cannot make laws (s.29(2)). These specifically include aspects of the constitution that relate to the Union of the Kingdoms of Scotland and England: Schedule 5(1).

[96] Electoral Commission, Referendum on Independence for Scotland: Advice of the Electoral Commission on the Proposed Referendum Question, p. 33.

[97] See also the Scottish Independence Referendum (Franchise) Act 2013, which confirmed the franchise as the same as for local government elections, but extended it to include any person aged 16 who fitted the registration requirements.

Future.[98] Some constitutional questions were relatively non-contentious: it was intended that Scotland would become a constitutional monarchy and retain a unicameral parliament on the basis already established, the outlines of which had been presented in a consultative draft Scottish Independence Bill in June 2014.[99] But many major issues, including those concerning defence, security, EU membership and currency union, remained contentious throughout the campaign.[100]

On a turnout of around 85 per cent, the referendum yielded a majority vote against independence (55.3% to 44.7%). That result, which led to the announcement of Alex Salmond's resignation as First Minister, does not mark the end of the constitutional question. On 5 August 2014 the three main UK parties had already issued a joint statement pledging to strengthen further the powers of the Scottish Parliament, especially in the areas of fiscal responsibility and social security.[101] It was therefore accepted that, in the event of a 'no' vote, the parties would propose the introduction of certain 'devo-plus' schemes.[102] It was anticipated that these would be presented in their 2015 election manifestos, but on 8 September, and with the unionist camp expressing concern about the growing strength of the independence campaign, former PM Gordon Brown announced an accelerated timetable that proposed the publication of draft legislation to achieve

[98] *Scotland's Future: Your Guide to an Independent Scotland* (Scottish Government, November 2013) (accessed at www.scotland.gov.uk/Resource/0043/00439021.pdf, 6 November 2014).

[99] *The Scottish Independence Bill: A Consultation on an Interim Constitution for Scotland* (Scottish Government, June 2014) (accessed at www.scotland.gov.uk/Resource/0045/00452762.pdf, 6 November 2014).

[100] The UK Government produced a series of documents over 2013–14 dealing with aspects of independence under the banner of Scotland Analysis. These were brought together in: *United Kingdom, United Future: Conclusions of the Scotland Analysis Programme* (Cm 8869, June 2014).

[101] Labour List, 'Labour, Tories and Lib Dems join together to promise further devolution ahead of first independence TV debate', 5 August 2014 (accessed at http://labourlist.org/2014/08/labour-tories-and-lib-dems-join-together-to-promise-further-scottish-devolution-ahead-of-first-independence-tv-debate/, 6 November 2014).

[102] See Iain McLean, Jim Gallagher and Guy Lodge, *Scotland's Choices: The Referendum and What Happens Afterwards* (Edinburgh: Edinburgh University Press, 2nd edn, 2014), ch. 4. See also the (Strathclyde) *Report of the Commission on the Future Governance of Scotland* (Scottish Conservatives, 2014) (accessed at www.scottish-conservatives.com/wordpress/wp-content/uploads/2014/06/Strathclyde_Commission_14.pdf, 6 November 2014).

'home rule' for Scotland by 25 January 2015.[103] This raises major constitutional questions because to this point devolution to Northern Ireland, Scotland and Wales has taken place with only the most marginal of adjustments to the Westminster system of parliamentary government. But the limit of incremental accommodation seems now to have been reached; any further devolution cannot sensibly take place without putting into question the foundation of the UK's entire constitutional architecture.

Conclusion

In February 2014, the Select Committee on the Constitution, recognizing that hung parliaments are likely to occur more regularly, issued a report entitled *Constitutional Implications of Coalition Government*. Despite this broad title, their report was devoted mainly to the need to make certain relatively technical adjustments to conventional rules in order to accommodate these changing political circumstances. These included instituting a twelve-day gap between the election and the first meeting of the new parliament, proposing that the PM remain in office until a new government is formed, and recommending that official support be given to parties involved in government formation negotiations.[104] It also reviewed the difficulties of maintaining the principle of collective responsibility under coalition arrangements and, highlighting the value of the convention, it recommended that in future a 'proper process should be set in place to govern any setting aside' of the convention.[105]

There are, however, certain broader constitutional implications that flow from the formation of coalitions between the parties. One obvious consequence is that it will be Parliament rather than the electorate that has the decisive role in determining who will form the government. Any programme for government negotiated between the parliamentary parties might deviate significantly from their manifestos and cannot easily be said to have a popular mandate. In addition, many

---

[103] See 'Gordon Brown unveils cross-party deal on Scottish powers', *Daily Telegraph*, 8 September 2014; also *Report of the Smith Commission for Further Devolution of Powers to the Scottish Parliament* (November 2014).

[104] Select Committee on the Constitution, *Constitutional Implications*, paras 26, 31, 40.

[105] *Ibid.*, para. 79.

of the commitments entered into by the parties under a coalition agreement are likely to be of vital significance for continued co-operation, so that, as we have seen, they will necessitate the quashing of any dissent through strong whipping of their parties in Parliament. Coalition agreements can accordingly result in the displacement of parliamentary scrutiny of governmental measures. Coalitions are likely to operate in ways that strengthen parliamentary action vis-à-vis popular action, and governmental action vis-à-vis parliamentary action. As the experience of the 2010–15 government shows, the structural logic of coalition governments may work contrary to the principles of open and popular government.

In this chapter, we have addressed a broader question than that of the impact of coalitions on the workings of the constitution. Our primary objective has been to examine and evaluate the achievements of the 2010–15 coalition government in delivering its programme of constitutional reform. The record is stark: no voting reform, no constituency equalization, no reform of the House of Lords, no use of the EU referendum lock provisions, and no reform or repeal of the Human Rights Act. The PM's discretionary power to dissolve Parliament has been curbed, though it is not self-evident that the fixed-term parliament reform will lead to an improvement in the British system of government. What is obvious is that it restricts the ability of governments to make what they conceive to be a timely appeal to the people. Finally, the government has promoted further measures to devolve legislative powers to Wales and Scotland, though the Scottish independence referendum – triggered at least in part by the collapse of Liberal Democrat support in Scotland – has most certainly placed that settlement in question.

From the procedural perspective, the most distinctive feature of the coalition government's constitutional programme has been their promotion of referendums. Does this policy mark a shift from parliamentary to popular government? The question highlights the ambiguities of constitutional reform in the British tradition. If, as Thomas Paine famously remarked, 'the constitution of a country is not the act of its government, but of the people constituting a government',[106] how can

---

[106] Thomas Paine, 'Rights of Man', in his *Rights of Man, Common Sense and other Political Writings* [1791], Mark Philp ed. (Oxford: Oxford University Press, 1995), pp. 83–331, at 122.

governments legitimately reform the British constitution? One answer is that constitutional questions should be resolved by popular referendum. But there are difficulties. If they are constitutional mechanisms, then as the Select Committee on Constitution recommended,[107] referendums must be reserved for constitutional questions. If the procedure is not to be manipulated by governments, it must be triggered by the adoption of clear advance criteria for its use. And if the referendum is to perform that constitutional role, the issue must be of fundamental importance, such that it will engage the active interest of the general public. Without these principles for their use being instituted, the suspicion must remain that the growing interest in the device is a consequence of governments' recognizing the potential of deploying populism as a tool of governmental policy.

Our conclusion, then, is that the experience of the 2010–15 coalition government highlights the dangers of a minority party seeking to use its leverage to bring about basic constitutional reform on matters for which there is no cross-party consensus. They may succeed in having those commitments recorded in a formal agreement but this cannot buck one of the most basic laws of parliamentary politics: that there exists a considerable gulf between promise and realization and without continuous active political support, both within Parliament and among the electorate, even the noblest of aspirations will count for little.

---

[107] Select Committee on the Constitution, *Referendums in the United Kingdom* (HL 99, Twelfth Report of Session 2009–10).

3 THE COALITION BEYOND WESTMINSTER

NEIL MCGARVEY

Coalition politics, while new, novel and unique in the village of Westminster in 2010, were already well-established governing forms, and are actually 'par for the course' and the anticipated governmental outcome post-election in Northern Ireland, Scotland and Wales. In each of these countries, post-devolution constitutional rules and electoral procedures all contained within them provision for a more proportional legislature. Despite coalition politics being the anticipated 'normal' politics in the Celtic periphery, the irony is that for the bulk of the 2010–15 period, both Scotland (SNP) and Wales (Labour) were governed by single parties.

Beyond Westminster, the prospect of minority government did not raise the same alarm that it did in London. The assertion that coalition was a necessity due to the UK's urgent economic crisis associated with spiralling public sector debt appeared rather manufactured. In 2010, Scotland had already experienced three years of stable minority government under the SNP. In Wales Labour governed as a minority during 1999–2000 and 2005–7. The Conservatives were only 21 seats short of a majority in the 650-member House of Commons; the SNP had been governing Scotland 18 seats short of a majority in a much smaller 129-member chamber. The notion of minority government being unstable was more a judgement of the internal politics of the Conservative Party, and reflected the biases of the Westminster political class.

An immediate effect of the Coalition Agreement was that the five-year fixed-term parliament ensured that the general election of 2015 would coincide with the scheduled devolved 2015 elections. Faced with the prospect of UK and devolved parliamentary elections taking place simultaneously it was agreed that the elections beyond Westminster be postponed until 2016.

The UK Government coalition effect, in terms of policy impact, was less tangible in Northern Ireland, Scotland and Wales: principally because devolution contained, as part of its design, an umbrella sheltering each territory from some parts of UK Government policy agenda they did not want to pursue. The UK Government's policies in areas like education, social and health care stopped at the English border. It became clearer in each area that, post-devolution, significant political power now lies beyond Westminster and Whitehall. There was no more vivid manifestation of that than on 18 September 2014, when the future sovereignty of Scotland was placed in the hands of the Scottish electorate for a day. The 2014 Scottish referendum focused the spotlight very much on Scotland with the potential break-up of the United Kingdom of Great Britain and Northern Ireland.

Three themes are outlined in this chapter: First, the coalition government carried on from its Labour predecessor in approaching territorial governance issues with flexibility. Unionist flexibility became a newly established operating code for UK government. Post-1999 in Northern Ireland, Scotland and Wales, there is a wealth of evidence of what could be termed flexible unionism. The trend continued by the government is of the UK being an ever-looser union with increased autonomy in the Celtic nations. The UK, when viewed from beyond Westminster, can no longer credibly be conceived of as a unitary state; it is now quite clearly a state of asymmetrical unions. Indeed, for a brief period in the September 2014 referendum campaign (after the first poll showing a Yes lead), there was the rather bizarre situation of Gordon Brown, a former Prime Minister and Labour backbencher, appearing to announce a timetable for the granting of new powers to Scotland. This was in a closed-doors Labour Party meeting in Midlothian, apparently with the consent of his party leader as well as the UK Prime Minister and his Deputy!

The coalition government inherited commitments to extend more devolutionary powers to Scotland and Wales and it carried forward on this commitment. In Scotland, it responded to the SNP's 2011 landslide election victory and manifesto commitment to holding a referendum on Scotland's membership of the United Kingdom by negotiating and agreeing on the terms of that referendum. In Wales, there was more stability, but the trajectory of travel was also enhanced autonomy. The knock-on effect of these developments in Northern Ireland meant that constitutional politics remained never far from its agenda.[1]

A second, notable development – that has largely gone under the radar – is that the legitimacy question has been removed from politics beyond Westminster. From the 1970s, politics was dominated, albeit in radically different ways, by notions of a democratic and political legitimacy deficit in Scotland, Northern Ireland and Wales. Different forms of politics, the inflexibility and weakness of the Conservative Party, as well as their perceived inflexible approach to the union, led to increasing demands for more autonomy. Post-2010 those legitimacy concerns were not heard. The combination of devolution and the Liberal Democrat inclusion in government has allowed the UK Government to claim an enhanced degree of legitimacy. The collective vote of the Conservatives and Liberal Democrats added considerable weight to its governing authority throughout the UK.

Pre-devolution, there was much talk of new politics and Westminster as a negative template; however, as devolution has evolved, the legislatures in both Scotland and Wales have gradually taken on more of the features of the Westminster arrangements.[2] Northern Ireland, with its own distinctive arrangements, has remained something of a case apart. However, the new legislatures in all three countries are now widely accepted as politically legitimate and democratically accountable bodies in all three nations. In Northern Ireland, the armed struggle republican tradition has been sidelined, with mainstream Irish republicanism now participating in relatively stable joint governance arrangements with the Democratic Unionist Party (DUP). Devolution has shifted perceptions amongst Northern Irish, Scottish and Welsh electorates about where political power and authority is and should be. Despite previous projections of the doomsday scenario of a Conservative-led Westminster government facing off to nationalist-led (or influenced)

---

[1] See, for example, Glenn Patterson 'All this talk of Scottish independence gave this man from Belfast the jitters', *The Guardian*, 27 September 2014.

[2] See Alan Trench, 'Wales and the Westminster model', *Parliamentary Affairs*, 63:1 (2010), pp. 117–33; Paul Cairney and James Johnston, 'What is the role of the Scottish Parliament?', *Scottish Parliamentary Review*, 1:2 (2013), pp. 91–130 (accessed at https://paulcairney.files.wordpress.com/2013/09/scottish-parliamentary-review-cairney-johnston-2.pdf, 7 November 2014).

administrations in the periphery, intergovernmental relations have remained cordial, with each side according the other a degree of respect oiled by the diplomatic skills of the UK Home and Northern Ireland civil service.

A final theme identified is the continuing constitutional tinkering that is now par for the course for British politics, with little effort made to identify any underlying principles. In Wales and Scotland two very different referendums were held. The Welsh one in 2011 was low key and labelled unnecessary.[3] The Scottish one in 2014, in contrast, was more fundamental to the issue of constitutional sovereignty. Together with the Alternative Vote (AV) referendum and the Conservative commitment to an in-out EU referendum in 2017, they highlight just how quickly referendums came to be established as conventional custom and practice in a Westminster constitutional order that until the 1970s had regarded them as alien.

The chapter has been structured around these three themes. In discussing each, reflections are made on developments in Northern Ireland, Scotland and Wales. Inevitably, as a result of size and the importance of the Scottish independence referendum campaign to the UK's political and constitutional future, much of the discussion focuses on developments in Scotland.

From a unitary state to a state of unions

The coalition government carried forward the trajectory of new flexible unionism in British politics. The constitutional conservatism of pre-1997 UK government was eschewed in favour of carrying on the trajectory of post-1997 territorial governance. Devolution has proved to be an ongoing process rather than a series of singular events in Northern Ireland, Scotland and Wales.

The 2012 Scotland Act[4] was a grudging, incremental adjustment to the 1999 devolution arrangements. It was always unlikely to promote stability. Indeed it already had a dated feel before it even reached the statute book, with the 2012 Edinburgh Agreement between

---

[3] Richard Wyn Jones and Roger Scully, *Wales Says Yes: Devolution and the 2011 Welsh Referendum* (Cardiff: University of Wales Press, 2012).

[4] See Table 3.7 for details.

the UK and Scottish Governments on the terms of the 2014 Scottish referendum signed in the same year. That agreement was designed to give a definitive answer to 'The Scottish Question'.[5]

In Wales, both the Liberal Democrats and Conservatives advocated extensions to devolution at the 2011 Welsh election. The Liberal Democrats advocated policing, justice and energy projects. The Conservatives advocated part of the latter too, though it should be noted that neither party was particularly vocal about these during campaigning.[6]

In Northern Ireland, there were no new Acts, referendums or significant constitutional developments. However, there did continue to be clashes around the politics of symbolism – flags, marches, language and the like. The point to be made is that the political process in each area was ongoing and much of it was independent of any coalition effect.

The UK coalition government faced governments in all three peripheries without any Conservative or Liberal Democrat representation. Despite the obvious potential for antagonism, intergovernmental relations remained relatively smooth. David Cameron had previously written of the union as a 'constitutional masterstroke'.[7] He also challenged the 'at best widespread ambivalence, and at worst prevailing animosity'[8] in England, as well as the campaigning tone of bullying Scotland into remaining in the UK for fear of the consequences of going it alone, suggesting the case for the Union must also appeal to the heart. Whilst in opposition Cameron had previously acknowledged 'small, independent and thriving economies across Europe such as Finland, Switzerland and Norway. It would be wrong to suggest Scotland could not be another successful, independent country.'[9]

This conciliatory tone was an implicit acknowledgement that the more inflexible unionism of the Thatcher and Major years was a mistake, and one that the Conservative Party beyond Westminster paid (and continued to pay in Scotland) a heavy electoral price for. It also reflected Conservative electoral weakness beyond its English heartlands.

---

[5] See James Mitchell, *The Scottish Question* (Oxford: Oxford University Press, 2014).

[6] Laura McAllister and Michael Cole, 'The 2011 Welsh general election: An analysis of the latest staging post in the maturing of Welsh politics', *Parliamentary Affairs*, 6:7 (2014), p. 175.

[7] David Cameron, 'Scots and English flourish in the union', *The Telegraph*, 11 April 2007.

[8] *Ibid.*   [9] *Ibid.*

Table 3.1 *The 2014 Scottish referendum result*

No	2,001,926	55.3%
Yes	1,617,989	44.7%
Turnout	84.5%	

The Scottish referendum campaign provided an illustrative example of the slippage of power from Westminster. The two parties of the coalition, whilst not bystanders, were supporting actors in the tribal war of attrition, led by Labour and the Scottish National Party on each side. David Cameron, Prime Minister, and Nick Clegg, Deputy Prime Minister, largely watched from the sidelines as the leading figures from the Scottish Labour Party such as Alistair Darling, Jim Murphy and Gordon Brown presented the case for remaining in the union.

The campaign itself, especially in its latter days, had an intensity rarely (if ever) seen in electoral politics in the UK. It was prone to much hyperbolic claim and counter-claim as regards the costs and benefits of the union and independence. At its height the Yes side boasted every Scot would gain £1,000 per year, while Better Together were claiming independence would cost £1,400 per annum. Both were claiming a vote for them was necessary to 'save the NHS'.

Better Together won a convincing 55–45 per cent majority (see Table 3.1) but were widely seen to have 'lost' the campaign despite winning the vote. Much of the Better Together campaign was labelled 'Project Fear', such was its negativity about the future of an independent Scotland, with no currency union, no EU membership, banks threatening to move head offices and retailers warning of price increases.[10] George Robertson, former Labour Defence Minister and NATO chief, outlined warnings of independence being cataclysmic for not only Scottish defence and security, but the whole of the western world![11] Some hyperbole referred to a Scottish decision to leave as a potential 'Suez moment' for the UK.[12]

[10] Julia Finch, Sarah Butler, Jill Reanor and Severin Carrell, 'Retailers under pressure to back no vote in Scottish Referendum', *The Guardian*, 11 September 2014.

[11] 'Scottish independence: Lord Robertson says Yes vote would be cataclysmic', *BBC News*, 8 April 2014 (accessed at www.bbc.co.uk/news/uk-scotland-scotland-politics-26933998, 7 November 2014).

[12] See James Forsyth, 'Without Scotland, England will be a weedy laughing stock', *The Spectator*, 5 July 2014.

There was a failure to articulate a positive future of the Union and the Better Together campaign fell into the Yes Scotland trap of contrasting Scotland with the UK. Perhaps this was a clear example of how different the approach may have been if Gordon Brown had won in 2010. Brown, as his interventions in the campaign demonstrated, had a clear and forthright message about Scotland's place in the union. In his book *My Scotland, Our Britain*[13] he articulates how 'it was Scottish ideas of solidarity that combined with English ideas of toleration and liberty to create a union that remains greater than the sum of its parts'. The Edinburgh Agreement signed by Salmond and Cameron may have taken a different form if Brown had retained office. The animosity and tribal nature of Scottish politics may have meant negotiations between an SNP First Minister and Labour Prime Minister would not have been so cordial.

The Better Together campaign was caricatured by Simon Jenkins: 'Horsemen of the apocalypse will descend from the Highlands bringing famine, terrorism and nuclear war. Vote yes, says Osborne, and old men will starve in the gutter and wee bairns erupt in boils.'[14] The aspiration of setting out a positive case for the union was lost and, for a brief period during the latter stages of the campaign, Scotland's union with the rest of the UK looked in serious jeopardy. Serious questions were being asked about the knock-on implications of independence or enhanced devolution for governance in Northern Ireland, Wales and the English regions. After the conclusive No vote, Cameron immediately seized the constitutional agenda by linking enhanced devolution to Scotland with 'English votes for English laws' and the potential for constitutional reform across the whole of the UK.[15]

Whilst devolution sheltered the Celtic periphery from much of the coalition government's social policy agenda, the politics of austerity and welfare reform were major issues in all three countries. Indeed, one could even argue that the UK government's welfare reform agenda had an enhanced saliency in the Celtic periphery because it remained the

---

[13] Gordon Brown, *My Scotland, Our Britain: A Future Worth Sharing* (London: Simon and Schuster, 2014).

[14] Simon Jenkins, 'Scotland's new era beckons regardless of how it votes in a stupid referendum', *The Guardian*, 29 May 2014.

[15] Oliver Wright and Heather Saul, 'Scottish referendum results: David Cameron pledges plans for "English votes for English laws" in January', *The Independent*, 19 September 2014.

only area of social policy where it can have an impact (the others being largely devolved). The umbrella of devolution has meant that many of the English reforms in the fields of education, health care, housing and other areas of local government did not have an impact. Probably the most visible (and politically controversial) of those that did was the 'bedroom tax' – the policy aimed at encouraging a more efficient use of social housing. Like the poll tax three decades previously, its official title was replaced in popular discourse by those campaigning for its abolition. The bedroom tax and other related welfare reforms tend to be narrated as Westminster-inspired cuts in welfare support in the periphery.[16] This reform had potentially a larger impact beyond Westminster as social housing was more prevalent in the devolved countries. In all three countries there were devolved legislature majorities in favour of its abolition and steps were taken to delay or negate its impact.

Although more reconciliatory in terms of territorial management and constitutional politics than the previous Conservative-led UK government, the 'bread and butter' coalition programme followed a rather Thatcherite agenda of fiscal austerity, public sector retrenchment, privatization (NHS, Royal Mail) and welfare cuts. Whilst such policies undoubtedly have constituencies of support, beyond Westminster there is generally a less receptive electorate to many of these issues.

Disillusionment with Westminster politics, the corrosiveness of their austerity agenda and dislike of the Conservative Party were a key strand of the Yes campaign's narrative in the Scottish referendum campaign. The coalition oversaw a period of state retrenchment and cutbacks that was unprecedented. Given the financial control the UK government continues to enjoy (as well as the City of London location of key banking and financial institutions), it is perhaps inevitable that most of the public blame for austerity in the periphery has been directed towards London. The Yes campaign in Scotland was able to capture the disillusionment with Westminster politics and utilize it to create a momentum behind their campaign.

In Northern Ireland David Cameron referred to his alarm at the 'East European' level of dependence on the public sector. Northern Ireland since the arrival of the welfare state in 1945 has been materially dependent on Westminster. From 2010 to 2015 the DUP–Sinn Fein

---

[16] See for example Peter Lazenby, 'This Tory-LD assault on welfare is battering Scotland and the North again', *The Guardian*, 29 March 2013.

devolved administration presided over a £4 billion reduction in public expenditure.[17] On one level this was 'normal' and the austerity cuts in line with those inflicted on other devolved administrations. However, Northern Irish politics remained somewhat dysfunctional and abnormal. The fundamentals of the nationalist–unionist divide remain institutionalized in the power-sharing arrangements at Stormont – they reflect more the communal parcelization of power and mutual vetoes than power-sharing between the two blocs.[18]

By 2015, it was looking even less like the unitary state that pre-devolution British politics textbooks conventionally labelled the UK. Relations with executives and legislatures in Northern Ireland, Scotland and Wales were continuing on the trajectory of increased detachment and autonomy.

A more legitimate UK government?

However, the increased flexibility in their approach to the union has allowed the UK coalition to firmly establish its constitutional and governing authority over the whole of the UK. Being a coalition government has actually helped in this respect. The existence of the Liberal Democrats in government has, at least, dampened the perception of an alien right-wing government imposing its will beyond Westminster. The Liberal Democrats, by being part of the coalition as a junior partner, enhanced its political legitimacy beyond Westminster. The awkward and potentially politically illegitimate governing position the Conservative Party found itself in in the 1980s and 1990s was avoided.

As Table 3.2 shows, in both Wales and Scotland, the dominance of Labour remained in terms of seats at UK general elections.[19] In Wales, the coalition could point to 46.2 per cent of the vote, but only 11 seats (out of 40). The 2010 general election was the Conservatives' best performance in Wales since 1992. For the Liberal Democrats, it was the best since the Liberal–SDP high point of 1983. In Scotland, the coalition parties gained 35.6 per cent of the vote, but only 12 seats (out of 59).

[17] Henry Patterson, 'Unionism after Good Friday and St Andrews', *The Political Quarterly*, 85:2 (2010), pp. 247–55.

[18] *Ibid.*, pp. 253–4.

[19] For further analysis of elections see chapter twenty-one, this volume.

Table 3.2 *2010 UK general election result in Northern Ireland, Scotland and Wales*

Scotland		
	% Vote	Seats
Labour	42.0 (+2.5)	41 (+2)
Liberal Democrats	18.9 (−3.7)	11 (−1)
SNP	19.9 (+2.3)	6 (−1)
Conservative	16.7 (+0.9)	1 (0)

Wales		
	% Vote	Seats[a]
Labour	36.2 (−6.5)	26 (−4)
Liberal Democrats	20.1 (+1.7)	3 (−1)
Plaid Cymru	11.3 (−1.3)	3 (+1)
Conservative	26.1 (+4.7)	8 (+5)

Northern Ireland		
	% Vote	Seats[b]
Sinn Fein	25.5 (+1.2)	5
DUP	25.0 (−8.7)	8
SDLP	16.5 (−1.0)	3
UCU-NF	15.2 (−2.6)	0
Alliance	6.3 (+2.4)	1

[a] In Wales, the minor party Blaenau Gwent People's Voice lost their only seat.
[b] Lady Syliva Hermon, ex-UUP, was elected as an independent unionist MP for North Down in 2010 having previously sat as MP for North Down as a UUP MP.

Importantly, there was an upward trajectory for both parties in Wales, as well as for the Conservatives in Scotland. Few questions were raised about their legitimacy to govern. In Northern Ireland, Sinn Fein and the DUP continued to benefit from the peace dividend, retaining 13 of 18 seats.

The 2010 general election result and the 2011 devolved election results were yet again reminders of how political party dynamics and electoral politics were diverging from the Westminster party 'norm'. As Table 3.3 demonstrates, the Conservatives have been in long-term decline in both Scotland and Wales, though in the latter some signs of revival have started to emerge. These results, due to the proportional perversities of the first-past-the-post electoral system, tend to mask the changing party political dynamics in devolved areas. Table 3.4 illustrates the changing party systems more sharply: the nationalist parties

Table 3.3 *General elections in Wales and Scotland 1979–2010*

	Labour Vote	Seats	Conservative Vote	Seats	SNP/Plaid Vote	Seats	Lib Dem[a] Vote	Seats
1979	%		%		%		%	
Scotland	41.5	44	31.4	22	17.3	2	9.0	3
Wales	47.0	21	32.2	11	8.1	2	10.6	1
1983								
Scotland	35.1	41	28.4	21	11.8	2	24.5	8
Wales	37.5	20	31.0	14	7.8	2	23.2	2
1987								
Scotland	42.4	50	24.0	10	11.0	3	19.4	9
Wales	45.1	24	29.5	8	7.3	3	17.9	3
1992								
Scotland	39.0	49	25.6	11	21.5	3	13.1	9
Wales	49.5	27	28.6	6	8.8	4	12.4	1
1997								
Scotland	45.6	56	17.5	0	22.1	6	13.0	10
Wales	54.7	34	19.6	0	9.9	4	12.4	2
2001								
Scotland	43.2	55	15.6	1	20.1	5	16.4	10
Wales	48.6	34	21.0	0	14.3	4	13.8	2
2005								
Scotland	39.5	41	15.8	1	17.7	6	22.6	11
Wales	42.7	29	21.4	3	12.6	3	18.4	4
2010								
Scotland	42.0	41	16.7	1	19.9	6	18.9	11
Wales	36.2	26	26.1	8	11.3	3	20.1	3

[a] Liberal Democrat vote in 1979 refers to the Liberal Party, and in 1983 and 1987 the Liberal/SDP Alliance.

Table 3.4 *Scottish Parliament and Welsh Assembly Elections 2011*

	Scotland Constit.	List	Wales Constit.	List
	%	%	%	%
Labour	31.7 (−0.5)	26.3 (−2.9)	42.3 (+10.1)	36.9 (+7.2)
Conservatives	13.9 (−2.7)	12.4 (−1.6)	25.0 (+2.6)	22.5 (+1.1)
Liberal Dems	7.9 (−8.3)	5.2 (−6.1)	10.6 (−4.2)	8.0 (−3.7)
SNP/P Cymru	45.4 (+12.5)	44.0 (+13.0)	19.3 (−3.1)	17.9 (−3.1)

Table 3.5 *The AV referendum vote in the UK, Northern Ireland, Scotland and Wales*

	Turnout	Yes	No
UK	42.2	32.1	67.9
Northern Ireland	55.8	43.7	56.3
Scotland	50.7	36.4	63.6
Wales	41.7	34.6	65.4

do much better in the more proportional election contests solely focused on their country.

During its first year – the honeymoon period – the coalition relationship between the Liberal Democrats and Conservatives was cohesive and reflected a unity of purpose. The novelty of governmental office and the goodwill engendered by the coalition agreement was evident. However, at the end of this first year there were important electoral contests: devolved elections and the Alternative Vote referendum. The honeymoon period ended abruptly on the evening of 5 May 2011. As outlined in Table 3.4, the Liberal Democrats' support collapsed in Scotland and significantly declined in Wales. In Wales the party suffered a 4.2 per cent decline in constituency vote share and 3.7 per cent in regional vote share. It only lost one seat, dropping from six to five. Interestingly the Conservatives' support actually increased in Wales (though it continued to fall in Scotland).[20]

The alternative vote (AV) referendum in the Celtic periphery was overshadowed by the parliamentary elections on the same day (although this did result in higher turnout). It is worth noting that the results in Northern Ireland, Scotland and Wales of the AV referendum were somewhat out of sync with the overall result with all three having more yes votes than the overall UK result – see Table 3.5. This may reflect that each country has had experience of more proportional electoral systems. Though noticeably 'no' was in the majority in every country.

Without the Liberal Democrats, the Conservatives would have been forced to appoint their only MP as Secretary of State for Scotland,

---

[20] See Alan Convery, 'Devolution and the limits of Tory statecraft: The Conservatives in coalition and Scotland and Wales', *Parliamentary Affairs*, 67:1 (2014), pp. 25–44; James Mitchell and Alan Convery, 'Conservative Unionism: Prisoned in marble', in D. Torrance, *Whatever Happened to Tory Scotland* (Edinburgh: Edinburgh University Press, 2012).

abandon having the post or appoint an MP from outwith Scotland. Instead of engaging with Scottish politics directly, the Conservatives chose the more politically astute option of devolving responsibility for Scotland to the Liberal Democrats, who held 11 of Scotland's 59 seats. The Liberal Democrats' initial choice of Secretary of State for Scotland Danny Alexander only served in post for eighteen days and was replaced by Michael Moore, with Alistair Carmichael taking over from him in October 2013. The latter change was widely reported as being about the coalition looking for a more robust, combative pro-union message. Ironically, Carmichael in 2010 had suggested the Scotland Office should be abolished as its role had changed from being a 'clearing house' between London and Edinburgh governments to being 'just a focal point for conflict'.[21]

The posts of Secretary of State for Northern Ireland, Scotland and Wales have themselves changed significantly since devolution. Although officially stated as being about representing the UK government in each country, in Scotland and Wales the post has become a key party political platform in constitutional politics.

The Conservatives had long struggled with their approach to devolution in Scotland and Wales. Until 1997, the party adopted an increasingly inflexible unitary unionist stance, refusing to engage in any meaningful way with the home rule agenda in both Scotland and Wales throughout the 1980s and 1990s. Post-devolution the party has engaged with the ongoing constitutional debate and worked with other parties. The Scottish party's 2014 Strathclyde Commission Report[22] highlights just how far the party has moved: it represents the most significant shift in any of the unionist parties' policy stances on devolution (see Table 3.6). In offering full income tax-raising powers the Conservatives allowed Labour to inherit the title of constitutional conservatives. This shift encapsulates how much better the Conservatives, as a party, have adjusted themselves to the reality of devolution than Labour. The new brand of Conservative unionism has an emphasis on decentralization, autonomy and – most importantly – fiscal accountability.

[21] 'Top experts give their views on the government reshuffle', *LSE Blog*, 10 October 2013 (accessed at http://blogs.lse.ac.uk/politicsandpolicy/archives/37039?utm_content=buffer64b41&utm_source=buffer&utm_medium=twitter&utm_campaign=Buffer, 7 November 2014).

[22] See www.scottishconservatives.com/2014/06/strathclyde-commission-scotland-full-powers-income-tax (accessed 7 November 2014).

Table 3.6 *Extending devolution if Scotland votes* No – *the unionist party positions*

Labour
- A default Scottish tax rate of 15% (covering all UK bands 20%, 40% and 45%) – rather than the 10% in the 2012 Scotland Act
- Devolution of housing benefit and attendance allowance
- New devolved powers in election administration, health and safety, employment tribunals, equalities policy, consumer advice and railways
- Report specifies that 60% of Scottish Parliament spending should be covered by UK block grant to secure 'key UK social rights' in Scotland

Liberal Democrats
- Income tax wholly devolved (including ability to vary rates and tax bands)
- Air Passenger Duty wholly devolved
- Assignment of Scottish share of corporation tax
- Approximately 55% of Scottish spending would be covered by devolved and assigned taxes

Conservatives
- Income tax wholly devolved (including power to set rates and thresholds)
- Examine the possibility of assigning a proportion of the proceeds of VAT
- Devolution of attendance allowance, housing benefit

Each unionist party offered separate further devolution offerings during the campaign. However, late in the campaign there was some attempt to manufacture consensus and a post-referendum timetable for further devolution. This established the Smith Commission which essentially merged these proposals into one (notably moving closer to the Conservative/Liberal Democrat than Labour's position on the devolution of income tax).[23]

As Convery notes, it marks a long journey for the Conservative Party in reconciling the competing ideological strands of conservatism and unionism.[24] The party's proposals express, at one and the same time, a belief in the union and measures designed to ensure more fiscal responsibility and discipline within devolved bodies. They were designed to solve the problem of the imbalance in the 1999 devolution settlement between social policy expenditure (almost wholly devolved)

---

[23] The Smith Commission, *The Smith Commission Report* (Edinburg: Smith Commission, November 2014); Centre on Constitutional Change, *Beyond Smith: Contributions to the continuing process of Scottish devolution* (Edinburgh: Future of UK and Scotland, 2014).

[24] Convery, 'Devolution and the limits of Tory statecraft'.

and tax (almost exclusively reserved). It was also thought that it could be useful in shifting the dynamic of devolved politics towards more natural Conservative terrain, placing more emphasis on achieving the correct balance between taxation and expenditure. To date, devolved politics has tended to focus almost exclusively on the latter. The social policy agenda of devolution has been dominated by issues that centre-left parties such as the Scottish and Welsh nationalists, Labour and Liberal Democrats feel more comfortable operating on. The welfare state has gradually taken on a different slant, with marketization given less emphasis and policies such as free school meals, free prescriptions, free personal care for the elderly, free university tuition all emphasizing difference from England.

What the new form of unionism projected by the Conservatives also did was allow the party to project itself as offering more (in terms of devolution) than Labour. The 2010 leadership contest within the Scottish Conservative Party had previously highlighted alternative visions of the future of the party in Scotland. Murdo Fraser, who finished a close second in the contest to Ruth Davidson, had campaigned for a new party in Scotland, allowing it to break away from the unionist London-periphery structure and re-invent itself. The party's previous Thatcherite unitary unionism and governing philosophy has been replaced. Cameron's post-2010 soothing rhetoric was generally well received, as was the internal diplomacy surrounding the 'Edinburgh Agreement' in 2012.[25] The Better Together campaign threw up some strange bedfellows, with the party's Scottish leader, Ruth Davidson, at one point sharing a platform with George Galloway.

The Conservatives remained a toxic brand in Scotland, and the Liberal Democrats suffered by their association with it. Post-devolution the most striking thing about the Conservative Party in Scotland is that there is little or no evidence of any potential for revival. However, the situation in Wales stands in contrast, with the Welsh Conservatives gaining votes and seats in 2011. Also, whilst the SNP in Scotland became a sole governing political party with independence dominating the political agenda, Plaid Cymru in Wales was in the doldrums – 2011 was its worst Assembly election result.

---

[25] See chapter two, this volume.

The Liberal Democrats, despite their status as coalition partners and holders of key UK ministerial posts, remained somewhat peripheral to developments at Scottish and Welsh levels. This reflects how Scottish and Welsh politics increasingly became autonomous from developments in Westminster politics. The Liberal Democrat effect, beyond giving the UK Government enhanced legitimacy, is rather difficult to demonstrate. The Liberal Democrats in Scotland and Wales have paid a heavy representational price at both the 2011 Scottish and Welsh parliamentary elections and the 2012 Scottish and Welsh local government elections. If Labour were seen as the natural partner at UK level,[26] this was doubly the case in both Scotland and Wales, where the parties had formed coalitions in 1999–2007 and 2001–3 respectively. The 'betrayal' of coalition with the Conservatives was felt most keenly in Scotland. Liberal Democrat willingness to enter formal coalition with the Conservatives in 2010 was contrasted with their lack of willingness to discuss coalition with the Scottish National Party in 2007. Beyond Westminster it had already ditched the perennial party of protest tag by serving in Scottish and Welsh administrations.

In Scotland, the party lost much of its geographical power base. From a party of local heroes in the Highlands, Borders and other parts of rural Scotland (the Liberal Democrats had a long tradition of long-serving MPs in such areas of Scotland), their representation at the Scottish Parliament and in local government was decimated. In Wales, whilst the downslide has not been so dramatic, there were similar tales of collapsing votes, lost seats, lost deposits and falling party morale. In 2015 in both countries they are largely on the periphery of mainstream politics. They face an uphill struggle to rebuild – the nationalist parties in both countries add another serious player to electoral competition, and even minority parties such as UKIP, Socialists and the Green Party have been known to squeeze their vote into lost deposit territory.

Katherine Dommett identifies trust, identity and influence as explanations for why the Liberal Democrats have been so badly affected by the coalition.[27] The inflated expectations engendered by pre-election

---

[26] Andrew Heywood, 'The loveless marriage: Making sense of the Conservative–Liberal Democrat coalition', 2013 (accessed at http://andrewheywood.co.uk/styled-8/index. html, 7 November 2014).

[27] Katherine Dommett, 'A miserable little compromise? Exploring Liberal Democrat fortunes in the UK coalition', *Political Quarterly*, 84:2 (2013), pp. 218–27.

2010 campaigning, reneging on high-profile commitments and their complicity in the austerity agenda fed directly into negative polling in the periphery. In Scotland their partnership with the tarnished brand of Conservatism led to revised perceptions of what the party stands for. Moreover, whilst their influence on the pre-2010 Scottish and Welsh devolved coalition administrations appeared obvious (for example in Scotland in key policies such as tuition fees and care for the elderly) it appeared negligible in the UK coalition. As Dommett suggested, 'the cost-benefit analysis of the coalition does not stack up for the Liberal Democrats as they are sacrificing key principles and pledges in return for limited rewards'.[28] Whilst Clegg spoke of 'anchoring Britain to the centre ground',[29] many previous voters in the Scottish and Welsh electorate deserted his party.

The image of the Liberal Democrats has been seriously weakened in both countries. Polling data and results throughout 2010–15 indicate a declining vote share. The Liberal Democrat experience of coalition 2010–15 somewhat mirrors the experience of Plaid, the junior partner in the 'One Wales' coalition 2007–11. However, such a squeeze should not be viewed as inevitable for a junior coalition partner. In Scotland between 1999 and 2007, whilst in coalition, the party actually grew.

The union in Northern Ireland appears more secure in 2015 than at any time since the 1950s – from a unionist perspective there is no UK Government pressing for change or Irish republican armed struggle any longer.[30] The DUP–Sinn Fein diarchy became further embedded. The clashes that have taken place are over identity issues and symbolic and traditional customs – the flying of the union flag over Belfast City Hall, the perennial marching season clashes and debates about the status of languages.

The coalition government faced governments in all three peripheries without any Conservative or Liberal Democrat representation. This represented a basis for antagonistic relations. However, the post-

[28] Katherine Dommett, 'A miserable little compromise: Why the Liberal Democrats suffered in coalition', *LSE Blog* (accessed at http://blogs.lse.ac.uk/politicsandpolicy/a-miserable-little-compromise-why-the-liberal-democrats-have-suffered-in-coalition, 7 November 2014).

[29] George Parker and Kiran Stecey, 'Nick Clegg says the Lib Dem aim is to bring down the two-party system', *Financial Times*, 18 September 2013.

[30] Patterson, 'Unionism', p. 254.

devolution pattern of parties and governments working together with the wheels oiled by the civil service has continued.

Continued constitutional tinkering

Smoother territorial relations also partly reflected the post-1997 constitutional flexibility of the UK Government. Referendums have established themselves firmly as part of the conventional constitutional landscape of British politics in a system that has traditionally viewed them with suspicion. The 2011 AV referendum was only the second UK-wide one ever held (the first being the 1975 'Common Market' – as the EU was then referred to – vote). In Northern Ireland, Wales and Scotland, they have been far more common. There were constitutional referendums in both Scotland and Wales in 1979 and 1997, a 2011 Welsh Referendum and a 2014 Scottish referendum. Devolution in Northern Ireland was preceded by two separate Good Friday Agreement consenting referendums in the twenty-six counties of the Republic and the six counties of the North.

What these referendums highlight is the ad hoc and often instrumental manner in which referendums are being used. Although often portrayed as being about issues of fundamental constitutional importance, they are more accurately viewed as political tools, a tactical device utilized by politicians to suit their needs in particular circumstances. The Welsh vote in 2011 was not about the principle of whether or not Wales should have legislative devolution. The 2006 Government of Wales Act had already established the *de jure* distinction between the National Assembly for Wales and the Welsh Assembly Government (since 2011 the Welsh Government).[31] Moreover, an interim legislative dispensation enabled the National Assembly of Wales to create primary legislation. The Rubicon of primary legislative powers was already crossed in 2007. The 2011 referendum was 'merely . . . sanctioning a move to another, more expansive, form of primary law making, rather than heralding a fundamental change'.[32]

It was a choice between two systems of granting primary law-making powers to the Welsh Assembly. The referendum was as a

---

[31] Wyn Jones and Scully, *Wales Says Yes*, p. 20. [32] *Ibid.*, p. 22.

consequence of internal politicking within the Welsh Labour Party and the coalition with Plaid Cymru (though it should be noted the Welsh Conservatives included a commitment to a referendum in their 2010 Welsh manifesto). Back in the 1990s Blair utilized the promise of referendums in Scotland and Wales to neutralize the Conservatives' unionist line of attack. Cameron, likewise, utilized the referendum promise to serve political purposes in Scotland and Wales.

Wyn Jones and Scully refer to the Welsh 2011 referendum campaign as 'generally uninspiring and at times dispiriting'.[33] This stands in stark contrast to the Scottish 2014 independence referendum campaign. The record 84.5 per cent turnout was reflective of the high levels of grass-roots activism, continual political debate via social media, community halls, cars, clubs, street corners and almost any arena imaginable. The 2014 Scottish referendum dominated the political agenda in Scotland for over two years. Almost every political issue came under its prism. Whilst the Scottish example is a textbook referendum concerning a fundamental constitutional principle, the Welsh one clearly was not. In Scotland the process itself served to legitimate the Scottish constitutional order post September 2014. In contrast, the Welsh one took place with little public debate and participation evident.

Whilst the two referendums were very different, both served to highlight the continuing shifting sands of devolution in both countries. The phrase 'devolution settlement' is both inappropriate and inaccurate in all three nations beyond England. The term 'settlement' is only appropriate in the sense that devolution appears now to be more fundamentally entrenched than it may have appeared in 2010. The coalition effect, in that sense, involved more instability and negotiation as regards the precise nature of devolution in each country. The previous settlements had not proved politically sustainable.

However, despite being much predicted – the consequences of the continual flux of devolution in the Celtic periphery – the governance of England remained largely untouched and stable, until after the Scottish referendum campaign was over. One hour after the declaration of the No victory, David Cameron placed the so-called 'English Question' at the centre of UK constitutional politics. The politics of the coalition of Conservatives and Liberal Democrats, and the serious complexities any

---

[33] *Ibid.*, p. 3.

serious examination of it would throw up, ensured it was kept on the sidelines of government purview until the 2015 general election campaign was on the horizon.

Also, at the end of 2014 the long-standing issues surrounding devolution funding and representation (commonly referred to as the Barnett formula and the West Lothian question respectively), untouched and unanswered for so long, were firmly on the UK political agenda. The durability of the Barnett formula, as the basis for calculating territorial increments (or decrements) in funding, remained contested. Its durability can be explained by the fact that it kept 'the potentially controversial issue of territorial finance out of the spotlight . . . and avoid[ed] the complex and angst-ridden discussions of (territorial) finance that we find in the USA and a range of other countries'.[34] That said, the Holtham Commission in Wales did suggest reform whereby the base level of UK Government funding would be protected but the method for funding distribution be reformed to be more reflective of need.[35] Debates over the reform of Barnett remained largely the preserve of academics, think tanks, newspaper columnists and minor political voices in each country. However, the promise of further devolution to Scotland had implications for governance in England, Northern Ireland and Wales.[36]

One of the overriding narratives of the Yes campaign was dissatisfaction with Westminster and the potential for Scotland to practise a different type of politics. This has echoes of the early days of devolution and the talk of 'new politics' in Northern Ireland, Scotland and Wales. The Better Together campaign involved the Conservatives, Liberal Democrats and Labour working together. Led by Alistair Darling, the former Labour UK Chancellor, the Better Together campaign had consistent murmurings of unhappiness about his leadership across all three parties. For much of the referendum campaign

---

[34] Paul Cairney and Neil McGarvey, *Scottish Politics* (Basingstoke: Palgrave, 2nd edn, 2013), p. 234.

[35] Jonathan Bradbury, 'Wales and the 2010 general election', *Parliamentary Studies*, 63:4 (2010), p. 728.

[36] See Adam Evans, 'While the Scottish people may be on the brink of the unknown, the Welsh continue to prefer familiarity', *LSE Blog* (accessed at http://blogs.lse.ac.uk/politicsandpolicy/wales-and-the-scottish-independence-debate, 10 November 2014) and Lucy Shaddock and Akash Paun, 'Further devolution to Scotland: What have the parties proposed?', *LSE Blog* (accessed at http://blogs.lse.ac.uk/politicsandpolicy/further-devolution-to-scotland-what-have-the-parties-proposed, 10 November 2014).

momentum was perceived to be with the 'Yes' side, with off-message mishaps more prevalent on the 'No Thanks' (it was rebranded in mid-campaign) side. For example, Philip Hammond's April 2014 gaffe that sterling would be up for negotiation (despite both the UK coalition partners and Labour previously presenting a united front in dismissing a potential currency union between Scotland and the rest of the United Kingdom). There was also a UK Treasury Report that extrapolated some research on setting up costs of government departments to arrive at a nonsensical figure for the cost of setting up government in a post-independence Scotland. Late in the campaign, in reaction to the first poll showing a Yes lead, Prime Minister's Question Time was cancelled so that all three unionist party leaders could spend the day campaigning in Scotland.

The almost universal criticism of the 'Better Together' campaign was its negativity and failure to narrate a positive vision of Scotland in the union. Despite a political consensus amongst unionists that Scotland was a viable economic and political unit (itself a significant change in tone post-devolution), there were constant dire warnings and projections of risk in terms of security and defence, the economy, pensions and employment, and the flight of nomadic businesses. Much of this, of course, is par for the course in terms of the tribalism and counter-claims of referendum and party campaigning, but part of the problem was the inconsistency in tone and message from the three parties of the union. The constant projections of uncertainty, instability and risk meant the more positive messages of common values, interdependence and shared history were diluted. At the same time, Yes Scotland were presenting a 'de-risked' version of independence. They talked of a shared social and economic union; it was 'only' the political one that would change. Scotland could be rid of the Westminster elite, austerity, Trident, the bedroom tax and, best of all, the Tories (a message that resonated well with Scottish Labour voters).

The toxicity of Conservatism, combined with its lack of appeal to the crucial swing constituency of Labour voters,[37] meant the incursions of Conservative ministers north of the border were minimal

---

[37] See Craig McAngus, Neil McGarvey and Arno Van Der Zwet, 'Advocates of Scotland's settled will? Labour elites, affiliates and the constitutional question in Scotland', Elections Public Opinion and Parties Conference, University of Edinburgh, 12–14 September 2014.

Conclusions

It has become a commonplace in discussions of the coalition to note that David Cameron may have been happier in coalition with Nick Clegg than with the right wing of his own party. Reflecting on the *Programme for Government*, it is easy to see that this might have been so. But it is equally true – and less often noted – that Nick Clegg might have been more comfortable in coalition with David Cameron than with the left wing of his own party. Both men had moved their parties to the middle in the period leading up to 2010. The Coalition Agreement – made possible only by electoral failure by both parties – gave them an opportunity to translate ideological convergence into political reality, and deliver the 'new politics' both had promised.

This chapter has outlined the story of the coalition 'before the coalition', an incipient coalition of ideas and personalities which though not in formal partnership were growing increasingly aligned with one another. Historical events are contingent, and though this chapter – written in the contemporary history approach – may appear teleological, what took place between 2005 and 2010 that facilitated coalition agreement (in both literal and metaphorical senses) between the Conservatives and Liberal Democrats was not inevitable. The process was not inexorable, however 'smooth' a journey this retrospective analysis might imply. It was the results of participants' decisions, individual and collective, and was subject to the law of unintended consequences. However, it is worth noting at this point that at least in part the story developed as it did because those participants themselves sought to present their *choices* as *inevitable*; political scientists such as Colin Hay describe this as the deployment of 'logics of inevitability',[125] perhaps most familiar in the form of Margaret Thatcher's famous pronouncement of 'there is no alternative'.[126] However, Thatcher – as one of the architects of neoliberal politics – was largely successful in winning her arguments.[127] Neither Cameron nor Clegg were able to do so decisively, either with the public or their own party memberships, though for brief moments both looked as if they might succeed at least in

[125] Colin Hay, *Political Analysis* (London: Palgrave, 2002).
[126] 'Margaret Thatcher: A life in words', *Daily Telegraph*, 8 April 2013.
[127] David Harvey, *A Brief History of Neoliberalism* (Oxford: Oxford University Press, 2005), pp. 22–3.

during the referendum campaign. Despite much goading from Salmond, Cameron avoided any televised debate with him, leaving the defence of the union largely to Darling and the Scottish Labour Party. At one point when he did campaign he even made reference to the fact that the referendum was not just a chance to 'give the effin' Tories a kick', emphasizing that the vote had a finality unlike a protest vote in a by-election or the like.[38]

Surprisingly little effort was made amongst the coalition part-ners to present a unified set of proposals on extending devolution in Scotland (see Table 3.6). The three major parties all launched their own quite different and separate visions of devolution after a 'No' vote. This was despite the fact that the Scotland Act 2012 was based on the three parties working together post-2007 in the Calman Commission. The UK parties, and indeed the UK Government, did not have a consensual unified message of what the process of devolution will involve post-2015. They did seek to project one in campaign-driven joint photo-opportunities and an agreement on a Gordon Brown-driven fast-track joint timetable for delivering more powers very late in the campaign (in response to the first poll suggesting the union was in jeopardy). Two days before polling they published a joint oath.[39] It was difficult for them to conceal the defensive, reactive nature of this 'offer' so late in the campaign.

However, in line with expectations, they emerged victorious. Prior to the final days of the campaign the question was not whether the unionist parties would win but how big the winning margin would be. A 'No' vote quickly moved from a foregone conclusion to being too close to call as the polls narrowed sharply in the final two weeks. When Cameron, Clegg and Miliband rushed north (having been previously, like the UK media, rather disengaged) they were projected – somewhat exaggeratedly – as either the three wise men coming bearing gifts of more devolution in order to save the union or the horsemen of the apocalypse symbolizing the dying days of the union. In the final days

---

38 Nicholas Watt, Severin Carrell, Terry Macalister and Julie Kollewe, 'Cameron: referendum is not just a chance to "give the effing Tories a kick"', *The Guardian*, 10 September 2014.

39 'David Cameron, Ed Miliband and Nick Clegg sign joint historic promise which guarantees more devolved powers for Scotland and protection of the NHS if we vote No', *Daily Record*, 16 September 2014.

Table 3.7 *The 2012 Scotland Act in summary*

- Introduces an ability of the Scottish Parliament to vary income tax by 10p in the pound and announce the Scottish rate annually.
- Devolves stamp duty and landfill tax.
- Allows the Scottish Government to borrow from the UK government up to £2.7 billion (£500 million in current borrowing and £2.2 billion in capital borrowing).
- Administration of Scottish Parliament elections, Scottish Parliament business.
- Devolution of policy regarding air weapons, drink driving limits, national speed limit.
- Formally renames the Scottish Executive as Scottish Government.
- Gives Scottish Government more responsibility for Gaelic broadcasting and appointment of one member of the BBC Trust.
- Various other amendments and provisions relating to Crown Estate, Antarctica, UK Supreme Court, European Court of Human Rights.[a]

[a] For a fuller outline see Cairney and McGarvey, *Scottish Politics*, p. 247.

of the referendum campaign the survival of Cameron as Prime Minister in the event of a Yes vote was even being questioned.[40] The campaigning desperation with which the Westminster class fought to maintain the union was indicative of how power over Scotland post-devolution had drifted away from the UK office-holders.

Whilst constitutional tinkering remained evident in Scotland and Wales, in Northern Ireland power-sharing, as Peter Mandelson had once remarked, remained 'the only show in town'.[41] The death of Ian Paisley in September 2014 was marked with reflections on how much he and the politics of Northern Ireland had changed. Working alongside Sinn Fein's Martin McGuinness, the sworn enemies had developed a genuine friendship and were labelled 'the chuckle brothers' by the Irish media, such was their predilection for smiling and laughing together in public.[42]

The five years of coalition government were marked with more stability in the Northern Ireland Assembly after its previous years of arrested development punctuated by periods of London direct rule. The Democratic Unionist Party and Sinn Fein both recognize that, despite their fundamental disagreement on Northern Ireland's constitutional

[40] George Eaton, 'Even if the union endures, the last vestiges of Westminster's authority have been washed away', *New Statesman*, 10 September 2014.

[41] R. Wilford, 'Northern Ireland: The politics of constraint', *Parliamentary Affairs*, 63:1 (2010), pp. 134–55.

[42] *Ibid.*, pp. 135–6.

future, power-sharing is the 'least worst' option available to them. The UK coalition government inherited the legacy of the arrangements put in place by the Belfast and St Andrews Agreements and it has largely retained a hands-off role that may reflect that the transitional period between armed conflict and 'normal' politics has ended.

Whilst the UK union was changing beyond Westminster it is worth noting in passing the issue of the other key union in UK politics, the European one. The EU, that great 'sleeper' issue of internal Tory Party politics – it sporadically appears, to cause strife and division – is one that is framed very differently in politics beyond Westminster. The 'ever closer union' of the EU is a subject that has conjured up issues for the ever-looser union of the United Kingdom. Cameron simultaneously campaigned for an EU Referendum at UK level in 2017, while he suggested that Scottish independence would leave it 'at the back of the queue to join the EU'.[43] It is worth noting that a Yes vote in the Scottish referendum was implicitly accepted as a yes to Scottish independence *and* Scottish membership of the EU.

Conclusion

Whilst the coalition effect on policymaking is immediately obvious when viewed through the prism of UK politics, it is less readily apparent when viewed from the Celtic periphery. In that respect the 'seismic change in the dynamics of British politics'[44] did not appear quite as such in the world beyond Westminster. Coalition and multi-party politics, fixed-term parliaments, referendums and the like were not novel in Northern Ireland, Scotland and Wales. Indeed they have become very much part of 'normal' politics.

Devolution in the UK was not born out of any constitutional or political ideology or principle. The three asymmetrical systems of devolution reflect political pragmatism and circumstance in each territory, both in terms of inception and development. The union is elastic. One of the problems the UK coalition faced was that the process of devolution and constitutional change has developed its own dynamic in each of the

---

[43] Nigel Morris, 'Scottish independence: Scotland "would be put at the back of the queue to join the EU" says David Cameron', *The Independent*, 3 June 2014.

[44] Dommett, , 'A miserable little compromise'.

Celtic countries. The constitutional changes set in motion by the previous Labour government mean that agenda control has slipped away from Westminster. Legally, devolution may mean power devolved is retained; however, politically, as the events of 2010–15 demonstrate, the political agenda in each territory has developed differing trajectories. These developments reflect political priorities, agendas and processes in Belfast, Cardiff and Edinburgh rather than London. This marginalized the coalition effect in devolved policy areas – although it should be acknowledged that the austerity effect on budgets was very apparent.

The direction of travel from 2010 to 2015 was that of increased devolution. In Scotland a 'No' vote was achieved at the cost of promises (by all three UK parties) to surrender more powers to the Scottish Parliament. Events of 2010–15 amply demonstrated that devolution was indeed a process rather than an event. The coalition has conceded more autonomy in both Scotland and Wales. Northern Ireland in this period was rather vividly described as 'something akin to a constitutional granny flat perched on the edge of the Union'.[45] As ever, politics in the six counties of the north of Ireland appeared remote and very different. However, both Scottish and Welsh politics also appeared more differentiated, as the extenuation and enhancement of the territorialization of UK politics triggered by devolution continued.

Both the Conservatives and the Liberal Democrats have felt the electoral cost of being in power at Westminster, the latter party much more keenly. Both coalition parties were minority players in Scottish and Welsh politics in 2010; by 2015 they had accentuated that status. The Liberal Democrats were approaching irrelevance in the devolved politics of both countries, and the Scottish Conservatives continued to struggle to extend their support beyond their base. Only the Welsh Conservatives showed signs of revival.

Devolution and territorial governance became even more firmly embedded in UK politics. Less than two decades after its inception, opposition to devolution in each territory was so small as to be politically inconsequential. The strident unionism of the Conservative Party 1979–97 is the constitutional politics of a bygone era.

---

[45] Esmond Birnie, cited in J. W. McAuley and J. Tonge, 'Britishness (and Irishness) in Northern Ireland since the Good Friday Agreement', *Parliamentary Affairs*, 63:2 (2010), p. 274.

There is some evidence that the Scottish independence referendum led to some reassertion of British identity.[46] Historically and comparatively, the notion of being British is an understated one: the Better Together campaign tended to steer clear from issues of identity, at least until late in the campaign, when the Scottish Saltire was raised above Downing Street – an indication that the politics of symbolism and flag-waving is not confined to Northern Ireland. The events of 2010–15 in Scotland, Northern Ireland and Wales give testimony to the pluralism of identities in the UK. The new unionism practised by the UK Government post-2010 was more flexible and legitimate. It may be one of the areas where Liberal Democrat influence was most apparent. Without them, questions of political legitimacy would undoubtedly have been raised beyond Westminster.

[46] Ben Riley-Smith, 'Scottish independence debate triggers rise in Britishness north of the border', *The Telegraph*, 11 August 2014.

4 THE COALITION AND THE EXECUTIVE

PETER RIDDELL

The way the United Kingdom is governed has changed substantially following the 2010 general election. The central executive looks very different four to five years on. This is partly due to the existence of the Conservative/Liberal Democrat coalition altering the familiar pattern of decision-making, but only partly. Many of the changes in the scale of central government, of the civil service based in Whitehall, were proposed, at least in outline, by the Conservatives in opposition before the 2010 election and were implemented after then with little input from the Liberal Democrats. This chapter will therefore address two questions: first, how the coalition is run within Whitehall; and, second, how the executive itself has changed since 2010.[1]

The coalition came into existence in May 2010 after thirteen years of two very different Prime Ministers, Tony Blair and Gordon Brown. Each, in their contrasting ways, personalized the office, relying on a group of personally appointed advisers to take forwards their wishes, sidelining many of their Cabinet colleagues. Senior civil servants in 10 Downing Street still had influence, notably Sir Jeremy Heywood, initially as principal private secretary to Blair and then as Permanent Secretary, Downing Street, to Mr Brown, and then to David Cameron, as well as foreign policy advisers like Sir David Manning. There were a number of innovations at the centre, such as the creation in 2001 of the

---

[1] There is a limited literature on many of the topics in this chapter. Apart from where there is a specific reference, many of the insights and conclusions come from my work with ministers and civil servants at the Institute for Government.

Delivery Unit and of the Strategy Unit, and, then in the wake of the international financial crisis of 2008, of the National Economic Council. Other new units came and went, though some have been re-invented under a different name, as discussed in the Institute for Government's report on such units.[2]

Pre-election plans

The House of Commons expenses scandal of 2009 led to demands to 'clean up' politics, in the hope of restoring the reputation of politicians and politics generally. The resulting recommendations were mainly directed at Parliament and at the ethical standards of MPs and ministers. But the Conservatives, and to a lesser extent the Liberal Democrats, produced proposals to change the way the UK was governed. The Conservatives promised in their 2010 manifesto

> to scrap Labour's failed target regime and instead require every department to publish a business plan, with senior management accountable to more rigorous departmental boards for their performance. We will make it easier to reward the best civil servants and remove the least effective. We will reform the Civil Service Compensation Scheme to bring it more into line with practice in the private sector. We will put a limit on the number of special advisers and protect the impartiality of the civil service.[3]

The Conservatives had a range of proposals to make the performance of the state more transparent and to cut its size, and, in particular, sharply to reduce the number of quangos or arm's-length bodies. Their manifesto promised to 'create a powerful new right to government data, enabling the public to request, and receive, government datasets in an open and standardized format'. In addition, central government job vacancies would be published online; all data would be published in an open and standardized format, with details of job titles, pay and expenses of senior officials, and anyone paid more than the Prime Minister in the public sector would have to have their salary signed

---

[2] Josh Harris and Jill Rutter, *Effective Support for the Prime Minister at the Centre of Government* (Institute for Government, July 2014).

[3] This and subsequent Conservative proposals are from *Invitation to Join the Government of Britain: The Conservative Manifesto 2010*.

off by the Treasury. The Conservative manifesto also promised sharp cuts in the 'quango state' on the principle that 'ministers should be responsible for government policy, not unelected bureaucrats'. So 'any quangos that do not perform a technical function or a function that requires political impartiality, or act independently to establish facts, will be abolished'. There were proposals to reduce the cost of procurement, notably in the handling of ICT projects and by publishing in full government contracts for goods and services worth over £25,000. The Conservatives also called for 'appointing senior private sector non-executives to departmental boards to deliver better value for money'. There were a number of recommendations to decentralize power locally, to local councils, neighbourhoods and individuals.

The Liberal Democrats touched on similar themes of a 'rotten' system which needed radical change, even though their specific recommendations differed, notably on electoral reform, party funding and broader constitutional change. While there were lengthy passages on voting, Parliament, lobbying and local government, the Liberal Democrat manifesto said relatively little about central government organization, as opposed to recommendations affecting particular departments. This later left the field open to the introduction of largely Conservative-inspired proposals for changing the operations of Whitehall.

None of these proposals – with the exception of the proposed limit on the number of special advisers – had any relevance to the formation of the coalition. It was a forbidden subject, notably, and understandably, because British politics operated, at least at a United Kingdom-wide level, on the assumption of a majoritarian, winner-takes-all system. The Liberal Democrats, while implicitly recognizing that their support for reform of the voting system would mean the creation of coalitions, were reluctant to talk about the issue, having been badly burned in the past, notably in the 1987 and 1992 general elections, when the possibility of a hung parliament had been raised in the later stages of the campaign, only to produce a swing back to the main parties by polling day. Nick Clegg referred carefully to talking first to the party with the largest number of MPs, thus avoiding any question of preference between the two main parties.

Consequently, there was virtually no public discussion about the politics of coalition, not only in the manifestos but also in the campaign, even though opinion polls increasingly pointed to a hung parliament with no party having an overall majority. As noted in the report, *Transitions: Lessons Learned* by Dr Catherine Haddon and myself,[4] a 'war game' was held in early 2010, with senior officials playing the roles of leading politicians. It was attended by Sir Gus (now Lord) O'Donnell, the then Cabinet Secretary; Sir Jeremy Heywood, then Permanent Secretary at 10 Downing Street and later Cabinet Secretary; Sir Christopher Geidt, the Queen's private secretary; and Sir Alex Allan, then in the Cabinet Office and a veteran of changes of government. In advance, some officials were sceptical, arguing that the civil service already knew the rules. However, the playing out of the scenarios showed their limitations. Scenario four in the exercise was just like the result which occurred in May 2010. Yet the civil servants role-playing it did not succeed in coming to a clear conclusion. This may have been a matter of temperament in that civil servants, perhaps fortunately, mostly do not think like politicians – between logic and emotion, natural caution and risk-taking. No one acted as boldly as Mr Cameron in the event did on the Friday after polling day.

After the election it was learnt that there had been some private discussions before polling day among a tight group in the top leaderships of both the Liberal Democrats and the Conservatives, not together but separately, as the books by Tory MP Rob Wilson and Liberal Democrat David Laws reveal.[5] Wilson notes that during the campaign, as the polls increasingly pointed to a hung parliament, George Osborne persuaded Mr Cameron of the need to do some very private planning for that possibility. So Oliver Letwin, in particular, started looking at Liberal Democrat policy proposals and what Nick Clegg had said during the campaign. But that was not with a view to a coalition government, which Mr Cameron and his colleagues then thought was an unlikely outcome, but rather to what understandings with other parties might be necessary to support a minority Conservative Government in the Commons – in particular, a confidence and supply arrangement. Laws records how a team was set up secretly by Mr Clegg in late 2009 to advise on strategy in a hung parliament and then to do the

---

4 Peter Riddell and Catherine Haddon, *Transitions: Lessons Learned, Reflections on the 2010 UK General Election – and Looking Ahead to 2015* (Institute for Government, October 2011).
5 Rob Wilson, *5 Days to Power: The Journey to Coalition Britain* (London: Biteback, 2010), pp. 52–4; David Laws, *22 Days in May: The Birth of the Lib Dem–Conservative Coalition* (London: Biteback, 2010), pp. 13–20.

negotiating. Most of the members of the team, with the exception of Chris Huhne, believed that in a Conservative-dominated hung parliament, the most likely outcome was a confidence and supply agreement, with the Liberal Democrats remaining on the opposition benches, while supporting a Conservative government on economic issues and on confidence votes in exchange for a commitment on some key policies. Mr Huhne pushed the coalition option.

Most of these pre-election discussions, particularly on the Tory side, were about negotiations, policy priorities and red lines. Paul Burstow, the Liberal Democrat Chief Whip, seems to have been about the only person to consider how a coalition government would be run, and what a coalition executive would look like. Reflecting the party's Scottish experience, he looked at issues such as the allocation of ministerial posts, arrangements for Cabinet committees, details of collective responsibility and whipping arrangements. There was virtually no other discussion about how a coalition would work as opposed to negotiating tactics and positioning.

Perhaps the most important factor in 2010 was that virtually no one, politician or civil servant, had worked in a coalition before. The only exceptions were Jim Wallace, Lord Wallace of Tankerness, who served as deputy First Minister for six years in the Lab–Lib Dem coalition in Edinburgh, and a scattering of civil servants, such as Philip Rycroft, who had worked for the Scottish Government until 2009 and after 2012 became Director General for the Deputy Prime Minister's team in the Cabinet Office.

Adapting Whitehall for a coalition

On election day itself, senior officials in the Cabinet Office expected a minority Conservative Government probably backed by the Democratic Unionists. As discussed in chapter one, civil servants then quickly adapted to the coalition that emerged five days later. O'Donnell and his team quickly produced proposals for the running of the government. But what is striking, in retrospect, is how the Whitehall machine was essentially adapting the familiar methods of working for single-party governments rather than re-thinking them for a very different political context of multi-party government. One Cabinet Office official noted that

> There has been no need to change any of the civil service guidance. We made one change to the Ministerial Code, about setting aside collective responsibility on those issues where the parties agree to disagree. There have been no ethics or propriety issues specific to the Coalition.[6]

One month after the election, the Cabinet Secretary sent a note round his fellow Permanent Secretaries:

> The role of the Civil service is to serve the Government of the day. This is of course no different for a coalition government, with majority and minority partners . . . Collective agreement through the Cabinet Committee clearance process is therefore of additional importance, as one means of making the Coalition work.[7]

At this period, there was great sensitivity to making sure both sides of the coalition were involved:

> In thinking about coalition issues, officials should consider the importance both sides of the Coalition attach to a no surprises culture . . . Civil service advice can flag the need to engage on a point of party political difference relevant to the functioning of the Coalition. Permanent Secretaries may also advise ministers that an issue should be taken to the Coalition Committee.

Such good intentions looked almost quaint from the perspective of the end of the parliament.

There was a sense of the provisional rather than the permanent, implicitly seeing whether the absence of a single-party majority government was merely temporary. Moreover, the conventions of Whitehall are for civil servants to work to a Prime Minister or to a Secretary of State, with no special role for other ministers. In Liberal Democrat eyes, this produced a bias in favour of the Conservatives since they occupied most of the main Secretary of State posts.

The Coalition Agreement[8] set out the formal arrangements for the working of the coalition. But it was a thin document, which left many issues unaddressed, some of which only emerged later. The agreement rested on two assertions. First, 'There is no constitutional difference between a coalition government and a single party Government, but working practices need to adapt to reflect the fact that the UK has not had a Coalition in

---

[6] Quoted in Robert Hazell and Ben Yong, *The Politics of Coalition: How the Conservative–Liberal Democrat Government Works* (Oxford: Hart, 2012), p. 66.
[7] *Ibid.*   [8] *Coalition Agreement for Stability and Reform* (Cabinet Office, May 2010).

modern times.' Second, 'Close consultation between the Prime Minister and Deputy Prime Minister, other Ministers and members of the Conservative and Liberal Democrat Parties in both Houses will be the foundation of the Coalition's success.' This was linked to the 'principle of balance' in the allocation of responsibilities, decisions on policy and the Government's legislative programme, the conduct of business and the resolution of disputes.

The formal procedures, in practice, constrained the freedom of the Prime Minister to appoint to the government. The initial allocation of Cabinet, ministerial, whip and special adviser appointments between the parties was agreed between Mr Cameron and Mr Clegg, on a roughly five-to-one ratio, reflecting the broad balance of the parties' numbers of MPs in the Commons. Any changes to the allocation between parties during the lifetime of the coalition would be agreed between the two leaders. And within this allocation, Clegg would nominate Liberal Democrat ministers, while no Liberal Democrat minister or whip could be removed on the recommendation of the Prime Minister without full consultation with the Deputy Prime Minister.

The effect of this agreement has been to discourage change in two ways. First, Mr Cameron's instinctive reluctance to alter departmental boundaries by reorganizing the machinery of government has been reinforced by the existence of the coalition. The abolition or merger of a department would upset the fine balance of allocation of ministries between the two parties. This is unlike the recent pattern, since previous Prime Ministers have regularly announced changes in the machinery of government. Second, the allocation of departments at Cabinet level between the two parties has not altered even though the personnel have changed. For instance, when Mr Laws and Mr Huhne had to resign, they were succeeded as Chief Secretary to the Treasury and Energy and Climate Change Secretary respectively by another Liberal Democrat (Danny Alexander and Ed Davey respectively), rather than a Conservative, since this would have triggered a complicated swopping of portfolios. This has not applied at below Cabinet level, where the Liberal Democrats have lost representation in some departments, such as the Foreign Office and Defence, and gained in others, such as DEFRA and International Development. But the division of the right to appoint between the two party leaders has meant that some junior ministers have been chosen who have different views from a Secretary of State of the other party.

The Liberal Democrats decided from the start that they would seek as wide a spread as possible across Whitehall rather than concentrate on a few departments, as happens in some coalition governments in the rest of Europe. They opted for breadth rather than depth. As one Liberal Democrat minister commented: 'I don't think you can be a party which is only interested in a limited number of issues and a restricted number of departments. To be credible coalition partners, you have to be engaged and involved across the whole patch.'[9] The roughly five-to-one ratio between ministers has meant that the Liberal Democrats have had no representation in some departments or only a junior minister in others.

The original coalition documents laid considerable stress on the role of Cabinet committees in ensuring that both sides' views were heard, in effect giving disproportionate numbers on committees to the Liberal Democrats. Matthew d'Ancona reported that, 'Fresh life was breathed into the Cabinet committee system, sluggish at best under Brown. Lib Dem ministers, being fewer in numbers, found themselves stretched by this revival: Alexander sat on 12 such committees. Cable on seven and Huhne on nine.'[10] Where there were clashes – for instance criminal justice and human rights – issues were often passed to the Home Affairs Committee chaired by Clegg. But this did not mean the debates there were necessarily Conservative versus Liberal Democrat, since Kenneth Clarke, the Justice Secretary, often sided with Clegg rather than with Theresa May, the Home Secretary. That changed in September 2012 when Clarke was replaced by Chris Grayling. Conservatives have complained that Mr Clegg has used the committee to hold up their proposals, preventing issues from being resolved.

The most notable, and less partisan, innovation was the creation of the National Security Council, chaired by the Prime Minister, which usually met each week on Tuesday, the same morning as the full Cabinet. This replaced previous Cabinet committees dealing with overseas and defence policy and included not only senior ministers but also the chief of defence staff and the three heads of the intelligence agencies. The aim was to provide a broader view of national security policy, though the council has been criticized for having too short-term a focus because of the Prime Minister's approach, and with a bias towards foreign rather than domestic

---

[9] Quoted in Hazell and Yong, *Politics of Coalition*, p. 43.

[10] Mathew d'Ancona, *In It Together: The Inside Story of the Coalition Government* (London: Penguin, 2013), p. 37.

threats. The council, and its supporting secretariat, would have been introduced by a single-party Conservative government.

The normal principles of collective responsibility were reaffirmed – frank and private expression of opinions and advice as decisions are reached which are then binding on, and supported by, all ministers. However, significant exceptions were specifically cited in the 'Programme for Government', the second and more important of the two policy agreements.[11] There were specific permissions to 'agree to disagree' on tuition fees, the building of new civil nuclear power stations and transferable tax allowances for married couples, and, less precisely, on the renewal of the Trident nuclear deterrent. In these cases, Liberal Democrat MPs could abstain, not vote against the Government. The difference was crucial, since abstention would just reduce a Conservative majority in a Commons division, while voting against could result in a defeat. The practice was in some cases different, with a distinction between Liberal Democrat ministers and backbench MPs, while strains over the interpretation of collective responsibility became increasingly apparent during the course of the parliament. Moreover, differences of view between the coalition parties were also reflected in the creation of two dozen policy reviews and commissions, which in some cases, such as a Bill of Rights, put off the underlying disagreement.

The Coalition Agreement had some significant omissions. The emphasis was on the centre, on Cabinet committees and on the interests of the government as a whole. 'The general principle will be that the Prime Minister and Deputy Prime Minister should have a full and contemporaneous overview of the business of government.'[12] But there were immediate problems. Previous Deputy Prime Ministers had been of the same party as the Prime Minister and their title was often largely symbolic, for internal party reasons, especially if they were also deputy leaders of their party. Mr Clegg's position was different. He headed a separate party with a fifth of the ministers in the government. His initial private office was small, in part because of a reluctance among senior civil servants to create a separate power base which might be seen to rival that of the Prime Minister. There was a deliberate desire to avoid the tensions which appeared in French governments in the 1980s and 1990s during

---

[11] HM Government, *The Coalition: Our Programme for Government* (Cabinet Office, May 2010).
[12] Coalition Agreement.

periods of 'co-habitation', when the President and the Prime Minister came from different parties. For instance, when the Institute for Government produced a report in September 2010,[13] only a few months after the election, arguing for an increase in support in Mr Clegg's office and more generally for Liberal Democrat ministers, the response from senior civil servants was distinctly cool. In time, they appreciated the problems faced by Mr Clegg. In 2011, more officials and special advisers (initially six, but then more in the following year) were appointed, mainly at the centre. Mr Clegg's office remained small, with Jonny Oates as chief of staff from August 2010, while there was a high turnover amongst other advisers, in part because both Polly Mackenzie and Lena Pletsch, amongst long-standing aides, had periods on maternity leave. A *de facto*, and then formal, policy unit developed in the Cabinet Office, servicing Mr Clegg's particular interests such as social mobility, city deals and constitutional reform, as well as providing advice across Whitehall.

This involved breaching the Conservatives' manifesto commitment to reduce the overall number of special advisers below the total appointed by Labour. But that pledge had been given on the assumption of a single-party majority government, and most ministers, including Conservatives, accepted that the change made sense in the context of a coalition where more advisers were needed to ensure fuller coordination within the parties. Indeed, some ministers believed that the 2010 manifesto pledge was misguided anyway, since they wanted to strengthen the political advice available to ministers.

In retrospect, there was some discussion about whether it would have been better for Mr Clegg to move into 10 Downing Street to be alongside Mr Cameron. That was never considered at the time, so Mr Clegg took over one of the office suites in 70 Whitehall, the home of the Cabinet Office, with an interlinked door to 10 Downing Street. Later, further underlining the separation, Mr Clegg's team moved further away from Downing Street, down Whitehall to Dover House, shared with the Liberal Democrat Scotland Secretary. However, in 2010 some Liberal Democrats did move into Number 10 to work, for a time, in the same offices as Conservatives, notably the senior policy advisers Steve Hilton for Mr Cameron and Polly Mackenzie for Mr

---

[13] Akash Paun, *Coalition Government in the UK* (Institute for Government, September 2010).

Clegg, who worked noisily alongside each other next door to the Cabinet room.

Other advisers worked together in 10 Downing Street in a small and under-powered unit under James O'Shaughnessy as Conservative head of the Policy Unit. Indeed, curiously in retrospect, some provided advice to both the Prime Minister and Deputy Prime Minister. That phase only lasted a few months. The problems were not primarily over political advice, but about being spread too thinly, and missing, or inadequately dealing with, very difficult issues such as the sell-off of forestry land and the long-running row over NHS reform. It was widely agreed that it was a mistake to scale back the Downing Street Policy Unit by so much. This was a Conservative decision by Mr Cameron and his advisers; in reaction to what they saw as an octopus-like Number 10 operation in the Blair and Brown years interfering in the work of departments, they wanted to stand back, setting goals for Secretaries of State under the Business Plans and allowing them to get on with it without 'man-marking' from the centre. The result was that some potential problems were missed at the centre in Downing Street until they had become urgent, and often public, headaches.

Otherwise, Mr Cameron followed the familiar pattern of previous Prime Ministers in retaining a close group of advisers who had served him in opposition, notably Ed Llewellyn as chief of staff, in a role akin to the one which Jonathan Powell occupied under Tony Blair for a decade, also with a particular interest in foreign affairs. Kate Fall continued as deputy chief of staff. Otherwise, there were few constants with, as noted above, Steve Hilton and James O'Shaughnessy departing before the half-way mark and Rohan Silva also going. Andy Coulson, as director of communications, was an enforced departure because of the phone-hacking scandal which later saw him jailed. He was replaced by Craig Oliver from the BBC, a more low-key figure. On the media side, Mr Cameron followed the practice of Mr Brown rather than Mr Blair in having a civil servant as his chief press spokesman, dealing day-to-day with the media, and then a director of communications. Andrew Cooper, a long-term modernizer and founder of the Populus polling firm, served from spring 2011 until autumn 2013 as Director of Strategy. As the election approached, the increasingly important figure was Lynton Crosby, the Australian strategist who had advised Michael Howard ahead of the 2005 general election and Boris Johnson in his mayoral campaigns. He was hired by the Conservatives midway through the parliament. George Osborne was also a constant, and crucial, presence in 10 Downing Street discussions. After the strains and rows of the Blair/Brown years, both Mr Cameron and Mr Osborne were determined to avoid any Treasury/10 Downing Street splits.

Mr Cameron also relied heavily on Sir Jeremy Heywood, for eighteen months as civil service head of the Downing Street operation, and then, from January 2012, as Cabinet Secretary. Sir Jeremy became a lightning rod for some of the Tory right's criticism of 10 Downing Street, and he was accused of acting as a counter-balance to some of Mr Hilton's ideas and being too cautious over universal credit. Also, Sir Jeremy was unfairly criticized for the advice he gave over the Andrew Mitchell affair. He was blamed by some MPs, and in the press, for easing Mr Mitchell out, when his strictly limited advice to Mr Cameron had the reverse impact, in ensuring that he remained in office for a few weeks longer before losing the confidence of Conservative MPs and having to resign. More generally, Tory MPs and the press criticized the Downing Street operation as a means of expressing their dissatisfaction over the recession and policy errors caused by wider political weaknesses in the government. Nonetheless, there was a widespread view that the leadership within Number 10 was not strong enough and did not provide sufficient direction.

The original, small political operation was replaced in 2011 by what became a larger policy and implementation unit of civil servants under Paul Kirby and Kris Murrin. That, in turn, lasted until early 2013, when Mr Cameron decided he wanted a more political outfit and Jo Johnson, a Tory MP, was brought in to head a unit of Conservative special advisers in 10 Downing Street, clearly separate and distinct from the civil service, while Mr Clegg has his parallel team of Liberal Democrat advisers based in first the Cabinet Office and then Dover House. Instead of working alongside each other, the two teams of advisers have negotiated with each other on behalf of their political masters, symbolizing the changing relationship between the two parties.

The formal agreement also paid insufficient attention to what happened within departments, especially where the Liberal Democrats were not represented. The assumption was that the Cabinet committee structure would address this issue, and it did to some extent. But this meant that potential problems were not addressed early enough. Various solutions have been tried by the Liberal Democrats, notably the use of whips attached to departments without a full minister, attending meetings and reporting back to the centre. As noted above, the most important change, brought in 2011 and 2012, was to increase the number of politically appointed special advisers. These were largely based at the centre, in the Clegg office, but were allocated specific departmental portfolios to monitor.

How the coalition parties worked together

As important as the formal procedures have been the personal relations between the senior members of the two coalition parties. There has been something like a pyramid with relations closest at the top – between Mr Cameron and Mr Clegg, Mr Osborne and Mr Alexander, and Mr Letwin and Mr Laws – and more strained the further you go down. Informal relationships at the top have been crucial to resolving differences when they have arisen. This has meant that the formal Coalition Committee has hardly met and tricky items have gone to the Quad – Messrs Cameron, Clegg, Osborne and Alexander – and in some cases just to the regular weekly bilateral meetings of the Prime Minister and the Deputy Prime Minister. The danger has been of loading too much onto the top, so that some issues do not get resolved.

Within departments, relations were, at least initially, and have often continued to be good, with some notable exceptions such as the Home Office and Education (towards the end of Michael Gove's period there). But much has depended on the personalities of ministers from the two parties. In some cases, a Conservative Secretary of State has treated a junior Liberal Democrat minister as he would other junior ministers – often meaning they are ignored – rather than as the representative of a partner in the coalition. The practice has varied considerably, with some junior Liberal Democrat ministers brought into the confidence of a Conservative Secretary of State, and, in other cases, not. The determining factor has been the attitude of the Secretary of State to the coalition. As discussed in other chapters, relations between the parties, and support for the coalition, has been even more critical, and increasingly hostile, amongst backbench MPs and local party activists and members.

Over time, broader relationships between the two parties have become strained and they have operated as two increasingly distinct groups, working together on the business of government, but suspiciously and warily with little co-operation on future plans. There have been three broad phases which have determined working relations within the coalition.

First, there was an initial euphoric phase, when the coalition was seen as more than the sum of its two parts. D'Ancona records:

> In the infancy of the new government, the Lib Dems had to 'own everything', so to speak. To do otherwise would have looked gutless and semi-detached, and given a bad name to coalition as a new and untested constitutional structure. The Lib Dems had to risk associating themselves with unpopular policies if they wanted to share credit with the Tories for popular measures. The party could not approach its participation in the alliance as a 'tick-box' exercise, in which Clegg and his colleagues applauded only those policies which were recognizably Lib Dem in inspiration.[14]

This phase was reflected in closer working relationships, as discussed above, and statements from ministers of both sides that they had much to learn from the other party.

Second, there was the phase of distancing. That began over the winter of 2010–11 with the controversies over the increase in tuition fees and NHS reform, when Mr Clegg came under increasing pressure from his own party. Mr Clegg faced unpleasant personal abuse over the rise in fees but still publicly supported the policy, which came from Mr Cable's Business Department. On health, pressures from the Liberal Democrats, and some discontented Conservatives, forced a pause in parliamentary consideration of the legislation and some amendments. The pivotal moment which led to a recognition of distinct rather than overlapping interests was over the referendum on the Alternative Vote in May 2011, when the Conservatives vigorously, ruthlessly and successfully campaigned against the change. That led to a counter-reaction against the Conservatives and the coalition within the Liberal Democrat party. Mr Clegg and his team felt let down by Mr Cameron over what was a central Liberal Democrat objective of, at least, one step towards electoral reform. The episode was seen by some Liberal Democrats as an eye-opener to the determination of the Conservatives not to compromise on their basic political interests. That was the start of differentiation, a conscious effort by the two parties to distance themselves from one another, particularly on the part of the Liberal Democrats, stressing where they had moderated or watered down the other party's approach, and highlighting their own achievements, such as raising the starting threshold for income tax and introducing the pupil

---

[14] D'Ancona, *In It Together*, p. 59.

premium. The Conservative response, particularly of ministers hostile to the coalition, was partly to ignore or brush aside the Liberal Democrats and to emphasize what they hoped to do on their own if only they were free of their tiresome coalition partner, notably on Europe and human rights.

Even in this chillier phase, government business was done; Mr Cameron and Mr Clegg managed to co-operate and sort out problems. But that spirit of even grudging co-operation did not reach everywhere in Whitehall. Typical of this phase was the autumn round of conferences, when each party had its own distinctive policies to announce, rather than joint ones. There was a sense of one party being allowed to announce its own favourite policies, followed by a competing list from the other party, with no real coordination and often scant attempt to cost the pledges. These competitive promises were to the despair of civil servants, who regarded such double-headed policymaking, or rather policy announcing, as counterproductive as well as expensive.

Third, the parties moved into a phase of prickly co-existence after a tit-for-tat series of exchanges over constitutional reform during the summer and early autumn of 2012. After Conservative MPs had ensured that no progress would be made on House of Lords reform, one of Mr Clegg's cherished constitutional priorities, the Liberal Democrats reacted by backing a blocking manoeuvre in the Lords which halted the planned changes to parliamentary boundaries. The proposed change in constituency boundaries, part of the legislation also authorizing the referendum on the Alternative Vote, had been widely seen as hitting the Liberal Democrats and benefiting the Conservatives – possibly by a sufficient margin to tip the balance between a minority and a majority government in a closely fought election. Either way, the Liberal Democrat support for blocking the boundary changes was denounced as a betrayal of the Coalition Agreement by the Conservatives. The political mood was soured and the parties became even less inclined to co-operate. There were two distinct camps, recognizing the need, not least for electoral reasons, to remain in coalition. But it was a joyless marriage of necessity.

In the fifth year of the parliament, the relationship between the coalition partners was commonly described as 'transactional' – that is, the parties did the necessary business of government. But there was no longer any desire to work together on new policy ideas since many on both sides did not think there would be a post-election coalition, nor really wanted one. Ministers and advisers met within their own party groups rather than jointly except when required by the business of government. Both parties put forward their own separate and often conflicting ideas for policy after the election, on Europe, human rights and welfare cuts. The mood was increasingly of frustration. The Conservatives ached to be free of what they saw as uncongenial and complaining colleagues, while the Liberal Democrats found increasing grounds for complaint in their coalition partners. Mr Clegg and his colleagues switched from lauding what had been achieved together to stressing, rather, what they had prevented the Conservatives from doing. The earlier restraint in comments largely disappeared, with open disagreements between senior ministers in the Cabinet. The parties voted in different lobbies – on European issues and over the so-called bedroom tax in 2014 – further straining the conventions of collective responsibility. The justification was that the votes were over future, party policies – not covered by the Coalition Agreement – rather than over current government commitments. This became an increasing cause of public division during the summer and autumn of 2014 as both the Conservatives and the Liberal Democrats set out and developed their distinct, and often sharply contrasting, plans for the 2015 parliament. Yet none of these exchanges imperilled the existence or operation of the coalition as such. Unity was more or less retained on the key question of deficit reduction and Mr Osborne and Mr Alexander continued to work closely together on the economy.

Because the experience of coalition was novel, there were none of the usual patterns of behaviour in the final year of a parliament seen in countries where coalitions were the norm. The experience of countries such as the Netherlands, Germany, Sweden and Ireland showed that, while politicians were increasingly in campaigning mode, looking ahead to the coming elections, they recognized the need for self-restraint in what they said. Politicians in countries with coalitions accepted that, while they would be competing against other parties in elections, they would also be potential partners in a post-election coalition. This affected what they said and what they promised. They were always aware of potential coalition negotiations. Many countries had developed special conventions for the final year to allow government to operate and for parties to obtain civil service advice, as discussed in various Institute for Government reports.[15] In particular, in

---

[15] Akash Paun and Robyn Munro, *Whitehall in Year Five of the UK Coalition: Lessons from Elsewhere* (Institute for Government, April 2014), and the same authors, *Separate Space: The Final Year of the Scottish Coalition, 1999–2007* (Institute for Government, April 2014).

Scotland, under the Labour and Liberal Democrat coalitions, a 'separate space' system was set up to enable parties to receive civil service advice during the final six months in 2006–7. None of these factors, or constraints, applied to the Conservative–Liberal Democrat coalition, largely because there was no tradition of coalitions. Moreover, many Conservative ministers did not want to give the Liberal Democrats the opportunity to receive civil service advice in areas outside their direct ministerial responsibilities, quite narrow in the case of many junior ministers. That naturally favoured the Conservatives, who held most Secretary of State posts and could seek whatever advice they wanted. However, the formal barries to the Liberal Democrats' getting broader advice were eventually relaxed towards the end of 2014.

An asymmetrical coalition

Some of the niggling problems of earlier years had developed, certainly on the Liberal Democrat side, into open complaints about the asymmetry of the coalition and the reassertion of the instincts and habits of single-party majoritarian governments. In particular, the flaws in the Coalition Agreement of May 2010 were highlighted: the failure sufficiently to recognize that the executive and patronage powers of the Prime Minister and Secretaries of State in making appointments and taking decisions, often under delegated statutory powers, had not been adapted to the existence of two parties. There was also the sense that the civil service naturally, and instinctively, defaulted to one-party government habits of behaviour, which, in practice, favoured the Conservatives.

As the parliament ended, there was therefore considerable discussion amongst senior Liberal Democrats about how arrangements should be altered in future if there was another coalition, either after the May 2015 election, or later. The widespread belief was that the Liberal Democrats should go into any negotiations with a much more detailed list of demands, not only over the allocation of portfolios but also about how government should be run. This would involve a more rules-based, prescriptive system on consultation over decisions and appointments. In effect, this amounted to a shift from the piecemeal 'coalitionizing' of government of the 2010–15 period to a formal adjustment of the processes of government, as in many other European countries, which always have coalitions. These pressures were resisted not just by the Conservatives – anyway in the most part reluctant to go into coalition again – but also, instinctively, by the civil service, who dislike rules and prefer ambiguity and flexibility. Nonetheless, a second coalition, or even a period of minority government, might lead to more lasting and profound changes in Whitehall practice. What had been provisional and ad hoc might become permanent and customary.

The implication of this debate is that if Britain reverted to a single-party government after the May 2015 election, then many of the ad hoc adjustments made to deal with the coalition would disappear. Obviously, the Prime Minister would regain total control over the right to appoint ministers and greater freedom in practice to change the machinery of government – though both are constrained by political circumstances and by internal party pressures. The Quad would disappear and there would be none of the elaborate processes of ensuring that both parties, or rather their leaders and advisers, were signed up to new policy initiatives. Again, this might mean less in practice since, even in single-party governments with big majorities, as between 1997 and 2005, the freedom of manoeuvre of even a powerful Prime Minister like Tony Blair was constrained, to his intense and frequent frustration, by the need to get the support of, or least remove obstruction by, Gordon Brown and the Treasury. A more intriguing question is whether the revival of collective discussion, both formally through Cabinet committees and, usually more important, informally through discussions between ministers would remain. The civil service would obviously be pushing in that direction. The dilemma was recognized by Robert Hazell: 'Of course the revival of Cabinet government might have happened anyway under a new Prime Minister with a commitment to collegiality. It is important to try to distinguish what is a necessary consequence of coalition government and what is merely contingent.'[16] Quite; and structures and patterns of behaviour would be different again if there were a sustained period of minority government. Much depends anyway on the personality and style of a Prime Minister, which itself usually changes and develops during the course of a premiership.

Another intriguing question is how far the running of government has been affected by the existence of the Fixed-term Parliaments Act introduced by the coalition. The fixed five-year term has given the process

---

[16] In Hazell and Yong, *Politics of Coalition*, p. 68.

certainty, though the impact can be exaggerated. In the past, governments ahead in the polls have usually called elections after four years (as in 1983, 1987, 2001 and 2005) before retaining power, while those in trouble have held on until around the end of the maximum five-year term (in 1997 and 2010) before losing office. The only recent exception was 1992, when, after the change of Prime Minister in November 1990, the Major government delayed the general election until just short of the five-year mark and won re-election. In the 2010–15 parliament, the Conservatives have been behind in the polls for most of the period and have done badly in elections, with the Liberal Democrats having single-figure poll ratings and suffering huge electoral losses. So neither party had any incentive to opt for an early general election, even if there had been no Fixed-term Parliaments Act. If one of the parties, or both, had seen an electoral opportunity, they could have used one of the override provisions of the Act, notably the provision for two-thirds of the Commons voting for a general election. In that sense the act only sets fixed terms because it is in the electoral interests of the governing party or parties to serve for five years. Nonetheless, by removing even the temptation, the act may have introduced some stability to the coalition. Of course, it is hard to reach firm conclusions since the act has only applied during a period of coalition rather than of single-party government. Sir Jeremy Heywood, the Cabinet Secretary, told an inquiry by the Political and Constitutional Reform Committee of the Commons that the act

> has definitely brought some stability. It has made it easier to plan . . . personnel issues, financial issues, legislative issues. It has definitely brought a lot of advantages. I would argue probably more so in years three and four of the Parliament than year five, but until we have been though the whole five years it will be difficult to give a completely comprehensive assessment. It has definitely led to a net improvement in planning, long termism, sequencing and so on, so we definitely support it.[17]

The shrinking of Whitehall

The existence of the coalition has, however, been only one part of the story of what has happened to the executive since May 2010. Indeed,

---

[17] House of Commons Political and Constitutional Reform Committee, *Fixed-term Parliaments, the final year of a Parliament* (HC 976, Thirteenth Report of Session 2013–14).

what has been described so far in this chapter can be seen as the necessary political underpinning for a far-reaching programme of economic and administrative change which the Conservatives anyway planned to introduce, and then, with the assurance of Liberal Democrat backing in the Commons, set about implementing. If you focus on the executive, the dominant theme since 2010 has not just been the existence of the coalition but the scale of the measures on deficit reduction and the accompanying reductions in the size of the civil service.

In one sense, paradoxically, central government looks much as it did in spring 2010. There have been few changes to the machinery of government, by contrast to the previous ten years. Some units have moved around a bit: the civil servants dealing with constitutional change have moved from the Ministry of Justice to the Cabinet Office to work under Mr Clegg. And some new functional units have been created in the Cabinet Office, notably the Major Projects Authority. But the architecture of departmental boundaries has remained largely unchanged, as noted earlier in the chapter, both because of Mr Cameron being persuaded that such changes were often costly and disruptive and because of the pressures against moves created by the existence of the coalition.

Yet behind this familiar organogram, there have been the most far-reaching changes to Whitehall for decades. The number of civil servants has fallen by around 17 per cent, or more than 70,000 since 2010, to just over 400,000. The goal is for a 20 per cent reduction to about 380,000 by the time of the 2015 election. This is the smallest total since before the Second World War, and before the foundation of the modern welfare state. The decline in civil service numbers has been further and faster than in the wider public sector, though not as much as in local government. Physically, the impact can be seen in the shrinkage in the size of the civil service estate: familiar landmarks such as Admiralty Arch, vacated by the Cabinet Office. The impact has been greatest at both the most senior and junior grades. The relative declines have been largest in the departments of Culture, Media and Sport (partly reflecting an exodus following the end of the 2012 London Olympics, partly offset by taking on responsibility for broadband), Communities and Local Government, Health (excluding the NHS itself), Work and Pensions, and Defence. The result has been a hollowing out of the senior civil service layers of many departments, with fewer civil servants at the second and third tiers.

These changes have been combined with significant central drives to reduce costs – by squeezing pay tightly in real terms, by reducing pension entitlements, by cutting operational, procurement, advertising and consultancy costs. And the number of quangos or arm's-length bodies has been cut, though not in a consistent pattern. These initiatives have been particularly associated with Francis Maude, the Minister for the Cabinet Office and historically unusual in being a minister for the civil service who both wanted and cared about the post. (By contrast, most civil service ministers in the Cabinet Office have been on the way up, or down, and have held the job for a very short period, making little impact.) Mr Maude has said that these and other cost-saving measures have produced cumulative savings of more than £14 billion by 2014.

Mr Maude has been committed to civil service reform since before the 2010 election, when he headed the Conservatives' implementation unit in opposition. He has been critical of the quality of civil service work in handling big projects, its use of information technology, procurement, outsourcing and commercial activities, and management information and financial leadership. Initiatives have been launched in all these areas to improve civil service skills and capability, notably via the creation of the Major Projects Authority to oversee, evaluate and assist with major reform and infrastructure schemes, and by pushing for the much more widespread use of digital transactions between the public and government. There has also been a big push to greater transparency and the provision of more data.

Mr Maude has sought to improve the operations of departments in other ways. First, he appointed Lord Browne of Madingley, the former chief executive of BP, to become the government's lead non-executive director and to help recruit successful private sector chief executives to serve on the revamped boards of departments. The recruitment of these neds, as they became known, was initially viewed sceptically by many permanent secretaries but, in general, they have welcomed the change as providing them with an additional source of advice as they seek to transform the running of their departments. The use made by Secretaries of State has varied substantially, depending on their personalities and their own, often limited, experience of working in large organizations.

The most controversial development has been Mr Maude's attempt to give Secretaries of State more say over the appointment both of their Permanent Secretaries and of advisers in their private offices. This has provoked worries over politicization, and resistance from the Civil Service Commission, which was forced to concede in late 2014 a final prime-ministerial choice between candidates short-listed on merit.

This largely recognized previous practice, since Secretaries of State have exercised strong preferences both over appointments of Permanent Secretaries and, in particular, of pushing some out. A number of Permanent Secretaries left Whitehall much earlier than expected during the 2010–15 parliament, though in virtually every case their replacements came from the existing ranks of the civil service.

The process has been difficult, with strained relations at times between Mr Maude and his team, and officials responsible for reform. In particular, following the retirement of Lord O'Donnell at the end of 2011, the innovation of splitting the posts of Cabinet Secretary, held by Sir Jeremy Heywood, and Head of the Civil Service, held by Sir Bob Kerslake until September 2014, never really worked. The problem was partly that Sir Bob combined the post of leading the civil service with being Permanent Secretary at the Department of Communities and Local Government, but he also never commanded the confidence of either senior ministers, such as Mr Cameron and Mr Maude, or, ultimately, of his fellow permanent secretaries. Sir Bob did push through important reforms, notably in improving skills, but progress was patchy, as various reports on the 2012 plan showed.[18]

Part of the problem was an inherent tension between an assertive centre seeking to control and, at times, override strong departmental interests embedded in the federal Whitehall structure. Officials at the centre also lacked the necessary authority. Consequently, in July 2014, the Prime Minister decided to change direction. Sir Jeremy resumed the dual titles of Cabinet Secretary and Head of the Civil Service, with Sir Bob returning to Communities and Local Government until his retirement in early 2015. Meanwhile, a chief executive of the civil service was sought from the private sector to drive forward reform and to run the various central units. The post was not really a CEO in the sense understood in the private sector, since departmental Permanent Secretaries would continue to be responsible to Sir Jeremy. But the new post would be crucial to further attempts to achieve change. In the event, John Manzoni, who had long experience at a senior level in BP and the energy sector, was chosen. He had the advantage of already being in Whitehall as head of the Major Projects Authority for eight months before becoming chief executive.

---

[18] *The Civil Service Reform Plan* (Cabinet Office, June 2012); *Civil Service Reform Plan: One Year On Report* (Cabinet Office, June 2013); *Civil Service Reform Plan Progress Report* (Cabinet Office, October 2014).

The striking feature about Mr Maude's initiatives and the changes to the civil service is how little, if any, involvement the Liberal Democrats had in them. These changes were primarily driven by a handful of Conservative ministers. So profound, lasting and probably irreversible changes to the size and shape of Whitehall took place almost as if the coalition had not existed.

Conclusions

The most striking point after four and a half years of the coalition is not only that it has survived but that it has functioned. Despite increasingly fractious public comments about each other, the leaders of the two parties have managed to work together on pressing issues – even if long-term policy problems have been increasingly deferred until after the 2015 general election. This has partly been a matter of machinery and support. But more important has been necessity, a recognition by Mr Cameron, Mr Clegg and their inner circles that keeping the coalition together was in their mutual interests, and certainly far better than the risk of splitting apart and an early general election (using one of the override provisions of the Fixed-term Parliaments Act). The close advisers to Mr Cameron in 10 Downing Street and to Mr Clegg as Deputy Prime Minister, and their offices, have worked well, and managed to co-operate with each other, despite carping from outside. Many of the adjustments in Whitehall have been provisional. But, however creaky, and however much the Liberal Democrats have complained about the system favouring the Conservatives, the system has worked. Moreover, much has been achieved. Far-reaching reforms have been introduced both within Whitehall and across the public sector, mainly Conservative-inspired. The coalition government has not been a lowest common denominator of minimalism. The executive has not only operated in a new, and unexpected, political environment, but it has also delivered.

The unanswerable question is whether the existence of the coalition has left a lasting impact on the way decisions are taken and Whitehall operates on a day-to-day basis. Few of the changes in working patterns appear permanent or irreversible. Rather, everyone – politicians and civil servants alike – has been waiting until May 2015 to see whether the outcome of the 2010 general election was an aberration, or the start of a new pattern of minority or multi-party governments.

5 THE COALITION AND PARLIAMENT

PHILIP COWLEY

By the time of the 2010 election, Parliament – and especially the House of Commons – was widely seen as a battered and bruised institution, 'on its knees' in the words of one article on the subject.[1] The expenses scandal of the year before had forced the Commons Speaker, Michael Martin, from office, and seen the institution suffer what his replacement, John Bercow, described as 'reputational carnage'.[2] 'I cannot think of a single year in the recent history of Parliament', Bercow claimed, 'when more damage has been done . . . with the possible exception of when Nazi bombs fell on the chamber in 1941.'[3]

Both the Commons and the Lords had rapidly taken measures to reform their expenses regimes, but given the widespread anti-politics mood that the scandal generated it was not surprising that all the main parties' election manifestos included further proposals for more widespread political reform, couched in terms of cleaning up politics.[4] The resulting post-election Conservative–Lib Dem Coalition Agreement

---

[1] Alexander Kelso, 'Parliament on its knees: MPs' expenses and the crisis of transparency at Westminster', *Political Quarterly*, 80 (2009), pp. 329–38.

[2] The sordid details of the expenses scandal are covered well (if somewhat *parti pris*) in R. Winnett and G. Rayner, *No Expenses Spared* (London: Bantam, 2009).

[3] 'Parliament in an anti-politics age: the outreach challenge', Political Studies Association/Hansard Society Lecture, 30 November 2009 (accessed at www.johnbercow.co.uk/content/political-studies-association-hansard-society, 18 November 2014).

[4] See, for example, the section entitled 'A new agenda for a new politics' in the Conservative manifesto (pp. 65–7); or the section 'Your say' in the Liberal Democrat manifesto (pp. 86–95).

included a sizeable section on political reform, of which much directly related to Parliament.[5] Had the Coalition Agreement been implemented in full, Parliament by 2015 could have looked very different from the institution elected in 2010. Elected to five-year fixed terms, the Commons would have been a smaller body with more equally sized constituencies. It could have been elected by the Alternative Vote, and would have had control over its own timetable. Members of the public would have had the power to initiate recall against MPs accused of wrongdoing and to initiate proceedings in the Commons, including bringing forward Bills. There would have been widespread all-postal primaries to select candidates for election. And there would have been the first steps towards a wholly or at least mainly elected House of Lords.

Almost none of this occurred. Most of the reforms died, from neglect or abuse. Where they survived, they were often a pale imitation of what had first been promised. But for all that the story of the coalition is of parliamentary reform frustrated, Parliament by 2015 was still different to that of 2010, and, moreover, the expenses scandal continued to be one of the main drivers of change during the period, with its legacy clear in much of what unfolded during the five years of the parliament. This was true, for example, in the very make-up of the Commons; it was true of the reforms that did occur; and it was true of the increasingly high-profile and controversial role of the Commons Speaker. The other driver for change was the coalition itself, which had a significant impact on the behaviour of both MPs and peers, raising the level of backbench dissent in the House of Commons and shifting the centre of gravity in the House of Lords.

The new parliament

One of the first and most obvious effects of the events of 2009 was a record number of retirements at the 2010 election, as MPs caught up in the expenses scandal chose to leave politics.[6] For some, their retirement

---

[5] *The Coalition: Our Programme for Government* (Cabinet Office, May 2010), pp. 26–8.

[6] Byron Criddle, 'More diverse, yet more uniform: MPs and candidates', in Dennis Kavanagh and Philip Cowley, *The British General Election of 2010* (London: Palgrave, 2010), p. 305.

included an unexpected spell in prison.[7] These retirements, combined with the Conservatives' successes at the polls, meant that more than a third of the MPs elected in 2010 were elected for the first time, a higher proportion than at any election since 1997. The rate of change was especially high for the Conservatives: almost half of Conservative MPs (48 per cent) were elected for the first time.[8]

Some of the new MPs were visibly different from those they had replaced. As a result of the changes to the Conservatives' selection procedures used between 2005 and 2010, there were more Conservative women MPs (forty-nine, up from seventeen in 2005) as well as more from ethnic minorities (eleven, up from just two).[9] Both were historic high figures for the party. The use of all-women shortlists on the Labour side of the House – for the third time in the last four elections – meant that although the number of Labour women MPs fell in absolute terms, their presence as a proportion of the PLP reached a record high (31 per cent). Combined with a handful of women MPs from other parties, the total number of women now reached a record 21 per cent of the House. There was also an increase in the number of MPs from ethnic minorities, almost doubling from fifteen to twenty-seven, including the first three Muslim women MPs, all Labour.

The majority of the House, however, remained disproportionately white and male, something which was especially true on the government frontbench. The Lib Dems in particular remained almost totally white and male, despite the party's exhortation towards diversity. Ironically, despite repeated claims of social exclusiveness which would dog the party throughout the parliament, the proportion of privately educated Conservative MPs after 2010 hit an all-time low – with the new intake splitting roughly evenly between those educated at state and private schools – but the privately educated were still heavily over-represented (and, again, especially on the frontbench). The near total absence of working-class MPs on the Conservative side of the House continued. The rare exceptions – such as Cameron's first Chief Whip, Patrick McLoughlin, a former miner – merely proved the broader

[7] Six MPs were found guilty of various offences, involving jail sentences of up to eighteen months.
[8] Criddle, 'More diverse, yet more uniform', pp. 306–7.
[9] See Sarah Childs and Paul Webb, *Sex, Gender and the Conservative Party: From Iron Lady to Kitten Heels* (London: Palgrave, 2011).

point. The Labour Party similarly saw yet another decline in the number of working-class MPs (or, more accurately, those with a background in manual work), down to record low levels.[10]

One of the interesting aspects of contemporary discussions of Parliament is that it is now widely accepted that all this matters. The days when it was commonplace to be told that it did not matter who MPs were, as long as they were 'the best person for the job', are now largely over. What Anne Phillips called 'the politics of presence' is now a widely, if not wholly, accepted part of political discourse.[11] All the major parties have signed up to the principle that MPs should (broadly) resemble the wider population, although they vary in the seriousness with which they take this. Equally strikingly, this concern now encompasses a much wider range of social characteristics than it used to. For years, politicians discussing this subject would talk about the sex and (more recently) the ethnicity of MPs. But recent discussions, beginning with the Speaker's Conference at the end of the 2005–10 parliament and continuing since 2010, have included representation of disability, sexuality, age and social class (the last the original piece of identity politics, albeit one that has been absent from discussion for decades).[12] As a result, the scope of the politics of presence is currently wider than it has been at any point since mass suffrage was introduced.

This debate has become entwined with another, about the rise of the 'political class' and the extent to which MPs do not share the aims and aspirations of 'normal' people. So-called career politicians still remain a minority of parliamentarians, but they are an increasingly large minority and one that enjoys fast-track career progression.[13] The three main party leaders during the 2010 Parliament had all been MPs for no more than five years when they were elected to the leadership of their parties.[14] This privileging of experience outside the Commons (as a

---

[10] Criddle, 'More diverse, yet more uniform', p. 328.

[11] Anne Phillips, *The Politics of Presence* (Oxford: Oxford University Press, 1995).

[12] Speaker's Conference (on Parliamentary Representation), *Final Report* (HC 239-I, 2010).

[13] See, for example, Peter Allen, 'Linking the pre-parliamentary political experience and political careers of the 1997 General Election cohort', *Parliamentary Affairs*, 66:4 (2013), pp. 685–707.

[14] Philip Cowley, 'Arise, novice leader! The continuing rise of the career politician in Britain', *Politics* 32:1 (2013), pp. 31–8. See more generally, Judi Atkins et al., 'The rise of the novice Cabinet minister? The career trajectories of Cabinet ministers in British government from Attlee to Cameron', *Political Quarterly* 84:3 (2013), pp. 362–70.

Special Adviser or similar) over experience in the Commons (as a back-bencher) has potentially serious consequences for the role played by the Commons as the training ground and talent pool of senior politicians. The political parties claim to take concerns about the political class seriously, and to want a wider pool of candidates for Westminster, but apart from measures to increase the number of women elected, remedial action remains largely exhortatory. The coalition's plan to introduce 200 all-postal primaries, part of a plan designed to open up politics, was one of the first reform proposals to be discarded.[15]

Coming into parliament after the expenses scandal, many of the new cohort of MPs certainly saw themselves as different, and some set out, somewhat self-consciously, to be different from the more established MPs. In many ways, however, they continued existing practices: they were, for example, just as constituency-focused. One study from the Hansard Society found that the newly elected MPs spent around 60 per cent of their time working in, or on, the constituency.[16] Constituency casework alone made up an average of 28 per cent of their working life. Many of the new MPs found the day-to-day reality of parliamentary life unfulfilling and frustrating, and the 2015 election saw the largest number of retirements of MPs who had served just one term of any parliament in the post-war era.

Reform and resistance

Not all of the coalition's plans for parliamentary reform failed. The Fixed-term Parliaments Act reached the statute book during the first session, as did the Parliamentary Voting System and Constituencies Act allowing for the AV referendum, albeit only for AV then to be comprehensively defeated in the resulting referendum (see chapter two). The latter piece of legislation also included measures to reduce the size of the House of Commons, but these – and the promised proposals for House of Lords reform – were later defeated as a result of intra- and inter-party

[15] It was first reported as dropped as early as late 2010. The grounds for abandonment appear to have been a combination of cost (all-postal primaries are not cheap) along with the realization that MPs chosen in this way may be worryingly independent-minded.

[16] Matt Korris, *A Year in the Life: From Member of Public to Member of Parliament*, Interim Briefing Paper (London: Hansard Society, 2011). Some of this 60% was spent at Westminster, but it was constituency-focused work.

coalition infighting (discussed further below). A draft Recall of MPs Bill was first published in December 2011; a revised Bill, much criticized for being too weak, was then introduced in the Commons almost three years later, in September 2014.[17] Other proposals – such as introducing a public reading stage for Bills – failed to make much of an impact.[18]

The most significant Commons reforms had their antecedents before the 2010 election. Gordon Brown's reaction to the expenses scandal had included establishing a Select Committee on Reform of the House of Commons, to be chaired by the then Labour MP, Tony Wright. The 'Wright Committee' (as it soon became known) was charged with investigating reforms to the appointment of select committees, the way business was scheduled in the House, and ways to enable the public to initiate debates. It was not immediately obvious why the effects of a scandal concerning MPs' expenses would be mitigated by reform to the way the House of Commons scheduled its business (as if they talk of little else in Grimethorpe), but Wright and his committee were determined not to let a crisis go to waste and jumped at the chance to propose reforms.[19] Their key recommendations, *Rebuilding the House*, were published in 2009, and received a largely positive reaction.[20]

The Coalition Agreement promised to implement Wright 'in full', beginning with proposals for a committee to control backbench business, with a full House business committee to cover the scheduling of government legislation to appear by the third session. The former was indeed established soon after the 2010 election, with control over backbench business on thirty-five days per session. Under its chair, Natascha Engel, the committee prioritized non-partisan business that it saw as important, of wide interest and which had not been debated recently.[21] These included debates on several high-profile issues, which made life awkward for one or both of the front benches, such as a referendum on EU membership, voting for prisoners and a

---

[17] The draft Bill was much criticized. See for example Political and Constitutional Reform Committee, *First Report: Recall of MPs* (HC 373, 2012).

[18] Public reading stages were applied to just three government Bills in the first four years of the Parliament.

[19] Meg Russell, '"Never allow a crisis to go to waste": The Wright Committee reforms to strengthen the House of Commons', *Parliamentary Affairs*, 64:4 (2011), pp. 612–33.

[20] House of Commons Reform Committee, *Rebuilding the House* (HC 1117, 2009).

[21] House of Commons Backbench Business Committee, *Second Special Report: Work of the Committee in Session 2010–12* (HC 1926, 2012).

Hillsborough inquiry. It was not long before the whips began to interfere.[22] The promised House business committee never appeared at all. Any lingering, half-hearted support those in government had for ceding control of the timetable of government business to MPs vanished once they saw how much harder their life had been made even by a backbench business committee.[23]

The Coalition Agreement's pledge to allow the public control over Commons debates, and to allow them to introduce Bills, also did not quite materialize in the form initially promised. In a curious hybrid arrangement, the government – not Parliament – established a petitions system in 2011, and petitions which reached a total of 100,000 signatories were then passed to the Backbench Business Committee to consider. The 100,000 signatures was often discussed as if it triggered debate; rather, it triggered consideration of a debate. Petitions, whether electronic or otherwise, were just one of the factors that the Committee considered in selecting matters for debate, and it explicitly ruled out debating any matter which did not otherwise meet its criteria, no matter how many signatures a petition had acquired. The Coalition Agreement's promise of Bills to be initiated by the public did not materialize at all.

More impactful were the Wright committee's recommendations for the membership of select committees. This encompassed both the chairs of committees (to be elected by the House by secret ballot) and their members (to be elected within party groups, but again by secret ballot). Substantively accepted before the 2010 election, these reforms then came into force shortly after the election.[24] The initial tranche of elections resulted in a handful of surprising elections, but the effect of the reform became clear later in the parliament in 2014, when Dr Sarah Wollaston and Rory Stewart were elected to chair the Heath and Defence committees respectively.[25] With just four years' experience in

---

[22] David Foster, 'Going 'Where angels fear to tread': How effective was the Backbench Business Committee in the 2010–2012 parliamentary session?', *Parliamentary Affairs* (online) 2013.

[23] The official justification was a lack of consensus on how to proceed. But doubts did not just exist within the government; several of Labour's party managers looked at the difficulties being caused by the backbench committee and, thinking about what might happen were they to win the 2015 election, had no desire to see the principle extended.

[24] Ironically, the method used for select committee chairs is the Alternative Vote.

[25] The runner-up to Sarah Wollaston in the race for the Health Select Committee was also a former doctor, also elected first in 2010.

the House each, having both been elected in 2010, but with widespread experience outside (as a doctor and a diplomat), both were exactly the sort of people who would not have prospered – at least so quickly – under the old system.

Several of the most high-profile events of the parliament took place in select committees, such as the Culture, Media and Sport Committee's investigation into phone hacking, taking evidence from the Murdochs, or Margaret Hodge's chairing of the Public Accounts Committee, which went after the tax affairs of several very high-profile companies. Press coverage of select committees more than trebled in the four years from 2008 to 2012.[26] No doubt some of this was due to the changes in membership caused as a result of the Wright reforms, but the mere fact of coalition also triggered an important shift in the dynamics within select committees. Although committees continued to have a 'government' majority, it was much less cohesive, and less able to move committees onto safer ground or to tone down criticisms. Conservative MPs wanted to put the boot into the Liberal Democrat bits of the government and Lib Dem MPs wanted to do the same to the Conservative bits. Labour MPs wanted to criticize both. After 2010, in other words, all MPs wanted to put the boot into someone.

These reforms were nowhere near as radical as those promised by the Coalition Agreement. But combined, they still acted as a significant reduction in the patronage available to, and the control enjoyed by, the party whips; and they raised the profile and effectiveness of the Commons. If they were not as significant as the coalition had initially agreed, the direction of travel was at least in the right direction.

The Speaker

Another legacy of the expenses scandal was the Speaker, John Bercow, elected in 2009 to replace Michael Martin. Bercow had been positioning himself to run for the Speakership at some point, but that he became

---

[26] Patrick Dunleavy and Dominic Muir, 'Parliament bounces back – how Select Committees have become a power in the land', Democratic Audit, 18 July 2013 (accessed at www.democraticaudit.com/?p=1106, 10 November 2014). See also M. Kubala, 'Select Committees in the House of Commons and the Media', *Parliamentary Affairs*, 64:2 (2011), pp. 694–713.

Speaker when he did, and how he did, owes almost everything to the expenses scandal. Some of his former Conservative colleagues distrusted Bercow, as a result of his shift from somewhere on the right of the Conservative Party to a much more socially liberal position.[27] Although elected by secret ballot, it is widely known that he enjoyed the support of relatively few Conservative MPs and secured his election largely thanks to the votes of a sizeable number of Labour MPs, who voted for him not least because they knew it would annoy Conservative MPs.[28] Even by the 2010 election, there was already talk of plots to depose him if the Conservative parliamentary party increased sufficiently in numbers, although these came to nothing. Had the expenses scandal not occurred when it did, or had Michael Martin hung on until after the 2010 election, there would have been fewer Labour MPs to back Bercow's bid for the Speaker's chair.

Moreover, his pitch, running on what he described as an explicitly 'reform prospectus', would also not have been as appealing but for the events of 2009. 'The next Speaker', he claimed, 'faces an unprecedented challenge – to help clean up politics, to place Parliament at the centre of an effective democracy and to build a relationship of mutual respect with the electorate. Above all, the Speaker must be part of the solution and must drive the process of renewal.'[29] Some of his reforming zeal manifested itself internally, such as his support for a parliamentary crèche (an idea long advocated, but previously going nowhere), and his support for ParliOut (a new LGBT network at Westminster). Neither particularly endeared him to some of the more traditional wing of his former party, nor did his decision not to wear the Speaker's traditional wig and robes. He was also a believer in working as what he termed 'an ambassador for Parliament', engaging with the world outside of Westminster, and was an enthusiastic advocate of parliament's outreach programme, overseeing a huge

---

[27] When MPs fall out with their former party, they often attempt to justify it on the basis that the party has changed, not them; John Bercow was unusual in being more accepting of the fact that it was he who had changed, not the party.

[28] Bobby Friedman, *Bercow* (London: Gibson Square, 2011), ch. 20.

[29] John Bercow, 'The Speakership in the Twenty First Century' (accessed at www.conservativehome.com/thetorydiary/2009/06/john-bercow-sets-out-his-3000-word-manifesto-for-a-21st-century-speakership.html, 18 November 2014). This 3,000-word document written in 2009 proved a good guide to what he went on to deliver as Speaker.

expansion of its work. In late 2013, he announced the establishment of a commission on digital democracy, to investigate how the parliament could 'embrace the opportunities afforded by the digital world'.

In the chamber he intervened regularly, and at length, during Prime Minister's Questions (PMQs); he was also prepared to allow the sessions to run over the thirty minutes formally allocated, adding on 'injury time' for interruptions. He behaved, argued one journalist, 'like a Victorian head teacher overseeing a noisy assembly'.[30] He argued repeatedly and vociferously that the behaviour seen at PMQs lowered public respect for the Commons, and would refer to the 'bucket loads' of letters he received on the subject from members of the public.[31] The fact that he continued to make such interventions throughout the Parliament, however, merely went to show how ineffectual the interruptions were. Although the number of questions dealt with at PMQs increased, behaviour during the session at the end of the parliament was not much better than it had been at the beginning. More significant was his granting of Urgent Questions, which hauled ministers to the House to deal with urgent developments. He granted seventy-three in the first (long) session, thirty-eight in the second, and thirty-five in the third. Michael Martin, by contrast, had granted two in the last twelve months of his Speakership. Many Ministers, perhaps understandably, did not approve, but the revival of UQs undoubtedly made the Commons a more significant focus of debate and scrutiny. Bercow himself saw these as the greatest impact made by his Speakership.

His critics, of whom there were a growing band by the end of the parliament, alleged two things. The first – heard almost exclusively from Conservative MPs – was that Speaker Bercow demonstrated anti-government bias. Always difficult to quantify or prove (not something many of his critics ever attempted), it was this, ironically, that ensured that he did at least have some supporters on the Conservative benches: many of the more rebellious Conservative MPs saw in the Speaker a champion of their rights, and of Parliament's, against the executive. The second criticism was one of pomposity and rudeness. His critics saw, in his constant interventions at PMQs, not an attempt to raise the importance and standing of

---

[30] 'Has John Bercow fulfilled his pledges as Speaker?', *Total Politics*, 7 March 2011.
[31] When, in late 2013, his correspondence on the subject was released, it revealed that this was clearly a small bucket: some sixty-one letters between July and November. But the tone of the correspondence backed up the Speaker's complaint that the public did not take kindly to the behaviour seen at PMQs.

Parliament, but an attempt to raise the importance and standing of John Bercow. It was often not the fact that he intervened, but how he did it and what he said. At times, it was almost as if he was going out of his way to be rude, especially to Conservative MPs, with whom he had several private and public fallings-out. There were also stories of his behaviour behind the scenes, where it was said he could be short-tempered with staff and some Members.[32] The (early) retirement in 2014 of the Clerk of the House of Commons, Sir Robert Rogers, became mired in allegations about Bercow's behaviour and there followed a row over the appointment of Rogers' successor, during which the Speaker was forced to retreat. By the end of the parliament, the contempt that some MPs, predominantly Conservatives, had for the Speaker was very public, and his position was less certain than it had been in 2010. For the Commons, however, the overall Bercow effect had been positive.

Intra-party splits

The parliament saw a record-breaking level of backbench dissent in the House of Commons. The first three sessions of the parliament, up to May 2014, saw coalition MPs vote against the party line on some 388 occasions, a rebellion by coalition MPs in 37 per cent of divisions, a level without precedent in the post-war era.[33] The previous post-war peak was 28 per cent, for the Parliament of 2005–10.[34] This figure is for the coalition as a whole but even the data for the parties separately demonstrate the scale of the problems that the party whips faced. Conservative MPs broke ranks in 25 per cent of votes, a figure higher than the rate of rebellion by government MPs in all but one post-war parliament.

Moreover, this high level of dissent ran for the entire parliament. Contrary to usual practice, there was almost no honeymoon for the new Prime Minister. First sessions, particularly first sessions after changes in government, usually see governments with authority: the

---

[32] Friedman, *Bercow*, p. 212.

[33] Philip Cowley and Mark Stuart, *The Four Year Itch: Dissension amongst the Coalition's Parliamentary Parties, 2013–2014* (Nottingham: University of Nottingham, 2014), pp. 2–3.

[34] Philip Cowley and Mark Stuart, 'In the Brown Stuff? Labour Backbench Dissent under Gordon Brown, 2007–2010', *Contemporary British History*, 28:1 (2014), pp. 1–23.

discipline of the election campaign is still strong; and the fact that the government is implementing its manifesto is usually enough to prevent many MPs, even those who may disagree with the policies, from dissenting. But the rate of rebellion in the first session (44 per cent) was higher than in either the second (27 per cent) or third session (31 per cent); indeed between September 2010 and February 2011, the rate of dissent consistently exceeded 50 per cent, with rebellion becoming the norm, cohesion the exception.

The Coalition Agreement specified that the Conservative Chief Whip would serve as the government's Chief Whip; the Government's Deputy Chief Whip would be the Liberal Democrat Chief Whip. Although the two parties would consult, they were responsible for the internal organization and discipline of their own MPs.[35] Throughout the parliament there were criticisms made of the whips – and especially the Conservative whips and/or the Number 10 machine – for mishandling relations with backbenchers. They were accused of being heavy-handed or aloof, of not listening or of only promoting MPs who had been to school with the Prime Minister or who were allies of the Chancellor. Some of these criticisms were valid, but they often failed to appreciate the broader structural difficulties that the party managers were working under. The Conservatives got through four Chief Whips during the parliament; each time a new Chief Whip took office there was discussion of how this would shake up the Whips' Office and solve the party management problems the party was facing; each time, it made little difference.[36]

What happened after 2010 did not come out of the blue; it was merely the most recent manifestation of a trend that was well established (even if many commentators often ignored it).[37] But it was exacerbated by a range of factors specific to the coalition. First, the government's MPs occupied a broader ideological range than any other government in the post-war era (even the broad churches that are British political parties are not quite as broad as the range between the left of the Liberal Democrats

[35] *Coalition Agreement for Stability and Reform* (Cabinet Office, May 2010), paras 5.1–5.4.
[36] Conservative Chief Whips were: Patrick McLoughlin, Andrew Mitchell (who resigned from the office less than two months after taking it up), Sir George Young (who, having just been sacked as Leader of the House, was then recalled to replace Mitchell) and Michael Gove. Lib Dem Chief Whips were: Alistair Carmichael and Don Foster.
[37] See for example, Philip Cowley, *The Rebels* (London: Politico's, 2005).

and the right of the Conservatives). Whatever it did, therefore, it was bound to alienate one wing or the other.[38] Second, many of the rhetorical weapons that would normally be deployed by the party whips (especially during the early stages of a parliament) were absent as a result of the coalition. It was, for example, no use the Conservative Party managers telling would-be rebels that they need to support legislation because it was in the party's manifesto – a traditional whipping tactic – because in many cases the coalition were doing things that were not in a party's manifesto, and sometimes indeed things that were the opposite of manifesto pledges. In some cases it was the would-be rebels who were able to claim the legitimacy of the manifesto.

Things were particularly bad for the Conservatives – one of the reasons why more of the significant backbench opposition came from Conservative MPs, rather than Liberal Democrats. It was difficult for Conservative whips to tell their MPs that they needed to support the Prime Minister who won them the election, another traditional whipping tactic, given that he had not. Indeed, some Conservative MPs blamed the Prime Minister for not winning the election, and did not see that they owed him much loyalty as a result.

And, third, whereas Lib Dem MPs had been part of a process to ratify the coalition – thereby binding them to it, even when they disagreed with policies – Conservative MPs were largely passive observers to the drawing up of the agreement, which was then presented to them as a *fait accompli*; they therefore felt more willing to ignore it when it suited them.[39] Then, fourth, there were the problems of managing such a large number of new Conservative MPs. It is hard enough to fill all the positions in government under normal circumstances. Trying to reconcile the demands of the newly elected for advancement with fair treatment for the longer-serving, especially those who have worked hard for the party in opposition, was near to impossible.[40] Matters were made

---

[38] One of the paradoxes of the 2010 coalition was that members of the public did not tend to think the Lib Dems achieved very much as a result of being in government, whereas many Conservative MPs would frequently blame them for preventing the government from being more right-wing. Both cannot be true.

[39] Kavanagh and Cowley, *British General Election of 2010*, pp. pp. 220–1.

[40] In 1997, one senior figure in the Parliamentary Labour Party, when discussing the problem of dealing with their large intake of new MPs, simply shrugged his shoulders and said: 'What the fuck do you do?' Conservative whips after 2010 found themselves thinking similar thoughts.

worse, fifth, by a pledge Cameron had given that by the end of his first term a third of his ministers would be female. When he made it (in 2009), people pointed out how difficult this would be to achieve, given the usual lag between initial election as an MP and ministerial office, and so it proved.[41] Throughout the 2010 parliament Cameron was routinely criticized by (some) male MPs for over-promoting women MPs and routinely criticized by (some) commentators for not having enough women on his frontbench and in Cabinet. He received little thanks or praise for his efforts to deal with the latter, and the former perception just stored up more resentment on the backbenches. Finally, sixth, it is not difficult to imagine the disgruntlement felt by Conservative MPs who had served their party loyally during Opposition and had expected a position in government, only then to discover that not only were they not going to get any such post, but they were going to lose out to a Lib Dem instead.

In common with other parliaments of recent years, most of the backbench rebellions that occurred were small and of little or no policy significance. But periodically they could be large, on major policy matters, and have serious consequences. The first significant Conservative rebellion of the parliament came in October 2011, when eighty-one Conservative MPs voted for a referendum on Britain's membership of the EU.[42] Although the government won, it was a sign of the trouble ahead: revolts on Europe by Conservative MPs were on average around double the size of rebellions on other issues. A year later, in October 2012, fifty-three Conservative MPs voted against their whip on an amendment calling for a reduction in the EU budget. Whereas the European referendum rebellion in 2011 had seen Labour join forces with the government to defeat the rebels, on this occasion Labour backed the amendment, and the combination of Official and backbench opposition was sufficient to defeat the government. David Cameron thus joined the list of Prime Ministers defeated in the House of

---

[41] See Philip Cowley, 'The Parliamentary Party', *Political Quarterly*, 80:2 (2009), pp. 214–21. The problem was made even worse by the presence of the Lib Dems, with even fewer women MPs, who thus lowered any percentages for the government as a whole.

[42] Discussed in more detail in Philip Cowley and Mark Stuart, 'The Cambusters: The Conservative European referendum rebellion of October 2011', *Political Quarterly*, 83:2 (2012), pp. 402–6.

Commons as a result of their own MPs rebelling, a line which dates back unbroken to Edward Heath.

The beginning of the third session of the parliament saw yet another threatened rebellion over a referendum on EU membership – this time on an amendment to the motion on the Queen's Speech.[43] Faced with the possibility of a very large rebellion, the Conservative leadership reversed its earlier opposition to a referendum and promised support for a private member's Bill on the subject.[44] Despite this, the rebels pushed ahead with their amendment, and faced with what would have been an enormous rebellion, the Conservatives allowed a partial free vote on the issue: Ministers would abstain, backbenchers could do what they liked. More than 110 Conservative MPs went on to vote for an amendment 'regretting' the absence of a referendum Bill from the Queen's speech. The amendment was defeated, as a result of Labour and Lib Dem votes, but the vote had achieved its goal.

The largest rebellion of the Parliament, at the point of writing, came in July 2012 not over Europe but over House of Lords reform. Some ninety-one Conservative MPs voted against the Bill's Second Reading, the largest rebellion by government MPs at the Second Reading of any Bill in the post-war era. With the support of the Labour frontbench, the Bill's Second Reading was secured relatively easily. But Labour's support did not extend to the Bill's programme motion, where the whips faced a similar-sized rebellion; knowing that they would go down to defeat, the government pulled the programme motion rather than see it voted down. Trying to legislate on Lords reform without control of the timetable would have been next-to-impossible – as Harold Wilson had discovered in the 1960s – and so shortly afterwards the Bill was abandoned. It will go down in the record books as a government withdrawal rather than defeat, but no one was in any doubt what would have happened had the vote gone ahead, and the effect was the same: the blocking by backbench MPs of a major part of the Coalition Agreement's plan for political reform.

---

[43] One aspect of this vote to which insufficient attention was paid at the time was the role of the Speaker in granting the Conservative backbench amendment. As Mark D'Arcy noted on his BBC blog, 'the Speaker was stretching the rules to accommodate a new multi-party politics'. He continued: 'Behind the scenes, the government was seething. And continues to seethe' ('Speaker cornered?', 12 November 2013).

[44] A Conservative backbencher, James Wharton, then introduced the European Union (Referendum) Bill.

The knock-on consequences of that vote, however, were equally important. Together with the announcement that the Lords Bill would be withdrawn came the announcement that the Liberal Democrats were, as a consequence, withdrawing support for the government's proposed constituency boundary changes. As a result, in January 2013, a vote to overturn a Lords amendment to the Electoral Registration and Administration Bill failed, and the Coalition Agreement's policy on reducing the size of the House of Commons bit the dust.

Perhaps the most significant rebellion of all, however, occurred in August 2013 over possible military action in Syria. Having recalled Parliament to debate the situation in Syria, the government whips discovered such unhappiness amongst a large number of its MPs over the possibility of military action that the government was forced to retreat, promising that no action would take place without a further vote – which left it in the curious position of having recalled Parliament to have a vote that would not achieve anything even had it been passed. But despite this retreat, thirty-nine coalition MPs – thirty Conservatives, nine Liberal Democrats – voted against a Government motion condemning the use of chemical weapons in Syria and planning for a further vote on the use of military force in the country. Others abstained. The government was defeated by 283 to 270 and abandoned all plans to intervene militarily in Syria. The crucial factor in distinguishing this vote from previous votes on military engagement – such as Iraq in 2003 – was the behaviour of the Official Opposition, who opposed the government on such votes for the first time since Suez. But Labour opposition was merely a necessary but not sufficient condition for defeat; defeat also required the rebellion by a sufficient number of government MPs. No British government has lost a comparable vote over matters of defence or military involvement since at least the mid-nineteenth century. The fact that the only comparable votes involve Lord Palmerston, Lord Aberdeen and even Lord North is a sign of just how significant the vote was as an indicator of the Commons' developing independence.

Taken together, these were not minor or insignificant matters. During the parliament, opposition from Conservative MPs derailed one part of the Coalition Agreement (in turn, consequently derailing another part), prevented the UK taking military action and significantly steered government policy towards the EU.

Inter-party splits and collective responsibility

The Coalition Agreement explicitly allowed for the governing parties in Parliament to take different positions on three issues: nuclear power, married tax allowances and student fees. In all three cases, the Liberal Democrats would be allowed to abstain – although the last only applied if the Lib Dems were not happy with the recommendations of Lord Browne's report on the subject.[45] The parliamentary arithmetic was such that *en bloc* Liberal Democrat abstentions like these would still allow the measures to pass the Commons. That there would be other issues which could divide the coalition was considered during its formation, but any additional differences between the parliamentary parties needed to be 'specifically agreed by the Coalition Committee and Cabinet'. Agreement would also be needed on which issues would be subject to a free vote, 'which will normally be the case for Private Members' Bills'.[46]

In the event, life was messier than the arrangements had anticipated. The first significant part of the agreement to come under pressure was the Lib Dem opt-out on tuition fees. Following the publication of the Browne report, it became clear that a sizeable number of Lib Dem MPs intended to vote against the measure, rather than abstain. At this point, the parliamentary arithmetic became trickier: if most Lib Dems abstained, as per the manifesto agreement, but a sufficient number of backbenchers voted against, then it was possible the reform might be defeated. The Lib Dem leadership felt that a government defeat, on something so high-profile so early in the parliament, could do irreparable damage to the prospects for the coalition. Despite considerable efforts to agree an all-party abstention, once it became clear that some Lib Dem MPs would vote against regardless, then it became too risky for the rest of the party to abstain.[47] As a result, on 9 December 2010 the Lib Dems split three ways: twenty-one Lib Dem MPs voted against allowing fees to rise, a further eight abstained or were absent, and the rest voted with the government.

---

[45] *Programme for Government*, pp. 17, 30, 32.
[46] Coalition Agreement, paras 5.1, 5.2 and 5.5.
[47] It also became clear that not all Lib Dems objected to Lord Browne's proposals. Some were supportive. The problem was that those who were supportive were prepared to abstain, but those who objected were not.

The most serious intra-party division, however, was not predicted, and it came after the withdrawal of the Bill on Lords reform. The crucial vote on the Electoral Registration and Administration Bill (mentioned above) saw the Liberal Democrats and Conservatives whipped in separate lobbies. In other words, government MPs were whipped, in different directions, and with the Lib Dems voting in direct contravention of the Coalition Agreement. This vote is sometimes described as a government defeat, although it is not clear that this is the right term, given that only one part of the government was defeated. There was also the possibility of something very similar then occurring in March 2013 over the issue of press regulation. The Liberal Democrats had indicated that they would be voting differently to the Conservatives, and another 'defeat' looked certain (aided in this case by a number of would-be Conservative backbench rebels). In the event, the Prime Minister conceded, rather than face a formal defeat.

There was a similar split over the Queen's Speech in 2013 (also mentioned above) where again the parties were in different lobbies: the Lib Dems were whipped, but Conservatives allowed a free vote for backbenchers. Rebellions on motions on the Queen's Speech like this are extremely rare. Even more rare – I can find no equivalent – are occasions where a modern government (or in this case the largest party of the government) *abstains* over the Queen's Speech. The Prime Minister declared himself 'relaxed' about the outcome of the vote, which is a curious position for a Prime Minister to take over a vote on the government's legislative programme, if an accurate acceptance of the political realities he faced.

Just as peculiar was an amendment to the Immigration Bill, in January 2014. Faced with a very large potential rebellion, the Conservatives allowed a free vote on the legislation, and whipped ministers to abstain. This was an amendment that previously the government had said was 'unworkable'. Governments occasionally duck out of parliamentary fights they know they cannot win, declaring themselves disinterested and making the issue a free vote, but it is novel to see a governing party declare itself disinterested in the outcome of unworkable legislation. The coalition parties again split, the Lib Dems joining with Labour in voting down the measure. Similar splits occurred *inter alia* over knife crime and the bedroom tax, both over private members' Bills, but where the parties were whipped.

A similar transformation occurred with the way the government approached motions emanating from the Backbench Business Committee. The government whips began the parliament approaching backbench business as if it was 'normal' business: that is, as resolutions in the House of Commons they should not endorse something contrary to the position of the government. But the nature of the issues the committee showed itself willing to discuss soon put this approach under strain. In February 2011, facing almost certain defeat over a Backbench Business Committee motion on voting for prisoners, the government decided to absent itself from the vote, ministers abstaining *en masse*, and allowing a free vote for backbenchers and PPSs. This is a tactic governments have used in the past, albeit only rarely, but as the parliament went on, it became one increasingly employed with backbench business. Having initially treated votes on backbench business as if they had to win, the government soon resorted routinely to shrugging their shoulders and admitting defeat.

The parties thus began the parliament with a relatively coherent and traditional approach to business in the House; as time went on, and the strains in the coalition became greater, so the approach became much more ad hoc. At times, one could be forgiven for thinking they were just making it up, vote by vote.

The House of Lords

If there is a part of the story where the reality did not match the promise, it was in the House of Lords. The Conservative manifesto had contained a pledge for 'a mainly-elected second chamber' (or, more accurately, it had contained a pledge 'to work to build a consensus' for such a chamber, which is a little less ambitious). The Liberal Democrat manifesto had pledged to create 'a fully-elected second chamber with considerably fewer members than the current House'. It is therefore ironic that the result of a coalition between two parties with such manifestos was not only the continuation of the mainly appointed status quo but its expansion, into a much larger, some would say bloated, institution.

Lords reform had long been an area where the Conservative leadership and its backbenchers parted company, with the results outlined above. The Coalition Agreement, however, also argued that in the interim, appointments to the Lords would 'be made with the objective of creating a second chamber that is reflective of the share of the vote secured by the political parties in the last general election'. The only way to do this – or anything close – was to appoint many more life peers, and the Prime Minister proved himself an eager user of his power of patronage, appointing peers at a faster rate even than Tony Blair (himself no slouch when it came to dishing out patronage). The result was that by late 2014, the Lords had grown in size by more than 15 per cent from its 2010 size, reaching around 850 eligible members. Complaints soon began about its bloated scale. The Lord Speaker admitted to finding it 'embarrassing to mention how many people are in this house'. 'I think', she said, 'the only larger house is the Chinese politburo.'[48] Partly in response, the House of Lords Reform Act 2014 was passed, a minor measure that allowed peers to resign (and allowed for the exclusion of those who had committed serious criminal offences), but such outflows will do little to mitigate the massive inflow. Calls for a moratorium on appointments until nature had taken its course – a sort of one-in, one-out arrangement – run up against the desire of Prime Ministers to reward loyalty and to attempt to increase their party's representation.[49] The Lords is still smaller than it had been prior to the reforms of 1999, when it had around 1,200 members, but this last figure was hugely inflated by peers who rarely if ever attended, and at its present rate of expansion, it won't be long until it is back where it began. Perhaps the most significant point about the 2014 reform is that it was the first legislative reform of the House of Lords since 1999. Even that minor reform was not achieved easily.

If it did little to reform it, the coalition did at least transform the balance of power within the Lords. Prior to 2010, the Liberal Democrats had been the pivotal voting bloc, determining whether measures passed or failed in what was otherwise a hung chamber.[50] The formation of the coalition created the potential for the Lords to become a *de facto* majority chamber. The result, however, was that the votes of crossbench peers, previously relatively unimportant, became more crucial. Their turnout in divisions increased and their votes came to matter

[48] *House Magazine*, 21 June 2013. She almost certainly did not mean the politburo, but rather the National People's Congress.
[49] Meg Russell et al., *House Full* (London: Constitution Unit, 2011).
[50] Meg Russell and Maria Scaria, 'Why does the government get defeated in the House of Lords? The Lords, the party system and British politics', *British Politics*, 2:3 (2007), pp. 299–322.

almost as much in terms of inflicting defeat as those of Labour peers.[51] The other development – also not helpful to the government – was that the party blocs in the Lords became less cohesive. Overt rebellion had been relatively rare under Labour: between 1999 and 2010 less than 30 per cent of divisions in the Lords saw a rebellion by a government backbench peer. But the equivalent figure for the first two years of the coalition was over 55 per cent. This was largely a result of the behaviour of Lib Dem peers, who in the Lords rebelled noticeably more than their Conservative partners (or their Lib Dem counterparts in the Commons).[52] Although the number of outright government defeats fell from its high point under Labour, with almost ninety government defeats in the Lords in the first four years of the parliament the Lords remained a difficult chamber for the government to pass legislation through.

Conclusion

The coalition effect in Parliament was therefore a pale imitation of what had been promised. Some of this was the fault of the parties, who found reform less appealing when in power than they had done when in opposition, but it was also partly (ironically) because of the power of Parliament, and in particular the willingness of backbenchers to defy their whips. A more malleable Commons might have done what it was told and passed Lords reform.[53] And in both the Commons and the Lords, the government found Parliament increasingly difficult to handle. On the government side of the House both MPs and peers were more independent, as were select committees in the Commons. The party whips lost influence and control, and, thanks in part to the Speaker, ministers found life tougher than before. This was all much less radical than the manifestos and the Coalition Agreement had promised; it was, perhaps, a more traditional, evolutionary, way to develop and change; perhaps more 'Westminster', but it was still useful.

---

[51] Meg Russell, *The Contemporary House of Lords* (Oxford: Oxford University Press, 2013), p. 120.

[52] Russell, *The Contemporary House of Lords*, pp. 115–16.

[53] Even if it had, it might have required a more malleable Lords for the measure to reach the statute book, but that is another story.

Part II

The coalition and policy

Morten Morland for The Times / News Syndication

6 THE COALITION AND THE ECONOMY

PAUL JOHNSON AND DANIEL CHANDLER

The 2008 financial crisis, which developed into the deepest recession experienced in the UK since before the 1930s, formed the backdrop to the 2010 election and the formation of the coalition government. In 2010, the coalition stated that its first priority was to 'reduce the deficit and restore economic growth'.[1] The story of fiscal retrenchment will surely be one of the main things for which this government is remembered: cuts to public spending on a scale unprecedented in modern times have, in the main, been successfully delivered. However, the return to growth proved more elusive, making the path to deficit reduction much slower and rockier even than predicted in 2010.

Indeed, the coalition government has had to steer a course through economically uncharted waters. The slowdown has lasted longer, and had a more profound impact on household incomes and productivity, than any since at least the 1920s. Despite healthy economic growth since 2013, wages and national income per capita remain lower than they were pre-recession. Employment, on the other hand,

The authors would like to acknowledge generous support from the Nuffield Foundation for a range of pre-election analysis at the IFS. Support from the Economic and Social Research Council (ESRC) through the Centre for the Microeconomic Analysis of Public Policy at IFS (grant reference ES/H021221/1) is also gratefully acknowledged. The views expressed are those of the authors and not necessarily those of the Nuffield Foundation or the ESRC. In addition, the authors would like to thank Rowena Crawford, Soumaya Keynes and Gemma Tetlow at the IFS for providing much of the data on the public finances contained in this chapter.

[1] Queen's Speech 2010, Lords Hansard, 25 May 2010, col. 5.

has held up astonishingly well. Despite the upturn since 2013, the economy remains far from 'recovered', with labour productivity 16 per cent below the level implied by the pre-crisis trend.[2]

Much lower-than-expected economic growth during 2010–12 means that deficit reduction has not gone to plan. The original expectation was that the 'structural current budget deficit' – that bit of the deficit that is not explained by spending on investment and that which will not disappear automatically as the economy returns to trend levels of output – would have been dealt with in time for the 2015 general election. That has not happened. That itself has profound political consequences. The coalition cannot go to the electorate saying 'job done' on the deficit. Rather, they have signed up to another very tough spending settlement for 2015–16 and the coalition government's plans imply further cuts to spending in 2016–17 and 2017–18. The state of the public finances creates an obvious challenge for whoever forms the next government.

On the overall scale of 'austerity' there seems to have been remarkably little disagreement between the coalition parties. A Liberal Democrat Chief Secretary to the Treasury was intimately involved in, and signed up to, both the 2010 Spending Review which set departmental budgets up to 2014–15, and the 2013 review which set budgets for 2015–16. There is little evidence either of a different set of views about the appropriate fiscal response to poor economic performance up to 2013 – notwithstanding some signs of discontent from the Business Secretary. The Labour opposition found it hard at times to communicate a clear stance, while changing economic circumstances quickly rendered their stated ambitions from their time in government effectively redundant.

The shape of austerity has inevitably been subject to more debate both within parties and between them, with, for example, the opposition decrying the scale of cuts to the working-age welfare budget, and some uncertainty as to whether a Conservative government unconstrained by coalition would have gone further. On the other hand, there has been significant cross-party consensus on the need to protect certain areas of spending, including on the NHS, schools and overseas aid.

---

[2] Alina Barnett, Sandra Batten, Adrian Chiu, Jeremy Franklin and María Sebastiá-Barriel, 'The UK productivity puzzle', *Quarterly Bulletin* (2014: Q2), pp. 114–28.

We start this Chapter with a very brief overview of the performance of the economy under the coalition government. We then turn to the two economic issues which have dominated public debate over the past five years: in the second section we look at the government's efforts to restore the public finances, while in the third section we chart the unprecedented squeeze on living standards since the 2008 recession. Finally, we turn to an assessment of policies to restore the economy to growth, noting the central role of the independent Bank of England.

The economy under the coalition

Figure 6.1 neatly encapsulates the background to the economy and the challenges faced by the coalition.

The top dashed line shows the official forecast for the growth path of the economy as at the March 2008 Budget, just before the scale of the subsequent recession became apparent. Instead a very deep recession followed. By the time of the coalition's first Budget in June 2010 (the

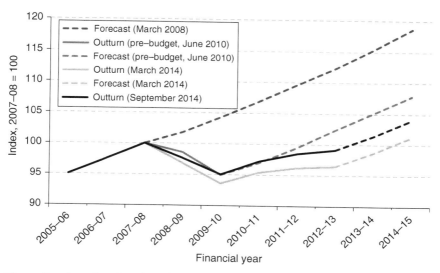

Figure 6.1 Actual and projected real national income (GDP)
Note: the most recent (December 2014) estimates of GDP are based on a new definition of GDP which cannot be directly compared to previous estimates (see footnote 3).
Source: author's calculations using GDP forecasts from HM Treasury (Budget: March 2008) and Office for Budget Responsibility (Pre-Budget forecast: June 2010, Economic and fiscal outlook: March 2014, and Economic and fiscal outlook: December 2014).

second and third lines in Figure 6.1) it was expected by both the newly created Office for Budget Responsibility and most independent forecasters that steady growth would return. But even then the expectation was that the economy in 2015 would be more than 10 per cent smaller than had been forecast back in 2008. The solid and dashed black lines show more recent estimates and forecasts of GDP since 2008, incorporating recent revisions to Office for National Statistics (ONS) measurement methods and to their definition of GDP.[3] It shows that growth was broadly in line with June 2010 expectations for the first year of the coalition (2010–11) but was more sluggish than expected in 2011–12 and 2012–13. The latest estimates suggest that the economy returned to its pre-recession peak at some point in Q3 2013. However, the growth in population means that, even by 2015, national income per head still lags behind its pre-recession level, with the unsurprising consequence that household incomes remain below their real-terms peak. The focus on living standards and the 'cost of living crisis', as the Opposition refers to it, is a direct consequence of this.

The first three years of coalition government were marked by a series of dramatic downwards revisions to official forecasts for the UK economy, reaching a nadir in the March 2013 Budget. It is important to recall just how difficult economic circumstances were in the early years of the parliament. Beyond dealing with the deficit the government was faced with uniquely challenging external circumstances and in particular a Eurozone crisis which at the time looked quite likely to result in a break-up – a possibility that only really receded after ECB president Mario Draghi made his famous promise 'to do whatever it takes to preserve the Euro' in July 2012.

As is often the way, though, just as everything seemed at its worst, so the recovery was in fact beginning. Office for Budget Responsibility

---

[3] In 2014 the ONS introduced major changes to its measurement methods and its definition of GDP (in order to implement the ESA 10 guidelines for the National Accounts), which it said were 'the most wide-ranging in more than a decade'. The biggest impact has been on estimates of the level of nominal GDP, which has increased by an average of 4 per cent a year for the period 1997–2012. The impact on growth in real GDP has been more muted: the ONS now believes that the downturn in 2008–9 was shallower than previously estimated and that subsequent growth was stronger, but they conclude that the broad picture for the recession is unchanged, and it remains the case that 'the UK experienced the deepest recession since ONS records began in 1948 and the subsequent recovery has also been the slowest' (Office for National Statistics (ONS), *Economic Review: September 2014*).

(OBR) forecasts in autumn 2013 and Budget 2014 finally moved in a positive direction, and the economic debate started to move away from its focus on the lack of growth and the role of fiscal policy in supporting or hampering growth. Moreover, revisions to ONS data in 2014 meant that things hadn't even been quite as bad as they had seemed: the lines at the bottom of Figure 6.1 represent estimates and forecasts of GDP in March 2014, while the solid black line represents estimates following these ONS revisions. The new estimates put real GDP growth between 2007 and 2012 0.5 percentage points per year higher than previous estimates.[4] The consequences of these errors in official statistics were perhaps not as grave as those created by erroneous estimates of borrowing requirements which were partially responsible for driving Chancellor Healey into the arms of the IMF in 1976, but they did not help the economic debate. In any case by mid-2013 a significant economic recovery was becoming apparent, and the last two years of coalition government have seen the UK economy outperform most other European and G7 economies. The OECD puts real GDP growth in the UK in 2014 at 3.0 per cent, compared to 0.8 per cent for the Euro area and 1.8 per cent for the OECD overall.[5]

Dismal economic growth in the initial years of the coalition translated into falling real earnings and falling living standards – an important theme we examine in more detail below. But what it did not translate into, to the surprise of most commentators, was mass unemployment or sustained high levels of long-term unemployment. Unemployment rose from a low of 5.3 per cent in early 2008 to a peak of 8.5 per cent in late 2011, falling back to 6.5 per cent in the middle of 2014.[6] The flip side of the very strong employment record has been a very weak productivity record. By 2014 the Bank of England estimated that hourly productivity was still below its pre-crisis peak and 16 per cent below its pre-crisis trend.[7]

All of this – slow growth, high employment, low wage growth, very poor productivity – was unanticipated by Chancellor and Treasury back in 2010. There are no parallels between this period of emergence from recession and the 1980s and 1990s. The deep recession at the start of the 1980s, for example, was followed by almost exactly the opposite

[4] ONS, *September 2014*.
[5] Annex Table 1, in OECD, *Economic Outlook*, vol. 2014, Issue 2.
[6] ONS, ILO unemployment rate, all aged 16–64 (LF2Q).
[7] Alina Barnett, Sandra Batten, Adrian Chiu, Jeremy Franklin and María Sebastiá-Barriel, 'The UK productivity puzzle', *Quarterly Bulletin* (2014: Q2), pp. 114–28.

set of economic indicators: robust growth, fast growth in wages and productivity but high and persistent levels of unemployment. So one of the stories of economic management over this period has been the extent to which fiscal, monetary and other policy has had to adapt to unexpected change.

Before moving on to some of the policy responses to this economic inheritance it is worth mentioning one important development in economic policy over this period, illustrated perfectly by the sourcing of Figure 6.1: the creation of the OBR. It was set up immediately after the 2010 election in response to concerns about the lack of independence from politically motivated wishful thinking in official economic and fiscal forecasts. It quickly became an accepted part of the political and economic landscape and by 2013 the Shadow Chancellor was calling for its powers to be significantly extended to enable it to cost the policies put forward by the major parties in their general election manifestos.

We will come on to a discussion of other aspects of the economy in later sections, not least the falls in real incomes and earnings, the robustness of the labour market, and the role of monetary policy. But for now we move on to look at the central plank of coalition policy – deficit reduction.

Fixing the public finances

A record deficit precipitated by the recession of 2008–9 formed the backdrop to the 2010 general election.[8] The opposition parties inevitably blamed the then government for racking up unsustainable levels of spending and borrowing. The government claimed that it was all down to the consequences of a global recession over which they had no control. There is some truth in both claims.

---

[8] Where possible, outturns and forecasts of the public finances in this chapter are based on the most recent (December 2014) OBR data, which incorporates the substantial revisions made by ONS in 2014 to their estimates of GDP (see footnote 3) as well as changes to their public finance statistics following the ONS Public Sector Finance review. These revisions increased estimates of nominal GDP, thereby reducing all ratios expressed as a share of GDP. The Impact on public sector net borrowing is more complex (positive in some years, negative in others) and is discussed in some detail in the OBR's Economic and fiscal outlook: December 2014 (London: Office for Budget Responsibility).

The UK was running a deficit of nearly 3 per cent of national income in 2007 at a time when the economy had, as the then Chancellor never tired of reminding us, been growing for the longest continuous period in centuries. The UK entered the recession with one of the biggest structural deficits in the OECD – having done less than most other advanced economies to reduce its debt and deficit over the preceding decade.[9] And the scale of fiscal consolidation now being carried out is one of the biggest in the OECD. The fiscal rules being followed pre-recession were inadequate, and were described as such by many commentators. Even then they were barely followed and the government's behaviour was enough to suggest that they weren't taken terribly seriously. In the words of the OBR:

> Having briefly delivered budget surpluses in the early 2000s, the then Government chose to increase public spending as a share of GDP into its second term in the belief that this would be paid for by a rise in receipts as a share of GDP. But – in line with the predictions of many external observers – receipts did not perform as strongly as the Government hoped and in the run-up to the crisis it consistently ran deficits that were larger than forecast and larger than in most other developed economies.[10]

The case for the defence is that nobody saw the crisis coming. On the basis of the best information then available, forecasts suggested that the public finances were sustainable into the medium term. Spending increases had largely been matched by tax increases. And even if the fiscal rules were sub-optimal and barely honoured in the breach, they did exert a real constraint on behaviour and ensured that neither government debt nor government borrowing looked unsustainable at the time.

The truth is of course not as black and white as either of these summaries would suggest. What is clear is that, just as happened in the late 1980s, a degree of hubris allowed the government to convince

[9] See for example Robert Chote, Carl Emmerson and Gemma Tetlow, *The UK Public Finances: Ready for Recession?* (IFS Briefing Note No. 79, 2008) (accessed at www.ifs.org.uk/bns/bn79.pdf, 11 November 2014).

[10] Jon Riley and Robert Chote, *Crisis and Consolidation in the Public Finances* (OBR working paper number 7, 2014) (accessed at http://budgetresponsibility.org.uk/wordpress/docs/WorkingPaper7a.pdf, 11 November 2014), para. 2.31.

itself that it had achieved what no government had previously achieved – in Nigel Lawson's case that the trend growth of the economy had risen to much higher levels and in Gordon Brown's case that he had abolished the economic cycle, or 'boom and bust' as he put it.

Looking back there are clear lessons here. 'Boom and bust' had not been abolished and economic policy should never assume that it has been. Relying on pro-cyclical revenue streams can create particular problems. Running substantial deficits on the basis that an ill-conceived backward-looking fiscal rule 'allows' it makes little sense. But even if all these mistakes had been avoided, a substantial deficit and subsequent consolidation could not have been. And it is worth remembering that before the crisis hit, the Conservatives in opposition signed up to supporting the then Labour government's spending plans, rather as the Labour Party in opposition had signed up to Conservative plans after the 1997 election and have again signed up at least to the plans for 2015–16.

In any case all three main parties entered the 2010 general election with 'plans' to fix the deficit. In fact there was little to choose between them in terms of their stated intentions with respect to the scale of deficit reduction intended. A detailed analysis by IFS researchers after the 2010 election manifestos had been produced, but before the 2010 election, concluded:

> As best we can tell from the statements they have made to date, all three parties aim to implement a fiscal tightening of 4.8% of national income, or £71 billion, by 2016–17. The only real difference is that the Conservatives would aim to get most of the job done a year earlier by 2015–16.
>
> This does not make an enormous difference to the total amount of government borrowing over the next few years or to the long-term profile for government debt. Over the next seven years (2010–11 to 2016–17 inclusive), Labour and the Liberal Democrats plan to borrow £643 billion, while the Conservatives would end up borrowing £604 billion, about £38 billion or just 6% less.[11]

[11] Robert Chote, Rowena Crawford, Carl Emmerson and Gemma Tetlow, *Filling the Hole: How do the Three Main UK Parties Plan to Repair the Public Finances?* (London: Institute for Fiscal Studies, 2010).

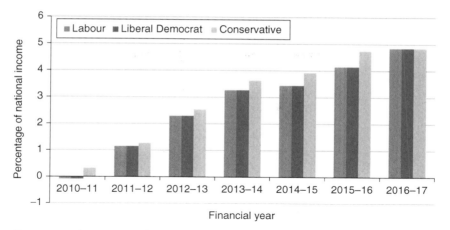

Figure 6.2 The timing and size of the fiscal tightening: the main parties' plans
Source: Figure 3.1 in R. Chote, R. Crawford, C. Emmerson and G. Tetlow, *Filling the Hole: How do the Three Main UK Parties Plan to Repair the Public Finances?* (London: Institute for Fiscal Studies, 2010).

To the extent that there were differences it was Labour and Liberal Democrat plans which appeared near enough identical and the Conservatives who were promising a modestly swifter tightening. This is all perhaps best illustrated in Figure 6.2, drawn from the same source.

There were bigger, but still not enormous, differences between the parties in the planned composition of the fiscal tightening. Based on analysis of their manifestos at the time, IFS researchers concluded that the Conservatives were planning £57 billion of spending cuts and £14 billion of tax increases, against £47 billion of cuts and £24 billion of tax rises by Labour. The Liberal Democrat plans at the time appeared to roughly split the difference, with a slight leaning towards Labour, planning £51 billion of spending cuts and £20 billion of tax increases. As we shall see in a moment any detailed differences were soon overwhelmed by the deteriorating economic situation.

Immediately post-election, though, deficit reduction was at the heart of the Coalition Agreement. Indeed, in the list of contents in the coalition's programme for government there is no heading for 'growth' or 'the economy' – just 'deficit reduction'. The new Chancellor, George Osborne, set out the coalition's headline fiscal strategy in an 'Emergency' Budget in June 2010, outlining plans for a consolidation in the region of 7 per cent of GDP, with 77 per cent of this coming from cuts to public spending (to 2015–16, and including plans inherited from the outgoing

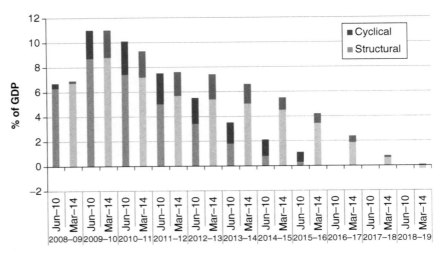

Figure 6.3 Structural and cyclical public sector net borrowing: March 2014 data compared to plans in June 2010 (% of GDP)

Note: excludes transfers relating to the Asset Purchase Facility (APF) and Royal Mail Pension Fund. We use data from the 2014 Budget ('March 2014'), rather than the more recent Autumn Statement in December 2014, because this is the last fiscal event where GDP and borrowing figures were provided on a basis consistent with those produced in June 2010. As a result, this figure does not reflect recent ONS revisions to the measurement and definition of GDP and public sector net borrowing (see footnote 8), or changes to the underlying borrowing forecasts between March and December 2014, which put borrowing higher in the initial years of the forecast and slightly lower from 2016–17 than was anticipated in March 2014 (see OBR Economic and fiscal outlook: December 2014).

Sources: OBR, *Economic and Fiscal Outlook: June 2010* and OBR Databank (May 2014).

Labour government). A range of tax measures were announced in the June Budget, including a hike in the VAT rate, with £20 billion of tax increases and £12 billion of cuts amounting to a net increase of £8 billion by 2014–15.[12] The budget was followed by a spending review, delivered at speed in November 2010, which set out the initial details of the substantial cuts to spending announced in the Budget, including a substantial increase in the amount coming from the working-age welfare budget.[13]

In its own terms, perhaps the greatest success of the coalition has been the successful delivery – indeed over-delivery – of those planned cuts (discussed in more detail below). However, in the face of the poor economic performance discussed above, the original plans proved nowhere

[12] Chote et al., *Filling the Hole.*   [13] See chapter twelve, this volume for more details

near sufficient to deal with the deficit. This is simply illustrated by Figure 6.3, which shows borrowing planned in June 2010 and outcomes and plans as of mid-2014 (based on data prior to recent ONS revisions – see footnote 8). By 2014–15 borrowing was more than 3 per cent of GDP higher than had been planned. Rather than implement additional cuts or tax increases, the coalition pushed the task of deficit reduction into the next parliament, announcing additional cuts for 2015–16 in a second spending review, with plenty more to come thereafter.

This deterioration in the planned state of the public finances was associated with what was probably the defining economic debate of the first three years of coalition government – the impact of austerity on growth. According to the government, deficit reduction was a necessary precondition for growth – a position which was broadly in line with the economic views of the Treasury. They argued that reducing the deficit and bringing debt onto a sustainable long-term path would create macro-economic stability, allow very loose monetary policy, keep borrowing costs low for the government, provide greater certainty about the trajectory of public spending, and leave room for private sector spending and investment. However, as economic conditions continued to disappoint, the government came under increasing pressure to change course, or ditch 'plan A'. The essential argument of the opposition was simple enough. The coalition was going 'too far, too fast' on spending cuts, resulting in lower economic growth and unnecessary damage to the economy. They held out the poorer-than-expected economic performance as evidence of this.

Even before the election, this question of the appropriate pace and scale of deficit reduction, and the likely impact on growth, was the subject of lively debate among economists. On 14 February 2010 the *Sunday Times* published an open letter to the (then Labour) government in which twenty respected economists called for faster action to reduce the deficit, and suggesting the government should seek to eliminate the 'structural' deficit in a single parliament. However, this was followed just days later by a reply, signed by a hundred similarly eminent economists and published in the *Financial Times*, which called on the government to prioritize returning the economy to growth, and warning against an accelerated programme of fiscal austerity. The debate continued through the first years of the parliament with a number of economists and commentators weighing in against austerity. As growth disappointed, the balance of opinion within the economics professions shifted towards the need for fiscal stimulus: when the *New Statesman* surveyed the twenty signatories to the original *Sunday Times* letter, nine urged some form of fiscal stimulus to promote growth, while just one repeated their endorsement of the coalition's fiscal plans.[14]

The coalition was probably coming under most pressure to reverse its fiscal policies in early 2013. In February, Moody's stripped the UK of its triple-A credit rating, citing the UK's weak economic performance. In March, the OBR reduced its growth forecast once again, cutting in half expected GDP growth for 2013, but suggesting the UK would (narrowly) avoid a 'triple dip' recession (in fact, revisions to the data now suggest there was no 'double dip'). In April, the IMF – which had enthusiastically endorsed the coalition's fiscal strategy in 2010 – highlighted the weak outlook for the UK economy. The IMF's chief economist Olivier Blanchard suggested the government was 'playing with fire' and urged the government to consider a loosening of austerity.[15] This period also saw perhaps the most direct criticism of the government's fiscal strategy from coalition ministers, as Business Secretary Vince Cable called for an expansion of capital spending and suggested that the changing economic climate might justify an increase in public borrowing.[16] Naturally the return to growth in 2013, at a rate which took everyone by surprise – OBR, Bank of England and Treasury alike – left the coalition to claim that its strategy had been vindicated. The counterfactual, of course, is extremely hard to determine.

According to the OBR, the shortfall in GDP relative to expectations was driven above all by lower than expected private investment, followed (in order of importance) by weak net exports and low real consumption growth. There were clearly a number of external reasons for this, including the Eurozone crisis, which resulted in slow growth and great economic uncertainty in the UK's key trading partner, the continued tightness of credit conditions, and high commodity prices (particularly in oil). While the OBR acknowledged that the

---

[14] George Eaton, 'Exclusive: Osborne's supporters turn on him', *New Statesman*, 15 August 2012 (accessed at www.newstatesman.com/blogs/politics/2012/08/exclusive-osbornes-supporters-turn-him, 11 November 2014).

[15] Ed Conway, 'IMF inflicts "double blow" on George Osborne,' *Sky News*, 16 April 2013 (accessed at http://news.sky.com/story/1078887/imf-inflicts-double-blow-on-george-osborne, 11 November 2014).

[16] Vince Cable, 'When the facts change, should I change my mind?', *New Statesman*, 6 March 2013.

government's fiscal consolidation may have had a bigger impact on growth than was expected in 2010, they argued that this did not seem to be the most likely explanation for the fact that the economy performed so much worse than expected.[17] In any case, it is worth remembering that – certainly into early 2011 – the expectation was that the Bank of England would be raising base rates in the foreseeable future, and a fiscal loosening could well have precipitated an offsetting monetary tightening.[18]

Perhaps more pertinent to ask, though, is whether the fiscal stance was really as tight as the rhetoric on both sides suggested. Look again at Figure 6.3. Both the headline and underlying deficits have been much higher than planned. The coalition did *nothing* to tighten fiscal policy in the face of failure to reduce the deficit anywhere near as fast as intended. Instead further tightening was pencilled in for future years – for the next parliament. This remained consistent with the Chancellor's main forward-looking fiscal target that there should be structural budget balance at the end of the five-year forecast horizon. That forward-looking rule has turned out to provide considerable flexibility in the face of poor economic performance. The Chancellor's supplementary target, stating that debt should be falling in 2015–16, looks likely to be breached, and the OBR has been forecasting a breach since late 2012.[19] The fact of this likely breach of his own fiscal rule seems to have come at little or no political cost to the Chancellor, perhaps because in economic terms the target itself had little to commend it.

In fact the government's forward-looking fiscal target allowed it much more freedom than the rules set by the Labour Party in government. The Fiscal Responsibility Act 2010, legislated by the last Labour government, imposed legally binding constraints on borrowing and debt. One of the Act's three provisions was that borrowing in 2013–14 should be half its 2009–10 level. That was not achieved. It is to be presumed that a Labour government would not have stuck to this target. But this is a good illustration of the difficulties in constructing counterfactuals as to what might have happened under an alternative

---

[17] Office for Budget Responsibility, *Forecast Evaluation Report* (London: Office for Budget Responsibility, 2013).

[18] Rowena Crawford, Carl Emmerson and Gemma Tetlow, 'Green Budget public finance forecasts', in Mike Brewer, Carl Emmerson and H. Miller (eds.), *Green Budget 2011* (London: Institute for Fiscal Studies, 2011), pp. 108–29.

[19] Office for Budget Responsibility, *Economic and Fiscal Outlook: December 2012* (London: Office for Budget Responsibility).

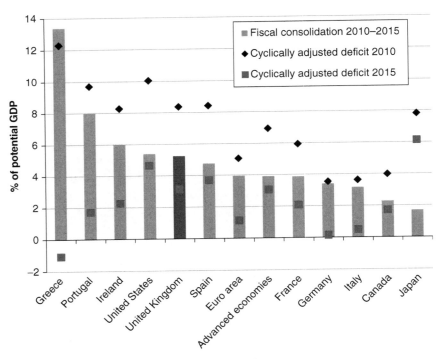

Figure 6.4 Fiscal consolidation in the UK compared to other countries, 2010–2015 (% of potential GDP)
Note and source: see Table 1.1 in IMF, *Fiscal Monitor*, April 2014.

government. One can also contrast the scale of the consolidation in the UK with that in other countries. This is illustrated in Figure 6.4. The scale of the UK's consolidation since 2010 has been only slightly greater than the Euro area average and leaves the UK with a cyclically adjusted Budget deficit well above the Euro area average.

The coalition's relative flexibility with respect to deficit reduction in the short run did nothing to change the fact that the poor economic performance required the total tightening to be greater than originally planned. The changing scale of the planned consolidation is illustrated in Figure 6.5 (incorporating recent ONS revisions – see footnote 8). It is notable not only that the scale of the fiscal problem rose over time but also that the scale of the planned consolidation increased even faster as the Chancellor announced his intention to achieve a budget surplus by 2018–19, and that all remaining fiscal tightening should come from spending cuts rather than tax increases. This pledge

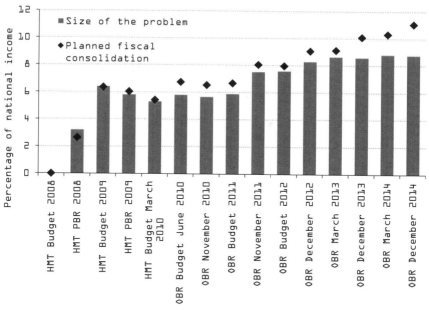

Figure 6.5 The changing size of the problem and cure
Note: estimated increase in medium-term cylically adjusted borrowing (excluding policy response) and the size of the policy response since March 2008.
Sources: Authors' calculations using all HM Treasury Budgets and Pre-Budgets between November 2008 and March 2010 (available at www.hm-treasury.gov .uk/budget_archive.htm) and all OBR Economic and fiscal outlooks between June 2010 and March 2014 (availlable at http://budgetresponsibility.org.uk/economic-fiscal-outlook-december-2014).

to some extent moved the fiscal goalposts, and kick-started the debate about fiscal strategy in the next parliament. While the coalition's fiscal mandate commits them to ensuring that government revenues are sufficient to pay for current spending only, i.e. excluding investment spending, this new target would require more spending cuts, requiring the revenues to cover investment spending too. Promises of an additional £7 billion of income tax cuts made at the 2014 Conservative Party conference will make this already stretching target even more difficult to achieve.

Shadow Chancellor Ed Balls has said he will target balance on the current budget during the next parliament – similar to the existing fiscal mandate, but without cyclical adjustment. The Liberal Democrats have committed to something very similar: promising to achieve a balanced current budget by 2017/18, after which they intend to aim for a 'cyclically adjusted balanced total budget, excluding capital spending that enhances economic growth or financial stability' – in other words, a (cyclically adjusted) balanced current budget.

The difference between the Conservatives on the one hand, and Labour and the Liberal Democrats on the other, is potentially substantial – as much as £25 billion in additional borrowing per year by 2019–20 (in 2015–16 prices).[20] Arguably, since the start of 2014 there has been more clear fiscal water between the parties than there was at the height of the rhetorical differences in 2012 and early 2013, and possibly more than there has been in the run-up to any election since at least 1992 and perhaps before. But whichever particular fiscal rule is targeted it is clear that much fiscal tightening will be required after the 2015 election. The Labour Party has already signed up to many of the additional cuts announced for 2015–16 and has no scope for additional spending commitments beyond that without tax increases to pay for them.

The spending cuts

The large majority of the fiscal consolidation in the period to 2015 was on the spending side. The Conservatives have said that further consolidation will also come entirely from controlling spending, not from any further tax increases. One can find an immediate explanation for that strategy in Figure 6.6. It shows, on the basis of plans laid out in the Autumn Statement 2014, how revenues and spending are expected to develop as a share of national income through to 2018–19, on the assumption that spending plans are met. Taxes will be at near enough their highest level as a share of national income since the late 1990s. Spending, will, as a share of GDP, be roughly back at its level in the early 2000s.

The pattern of spending in the chart is in part explained by the collapse in national income in 2008–9: as national income fell, public spending as a fraction of it rose. As national income has failed to recover as hoped, so less spending is possible. The scale of real-terms cuts has been genuinely unprecedented – of an entirely different scale and magnitude to those seen in the 1980s, for example.

[20] Rowena Crawford, Carl Emmerson, Soumaya Keynes and Gemma Tetlow, *Fiscal Aims and Austerity: The parties' plans compared* (IFS Briefing Note BN158, 2014) (accessed at www.ifs.org.uk/uploads/publications/bns/BN158.pdf, 5 January 2015).

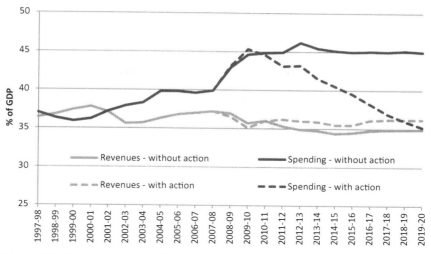

Figure 6.6 Texation and spending without policy responses, as % GDP (2007 onwards)

Notes: Revisions to the method for calculating GDP mean that figures for the level of revenues and spending as a share of GDP are now substantially lower than the figures that were published a few years ago. As a result, it is not sensible directly to compare outturns for revenues and spending as a share of GDP to the forecasts produced in March 2008. Instead we scale the March 2008 forecasts by the difference between the outturn for spending/revenues in 2006–7 as was estimated in 2008 and the latest estimated outturn.

Sources: Figures up to 2007–8 and figures for 'with action' from 2008–9 onwards are calculated using ONS series for total managed expenditure (KW5Q) and revenues (JW20) divided by GDP (series BKTL). Figures from 2008–9 onwards 'without policy' are authors' calculations based on the estimated impact of discretionary policy measures enacted since the March 2008 Budget.

The scale of the cuts in some areas has been driven in part by the protection afforded to some of the biggest elements of spending, notably health and schools on the public services side, and state pensions within the benefits bill. There has been essentially no disagreement between the main parties on the protections afforded to the NHS and schools budgets, reflecting their widespread public support across the political spectrum, and the sheer practical difficulties of reducing spending, particularly for an NHS struggling to cope with an ageing population. For the Conservatives in particular, preserving hard-won public trust in their stewardship of the NHS was an important political priority.

In any case, this was a huge, fiscal decision with important consequences for the distribution of public spending. Spending on the NHS, schools and overseas aid (which has grown with cross-party support) accounted for 39% of total departmental spending in 2010–11 and 46% by 2015–16. If they continue to be protected through to 2018–19 they could account for half of the total. Meanwhile, as of Budget 2014, real cuts to 'unprotected' departments are expected to have averaged 4.6% per year over the course of the parliament (2010–11 to 2014–15), amounting to a cumulative cut of just over 17%.[21] Further cuts in departmental budgets were announced for 2015–16 in a second spending review held in July 2013, taking the total planned cuts to unprotected departments over the five years since 2010–11 to around 19%. By the end of 2015–16 spending by the Departments for Communities and Local Government; Culture, Media and Sport; Work and Pensions; Justice; and DEFRA will be down by 30% or more on 2010–11 levels, with Home Office spending down by 29%. The fact that spending cuts of this scale have been achieved with relatively little public outcry has surprised many observers and, perhaps, convinced Treasury ministers and leading members of the coalition of the possibility of quite radical reductions in the size of the public sector.

Within spending on public services, a significant fraction of the savings has inevitably come from the workforce – pay making up about half of total non-investment spending by departments. The bulk of savings has come from reductions in employment, though reductions in real pay – resulting from a pay freeze followed by a cap of 1 per cent on increases for most public sector workers – have also played a role.[22] Such potentially contentious cuts have been made easier by broader labour market trends. Employment levels overall rose substantially, allowing the Chancellor to boast that reduced numbers of public sector employees had been more than offset by increased employment in the private sector in every region.[23] This strong employment growth in the private sector was accompanied by very weak earnings growth, which has also made the public sector pay freeze look sustainable. In fact, the

[21] Gemma Tetlow, 'Economy bouncing back more strongly but policy choices have increased long-run risks to the public finances', Institute for Fiscal Studies, 20 March 2014 (accessed at www.ifs.org.uk/publications/7153, 11 November 2014)

[22] Rowena Crawford, Jonathan Cribb and Luke Sibieta, 'Public spending and pay', in Carl Emmerson, Paul Johnson and Helen Miller (eds.), *Green Budget 2013* (London: Institute for Fiscal Studies, 2013), pp. 149–80.

[23] Jonathan Cribb, Richard Disney and Luke Sibieta, *The Public Sector Workforce: Past, Present and Future* (London: Institute for Fiscal Studies, 2014).

public–private wage differential actually increased during the recession, and as of mid-2013 it remained above its estimated level in 2007–8.[24] As real wages in the private sector, presumably, grow through the next parliament, savings from the public sector workforce will become less easy to access.

Despite the scale of these changes, within the coalition it seems that the main source of disagreement has been over the scale of cuts to social security spending. Given the size of the budget (social security benefits and tax credits comprised 30 per cent of total spending in 2010–11),[25] any programme of austerity was almost bound to include significant cuts in this area – though the commitment to protect pensioner benefits meant that cuts have come almost entirely from working-age benefits. Controversy deepened as the deteriorating economic situation led to the need for further spending cuts, with opposition to further welfare cuts appearing to come not just from the Liberal Democrats but also, at times, from Iain Duncan Smith, the Secretary of State for Work and Pensions.

The protection of key pensioner benefits emerged as a particular flashpoint. In the wake of the 2011 Autumn Statement, which confirmed that austerity would continue for two more years than originally planned, Deputy Prime Minister Nick Clegg called for certain pensioner benefits, such as free TV licences and bus passes, to be means-tested. However, with the Prime Minister unwilling to reopen this question, the debate shifted to the extent to which further cuts could be made to working-age benefits. Significant further cuts were announced in the Autumn Statement of 2012, as the Chancellor limited increases to most working-age benefits to 1 per cent per year for three years (saving £3.1 billion by 2017–18), though Clegg claimed to have halted some of the 'more extreme reforms that had been put on the table'.[26] In the run-up to the 2015/16 Spending Review, Danny Alexander confirmed Liberal Democrat opposition to further welfare cuts, while Philip Hammond made a public plea for further cuts to welfare in order to spare other budgets, including (his own) defence budget. In the event, relatively

[24] *Ibid.*

[25] Office for Budget Responsibility, *Budget Forecast: June 2010* (London: Office for Budget Responsibility, 2010)

[26] Quoted in Rajeev Syal, 'Nick Clegg risks Lib Dem–Tory coalition by spelling out differences', *The Guardian*, 17 December 2012.

small welfare cuts (amounting to less than half a billion pounds) were announced, alongside a cap aimed at limiting future spending on most working-age benefits.

Looking forward, the biggest change in spending plans since the October 2010 spending review has been the extension of the period of spending reductions well beyond the 2015 election. Details of these cuts, at least for the financial year following the planned election (2015–16), were set out in a second spending review in July 2013. Despite substantial additional cuts planned for most departments this additional spending review would appear to have created remarkably little inter-party disagreement either between the coalition parties or between the coalition and the Labour Party, which has signed up to the proposed spending envelope for 2015–16, if not the detailed distribution of the cuts.

Beyond 2015–16, although we now know something of the different parties' broad fiscal plans, we know next to nothing of their specific plans to cut spending. The Budget Red Books have set out the fiscal plans as though all the additional savings will come from departmental budgets. If the NHS, schools and overseas aid continue to be protected, this would imply remarkably deep cuts in unprotected areas – averaging more than a third between 2010–11 and 2018–19. The Conservatives have intimated that they would look to protect departments from such swingeing cuts by cutting the social security budget further. George Osborne has come close to ruling out tax rises, saying to the Treasury Select Committee in July 2013 'I am clear that tax increases are not required to achieve this', while David Cameron unveiled proposals for substantial income tax cuts at the 2014 Conservative Party conference, cuts which might well mean that even greater spending reductions will be required if the Conservatives' fiscal targets are to be met.

Tax changes

While tax increases formed an important part of the initial consolidation, the overall plan is to rely much more heavily on spending cuts to address the deficit. But the coalition has also been active in tax policy. Indeed, in the context of such a major fiscal tightening some of the choices made have been quite remarkable, with very large tax *cuts* in some areas, most notably the very big increase in the income tax personal allowance. This pledge was a key plank of Liberal Democrat policy in their manifesto which appeared in the Coalition Agreement and has been consistently pushed through. A constant theme of Budgets over the parliament has been one of how to pay for some of these tax cuts whilst sticking to the overall fiscal path.

The coalition inherited some substantial tax increases on those on the highest incomes implemented immediately before the election, including of course the new 50p rate of income tax on incomes over £150,000. Rather less salient was a new 60 per cent rate on incomes in a band over £100,000, proposed reductions to the generosity of pension tax relief and an increase in stamp duty on expensive properties. While the 50p rate has been reduced to 45p, the other measures hitting 'the rich' have been maintained or even, in the case of stamp duty and cutting pension tax relief, extended.

Easily the most substantial additional tax increase has been the rise in the standard rate of VAT from 17.5 to 20 per cent announced in the June 2010 Budget and implemented in January 2011. This passed with apparently little internal dissent within the coalition. In the search for additional revenue it was judged the least politically and economically damaging. One cannot know what a Labour government would have done, but we do know that Alastair Darling came very close to announcing an increase in VAT even before the election, before opting instead for a rise in National Insurance Contributions.

Beyond the extraordinary £11 billion a year or so that is now being invested in raising the income tax personal allowance the coalition has also pushed through big reductions in the main rate of corporation tax, with considerable enthusiasm for this on the Conservative side. Less strategic has been a substantial reduction in the real rate of fuel duty as the Chancellor has continually bowed to pressure from his own backbenches to delay and cancel planned upratings. This is beautifully illustrated in Table 6.1, which shows how each planned uprating has been gradually pushed back and eventually cancelled. Of course the government have compared their generosity to motorists with the significant increases planned by the Labour government and set out in their pre-election Budget. In fact the pattern illustrated in the Table almost replicates the behaviour of the last government whilst in office. Even maintaining the real value of fuel duties seems to have become close to politically impossible.

Table 6.1 *Actual and announced fuel duties since 2011*

Dates uprating originally due	Dates uprating due following policy announcement					
	Budget 2011	Autumn Statement 2011	June 2012	Autumn Statement 2012	Budget 2013	Autumn Statement 2013
Apr 2011	Jan 2012	Aug 2012	Jan 2013	*Cancelled*	*Cancelled*	*Cancelled*
Apr 2012	Aug 2012	*Cancelled*	*Cancelled*	*Cancelled*	*Cancelled*	*Cancelled*
Apr 2013	Apr 2013	Apr 2013	Apr 2013	Sep 2013	*Cancelled*	*Cancelled*
Apr 2014	Apr 2014	Apr 2014	Apr 2014	Sep 2014	Sep 2014	*Cancelled*
Apr 2015	Apr 2015	Apr 2015	Apr 2015	Sep 2015	Sep 2015	Sep 2015
Apr 2016	Apr 2016	Apr 2016	Apr 2016	Apr 2016	Apr 2016	Apr 2016

Politically, of course, the big tax story of the parliament has been the decision over the top 50p, now 45p, rate of income tax on incomes over £150,000. The 50p rate was announced by Chancellor Darling in Budget 2009 and introduced in April 2010 immediately before the election. This of course ensured that it was almost completely ineffective in its first year of operation because it gave those with very high incomes plenty of notice and allowed them to rearrange their affairs to take income early. This gave the coalition a problem. Convinced that this level of tax was likely to be economically damaging and would raise little additional revenue, the Conservatives did not want it as a long-term feature of the tax system. But politically, reducing a tax paid only by those on incomes over £150,000 – the top 1 per cent of taxpayers – was never going to be easy for a government claiming we were 'all in it together' and stung by accusations that they were out of touch with mainstream voters.

In the event an analysis was commissioned from HMRC to assess how effective the top rate had been in raising revenue. While stressing the great uncertainty around estimates based on only two years of data, HMRC concluded that only about £1 billion of additional revenue was being raised – rather less than the £2.7 billion originally envisaged and well short of the £6.8 billion a year that would have been raised if there had been no behavioural response. Their analysis also suggested that cutting the top rate from 50p to 45p would cost only around £100 million. The OBR signed these off as reasonable estimates and in his 2012 Budget the Chancellor acted to announce a cut from 50p to 45p from April 2013. At the same time, and at the insistence of the Liberal Democrats, a big increase of more than £1,000 in the personal allowance was announced.[27] The horse-trading required that the two changes be made at the same time. Just as the previous government had made the fiscally expensive mistake of announcing the introduction of the 50p rate well in advance, so the coalition made the same mistake in reverse – announcing its demise well in advance. In each case the billions of pounds of income were shifted between financial years by those on high incomes seeking to take advantage of differential tax rates. The Labour Party has subsequently announced that it would, in office, return the top rate to 50p.

The immediate aftermath of the 2012 Budget was, however, dominated by controversy over a range of other smaller tax measures, largely aimed at recouping some of the costs associated with the big increase in the personal allowance. These included the phasing out of the additional income tax personal allowance enjoyed by pensioners – in a move dubbed the 'granny tax' – and a small movement in the VAT boundary to bring any food sold above room temperature into the VAT net. Bizarrely (at least bizarrely if looked at from any rational point of view) this small extension of VAT, which quickly acquired the name 'pasty tax', drew far more political flack than the massively more significant hike in the main rate which had come in only just over a year earlier, and was partially reversed.

More radical reform has been eschewed by the coalition. The need to repair the public finances has quite definitely not been used to force through measures such as a broadening of the VAT base,[28] which might have improved the efficiency of the tax system whilst also offering the potential for additional revenue. In many respects there has been considerable continuity with the (lack of) strategy pursued by the previous government. This lack of radical reform stands in stark contrast to policy on the spending side of the balance sheet. Perhaps some of that has come from difficulties in agreement across the coalition. The Liberal Democrats might well have imposed a 'mansion tax' – a higher council

---

[27] See Matthew d'Ancona, *In It Together: The Inside Story of the Coalition Government* (London: Penguin, 2013), p. 231.

[28] See the Mirrlees Review (James Mirrlees, Stuart Adam, Tim Besley, Richard Blundell, Stephen Bond, Robert Chote, Malcolm Gammie, Paul Johnson, Gareth Myles and James Poterba, *Tax by Design: The Mirrlees Review*, Oxford: Oxford University Press for IFS, 2011) for a comprehensive analysis and setting out of a tax strategy. Paul Johnson, 'Tax without design: recent developments in UK tax policy', *Fiscal Studies*, 35:3 (2014), pp. 243–73 analyses the coalition's record in more detail.

tax charge on very expensive properties. But there has been little sign that either coalition partner has been interested in more fundamental reform of tax policy.

From the perspective of 2015, though, three aspects of coalition tax policy stand out. The first two we have already alluded to: the expenditure of colossal amounts of money on three measures – the personal allowance, corporation tax and fuel duties – and the general lack of any clear strategy for reform beyond one or two narrow areas. The third is the distributional consequences – the incomes of those in the middle to upper-middle parts of the household income distribution have been quite effectively protected from the direct effects of the tax and benefit changes introduced since January 2010. Taking tax and welfare changes into account, analysis by IFS researchers suggests that losses have been concentrated in the bottom half and the top 10 per cent of the income distribution. 'Middle England' has suffered remarkably little on average from tax and welfare changes over this period.[29]

Living standards

For most people of working age it has not been changes to tax policy which have hit their incomes, rather it has been a historically unprecedented and long-lasting fall in real earnings. Figure 6.7 illustrates just how remarkable the period since 2008 has been by comparing the path of real hourly wages with their paths after the 1979 and 1990 recessions. The failure of wages to grow continued right through 2014 as economic recovery, as measured by national income, continued apace. Economic recovery was not leading to a recovery in earnings and living standards.

Largely as a result of this fall in earnings, real household incomes in 2015 remain well below their 2010 and pre-recession levels. To go such a period without a recovery in living standards is historically unusual if not unprecedented, at least since the last war. The political challenge created by this fall in living standards has been defined by its widespread nature. In complete contrast to the 1980s, when high

[29] David Phillips, 'Personal tax and welfare measures', Institute for Fiscal Studies, 2014 (accessed at www.ifs.org.uk/budgets/budget2014/personal_measures.pdf, 11 November 2014)

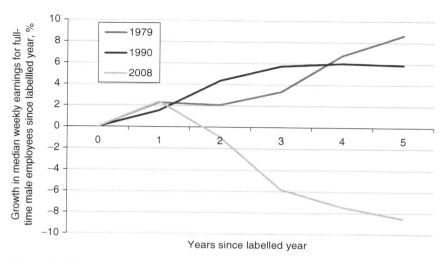

Figure 6.7 Changes to average real hourly wages in the UK, by recession
Note: median gross weekly earnings for adult full-time male employees in Great Britain whose pay for the survey period was not affected by absence. We have not looked at men and women combined because data is only available from 1984. Source: 1970–1997 New Earnings Survey, 1997 onwards Annual Survey of Hours and Earnings. See www.ons.gov.uk/ons/about-ons/business-transparency/freedom-of-information/what-can-i-request/published-ad-hoc-data/labour/december-2012/gross-weekly-earning-1968-to-2013.xls.

unemployment hit a minority and earnings, especially for high earners, rose swiftly, the fall in income over this parliament has been experienced across most of the distribution. Employment has risen and earnings have fallen. Up to 2013 at least this has been a period of falling income inequality. Much more than the 1980s at least we are 'in it together'. But for many people in work that has been a very uncomfortable experience as their living standards have fallen. And while the gap between rich and poor has not widened, the gap in experience between old and young has been quite dramatic. While the incomes of those over state pension age have continued to rise, 31–59-year-olds suffered an average 11 per cent fall in real incomes (measured after housing costs) between 2007–8 and 2012–13, and those in their 20s saw their incomes fall by an average 20 per cent.[30]

---

[30] Chris Belfield, Jonathan Cribb, Andrew Hood and Robert Joyce, *Living Standards, Poverty and Inequality in the UK: 2014* (London: Institute for Fiscal Studies, 2014).

Some of the tax cuts described above were more or less deliberate attempts to help ameliorate the effects of falling earnings. The increase in the personal allowance has been particularly valuable for those on modest to middle earnings – at least up to £40,000 or so, where higher-rate tax starts to bite. Fuel duty freezes were explicitly linked to concerns about the cost of living, as have been council tax freezes. Beyond that the government has struggled to respond. With GDP per person still well below pre-recession levels it is in truth no surprise that income per person has not recovered.

One feature of the period has been the fact that lower-income households have faced higher effective inflation rates than those on higher incomes, in part because energy and food prices rose particularly quickly, especially over the first part of the parliament. Adams et al., for example, calculate that low-income households faced an effective inflation rate 1 per cent higher each year between 2008–9 and 2013–14 than did high-income households.[31]

Reflecting these concerns, the Labour Party moved from talking about the 'cost of living crisis' to offering at the 2013 party conference to freeze energy bills. This arguably represented a radical shift in the terms of political and economic debate. A promise of such direct political intervention in a market to control prices appeared to sit well outside not only the coalition's economic policy framework but also that of the previous Labour government. The opposition followed a similar theme in later proposing some limited control of rents in the private rental sector.

Responding to concerns about energy bills the 2013 Autumn Statement included a set of measures to reduce the effect of 'green' taxes and levies, designed to reduce household energy bills by £50 a year. This response itself represented a compromise within and between the coalition parties over the importance of green policies.[32]

The other significant policy initiatives, driven significantly by concerns about living standards, have been controversial interventions in the owner-occupied housing market. With the banks, in the wake of the financial crisis, making few mortgages available to buyers with deposits of less than 20 per cent of the purchase price, owner-occupation was

[31] Abi Adams, Andrew Hood and Peter Levell, 'The squeeze on incomes', in Carl Emmerson, Paul Johnson and Helen Miller (eds.), *Green Budget 2014* (London: Institute for Fiscal Studies), pp. 90–125.

[32] See chapter seven, this volume.

becoming unaffordable for many potential first-time buyers. Home ownership rates among those in their 20s and 30s had fallen to much lower levels than had been the case a decade or two decades previously. For those in their mid-20s ownership rates had halved.[33]

The government responded by announcing the 'Help to Buy' scheme in the March 2013 Budget, aimed at both stimulating the market and reducing the upfront deposit costs of ownership. The policy has two parts, both of which are set to run for three years: 'help to buy: equity loan', launched in April 2013, provides interest-free government loans of up to 20 per cent to purchasers of newly built homes while 'help to buy: mortgage guarantee', launched in January 2014, allows mortgage lenders to purchase government-backed insurance for high loan-to-value (LTV) mortgages on all new and existing properties worth less than £600,000. The scheme represents a significant expansion of previous initiatives, with the government committing to provide £3.5 billion in equity loans over three years from April 2013, and insurance guarantees sufficient to support as much as £130 billion of high LTV mortgages insurance over three years from January 2014.

The equity loan scheme has been broadly welcomed as an attempt to increase access to the housing market while also stimulating the construction of new builds, addressing long-standing concerns about the inadequacy of new supply. While housing construction has picked up, there has been no evaluation of how far the equity loan scheme contributed to this change (NAO 2014). The mortgage guarantee scheme, on the other hand, has been subject to more criticism on grounds that, by stimulating demand without any direct link to new supply, it risks stoking a house price bubble which could put the recovery at risk. Whatever the role of these policies the pick-up in house prices, especially in London, has raised fears of a house price bubble, with the IMF and Bank of England, among others, seeing it as a potential threat to economic recovery.

Getting back to growth

Deficit reduction and living standards have dominated public debate over the parliament. As we have seen, the unexpectedly poor

---

[33] Belfield et al., *Living Standards*.

performance of the UK economy in the first three years of the period has underpinned both the difficulty of bringing down the deficit, and the continued squeeze on living standards. Unsurprisingly, then, there has also been considerable pressure on the coalition to 'do something', beyond deficit reduction, to restore the economy to growth and to make good on early promises about delivering a more sustainable and balanced model of growth.

In many respects the Bank of England has led the way, engaging in a remarkable policy of 'quantitative easing' whilst maintaining interest rates at their lowest level in history. From the Chancellor's point of view it was his fiscal discipline that was a prerequisite for effective monetary activism. The Bank has also worked very closely with the Treasury at times – the funding for lending scheme, for example, being a joint effort by Bank and Treasury to increase the supply of credit in the economy. Beyond that, while the coalition has put in place a range of specific policies spanning tax policy, planning, schools, welfare, infrastructure and industrial policy, and financial reform, it is difficult to discern a coherent 'growth strategy', in particular one aimed at the long-term goal of 'rebalancing the economy'. As economic historian Nicholas Crafts has pointed out, the absence of a wider economic strategy is thrown into sharp relief by comparison to the radicalism of governments in the 1930s and 1980s.[34]

Monetary policy and the Bank of England

Although the Bank of England has been independent since 1997 (one of Gordon Brown's first acts as Chancellor), and is therefore formally outside the remit of political influence and government policy, it is impossible to understand economic policy without it – particularly over the past five years.

As the severity of the recession unfolded between 2007 and 2009, the Monetary Policy Committee pursued an unprecedented loosening of monetary policy. In October 2008, central banks around the world, including those in the UK, USA, Canada, China and across

---

[34] The 1930s are associated with both loose monetary policy and a boom in housing construction, while the 1980s saw a range of radical supply-side reforms. For a summary and discussion, see Nicholas Crafts, 'Returning to growth: Policy lessons from history', *Fiscal Studies*, 34:2 (2013), pp. 255–82.

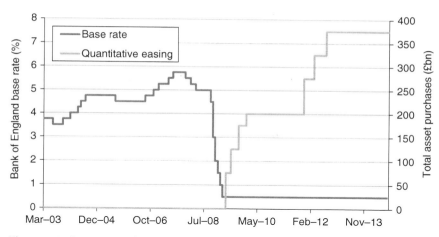

Figure 6.8 Conventional monetary policy and central bank asset purchases
Source: Bank of England

the Euro area undertook a coordinated cut in interest rates. As Figure 6.8 shows, the Bank of England cut its base rate by four and a half percentage points in just six months, from 5% in October 2008 to just 0.5% in March 2009 – the lowest rate in its more than 300-year history. In late 2014, the bank rate remains at this unprecedentedly low rate.

Despite the dramatic reduction in interest rates, the depth of the economic downturn persuaded the Bank that further monetary loosening was required and, along with a number of other central banks, it turned to 'unconventional' monetary policy measures, of which quantitative easing or QE is the most significant. This involves the Bank creating money to purchase (mainly) government bonds. The Bank first announced that it would undertake a policy of QE in March 2009, purchasing £75 billion of assets using money it would create. A series of announcements during 2009 more than doubled the scale of QE to £200 billion, a sum that was raised further as the economic situation continued to deteriorate between 2010 and 2012, reaching a peak of £375 billion in May 2012. The Treasury saw a clear 'implicit contract' involving fiscal credibility on the one side and monetary activism on the other.

Some gloomy speeches by governor Mervyn King in Autumn 2012,[35] in which he speculated about the limits of monetary policy,

---

[35] For example here: www.bankofengland.co.uk/publications/Pages/speeches/2012/613. aspx (accessed 12 November 2014).

were seen by some as threatening this implicit contract. Mark Carney, the replacement Chancellor Osborne had been wooing for some time, was more positive about what central banks could do. Initial speculation about whether the inflation target might be changed in any way was quashed in Budget 2013 and Carney sought to reassure the markets that interest rates would not rise in the short term by announcing a policy of 'forward guidance', suggesting that interest rates would remain low until unemployment fell below 7 per cent (an announcement the Bank subsequently revised in light of better-than-expected labour market performance).

The Chancellor will always be the key player in determining who will be the Governor of the Bank of England, though in this case the focus on securing a particular candidate was perhaps unusual. But the whole period has tested the theory of central bank independence. The funding for lending scheme, launched in July 2012 and designed to deal with the lack of credit supply by incentivizing banks to lend, was explicitly badged as a joint Bank/HM Treasury initiative. In the event the design of the policy incentivized more lending to households than to the main intended focus, business and especially SMEs. In fact it was the newly formed Financial Policy Committee of the Bank of England which in Autumn 2013 ensured that the policy was skewed away from lending to households because of concerns about its effect on the housing market – an effect potentially magnified by the 'Help to Buy' scheme described above, which acted on the demand side of the credit market.

Coalition policies for growth

Monetary policy, led by the Bank of England, albeit with the support of the government, has been the primary tool for returning the UK economy to growth. The Treasury would argue that it is tight fiscal policy which has provided the necessary space for this monetary activism. Given the severity of the recession, the coalition has been under pressure from the start to develop a wider growth strategy. Indeed, David Cameron used his first speech as Prime Minister to emphasize that the economy was the 'first priority' for his government, in terms of both the immediate priority of achieving growth and delivering a more sustainable and balanced model of growth for the long term.

Of course the government has seen the deficit reduction programme itself as a 'necessary precondition for sustained growth'.[36] The one element of that which came under most sustained attack in the early years of the coalition was the sharp cut in investment spending – a cut in fact inherited directly from the Labour government's plans. Critics of the coalition's fiscal strategy argued that it should take advantage of historically low interest rates by borrowing more to invest in infrastructure, providing both a short- to medium-term stimulus and investment which would improve long-run economic performance. Responding to these pressures, the government announced £5 billion of additional infrastructure spending (funded by cuts elsewhere) in the 2011 National Infrastructure Plan to be spent over the next three years. Despite concerns within the Treasury that turning on the investment spending taps at any speed was actually remarkably difficult, pressure to increase capital spending further continued to mount over 2012 and 2013, with the IMF suggesting that the government increase borrowing to bring forward infrastructure projects in the region of £10 billion (to be paid for by cuts later on). Internal coalition debates were publicly aired ahead of the 2013 Budget as Nick Clegg suggested it may have been a mistake to cut capital spending so fast and Vince Cable proposed an increase in government spending on house-building of the order of 1 per cent of GDP.[37] The government announced further spending on infrastructure in the 2013 Budget and Spending Review later in the year, but again this was to be paid for by cuts elsewhere, and additional spending was not planned to begin until 2015–16. In any case the scale of the increases in planned infrastructure spending has been small relative to the initial cuts the government inherited.

Beyond this, the coalition has at times been at pains to demonstrate that it has a more comprehensive growth strategy. Following the 2010 Autumn Statement, it announced a wide-ranging Growth Review, published in two phases alongside the 2011 Budget and Autumn Statement. The review sought to shift the focus beyond short-term recovery and towards longer-term goals, stating that 'The Government's

---

[36] HM Treasury, *National Infrastructure Plan 2010* (London: The Stationery Office, 2010).

[37] 'Clegg says coalition was wrong to cut capital spending', *BBC News*, 25 January 2013 (accessed at www.bbc.co.uk/news/uk-politics-21190108, 12 November 2014); Patrick Wintour, 'Senior Liberal Democrats rebuff Vince Cable over plea for capital investment', *The Guardian*, 10 March 2013.

economic policy objective is to achieve strong, sustainable and balanced growth that is more evenly shared across the country and between industries.' In total, the growth review, plus the National Infrastructure Plan published alongside the 2011 Autumn Statement, set out more than 250 economic reforms and investments in infrastructure,[38] with the broad aims of improving the competitiveness of the UK tax system, encouraging investment and exports, making the UK an attractive place for entrepreneurs, and creating a more educated and flexible workforce. Specific reforms (sometimes building on previous announcements) included significant cuts to corporation tax, a £1 billion Regional Growth Fund to support growth in areas heavily dependent on the public sector, the removal of a range of regulations faced by businesses, a simplified planning regime, a range of policies to support small businesses including an extended business rate holiday, and increased funding for apprenticeships.

Few of these, with the possible exception of the remarkably large cuts to corporation tax, are likely to have had much short-term effect on growth. That is not a criticism. Growth policy is long-term by its nature. As ever, longer-term effects are hard to predict, though if the planning reforms with their presumption in favour of 'sustainable development' do lead to a change in behaviour and culture they might prove effective.

The period since the financial crisis has also seen a revival of interest in so-called 'industrial policy', which broadly refers to government policies to support or develop certain industries in order to support economic growth. The 'Growth Review' encompassed a range of 'horizontal' policies – policies aimed at improving the economic conditions for industry rather than supporting specific sectors directly – while Business Secretary Vince Cable has outlined a wider industrial strategy, including support for key sectors and technologies, improved access to finance, policies to develop certain types of skills and proactive use of government procurement to generate opportunities for UK firms and supply chains.[39] From time to time the coalition has also expressed ambitions to decentralize power and to spur economic growth at a more local level, despite abolishing the regional tier of government built up

---

[38] HM Treasury, 'Budget 2012' (accessed at http://webarchive.nationalarchives.gov.uk/20120403141350/http:/www.hm-treasury.gov.uk/budget2012.htm, 12 November 2014).

[39] Chris Rhodes, *Industrial Policy since 2010* (House of Commons Library, 2014).

under Labour, including the nine Regional Development Agencies. The most radical voice on decentralization has been that of Lord Heseltine, whose report on the issue in 2012 'No stone unturned: In pursuit of growth' recommended a strengthening of local leadership combined with a radical devolution of powers and funding to the local level. This was probably the high point of enthusiasm for devolving economic power, though the close call on Scottish independence and the additional powers promised to Holyrood reawakened some more general calls for devolving tax and spending powers. Other announcements aimed at increasing growth around the country seem to have focused on the possibility of big long-term infrastructure projects such as HS2.

If it is hard to see a clear growth strategy and narrative in all of this, that is unsurprising. Whatever the merits of specific policies among those listed above there is little here that could be said to constitute a really substantial change to economic policy or the supply-side potential of the economy to match the big movements towards greater competition, labour market flexibility, openness to global markets, including global labour markets, and increased access to higher education, which characterized the previous decades. Nor has there been much movement to overcome some of the institutional barriers to growth identified by, for example, the LSE Growth Commission.[40]

A final area worth touching on is reform of the financial sector – an obvious priority in the wake of the financial crisis that precipitated the recession. This has been an area of substantial activism and one perhaps deserving of a chapter of its own. The whole regulatory architecture has been overhauled. Responsibility for prudential regulation has been returned to the Bank of England, the Financial Services Authority wound up and the Financial Conduct Authority created. A new independent Financial Policy Committee of the Bank of England has been created with an objective to manage systemic risks, and a secondary objective to support the economic policy of the government.

An early decision of the coalition, indeed a commitment in the Coalition Agreement, was to establish an Independent Commission on Banking, led by Professor Sir John Vickers, to examine the case for structural reforms to the financial sector, including the need to address

---

[40] *Investing for Prosperity* (LSE Growth Commission, 2013) (accessed at www.lse.ac.uk/researchAndExpertise/units/growthCommission/documents/pdf/LSEGC-Report.pdf, 12 November 2014).

the problem that certain banks were 'too big to fail'. In part the setting up of a commission was intended to help deal with differences between the coalition parties over the extent and type of reform required. The Commission published its final report in September 2011, advocating the ring-fencing of British retail banks (separating deposit and lending functions from investment banking) among other reforms. Following the public outcry over fixing of the LIBOR interest rate benchmark in 2012, a Parliamentary Commission on Banking Standards was established with a wide-ranging remit to look at professional standards and culture in the UK banking sector. The Commission made a series of recommendations to improve accountability and standards, including a tougher licensing regime for bankers and the proposal that bankers be jailed for 'reckless misconduct'. The key recommendations of both groups – including the ring-fence, tougher licensing and criminal sanctions for misconduct – were brought into law via the Banking Reform Act 2013.

Conclusion

So how will the coalition be judged on its handling of the economy?

In its own terms its progress on deficit reduction must be seen as the defining issue. In the event, disappointing economic growth has meant that much less progress has been made than was planned. This despite the fact that George Osborne stuck to 'plan A', withstanding very considerable pressure to slow the pace of spending cuts in the first years of the parliament. For while he may not have deviated from 'plan A' in terms of planned spending cuts (and tax rises) he proved more flexible in his plans to eliminate the deficit than is often acknowledged: the forward-looking fiscal rule has allowed additional tightening to be put off into the next parliament. And this is the context that frames the 2015 election. The next parliament will be characterized by austerity on a comparable scale to that seen since 2010 – not at all the original intention of a Chancellor aiming to have the deficit all but eliminated in time for the 2015 election.

Indeed some very big fiscal and economic questions remain unanswered. It looks like the shape of the state in 2020 will be dramatically different to its shape pre-recession. It will be different not so much because of a change in its absolute size as a share of spending in the economy, but in the distribution of that spending. Health, pensions and debt interest will take up a much larger share of the total. Nearly all other aspects of public spending will be much reduced.

There is little explicit sign of serious debate about these decisions, though one can read some substantial differences into the stances of the main parties as they enter the 2015 election. The Conservatives are committing to a combination of a balanced budget by 2018–19, protecting health spending and pension spending, and tax cuts. Labour is promising a budget balance only on the current budget – a significant difference made the greater by the Conservative tax promises.

In the end this period of government has been merely Act 1 of what looks like being at least a two-part process of fiscal consolidation. Act 2 could well be considerably tougher and bloodier than the opening act. It will perhaps be only at the end of the second act that we will be able to judge the long-term consequences of events so far.

As for the rest, the government has had to deal with an economy which continued to behave in unexpected ways. Growth was initially much lower than anticipated and even when recovery arrived it sprang surprises of its own. Employment has been much stronger than anybody expected. Productivity, wages and household incomes have suffered badly. The Bank of England, itself wrong-footed by the unexpected behaviour of the economy, has played a central and activist role, keeping interest rates at their lowest ever for far longer than anticipated, engaging in a huge programme of quantitative easing, and using a range of other unconventional monetary tools.

The Chancellor has cut corporation tax rates remarkably aggressively and a new totem has arisen in the income tax system – the level of the tax-free personal allowance apparently replacing the basic rate of income tax as the focal point of policy. Otherwise, beyond changes to the taxation of pensions, there has been little memorable on the tax reform front. As far as 'rebalancing' the economy is concerned, there has been a big shift in jobs from public to private sector. Some supply-side reforms, notably to corporation tax and perhaps to the planning regime, may bear long-term fruit. The challenge to find more coherent and effective long-term supply-side economic policy remains.

7 THE COALITION AND ENERGY POLICY

DIETER HELM

The coalition came to power with a ready-made energy policy developed under Labour. The Secretary of State was Ed Miliband, and his policy as it played out under the coalition was to prove the basis of a return to a level of state intervention not seen since the days of the CEGB, British Gas and the nationalized industries. By the general election in 2015, an almost complete U-turn had been performed, abandoning most of the liberalized and competitive structures that had been the hallmark of British energy policy for a quarter of a century.

How did a Conservative-dominated government come to preside over such a profound reversal to their policy heritage from the Thatcherite years? Why did they allow this to happen? The answers lie in the path dependency which Labour had created towards ever-greater intervention and the ceding by the Conservatives of energy policy to the Liberal Democrats as part of the price of coalition. It was something the Conservatives would come to regret, forcing the Chancellor and his allies to fight a rearguard action. Worse still, the coalition was to preside over a big increase in the coal burn, a rise in carbon dioxide emissions in 2013, a political rebellion on prices, and come perilously close to provoking a security of supply crisis. No one could describe coalition energy policy as a success.

The Labour legacy

Labour in government had agonized over energy policy. Having reviewed regulation following the 1997 election, there were major

Research assistance from Andrea Caflisch is gratefully acknowledged. All errors remain mine.

energy policy reviews after both the 2001 and the 2005 general elections. The 2001 policy review came after the Royal Commission on Environmental Pollution (RCEP) had recommended a 60 per cent cut in emissions over the next fifty years. The 2005 review was a battle as much about the role of nuclear (which Blair favoured) and finding a way back for coal on security of supply grounds as it was about climate change. The EU put in place a climate change package in 2008 centred on three targets, all adding up to the magic number 20. By 2020, emissions were to be reduced by 20 per cent, renewables were to make up 20 per cent of energy, and energy efficiency would contribute 20 per cent too.

Although Britain ended up with a 15 per cent renewables target, the EU directives and the commitments made following the 2000 RCEP report left the Labour government with a profound problem, which would continue to dog the coalition. How exactly were all these ambitious targets to be met?

Labour's answer was the Climate Change Act 2008, overwhelmingly supported by all the main parties, creating a set of rolling five-year carbon budgets, and Energy Market Reform (EMR). The carbon budgets tied government's hands, as they were meant to do. Short of repealing the Act, there was little wriggle room. The EU Renewables Directive (to meet the 20–20–20 targets) forced through a crash programme in wind and solar power, and eventually biomass.

Ed Miliband, in a speech in 2008 on energy policy,[1] argued that the market approach was not up to the challenges ahead, and endorsed a much more interventionist approach. In fact he and his successors had little choice. The die was cast by the twin straitjackets of the EU Renewables Directive and the Climate Change Act. Though it was already obvious that Britain faced a substantial challenge to meet the coming energy demands even after the economic crisis cut demand, the 2020 imperatives and the carbon budgets dictated the priorities.

In opposition the Conservatives had tried to come to terms with energy policy, and a policy paper was duly produced by the shadow secretary of state, Greg Clark, advocating a more market-orientated approach generally and a more sympathetic approach to nuclear in

---

[1] 'The rise and fall and rise again of a Department of Energy', lecture by Miliband, Imperial College London, 9 December 2008 (accessed at www3.imperial.ac.uk/pls/portallive/docs/1/54221696.PDF, 18 November 2014).

particular.[2] But much of it was tinkering, moving the tiller a bit towards markets. In any event, nuclear was not included in the EU renewables definition and could not make much impact before 2020.

The Coalition Agreement

The Liberal Democrats in 2010 were the closest thing Britain had to a mainstream green party. They liked renewables, and prioritized climate change. Wind and solar fitted their political philosophy. Both were local and small-scale, and the idea of community-based energy fitted with their ideas about decentralized societies.

As with other green parties in Europe, the prize in a coalition was to be the energy department. The German Greens had taken that path, the Irish Greens followed, and even Hollande's socialists in France found it convenient to endorse renewables as a way of binding in green votes.

There was, however, one very difficult issue in the coalition negotiations. The Conservatives were in favour of nuclear, and the Liberal Democrats manifesto was against. Whilst the Liberal Democrats could not fudge the abandonment of their pledge not to support university tuition fees, they found a convenient way to hide the volte-face on nuclear. Chris Huhne, the first coalition Secretary of State for Energy and Climate Change, claimed that he was not opposed in principle to nuclear, but rather he had doubts on economic grounds. Provided nuclear received no public subsidies, the Liberal Democrats would not stand in nuclear's way. The fact that many in the Liberal Democrats were opposed to nuclear full-stop, as were many in the green NGOs, could be conveniently glossed over. For since Huhne thought nuclear would not be economic, all that was needed to hold the line was to prevent the coalition from subsidizing it (and indeed the Conservatives had said as much in their manifesto on the undesirability of subsidies). If Huhne was right, then there would be no nuclear programme, satisfying all factions in his party. But eventually his party would go much further, embracing nuclear at a party conference in 2013.

---

[2] *Rebuilding Security: Conservative Energy Policy for an Uncertain World* (Conservative Party, 2010).

The rest of the energy policy part of the Coalition Agreement was plain sailing, with a heavy endorsement of renewables, and an explicit commitment to introducing a carbon floor price was included. What the agreement meant in practice was that Huhne could press on with renewables, and George Osborne could push for nuclear. It was an unstable political balancing act.

Picking winners and the renewables

The balancing act began in earnest with EMR, as it was inherited from Miliband. What Huhne wanted was a way of improving on the Renewables Obligation and the Renewable Obligation Certificates (ROCs), again inherited from Labour, to expand the ambition and reduce the costs. The Feed-in Tariffs (FiTs) were the way to do this, since instead of both being paid for the ROCs *and* receiving the wholesale electricity price as well, renewables would now go onto fixed-price tariffs. These would be related to the wholesale price by a contract for difference (CfD), bringing a massive amount of complexity neither necessary nor with much effect. The important point was that FiTs fixed the price the renewables got.

For Osborne and the Conservatives the move from ROCs to FiTs had a special appeal. The ROCs were for renewables only. FiTs could include other low-carbon technologies, and crucially nuclear. Both Huhne and Osborne could have what they wanted. Except Osborne was not prepared for customers to write an open-ended cheque for the wind farms and solar panels, and he inherited a policy instrument which would in time allow him to tighten the noose around the renewables. It was called the Levy Control Mechanism (LCM), and it fixed the total amount of subsidy over and above the wholesale price.[3]

Few at the time understood the effects this would eventually have, because it was a conventional assumption of the renewables lobby that the oil and gas prices were going to go up significantly. Miliband, Huhne and his successor Ed Davey all agreed. And since they 'knew' that oil and gas prices would rise sharply, they could complacently assume that by around 2020 wind and solar would be cost-competitive

[3] HM Treasury, 'Control framework for DECC levy-funded spending' (March 2011).

with the fossil fuel generators, and hence the subsidies could wither away. Unlike the fossil fuel-dependent United States, under George Bush, the renewables would, they believed, usher in an era of competitive and *relatively* cheaper wind and solar power. Huhne in particular was initially convinced that shale gas would not go far, and in any event would have no effect over here.

Knowing the future course of oil and gas prices – and assuming that coal would follow the same path – meant that Huhne could pick certain winners. He basked in the approval that the formidable renewables lobby heaped upon him. It was at least good politics, if terrible economics. But the trouble with knowing the future is that such certainty can be misplaced. Prices can go down as well as up. Despite all the traumas of the Arab Spring in Libya and Egypt, the terrors of Syria, the coming of ISIS in northern Iraq, and the Russian annexation of Crimea and destabilization of eastern Ukraine, prices remained remarkably stable. In the first half of 2014, gas prices in Europe halved, and later in the year oil prices eased too.

This was not in the Liberal Democrat script. Nor was the collapse of coal prices and the increase in coal's competitiveness against gas. More generally, and perhaps more remarkably, Huhne and Davey, his successor, failed to appreciate that the consequence of the FiTs and falling coal prices would be to push the wholesale price of electricity down, not up. Indeed as late as autumn 2014, Davey was still relying on a DECC-forecast doubling of wholesale prices to £92 per megawatt hour by the mid-2020s. This is where the LCM came in. It limited subsidies relative to the wholesale price. If the wholesale price went up, then the constraint would not bind. But if it went down, a yawning gap would open up, and the renewables might be rationed off. Looking ahead, such a collision between the renewables and the LCM looked inevitable. Wholesale prices in northern Europe were much lower – in the middle of 2014 they were around half the British level. Renewables are typically zero marginal cost, receive FiTs and hence can bid in zero to force themselves onto the system without affecting their revenues. More renewables meant lower wholesale prices. Falling coal gas prices would do the rest. Year by year the potential for the LCM to bind might therefore increase, thereby tightening the Treasury noose around DECC's subsidies.

Neither side was willing to push this to its logical conclusion – that either the LCM or the renewables directive would have to give.

They only fixed the LCM for the short term anyway. The impact of nuclear after 2020 was for another, post-election day. Furthermore, the coalition had discovered biomass, catching up with Europe, where biomass was fulfilling half the renewables directive. Converting old coal-fired power stations like Tilbury and DRAX would produce lots of electricity. Not all biomass was quite so green as some of its advocates pretended, but this did not matter since the renewables directive had nothing to do with net carbon emissions. It was a directive about promoting specific technologies and biomass was included.

Picking winners proved a complex task, not least because there were some obvious economic losers. The Conservatives were noticeably hostile to onshore wind farms, facing a lot of resistance in their rural constituencies to what were widely regarded as blots on the landscape.[4] Offshore wind had the advantage of being at least out of sight. It was, however, horribly expensive. Even excluding all the costs of its intermittency, and the offshore cabling, it required a subsidy of more than three times the wholesale price. The renewables could therefore not be allowed to bid against each other if offshore wind was to have any chance, and each would therefore require its own tailored subsidy. What is more, these subsidies could be repeatedly fine-tuned, and from time to time the availability of the subsidies could be arbitrarily withdrawn.

Gas, security of supply, and the politics of fossil fuels

The trouble with intervention is that it is rarely economically or politically static. It is hard to be a bit pregnant, and ministers found that once they were picking the winners and fixing prices on a technology-by-technology basis, they would eventually have to fix them all. This is where gas came in.

Huhne had dismissed shale gas as largely irrelevant to Britain, worried about the environmental impacts of hydraulic fracturing and stressed the differences between Britain and the US, warning that the UK

---

[4] See for example the letter to the PM from Conservative backbenchers, Chris Heaton-Harris et al., 30 January 2012 (accessed at www.telegraph.co.uk/earth/energy/wind-power/9061554/Full-letter-from-MPs-to-David-Cameron-on-wind-power-subsidies.html, 18 November 2014).

'should not bet the farm on shale'.[5] The green NGOs were not so sure about shale's prospects, and they saw shale gas as a serious threat to their favourite renewable technologies. Having got cold feet over bio-mass (and biofuels), and wobbled over nuclear, the problem for the green NGOs with shale gas was that it might be so cheap as to set a path to reducing carbon in the short run, and undercutting renewables. Switching from coal to gas in the short run is a very effective way of quickly getting emissions down.[6] This is indeed what happened in the US: the immediate effects were that it had rising oil and gas production, falling gas prices, and broadly falling carbon emissions. In contrast, Britain had falling North Sea production of both oil and gas, higher prices and, with an increasing coal burn, rising emissions. Cheap gas had put paid to the nuclear renaissance in the US that George Bush had encouraged. The fear amongst the NGOs and the renewables lobby was that it might put paid to wind farms here.

The coalition discovered that Britain might have lots of shale gas too.[7] But what to do? The green NGOs were strongly opposed, as were rural constituencies in the south, where both coalition parties had votes at stake. Britain is a small, crowded island with very different property rights to those of the open US landscapes. It was never going to be easy, but the Chancellor and the Prime Minister were determined to push for a rapid development of Britain's shale gas. Legislation tried to speed the process, but political consent proved difficult, and in the end Davey, Osborne and Cameron made remarkably little progress. Shale gas was destined to be a post-2015 energy source, if at all.

The gas problem was not, however, just about shale. There was also the problem of gas-fired power stations, which were being moth-balled because of a combination of cheap coal and renewables. Just when gas would be needed to plug the gap of the coal closures (forced through by the EU Large Combustion Plant Directive 2001 and its successor the Industrial Emissions Directive 2010), existing gas plant

---

[5] Chris Huhne, 'Britain can't afford to bet its future on shale gas – wind turbines are here to stay', *The Telegraph*, 8 November 2012. See also for Labour's position, Caroline Flint, 'The shale myth', *Prospect Magazine* (October 2014).

[6] See Dieter Helm, *The Carbon Crunch* (New Haven: Yale University Press, 2012), ch. 10.

[7] Department for Energy and Climate Change, *Next Steps for Shale Gas Production* (2013) (accessed at www.gov.uk/government/news/next-steps-for-shale-gas-produc-tion, 11 November 2014).

was being taken out, and nothing new was being built, bar a single station at Carrington.

Having fixed everything else, DECC now had to fix gas, too, to keep the lights on. The result was another major intervention – the capacity mechanisms. There would be long-term rolling capacity auctions for everything not covered by the FiTs. But again, the market was not to be trusted. Rather than an open auction of all the options, DECC split the auction up into several parts. Old stations which might invest to lengthen their lives would have a short-term auction, whilst new (gas) plants would have a separate fifteen-year auction.[8]

To this complexity, two more capacity mechanisms had to be added to deal with a more imminent threat to security of supply. In 2013 Ofgem warned that the capacity margin might go as low as 2 per cent in the winter of 2015/16.[9] This was far too close for comfort and the press ran headlines about possible power cuts. National Grid was given the power to pay large customers to turn off their demand at short notice and to pay some existing power stations to enter a strategic reserve and hence call back mothballed plants. The resulting set of capacity mechanisms is mind-blowingly complex.

With these and the FiTs, and without intending to do so, DECC had become the micro-manager of the electricity system. By 2014 almost every investment in electricity generation would be determined by the government. It had become a central buyer – doing a similar job to that once done by the CEGB.

The nuclear saga

If the FiTs and capacity mechanisms were complex, it can at least be said that the coalition forced them through, and legislated in the Energy Act 2013 to take sweeping powers. The nuclear saga had in the meantime run on and on. It had all started with Labour's U-turn from the anti-nuclear politics of Margaret Beckett and Patricia Hewitt, who effectively killed any hope of a nuclear renaissance back in 2003, to

---

[8] Department for Energy and Climate Change, *Implementing Electricity Market Reform (EMR): Finalised Policy Positions for Implementation of EMR* (London: DECC, 2014).
[9] *Electricity Capacity Assessment Report 2013* (London: Ofgem, 2013) .

John Hutton's white paper in 2008.[10] By the time of the 2010 general election, Labour was definitely in favour.[11] So were the Conservatives, but not, as noted above, the Liberal Democrats.[12]

The Coalition Agreement required that there be no public subsidy for nuclear, and ways had to be found to meet the letter, if not the spirit, of the undertaking. FiTs got nuclear inside the subsidized technologies, and the wording soon became, no public subsidy *relative* to the other low-carbon technologies. Since virtually anything – including nuclear –was cost-competitive against offshore wind, this was safer territory. But of course they were all subsidized, and nuclear could never – and had never – survived in a purely private market. Its risks and liabilities are not ones that admit of a limited liability company, and the long construction and operational lives require long-term government-backed contracts. And so it proved.

Building a new nuclear power station requires a lengthy, complex and expensive process just to get to the starting line. In 2009, Labour had auctioned a number of sites for future developments near existing nuclear stations. Replicating the approach taken in the 1970s,[13] the coalition pursued the idea that there should be competing nuclear power stations. So it encouraged the formation of several consortia. EDF was always in the lead, but Westinghouse and Hitachi were also in the new nuclear game, and a number of European energy utilities fancied their chances in the new British nuclear market. EON and RWE teamed up, Iberdrola and GDF joined in, and soon new-build nuclear proposals mushroomed.

The early enthusiasm proved misplaced for the German companies, and the nuclear exit post-Fukushima in Germany and other European countries led to a reappraisal. EDF remained true to its

---

[10] Department of Trade and Industry, *Our Energy Future* (Energy white paper, 2003); Department for Business Enterprise and Regulatory Reform, *Meeting the Energy Challenge: A White Paper on Nuclear Power* (2008).

[11] Labour's manifesto stated, 'We have taken the decisions to enable a new generation of nuclear power stations.'

[12] The Conservative manifesto included a commitment to 'clearing the way for new nuclear power stations – provided they receive no public subsidy' and the Liberal Democrats 'reject a new generation of nuclear power stations; based on the evidence nuclear is a far more expensive way of reducing carbon emissions than promoting energy conservation and renewable energy'.

[13] See Dieter Helm, *Energy, the State and the Market: British Energy Policy since 1979* (Oxford: Oxford University Press, 2014).

ambitions and pushed on with its Hinkley twin reactor proposal. Its partner Centrica pulled out, leaving it dependent on the Chinese to carry the project forward. The coalition declined the possibility of directly investing, to create a French–British nuclear industrial partnership.

Instead the coalition offered Hinkley a FiT contract for thirty-five years and a Treasury guarantee over the finance for construction. The project would, as a result, earn around a 10 per cent real rate of return, despite the government guarantees. Just over 3 GW of new nuclear generation would, as a result, cost around £16 billion. Unsurprisingly the European Commission decided to investigate the contract on state aid grounds, as indeed it did for other finance guarantees (such as that extended to DRAX) and for the EMR subsidies and capacity mechanisms more generally, though with limited effect.

After four years, the coalition was edging towards an agreement that would stick, and then it would be left to EDF to deliver. The initial starting date for generation in 2017 had by then been pushed back to 2022 at the earliest. As for the rest of the nuclear new-build programme, others are pursuing their particular technologies, with Westinghouse and Hitachi working their way forward towards regulatory approvals for designs and eventually their own FiTs. The coalition is on course to repeat the timescale of the last major programme of ten new reactors announced in the House of Commons in 1979,[14] then to be carried out by the state-owned CEGB. In that case only one reactor, Sizewell B, came online fourteen years later. In the case of Hinkley, setting the starting date back with Hutton's white paper in 2008 would mean that Hinkley might come online 14 fourteen later too. Whether any others follow remains to be seen – as indeed does the completion of Hinkley.

The great price and tax rebellion

Whilst the renewables programme continued to be rolled out, so too did the consequent levies to pay for all the interventions. Huhne and Davey were, however, unconcerned about the impact on consumer bills for two reasons. First, as noted, they knew that fossil fuel prices were going to go up, thus rendering their favoured technologies eventually

[14] See again Helm, *Energy, the State and the Market*.

economic. Electricity might end up expensive but it would, they were sure, be relatively cheap even if absolutely more expensive. Second, and this was their ace card, they were convinced that energy efficiency would go up so much as a result of their policies, that although the unit price of electricity would go up, the number of units demanded would go down. Davey therefore confidently predicted that bills would be 11 per cent lower relative to business-as-usual as a result by 2020.[15] Energy was going to be both greener and relatively cheaper. The muddle over energy efficiency was profound, shared by all the parties, and common across Europe. All think that the demand for energy is going to keep on going down.

It was taken as given that there were enormous opportunities to improve energy efficiency, and the coalition was especially keen to promote it. They inherited a number of schemes from Labour, including the Carbon Reduction Commitments, the Climate Change Agreements and the Carbon Emission Reduction Target. The centrepiece of the coalition's efforts was to be the Green Deal. This was to be a win-win-win policy. Customers would get lower bills, 250,000 jobs would be created, and the renewables costs could be absorbed without a relative bill increase. Huhne described the Green Deal as 'a massive new business opportunity which has the potential to support up to a quarter of a million jobs as part of our third industrial revolution'.[16]

The Green Deal was designed on the assumption that this would all have positive returns to customers. Therefore they could borrow and get repaid in lower bills. The innovation was to tie the loan to the house rather than the individual current occupiers. A complex implementation architecture was put in place. There would be energy assessments by certified assessors, there would be loans, and the work would be carried out by approved contractors. So confident was DECC that this would prove an economic bonanza that there was much hype about street-by-street energy efficiency upgrading.

The reality proved soberingly different. Take-up was very low, with only 3,234 Green Deal plans in progress at the end of June 2014,

[15] Department of Energy and Climate Change, *Estimated Impacts of Energy and Climate Change Policies on Energy Prices and Bills: March 2013* (London: DECC, 2013).
[16] Department of Energy and Climate Change, *Green Deal to Create Green Jobs* (London: DECC, 2010).

of which 1,587 had been fully completed.[17] The problems lay with the underlying assumptions. Just as Huhne and Davey 'knew' that fossil fuel prices were going up, they 'knew' that there were a vast number of positive net present value energy efficiency investments. But there were not: once the full costs of refitting the ageing British housing stock were taken into account, and the 8 per cent return demanded for the loans, it looked very different. Energy efficiency policy gradually drifted back to being a subsidized activity targeted primarily at the poor and paid for by levies on all customers, in particular the Climate Change Levy, off the back of utility obligations. The main effect came, predictably, from higher energy prices, which increased the economic returns to energy efficiency measures, not the Green Deal.

Alongside the Green Deal, the coalition pursued smart metering, and set ambitious targets for installing smart meters in all houses by 2020. The trouble here was again one of hype. Central planning of a large-scale roll-out programme was based upon the assumption that DECC knew the best way of doing this. In practice it was very vulnerable to lobbying by companies that wanted to use the meters to capture and hold customers. Centrica led the way, as it had on the Green Deal, as part of its strategy of expanding its household services business.

The results have not been good. DECC picked a central Data and Communications Company (DCC). But, as with the renewables, picking technologies was not an area where government had a comparative advantage, especially in an area experiencing rapid technical change. There were also significant data-related issues, notably privacy and data access. Unsurprisingly, the Public Accounts Committee found in late 2014 that the programme was not likely to yield the consumer benefits DECC has predicted, and that it was seriously flawed.[18]

The Green Deal and smart meters made little or no difference to prices. One additional policy intervention made matters worse on the industrial side – the carbon floor price. Whilst there is a very powerful case for a carbon tax over an emissions trading scheme like the EU Emissions Trading Scheme (EUETS), the coalition faced the fact that the EUETS was here to stay. It produced a very low price, partly because the

---

[17] Department of Energy and Climate Change, *Domestic Green Deal and Energy Company Obligation in Great Britain, Monthly Report* (London: DECC, 2014).

[18] House of Commons Committee of Public Accounts, 'Update on preparation for smart metering', September 2014.

EU target of 20 per cent emissions reduction proved easy to meet as the economic crisis bit hard into European energy demand, and because of de-industrialization. But the coalition had endorsed Labour's *unilateral* national carbon target under the Climate Change Act. So the low EUETS carbon price was a problem, and a floor price of carbon, gradually rising over time, would ensure that the aggregate carbon price would bind on company decisions.

The carbon floor price provoked significant hostile lobbying from industry, arguing that it did not achieve its objectives, as production was displaced to the EU. In effect, industry argued that carbon price arbitrage would take place. However, the fact that industry was right was less an argument against the floor price of carbon and more one against the unilateral carbon target. It was this target which drove up British costs relative to Europe, and the floor price was merely the messenger. This could not of course be admitted by a coalition wedded to its 'climate change leadership', and repealing the Climate Change Act was unthinkable. Thus the Chancellor bowed to the industrial lobbying and capped the carbon price at £18 until 2020. The politics of prices would not, however, go away, and as the policies – the Green Deal, smart meters and the carbon floor price – all failed to deliver lower prices, the Opposition jumped in and proposed a price freeze.

The politics of prices and competition

As it became more and more apparent that the coalition's energy policy could not produce the cheap energy it promised, consumers took note. They began to rebel, as opinion surveys kept showing energy bills were a high priority. The government was forced onto the back foot by a populist move by the Labour leader. Miliband promised at his party conference in autumn 2013 that: 'if we win the election 2015 the next Labour government will freeze gas and electricity prices until the start of 2017. Your bills will not rise. It will benefit millions of families and millions of businesses. That's what I mean by a government that fights for you.'

Miliband's move was a long time coming. Electricity prices had been a focus of political attention through the recession. The Prime Minister intervened early on to demand that everyone was put on the cheapest tariff, showing a remarkable naivety about how competition and markets worked. If ever there was a proposal to kill customer-switching and stop the search for tariffs shaped for different customer needs, this was it. The regulator OFGEM joined it, trying on the one hand to increase switching and on the other to confine the suppliers to just four types of tariff, and in the meantime exempting small competitors from having to pass through some of the policy levies. The politicians and the regulator had finally rigged the market. It made good politics and very bad economics.

When Miliband made his price freeze announcement, the coalition government reeled as a result of this overwhelmingly popular policy. It took two tracks. First, it shifted some green levies, such as those financing the Energy Company Obligation, from customers to the taxpayer, announcing a £50 price reduction. Second, it joined the scapegoating game of blaming the incumbent Big Six companies. It became open season on their executives and the regulator joined in effectively demanding price reductions. After endless 'probes' into the electricity and gas markets, OFGEM referred the industry to the Competition and Markets Authority (CMA), on grounds of the loss of public confidence rather than any hard evidence of market abuse or discrimination. The companies had been tried in the court of the media, and they had the misfortune to have to pass on the levies and policy costs to their customers. Having knocked the stuffing out of competition, the government and the Opposition now demanded that the incumbents prove they were behaving competitively. It was politically convenient that this inquiry would span the coming general election, and hence kick into touch a difficult problem. The companies could be politically assumed to be 'guilty' without the inconvenient facts being revealed by the CMA in advance of the election.

An unsustainable outcome

An initial audit of the coalition's energy policy makes very grim reading. It had failed on all fronts in trying to achieve its stated objectives, despite an economic depression that cut demand and should have given it a comfortable breathing space. Not that this is the impression given by Davey and DECC. On the contrary, they think it is a roaring success, and that it shows not only that competitive markets are working but that the coalition's policies all along have been market-orientated.

Davey proclaimed as late as July 2014 that Britain had the world's leading competitive low-carbon market and was still convinced that the results would be more security, and competitiveness too. It was as if there were two parallel universes – one in which carbon emissions are rising, the coal burn has gone up, and the capacity margin might fall to 2 per cent within a year or two; and the other in which emissions were falling, the British energy market was one of the most secure in the world, and customer prices were falling.

The problem any government committed to spinning a message based upon underlying 'certainties' has is that, however inconvenient, the facts will not go away. Stuck in a mid-2000s paradigm, with its own internal logic, these inconvenient facts have kept forcing the coalition to redouble its efforts. It has been dragged into one intervention after another, with the result that the emerging energy sector has metamorphosed into something very different – a central buyer and increasingly central planning model.

Though most of the blame lies with those who controlled energy policy at DECC – the Liberal Democrats and their Labour predecessors – it remains a mystery as to why the Conservatives acquiesced in such a profoundly non-market transformation. One explanation is that they thought this a price worth paying for forming the government and staying in power. Another is a cynical one that the Conservatives thought that the Liberal Democrats would get the blame. A third is that the Conservatives were not really in favour of competitive energy markets either, as witnessed in their determination to drive the nuclear programme forward. Whichever explanation is correct – and probably all three have some force – the result is that Britain's energy market is not on a convincing low-carbon path and faces customer revolt. It will be left to a future government to have the political courage to decide how far it wants customers and taxpayers to pay for some of the most expensive technologies for making marginal carbon reductions.

8 THE COALITION AND INFRASTRUCTURE

JULIAN GLOVER

This was the government that liked to dress in Dayglo orange, hard hats and safety boots. The outfit became such a staple of ministerial visits that some began to speculate whether the Chancellor left London wearing anything else.[1] The look was an obvious visual cue for the much talked-of 'long term economic plan'– hard work, investment and skills in one simple, optimistic shot, endlessly repeated at road schemes, rail yards and businesses all over Britain.

But there was more to it than marketing. After the success of the London 2012 Olympics Britain began to believe once again in the power of building big things. The need to restart economic growth opened minds to new approaches. The word 'infrastructure' took on totemic power as a route to post-crash recovery. The BBC started to show long series in prime time about projects such as Crossrail.[2] Broadband and mobile networks became fundamental to commerce and leisure – and the lack of them in parts of rural Britain and the lack of speed and reliability in many other places a long-running sore. There was a sense that communication networks of all kinds, as well as engineering, manufacturing and the apprenticeships which could be linked to them, mattered to national strength as they had not in recent

---

[1] See for instance www.theguardian.com/politics/gallery/2013/sep/05/hi-vis-george-osborne-pictures.

[2] 'The BBC goes behind the scenes for Crossrail documentary series', 7 July 2014 (accessed at www.crossrail.co.uk/news/articles/the-bbc-goes-behind-the-scenes-for-crossrail-documentary-series#, 12 November 2014).

decades, when finance had seemed to hold most of the cards. The term 'industrial strategy' began to be dusted down.

The state of infrastructure in 2010

It is true that before May 2010 there were stirrings of change. These came partly from Lord Adonis, the energetic Labour policymaker whose appeal – and past – straddled parties. Although he was the Transport Secretary for less than a year before the election, as a junior minister at the department from October 2008 he had thrown himself into promoting transport as a radical driver of social and economic progress. He led the shift at the Department towards rail electrification, for instance – previously blocked.[3] His legacy as a reformer – as at education before – lasted long into the coalition government. And even before his arrival at transport, High Speed 1 had been launched and without much fanfare a Hybrid Bill eventually passed Parliament to allow Crossrail to be built, if funds could be found. But neither Tony Blair nor Gordon Brown sought to identify as closely as coalition ministers came to do with big infrastructure projects. Nor did either of them show much personal interest in transport.

The caution was unsurprising. Though Margaret Thatcher authorized the Channel Tunnel, John Major the Jubilee Line extension and Labour HS1 to St Pancras, infrastructure had long been at the unfashionable end of government activity. Previous volumes in this series said little on the subject; perhaps that was because there was not much positive to say.[4] With the exception of a handful of heroic politicians such as Lord Heseltine and Lord Adonis whose appeal went beyond and sometimes defied their respective parties it was not something that troubled politics or the political media. Good infrastructure

---

[3] Electrification is hardly mentioned in the otherwise significant 2008 Eddington Transport study, for instance: see http://webarchive.nationalarchives.gov.uk/20090104005813/http://www.dft.gov.uk/about/strategy/transportstrategy/eddington-study (accessed 12 November 2014).

[4] See Dennis Kavanagh and Anthony Seldon (eds.), *The Thatcher Effect* (Oxford: Clarendon Press, 1989); Dennis Kavanagh and Anthony Seldon (eds.), *The Major Effect* (London: Macmillan, 1994); Anthony Seldon and Dennis Kavanagh (eds.), *The Blair Effect 2001–5* (Cambridge: Cambridge University Press, 2005); Anthony Seldon (ed.), *Blair's Britain, 1997–2007* (Cambridge: Cambridge University Press, 2007).

was thought to be something other European nations did. British stories were about schemes being delayed or going over budget.

As a result, the Transport Secretary's post had been something politicians held as briefly as possible on the way up or the way down or (like Alistair Darling) when nudged intentionally into invisibility. Once, asked what he learnt in the job, Darling replied 'to drive at 69.5 miles an hour for hours at a time'[5] – speeding on motorways being disturbingly newsworthy. There were reputed to be more former Transport Secretaries alive than the holders of any other Cabinet post. Patrick McLoughlin, the third of the coalition ministers to hold the job (and for whom this author worked as a Special Adviser) was on course at the time of writing to become the longest-serving Conservative holder of the Transport job since Ernest Marples in the 1950s – a sign of how short the careers of the others had been.[6]

What changed from 2010 to 2015?

Under the coalition, and somewhat to the government's own surprise, the state emerged in a muscular and ambitious role as the instigator, funder and champion of infrastructure projects of many kinds. The coalition intended to write its legacy in concrete, steel and fibre-optic lines.

Each budget and autumn statement sought to extend the one that had come before. In 2013, for instance, the government committed to working with private providers to make sure superfast broadband reached 95 per cent of customers by 2017.[7] By the summer of 2014 the Chancellor was promising not just a High Speed Two Railway to the north, but possibly High Speed Three between major cities – supporting a new northern 'powerhouse'.[8] An Infrastructure Bill was a major part of the pre-election Queen's Speech.[9] The last Cabinet before the

---

[5] Heard by the author.
[6] Marples, like McLoughlin, began his career as a coal miner.
[7] www.gov.uk/broadband-delivery-uk (accessed 12 November 2014).
[8] George Osborne, 'We need a Northern powerhouse', Speech in Manchester, 23 June 2014 (accessed at www.gov.uk/government/speeches/chancellor-we-need-a-northern-powerhouse, 12 November 2014).
[9] 'Infrastructure bill', 6 June 2014 (accessed at www.gov.uk/government/news/infra-structure-bill, 12 November 2014).

2014 summer recess – and the first after a significant reshuffle – opened with a long discussion of infrastructure plans.

The Olympics also bred a generation of nationally respected project engineers and financiers, some of whom took on government jobs. Sir David Higgins, previously chief executive of the Olympic Delivery Authority, ran first Network Rail and then HS2. Lord Deighton, Chief Executive of the London Organising Committee, became a Treasury minister with responsibility for Infrastructure. Sir John Armitt, previously Chairman of the ODA, became a member of the Airports Commission. Their voices were listened to.

Yet the coalition's accelerating interest in infrastructure rested on a series of paradoxes. The most obvious was that a government whose defining opening challenge was a reduction in state spending found itself committing increasingly large sums of public money to capital investment (much of it allocated ahead, to the years after 2015, when the public finances were thought to be able to afford it, but also within the life of the parliament, too). The cost of a scheme was often quoted approvingly in the media as evidence of its scale and impact.

This had the unavoidable result that a government that set itself as a sceptic of state command (opposed at the outset, for instance, to the unelected Infrastructure Planning Commission inherited from Labour) became by 2015 a champion of government action on infrastructure.[10] There was some devolution of decisions on local transport funding to Local Enterprise Partnerships under reforms backed by Lord Heseltine and also growing independence for London.[11] But by and large big public sector projects came with a great deal of Whitehall activity. This was true especially of High Speed Two. Although it won the strong support of some of the most powerful local authorities outside London, it was directed from the centre.

These paradoxes were followed by others. A government that wanted to simplify planning and speed up growth found itself caught just like its predecessors in a seemingly endless round of consultations, environmental assessments and judicial reviews long before any

[10] For the IPC see www.gov.uk/government/organisations/infrastructure-planning-commission (accessed 12 November 2014).

[11] Lord Heseltine's report, 'No stone unturned: in pursuit of growth', is worth reading in particular for its foreword on the role of the state in economic development: www.gov.uk/government/publications/no-stone-unturned-in-pursuit-of-growth (accessed 12 November 2014).

building could begin. This led to regular outbursts of ministerial frustration – as well as an effective intervention from the Cabinet Office minister Oliver Letwin, whose challenge to build a road in a year led if not to that, then at least to a quickening of pace at the Highways Agency. But there was no fundamental reform to speed up infrastructure planning alongside the extra investment. (A single Great Crested Newt – and the fact that its proposed new home was judged inadequate by English Nature – helped to delay the opening of a modest new station in Ilkeston, Derbyshire, by months, for instance.)

Nor was there reform of private financing. If anything, there was a step away from what had gone before. The new government ceased to use the extremely costly forms of semi-private funding that had allowed Gordon Brown to build hospitals on someone else's credit card and nominally off the government books (and which earlier had led to a disastrous experiment with a public–private upgrade of the London Underground). But although the coalition wanted to see the private sector expand and the public sector shrink – and saw this happen in the national economy – it made little progress in finding new ways to do this when it came to infrastructure.

David Cameron gave a significant speech on infrastructure in March 2012, describing it as 'the magic ingredient in so much of modern life ... it is, if you like, the platform for active citizenship ... its value lies in its ability to make things possible tomorrow that we cannot even imagine today'.[12] But his proposal 'to use the power of the state to unlock the dynamism of the market' – and in particular to get private money into improving the road network – ran into challenges. It was also partly overtaken in the short-term by increased direct funding from the Treasury, which allowed schemes to go ahead without new sources of income.

Meanwhile the movement was partly the other way. Network Rail's large debt came onto the government books in September 2014 as a result of a reassessment by the Office of National Statistics. Private finance initiative road schemes were replaced by state-funded ones. In this regard, at least, the coalition was more Keynesian in its support for funding public works than either its supporters or its critics chose to say. Reform was left as an issue for a future government to resolve.

[12] 'PM speech on infrastructure', 19 March 2012 (accessed at www.gov.uk/government/speeches/pm-speech-on-infrastructure, 12 November 2014).

A final paradox stands out too. A government in search of popularity stuck (to the fury of some of the supporters of its leading party) to schemes like HS2 or a possible new southeast runway that threatened to become very unpopular indeed. There were of course benefits to the coalition in being seen to have a purpose and a plan, however controversial. But away from roads it was questionable whether the government gained many votes from the things it chose to announce. UKIP tried to exploit this – though the fact that the Eurosceptic party had backed three new high-speed rail lines in its 2010 manifesto blunted the attack.[13] An impression that the government stuck to unpopular schemes added weight, at least, to the claim the coalition was doing what it thought necessary, and not just what might win it support.

Why did it change?

Where did this energy for new infrastructure come from? In part, the personal enthusiasm of the Prime Minister and especially the Chancellor. They shared a commitment – that grew during the parliament – to big, nation-changing projects that could match what they both saw being built on visits abroad, especially in Asia.

The psychoanalysis of government and party is a tentative business but it might be speculated that none of the coalition leadership had entered politics to cut and cancel things, yet all of them now had to embrace austerity. Amid a ceaseless and noisy national conversation about deficit reduction there was perhaps a hankering for positive ideas and actions. Capital projects, particularly those that that could be represented as investment for the future, business-friendly and complementary to the free market, combined vision and generosity with hard-headedness. They were also relatively cheap in the early stage, the bulk of costs coming later.

But the interest in infrastructure was driven forward, too, by the simpler fact that this was something the two coalition parties could mostly agree on (if not always the detail or location of schemes). As a

---

[13] UKIP *Manifesto* (April 2010), p. 11. Proposals included: 'a new line between London and Newcastle with a spur to Manchester, a London–Bristol–Exeter line and a linking route via Birmingham'.

result it was one of the themes that gave their government a uniting sense of progressive purpose.

At the Treasury the Liberal Democrat Chief Secretary, Danny Alexander, pushed for progress alongside the Chancellor and if some Liberal Democrats had doubts about the consequences of road schemes or airport expansion other MPs lost no ground asking for improvements in their constituencies. There was a similar congruence of interest in London, where the Conservative Mayor Boris Johnson ran his own transport policy – even extending to a plan for a new estuary airport – and used his post to lobby, often successfully, for more funding and bigger schemes.[14] In opposition, Labour also launched its own review of infrastructure,[15] which called for schemes to be more independent of politics – although that ambition fell short almost immediately when the Shadow Chancellor, Ed Balls, turned against High Speed Two. A political infrastructure arms race began to build up – to the dismay of some economists, who asked whether the belief that ever bigger schemes led to growth rested on evidence, or just hope.

If all parties were showing a growing interest in infrastructure, then, what difference did coalition government make to policy, against possible majority-party rule? In this area, at least, the answer must be surprisingly little. Most of the big early decisions about transport and broadband infrastructure would almost certainly also have been taken by a majority Conservative government. Transport issues, after all, straddled parties more than many others. In May 2010 one of the things that united the Conservative and Liberal Democrat manifestos was shared opposition to the construction of a third runway at Heathrow Airport. In some ways, it was a defining item in their lists of hopes for government and a clear rallying point for coalition. Both parties were also committed to high-speed rail in opposition. And both had emphasized the need to reduce carbon emissions from transport.

As a result, the coalition programme for government called for investment in a national superfast broadband network, high-speed rail and a national network of electric vehicle charging points.[16] It also backed Crossrail in London, High Speed Two and rail

[14] 'London orbital railway on mayor's £1.3tn wish list', *The Guardian*, 30 July 2014.
[15] See www.armittreview.org (accessed 12 November 2014).
[16] *The Coalition: Our Programme for Government* (London: Cabinet Office, 2010).

electrification. All this pointed to advance. But the agreement also stood clearly against a third runway at Heathrow or expansion at Gatwick or Stansted.

In 2010, therefore, the coalition government came into office with a choice. It could accelerate infrastructure investment as a government priority. Or it could pause on schemes that had been announced – if not funded – under Labour and focus its energies on deficit reduction and generating growth by other means. The starting point in deciding the answer – but only the starting point – was money.

When the coalition government was formed, Philip Hammond – who in opposition had been shadow Chief Secretary – became Transport Secretary. It was not a post he had expected. He brought with him an understanding of Treasury processes and a grip on finding savings from inside the Department – cuts that later took physical form when half the Department's London offices were sold to be converted into flats (visitors continued arriving at the old entrance for years, to be surprised by the lavish new furnishings). But Hammond also negotiated a spending review settlement that provided the basis for capital investment to come.

The story was not straightforward. In 2010 the coalition inherited a series of substantial proposals including HS2, Crossrail and a roads programme from Labour. But it did not inherit a plan to pay for them all: they were in part Potemkin schemes, impressive only from a distance. Under spending plans set out by Alistair Darling, the Department for Transport's capital spending allocation was boosted, exceptionally, by £1 billion in the last full year of Labour rule, 2009–10, to £8.3 billion. But it was then set to be reduced very sharply under Darling's plans in 2010–11, to £7.3 billion. Whoever won the election would have had to reduce previously announced programmes or reverse this cut. The question was by how much.

The answer came soon enough. Immediately after the election the 2010–11 allocations were reset by the Treasury. Alongside a substantial cut in resource spending (managed without obvious difficulty) the Department for Transport ended up with a small increase in capital funding (though the total remained lower than the year before). Several road schemes inherited without funding were removed from the programme, including an upgrade of the A14 in Cambridgeshire and the A1 near Newcastle. Both were later reinstated, under revised plans.

The full Spending Review that followed in October 2010 laid out an intended settlement for the rest of the parliament.[17] In transport, this was to see budgeted capital spending increase each year in cash terms from the figure inherited from Labour in 2010–11 – but not by enough to return to the particularly high level of 2009–10. Played one way, this was a cut in capital spending under the new government. Played the other, this was a generous increase on the level left by Darling. Either way, it turned out to be only the start of greater investment to come.

The reason for this is that every Autumn Statement increased the level of transport capital spending from that initially planned. This took time to take effect: in the first years of the government, spending was slow. But by 2013–14 the Department's capital programme was almost £1 billion higher than initially announced in 2010 and by 2014–15 it was £9.2 billion against £7.5 billion planned in 2010. It was said, informally, by officials that at times the national roads programme rose from spending £1 million a day to £4 million. And from that followed an increase in ambition.

The Department's capital settlement up to 2015 was also only one part of the story. Plans for the future also shaped decisions on infrastructure. In June 2013, alongside the spending round, the Treasury set out proposed funding for infrastructure investment in a handful of particular areas running to 2020.[18] In a joint foreword to a Treasury document, the Chancellor and the Chief Secretary described a recent failure of national ambition on infrastructure that was 'not the fault of any one party or any one government [but] a collective national mindset that has privileged the short term over the long term'.[19]

Their response included £70 billion for transport schemes and matching funding for private sector investment in things such as broadband infrastructure. Though some of the money was to flow in the next parliament – and so be subject to possible revision after the election – it was a very clear marker of the government's intention. Rarely before

[17] HM Treasury, *Spending Review 2010* (accessed at www.gov.uk/government/uploads/system/uploads/attachment_data/file/203826/Spending_review_2010.pdf, 12 November 2014).

[18] HM Treasury, *Investing in Britain's Future* (June 2013) (accessed at www.gov.uk/government/uploads/system/uploads/attachment_data/file/209279/PU1524_IUK_new_template.pdf, 12 November 2014).

[19] *Investing in Britain's Future*, p. 3.

had the Treasury been pinned down even to promise such sustained investment. Any retreat later would be all the more obvious as a result.

The most visible consequence was a new system of long-term funding for a reformed and more independent Highways Agency, to be established by the Infrastructure Bill introduced in 2014. This was intended to put roads on a similar footing to rail infrastructure, which had an established cycle of five-year investment plans. The aim, as with rail, was to create a clear list of schemes and the budget to pay for them – rather than the stop–start funding that had bedevilled national roads and left the Highways Agency with repeated underspends that it could not carry over.

But it was rail that saw the bigger investment. Under the coalition, Network Rail's capital investment continued to climb sharply. This was championed by government as the biggest increase since the Victorian age (and it was, particularly if HS2 and London were taken into account). This Network Rail capital funding was initially a mix of government grant, revenue from operations and commercial borrowing: the latter counting as additional government borrowing from September 2014.[20] It provided the basis for the first national programme of electrification in two decades, to Bristol and Cardiff as well as – eventually – on the Midland Mainline. Britain, alone in the world in running a large network of high-speed intercity diesel services, was catching up.

For transport, all this capital spending amounted to something close to largesse: suddenly the challenge was not a lack of investment but spending it efficiently and quickly. But this came with a catch. Departmental finances increasingly took on two flavours: resource spending, which was seen as wasteful and in need of rapid reduction; and capital, which was regarded as healthy investment and grew. The difference was not always so clear-cut internally – it took resource to maintain capital assets and resource to plan capital schemes. It also took resource to fund new trains to run on electrified routes. And in the end it was all counted in the same currency, however badged.

How did the government machine respond to this resurgent interest in infrastructure? Treasury officials, in particular, took time to warm to the new way of thinking (and some never did). Many did not like to see the state build things or pay for them – or at least for things

---

[20] The reclassification by the ONS was retrospective and a result of accounting changes, not a government decision.

other than roads, which brought revenue in the form of fuel duty. One senior official reportedly encouraged the *Financial Times* over lunch to oppose HS2 in what was seen as a calculated attempt to stop the scheme in its tracks.[21] Some officials may also have assumed in 2010 that London's Crossrail would be cancelled or postponed by the new government (since it had not been formally funded by the previous one). 'Don't forget, the Treasury opposed the M25,' the Chancellor was reported to joke when asked about such doubts.[22]

Assessment of the success of infrastructure policy

The first big decision the coalition government took on infrastructure was to step back from expansion at Heathrow. For new ministers the decision was clear. 'The third runway at Heathrow is not going ahead, no ifs, no buts,' David Cameron had said in 2009[23] – a promise that held for the parliament. As a result, on 12 May 2010 the new government withdrew its support for expansion.

This commitment was the one with the most immediate consequence. Airport expansion in the southeast had been a source of anxiety and equivocation for decades. In 2009, the Labour government had given its support to the construction of a third runway at Heathrow, to be completed in or around 2015. The scheme, which would have seen a shorter runway for regional flights built north of the two main intercontinental ones, was intrusive and controversial both because of noise and pollution. It was also popular with business.

Ed Miliband, the environment secretary, was said to have come close to resignation over the issue on the day it was announced.[24] Lord Adonis, at transport, was at least as interested in plans for a high-speed railway to the north, which he also announced on the same day. (The third runway and HS2 continued to be associated: supporters of the former often emerging as opponents of the latter. Asked in a *Times* quick quiz which he preferred, Ed Balls named the runway – even

---

[21] 'Internal Treasury concerns mount over HS2', *Financial Times*, 20 August 2012.
[22] 'George Osborne puts faith in High Speed Two being engine for growth', *Financial Times*, 20 August 2013.
[23] Speaking at Christ's School, Richmond on 21 October 2009.
[24] Claimed by former adviser Damian McBride in *Power Trip* (London: Biteback Publications, 2013).

though by that point Labour had formally moved to oppose Heathrow expansion, while still supporting HS2.)[25]

Following the 2010 decision, Heathrow retreated, but the issue of airport capacity did not. The feeling grew that expansion, if not at Heathrow, was inevitable. As the early days of coalition passed, pressure grew to drive economic growth. London's Mayor, Boris Johnson, strongly opposed to expansion at Heathrow, had long been promoting an alternative new airport site somewhere in the Thames Estuary.[26] Others pointed to growth at Gatwick or continued to champion Heathrow. Whoever was right, inaction was becoming difficult for a government that by 2012 was repeatedly talking of Britain's need to compete in what the Prime Minister called 'the global race'[27] and by 2014 had raised to a 'long-term economic plan'.

The result was that the government moved. In October 2012 the newly arrived Transport Secretary Patrick McLoughlin announced that an independent Airports Commission under the leadership of the economist Sir Howard Davies would investigate the issue of airport capacity in the southeast of England. The Commission was asked to produce an interim report and a shortlist of options before the election and a single option for expansion immediately after it. The Commission was seen by some as a delaying tactic; by others as a cover for actually doing something about the issue – but it soon won a reasonable degree of respect for its membership and work and at least grudging backing from all three main parties and industry. 'Few commentators failed to point out that ours was the latest in a long series of so far largely fruitless attempts to grapple with the problem of airport capacity in a densely populated island,' Sir Howard wrote in the foreword to the Commission's interim report, a year after the Commission came into being.[28]

This first report confirmed that 'there is a clear case for one net additional runway in London and the southeast, to come into operation by 2030'. It also narrowed the options for expansion more tightly than some had expected. The choice it presented was between a second runway at Gatwick, a third runway to the northwest of Heathrow

[25] 'Saturday interview: Ed Balls', *The Times*, 21 September 2013.
[26] See for instance 'London Mayor Boris Johnson argues case for new airport', *BBC News*, 21 November 2011 (accessed at www.bbc.co.uk/news/uk-england-london-15817520, 12 November 2014).
[27] See, for instance, the PM's speech to the CBI, 19 November 2012.
[28] Airports Commission, *Interim Report* (December 2013).

(and on a different site to the previous third runway proposal) or an innovative plan to extend one of Heathrow's existing runways to allow double operations. The Commission also said it would carry out further work on the potential of a new airport to the east of London – the scheme backed by the Mayor – and would include this among the final options for consideration only if the evidence merited it. The Mayor welcomed this, perhaps through gritted teeth. In the event, the Commission announced in September 2014 that the estuary airport option would not be included in the final shortlist.

By the 2015 election, therefore, the coalition's position on airports in the southeast of England had evolved: from clear opposition to expansion to investigating the options. If expansion does eventually take place, the Commission process will have done its job. But airport expansion was only one of three contentious infrastructure issues that faced the new government in 2010. The other two involved rail schemes: Crossrail in London and High Speed Two to the north.

Of the two, it was Crossrail that proved easier and quicker to resolve. The scheme, whose origins lay in the 1974 Central London Rail study and which had repeatedly been backed by governments since 1989 but not funded, linked mainline stations at Liverpool Street in the east and Paddington in the west.[29] It partnered the less heralded but also hugely significant Thameslink upgrade between north and south mainline routes, also due to be completed around 2018. Together, they would when completed transform travel into central London – a city whose population and economy was growing fast.

In May 2010 Hammond confirmed after the first coalition Cabinet meeting that Crossrail would be constructed – although savings were found by redesigning sections and slowing construction by a year. This was a significant moment. Alongside – and after – the London 2012 Olympics, Crossrail became a showpiece for Britain's growing ambitions in infrastructure. It was the biggest construction project wholly in Europe. It threaded its way through some of the most built-up areas anywhere in the world. It remained on time and on budget – winning a rare flattering verdict from the National Audit Office in 2014.[30] It made rapid progress, with the majority of tunnelling

[29] See www.crossrail.co.uk/route/crossrail-from-its-early-beginnings (accessed 12 November 2014).
[30] National Audit Office, 'Crossrail', 24 January 2014.

completed by the start of 2015. And it led the way in developing skills and youth training, with a Tunnelling Academy in Newham in east London and an apprenticeship programme that did a lot to encourage political support for infrastructure investment more widely. So did the cathedral-like scale of the stations being built underground. Impressed by visits to them, who could not want more?

The obvious next step was to expand new rail services to the Midlands and the north of England with High Speed Two. Of all the infrastructure projects that defined the coalition, this was the biggest and most controversial. It was intended to cost more than any other – a budget in 2014 of £40.6 billion in total, and spending of £900 million in the 2010–15 parliament and a budget of £16 billion in the next. It was longer than any other – 330 miles in total and 140 on phase one to the Midlands. It took more ministerial time and more planning effort than any other – the Hybrid Bill for Phase One was 55,000 pages long, the biggest Parliamentary Bill ever.[31] And it led to more opposition than any other, though the strongest feelings were expressed by those directly affected, with polling suggesting that most of the nation was indifferent and many city authorities (though not all) were in favour. In Parliament all three main parties officially backed the scheme but there were plenty of MPs who did not.

High Speed Two was therefore both a test of political determination and a test of Whitehall's skill in project management. The new government arrived equipped with broad Conservative and Liberal Democrat support for the principle of high-speed rail – the Chancellor had first backed it in an interview in opposition on a Japanese Bullet train and Conservative policy was confirmed at the 2008 party conference. In 2009, Adonis had set out the Labour government's plan for a Y-shaped route, running from Euston northwest to Birmingham and on in two arms to Manchester, the East Midlands and Yorkshire. This route, with variations, remained at the core of the scheme throughout the parliament, though it was reviewed by the new government in 2010.

By early 2011 the government had announced an intended route of the first phase to Birmingham, running through the Chilterns: symbolically it was discussed at a Cabinet held at the newly built Olympic Park. By early 2012, ministers had set out a possible route

[31] See www.hs2.org.uk/hs2-phase-one-hybrid-bill/hybrid-bill (accessed 12 November 2014).

for the second phase, too. But it was the initial section – and rising costs – that proved the greatest challenge. Opposition in the Chilterns was particularly strong, which led to an increase in expensive sections of tunnelling. And by June 2013, following a decision to increase the contingency reserve alongside the formal Treasury allocation of a budget until 2020, the scheme was running into strong opposition at Westminster, too.

That was the lowest point of the coalition parliament for the project. News that the budget had reached £42.6 billion led to a restless summer and party conference season. Neither Downing Street nor the Treasury wanted to shift ground, though by the autumn of 2013, with the Shadow Chancellor openly expressing doubts, Labour had it in its power to bring the project down.

In October 2013 Cameron warned the opposition that HS2 'could not go ahead without all-party support'[32] – and for a moment, it looked like it might well have been dropped. But helped by confident leadership from the project's new Chairman Sir David Higgins (who had overseen construction of the Olympic Park) 2014 saw HS2 fade as a frontline political issue.[33] The government secured a 10–1 majority for the second reading of the Hybrid Bill in April 2014 and the select committee began its mammoth task of considering the route in detail in July.

As parliament began its work in London things began to change in the midlands and the north, too. The balance of infrastructure funding between London and the rest of the country had long been a source of controversy: with the north arguing its economic growth was held back by the concentration of capital investment in the southeast.[34] The debate about High Speed Two evolved during 2014 into a wider discussion about the role of infrastructure in economic growth.

The first Higgins report, in March, emphasized the importance of links between northern cities. It was followed by a series of interventions by the Chancellor, who commissioned a second report, published in the run-up to the Autumn Statement, with an emphasis on

---

[32] 'Cameron warns Labour: if you oppose HS2, we'll cancel it', *New Statesman*, 25 October 2013.

[33] David Higgins, *HS2 Plus*, March 2014 (accessed at http://assets.hs2.org.uk/sites/default/files/inserts/Higgins%20Report%20-%20HS2%20Plus.pdf, 12 November 2014).

[34] Henry G. Overman, 'Investing in the UK's most successful cities is the surest recipe for national growth', *British Politics and Policy at LSE*, 26 January 2012.

east–west links between Liverpool, Manchester and Leeds. What began as a new line from London ended the year as a much wider project to address national imbalances in transport infrastructure.

Whether this enthusiasm for regional development can be sustained will depend on future political commitment. Under the coalition, rhetorical interest in devolution at times ran into the complexity of multiple local authorities and transport providers. Neither Birmingham nor Manchester could match the clout of Transport for London. But Manchester – guided in part by its long-serving and determined Chief Executive Sir Howard Bernstein – made progress, expanding the Metrolink tram network to 60 miles and building a second cross-city route. The city was also at the centre of what became the Northern Hub of rail improvements, electrifying and accelerating east–west links.

Bernstein also championed progress on HS2, serving as deputy chair of a Growth Taskforce under the guidance of the Treasury Commercial Secretary, Lord Deighton. But many decisions about the project, especially about the nature and funding of the second phase, remained for the next parliament. If the line is completed, it will be one of the most tangible legacies of the coalition. But completion is not yet a certainty. If it happens, Hammond's early steady nerve on the project and McLoughlin's amiably unwavering support will certainly be among the reasons.

High Speed Two also exemplified the frustration of much infrastructure planning. Some of the costs and many of the controversies are immediate but the benefits do not come until later. This seemed particularly true in Britain: though the first intercity railway north from London was built in less than a decade in the 1830s and the first sections of the motorway network went from design to opening in less than three years in the 1950s,[35] High Speed Two, admittedly a much larger scheme, was not intended to be complete until the 2030s. In 2010 the coalition inherited the newly created Infrastructure Planning Commission, which was intended to accelerate the approval of significant schemes. This was quickly merged into the Planning Inspectorate by the new government, as part of a promise to increase political oversight – but the challenge of identifying significant infrastructure schemes and taking them to fruition remained.

---

[35] The contract for the first section of the M6, the Preston bypass, was awarded in early 1956 and the road opened in December 1958.

One answer was the creation of a National Infrastructure Plan, overseen by a Treasury unit, Infrastructure UK. This brought together a summary of the largest public and private infrastructure projects thought necessary to promote growth. According to the foreword of the 2013 edition of the plan, 'the government's ambition is to reverse the effects of . . . historic underinvestment and equip the UK with world-class infrastructure, which rivals that of all its Organization for Economic Co-operation and Development (OECD) counterparts in every sector and ensures the country can compete in the global race'.[36] The breathless language disguised what some critics thought was nothing more than a to-do list, including many schemes already under way. But it was at least an indication of government priorities, just as the creation in the Cabinet Office of the Major Project Authority was an attempt to improve the management of schemes.[37] To some of those affected, however, the MPA seemed less a source of clarity than another layer of control that added to an already over-complex regime.

For rapid action, the coalition had to point to smaller schemes: especially the programme of pinch-point alleviation on local roads and some of the work of the Local Sustainable Transport Fund – a coalition innovation that sought to broaden infrastructure spending into new areas such as cycle parks at stations. With increased certainty over funding, the Highways Agency also began to pick up the pace. The agency began twenty-five schemes on the trunk road network under the coalition that were due to be completed by 2015 and it continued with another thirteen. These included long sections of four-lane running on previously three-lane motorways, taking the hard shoulder into use and regulating traffic flow – and sometimes speeds – by digital control.

That was one sign of new technology intruding into infrastructure. But set against some other areas of the economy, technological change in transport was limited. Even high-speed rail drew on established standards. Progress towards clean vehicle technology was steady at best: heavy investment in electric charging points and subsidies for electric

[36] HM Treasury, *National Infrastructure Plan 2013* (accessed at www.gov.uk/government/uploads/system/uploads/attachment_data/file/263159/national_infrastructure_-plan_2013.pdf, 12 November 2014).

[37] See www.gov.uk/government/groups/major-projects-authority (accessed 12 November 2014).

vehicle costs was not, at the start, matched by enthusiastic take-up, although both sales and industry investment accelerated rapidly in 2014.

What people did want unequivocally was a better digital infra-structure: especially faster broadband and stronger mobile signals. This, too, was a coalition ambition in 2010 and what often seemed to be the slow pace of progress was a repeated frustration to government. In 2011, the Culture Secretary, Jeremy Hunt announced that 90 per cent of premises in every local authority area of the UK should have access to internet speeds above 24 megabits per second by May 2015 and a minimum of 2Mbps for others.[38] Making this a reality proved hard. In some rural areas, such as Cumbria, there was enthusiastic public sup-port for self-help schemes, with people digging ditches for cables and linking homes.[39] But limited competition for government funding saw contracts for rural broadband won entirely by BT, amid plenty of criticism.

There was in fact reasonable progress – more than some real-ized. By late 2013 23 per cent of homes had access to broadband speeds above 30Mbps,[40] and average speeds had tripled since May 2010. Ofcom, the communications regulator, could just about point to the fact that by 2015 Britain would have the 'best' broadband in Europe – but it did so by scoring availability and use above speed.[41] And the quality of mobile signals remained a contentious point. Demand for mobile data rose at least as quickly as supply, though the decision to require one of the winners of the 4G spectrum competition, which allocated space for faster mobile data and voice services, to cover 98 per cent of the population by 2017 – rather than the previous 95 per cent commitment for slower 3G – offered the hope of better connections for some of the hardest places to reach. Meanwhile cover-age in many places remained patchy. Strong progress on turning things

[38] See www.gov.uk/government/news/90-per-cent-of-homes-and-businesses-should-have-superfast-broadband-by-2015 (12 November 2014).

[39] Rory Stewart, 'The trench warfare that built the Big Society', *Daily Telegraph*, 4 April 2012.

[40] 'Broadband speeds research shows "superfast" surge', *Ofcom*, 15 April 2014 (accessed at http://consumers.ofcom.org.uk/internet/broadband-speeds/broadband-speeds-april-14, 12 November 2014).

[41] 'UK overtakes major EU nations for superfast broadband', *Ofcom*, 12 March 2014 (accessed at http://media.ofcom.org.uk/news/2014/european-broadband-scorecard, 12 November 2014).

around was made from 2014, when the new Culture Secretary Sajid Javid forced the pace, working with operators to improve coverage.

Conclusion

The reality of infrastructure planning under any government is that cost and controversy come before results. The coalition was no different in this. Its growing interest in infrastructure did not lead to a slew of popular openings. Most of the projects it began were of necessity unfinished at the election. Future ministers and a future Mayor of London will cut the ribbon on Crossrail, for instance.

But on the terms on which it asked to be judged as it left office – its commitment to the much-mentioned 'long-term economic plan' – the coalition had a good case to make. On most fronts, there was advance – sometimes spectacular. Crossrail led the way. But High Speed Two – if completed – followed close behind. Both were massive projects of a kind Britain had shied from in recent decades. On the existing rail system Network Rail pressed on with an investment programme larger than at any time under British Rail. On the strategic road network the Highways Agency was encouraged to promote the largest programme in two decades. On the question of airport capacity in the southeast there was at least a plan to unlock things in the form of the Davies Commission. The coalition's enthusiasm for state-led schemes should also not overshadow progress made on infrastructure projects led by the private sector (the Thames super-sewer, for instance). On balance, the coalition did better in this than many of its predecessors. There was no great start-stopping of projects. There was obvious and consistent ministerial commitment. Investment and ambition gathered pace.

Where there is room for doubt is how much of this will be sustained without wider reform of funding, project management and planning. The increase in ambition will also need to be matched by an increase in the training of engineers and the capability of the construction industry if projects are to stick to planned timetables and budgets. But if this can happen, then in the decades ahead many schemes will come into operation that owe their origins at least in part to the coalition's interest in infrastructure. Whether it will be remembered – or thanked – for this is another matter.

9 THE COALITION AND SOCIETY (I): HOME AFFAIRS AND LOCAL GOVERNMENT

TONY TRAVERS

The coalition partners brought different approaches to their recent policies on home affairs and local government. The Conservatives, particularly during the Thatcher years, had taken steps to centralize control within British government, albeit from a relatively centralized starting point in 1979. In some ways Mrs Thatcher was maintaining the approach of earlier post-war Tory governments, which had been happy to consolidate the development of a nationally directed welfare state brought together by Labour between 1945 and 1951. The autonomy and discretion of local government in Britain had been in decline since the late 1930s.[1]

The Liberal Democrats and their predecessor parties, having been in opposition continuously since 1945, had evolved a relatively decentralist position as compared with the Conservatives and Labour. By the 2000s the party was strongly in favour of regional devolution, stronger local democracy and, indeed, a local income tax with locally-determined rates. The commitment to the last policy in particular put the Lib Dems in a very different position from the other major parties, who were wedded to the council tax which had been introduced by John Major after the fiasco of the poll tax.

Liberal Democrats had styled themselves as the party of civil liberties, opposing aspects of the Blair government's anti-terrorism laws.

---

[1] See, for example, M. Loughlin et al., *Half a Century of Municipal Decline* (London: Allen & Unwin, 1985).

Being by far the most pro-European of the major parties, the Lib Dems had been strong supporters of the adoption of European human rights legislation. The Conservatives had been more naturally drawn to English 'Bill of Rights'-style liberties.[2] Traditionally the Tories supported a tough approach to law-and-order, while the Liberal Democrats were more likely to support policies such as penal reform and limits on the use of 'stop and search' powers. As a result of New Labour's willingness to implement tough criminal justice policy, the Liberal Democrats' 'liberal' positions on many aspects of home affairs were relatively isolated within national politics.

Thus a coalition between the Conservatives and Liberal Democrats had, when it came to local government and home affairs, little common ground. Where a majority Liberal Democrat government might have introduced regional government for England, the Conservatives were opposed to all aspects of regional policy. The Tories might have been expected to encourage the privatization of local services, where the Lib Dems were far less enthusiastic about such an approach. The Conservatives had signalled an aggressive approach to limiting council tax increases, where the Liberal Democrats wanted new and progressive local taxation. On the other hand, and this difference was to be significant for local government, the Conservatives had committed themselves during the 2010 election to protecting the NHS from real-terms cuts, and no major reorganization, while the Lib Dems made no such promises.

The Coalition Agreement suggested the government wished to devolve power from the centre, promising 'a fundamental shift of power from Westminster to people. We will promote decentralization and democratic engagement, and we will end the era of top-down government by giving new powers to local councils, communities, neighbourhoods and individuals.'[3] The document went on to promise a review of council funding, greater financial autonomy, neighbourhood planning powers, a new planning framework, a 'general power of competence' for councils, mayors for the twelve largest cities, a community right to buy assets, and a freeze of council tax. Planned reforms to the structure

[2] 'Cameron promises UK bill of rights to replace Human Rights Act', *The Guardian*, 26 June 2006.
[3] HM Government, *The Coalition: Our Programme for Government* (London: Cabinet Office, 2010), p. 11.

of local government in Norfolk, Suffolk and Devon and regionalization of the fire service were to be abandoned. Greater local control of public health was promised, although control of schools was to be put in the hands of parents and governors rather than councils. Finally, the government committed itself to a full review of the terms and conditions of police officer employment.

The policies outlined in the Coalition Agreement proved to be a fair prediction of government activity in the five years that followed. While there was a commitment to a shift of power towards neighbourhoods and communities, this move was self-evidently designed to take power away from councils and give it to smaller, voluntary bodies. The creation of more academies and 'free schools' was similarly intended to remove power from town halls and put it in the hands of head teachers, parents and governors. The proposed freeze on council tax, as it was operated, amounted to a reduction of local freedom.

There were other proposals which suggested an intention to strengthen local councils themselves, notably the removal of 'ring-fences' from some of the grants paid by central departments to local government, the general power of competence and the removal of regional bodies. In addition, most of the previous Labour government's public service targets and the 'comprehensive area assessment' regime (which judged council and other local service quality) were abandoned.

However, the financial position of local government was to prove to be the single most important feature of policy towards local areas in the five years that followed.

Public expenditure and 'austerity'

One of Chancellor George Osborne's first initiatives was to undertake a 'comprehensive spending review' to determine the total of public expenditure and departmental allocations for the years 2011–12 to 2014–15. Osborne had decided to reduce the government deficit by a combination of spending cuts and tax increases in the ratio 4:1. As a result, overall 'total managed expenditure' had to be reduced in real terms. Nevertheless, the Conservative commitment to sustain NHS spending in real terms was embedded in the plans, as was protection for schools' budgets. International development expenditure, which the

Tories had promised to raise substantially, was shown as increasing by 37 per cent in real terms between 2011–12 and 2014–15.[4]

The review suggested that welfare expenditure was expected to rise in the years after 2011–12. With an increasing pensioner population and the long recession expected to push up benefit costs, the social security budget was shown as continuing to rise in cash and real terms. So, international development, NHS and schools spending were either increasing or flat in real terms, while welfare was being pushed up by demand. As a result of this set of decisions two-thirds of public expenditure was ring-fenced.

Thus the fate of local government and the Home Office, which had not been protected in any way, was decided. The coalition was to concentrate severe spending reductions on councils and on parts of Whitehall, including the Home Office and the Department of Justice.

The spending review showed local authority funding from central government plunging by 27 per cent between 2011–12 and 2014–15.[5] These grants amounted to broadly half of councils' income. The other half was derived from council tax, which was to be capped. The overall effect of these measures was shown as reducing local government expenditure, falling by 14 per cent in real terms over the years to 2014–15. Nothing as severe as this reduction had been attempted since 1945.

At first the response from councils and their representatives was stunned shock. Although commentators had made pre-election predictions about the scale of cuts likely to be visited on local government in England,[6] most councillors and officers privately believed that reductions on this scale could never be achieved. Seeing the Treasury's figures in black and white, while shocking, did not produce a particularly anguished response. Fatalistic acceptance was closer to a fair description of local government's initial view. The Home Office and Justice Department also faced a significant real reduction in their funding over four years.

In Scotland, Wales and Northern Ireland devolved administrations are responsible for local government funding and policy. Grants to

---

[4] *Spending Review 2010* (Cm 7942), Table 1.   [5] *Ibid.*
[6] Nick Hope and James David Chapman, *Scanning Financial Horizons: Modelling the Local Consequences of Fiscal Consolidation* (New Local Government Network, 2010).

these governments are made on the basis of the Barnett formula, an arrangement first put in place for Scotland in 1978 (and subsequently extended to Wales and Northern Ireland) to adjust funding for the UK nations outside England so as to reflect changes within England.[7] Decisions made in Edinburgh, Cardiff and Belfast about the budgets of councils in Scotland, Wales and Northern Ireland generally led to zero real-terms funding settlements. Thus, local government in the devolved nations enjoyed rather more generous treatment than in England, though by 2014–15, Welsh local authorities were facing cuts of a similar size to those in England.[8]

Early moves

In the summer of 2010 Communities and Local Government Secretary Eric Pickles announced that the Audit Commission was to be abolished. He also made it clear that the regional machinery of government would be dismantled. The previous government had relied on the Commission to deliver a series of league table assessments of councils' performance. Labour had developed a series of institutions in the English regions, including outposts of Whitehall departments, economic development agencies, arts boards and regional 'assemblies' of councils which had been given planning powers. The entire panoply of regional governance would be abolished.

The decision to scrap the Audit Commission was particularly surprising because the organization had been set up by Mrs Thatcher's government in the early 1980s to provide improved probity and value for money. In the run-up to the 2010 election, the press had run a story about the Commission suggesting it had employed consultants to 'handle' Eric Pickles in Opposition.[9] It is hard to believe this news had endeared the Commission to the new minister. But it took five years to close it down.

---

[7] *The Barnett Formula* (House of Commons Research Paper 01/108, 2001).

[8] Welsh Government, 'Local Authority funding announced', 16 October 2013 (accessed at http://wales.gov.uk/newsroom/localgovernment/2013/131016-local-authority-funding/?lang=en, 12 November 2014).

[9] 'Minister says abolition of Audit Commission was a "logical step"', *Public Finance*, 17 August 2010.

Regional governance was also abolished. Labour had created a profusion of weak, regionally based institutions between 1997 and 2010. The Liberal Democrats, as part of the coalition, evidently did not feel these unelected institutions were worth preserving. Conservatives had long been antipathetic to regional governance. Elected councils in cities and counties, which collectively and individually had substantially bigger budgets than any of the regional bodies, were not particularly sad to see them go. In particular, councils objected to so-called 'regional spatial strategies', including housing targets, whereby unelected regional authorities could dictate planning policies to elected local authorities.

Moreover, towards the end of the Labour government, models of 'city regional' government were beginning to emerge, notably in Greater Manchester. These bottom-up groups of councils working together had support from Labour ministers and were immediately embraced by their coalition counterparts. The evolution of this policy is considered in greater detail below.

The Big Society

David Cameron, in seeking new policies for the 2010 election, published plans for a 'Big Society' initiative. Although not spelled out in detail, the Big Society was intended to allow citizens, neighbourhoods, voluntary organizations and mutually owned bodies to assume greater control over what had traditionally been public services. Such policies would fill in gaps left by the shrinking state. Better still, the Big Society would 'give citizens, communities and local government the power and information they need to come together, solve the problems they face and build the Britain they want'.[10]

In this outline of the coalition effect on local government and home affairs the new government was committed to a 'localist' approach to governance, but it clearly interpreted the word 'local' as meaning an unplanned mixture of councils, neighbourhood societies, local charities, school governors, hospitals, 'commissioning' groups of

[10] HM Government, *Building the Big Society*, May 2010 (accessed at www.gov.uk/government/uploads/system/uploads/attachment_data/file/78979/building-big-society_0.pdf, 13 November 2014).

GPs, universities, colleges, museums, civic societies, heritage agencies and any other institution which could be seen to have legitimacy in delivering services and support within localities. Local government was merely one of a number of institutions within this set of organizations.

The Localism Act 2011

The Conservatives and Liberal Democrats each had a tradition of supporting local community organizations. Indeed the Lib Dems famously used 'pavement politics' to build their way back into many councils and Westminster constituencies. The Tories had long been the party of voluntary action and 'grass roots' in the shires. There was little disagreement, therefore, about the introduction of a number of powers within the Localism Act, 2011, designed to give neighbourhoods, parishes and other community groups the opportunity to have a more direct input into planning, local services and the management of certain community assets.

Communities Secretary Eric Pickles claimed that for 'too long local people have had too little say over a planning system that has imposed bureaucratic decisions by distant officials in Whitehall and the town hall'.[11] Neighbourhood planning would allow parishes, town councils or new local forums to be created which could generate neighbourhood plans, which, if agreed in a local referendum, would influence the local council's planning decisions. Neighbourhood plans would have to take account of the council's own planning framework, but the government hoped that by giving local residents a more powerful voice in the planning process, they would be less likely to resist new housing and other development.

By 2014 there was little evidence that neighbourhood planning produced any radical shift towards more or better development. According to the government, by mid-2014, about 1,000 communities had taken the first formal steps towards producing a neighbourhood development plan, 80 full draft plans had been produced for consultation and 13 neighbourhood plans had been passed at community

---

[11] James Derounian, 'Neighbourhood plans – democracy in action or just a sham?', *The Guardian*, 28 November 2011.

referendums.[12] In a country with some 8,500 parish and community councils, plus the many urban areas without such elected bodies, progress towards active planning has been less rapid than ministers might have hoped.

Other aspects of the government's localism policy in the Localism Act, 2011, included the 'community right to build', the 'community right to challenge' and the 'community right to bid'. Each of these initiatives was intended to allow local residents to become involved in actions where they took greater control of local assets and services.

The 'community right to build' gave local communities powers to undertake small-scale, site-specific, community-led developments. Such schemes might include residents delivering 'new homes, shops, businesses or facilities where they want them, without going through the normal planning application process'.[13] The 'community right to challenge' was supposed to give power to local people 'allowing voluntary and community groups, parish councils and local authority staff to express an interest in taking over the running of local authority services, making services more responsive to local needs and delivering better value for money'.[14]

Finally, the 'community right to bid' was designed to give community groups 'a fairer chance to save assets that are important to them'.[15] This right to save facilities could extend to village shops, pubs, community centres, children's centres, allotments, libraries, cinemas and recreation grounds. The right to bid included private as well as public assets.

Each of these new rights was intended to allow local communities to be more active in creating assets, delivering services and taking over facilities important to them. Most of the rights given to people were to challenge local government: the NHS was specifically excluded from the original challenge proposals. There is little evidence that major service departments within Whitehall were willing to allow their

[12] Department for Communities and Local Government, 'Giving communities more power in planning local development', 23 May 2014.

[13] Department for Communities and Local Government, 'Community right to build', 7 November 2012.

[14] Department for Communities and Local Government, 'Community right to challenge comes into force', 27 June 2012.

[15] Department for Communities and Local Government, 'Community right to bid', 2014.

institutions to be affected by the Department for Communities and Local Government's policy.

Nor was there substantial evidence that local communities were able to use their new powers to effect radical change. The 'right to challenge' proved harder for smaller and voluntary bodies to use than the government assumed: 'the procurement process may inherently disadvantage newly-formed, smaller challenger organizations, which may lack the necessary skills, resources and financial history to match better established players'.[16] The 'right to bid' had greater impact, enabling the purchase of a pub in south London, the chance for people in Portland to bid to buy 'The Old Post Office' and for the Cold War relic of the Greenham Common Air Base control tower to be transformed into a community venue.

Many local authorities delayed or refused planning permission for community assets where a case was made to bid for them. In the first year of the new powers local people successfully nominated over 1,000 'Assets of Community Value' across England. Football grounds, pubs, post offices, swimming pools, libraries, arts centres, theatres, a control tower and Turkish baths were all listed by local authorities.[17] The 'right to build' achieved modest success, with a number of housing associations working with local communities to bring forward schemes.[18]

The overall impact of the rights to build, challenge and bid was limited. Little research was undertaken by the government to see how far local people appreciated the new powers they were offered. For a small number of neighbourhoods the Localism Act 2011 provided a toehold on the often complex institutions of the state. But the impact of the legislation fell far short of a revolution. It is likely that most people do not have an appetite for being involved in the formal mechanisms required to take over public services, build houses or take responsibility for planning, and ministers were still willing to intervene to impose

---

[16] Kristian Scholfield, 'Is the community right to challenge in danger of falling by the wayside?', *The Guardian*, 29 April, 2013.

[17] 'Pubs, sports grounds and libraries are top "Assets of Community Value"', *Locality*, 20 May (accessed at http://locality.org.uk/news/pubs-sports-grounds-libraries-top-assets-community, 13 November 2014).

[18] HACT (Housing Associations' Charitable Trust), 'Community Right to Build case studies' (accessed at http://hact.org.uk/community-right-build-case-studies, 13 November 2014).

national decisions on local areas.[19] But the powers offered will, over the longer term, allow neighbourhood and community groups a chance to extend their capacity to influence local public policy.

Another local government funding review

The Coalition Agreement promised a review of council funding. It would be hard to exaggerate how little was expected of such an exercise. As recently as 2007 the Lyons Inquiry's report had been published,[20] making a number of modest proposals for the reform of local government finance, including a revaluation of the council tax base, additional valuation bands and freedom to set the rate of tax. The Labour government rejected almost all of these proposed reforms out-of-hand on the day the report was published. In 1976, the Layfield Report had suggested more radical changes, including the introduction of a local income tax to supplement rates.[21] These proposals were also rejected by the (again Labour) government of the day. In the years between these official inquiries, the country had seen the Conservatives introduce and abandon the community charge, one of the biggest policy blunders of contemporary British history.[22]

Council tax operated, as it still does, on the basis of 1991 property values. In the years from the early 1990s to 2010 there had been substantial changes in the relative value of homes from one place to another. None of these house price movements had been taken into account because the council tax continued to operate on 1991 values. Moreover, because council tax bills were sent annually to every household in Britain, people understood not only how much they paid, but also changes from year to year. Thus, although council tax accounts for less than 5 per cent of UK taxation, it is by far the most visible of all taxes. Finally, it is regressive: less affluent households pay a larger share of their income in council tax than richer ones.

---

[19] 'Don't let Nimbys halt Nick Boles' planning revolution, business leaders say', *Daily Telegraph*, 23 March 2013.

[20] *The Lyons Inquiry into Local Government* (London: The Stationery Office, 2007).

[21] *Local Government Finance Report of the Committee of Inquiry* (Cm 6453, London: HMSE, 1976).

[22] David Butler, Andrew Adonis and Tony Travers, *Failure in British Government: The Politics of the Poll Tax* (Oxford: Oxford University Press, 1994).

Conservative shadow ministers had between 2005 and 2010 operated a highly effective media campaign against the redistributive consequences of real or imagined council tax reforms.[23] Local taxation had become toxic at the time of the community charge and the Tories battered Labour over both increases in council tax and a potential tax-base revaluation.

The coalition set up a 'Local Government Resource Review' in March 2011. The title of this exercise is immediately suggestive of its limited nature. It was not a review of local authority taxation. Rather it looked at the various resources available to councils, including council tax, business rates and grants from the centre. The review's terms of reference were strictly limited, stating:

> the Review will consider the way in which local authorities are funded, with a view to giving local authorities greater financial autonomy and strengthening the incentives to support growth in the private sector and regeneration of local economies ... The Review will include consideration of changes to the business rates system, and focus in particular on: a) the optimum model for incentivising local authorities to promote growth by retaining business rates.[24]

The terms of reference included the need to examine redistribution mechanisms to accompany any business rate reform, 'tax increment financing' and 'the scope for further financial freedoms'. There was no commitment to modernize or reform council tax. On the other hand the review was framed in such a way as to shift the orientation of local government funding in a radical way.

For many decades grants had been paid to local authorities so as to 'equalize' for differences in both their spending needs and the size of their local tax base. The coalition's resource review was signalling that, in future, councils would be incentivized to build up their revenue base. The orientation of local government would move away from a requirement annually to lobby central government for additional

---

[23] See, for example, 'Website "spy" will increase council tax', *Daily Express*, 29 January 2008 or 'Council tax "snoopers" to revalue homes', *Daily Telegraph*, 20 August 2007.

[24] *Local Government Resource Review: Terms of Reference*, Department for Communities and Local Government, 2011.

resources to a system where they would, in effect, earn extra money by giving planning permission for additional development. Under the previous arrangements, there were (because of equalization) no financial incentives for councils to build up the value of their business rate or council tax tax base.

Under the arrangements foreshadowed by this review councils were able to keep 50 per cent of any growth in their business rate base and were given a 'New Homes Bonus' (equivalent to keeping the extra council tax generated) for each additional new home in their area. As the 2011 review made clear, the objective of these reforms was to drive local economic development. But it was hard to differentiate between development directly generated by the new tax-base incentives and growth that would have occurred anyway.

The technical details of the 'business rate retention' scheme were, as with all local government reforms in England, baroque in their complexity. There were to be 'pooling' arrangements, 'top-ups' and 'tariffs', 'levies' and an array of other operational mechanisms which made comprehension virtually impossible. It is hard to believe that the intended incentive effects were sharpened by these redistributive add-ons to the basic scheme. As with any reform to Britain's top-down local government finance arrangements, efforts to counteract resource redistribution on Day 1 of a new system become so incomprehensible that the original purposes of the reform become less important than perfecting transitional damping machinery.

A report from the National Audit Office[25] and subsequent Public Accounts Committee hearings led the PAC chair, Margaret Hodge, to comment:[26] 'The New Homes Bonus was introduced as a financial incentive for local authorities to encourage the building of new homes ... It is ... disappointing that after more than two years of the scheme being up and running, no evaluation is in place and no credible data is available to show whether the scheme is working or not.' The Permanent Secretary at the Department for Communities and Local Government (DCLG), Sir Bob Kerslake, went public to disagree with

[25] National Audit Office, *The New Homes Bonus* (HC 1047, Session 2012–13, 27 March 2013).

[26] 'No credible data to show New Homes Bonus is working', Press Notice accompanying *The New Homes Bonus* (HC 114, Twenty-ninth Report of Session 2013–14, 23 October 2013).

the PAC's report,[27] promising to review the New Homes Bonus by Easter 2014.

The economic impact of business rates retention, which was implemented in 2013, will take some years to test. But in advance of the reform DCLG undertook research which suggested there might be additional GDP in the (admittedly wide) range of £1.7 billion to £19.9 billion over seven years.[28] The methodology used for this calculation was externally reviewed and endorsed by Professor Henry Overman of the LSE.

Other reforms discussed early in the coalition's life included the removal of ring-fences from a number of the grants paid to councils. From the earliest months of the new government, grants to local authorities had been reduced as one of a number of efforts to cut the national budget deficit.[29] The government was devolving some of the more difficult decisions about where to make cuts by taking away restrictions on the use of particular funding streams. Of course, grants for schools and public health, which Whitehall spending departments saw as important to their core purposes, continued to be ring-fenced.

Council budgets

The coalition's 2010 spending review was explicit in targeting the deepest expenditure reductions at local government, the Home Office, the Department of Justice and capital expenditure. Between 2010 and 2015 council expenditure and employment had fallen faster than in any period since 1945. Average real spending by councils in England was down by 15 to 20 per cent in real terms. Major cities such as Newcastle, Liverpool, Manchester, Birmingham and inner London faced steeper reductions. Local authorities in Scotland, Wales and Northern Ireland were to some extent protected by their governments, but Scottish

---

[27] 'Civil service chief hits back at MPs' criticism of new homes scheme', *The Guardian*, 31 October 2013.

[28] Department for Communities and Local Government, *Business Rates Retention Scheme: The Economic Benefits of Local Business Rates Retention* (May 2012).

[29] Letter from Eric Pickles to the leaders of all English councils, 20 October 2010 (accessed at www.gov.uk/government/uploads/system/uploads/attachment_data/file/5656/1745945.pdf, 13 November 2014).

councils found their council tax frozen every year, making them ever more dependent on Edinburgh.

In 2011 and 2012 there was a sustained response from councils, public sector unions and the Labour Party to the expected consequences of reduced local authority funding. A number of exercises were undertaken to measure the job losses and service cuts affecting services and places.[30] There were occasional strikes over public sector pensions and budget reductions. Alarming reports were published about the scale of local government employment losses.[31] Library closures, in particular, attracted the attention of celebrities.[32] Barnet council memorably produced a 'graph of doom' which showed that within a few years the council would have sufficient resources to fund only a bare minimum of statutory social care.[33]

The perceived impact of five years of budget reductions was by 2015 surprisingly modest. There had been such startling predictions of service failure and social breakdown that the results inevitably proved less shocking than original expectations. In addition, local government was far more adept at managing reduced resources than other parts of the public sector. In late 2013 the BBC commissioned polling which suggested 'Many people in the UK think the quality of public services overall have [sic] been maintained or improved in the past five years despite government cuts.'[34] Evidence subsequently produced by pollsters did not suggest a tipping-point had been reached during 2014–15.

Council employment dropped by over 550,000 between the spring of 2010 and late 2014,[35] with every indication it would fall by a further 100,000 or more during 2015. Central government employment, by contrast, was unchanged over this period. Virtually the entire net effort of reducing public employee numbers was borne by local government, though the core civil service was cut significantly. Central

---

[30] See, for example, Amelia Gentleman, 'Public sector cuts – the truth', *The Guardian*, 25 March 2011 or Simon Rogers, 'Local authority cuts: the North–South divide mapped', *The Guardian*, 16 November 2011.

[31] *Spending Review One Year On*, Price Waterhouse Coopers, October 2011.

[32] 'Zadie Smith joins campaign to save her local library', *The Guardian*, 30 March 2011.

[33] 'Graph of Doom a bleak future for social care services', *The Guardian*, 15 May 2012.

[34] 'Public service cuts – did we notice?', *BBC News*, 9 October 2013 (accessed at www.bbc.co.uk/news/uk-24454006, 13 November 2014).

[35] Office for National Statistics, *Public Sector Employment Q2* (September 2014).

government found it hard to rein in the budgets of services for which it was directly responsible.

Local enterprise partnerships

The coalition's decision to abolish all forms of regional governance in England left a vacuum where regional development agencies had once operated. The sub-national coordination of policy on economic development would, if nothing new were created, disappear. The government proposed that new bottom-up groupings of council areas should be the basis of 'local enterprise partnerships' (LEPs). These organizations would have boards which businesses would chair and provide at least half their members, but where councils and other civic partners would also have a major role. Once they had been created, a pot of public money, the Regional Growth Fund, would be made available for LEPs to bid for.

Lord Heseltine, the veteran Conservative politician, was appointed not only to take responsibility for allocating the resources, but also to produce a report about the future of local economic development. This report, entitled 'No stone unturned', proposed that a large proportion of Whitehall resources for skills training, economic development, infrastructure and land improvement should be pooled and made available through a bidding process.[36] LEPs and their constituent local authorities would thus have access to a larger amount of resources which they could use locally.

Heseltine believed, as he had since the 1970s, in a form of managed localism. He had, as the result of his development and regeneration work in Liverpool and other cities during the 1980s, become something of a hero in northern cities. Few Tories were seen in this way outside the southeast. Moreover, he worked with Labour peers such as Richard Rogers and, particularly, Andrew Adonis, to pursue a bilateral approach to sub-national economic policy.

Greg Clark, a minister in the Department for Communities and Local Government, the Cabinet Office and then the Treasury, was another key figure in developing devolutionary policy for LEPs and city

---

[36] The Rt Hon the Lord Heseltine of Thenford, 'No Stone Unturned: in pursuit of growth' (Department for Business Innovation and Skills, October 2012).

regions. Clark, unlike a number of ministers concerned with local government, adopted an emollient and evidence-based approach to urban policy. Deputy Prime Minister Nick Clegg was another minister who played an important role in such matters. The impact of LEPs, like regional development agencies before them, was hard to measure. Major differences in GDP per head of cities and regions persisted in the 2010–15 period. Labour, however, did not commit themselves to abolish LEPs.

City regions

The Blair government had attempted to devolve powers to English regions following the success of devolution to Scotland and Wales. But the limited nature of the powers on offer meant that when the northeast of England voted on the issue in 2004, regional government was rejected by three to one.[37] Thereafter, no effort was made to resuscitate the policy. Outside London there was no devolution within England, although a number of non-elected regional institutions continued to function until the coalition abolished them all.

In the vacuum left by Labour's failed English devolution policy, a number of 'city regional' mechanisms emerged. In particular the ten councils in Greater Manchester started to work together to produce an economic plan.[38] Legislation was passed which made it possible for councils to create a combined authority which gave the force of a legal arrangement to what would otherwise have been a voluntary joint committee. The Greater Manchester city region became the prototype for others in the areas surrounding Liverpool, Leeds and Sheffield. By 2014 counties such as Derbyshire were taking steps to create combined authorities with their districts.

The Cabinet Office, and ministers Nick Clegg and Greg Clark, led the coalition's drive to empower cities.[39] A number of 'city deals' were struck with urban authorities, and later 'growth deals', which

---

[37] Tony Travers, 'Local and central government', in Anthony Seldon (ed.), *The Blair Effect 2001–5* (Cambridge: Cambridge University Press, 2014), pp. 68–93.
[38] See *GM Growth and Reform Plan*, Association of Greater Manchester Authorities (accessed at www.agma.gov.uk, 13 November 2014).
[39] *Unlocking Growth in Cities* (Cabinet Office, December 2011).

included non-urban areas. Authorities bid for new powers to direct and administer skills projects, transport, regeneration and other services linked to economic growth. They also bid for the Regional Growth Fund resources. Some deals allowed councils to undertake investments which would generate additional business rates which could be used to re-invest in infrastructure. Greater Manchester secured an 'Earn Back' deal which allowed it to benefit financially from growth in the wider yield of taxation (i.e. including national revenues) generated by investment in transport and other assets.[40] This process is still one where central government makes many of the important decisions, and which requires much effort by local civic leaders to make their case for a limited amount of local discretion.

A number of publications supported devolution to city regions, notably the report of the London Finance Commission,[41] appointed by London Mayor Boris Johnson in 2012, and one from the Communities and Local Government Select Committee in 2014.[42] The Centre for Cities, whose chief executive Alexandra Jones had been one of the most consistent supporters of city regional governance, also outlined proposals for devolution.[43] Other think tanks, notably ResPublica, published reports arguing for city regional devolution.[44]

Following the Scottish referendum in the autumn of 2014, devolution to city regions became a popular vehicle for potentially delivering a new kind of within-England devolution of power. The longer-term constitutional implications of the post-referendum UK settlement appeared likely to include at least modest changes to the centralized nature of English government, notably including the transfer of some powers to city regions and to local government.[45]

---

[40] See GMCA, *Greater Manchester City Deal* (accessed at www.gov.uk/government/uploads/system/uploads/attachment_data/file/221014/Greater-Manchester-City-Deal-final_0.pdf, 13 November 2014).

[41] *Raising the Capital: The Report of the London Finance Commission* (Greater London Authority, 2013).

[42] Communities and Local Government Committee, *Devolution in England: The Case for Local Government* (HC 503, First Report of Session 2014–15, 9 July 2014).

[43] Zach Wilcox, Nada Nohrova and Maire Williams, *Breaking Boundaries: Empowering City Growth through Cross-border Collaboration* (Centre for Cities, March 2014).

[44] Philip Blond and Mark Morin, *Devo Max – Devo Manc: Place-based Public Services?* (ResPublica, 2014).

[45] See, for example, Andrew Blick, *Devolution in England: A New Approach* (Federal Trust, 2014).

NHS reform and public health

The coalition, in common with many earlier governments, reformed the structure and operation of the NHS. This issue is covered fully in chapter eleven. But there were a number of consequences for local government. Most importantly, the reforms created Health and Well-being Boards, which were intended to establish a degree of local accountability for health services. These new bodies were led by local councils.[46] Although the extent of local powers was limited, councils had been offered the possibility of developing a wider role within the NHS. The power of other health bodies, notably clinical commissioning groups, teaching hospitals and NHS England was such that local government had relatively little power. Nevertheless, councils are now part of the fragmented system of health accountability.

Public health, which had been a local government responsibility until 1974, was transferred from the NHS to councils in April 2013. Although initially funded from a ring-fenced central grant, local authorities happily accepted their new responsibilities. Council leaders privately observed that the budgets they had inherited were generous by the standards of analogous local government provision. The devolution of public health powers created the potential for greater innovation and experimentation in an important field of public policy.

Community budgeting

The previous Labour government had had a 'total place' policy intended to bring together a number of local public services and their budgets so as to allow 'joined-up' provision. The coalition renamed the policy 'community budgeting'. However, Eric Pickles and other ministers supporting this policy found, as their predecessors had, that many of their colleagues in central government were unwilling to pool their services or spending. Opportunities for creating consistent local provision and improved efficiency were undermined by the baronial departments of Whitehall.[47]

---

[46] *A Short Guide to Health and Wellbeing Boards* (Department of Health, 2012).

[47] House of Commons Communities and Local Government Committee, *Community Budgets* (HC 163, Third Report of Session 2013–14, London: TSO, 2013), pp. 11–13.

The Department for Communities and Local Government introduced one policy which was successful in delivering a 'community budget'-type advantage. The Troubled Families Initiative, although it was initially criticized by some for stigmatizing a minority of families, proved a success. It worked by offering councils additional funding in recognition of successful joint working with other parts of the public sector to improve provision and cut costs.[48]

Towards the end of the coalition, efforts were made to bring council and NHS social care budgets together. The Better Care Fund was a chunk of NHS money which was, to a small extent, transferred to local government (by way of another bidding process) so as to create a pool of resources which could be used jointly by the health service so as to deliver better services. Despite evidence that there was concern about the risk to NHS resources,[49] the concept was one which created a potential precedent for other jointly funded provision.

Housing

Another local government activity where there was continuity between Labour and the coalition was the reform of the Housing Revenue Account (HRA). The HRA had operated for many years: councils were required by law to keep their housing activities financially separate from their general fund. Some authorities had sold off their council housing and were, by the late 2000s, running their HRA at a surplus. Other councils were still burdened by the debts of housing constructed in the 1960s and 1970s, some of which had been knocked down. Labour, and then the coalition, put forward plans to bring together the surpluses and deficits of councils across the country so as, in effect, to pool them. Once this pooling had been achieved, it was proposed that all authorities would be free to undertake new housing activity on the basis of 'prudential borrowing' rules. In the event, DCLG ministers decided to constrain the capacity of councils to use their new freedoms to build housing. Because of the coalition's overriding requirement to reduce the

---

[48] *Ibid.*, pp. 30–5.

[49] House of Commons Health Committee, *Public Expenditure on Health and Social Care* (HC 793, Seventh Report of Session 2013–14, London: TSO, 2014), paras. 59–64.

deficit, the Treasury was not prepared to operate a system where any additional spending on housing would add to public expenditure and borrowing.

Local government house building was heavily constrained throughout the years of the coalition government. Additional social and 'affordable' housing was provided by housing associations, though even with their contribution included, the overall public sector housing contribution remained modest by longer-term standards. Overall house building was generally in the range 120,000–180,000, which was short of the number required to cope with a UK population rising by 400,000 to 450,000 per annum.[50] House prices and rentals rose sharply between 2010 and 2015, particularly in London. By 2015 all parties were committed to substantially increasing the construction of new homes, particularly in the southeast.

Changes to the welfare system

Changes to the welfare system had a number of controversial effects for social housing tenants and thus local government. First, a policy change which came to be known variously as the 'bedroom tax' or the 'spare room subsidy' meant that working-age social tenants in receipt of Housing Benefit experienced a reduction in their benefit entitlement if they lived in housing deemed too large for their needs.[51] The elderly, the disabled, military families and foster carers were exempt from the change. The government's key stated aim in cutting housing benefit for people with spare rooms was to get them to move, thereby freeing up homes for families living in overcrowded properties. There was little evidence for the delivery of such an outcome, but housing organizations reported a rise in rent arrears.[52]

---

[50] Department for Communities and Local Government, *House Building: June Quarter 2014, England* (accessed at www.gov.uk/government/uploads/system/uploads/attachment_data/file/345947/House_Building_Release_-_June_Qtr_2014.pdf, 13 November 2014), Figure 2; KPMG and Shelter, *Building the Homes We Need* (2014).

[51] 'Under-occupation of social housing: Housing Benefit entitlement' (House of Commons Library Standard Note SN/SP/6272, 3 June 2014).

[52] 'Impact of housing benefit changes "worse than feared"', *BBC News*, 1 July 2013 (accessed at www.bbc.co.uk/news/uk-23122369, 13 November 2014).

Second, the coalition announced its intention to cap total household social security benefits at £500 per week for a family and £350 per week for a single person with no children from April 2013, though the implementation of this latter policy was subsequently delayed. The benefit cap was intended to contribute towards the reduction of the deficit. Statistics released by the DWP in March 2014 stated that a cumulative total of 38,600 households had had their benefits capped by January 2014. Later it was announced that 9,200 households, having had their benefits capped, had moved into work or reduced their benefit claim beneath the cap.[53] It was argued that some households would have to leave expensive areas, particularly inner London, for lower-cost locations.[54]

A third controversial reform was the abolition of council tax benefit (CTB) and its replacement by a localized system of support operated by local authorities, though pensioner households were exempt from any change. The grant given to councils to pay for this support in 2013–14 was 10 per cent smaller than the cost of the CTB system in its final year, 2012–13. From 1 April 2013 local authorities in England were responsible for administering their own 'council tax reduction schemes'. Some authorities (generally Conservative-controlled) chose to adopt a default scheme mirroring the former CTB arrangements, while others (generally Labour-controlled) reduced entitlement as compared to the previous arrangements.

By the second year of council tax reduction schemes, research showed that 244 out of 326 English authorities required everyone to pay at least some council tax regardless of income.[55] The Scottish and Welsh Governments decided to devise centralized council tax support schemes rather than devolve policy to local authorities as in England, though administration of the schemes rests with local authorities within the devolved nations.

These welfare changes were high-profile in the media coverage they received. The Labour Party strongly opposed all three reforms, though opinion polling suggested that the coalition's welfare policies

53 'The household benefit cap' (House of Commons Library Standard Note SN/SP/6294, 27 March 2014).
54 Amelia Gentleman, 'The families priced out of their London homes by benefit cap', *The Guardian*, 5 March 2014.
55 'Council tax reduction schemes' (House of Commons Standard Note SN/SP/6672, 12 May 2014).

were popular.[56] A minority of predominantly lower-income households were affected by the 'bedroom tax', the benefit cap and localization of council tax benefit. Ministers hoped to reduce dependency and encourage people back into work. The impact of these policies was hard to assess by 2015 and is likely to have been marginal as compared with the wider impact of the delayed Universal Credit reforms. However, for individual households, the financial impact was in many cases significant.

Structures and mayoral reform

The coalition undertook virtually no structural reform of local government. A number of 'combined authorities' were created, mostly involving city regions, although proposals also came forward in 2014–15 for combined authorities based on counties.[57] Eric Pickles, as Secretary of State for Communities and Local Government, was opposed to changing structures.

A number of referendums were held in May 2012 as to whether major cities in England should adopt a mayoral government model. Leicester and Liverpool had already decided to introduce mayors following resolutions by their respective city councils. A third city, Bristol, voted 'yes' in the 2012 referendum and elected its first mayor in November of that year. The remaining nine cities, including Birmingham, Manchester, Leeds, Nottingham and Newcastle-upon-Tyne, rejected the mayoral system in the May referendums.[58] George Ferguson (Bristol), Joe Anderson (Liverpool) and Sir Peter Soulsby (Leicester) proved successful additions to the small number of directly elected mayors.

Police

The coalition made a number of important changes to the police. Most importantly, police authorities were abolished and replaced by directly

---

[56] 'Voters back George Osborne's welfare crackdown, finds poll', *Daily Telegraph*, 29 June 2013.

[57] 'Derbyshire is set to form first non-metropolitan combined authority', *Local Government Chronicle*, 29 September 2014.

[58] 'Directly elected mayors' (House of Commons Standard Note SN/PC/5000, 16 July 2013).

elected 'police and crime commissioners' (PCCs). The first elections took place in November 2012 and were notable for their low turnout, around 15 per cent overall.[59] The functions of the PCC were similar to those of the police authorities they replaced. They appoint, and if necessary remove, the chief constable; they determine the police budget and the council tax precept; and set local policing priorities.[60] Chief constables remained responsible for operational decisions. In London the mayor, operating through the Mayor's Office for Policing and Crime, took over police authority functions.

PCCs were not a success. The low turnouts in the original elections and the 10.3 per cent turnout at a by-election in the West Midlands during 2014 self-evidently undermined their legitimacy.[61] A number of commissioners received adverse publicity.[62] Labour committed itself to abolish commissioners and to encourage voluntary mergers of police forces. The coalition did not pursue policies to reduce the number of forces, as the Blair government had.

Home Secretary Theresa May set about reforming police terms and conditions. She started the process of tacking abuses that had been revealed within police forces and the Police Federation. In a speech delivered in 2014, after listing a series of scandals involving police forces, she stated '[the Police Federation] needs to change from "top to bottom". We've seen accusations of bullying, a lack of transparency in the accounts, questionable campaign tactics, infighting between branches, huge reserve funds worth millions of pounds, and a resounding call for change from your members – with 91% saying things cannot go on as they are'.[63]

The Home Secretary, who had already initiated a College of Policing, also promised more powers and resources for the Independent

---

[59] The Electoral Commission, 'Police and Crime Commissioner elections in England and Wales', March 2013.

[60] 'Police and Crime Commissioners' (House of Commons Standard Note SN/HA/6104, 7 November 2013).

[61] 'Only one in ten voters take part in West Midlands police commissioner election', *The Guardian*, 22 August 2014.

[62] See, for example, 'Paris Brown: Kent youth PCC resigns after Twitter row', *BBC News*, 9 April 2013 (accessed at www.bbc.co.uk/news/uk-england-22083032, 13 November 2014).

[63] Theresa May's speech to the Police Federation, 21 May 2014 (accessed at www.gov.uk/government/speeches/home-secretarys-police-federation-2014-speech, 13 November 2014).

Police Complaints Commission, direct entry by graduates into senior police ranks and a radical overhaul of terms and conditions. Theresa May's willingness to confront the police in this way, and to take direct control over the Border Agency and, later in 2014, the Passport Office, showed her to be one of the toughest and most effective members of the coalition government, albeit one who was happy to centralize power to her office.

Standards and Audit

In August 2010 Eric Pickles had announced that the Audit Commission was to be abolished. The Commission had been created during Mrs Thatcher's government and had been responsible not only for the regulation of local government audit but also for 'value for money' studies. Its original remit had been extended to cover not merely local authorities but also other institutions such as schools and NHS bodies.

The coalition government's detailed proposals for abolition of the Audit Commission were published in August 2010.[64] Pickles stated:

> The Audit Commission's responsibilities for overseeing and delivering local audit and inspections will stop; the Commission's research activities will end; audit functions will be moved to the private sector; councils will be free to appoint their own independent external auditors from a more competitive and open market; and there will be a new audit framework for local health bodies. This will save council taxpayers' money and decentralize power.

There were to be new powers for the National Audit Office, a requirement for councils to appoint private auditors and other new safeguards. One such was a demand that councils publish details about their spending.

Eric Pickles later stated he hoped 'armchair auditors' would hold councils to account. Local authorities were to be required to publish details of all payments and contracts worth over £500

---

[64] 'Eric Pickles to disband Audit Commission in new era of town hall transparency', DCLG Announcement, 13 August 2010 (accessed at www.gov.uk/government/news/eric-pickles-to-disband-audit-commission-in-new-era-of-town-hall-transparency, 13 November 2014).

which would encourage 'a new wave of local scrutiny by citizen journalists, microbloggers and armchair auditors ... [a] "citizen samizdat"'.[65]

An ad hoc Parliamentary committee examining the draft Local Audit Bill, chaired by Public Accounts Committee chair Margaret Hodge, was critical of the government's proposals:

> The Committee is concerned that the proposed new arrangements ... will result in a more complex and fragmented audit regime. We believe that the principle of independent audit ... could be undermined ... It will become more difficult to ensure value-for-money if provisions in the Bill are not strengthened so that appropriate data which enables proper analyses and comparisons to be made are required by statute.[66]

As with many of the coalition's reforms involving local government, it was hard to judge their full impact by 2014–15. Commenting on the 'armchair auditor' proposals, Neil O'Brien of Policy Exchange noted that many of the data published by the government were in an 'unusable format and if they want that to be a serious driver of transparency they need to enable users to use it in a simpler way'.[67] Like the neighbourhood and community policies, the consequences of the audit reforms will take some years to have an effect.

The Audit Commission continued in a zombie-like fashion till March 2015. After this point contracts for audit services were to be managed by an independent, private company to be created by the Local Government Association (LGA). The longer-term consequences of the Commission's abolition are likely to include a future government re-visiting the broader issue of how to audit an increasingly fragmented and complex public sector.

---

[65] 'Armchair auditors are here to stay', DCLG Announcement, 8 July 2011 (accessed at www.gov.uk/government/news/armchair-auditors-are-here-to-stay, 13 November 2014).

[66] Margaret Hodge, MP, speaking at the launch of the *Draft Local Audit Bill: Pre-legislative Scrutiny* (HC 696, Report of Session 2012–13, 13 January 2013).

[67] 'Government online data ignored by "armchair auditors"', *BBC News*, 9 November 2012 (accessed at www.bbc.co.uk/news/uk-politics-20221398, 13 November 2014).

Snoopers, dustbins, yellow lines and 'town hall *Pravdas*'

The Department of Communities and Local Government (DCLG) and the Home Office were both targeted for substantial expenditure reductions between 2010 and 2015. The political decision to increase or protect international development, health, schools and parts of social security meant that unprotected programmes had to be reduced by 15 to 20 per cent in real terms. Councils, the police and fire services were affected by budget cuts throughout the years of the coalition.

DCLG ministers operated a policy of active confrontation with local government. Eric Pickles, in particular, was happy to challenge council leaders with attacks about profligacy, high officer salaries and over-zealous behaviour. He sustained a series of media assaults on councils about the way they used their powers, notably over 'snooping' on citizens with surveillance cameras, refuse collection, parking fines and 'Pravda-like' council newspapers.[68]

The purpose of these high-profile campaigns was, it must be assumed, to deflect attention from the fact that councils faced disproportionate cuts. When a 2011 survey suggested that local government employment would fall by 140,000 in the coming year, Pickles dismissed this calculation as done 'on the back of a fag packet'.[69] In fact council employment fell by 147,000,[70] but the original 'fag packet' comment was reported, not the eventual reality. In the end, Pickles' remark turned out to be an ear-catching dismissal of what had proven to be a conservative estimate.

At other times DCLG ministers publicly criticized councils for their refuse collection policies. A number of authorities moved from weekly kerbside refuse collection to alternate-week collections, generally with a second collection of recyclables in the intervening week.[71]

---

[68] See, for example, 'Time called on Town Hall snoops', *Sunday Times*, 22 August 2010; 'Eric Pickles warns councils over weekly bin collections', *BBC News*, 22 November 2012 (accessed at www.bbc.co.uk/news/uk-politics-20449141, 14 November 2014); 'I'll help residents to get rid of yellow lines on their roads, promises Pickles in crackdown of "over-zealous" parking policies', *Daily Mail*, 30 August 2014.

[69] 'Spending cuts: Councils "to lose 140,000 jobs"', *BBC News*, 25 November 2010 (accessed at www.bbc.co.uk/news/uk-politics-11840648, 14 November 2014).

[70] Office for National Statistics, *Public Sector Employment Q2* (September 2014), Table 1.

[71] See, for example, 'Pickles publishes "bins bible" to encourage return of weekly rubbish collection', *Daily Telegraph*, 27 December 2013.

Ministers attacked reductions in the frequency of bin-emptying as an infringement of basic rights and were able to gain significant press attention in doing so. They did something very similar over fines for parking infringements and yellow lines limiting parking outside shops. This approach was populist 'centralist localism'.

It is a measure of the condition of British democracy that government ministers now busy themselves with the minutiae of municipal activities. In fairness to ministers Eric Pickles and Brandon Lewis, their Labour predecessors had had form in neighbourhood-level meddling. As the UK's international power has declined, senior national politicians have increasingly turned to the regulation of parochial issues.

London

London was the only part of England to be given a measure of devolution by the Blair government's late-1990s reforms. Boris Johnson had defeated Ken Livingstone to become mayor of London in 2008 and repeated his victory in 2012. The Localism Act 2011 marginally strengthened the powers of the mayor and the London assembly, though the original government model was broadly unchanged. Johnson, who had long been seen as having ambitions within national politics, made it clear he would not seek a third term as mayor and also that he would try to return to Parliament in 2015.

The most remarkable feature of London between 2010 and 2015 was that, despite the recession which affected the coalition's early years, the capital's economy roared ahead. Overseas property buyers saw London property as a safe haven and continued to invest in the city in such a way as to sustain ever-higher house prices. By the 2015 election housing supply had replaced transport as the number-one issue facing London politicians. Indeed the balance of the UK economy between the London region and the rest of the UK had increased in importance as a national political issue.[72]

---

[72] See, for example, 'High-speed rail link needed to boost north – Osborne', *BBC News*, 23 June 2014 (accessed at www.bbc.co.uk/news/uk-27969885, 14 November 2014).

Scotland, Wales and Northern Ireland

Local government is a devolved responsibility in Scotland, Wales and Northern Ireland. Each of the systems operated in these nations was, as in England, relatively centralized. The Scottish Government froze council tax from 2007 onwards. In Northern Ireland, where local authorities have traditionally had fewer responsibilities than elsewhere in the UK, a structural reform cut the number of councils from twenty-six to eleven by 2015. Some powers will be transferred from Belfast to the new, larger, authorities. The Welsh Government proved willing to intervene directly in its local authorities on a number of occasions, notably in Torfaen and Blaenau Gwent, but most dramatically with the temporary imposition of commissioners to replace councillors in Anglesey,[73] on the grounds that factionalism between councillors had undermined good government.

Financial austerity had a less severe impact in Scotland, Wales and Northern Ireland than in England between 2010 and 2013. But by 2014–15 councils in Wales were being subjected to cuts similar to those in England.

The Scottish Government reformed both the fire and police services, in each case creating a single force for the whole country. Devolution in Scotland and Wales was to each of the governments in Edinburgh and Cardiff rather than from the devolved institutions down to local government. The period from 2010 to 2015 saw further evolution of centralization within at least three of the four UK nations. In Northern Ireland, where there was some decentralization, the number of councils was sharply reduced.

Conclusions

The coalition effect on local government owed far more to the traditional approach of the Conservative and Labour parties than to the Liberal Democrats' devolutionary enthusiasms. The eradication of the deficit, while protecting the funding of the NHS, schools and international development, was from the start a core element of the

---

[73] Welsh Government, *Road to Recovery: An Independent Evaluation of the Anglesey Intervention* (Social Research Number 85/2014, 2014).

agreement between the coalition partners. Once this set of priorities had been put in place, local government and Home Office services were bound to be cut significantly.

The removal of 'ring-fences' around grants and the abolition of Labour's many public service targets in England gave councils, the police and fire authorities slightly greater discretion, albeit the discretion to decide how to make cuts. There was no structural reorganization within England, though moves to reduce the number of councils were made in Wales and Northern Ireland. Scotland created national police and fire services, a move away from more localized services.

Ministers at both the Department for Communities and Local Government and, to a lesser extent, the Home Office continued to intervene in local matters. While there was some evidence that 'localism' policies in England had given neighbourhoods and communities a toe-hold on local planning, other initiatives, such as 'armchair auditors', had had little perceptible effect. The governance of schools shifted decisively from town halls to Whitehall, though public health was transferred the other way. The coalition attempted to merge funding for aspects of NHS and council social care, though this process met resistance from within the health service.

By 2015 the United Kingdom remained one of the most central-ized of all the world's large democracies. The constitutional fall-out from the Scottish independence referendum will lead to changes in the government of Scotland and Wales. It may lead to pressures for a greater measure of devolution within England, which again will be resisted by many parts of central government, both ministers and civil servants. A period of uncertainty for the UK's sub-national government would appear to be the coalition's main legacy.

10 THE COALITION AND SOCIETY (II): EDUCATION

ALAN SMITHERS

The accelerating pace of educational reform since the 1988 Act quickened still further in the 2010–15 parliament. There were three new acts, but also many of the powers acquired by previous acts were put to use. The heightened activity was partly because the programme had to embrace the ambitions of two parties. But the main impetus came from the new Secretary of State, Michael Gove, who in his three years shadowing the post had developed very clear ideas about what he wanted to achieve. In post, he pressed hard, anxious to embed as many of the desired changes as he could while he still held the reins.

Education was prominent in the 2010 manifestos of both the Conservative and Liberal Democrat parties.[1] Both envisaged more freedom for schools and extra money to raise the attainment of pupils from low-income families (the pupil premium). They also agreed on the need to improve the quality of teaching, proposing to increase school-led teacher training and expand the Teach First scheme.[2] But there were differences in emphasis, with the Conservatives placing more on new

[1] The Conservative Party, *Invitation to Join the Government of Britain: The Conservative Manifesto 2010* (London: Conservative Party, 2010); Liberal Democrats, *Liberal Democrat Manifesto 2010: Change That Works for You* (London: Liberal Democrats, 2010).

[2] A scheme whereby top graduates from leading universities would teach in difficult schools for at least two years. See Brett Wigdortz, *Success Against the Odds: Five Lessons in How to Achieve the Impossible; The Story of Teach First* (London: Short Books, 2012).

schools, higher standards and improved discipline, while the Liberal Democrats stressed fairness.

Inevitably, with two parties in government there have had to be compromises, but in the field of education, given the similarity of the manifestos, it was relatively easy to reach agreement, with one notable exception. Some of the compromises resulted in better policy. The Liberal Democrats pushed the pupil premium higher up the agenda than it might have been, and the Conservatives were so pleased with it that they let it be thought it was their policy. They were much less keen on Nick Clegg's free lunches for all infant school pupils, which had to be afforded a tightly constrained budget, with the additional expense of new kitchens.[3] Some compromises proved unworkable. In the reform of the examinations, where the Conservative wish for greater rigour clashed with the Liberal Democrat pursuit of fairness, the initial compromise was to have tougher exams, but without tiers. This would have left more failing so was softened to allow some subjects, like maths, to retain tiers.

But one compromise proved difficult and disastrous. The Liberal Democrats had campaigned very vigorously on tuition fees. All their candidates signed and publicly paraded a National Union of Students pledge to vote against any proposed increase. Labour as a potential coalition partner was ready to commit to this.[4] But the Conservatives stuck to their manifesto formula of 'considering carefully' the recommendations of the Browne Review convened by the outgoing Labour government.[5] Since there had been an interim report in March 2010 it was no great surprise when in October 2010 the Review recommended freeing up universities to set their own fee levels. This delighted the Conservatives, but was lose-lose for the Liberal Democrats. A compromise was hammered out involving a maximum fee of £9,000, conditions that would apply to universities, and generous loans and repayment terms. Anticipating that a compromise on tuition fees would be extremely difficult, the partners, as part of the coalition agreement, accepted that Liberal Democrat MPs would be able to

---

[3] Nick Clegg demanded free school meals for all infant school pupils to be in the 2013 Budget as a quid pro quo for the Conservatives' marriage tax allowance.

[4] Andrew Adonis, *5 Days in May: The Coalition and Beyond* (London: Biteback Publishing, 2013), p. 184.

[5] *Securing a Sustainable Future for Higher Education: An Independent Review of Higher Education Funding and Student Finance*, 12 October 2010.

abstain in any vote. When it came to the point in early December 2010, twenty-eight of the fifty-seven Liberal Democrats, including Nick Clegg, voted for the new fee arrangements. Going back on such an explicit pledge seriously damaged the credibility of the Liberal Democrat party, which it has yet to recover. But, as we shall see in the section on higher education, the compromise was also disastrous for the tax-payer, because the scheme saves very little and results in a large and uncertain charge on the public finances.

One of the first actions of the new government was to rename Michael Gove's department the Department for Education (DfE), although, rather surprisingly, it did not re-designate its responsibilities. Gordon Brown on coming to office in 2007 had split higher education off from schools in his administration. It was an unfortunate separation cutting right across further education. It was made worse when the universities were shuffled into the Department for Business, Innovation and Skills. If the Conservatives had gained a majority, higher education would have gone back into the DfE, but the move was blocked by the Liberal Democrat Secretary of State, Vince Cable.[6] Under the arrange-ments which emerged, the DfE retained responsibility for children's services, which gave rise to tensions that spread across party lines.

In the government's first major reshuffle two years into the parliament, both the Liberal Democrat children and families minister, Sarah Teather, and her Conservative junior, Tim Loughton, lost their jobs, along with the minister for schools, Nick Gibb. All three appeared before the Education Select Committee in January 2013.[7] It was evident that Tim Loughton, who had shadowed the brief for nearly a decade and was highly respected in the field, was particularly upset. He said, 'it was difficult for the children and families agenda to get a look in, in the bulldozer that was the schools reform programme', and he accused the department of having 'an upstairs downstairs mentality'. Sarah Teather agreed that the Secretary of State was focused on schools reform, but said he 'had regularly "gone into bat" to support her in pushing forward changes in her area'. It emerged, however, that she had become very disillusioned with other aspects of government policy. In contrast, the third minister, Nick Gibb, was relaxed about being asked to make

---

[6] This chapter has benefited greatly from conversations with insiders.
[7] Corrected Transcript of Oral Evidence taken before the Education Committee, Former Department for Education Ministers (HC 851-I, 16 January 2013).

way for the returning senior Liberal Democrat, David Laws, and so maintain the agreed balance in ministerial positions. He continued to be used by the government as a schools spokesman and returned to be an education minister in July 2014.

The three ministers were not the only early departures from the DfE. Four senior civil servants, including the permanent secretary, Sir David Bell, left during 2011. They all went to senior posts, with Sir David becoming vice chancellor of Reading University. But it was also reported that the Secretary of State was not sorry to see them go because he had become frustrated by what he saw as passive resistance from officials, particularly at the junior level, close to the left-leaning education establishment.[8] If Michael Gove sensed resistance in the department, little came from the Labour Party. All through the 2010 Parliament they struggled to find a distinctive alternative narrative for schools. In truth, their 2010 manifesto proposals for education did not differ markedly from those that were agreed by the coalition. But there were also frequent changes of shadow secretary: Ed Balls lasted five months; Andy Burnham, a year; Stephen Twigg, two years; and the present incumbent, Tristram Hunt, nineteen months, if he survives to the end of the parliament. The coalition phased out or neutered a number of Labour's cherished schemes, including the Children's Plan, specialist schools, dedicated gifted and talented funding, careers advisers in schools, Education Maintenance Allowances, and young apprenticeships, without much in the way of protest. The government also scrapped or merged a number of quangos, including in the field of education the General Teaching Council, the Training and Development Agency for Schools, the National College for Leadership of Schools and Children's Services, and the Qualifications and Curriculum Development Agency. Some of these functions were taken in-house, literally into the headquarters in Great Smith Street, which became very crowded, with hot-desking the norm and few meeting spaces. These conditions probably contributed to the frenetic atmosphere as the reforms were driven forward.

The DfE provided a detailed statement of its far-reaching aims in a white paper,[9] *The Importance of Teaching*, in November 2010. In a

---

[8] Jack Grimston, 'Gove at war with school mandarins', *The Sunday Times*, 16 October 2011.

[9] Department for Education, *The Importance of Teaching: The Schools White Paper 2010* (London: The Stationery Office, Cmnd 7980, November 2010), pp. 3–5.

joint foreword, David Cameron and Nick Clegg identified three main areas for action: raising the standards and status of teaching; 'devolving as much power as possible to the front line, while retaining high levels of accountability'; and narrowing the vast gap in the educational performance of the rich and poor. All were taken forward, but it was the second of these, Autonomy and Accountability, that came to dominate.

Autonomy

In the foreword also, David Cameron and Nick Clegg explained why they thought urgent and radical reform of England's education was essential: 'What really matters is how we're doing [in education] compared with our international competitors ... The truth is, at the moment we are standing still while others race past.'[10] This view was based mainly on their interpretation of England's performance in cross-country comparisons of attainment in reading, maths and science. They argued strongly that we must learn the lessons of others' success. In particular they noted that the countries which did best, like Finland and South Korea, coupled school autonomy with clearly defined and challenging standards.

As Adonis recounts in his book, *Education, Education, Education*, under David Cameron's leadership from 2005 (having been briefly shadow Secretary of State for education), the Conservative Party became increasingly attracted to Labour's academies programme as the basis for an autonomous schools system.[11] In a speech to the CBI in May 2007 David Willetts, then shadow education secretary, went as far as to say that his party saw academies rather than grammar schools as the engine of social mobility.[12] His successor in July 2007, Michael Gove, pledged that a Conservative government would enable all successful schools to achieve academy status and also introduce a new kind of academy, the 'free school', to be established by parents.

[10] Responsibility for education in Scotland, Northern Ireland and Wales rests with the administrations of those countries.

[11] Andrew Adonis, *Education, Education, Education: Reforming England's Schools* (London: Biteback Publishing, 2012), p. 118.

[12] It was a claim too far for his party and he was replaced by Michael Gove on 7 July 2007.

The Conservative Party's passionate commitment to academies went beyond the assumed virtues of autonomy; they offered the prospect of completing some unfinished business. Local authorities had run state education from the beginning, since it was they who were empowered to raise the money for it through the rates. Schools were completely answerable to them, and central government contented itself with the legislative framework. Kenneth Baker (now Lord Baker), Conservative Secretary of State from May 1986 to July 1989, wanted to change all that. He began the process of redistributing power by requiring in the Education Reform Act of 1988 local authorities to pass on most of the education grant they received from central government to schools. The act also enabled schools to opt out of local authority control and become grant-maintained, running themselves and able to set their own admissions criteria. John Patten, Conservative secretary of state 1992–4, was so confident of their appeal, that following a further Act in 1993, he boasted that: 'I will eat my academic hat garnished if by the time of the next election we haven't got more than half England's secondary schools grant-maintained.'[13] Unfortunately, schools were a lot less willing to leave local authorities than he thought – only 19 per cent of secondary schools, 3 per cent of primary schools and 2 per cent of special schools had made the change. Patten never honoured his boast, even though *The Guardian* attempted to deliver a nice mortarboard-shaped cake which they had had baked for him. The Blair government brought opting-out to a halt when it abolished grant-maintained status in the School Standards and Framework Act of 1998.

Blair's second administration, however, was to create its own version of autonomous schools: city academies, later just academies. It had tried everything it could think of to deal with some intractably difficult schools, when it had the idea of reviving the model of Kenneth Baker's city technology colleges. In part, this involved building some eye-catching new premises, often on the sites of the old failing schools. But, crucially, they had to have a sponsor to provide a modest amount of capital funding, and more importantly to set the tone of the school through the governing body. Excellent head teachers were found, among them Michael Wilshaw, who was to become Chief Inspector of Schools. At first, the academies programme focused on quality rather

[13] Alan Smithers, 'Education', in Anthony Seldon and Dennis Kavanagh (eds.), *The Blair Effect 2001–5* (Cambridge: Cambridge University Press, 2005), pp. 408–9.

than quantity: three opened in 2002, nine in 2003 and five in 2004, with 203 in total established by the time of the 2010 election.[14]

Conservatives, on returning to power, still harboured the desire to see all schools independent of local authority control. Backed by their interpretation of the international evidence and with the support of the Liberal Democrats, they radically changed and extended Labour's academies programme. The Academies Act 2010 was the first piece of legislation from the new government, passing all its stages in under three months. The Department for Education had agonized over what new powers it needed to implement the new government's wishes. It found that it was already able to do most of the things, including enabling successful schools, and forcing failing schools, to convert to academy status. These powers were reinforced in the Act, but its main point was to remove the requirement to consult with local authorities, which it feared would lead to massive delays.

By November 2014, 4,299 schools had become or were in the process of becoming academies. Of these, 3,032 were converter academies. An analysis by the House of Commons Library showed that in November 2014, 1,343 secondary schools had converted, 41 per cent of the total.[15] When the 459 sponsored secondary academies are counted in this becomes 55 per cent of secondary schools. More primary schools are now becoming academies than are secondaries, and they currently comprise 9 per cent of the total. Special schools, Pupil Referral Units, all-through schools and 16+ institutions are also converting. The reason most often given for making the change was that it would bring in extra funding.[16]

A particular kind of academy is the 'free school', originally intended to be set up by groups of parents, but more often in practice by teachers, charities, existing schools or other organizations. By September 2014, there were 251 free schools, with a further 76 in the pipeline.[17] The Public Accounts Committee, in its report *Establishing*

[14] Stephen Machin and James Vernoit, 'A note on academy school policy' (Centre for Economic Policy Briefing, July 2010).

[15] Paul Bolton, 'Converter academies: statistics (House of Commons Library Standard Note SNSG/6233, 24 November 2014).

[16] Dale Basset, Gareth Lyon, Will Tanner and Bill Watkin, *Plan+: Unleashing the Potential of Academies* (The Schools Network and Reform, March 2012).

[17] Department for Education, *Free Schools: Open Schools and Successful Applications* (28 October 2014).

Free Schools, expressed concern that only about a fifth of secondary free schools were in areas where there was a shortage of places.[18]

Academies can be claimed as a political success, but to what extent are they fulfilling Cameron's and Clegg's ambition of creating a world-class education system? The short answer is: we do not yet know. As is evident from the contrasting origins, the term academy embraces at least two types of school: failing schools that were forced to become academies (sponsored) and successful schools that opted to do so (converter). Only the former have been in existence for long enough to investigate whether they are making a difference. But they are distinctive in having more pupils from lower-income homes, more from ethnic minorities, more with special needs, and lower GCSE achievement. Findings for the sponsored cannot therefore be generalized to all academies.

The National Audit Office (2010) found a significant improvement in the pupil performance of the first sponsored academies compared to matched schools remaining in local authorities, attributing the difference mainly to changes in the pupil intake consequent upon becoming an academy.[19] Andrew Eyles and Stephen Machin examined this further in a study of 133 of the 203 sponsored academies established under the Labour government.[20] They reported an improvement in performance over and above the changed intake, which they linked to the freedoms granted – setting teacher's pay and conditions, adapting the national curriculum, and varying the school day. As far as converter academies are concerned, the strongest evidence that the DfE has so far been able to put forward is that primary academies (35 per cent) are more likely to retain their outstanding rating than non-academies (25 per cent) in the new, more rigorous Ofsted inspections.[21]

A difficulty for policymakers and commentators alike is that conclusive evidence on the effectiveness of education policies is hard to come by. In the physical sciences, the commonsense view that the earth is flat, stationary and at the centre of the universe is demolished by the

---

[18] Public Accounts Committee, *Establishing Free Schools* (HC 941, Fifty-sixth Report of Session 2013–14, May 2014).

[19] National Audit Office, *The Academies Programme* (HC 288, 10 September 2010).

[20] Andrew Eyles and Stephen Machin, 'The introduction of academy schools to England's education' (Munich, CESifo Area Conference on Economics of Education, 12 September 2014).

[21] Evidence from the Department for Education to the Education Select Committee, 5 February 2014: www.bbc.co.uk/democracylive/house-of-commons-26047873.

evidence, so we have to accept the much less comfortable picture of a small spinning spheroid in the vastness of space. Evidence about education is not like that. More often than not it can be just swept up into whatever is the preferred narrative. The evidence on autonomy and academies is no exception. Indeed, the very basis of the converter-academy policy is contestable. It can be shown that England's position did not decline relative to other countries in the international comparisons;[22] Andreas Schleicher, who was in charge of the PISA international tests, cautioned that autonomy on its own is not a way of improving schools;[23] and Tom Benton found that when PISA data for independent and government-run schools were analysed separately any suggestion of an autonomy effect disappeared completely.[24]

While it is too soon to know if academies will be the success the government hoped, a number of practical problems have come to light. They centre on how the individual schools are to cohere as a system. The 2010 white paper envisages this will come from the schools themselves working together as a self-improving system.[25] A great variety of partnerships and forms of co-operation and collaboration have emerged ranging from those with legal underpinning, as in federations, trust schools and academy chains, to the looser collaboration and informal school-to-school support of teaching schools and challenge partners. Ironically, some schools have less autonomy as academies than they did as local authority schools. Those becoming members of Multi-Academy Trusts (MAT) cede the running of the school to the trust and have governing bodies only insofar as the trust will delegate decision-making powers to them. Schools cannot at present choose to exit these trusts. The Chief Inspector of Schools wants powers to inspect academy chains, but is so far only able to inspect the schools, not the MAT itself.[26]

At first, the government seemed content to facilitate the various forms of partnership and co-operation, and allow a system to evolve.

[22] Alan Smithers, *Confusion in the Ranks: How Good are England's Schools?* (London: Sutton Trust, February 2013).
[23] Sean Coughlan, 'Academies "promising trend" says OECD', *BBC News*, 8 March 2014.
[24] Tom Benton, *A Re-evaluation of the Link Between Autonomy, Accountability and Achievement in PISA2009* (Cambridge Assessment, January 2014).
[25] Department for Education, *The Importance of Teaching*, para. 7.4.
[26] Sally Weale, 'Nicky Morgan told to clarify Ofsted's powers to inspect academy chains', *The Guardian*, 22 October 2014.

But over the parliament it has become increasingly clear that some means of oversight is essential.[27] Some academies have failed Ofsted inspections, there have been instances of conflict of interest in the awarding of contracts by schools,[28] and some academies have used the freedoms in ways that were never envisaged, as with the allegations of 'Trojan Horse' extremism in Birmingham schools.[29] Central government, through its direct relationship with academies, cannot be expected to monitor and intervene in over 4,000 schools, let alone if, as it wishes, all schools eventually become academies. There has to be something in between. There is, of course, a ready-made set of structures in the shape of the local authorities. But that would defeat one of the purposes of the programme. Local authorities have been left with the responsibility of securing enough school places, without the power to intervene in academy schools or to set up new schools of their own. The mechanism for oversight that the government came up with in December 2013 was to create eight Regional School Commissioners (RSC) reporting to the Schools Commissioner, whose role has become focused on academies. Each RSC is supported by a Head Teacher Board, but the areas they cover are vast and, moreover, do not coincide with Ofsted's regions, making liaison difficult. At first, it was envisaged they would promote the benefits of academies, but more recently the responsibilities have been reordered, with taking action on underperformance the priority.[30] While the academies are now firmly embedded, it is evident that there is still much to be done to ensure that they function optimally as, or within, a schools system.

Accountability

Accountability is the essential counterpart of autonomy. If a school has been granted freedoms, it is important to know how they are being

[27] National Audit Office, *Academies and Maintained Schools: oversight and intervention* (HC721, Session 2014–15, 30 October 2014).

[28] Toby Greany and Jean Scott, *Conflicts of Interest in Academy Sponsorship Arrangements: A Report for the Education Select Committee* (September 2014).

[29] *Birmingham Mail*, www.birminghammail.co.uk/all-about/trojan-horse (accessed 5 December 2014).

[30] Department for Education, *Regional Schools Commissioners* (updated 27 October 2014).

used. Independent schools – which are truly autonomous – are held to account mainly by parents. If a school consistently fails to provide the quality of education that parents expect, then it faces going out of business. Attempts to simulate something similar for state schools have faltered because it is often the schools choosing the pupils. The accountability of state schools rests mainly on outcomes and inspections. Both have changed considerably during the lifetime of this government.

Outcome measures

The publication of schools' results came about in the wake of the Conservatives' Education Reform Act of 1988, but they were turned into an accountability measure by the Blair government, which imposed sanctions on schools not reaching specified standards. The consequences for a school failing to meet the floor standard could be dire. It would trigger an inspection which could lead to the school being placed in special measures. As a result, the head and some teachers might be dismissed, the governors replaced, and the school merged or even closed.[31] Not surprisingly, schools pulled out all the stops to get a score that would secure their safety.

When the coalition government came to power in 2010 the basic accountability measure for secondary schools was framed in terms of the percentage of pupils achieving at least grade C in five GCSEs, or their equivalent, including English and maths. Schools, especially those potentially on the borderline, adjusted their behaviour accordingly.[32] A lot of effort went into boosting the performance of pupils from grade D to grade C, with the pattern of results showing a distinct 'cliff edge' at that point. Less attention was given to those who were safe or had no hope of passing, both of which with more preparation might have done better. The schools also found vocational qualifications had been given generous equivalences and strategically moved pupils on to them to boost the accountability score, seemingly without much regard to the pupils' futures.

---

[31] The government reinforced its powers in the 2010 Act to turn failing schools into academies.

[32] Warwick Mansell, *Education by Numbers: The Tyranny of Testing* (London: Politico's Publishing, 2007).

The coalition government adopted the view that accountability was best served by putting as much data as possible in the public domain. It attempted to counteract the cliff-edge effect by publishing data on the progress of very able, average and less able pupils separately. It also tried to nudge schools into concentrating on core academic subjects by introducing an English Baccalaureate (Ebacc) measure – consisting of English, maths, at least two science GCSEs, a foreign language, and history or geography. The old measure, while retaining its pre-eminence, came under attack from two directions. The Wolf Report challenged the equivalency to GCSEs of the vocational qualifications for 14–16 year-olds,[33] and Graham Stuart, Chairman of the Education Select Committee, campaigned energetically against the perverse incentives of the accountability measure.[34] The government listened and stripped out many of the quasi-vocational qualifications and reduced the weighting of those remaining. In 2013, it formally consulted on proposals for smarter accountability measures, and decided that beginning with the 2016 examination results there will be five indicators of a secondary school's performance: progress across a suite of eight subjects, with English and maths double-weighted; attainment in the eight subjects; the percentage achieving at least a C grade in English and maths; the EBacc; and, hopefully, a destinations measure which is being trialled.[35] The 'Progress Eight' measure, as it is called, will be used to set floor standards. The government hopes that by using a range of indicators and taking the performance of all pupils into account it will create a more rounded picture of a school's performance.

Ofsted

The other arm of accountability is Ofsted. This has an extremely wide remit. As well as inspecting schools, colleges and teacher training providers, it is responsible for the inspection of nurseries, children's centres, children's homes, child minders, adoption and fostering agencies, local authority children's services, work-based learning and skills providers,

[33] Alison Wolf, *Review of Vocational Education – The Wolf Report* (DfE, March 2011).
[34] Graham Stuart, 'Transforming GCSE rankings is an educational breakthrough', *The Guardian*, 15 October 2013.
[35] Department for Education, *Reforming the Accountability System for Secondary Schools: Government's Response to the February to May 2013 Consultation on Secondary School Accountability* (October 2013).

adult and community learning, and education and training in prisons; it also monitors the work of the Independent Schools Inspectorate. In March 2013 it employed 1,275 people, having lost 176 in the previous year due to cost constraints. In that year it had conducted 8,328 inspections of schools, colleges and adult learning and skills.

The government was fortunate (though it did not always see it that way) to be able to recruit an excellent new chief inspector, Sir Michael Wilshaw, who took up the post on 1 January 2012. Not only was he the founding head teacher of the highly successful Mossbourne Academy (built on the site of the notorious Hackney Downs school in Hackney[36]), whose success had convinced ministers of the rightness of academies, but he was independent, forthright and not afraid of challenging ministers.[37] He had urged the Secretary of State to retain Baroness Morgan as the chair of Ofsted, but she was not offered a further term and her removal was widely seen as political. He has continued to press for the power to inspect academy chains, which the government seems reluctant to grant him (perhaps through fear of putting off sponsors). He had the grace to admit that he had overstepped the mark in his vehement protests that the Department for Education was using two critical think-tank reports on Ofsted to brief against him, 'but it was a spontaneous burst of fury'.[38]

Under his leadership, a new and simplified framework for inspection, developed by his predecessor, Christine Gilbert, on a steer from government, was implemented and revised.[39] The main criteria for judging a school became pupil achievement, teaching quality, behaviour and safety, and leadership and management. The importance of teaching is underlined by making a grade of outstanding for it a requirement for the school to be judged outstanding overall. Under Sir Michael's leadership, the grade 'satisfactory' was replaced by 'requires improvement', signalling to schools that they could not rest on their laurels. He has sought to increase the proportion of inspectors with recent and relevant experience of the settings in which they operate and he has

[36] Fran Abrams and Judith Judd, 'A school that fell from greatness', The Independent, 28 July 1995.

[37] Peter Wilby 'Is Mossbourne Academy's success down to its traditionalist headteacher?', The Guardian, 5 January 2010.

[38] Richard Garner, 'Chief school inspector urged Michael Gove not to sack Baroness Sally Morgan', The Independent, 12 February 2013.

[39] Ofsted, The Framework for School Inspection, Reference No. 120100, July 2014.

appointed eight regional directors to improve Ofsted's regional performance (whose areas are not coterminous with the DfE's subsequent
Regional School Commissioners). Ofsted in its current form is unwieldy,
but rather than accepting advice to divide it, with one inspectorate
focusing on education and the other on children's services,[40] the government has been adding to the demands made upon it. In recent months
Ofsted has become something of a 'hit squad', descending on schools
against which allegations of extremism have been made. There have
also been reports of Ofsted marking down schools with predominantly
White British intakes and also Christian schools for not giving enough
attention to diversity.[41] The political agenda of 'British values' must be
one of the most difficult things Ofsted has had to handle.

Examinations, tests and the curriculum

Examinations and tests

The coalition government embarked on major changes to the content and
form of GCSE and A-levels. This seemed to be very much a personal
crusade on the part of Michael Gove, when he was the Secretary of State.
He had benefited greatly from an excellent education and wanted an
education of similar quality to be available for all children. He could
recognize an authentic examination and curriculum when he saw them,
and he felt passionately that those that were in place were not them. The
outgoing Labour administration had left him a vehicle for bringing about
the changes he sought. In 2007 it had announced its intention of budding
off the exams regulatory functions of the then Qualifications and Curriculum Authority into a separate body. This was confirmed by the Apprenticeship, Skills, Children and Learning Act 2009, which established Ofqual
as an independent body reporting to Parliament rather than ministers.

    The new regulator was slow to find its feet, but in March 2011 the
government made another excellent appointment in Glenys Stacey, a

---

[40] House of Commons Education Committee, *The Role and Performance of Ofsted*,
Volume I, HC 570-1 (The Stationery Office, 17 April 2011).

[41] 'Ofsted criticises school for lack of diversity', *BBC News Lincolnshire*, 20 November
2014; Sarah Harris, 'Christian school claims it faces closure for failing to invite imams
to assembly in line with new government policy promoting "British values"', *Mail
Online*, 25 October 2014.

solicitor by training with wide experience of running public bodies. As Head of Animal Health (formerly the State Veterinary Service), she had played a major part in minimizing the spread of foot and mouth disease during the potentially serious outbreak of 2007. Arguably even greater skills would be called upon to see through the exam reforms which the government wanted at breakneck speed. Peter Wilby summed her up neatly in a *Guardian* profile: 'a soft voice and great charm, but there is an underlying sternness'.[42]

She had a difficult initiation. Ofqual found itself in the eye of a storm over the 2012 GCSE English results.[43] The government let it be known to Ofqual that it wanted it to bear down on the ever-rising exam grades. In A-levels they had risen every year since 1982, and in GCSEs every year since their inception in 1988. Ofqual found it could do this by pinning GCSE outcomes to the Key Stage 2 results of the cohort, and A-level grades to those for GCSE. English GCSE results, a cornerstone of accountability, dropped sharply in 2012, provoking loud protests from schools. An interim report by Ofqual published in August 2012 found that the grade boundaries used for modules submitted in January had been over-generous, leading schools to expect better results than they received. The boundaries had been corrected for the June modules with a consequent lowering of the pass rate.[44] The complaint now became that different standards had been applied within the same examination. Meanwhile, Wales had conducted its own inquiry,[45] as a result of which the Welsh examination board was ordered to remark its GCSE English exams so that the results were comparable to 2011. It all got very heated and an alliance of professional bodies, teachers, pupils and councils applied for, and was granted, a judicial review against Ofqual and two exam boards, AQA and Edexcel. It was held in December 2012 and reported in February 2013, when it essentially vindicated Ofqual, and this defused a tense situation.[46] But a rift had developed between the regulators in England, Wales and

---

[42] Peter Wilby, 'Exam regulator in the front line', *The Guardian*, 2 July 2012.

[43] Covered in detail in House of Commons Education Committee, *2012 GCSE English Results* (HC204, First Report of Session 2013-14, 11 June 2013).

[44] Ofqual, *GCSE English Awards 2012: A Regulatory Report*, August 2012.

[45] Welsh Government, *GCSE English Language 2012: An Investigation into the Outcomes for Candidates in Wales*, September 2012.

[46] Judicial Review before Lord Justice Elias and Mrs Justice Sharp, Neutral Citation Number: [2013] EWHC 211 (Admin), Case Nos. CO/11409/2012 and CO/11413/2012, Date 13/02/2013.

also Northern Ireland, with the risk that the qualifications in the three jurisdictions, though with the same name, will become increasingly different.

Having come through largely unscathed, Ofqual embarked on some immediate changes. In advance of the full exam reforms it announced that January units would be graded at the same time as the June units, marking tolerances would be tightened and, after consulting, removed the teacher-marked speaking and listening element from the overall English grade because there was no written evidence that could be checked. But the main thrust of its work was to see through the substantial reforms the government wished to make to GCSEs, A-levels and vocational qualifications. This is an intrinsically lengthy process involving determining the content, Ofqual drawing up assessment structures and grading arrangements, and the Awarding Bodies devising examinations to be submitted to Ofqual for accreditation and regulation. Once ready the exams would need to be in schools a year before first teaching, with in the case of GCSEs and A-levels the first examination two years later. Even with speed being of the essence, on current plans, the last A-level in the present round of reforms – maths – is not due to be taken till 2019.

The process has been further complicated in a number of ways. To speed up reform, GCSEs and A-levels are being revised at the same time when, since the latter builds on the former, it might have seemed logical to do so in sequence. The reason why maths is not to have its new A-level examined till 2019 is that the substantial changes to the GCSE have been accepted as making this necessary. The government has changed its mind on several occasions. It had originally wanted the new qualifications in the EBacc subjects to be called English Baccalaureate Certificates, which would exist alongside GCSEs in the other subjects, and it flirted with the idea of having just one awarding body for each subject. Both proposals were dropped. There were, however, to be major structural changes. GCSEs and A-levels were to be mainly examined at the end rather than in modules, and by external papers rather than teacher assessment. Science practicals are to be dropped from the grading of science A-levels, because the assessment is not thought to be robust enough to withstand the pressure of league tables. Grades for GCSEs are to be changed from A*–G to 9–1, with some statistical juggling involved in establishing the equivalence to the old scale at the generally accepted passing grade of 'C'. Since some revised GCSEs will be in use before the others, at least two cohorts will be graded in two ways. AS-levels are to be decoupled from A-levels so that, although they can be taught alongside each other, the AS does not count towards the A-level. This change has been criticized by some of the leading universities, especially Cambridge, which has urged schools to continue to enter pupils for the AS.[47] The Labour Party has said that if elected in 2015 it would reverse this decision. The rate at which the reformed qualifications are to be brought in has meant that the better textbooks which the government wishes to see are unlikely to be ready on time.

A major issue in revising the content of subjects beyond the EBacc and the core A-levels is how it is to be arrived at. The DfE managed, directly or indirectly, the process of deciding the subject content of the first tranche of reforms. It was settled for the EBacc GCSEs in-house and for the core A-levels on the advice of the Smith Review and the A Level Content Advisory Board (ALCAB) formed by the Russell Group of Universities.[48] But neither the government nor ALCAB wants to take responsibility for the remaining GCSEs and A-levels. With nothing replacing the curriculum half of the old Qualifications and Curriculum Authority, Ofqual is considering asking the awarding bodies themselves to propose content. A similar issue arises with vocational qualifications, including the new TechBacc, where reform has been lagging. Given the huge variety of technical and vocational qualifications, Ofqual has dropped the requirement for prior accreditation and is consulting on abandoning the Qualifications and Credit Framework to make regulation more flexible.[49]

If all this were not enough, Ofqual is also required to keep the Key Stage 2 tests under review. These are not only important in themselves, but also as a baseline for the progress measure by which in future secondary schools will be judged. The Key Stage 2 tests are devised by the Standards and Testing Agency, an executive arm of the DfE. Key

[47] Katherine Sellgren, 'Cambridge urges schools to enter students for AS-levels', *BBC News*, 6 November 2014.

[48] Mark Smith, *Results of the Consultation on Revised A Level Subject Content. Recommendation for the Secretary of State*, March 2014 (accessed at www.gov.uk/government/consultations, 5 December 2014).

[49] Glenys Stacey, 'Putting validity at the heart of what we do', Speech to the Federation of Awarding Bodies, Leicester, 14 October 2014.

Stage 2 tests have also been reformed. Following the Bew Report,[50] published in June 2011, schools with primary-age pupils are required to administer Level 3–5 tests in grammar, punctuation and spelling, reading and maths, with composition assessed by teachers. There are also separate Level 6 tests, but there have been relatively few takers and an extremely low pass rate, leading Ofqual to express doubts about them in their current form. New Key Stage 2 tests are due to be introduced in 2016 which will be more demanding, with higher and more ambitious standards.

National Curriculum

The sheer scale and variety of the changes to GCSEs, A-levels and vocational qualifications reduced those who will have to deliver them to near silence; not so the national curriculum.[51] As Kenneth Baker, the father of the first national curriculum, found, specifying the required content of subjects, even maths, raises hackles. In the 2010 white paper the government announced it intended to review and reform the whole national curriculum. It was going to set down the essential knowledge and understanding and free teachers to teach it and around it, so that it became 'a rigorous benchmark ... rather than a prescriptive strait-jacket'.[52] The review was formally announced in January 2011, setting up an Advisory Committee advised by an Expert Panel. The Panel produced an interim report in December 2011 full of the complexities which the government detested. After a long delay, Michael Gove sent the government's response congratulating the Panel on its 'superb work', but not committing to the recommendations.[53] Instead, at the same time, it published draft programmes of study for the core subjects at Key Stages 1 and 2. These included more demanding curricula for English, maths and science, and detailed specifications in the basics such as spelling. The Expert Panel was appalled and two wrote to resign in October 2011, but were persuaded to stay till December 2011. When

[50] Lord Bew, *Independent Review of Key Stage 2 Testing, Assessment and Accountability*, Final Report, June 2011.
[51] Nerys Roberts, *National Curriculum Review* (House of Commons Library Standard Note SN 06796, 1 May 2014).
[52] Department for Education, *The Importance of Teaching*, p. 10.
[53] Letter from Secretary of State for Education to Tim Oates, Chair of the Expert Panel, 11 June 2012.

the June 2012 proposals came out, they took to the press and electronic media to rubbish the proposals.

They rather naively claimed that the schools minister, Nick Gibb, had had a 'significant influence',[54] while thousands of consultation responses had been disregarded. Nick Gibb has a very public enthusiasm for systematic synthetic phonics, having been the first politician in England to recognize the significance of the seminal work in Clackmannanshire.[55] It is perhaps not surprising, therefore, that this should be specified as the method of developing word reading skills and there should be a phonics check at the age of 6 (controversially including some non-words). As a minister, he was also known to be a stickler for correct punctuation and spelling, often staying late to correct the letters that had been drafted for him. So the primary English curriculum does bear his imprint, but as Minister for Schools that had been his privilege. Apart from phonics, the government has been very clear it has no wish to tell teachers how to teach. In order to provide them with a 'tool kit' of what works best and research evidence, Michael Gove in November 2010 announced an Education Endowment Fund of £110 million,[56] later raised to £125 million, which was won by the Sutton Trust in association with the Impetus Trust.

The process of formal consultation on the curriculum was begun in February 2013 with, for the first time, draft programmes of study for foundation subjects, such as history, geography and music at Key Stage 1 and 2, together with all the secondary programmes with the exception of English, maths and science at Key Stage 4. Again there was an outcry. *The Independent* published a letter from 100 academics in March 2013 criticizing the Secretary of State for expecting too much too young and the 'endless lists of spellings, facts and rules'.[57] Michael Gove hit back strongly in the *Daily Mail*, dismissing the signatories as 'enemies of promise' and

[54] William Stewart and Helen Ward, 'Experts wanted to quit curriculum panel over "prescriptive" proposals', *Times Education Supplement*, 22 June 2012.

[55] Rhona Johnston and Joyce Watson, *A Seven Year Study of the Effects of Synthetic Phonics on Reading and Spelling Attainment*, Insight 17 (The Scottish Government, 11 February 2005).

[56] DFE and Michael Gove, 'New endowment fund to turn around the weakest schools and raise standards for disadvantaged pupils', 3 November 2010 (www.gov.uk).

[57] Letter from Michael Bassey and 99 others, 'Gove will bury pupils in facts and rules', *The Independent*, 20 March 2013.

saying, 'I refuse to surrender to the Marxist teachers hell-bent on destroying our schools.'[58] This is so unlike his reputed private persona that one wonders whether he in fact wrote it. But it is consistent with his more aggressive journalistic self.

In July 2013 the DfE issued a report summarizing the consultation responses and in view of the changes it had made it announced another consultation. In September 2013 it reported on this and released the programmes of study to be introduced in September 2014.[59] The long struggle looked to be over, but the impact may be less than supposed since the 4,000-plus academies, free schools, university technical colleges and studio schools do not have to teach the national curriculum, but a broad and balanced curriculum including English, maths, science, plus religious education and personal and relationships education.

Education 16–18

Although the government was very clear about its intentions as regards autonomy, accountability, examinations and tests, and (as we shall see) teacher training, it does not appear to have fully thought through the final years of secondary schooling.[60] It accepted Gordon Brown's policy of raising the participation age to 17 in 2013 and 18 in 2015 legislated in the 2008 Education and Skills Act, while removing the sanctions for non-compliance.[61] Raising the participation age is not the same as requiring pupils to stay at school. It could also involve work-based learning such as an apprenticeship, or full-time work or volunteering provided they included part-time training leading to a qualification. Systematic provision of this kind could, as advocates maintain, provide the qualifications and occupational skills young people need as a basis for their futures.

[58] Michael Gove, 'I refuse to surrender to the Marxist teachers hell-bent on destroying our schools', *Daily Mail*, 23 March 2013.

[59] Department for Education, *Reforming the National Curriculum in England*, 11 September 2013.

[60] Kenneth Baker, *14–18: A New Vision for Secondary Education* (London: Bloomsbury, 2013).

[61] 'School leaving age set to be 18', *BBC News*, 12 January 2007.

Different routes imply choices. But the government has not provided clear pathways, nor has it been consistent in the age at which decisions have to be taken. Moreover, it has weakened the advice available to parents and pupils in making choices. The government is ambivalent about the appropriate age for deciding between the different directions. On the whole, it seems to favour sixteen. It has devised the EBacc indicator to signal to schools that pupils should study the same core of academic subjects through to Year 11. It received support from the Wolf Report which found that vocational qualifications below the age of sixteen were of very poor quality and that international evidence showed countries were tending to converge on sixteen as the age at which young people went in different directions. These are not, of course, conclusive. The fact that many current vocational qualifications pre-sixteen were no good does not mean that they cannot be good. And since children in many countries start formal education later than in this country, in terms of years of schooling age fourteen or fifteen here is the equivalent of sixteen there. The key point is that we have just two years for upper secondary schooling compared to three or four in most of those countries. The government seems to have recognized this and has supported the development of university technical colleges and studio schools from the age of fourteen, and enabled further education colleges to admit from age fourteen.

Not only is the decision point unclear, but the government has not put in place the means by which parents and pupils can make informed choices. In fact, it has taken it away.[62] The 2011 Education Act transferred responsibility for careers advice to schools from Connexions, a DfE-funded independent careers advice service. Connexions was cut back to a phone and online facility unable to provide face-to-face guidance, and its remit as the National Careers Service does not extend to schools. At the same time, schools were released from their statutory duty to provide careers education and work experience. Whether teachers have the necessary expertise to provide sound advice about the full range of occupational opportunities and the state of the labour market is open to question. Moreover, schools are funded on

---

[62] House of Commons Education Committee, *Careers Guidance for Young People: the Impact of the New Duty on Schools* (HC 632-1, Seventh Report of Session 2012–13, 15 January 2013).

pupil numbers so there is a major incentive for schools to advise pupils to stay with them.

Even more important is the lack of an array of attractive options leading on from school. The government has been working hard to establish a successful modern apprenticeship system, hoping to capitalize on the prestige of traditional apprenticeships. A scheme using the name was launched in 1994 by the Major government, with the apprenticeship as a container for a stipulated mix of national vocational and other qualifications. The present government has attempted to make apprenticeships more demanding. In 2012 it announced that all apprenticeships must have a minimum duration of at least a year and, in 2013, following the Richard Review,[63] it held consultations on standards, assessment and funding. An apprenticeship became defined as a job that requires substantial and sustained training, leading to the achievement of an apprenticeship standard and the development of transferable skills. Although often seen as for 16–18-year-olds, provisional figures for 2013–14 show 117,820 starts for young people in that age group compared with 314,580 starts for those who were older. There is more funding for 16–18-year-olds, but since payments to providers are based on the competences developed rather than the training undertaken, people already in work are a safer bet. Another important factor is that there is no clear jumping-off point from school into apprenticeships. The main qualification seems to be doing less well at GCSE than is required to go on to A-levels. The present government scrapped the young apprenticeships for 14–16-year-olds which served as a springboard, and the traineeship that it has introduced is catch-up provision post-16 for those whose GCSE results are even lower. In a sense the government's sparkling new apprenticeships are a castle in the air, floating above the school system and only loosely connected to it.

There has to be a suspicion that failure to use the opportunity of raising the participation age to create clear pathways from school to training and employment is because it was more about reducing youth unemployment than what it actually provided. At a stroke, it reduced the number of NEETs (Not in Education, Employment or Training),

---

[63] Doug Richard, *The Richard Review of Apprenticeships* (London: School for Startups, November 2012) (accessed at www.schoolforstartups.co.uk/richard-review/richard-review-full.pdf, 5 December 2014).

where the annual figures have been a continual source of embarrassment to successive governments. Raising the participation age will
only bring the benefits which Alan Johnson,[64] as the then Secretary of
State for Education and Skills, claimed when he announced it, if the
provision is well-designed and of a quality to enhance young people's
lives. Young people vote with their feet. Already there is a high truancy
rate among Year 11 pupils who feel there is nothing in school for
them. Young people will only freely participate in more education and
training if it genuinely gives them something.

Teachers and Teacher Training

Michael Gove has never been very popular with teachers. In a pre-2010
election debate at the Institute of Education between the education spokesmen of the three main parties David Laws was voted as having the best
policies, followed by Ed Balls, with Michael Gove a poor third. But since
he took office things have only got worse. The changes that he set in train
have been very unsettling. It has also been about money, with teachers
having their salaries held down. In primary schools the greatly increased
pupil numbers have led to over-crowding and discomfort. David Laws,
the senior Liberal Democrat, who since September 2012 has combined the
posts of minister for schools and minister in the Cabinet Office, where he
has a cross-party role overseeing the implementation of the Coalition
Agreement, played a very straight bat on school places, listening to the
arguments, providing measured responses and initiating action, so it never
really took off as a grievance as it might have done.

    At the heart of the teachers' disaffection has been the belligerent
stance Michael Gove has taken. In my (very few) encounters with him,
he has been charming, courteous and amusing. But, egged on by some
of his advisers, he seems to have become bewitched by the metaphor of
'the Blob', first used by Sir Christopher Woodhead, to characterize the
education establishment at a time when he was wearied by his experiences as Chief Inspector of Schools. It is taken from a 1958 film about a
giant amoeba-like alien that seeped everywhere and became stronger
through all the initial attempts to destroy it. Michael Gove apparently

---

[64] 'School leaving age set to be 18', *BBC News*, 12 January 2007.

feels that something similar has been happening in schools in obstructing the government's reforms. We saw how sharply he bit back at the 100 academics who dared to question his curriculum changes. In the film, Steve McQueen defeats the Blob by freezing it, but coldness towards the teachers has only alienated them further. Since these are the very people on whom the successful implementation of the reforms rests, this hardly seems the best strategy. Teachers have expressed their anger in a series of strikes over pay, pensions and conditions. On Michael Gove's removal to be Chief Whip, a comment online in response to *The Guardian* article about it simply said. 'I can hear thousands of teachers around the country all cheering very loudly!'[65]

Amongst those most unsettled by the government's education reforms have been the university teacher trainers. The 2010 white paper clearly stated that the government intended to 'provide more opportunities for a larger proportion of trainees to learn on the job by improving and expanding the best of current school-based routes'.[66] This was seriously bad news for the university departments of education, where funding of teacher training was a stable source of income, in part subsidizing the research. Now their allocation of funded training places was to be progressively reduced and made available to schools consortia. The one ray of comfort was that the schools would have to seek out partnerships with institutions through which the money would be channelled. In the end the new arrangements benefited the popular and successful university providers, who were able to increase their intakes, but some of the less well regarded were left struggling. The government's creation of School Direct, as it is called, accords with the research evidence. School-led programmes have had higher entry rates into teaching and tend to be rated more favourably by newly qualified trainees.[67] But given their fears the university departments have been gleefully pointing to impending teacher shortages. It appears that schools are applying higher standards in selecting trainees, tending to view them as future colleagues. University departments, on the other hand, tended to aim to fill their allocated places with the best available

[65] Nicholas Watt and Patrick Wintour, 'Michael Gove demoted to chief whip as Cameron shows no sentimentality', *The Guardian*, 15 July 2014.

[66] Department for Education, *The Importance of Teaching*, para. 2.21, p23.

[67] Alan Smithers, Pamela Robinson and Mandy-D. Coughlan, *The Good Teacher Training Guide 2013* (Buckingham: CEER, 2014).

applicants, whatever their qualifications and capabilities, so as to draw down the full funding. However, if the gloomy predictions are borne out, teacher supply will be on the agenda once more.

Higher Education

In the run-up to the 2010 election the Conservatives had a vision of the kind of higher education system they wanted. They were confident that the Browne Review would recommend removing the cap from tuition fees. With the students making a larger contribution towards tuition costs, there did not have to be the same limits on home-domiciled student numbers. Universities could be freed to determine their own student intakes and more institutions could be accorded university status, including private providers. A genuine market would emerge which would drive up quality.

They did not, however, win power, and their Liberal Democrat partners had made a cast-iron pledge during the election campaign to oppose any increase in tuition fees and aim to abolish them, underlined by each candidate being photographed holding aloft a large signed card. It was a hard compromise to make, but for the greater good the Liberal Democrats agreed to make it. The two parties settled on working within the legal framework that the Blair government had put in place, in order to ease passage through Parliament. In early December 2010 about half the Liberal Democrat MPs (28 out of 57), including Nick Clegg and Vince Cable, whose department was to administer them, voted for the new arrangements. But the Liberal Democrats had driven a hard bargain to ameliorate the impact on students from low-income backgrounds: there would be higher tuition fees but capped, to be funded through student loans; the earnings threshold before payments became due would be higher at £21,000; interest rates would be dependent on earnings; and the repayment period would be increased from twenty-five to thirty years, after which any remaining balance would be written off. The coalition also adopted Labour's two-tier fee cap, with the lower level set at £6,000 and the higher at £9,000. In order to charge at the higher rate universities had to make access agreements with the Office for Fair Access (OFFA) on bursaries and admission of students from certain backgrounds. Charging the maximum fee was anticipated to be an exception, but in the event it became the norm. The teaching grant to universities was abolished for all but the most expensive subjects.

The compromise satisfied no one. The Liberal Democrats were vilified for going back on their word and still bear the scars. Students did not at first grasp how generous the loan arrangements were and took to the streets in protest. The government now has to tolerate greater uncertainty over the considerable cost of funding higher education. If there are winners they are the universities which have received extra money, but in return for dancing to the tune of a beefed-up OFFA.

The government's loan arrangements for students have been criticized by the National Audit Office, two Select Committees and at least two independent institutes. In essence, the criticism is that the student loan scheme, as presently constituted, is building up a massive amount of public debt which the Department for Business, Innovation and Skills (BIS) is unable to forecast accurately. The National Audit Office concluded that BIS has no transparent and readily understandable forecast for the amount it expects to be collected each year, does not have a collections performance target, does not know whether non-payers are earning enough to repay, and does not do enough to chase borrowers living overseas.[68]

The Public Accounts Committee found that the amount of outstanding debt is likely to rise to £200 billion in 2013 prices by 2042, of which 40 per cent (£70–80 billion) is unlikely to be repaid.[69] It found that BIS was consistently overestimating what is due to be repaid by about 8 per cent a year. By July 2014 the predicted amount of outstanding debt in 2044 at 2014 prices was reported by the BIS Select Committee to be £330 billion.[70] The BIS Select Committee report also includes evidence from the Higher Education Policy Institute (HEPI) that the original projection was for 28 per cent of debt not to be repaid, but this has been continually revised upwards until it now stands at 45 per cent. The Institute for Fiscal Studies has calculated that the cost to the taxpayer of the new arrangements which came into operation in September 2012 was only 5 per cent less than it would have been under the scheme that it replaced.[71] The income per student to universities for teaching

[68] National Audit Office, *Student Loan Repayments* (HC 818, 27 November 2013).
[69] Public Accounts Committee, *Student Loan Repayments* (HC 886, Forty-fourth Report of Session 2013-14, 10 February 2014).
[70] Business, Innovation and Skills Committee, *Student Loans* (HC 558, Third Report of Session 2014–15, 22 July 2014).
[71] Claire Crawford, Rowena Crawford and Wenchao Jin, *Estimating the Public Cost of Student Loans*, IFS Report R94 (Institute for Fiscal Studies, April 2014).

was, however, boosted by 27.6 per cent. The government had hoped to sell part of the student loan book to recoup some of the money, but this has for the moment been put on hold because internal estimates show that it would only raise £2 billion against the hoped-for £12 billion.[72]

The loan arrangements are potentially rescuable by reducing the payment threshold to what it was before and holding it there. But will any government be brave enough? HEPI has produced a very interesting comparison between student loans in Australia and England.[73] It argues that the Australian scheme is better designed and there graduates pay back their loans more quickly. A student loan scheme is thus practicable and manageable. But the government in its required response to the BIS Select Committee has ruled out 'a formal review of the sustainability of the student loans system in England'.[74]

Coalition compromises over higher education have had another consequence. They have greatly strengthened the hand of the Office of Fair Access (OFFA). In order to set a tuition fee above £6,000 universities have had to make an annual access agreement with that body. These agreements have had to show that the university was moving towards levels of recruitment from identified groups to the extent calculated by the Higher Education Funding Council for England. In particular, they were expected to reach specified proportions of students from state schools, low-income postcodes and low-participation neighbourhoods. They found themselves being continually exhorted by SPA (Supporting Professionalism in Admissions), a body set up by HEFC(E), to contextualize admissions.[75] This means essentially admitting on potential rather than examination results, which would be a good idea if there were a measure of potential, but it has not been possible so far to devise one that provides information as good as A-levels. In seeking to comply with OFFA's requirements universities can find themselves having to put social factors above talent. HEFCE's own research has shown that students from more prosperous postcodes are more likely to get a good

[72] John Morgan, 'Student loan system "needs urgent review", say MPs', *Times Higher Education*, 22 July 2014.

[73] Nick Hillman, *A Comparison of Student Loans in England and Australia*, HEPI Report 66 (HEPI, April 2014).

[74] Chris Parr, 'Government rules out loans review', *Times Higher Education*, 6 November 2014.

[75] Kath Bridger, Jenny Shaw and Joanne Moore, *Fair Admissions to Higher Education* (Cheltenham: SPA, February 2012).

degree than those from the low-income postcodes whose case is being pressed.[76] Similarly, some universities in their access agreements are committing to raising the proportion of students from ethnic minorities, but HEFC(E)'s research shows that White entrants are much more likely to get a good degree than Black or Asian entrants. Deciding which students to admit to university where there are many more applicants than places is difficult enough without having to take into account group characteristics over individual abilities.

David Willetts, the thoughtful and popular Minister of State for the Universities and Science in BIS, was another casualty, along with Michael Gove, in the July 2014 reshuffle, possibly as a scapegoat for student loans or for having strongly opposed the Home Office over the inclusion of international students in migration figures. He was certainly highly regarded by the science community. Sir Paul Nurse, President of the Royal Society, said he had been 'an outstanding science minister, respected not only in the UK but throughout the world'.[77] He is widely appreciated for getting the science budget ring-fenced at a time of austerity, though he was going with the grain since the Treasury has been predisposed to be helpful to science since Gordon Brown's time there. What the universities made of Willetts' contribution to 'fair access' we do not know, since they have held their tongues in complying with the requirements of what is still their monopoly customer, the government.

Funding

The fundamental problem that the coalition government has had in education, as in all the departments, is that there has not been enough money for all that it wanted to do. The DfE fared better than most in the October 2010 Spending Review,[78] being asked for cumulative savings in real terms of 3.4 per cent by 2014–15. Within the overall figure the 5–16 schools budget, including a new £2.5 billion pupil premium, was

---

[76] Higher Education Funding for England, *Differences in Degree Outcomes: Key Findings*, Issues Paper 03 (Bristol: HEFCE, March 2014).

[77] Quoted in 'David Willetts quits as universities minister', *Times Higher Education*, 14 July 2014.

[78] HM Treasury, *Spending Review 2010* (Cm 7942, The Stationery Office, October 2010).

set to rise by 0.1 per cent each year. This meant, however, that real-terms savings of 12 per cent were looked for in the non-schools budget, to be achieved by cutting administration costs, reducing 16–19 unit costs, and rejigging the Education Maintenance Allowance. Labour's Building Schools for the Future programme was ended, reducing the capital settlement by 60 per cent over the period of the Spending Review. Although education had got off comparatively lightly in the circumstances – BIS was asked to make cumulative savings of 23 per cent – the reduction felt worse than it actually was because in the decade to 2010 public spending on education grew by 5.1 per cent per year in real terms. As a percentage of GDP, it rose from 4.5 per cent to 6.4 per cent over the decade.[79] The Spending Review reversed this, but the impact has been somewhat softened by the Department for Education's habit of underspending.

Within its constrained budget the DfE has had to find in previous years the money for its planned reforms. By far the biggest increase in costs came from the academies programme. The National Audit Office looked at the first two years of the programme, when the number of academies had risen tenfold from 203 to 2,309.[80] It found that about a billion of the spending was additional cost, largely because the funding system set up for a small number of academies could not cope effectively with the expansion. About a third of the overspend was due to money wrongly given to local authorities which the DfE was not able to recover to offset against academy funding. Premises for free schools have had to come from the greatly reduced amount allocated to capital spend. The National Audit Office in December 2013 found that 8 per cent of the Department's capital budget had been earmarked for this purpose.[81] By September 2013, 174 free schools had been opened at estimated capital spend to March 2014 of £743 million, about double what had been assumed.

If money was found for academies, free schools, the pupil premium, and later free school meals for all infant school children, reductions in other areas had to compensate. Teachers' pay was frozen

---

[79] Haroon Chowdry and Luke Sibieta, *Trends in Education and Schools Spending*, IFS Briefing Note BN121 (Institute for Fiscal Studies, October 2011).

[80] National Audit Office, *Managing the Expansion of the Academies Programme* (HC 682, 21 November, 2012).

[81] National Audit Office, *Establishing Free Schools* (HC 881, 21 November, 2012).

from 2011 to 2013, followed by 1 per cent rises in 2013 and 2014. The DfE has had to plan for a reduction in administration costs by half between 2010 and 2015. The closing of, or staff reductions in, quangos has contributed some savings. Even the Education Funding Agency, which, among other things, has responsibility for monitoring the finances of academies and free schools, had its budget cut by 15 per cent in spite of the rapid expansion of these schools. Ofsted, too, had its budget cut. School Direct received less funding per place than the highly successful Graduate Teacher Programme which preceded it, and this may have slowed its take-up. Providing for participation to age 18 has been hamstrung by financial constraints. FE budgets for education 16–18 have been cash-limited with no allowance for inflation and course funding has been cut by up to 3 per cent a year. The funding gap between pre-16 and post-16 education has been estimated at 22 per cent.[82]

In its 2010 white paper the government announced proposals for introducing a national funding formula for schools. It had found that in an internal analysis of seventy-two similar schools without sixth forms outside London, the amount received per pupil varied by as much as 50 per cent.[83] The government formally consulted in April 2011 and July 2011, issued a next steps document in March 2012[84] and consulted again in March 2014, this time on arrangements for 2015–16.[85] It had become evident that applying a fairer funding formula was not going to be easy, because of the turbulence it would cause in councils and schools with high current levels of funding which stood to lose a large slice of it. In the March 2014 consultation it claimed that, in 2014–15, local authorities were allocating 90 per cent of schools funding based on the needs of pupils, compared with 71 per cent in 2012–13. The steps outlined for 2015–16 would involve calculating the amount of money a local authority could expect to receive from a formula based on five pupil characteristics (age, deprivation, care status, low prior attainment, and English as a second language) and three school criteria (lump sum,

[82] Julian Gravatt, *The Department for Education Budget after 2015* (Association of Colleges, May 2014).

[83] Department for Education, *The Importance of Teaching*, p 79.

[84] 'School funding: moving towards a national funding formula' (House of Commons Library Standard Note SN/SP/6702, 14 August 2013).

[85] Department for Education, *Fairer Schools Funding: Arrangements for 2015–2016*, July 2014.

small school factor and area cost). An extra £350 million was made available to be distributed to fund schools in the least fairly funded authorities. Those authorities would then distribute the money to their schools according to their own formulas. Not a national formula, but at least a first step.

Unfinished business

The coalition government has left significant unfinished business. The shape of the future schools system is still unclear. Is it envisaged that all state schools will eventually become academies, and if so how will they be coordinated, regulated and administered? GCSEs and A-levels are being reformed on a very tight timetable with the risk of slippage as the details of what is involved are fully taken on board. The attention given to academic qualifications has meant that the reform of vocational qualifications is only just getting under way, and the flagship apprenticeship programmes are left without clear ladders to them from schools. There has been no real attempt to redesign education 14–18 to optimize the benefits of raising the participation age to 18. The switch from university-led to school-led teacher training runs the risk of teacher shortages in the short term, and with the training now so devolved it is harder to obtain the data to get the picture clear. The separation of higher education from school education in government departments has left further education neglected. We still await a Fair Funding Formula for distributing money equitably to schools. The finances of higher education will become an incubus for future governments if the student loan arrangements are not sorted out.

The coalition embarked on the final year of the parliament with new people at the helms of education and higher education. On 14 July 2014 David Cameron began the reshuffling of his Conservatives ministers to form what, barring accidents, will be his line-up for the May 2015 election. Among the prominent casualties were Michael Gove and David Willetts. They had been the pivotal ministers in the government's drive to improve the education system. Of the two, David Willetts' departure was the more surprising. He had been a very popular science minister and if he was being blamed for the student loans disaster that is not entirely fair since he was only the minister of state and it was his boss, Vince Cable, who was ultimately responsible. But Vince Cable is a Liberal Democrat in a post which under the coalition agreement is within the gift of the leader of his party.

Much less surprising, in retrospect, was the demotion of Michael Gove. Many supported his aims of better teachers, more freedom for the front line, better exams, a core rather than a prescriptive curriculum, and smarter accountability. But his increasingly pugilistic and mistrusting style alienated even those who wanted the same ends. So why did it end in tears? Perhaps it was his utter frustration at how long the changes were taking. Not realizing how difficult it was to speed up some of the things for which he was asking, he seems to have interpreted the delays as subversive opposition. Perhaps he was fired up by advisers as passionate, or even more passionate, about the reforms. In particular, Dominic Cummings, the best-known and most influential adviser on schools in fifty years, was verbally ferocious. He was contemptuous of those who did not fully appreciate the 'cultural revolution' that they were bringing about. He is on record as having described the prime minister as 'a sphinx without a riddle'[86] and the deputy prime minister as 'self-obsessed, sanctimonious and dishonest'.[87] If this was the atmosphere surrounding Michael Gove, it is not difficult to see where the overblown rhetoric may have come from. But as a highly successful former journalist Michael Gove must have realized how counterproductive it would be. His own emotions seem to have taken over. On the eve of the Queen's Speech in June 2014, he got into a very public spat with Theresa May, the Home Secretary, over who was to blame for the failure to combat extremism in schools. An immediate inquiry by the Cabinet Secretary, Sir Jeremy Heywood, concluded that Michael Gove was to blame, and he was forced to issue an abject apology. David Cameron had had enough and, in July, asked his good friend to step down to become Chief Whip.

Gove's and Willetts' successors seem to have been asked to play mainly holding roles. The new minister for universities and science, Greg Clark, is keeping such a low profile that he remains almost unknown to the general public. But Nicky Morgan, Gove's

[86] Ben Quinn, 'Michael Gove ally Dominic Cummings in personal attack on David Cameron', *The Guardian*, 16 June 2014.
[87] Steven Swinford, 'Nick Clegg is a "self-obsessed, revolting character"', *The Daily Telegraph*, 27 April 2014.

replacement, was determined on a fresh start. She immediately had the Permanent Secretary sack Gove's then three special advisers (Cummings had left in January 2014 but had still been a frequent visitor),[88] although it might have been expected that at least one would be asked to stay on to smooth the transition. She has been out there battling to keep the reform agenda on course, but with some rebalancing. Between September 2014 and January 2015 she appeared four times before the Education Select Committee, submitting to grillings from well-briefed MPs on extremism in schools, academies, exams and careers, unusually without requiring the protection of the Permanent Secretary or junior ministers. The sessions revealed the enormity of the brief with which she has been coming to terms. But she has also wanted to set a different tone. In her speech to the Conservative Party Conference she announced a new £5 million fund to support innovative ideas to help schools and young people to develop character: 'For too long there has been a false choice between academic standards and activities that build character and resilience. But the two should go hand in hand.'[89]

In some ways the Coalition government has had an easy ride on education. It has been largely unchallenged by a Labour Party which does not seem to have a vision of its own. The opposition has contented itself with highlighting particular issues such as unqualified teachers, the decoupling of AS from A-levels, and the divide between state and private schools. The coalition has become increasingly confident that its education reforms will become enduring, not easily overturned by a future government, but there is still a lot of unfinished business. Whichever government takes power in 2015 will still have a great deal to do to make England's education world class.

---

[88] Steerpike, 'Nicky Morgan hides in office as civil servant sacks Gove's special advisers', *The Spectator*, 21 July 2014.

[89] Nicky Morgan, Speech to Conservative Party Conference 2014 (accessed at http://press.conservatives.com/post/98807929855/nicky-morgan-speech-to-conservative-party, 5 December 2014).

11 THE COALITION AND SOCIETY (III): HEALTH AND LONG-TERM CARE

HOWARD GLENNERSTER

The inheritance

Whatever Labour's failings in economic policy it left behind a much improved National Health Service (NHS).

- The share of the nation's resources devoted to health care had risen from one of the lowest among advanced economies to near parity. The share of the GDP devoted to health care – public and private – had risen from 6.6 per cent when Blair took office to 9.6 per cent in 2010.
- The length of time patients had to wait for non-urgent procedures had fallen dramatically. It had never been so low. The number waiting for more than six months had fallen from 400,000 in mid-1998 to essentially nil by 2010 and those waiting three months from 700,000 to 7,000. Staffing levels had risen and physical plant had been modernized on a scale not seen since the 1960s.
- There was even *some* reduction in *some* health inequalities.[1]

As a result the NHS was enjoying unprecedented public support. The British Social Attitudes Survey showed overall satisfaction with the NHS was standing at 74 per cent in 2010 compared to only 39 per cent in 2001.[2]

---

[1] Polly Vizard and Polina Obolenskaya, *Labour's Record on Health (1997–2010)*, Social Policy in a Cold Climate Working Paper 2 (London: CASE, London School of Economics, 2013).

[2] *Ibid.*, Figure 14.

This posed a challenge to any incoming government bent on curbing public spending. But it also eased their task somewhat. The NHS was not on the rocks. It had some room for doing things more effectively.

The party manifestos

The Conservative manifesto promised that a future Conservative government would 'increase health spending in real terms every year'.[3] It would 'strengthen the powers of GPs as patients' expert guides through the health care system . . . putting them in charge of commissioning local services'.[4] It would 'scrap politically motivated targets'.[5] It would 'create an independent NHS board to allocate resources and provide commissioning guidelines'.[6]

The Liberal Democrats promised that they would 'Cut the size of the Department of Health by half' and 'scrap Strategic Health Authorities'.[7] They would 'integrate health and social care to create a seamless service'.[8] They would reduce central targets.[9] Crucially they would introduce elected Health Boards to take over the role of Primary Care Trusts and commission local health services.[10]

There was therefore some overlap between the two coalition partners' intentions but not much.

What change?

Over the period of the coalition government:

- The *English* health service underwent a change to its *organizational structure* so significant that 'you could actually see it from space' as

---

[3] Conservative Party, *Invitation to Join the Government of Britain: The Conservative Manifesto 2010* (London: Conservative Party, 2010), p. 45.

[4] *Ibid.*, p. 46.   [5] *Ibid.*   [6] *Ibid.*

[7] Liberal Democrats, *Liberal Democrat Manifesto 2010* (London: Liberal Democrats, 2010), pp. 40, 41.

[8] *Ibid.*, p. 41.   [9] *Ibid.*, p. 42.   [10] *Ibid.*, p. 43.

the service's Chief Executive put it.[11] Competition was placed at the heart of its legal framework.

- At the same time the NHS was to be 'protected' in financial terms but expected to do more with roughly the same resources.
- A new 'duty of candour' was placed on all NHS providers in England and all those who are contracted to provide care with NHS funds. This requires such organizations to disclose all errors in treatment that result in moderate or severe harm or death. This move arose directly from the abuses that occurred in the Mid Staffordshire Foundation Trust, which were extensively examined at a public enquiry chaired by Robert Francis QC.[12]
- Legislation was passed that will change the rules under which many individuals in *England* have to pay for their own long-term care.

Who was responsible?

There can be little doubt as to who was initially responsible for the train of events that led to the Health and Social Care Act 2012. It began life as the brain child of Andrew Lansley, the Conservative Party's shadow health spokesman from 2004 to 2010. He became Secretary of State for Health from the beginning of the new government in May 2010 and lasted in that post until September 2012. He not only initiated the ideas but drove through the legislation. His key role was explained to me by one insider:

> In the Conservative Party concern with the NHS is a train spotters' sport. No one had really felt the need to understand what Andrew Lansley was up to. He was a one man think tank – an NHS lover who was left alone and trusted.[13]

David Cameron had set the theme for Conservative health policy: 'We care about the NHS and will protect it.' The detail he left to a trusted expert and his old boss at Conservative Central Office.

---

[11] David Nicholson's address to the NHS Alliance Conference, 18 November 2010.

[12] *Report of the Mid Staffordshire NHS Foundation Trust Public Enquiry*, House of Commons (HC 947, London: The Stationery Office, 2013). The General Medical Council already places an ethical duty on individual clinicians to inform patients if anything goes wrong during their treatment and to remedy it insofar as is possible.

[13] Private information.

Yet it is clear from Nicholas Timmins' detailed account that anyone who had listened to Andrew Lansley's speeches as shadow minister should have known that something big was afoot. [14] He had devoted much of his tenure in that post to preparing his plans for government. It is clear from remarks he made afterwards that he was determined that his legislation should be far-reaching, detailed and so fundamental that it would be 'irreversible for a political generation'. No future Secretary of State would be able to simply walk in and do things differently.[15] The Department of Health certainly knew the outlines of the Conservative plans and were working on them in detail in case of a Conservative victory.

Why then did the legislation, and the explosion it caused, come as such a surprise, even to leading members of the Conservative Party as well as to Nick Clegg and the Liberal Democrat negotiators?[16]

One answer is that these intentions had been deliberately hidden from wider view, especially in the period when they were most likely to have been under scrutiny – in the run-up to the election. When Andrew Lansley explained his plans to medical consultants during the election campaign they were told that they would be freed of central targets and left to get on with their professional tasks. GPs were told that they would be running their own budgets much as GP fundholders had in Mrs Thatcher's time.

The carefully spun Conservative line at the election was that the 'New Cameron Conservatives' loved the NHS and that 'there will be no more of these pointless reorganizations that aim for change but instead bring chaos' as Cameron put it.[17] The pledge on 'no reorganization' was always carefully qualified. Reorganization would merely be 'not top down' or 'pointless', if you read the texts carefully.

In the run-up to the election all talk of major change was blanked out of the party's election pitch. As Andrew Lansley himself put it to Nicholas Timmins, 'I can remember it being said explicitly to

---

[14] Nicholas Timmins, *Never Again? The Story of the Health and Social Care Act 2012: A Study in Coalition Government and Policy Making* (London: King's Fund and Institute for Government, 2012).

[15] Timmins, *Never Again?*, pp. 38, 60, 63.

[16] George Osborne is reputed to have said 'Nobody told me this was coming. *Nobody*': Matthew d'Ancona, *In It Together: The Inside Story of the Coalition Government* (London: Penguin Books, 2014), p. 99.

[17] Timmins, *Never Again?*, p. 35; d'Ancona, *In It Together*, p. 103.

me that our presentation would be radical reform on education and reassurance on health.'[18]

It worked. The NHS barely featured in the 2010 election campaign. The sharp-eyed might have noticed that the promise of 'no reorganization' did *not* appear in the Conservative Manifesto. Reform was merely described as 'strengthening the power of GPs to commission services', something that sounded as if it were no more than Labour had been trying to do with 'practice-based commissioning'. Some examples were given of the wider freedoms local services would enjoy. But that was all.

Thus when the Liberal Democrats went into coalition discussions immediately after the election they clearly thought that what was on offer was continuing incremental change much on the lines set by the Labour government, at least during the Blair period. When the negotiators came to discuss the coalition programme the NHS was barely mentioned. It ranked a sentence in the Coalition Agreement. Its budget would be given protection from further cuts, an important pledge but not a revolution.

When, however, it came to agreeing the detailed legislative programme a week after the Coalition Agreement was published, there were problems. The Liberal Democrats wanted more local authority say in NHS decisions, the Conservatives did not. Those drawing up the more detailed legislative programme, notably Oliver Letwin and Danny Alexander, had little or no experience of health policy. Moreover, those in charge of the broader negotiations on the Liberal Democrat side were all 'Orange Book' sympathizers.[19] They favoured more public service competition. This seemed to be the general direction the NHS was going anyway under Labour. But the official Liberal Democrat policy had proposed *elected* health boards and a stronger voice for local government in the running of the NHS. This was not something the Conservatives supported.

What emerged from the negotiating team was to be what one insider called 'a spatchcocked mess'. Primary Care Trusts were to be elected partly by local voters and partly nominated by local authorities with chief officers and lead officials appointed by the Secretary of State.

[18] Timmins, *Never Again?*, p. 34.
[19] Paul Marshall and David Lawes (eds.), *The Orange Book: Reclaiming Liberalism* (London: Profile Books, 2004).

As one civil servant put it to Nicholas Timmins, 'Every single element of this proposal is crazy, really.'[20]

There was no mention of Strategic Health Authorities, which the Liberal Democrats wished to abolish. GPs would have more commissioning power. Yet the pledge, so carefully left out of the Conservative Manifesto, reappeared: 'We shall stop top down re-organization.'

The whole thing made no sense to anyone who knew anything about the NHS. What it provoked was an even more far-reaching set of changes than even Lansley had been envisaging.

The Department had to go back to square one. It was struggling, not only trying to make sense of the reform plans but also to make very large savings. Andrew Lansley's plans had been drawn up in the years of plenty. Neither Primary Care Trusts nor Strategic Health Authorities had many friends. They employed significant numbers of staff. A major cull would help reach the tight spending target. The Liberal Democrats were in favour of abolishing the Strategic Health Authorities, which opened the way to major structural change. The Treasury were unhappy about handing public money to groups of GPs with no clear statutory framework.

To cope with both the Liberal Democrats' structural demands and the need to save money the policy then took on an even more radical shape. The coalition programme on health was effectively torn up and the abolition of virtually all existing administrative bodies proposed. How might George Osborne and David Cameron react? 'Leave them to me to sort out – they all used to work for me' (in Conservative Central Office) was, evidently, Andrew Lansley's reply.[21]

At the very centre of his strategy was a determination to strip the Secretary of State and the Department of Health of its capacity to interfere with the running of the service and to take from the Secretary of State any capacity to reverse the steady move to patient choice and provider diversity he thought essential. Once you did that, other institutions had to be created to run the service, at arm's length from politics, as a regulated market. The Labour government had ended the exclusion of health from European competition rules. But the resulting role of European competition law in commissioning health services was less than clear. Now that had to be firmly established.

---

[20] Timmins, *Never Again?*, p. 53.   [21] *Ibid.*, p. 64.

A monster emerges

Andrew Lansley's original ambitions, the need to produce a compromise with the Liberal Democrats and the expenditure constraint the Department was under together produced what evolved into a legislative monster. This was a joint product and it is difficult to assign proportionate blame.

A white paper was published very soon after the election, in July 2010.[22] (Here, as elsewhere, the coalition wanted to avoid Blair's 'mistake' of not getting on with major change early.) The white paper set out the elements of the proposed new structure:

- A new central commissioning board would effectively take over strategic, and in many instances direct, control of who would actually provide local services. Later become any 'qualified provider'.
- Wide powers would be devolved from the Secretary of State to this new body, disengaging the Secretary of State from responsibility for services.
- A new economic regulator would promote competition in health services.
- Patients would be given the choice of 'any willing provider' to treat them – public or private. Later became any 'qualified provider'.
- Strategic Health Authorities and Primary Care Trusts, who had in combination commissioned and planned services for their local populations, would go. GP-led commissioners would authorize contracts for services their patients could use in ways approved by the national commissioning body.
- Public health functions would pass back to local authorities, which had undertaken these duties before 1974.
- Joint Wellbeing Boards would try to link local authorities and the new GP-led commissioning groups – a Liberal Democrat idea.[23]

This list of aims set many alarm bells ringing across the service and more widely, but it was not until the Bill was published the following January that many organizations woke up to its scale and

---

[22] Department of Health, *Equity and Excellence: Liberating the NHS* (Cm 7881, London: The Stationery Office, 2010).
[23] D'Ancona, *In It Together*, p. 107.

implications. It was over 500 pages long and had an explanatory memorandum as long again.

One of those alerted to its scale and significance was Shirley Williams (Liberal Democrat peer), who was shocked. As an ex-Labour minister and 'traditional social democrat at heart' (as she once put it to me), the proposals offended her core beliefs about the kind of institution she felt the NHS should be. She argued that there was no public call for change; on the contrary the NHS was enjoying unprecedented public support.

With ready access to the Liberal Democrat leadership Baroness Williams set about finding out what the professional and client group organizations felt. 'I had something like 60–70 meetings with every possible health organization,' she told Nicolas Timmins.[24] In short, she acted as a kind of parallel opposition spokesperson in the House of Lords. She gathered considerable support both on the crossbenches and from Liberal Democrat local parties. David Owen, her partner in setting up the Social Democrat Party in the 1980s, acted on her left flank. He had been health minister under Barbara Castle in the 1970s and had originally trained as a doctor. He believed the Bill was a major error. Norman Lamb, who had been Liberal Democrat spokesman on health before the 2010 election, also thought the Bill a fatal mistake.

Having amassed considerable local Liberal Democrat support and professional backing the rebels took their case to the Liberal Democrats' Spring Conference, which rejected the Bill's approach. This was followed by a special meeting of the BMA which did the same. A storm of opposition broke out in the 'new' media including the new '38 degrees' campaigning group.

This was enough for Nick Clegg to be able to say to David Cameron, 'I cannot get this through my party.' It was only at this point that coalition politics 'Borgen style' began in earnest. It was a contest *within* one of the coalition parties as much as between them.

David Cameron responded by proposing a 'pause' in the legislative process at the end of the Commons Committee stage of the Bill in March 2011. There was a scramble to decide what that might mean. The Department of Health came up with the idea of a small group that

[24] Timmins, *Never Again?*, p. 86.

would take evidence from those who objected but could suggest changes to the Bill that would meet 'well grounded' objections – 'The Future Forum'.

It can be seen as a pale imitation of the process used by Alan Milburn in 2000 when he changed the direction of Labour's health policy. But that had been undertaken with considerable care and cleared with the major interested parties long before any plans were announced. Moreover, that exercise had been undertaken by a party with a large majority. This 'consultation' was essentially a face-saving measure designed to placate a coalition partner.

The Forum reported on 13 June 2011 and its suggested changes were accepted, virtually in full, the next day. Some were a mere semantic gloss, others more substantive. None changed the fundamentals.

- 'Monitor', the financial regulator, was to 'promote integrated care', not defined, not just deal with competition.
- Monitor would not 'promote competition' but prevent 'anti-competitive practices'.
- The new local commissioning groups would include a hospital consultant and a nurse. These bodies would be given a proper governance structure, an important and a substantive change.
- These agencies would have to consult widely with a range of local bodies, notably a new Health and Well Being Board that would include local authority and health representatives. Liberal Democrats' wish to strengthen the local authority role was thus given a bit more substance. But such bodies had been ineffective in the past.

Legislative disharmony

Though these changes did not remove the key goals of the legislation, they did make the machinery even more cumbersome and complex. Nor did they satisfy the most critical Liberal Democrat or crossbench Peers, who pressed for more changes. An unusually large number of amendments were made at committee stage to tighten and clarify what many Lords from all parties thought was a shoddily drafted Bill. In particular the House of Lords Constitution Committee worried about the diminished accountability to Parliament the Secretary of State would have. This was discussed in detail in a series of 'seminars'. As a result, a series of amendments strengthened the Secretary of State's responsibilities and parliamentary accountability. But the new 'NHS England' would remain essentially at arm's length from government. Other changes were made:

- 'Medical' Peers worried about responsibilities for medical training and research. These were included in the Secretary of State's remit.
- The original draft bill was worded in such a way that prices would be open to local negotiation – price competition. This had attracted a lot of criticism, notably from economists, who pointed to the likely perverse results of price competition in a market where quality was difficult to measure. The wording was tightened to make it clear that those providing services for the NHS would be paid at a set NHS tariff. Competition should be on quality not price, but in practice there was wriggle room that enabled some local price variation.
- Hospital trusts' capacity to earn private fee income was increased, although by less than Andrew Lansley had originally proposed. It had to be less than half their total income, which was important in defining their status in competition law.

At this point Baroness Williams felt this was as much 'give' as was politically possible within the coalition. Lord Owen continued his opposition. Some significant positive changes had been made to the Bill as it passed through the Lords. But the resulting set of changes were much more far-reaching and complex because of the need to compromise with Liberal Democrat intentions and to cope with that party's internal divisions.

Andrew Lansley was relieved of his post in September 2012 and Jeremy Hunt took over. He had the task of soothing professional wounds and engaging with the public in a way his colder, technocratic predecessor could not. This led him to take on the role of being 'on the side of patients'. He responded to the Mid Staffordshire scandal vigorously in ways we discuss later. He was even involved in issuing guidance on how hospitals should deal with parking charges!

Detailed regulation and 'command and control' functions of the centre are now in the hands of regulators and NHS England. Whether they will be seen as any less intrusive by professionals we must wait and see.

What did not change

Before discussing what this may all mean for the future of health care in England it is important to step back and note what did not change.

- Health care remains largely free at the point of use throughout the UK.
- It remains predominantly funded out of general taxation. In that respect it is an outlier internationally.
- The way hospitals, general practice and other health services actually operate changed little, though some experiments are now under way, as we shall see.
- Outside England little or no organizational upheaval took place. If anything Scotland, and to some extent Wales and Northern Ireland, reverted to a 1948 vision of the Health Service. There competition and choice were minimized or rejected. Prescription charges were abolished in Scotland in 2011 and in Northern Ireland in 2010, as had already happened in Wales in 2007.

We should not let the English obsession with organizational 'reform' delude us into thinking that this is a shared, United Kingdom-wide phenomenon. Indeed, the Scottish Nationalists used what they claimed to be the privatization of the service in England to back their argument that the Scots should break free from those trying to destroy an institution that embodied 'Scottish' values.

How to judge the 2012 Act

Views on this massive legislative and administrative endeavour are sharply divided.[25] They can be roughly divided into three camps.

A tragic misdirection of effort

Looming in the background, and rapidly gathering in significance through this period, has been a demographic transformation. Each generation since the Second World War has been living longer. But

---

[25] 170 organizations have been closed and 240 new organizations created: National Audit Office, *Managing the Transition to the Reformed Health System* (London: National Audit Office, 2013).

from 2010 this 'ageing' effect was to be greatly amplified. The reason lies in a surge in the number of births occurring in the two decades immediately after the Second World War. These 'baby boomers' would now retire and live to ages at which the health resources they require more than *treble*. The factors lying behind this were highlighted by a cross-party committee of the House of Lords.[26] Evidence given to that committee found that, between 2010 and 2030:

- Numbers of those with dementia (moderate or severe cognitive impairment) were likely to rise by 80 per cent to nearly two million.
- Numbers suffering from arthritis, coronary heart disease and stroke were likely to rise by over 50 per cent each.
- The number of those with moderate or severe needs for social care may well rise by 90 per cent.

The NHS will have to change from what was a predominantly short-term *curing* service to a predominantly long-term *caring* one. It will face unprecedented increases in demand and generally higher medical costs. But these pressures will not only fall on the national public purse – something most commentators fail to see. The scale of the challenge facing local social services departments and individual family carers will be even greater.[27]

So, against this background it may be argued:

- The whole 'reform' process was a colossal waste of political capital and managerial energy. This should instead have been devoted to finding ways to fund services for an ageing population and solving the perverse incentives created by the separation of health and social care.
- The Act created a managerial structure that is so complex and lacking in strategic direction that the kinds of changes needed are difficult to implement. (Look for example at the King's Fund's diagram of the decision process required to produce a coherent

---

[26] House of Lords Select Committee on Public Service and Demographic Change, *Ready for Ageing?* (HL 140, Session 2012–13; London: The Stationery Office, 2013). It should be noted I was a Special Adviser to that committee.

[27] See, for example, House of Lords, *Ready for Ageing?*, Annex 15; David Oliver, Catherine Foot and Richard Humphries, *Making our Health and Care Systems Fit for an Ageing Population* (London: King's Fund, 2014).

pattern of services in London. It looks like a ball of wool some kitten has been playing with.)[28]

- Political capital should have been spent instead re-engineering the responsibilities for old people's care across the NHS, local authority and social security divides. The kinds of issues that needed addressing here, and some far from palatable choices, are discussed in a recent King's Fund Commission Report.[29]

Furthermore, the notion that Secretaries of State could somehow divorce themselves from the day-to-day consequences of the work of the NHS was dispelled while the ink on the Act was barely dry. A series of scandals, mostly involving the care of elderly patients, produced a series of inquiries. The Mid Staffordshire case was the most widely discussed. It occurred under the previous Labour administration but continued to have repercussions long after.

The resulting Francis Report[30] may become, in the long run, more important in shaping organizational practice than the much fought-over legislation. The Secretary of State was forced to intervene – drawing up good-practice rules and laying a duty on professionals to report poor treatment and, in February 2014, agreeing to dissolve the Hospital Trust in question. For the Secretary of State to wash his hands of it all was, as Stephen Dorrell, a past Conservative Secretary of State, had foreseen, a pipe dream. The new Secretary of State, Jeremy Hunt, became 'in some people's eyes the most interventionist of health secretaries on record'.[31] He both found it necessary in the summer of 2014 to tell local hospitals how to organize their car parking charges *and* improve their meals.

In short, the legislation was a tragic distraction from the real issues.

[28] Chris Ham, Nigel Edwards and Beatrice Brooke, *Leading Health Care in London: Time for a Radical Response* (London: King's Fund, 2013), p. 19.

[29] King's Fund Commission on the Future of Health and Social Care in England, *A New Settlement for Health and Social Care: Final Report* (London: King's Fund, 2014).

[30] House of Commons, *Report on the Mid Staffordshire NHS Foundation* (HC 947, London: Stationery Office, 2013).

[31] Nicholas Timmins, 'Happy returns for the health reforms?', Institute for Government blog, 1 April 2014 (accessed at www.instituteforgovernment.org.uk, 17 November 2014).

The end of the National Health Service

Others are even more critical. They think that the Health and Social Care Act 2012 spells the end of the National Health Service.[32] It is founded on the principle that health care is like any other commodity. Health care providers should be subject to competition law just like any other contractual arrangement. Existing public agencies should not be 'preferred providers'. In particular it is argued by these critics that:

- The NHS embodies a set of altruistic non-commercial values. The core of the Act is to frame health care as just another commodity. This will ultimately remove a major source of altruistic motivation in our society.
- The new institutional and legal framework has already begun to result in a higher share of *new* contracts being awarded to private organizations, even if the total budget share is still small.[33] The share of community and mental health services provided by private and voluntary organizations is already quite large – one-third and increasing.[34]
- The end result will be the complete reversion of health care to profit-maximizing institutions.
- This process was originally set in train by the decision the Labour Government in 2008 took not to exempt health care from European competition rules. This whole approach should now be rejected and the Act repealed by an incoming Labour government.

Necessary medicine

At the other extreme many Conservatives, some Liberal Democrats and some Labour experts want to see the NHS evolve into something much

---

[32] Jacky Davis and Raymond Tallis (eds.), *NHS SOS: How the NHS was Betrayed – and How we can Save it* (London: One World, 2013); Allison Pollock, David Price and Peter Roderick, 'How the Health and Social Care Bill 2011 would end entitlement to comprehensive health care in England', *The Lancet*, 6736:1, 26 January 2011.

[33] One-third of NHS contracts since reorganization have been awarded to private-sector organizations. They amounted to 6.1 per cent of the NHS budget, up from 5.5 per cent in 2012/13 and 4.4 in 2009/10 ('A third of NHS contracts awarded to private firms – report', *BBC News*, 10 December 2014, accessed at www.bbc.co.uk/news/health-303977329, 10 December 2014).

[34] Sara Lafond, Sandeepa Arora, Anita Charlesworth and Andy McKeon, *Into the Red? The State of the NHS' Finances* (London: Nuffield Trust, 2014).

nearer to a continental European model. Services would continue to be provided free but by a range of public and private suppliers. In the short run:

- The NHS has to increase its productivity dramatically to survive the fiscal and demographic pressure it will be under. New entrants to the health and care market are necessary to achieve this. They are especially needed to pioneer new ways to serve the elderly, long-term sick and disabled. Service boundaries need to be broken down. The statutory services have failed to do this in any lasting effective way.

- There are signs that some of the new commissioning groups are beginning to pioneer new approaches. For example, Cambridge and Peterborough have agreed a combined contract for older people's health and the provision of adult care based on achieving agreed results. Others are also basing their contracts for particular patient groups on rewarding those who succeed in achieving integrated care. The contracts and payments reward integration and good *outcomes* of care.

It will be clear that my primary sympathy lies with the first view, but there is some force in both the other, apparently contradictory, views.

It is possible that the legal and regulatory framework that has been created will permit the gradual transformation of health care into a commercial service industry, perhaps dominated by large private suppliers. If future governments favoured this route the structure is in place to enable it.

But this is not a necessary outcome. The Treasury, for one, has always been fearful of just such a prospect. Powerful provider lobbies could prize open the public cash box. Its tight control of the NHS budget now makes it far less attractive to any profit-seeker than the United States market.

Exactly what constitutes an 'economic undertaking' is far from clear-cut in European Commercial Law. How far local commissioners will be interpreted as performing a 'social solidarity function' and how far they will be seen as awarding commercial contracts has yet to be decided in the courts. Your average GP-led Commissioning Group does not see itself as driven by pure cost-minimizing criteria. There are many legal and political battles to be fought here. Yet the very scale of the legislation and the hostility it provoked may have endangered precisely the kind of trends Lansley wished to foster.

Conversely there is a need for a major improvement in NHS productivity and innovation, especially in the way services are commissioned. New entrants with new ideas are badly needed.

Despite the political sound and fury, the organizational structure of the NHS is not what primarily concerns voters. What matters to them is the quality and responsive speed of the services on which they depend. How has that changed in a period of financial stringency?

Broader outcomes

Budget protected?

The coalition agreed at the outset that the NHS budget should be 'protected'. But even before the coalition took office the NHS Chief Executive (David Nicholson) had warned that the service would have to make major 'efficiency savings' in the period up to 2014 to keep within the likely public spending limits that any government would set.[35]

Given additional demands and price increases, local health services in England would need to increase their 'productivity' by 4 per cent a year to deliver constant outcomes over the period 2010–21 – a productivity improvement the NHS had never remotely achieved before.[36]

To achieve this, a formal programme of 'efficiency improvement' was set in train. It was to be achieved in two phases – up to 2014/15 there would be hoped-for 'efficiency gains' of 3.0 per cent a year and then until 2020/21 these would have to grow to 4.7 per cent a year. That was a hugely ambitious goal.

In the early years of the coalition, savings were achieved by cutting the prices paid by local commissioners for each phase of treatment that local hospitals undertook. This single measure amounted to nearly half the 'savings' made in 2012/13. The next largest 'savings' came from a pay freeze and substantial reductions in administrative and

[35] 'We should also plan on the assumption that we will need to release unprecedented levels of efficiency savings between 2011 and 2014 – between £15 billion and £20 billion across the service over the three years': David Nicholson, *The Year: NHS Chief Executive's Annual Report 2008/09* (London: NHS, 2009), p. 47.

[36] Nuffield Trust, *A Decade of Austerity? The Funding Pressures Facing the NHS from 2010/11 to 2021/22* (London: Nuffield Trust, 2012).

clinical support staff.[37] It is difficult to see the prices paid for treatment being cut again by even more. Previous experience of pay freezes suggests that they end in a strong reaction – pay catches up with other earnings. That may be delayed this time, as the economy and private workers' pay take longer to rebound – but rebound they will at some point.

What, then, happened to the total resources available to the NHS?

The government's 2010 spending review planned for an annual real growth in spending over the whole period up to 2014/15 of 0.4 per cent. In fact, lower price rises than predicted and later revisions suggest that real expenditure has increased rather more than predicted. It should amount to a cumulative gain of just short of 5 per cent over the whole period of the government.[38] That would compare to a *70 per cent* increase in real resources during Labour's period in power. But that was a different world!

So, did the coalition keep to its pledge to increase real spending year on year? The answer is yes – but. If we take into account the changing age structure of the population, the answer is no. Older people cost several times as much to look after as younger people, as we saw earlier. Various attempts have been made to estimate real levels of spending per head of population taking account of the changing age structure.

The IFS saw real planned NHS spending as likely to be essentially stable from 2010 to 2018. But they estimate that to take account of the higher costs of older people real spending should be rising by 1.2 per cent a year.[39] Others produce a slightly higher figure but agree that real spending per head on an age-adjusted basis will have *fallen* over the parliament.[40]

---

[37] John Appleby, Amy Galea and Richard Murray, *The NHS Productivity Challenge: Experience from the Front Line* (London : King's Fund, 2014), p. 18.

[38] Polly Vizard and Polina Obolenskaya, *The Coalition's Record on Health* (London: CASE, London School of Economics, 2015).

[39] Carl Emmerson, Paul Johnson and Helen Miller, *IFS Green Budget 2014* (London: Institute for Fiscal Studies, 2014), Table 2.6, p. 45.

[40] Vizard and Obolenskaya, *The Coalition's Record*; The Nuffield Trust, 'The population time bomb: can NHS spending keep pace?' (accessed at www.nuffieldtrust.org.uk/blog/population-time-bomb, 25 November 2014).

The basic story is, however, clear. The NHS has been protected from the kinds of cuts most other services have suffered, but it has not escaped unscathed if we take account of the age of those it is serving.

This curb on health spending looks likely to continue. Indeed, the cuts to other services that continued 'protection' would imply are so great that the NHS budget must be at risk. Even on current plans the NHS budget will probably fall back to 6 per cent of GDP by 2021[41] – the kind of levels that provoked so much public disquiet in 1997. And the population it will have to serve will be much older. This translates into a potential funding gap of £30 billion by 2021 in the absence of continuing 'efficiency gains'.[42]

So, *have* local service providers managed to use their resources more efficiently to sustain service quality despite the pressures? Let us examine some evidence.

Time waiting to get hospital treatment

Given the circumstances, general non-acute hospital waiting times have remained remarkably stable, though they are now beginning to creep up.

- Median 'referral to treatment' times for non-urgent care hovered around the eight-week level after 2008 and on after the election. But by September 2014 they were rising again and had reached 9.5 weeks. A dangerous sign.
- The percentage of people in accident and emergency rooms seen, and treatment or discharge decided, within four hours fell from 98% to 96% when a new, lower target of 95% was introduced in 2011. In July–September 2014 it was 95%. But in November it had fallen below the target; in the second week of December it fell below 90%.
- The minimum two-week waiting time for outpatient screening for suspected cancer has remained little changed and so has the wait for

---

[41] Appleby et al., *The NHS Productivity Challenge*, p. 11.
[42] Monitor, *Closing the NHS Funding Gap: How to get Better Value Health Care for Patients*, 10 October 2013 (accessed at www.gov.uk/government/publications/closing-the-nhs-funding-gap-how-to-get-better-value-healthcare-for-patients, 17 November 2014).

treatment after diagnosis for breast cancer, but some other waits have risen.[43]

- Overall these figures are open to some manipulation, but they suggest the system has held up better than we might have feared, with some worrying signs emerging.
- Mental health has been exempted from central pressure to meet the waiting time targets. A Mind survey estimated that over 12 per cent of those referred by a GP have to wait longer than a year and 54 per cent more than three months for any specialist care.[44] Waiting targets are now to be extended to mental health care in some form but this will require resources and specialist staff.

Access to GP

The number of GPs per head of population has fallen from just over 90 per 100,000 to just below that, while the number of older people, who use their GP much more intensively, has grown faster than the general population. So primary care is under pressure. This is beginning to show up in the satisfaction levels for GP services.

- In 2011/12 88 per cent of respondents to the GP user survey classed their experience as good. By 2013/14 this was just below 86 per cent. Some tribute to GPs.
- But only three-quarters of out-of-hours experience was described as good. That was a fall of 4.6 per cent on two years before.[45] More worrying.

Satisfaction with quality of care

Public satisfaction with the NHS rose from relatively poor levels in 1997 to its highest recorded level in 2010. Overall satisfaction had only been expressed by 39 per cent of respondents to the British Social Attitudes Survey in 2001 but rose to 70 per cent in 2010. By 2013 this

[43] 95 per cent of patients got to be screened within two weeks of referral in 2013/14, the same figure as for the second quarter of 2010/11. For more details see www.england.nhs.uk/statistics.

[44] Mind, *We Still Need to Talk* (London: Mind, 2013).

[45] See www.england.nhs.uk/statistics/2014/07/03/gp-patient-survey-2013-4, accessed 19 September 2014.

figure had fallen back to about 61 per cent – still higher than most other British institutions but a significant fall even so.

But this is a survey of the whole population and for much of their lives most people have little intense contact with the NHS. In old age this changes. Here surveys of actual users are much more worrying.

The Care Quality Commission uses an Annual Inpatient Survey to look for danger signals and measure quality trends. Colleagues' analysis of these returns shows that older people, and especially older women, report that they did not receive help eating when they needed it.[46] Only 40 per cent of those women over 80 with a long-standing disabling condition received the help they felt they needed. Many other disturbing indicators emerged that were not confined to a few 'bad institutions'.

Mental health

In her latest annual report the Chief Medical Officer for England paints a deeply worrying picture of mental health care coverage. Her account covers a period both before and after the coalition came to power. Across Europe an estimated 75 per cent of those with mental illness receive no treatment at all. In the period 2005/6 to 2012/13 estimates of the numbers of adults receiving state-funded social care fell by 48 per cent in England, by far the worst-affected group of users.[47]

Particularly worrying is the 'extensive disinvestment' in specialist child and adolescent mental health services since 2011. This is at a time when there has been a significant rise in both young people presenting and the severity of their problems.[48]

The 2012 Act laid a duty on the Secretary of State 'to secure an improvement in the physical and mental health of the people of England

---

[46] Polly Vizard and Tania Burchardt, *Older People's Experience of Dignity and Nutrition during Hospital Stays Using the Adult Inpatient Survey: CASE Report* (London: CASE/London School of Economics, forthcoming).

[47] Graham Thornicroft and Mary Docherty, 'Mind the gaps – treatment, funding, access and service provision', in *Annual Report of the Chief Medical Officer 2013, Public Mental Health Provision: Investing in the Evidence* (London: The Stationery Office, 2014).

[48] Tamsin Ford, Oana Metrofan and Miranda Wolpert, 'Life course: children and young people's mental health', in *Annual Report of the Chief Medical Officer 2013, Public Mental Health Provision: Investing in the Evidence* (London: The Stationery Office, 2014).

and in the prevention, diagnosis and treatment of physical and mental illness'.[49] Mental health does not yet appear to have received equal priority.

Local involvement

It is too early to say if the local Wellbeing Boards are involving local actors more in health service decisions. Past experience suggests such joint boards achieve little.

International comparisons

We have to recognize that other health care systems are in trouble too and many to a greater degree than the NHS. A United States health care think tank (The Commonwealth Fund) regularly undertakes surveys of leading economies' health care systems, polling both users and practitioners in several countries.[50] Their criteria include ease of access, timeliness and quality of care as well as cost effectiveness. The NHS has always done well on these comparative rankings. It was second in 2010 and rose to the top ranking in 2014. But it has always done markedly less well on health outcomes, not only in this study but on a wider range of such measures. The NHS remains stuck midway down international rankings, or worse. This has not changed. Such indicators include fatality from stroke and heart disease, cancer survival and infant mortality rates.[51]

But life expectancy has gone on improving gradually. It is now higher in England (79) than in France (78.4) or Germany (77.7), but is much lower in Scotland (76.5).[52]

There are no trends yet reported in healthy life expectancy during the coalition period, but inequalities remain strikingly high despite the new duty laid on the Secretary of State to 'reduce the inequalities in the benefits from the health services' in England (Section1C).

[49] Section 1.
[50] Karen Davis, Kristoff Stremikis, David Squires and Cathy Schoen, *Mirror, Mirror on the Wall: How the US Care System Compares Internationally* (New York: The Commonwealth Fund, 2014).
[51] Vizard and Obolenskaya, *Labour's Record on Health* and *The Coalition's Record*.
[52] Office of National Statistics, 'National life tables 2010–12', *Statistical Bulletin* (London: The Stationery Office and ONS website, March 2014).

The Office for National Statistics (ONS) produced figures in 2014 that showed that on average those living in the most deprived parts of England (the bottom tenth) could only expect to enjoy fifty years of healthy life. Those in the richest areas (top tenth) could expect just over seventy years.[53] This presents as much a challenge to social policy as to the health services. It will take a long time to change, if it ever does.

Long-term care

Compromise

Before the election there had been a cross-party attempt to resolve the long-running issue of how to fund long-term care in England. That attempt broke up with the Conservatives rejecting one option on the table – deferring the means-tested charges for local services until after the individual died. A 'death tax', they claimed.

The Liberal Democrat Manifesto had proposed setting up a commission to look at the question. The Conservatives favoured promoting private long-term care insurance – a market that had never taken root and for good reason. The risks for an insurer are uncertain and the foresight young individuals need to buy such insurance is largely absent.

Most economists never saw the Conservative private insurance route as a real option without some government involvement to limit insurers' risks. The Liberal Democrats' idea of an independent commission was included in the Coalition Agreement. The Liberal Democrats were given ministerial responsibility for social care.

The funding problem

Funding the long-term care of older people had become a political conundrum. Most people believe that the state will care for them, or their parents, free of charge when they need it, much as the National Health Service does. That is if they think about the issue at all. But that has never been the statutory situation.

[53] *Healthy Life Expectancy at Birth by National Deciles of Area Deprivation 2009–11* (London: Office of National Statistics, 2014).

Care has always been subject to a means and asset test from the days of the Poor Law, whose financial rules local authorities inherited in 1948. If you had assets of any size you were always responsible for financing your own care. After the Second World War these rules affected relatively few people. Most old people did not own their own houses and had very little savings.

Over time two things changed. Owner-occupation became the norm. The value of assets you could possess and still receive free care rose much more slowly than house prices.[54] More and more people had to pay. This became a growing political irritant. The middle class are all in favour of means tests when they apply to the poor but not when they begin to apply to them.

This situation also made it more difficult to achieve the integration of health and social care services. The NHS would like to move people out of hospital as soon as possible after they have suffered a fall or stroke. Neither the local authority nor the family who may have to pay for alternative care are as keen to see this happen.

These issues had been bubbling to a boil over several decades. Blair appointed a Royal Commission to examine the issues. It suggested funding long-term care in the same way as the NHS – out of taxation.[55] The underpinning logic of this case was that the health, nursing and personal care of older people were so intertwined and difficult to distinguish at the margins that they should be funded in the same way. Since the NHS was tax-funded, one solution was to move all funding in that direction.

The Blair Government rejected this route for England but the newly devolved Scottish Parliament adopted it for Scotland. In England only *nursing* costs in residential homes were to be met from tax funds and only up to a low limit. Hence the issue continued to fester outside Scotland.

In June 2010 Andrew Dilnot, an economist and formerly head of the Institute for Fiscal Studies, was asked to take on the task

[54] John Hills and Howard Glennerster, 'Public policy, wealth and assets: A complex and inconsistent story', in John Hills, Francesca Bastagli, Frank Cowell, Howard Glennerster, Eleni Karagiannaki and Abigail McKnight, *Wealth in the UK: Distribution, Accumulation, and Policy* (Oxford: Oxford University Press, 2013).

[55] *With Respect to Old Age: A Report by the Royal Commission on Long Term Care* (Cm 4192, London: The Stationery Office, 1999).

of resolving this issue. He was to chair a small commission.[56] His remit was narrowly drawn. He was not to be concerned with the scale of future funding nor with the organization of long-term care. He was merely charged with considering how far people should continue to be responsible for funding their own care. He proposed a compromise. Individuals, subject to a more generous asset test, should be expected to shoulder the cost of their own care up to the point that these costs became 'catastrophic'.

He proposed setting a cap on the total accumulated value of *care* an individual or household should be expected to meet, excluding living costs. He suggested that figure should be set at £35,000 over a person's lifetime. The government, presumably on Treasury insistence, set a higher figure of £72,000. The hope was that clear individual responsibility for the first tranche of care costs would encourage a market in long-term care insurance – the original Conservative hope. In addition Dilnot suggested raising the amount of savings and assets someone would be permitted to own before having to pay for their care. He suggested an asset limit of £123,000, which was £100,000 higher than the situation before he reported. But it was still well below the average price of a house in most parts of the country. Most single owner-occupiers would thus still have to pay for their own care and the residential costs resulting from living in an old persons' home.

The Minister of State responsible for this area of policy was a Liberal Democrat, Norman Lamb. The package proved enough of a compromise to gain grudging support across both the Coalition and the Opposition.

The Care Act 2014, after a long passage through Parliament, not only gave legislative force to these proposals that were to come into force in 2016, it introduced a wide range of other measures designed to give people rights to a national standard assessment of needs, safeguards against abuse and a duty of candour on employees to inform the authorities if they saw abuses. There was also a duty on local authorities to integrate their services with the NHS. That was no more than the Labour government of 1976 had tried with little success!

---

[56] Commission on Funding of Care and Support, *Fairer Care Funding – The Report of the Commission on Funding of Care and Support* (London: The Stationery Office, 2011).

But these measures left unresolved the two central policy questions:

- How to get enough additional resources to fund the growing pressure on services for the elderly. Indeed, the Dilnot changes will make long-term care more costly for the taxpayer and exacerbate this policy dilemma.
- How to better integrate long-term health, social care and specialist housing provision as well as other public services for elderly people.

A King's Fund Commission, as we have seen, did later address these issues and made a series of far-reaching and none-too-palatable recommendations.[57] This subject will not go away and will be firmly on the plate of any government that succeeds this coalition.

Resources

During the coalition period a severe squeeze has been put on local authority grants from central government and their capacity to raise Council Tax (see chapter nine, this volume). This has produced a sharp reduction in total spending by local authorities. Real spending on the personal social services (old age, sickness and disability elements) had risen steadily through the first decade of the century. It fell in the first three years of the coalition. If we include transfers from the NHS budget to local authorities in England and 'winter pressure transfers', real spending fell by 5 per cent.

As in the case of health care, though, this only tells part of the story. The number of people 'at risk' has been rising in recent years. Over the whole coalition period total real spending is likely to fall by 11 per cent. During the same period the number of those over 65 will have *risen* by 11 per cent and the number of over 85s by 9 per cent.[58]

The result is that to get any help at all from local social care services requires a higher and ever-rising level of 'assessed need'.

---

[57] King's Fund Commission, *A New Settlement for Health and Social Care.*
[58] Polly Vizard, Tania Burchardt, Alex Roberts and Polina Obolenskaya, 'Social care under the coalition', Social Policy in a Cold Climate Paper (London: LSE/ CASE, 2015).

The story beyond England

We must end by reminding ourselves that organizational turmoil in health care really only applied to England. Scotland, Wales and Northern Ireland chose to leave their health and long-term care services structurally unchanged during this period. Both Scotland and Wales had already chosen not to go down the quasi-market path set by the Thatcher and Blair administrations. They abolished the split between purchasers and providers, discouraged competition and the entry of private providers.

The Scots chose to make their long-term care free soon after devolution. Scotland also chose to pioneer a series of public health measures such as minimum pricing for alcohol and smoking bans before England. It chose not to significantly change its administrative structures after 2004 but it did improve its management review procedures with some success. This is not the place to undertake a detailed comparison of English versus Scottish and Welsh health policy.[59] The material point for this chapter is that despite each country following strikingly different organizational paths for the past decade, the *trends* in health outcomes in the four countries look remarkably similar. Perhaps English politicians should stop obsessing about structures.

Coalition effect?

So what does this account tell us about how coalitions work in British politics? A standard view is that coalitions temper extreme policy choices and result in *gradual* policy evolution. That is not a good summary of the events we have just outlined.

A Conservative minister with a major reform programme drove his original ideas through Parliament, but they were made more far-reaching in an attempt to accommodate Liberal Democrat ambitions.

In the original allocation of ministerial portfolios Conservative politicians took charge of policy areas where the Conservatives had

---

[59] For such a study see Gwyn Bevan, Marina Karanikolos, Jo Exley, Ellen Nolte, Sheelah Connolly and Nicholas Mays, *The Four Health Systems of the United Kingdom: How do they Compare?* (London: The Health Foundation and Nuffield Trust, 2014).

ambitious changes in mind. Liberal Democrats were given lower-profile areas where there was more chance of compromise or where compromises had already been struck across parties – pensions is the obvious case. This twin-track approach certainly applied to health and long-term care.

The big structural changes legislated in 2012 have now been put into operation and new contractual rules are being applied. The scale of 'privatization' this may produce is as yet unclear. But a new and imaginative choice has been made for the post of Chief Executive of NHS England – Simon Stevens. He was trained and worked as an NHS manager, was health adviser to Tony Blair and then worked for an innovative health organization in the USA. If the service is to be steered between the advantages of innovation and the dangers of profiteering he looks like a good choice. His first five-year 'forward view' for the NHS has won support.[60]

On service standards the best that can be said is that they have not fallen as much as might have been feared in 2010. But cracks are beginning to show, for example in some lengthening of non-emergency waiting times. Mental health services and support for elderly people are showing worrying and growing deficiencies. Big resource gaps are about to open up.

Someone of my age sees close friends who were dynamic local residents or brilliant professional colleagues now changed personalities. They require twenty-four-hour care from loving partners who are under severe emotional pressure. They have little support.

The big failure of this period has been to effectively tackle two key problems – an ageing population and the inadequacies of mental health provision. They require new sources of funding and the fusion of health and social care. A vast reorganization took energy and political capital that should have been deployed elsewhere. Looking back on the coalition's health policy from the vantage point of 2025 that, surely, will be the lasting judgement.

---

[60] NHS England, *Five Year Forward View* , October 2014 (accessed at www.england. nhs.uk/ourwork/futurenhs, 2 December 2014).

12 THE COALITION AND SOCIETY (IV): WELFARE

NICHOLAS TIMMINS

Introduction

For most of the history of Britain's welfare state from 1948, benefit payments rode under the banner of social security. Over the past couple of decades, however, social security has more or less fallen out of the political lexicon. It has been replaced by the Americanism 'welfare'. In the United States, however, welfare has a narrow meaning. It applies chiefly to means-tested out-of-work support for lone mothers. It has nothing to do, for example, with the decidedly generous and popular US federal pension system.

In the UK, 'welfare' is occasionally used with a degree of precision to cover means-tested help for the workless – although even here its meaning has been more or less turned on its head to become a term of abuse, implying cash hand-outs to a far from always deserving poor, in a rhetoric that divides society into 'strivers vs scroungers'.

More often these days, 'welfare' is used indiscriminately to cover the whole of a social security budget which in 2010 totalled some £190 billion. It had – and still has – many different purposes. Getting on for half of it was spent on pensions, the bulk of which depend on people having paid sufficient national insurance contributions to qualify. Other significant elements included child benefit, a universal payment to recognize the additional costs of children; tax credits to support people in lower-paid work, who are anything but the feckless poor; and money to recognize the extra costs of disability. Roughly half the spending went to people of working age. But only about one-fifth of the £190 billion was being spent on people of working age who were out of work for whatever reason – the unemployed, lone parents, the sick and the disabled and those who cared for them.

The use of the term 'welfare', with its implication of means-testing for everything and chiefly for those out of work, has muddied the debate about the purposes and the effects of this largest single element of public expenditure – some 30 per cent of the total – and the public's understanding of it. The point is illustrated in a very minor way by the fact that in the commissioning of this book a discussion had to be had about just what was to be embraced by a chapter on 'welfare'.

It is taken here to include not just benefits for the workless and the programmes aimed at getting them back into work, but also payments to those in work, pensioner benefits and pensions for public sector workers. Those last are not part of the social security budget and are not included in the figures quoted above. But they are heavily dependent on taxpayer contributions.

One starting point for an account of social security under the coalition government is 26 March 2010, less than five weeks from polling day. David Cameron, the Conservative leader, made a pledge that took many independent commentators aback. The winter fuel payment, free bus passes and free TV licences for the over-75s, along with the pension credit, would be protected, he declared.

'You have my word', he told pensioners, that 'these vital benefits will not be cut under the Conservatives.'[1] Worried about the grey vote and by what the Conservatives saw as Labour 'lies' in their leaflets that these benefits would be under threat if the Tories won, the putative Prime Minister had just ring-fenced some £12 billion of public spending from the deluge of cuts that had become inevitable in the wake of the global financial crisis.

In a small but significant way, that was to set the tone for what was to happen under the coalition government. Protection – at least in the short term – for pensioners. Big cuts, and bigger ones thanks to that promise, for most other government programmes, including the other recipients of 'welfare'.

---

[1] 'Conservatives announce pensioner pledge' (accessed at www.webarchive.org.uk/wayback/archive/20100630001626/http://www.conservatives.com/News/News_stories/2010/03/Conservatives_announce_pensioner_pledge.aspx, 17 November 2014).

The promise also highlighted one of the least honourable elements of the 2010 campaign – a profound reluctance by all three main political parties to spell out just what would be involved in the spending reductions to come.

Cameron, to be fair, had long stopped talking of 'sharing the proceeds of growth' between tax cuts and spending increases. He had underlined that an 'age of austerity' was on its way. But the Conservatives were much clearer about what they would keep – a pledge of real-terms increases for the National Health Service, for example – than about what would go. Labour, under Gordon Brown, had provided no more detail. The Liberal Democrats were a tad more transparent, though they had little to say on welfare other than a hint that they would cut the winter fuel payments that Cameron was pledged to protect.

The state of play in 2010

The coalition government did not, of course, arrive to a blank sheet of paper. Labour, in its thirteen years in power, had been highly active in all these areas. One of the big strategic shifts it had made was to recognize that in an increasingly globalized economy huge pressure was being applied to wages in lower-paid jobs. Rather than just using taxpayers' money to support people out of work, it began to use it on a far larger scale to support people in work – through, for example, the introduction of tax credits, underpinned by a minimum wage intended to stop employers pushing wages down further so that more people became entitled to means-tested benefits at the taxpayer's expense.

Labour had adopted a pledge to end child poverty – a neat way of harnessing public support for one of its traditional aims, a policy of at least some redistribution. If the British Social Attitudes Survey – the annual snapshot of who we are and what we think – is to be believed, Britons have for three decades now consistently believed, and by large margins, that the gap between the rich and poor is too large. But when Labour took power in 1997, support for the government spending more on benefits for the poor, if this meant raising taxes, had been in decline for a decade – as indeed had support for redistribution.[2] No one,

[2] British Social Attitudes Survey, 1987–2013 (www.britsocat.com).

however, was likely to proclaim themselves in favour of having lots of poor children. But children live in families. So Labour was able to use its crusade to end child poverty as cover for helping less well-off families, while, by and large, avoiding talk of redistribution.

This extra help – notably new child tax credits and working tax credits – came at a price. Labour proclaimed it would make the welfare state an active one, providing 'a hand up not a hand out' while declaring that 'work is the best form of welfare', phrases still heard today from politicians of all parties. So 'welfare to work' arrived alongside this more generous help for those both in and out of work if they had children. Building on small initiatives under the previous Conservative administration came first the New Deal and later the Flexible New Deal, which saw the longer-term unemployed required to undertake much more active job search or training. Private providers were brought in to run these programmes. Their payments increasingly depended not just on taking people on, but on getting them into work and then helping to keep them there. In Labour's later years those on disability benefits were drawn into these requirements, while the age at which lone parents had to at least attend interviews to discuss training or job prospects, even if they did not all yet have actively to seek work, was progressively lowered – by 2010 it was due to apply to mothers with children as young as seven. In other words, more conditions were being attached to the receipt of out-of-work benefits. Under Labour's tenure, real incomes for childless out-of-work adults fell sharply – on the grounds that they should be working, not claiming.

On pensions, the coalition inherited the work of the Turner Commission. By the mid-2000s, pension policy was seen to be in deep crisis. Life expectancy had been rising sharply – far faster than the actuaries had been predicting. For a host of additional reasons, final salary schemes in the private sector, which at their peak had eight million members, were closing in droves: first to new members, and then to continued contributions from existing ones. Employers and indeed employees were putting much less into the defined contribution or money purchase pensions that replaced them. Millions in the private sector had no access to an employer-supported pension. And the value of the basic state pension was progressively eroding. Since 1981 its annual increase had been linked only to prices, not earnings, which, in normal times, grow faster. As a result, growing numbers were becoming reliant on the means-tested pension credit, with projections suggesting that by the middle of the twenty-first century more than 70 per cent of pensioners would be entitled to it. The basic state pension had ceased to be one that provided a minimal standard of living – a platform on which people could with confidence build their private saving. Instead by 2010 the basic state pension had become worth some £30 a week less than the means-tested provision – which meant that those in lower-paid jobs could no longer be certain that they would gain over what they would anyway get from the state, if they saved for their old age.

The initial diagnosis of the three-strong commission chaired by Adair (Lord) Turner in 2004 was that if future pensioners were not to be poorer then one of three things had to happen. People would have to work longer, or save more, or taxes would have to rise to fund better state pensions.[3] Their solution in 2005 was a mix of the three. The earnings link should be restored, but state pension age should rise progressively in the face of greater longevity to help pay for that. A low-charge national pensions saving scheme, with a compulsory employer contribution, should be introduced to give some nine million employees new access to a private pension. Employees would be automatically enrolled – either into this new national scheme, which became known as NEST, or into an equally good new or existing employer scheme. Individuals – though not employers – would remain free to opt out.

Labour legislated for all that. Little of it had actually been implemented, however, by the time of the general election. Labour had promised to restore the earnings link in 2012, subject to affordability, but certainly by the end of the forthcoming parliament. State pension age, already 65 for men and due to reach that for women in 2020, was to rise progressively – to 66 by 2026, then to 67 and to 68 by 2046. Automatic enrolment was due to be phased in over five years, starting in 2012 with the largest employers. The minimum level of contribution, which covered only a band of earnings, not all of them, would also be phased. It would start at 1 per cent for employers and 2 per cent for employees, eventually reaching a combined total of 8 per cent by October 2017.

---

[3] Pensions Commission, *Pensions: Challenges and Choices. The First Report of the Pensions Commission* (London: The Stationery Office, 2004).

The manifestos, the coalition agreements and the ministers

It was against that background that the Liberal Democrats and Conservatives published their manifestos. Both parties pledged to restore the earnings link for pensions. The Liberal Democrats went further, proposing a 'triple lock' – that the state pension would rise by the highest of earnings, prices or 2.5 per cent. That extra guarantee – the 2.5 per cent – was prompted by sore political memories of a quirk in the inflation figures which saw pensioners get only a 75p rise – a 'bag of peanuts' increase – in 2000.

The Conservatives said they would sharply bring forward the increase in state pension age to 66, without being precise about the date. Both parties pledged to end the requirement to buy an annuity at age 75, and the Liberal Democrats declared a 'long term aim' of creating a 'citizen's pension' paid at the level of the pension credit. The Tory manifesto provided support for auto-enrolment but the Liberal Democrats were silent on the issue. Conservatives promised to cap at £50,000 a year public sector pensions – those, for example, for NHS staff, the civil service, the police and local government – while the Liberal Democrats promised an independent review of them to ensure that they 'are sustainable and affordable for the long term'. The Liberal Democrats said they would cut tax relief on pension contributions to the basic rate, and promised to allow people early access to their pension pot, for example in times of financial hardship.

On welfare, the Conservative manifesto made no mention of universal credit – the huge benefit reform that was to absorb much of Iain Duncan Smith's time at Work and Pensions. Tougher sanctions of up to three years' loss of benefit for those who refused to accept reasonable job offers were proposed, and the Conservatives promised to continue Labour's 2008 policy of moving the 2.6 million people on incapacity benefit onto a new Employment and Support Allowance. This involved a more rigorous medical assessment, first for new claimants and then for existing ones. Those who failed were to be moved to Jobseeker's Allowance, with all its requirements actively to seek work. The most disabled would receive unconditional support. But for the first time an intermediate 'work-related activity' group would face sanctions if they did not take part in various forms of preparation for work.

The Conservatives also promised to scrap all of Labour's existing 'welfare to work' programmes. They were to be replaced by a new Work Programme in which the payments to private providers would rely even more heavily on getting people into work and keeping them there – reducing and eventually eliminating the existing up-front payments merely for taking them on. Drawing on New Labour language, the Conservatives promised that their plans 'will give unemployed people a hand up, not a hand out'. The manifesto also proposed a few very minor benefit cuts, including an end to paying tax credits to families on incomes of more than £50,000 a year. The Liberal Democrat manifesto had rather less to say on welfare, other than promising to target tax credits on 'those who need them most' while hinting that the better off would cease to get winter fuel payments.

The Coalition Agreement, hammered out over the famous 'five days in May', agreed to introduce the Work Programme, to set a date for bringing forward the increase to 66 in state pension age, and to scrap the requirement to buy an annuity at age 75.[4] The more detailed 'programme for government' which emerged twelve days later adopted the Liberal Democrat promise of the 'triple lock' on pensions and a review of public sector pensions. It promised to 'support' auto-enrolment. And it pledged to 'protect' the 'key benefits for older people' that Cameron had outlined, including free prescriptions. Perhaps more tellingly, the very first hint of universal credit emerged. 'We will investigate how to simplify the benefit system in order to improve incentives to work.'[5]

In all this there was huge continuity with what Labour had been doing. The headline might be that the coalition was going to scrap Labour's welfare-to-work programmes and replace them. But the idea of active welfare-to-work in which suppliers were increasingly paid by results remained. People with disabilities were to continue to be pushed, wherever possible, towards the labour market. The long history under Labour of placing increasing conditions on benefit receipt continued. And in pensions, auto-enrolment was to be supported, and the state pension age increased, though faster.

By the time the programme for government emerged, the department had got its ministers. They included the Liberal Democrat Steve Webb as pensions minister. An economist by training, a former Institute for Fiscal Studies researcher, he was – that rare thing in the

---

[4] *Coalition Agreement for Stability and Reform* (London: Cabinet Office, May 2010).
[5] *The Coalition: Our Programme for Government* (London: Cabinet Office, May 2010).

post – a pensions expert in his own right. Chris Grayling became employment minister, having spent a spell in opposition as the work and pensions spokesman, during which time he had developed the Work Programme. David Freud – Lord Freud, to whom we will return – was in charge of welfare reform. Iain Duncan Smith, known universally as IDS, became secretary of state. After losing the Conservative Party leadership in 2003, IDS had founded a think tank, the Centre for Social Justice, which had come up with radical ideas for benefit reform. As news of his surprise appointment emerged, its website reputedly crashed as departmental officials scrambled to understand what their new boss might get up to.[6]

Intentionally or not, the appointments set out what were to prove to be the key spheres of influence for the two parties – pensions for the Liberal Democrats, the Work Programme for the Conservatives, and what was to become universal credit for IDS. Plus, of course, a joint responsibility for the welfare cuts to come.

The origins of Universal Credit

The appointment of Duncan Smith, who had not been on the Conservative front bench in opposition, took aback both the man himself and his department.[7] The department had been expecting Theresa May, who had shadowed the department most recently. Her key concern in the pre-election talks had been around the Work Programme, not radical reform of the benefits systems. IDS arrived with a very different agenda. He came clutching an inch-thick 372-page document entitled *Dynamic Benefits*,[8] telling officials that was, pretty much, precisely what he intended to do.

Dynamic Benefits had emerged from IDS's journey during and after his leadership of the Conservative Party. While leader in 2002 he had visited the grim Easterhouse housing estate in Glasgow. He had been both shocked and inspired. Shocked by what he was to describe as

---

[6] Unattributable ministerial and official interviews.

[7] *Ibid.* Also Matthew d'Ancona, *In It Together: The Inside Story of the Coalition Government* (London: Penguin, 2014), pp. 25–6.

[8] *Dynamic Benefits* (Centre for Social Justice, 2009) (accessed at www.centreforsocial-justice.org.uk/publications/dynamic-benefits, 17 November 2014).

the effects of 'illiteracy, desertion and addiction'. Inspired by the fact that despite the social devastation, parts of the community struggled to help other parts. The visit was later to be popularized as the 'Easterhouse epiphany'. His then adviser, Tim Montgomerie, says that 'something suddenly clicked. He realized here was his personal mission and a mission for the Tory party.'[9] The Conservatives, IDS declared, had to become "the natural party of those who want to make a better life for themselves and their children', and one that 'doesn't just drive past Easterhouse on the motorway'.[10]

In 2004 he founded the Centre for Social Justice, which produced a string of reports, notably *Breakdown Britain* and *Breakthrough Britain*, that helped provide some of the soundtrack for Cameron's pre-election claims about 'Broken Britain', along with some 350 recommendations around family breakdown, education, addiction and more to tackle what he dubbed an 'emerging underclass' who were 'trapped by dependency and left behind by society'.[11] He'd come eventually to the view that 'the biggest barrier to those entering work for the first time was the benefit system itself'.[12] It needed fundamental reform to ensure that work paid. *Dynamic Benefits* spelled out a way to do that.

In fact, Labour's extensive programme of benefit reform had more or less ensured that work did, at least technically, pay. But it was far from always easy for DWP staff, let alone the claimant, to work that out. Claimants faced a complex mix of sometimes overlapping benefits from various forms of Jobseeker's Allowance, disability benefits, lone parent, housing and council tax payments plus tax credits, all of which meant many had to deal with DWP, HMRC for their tax credits and their local council for housing and council tax benefit. There were complex rules around which benefit kicked in when, depending on hours worked. It could take an expert adviser 45 minutes to do a 'better off in work' calculation. And while the gains were very real for most, for others they could be highly marginal. The interaction of the benefit and tax systems and the differing rates at which benefits were withdrawn as

---

[9] 'Profile: Work and Pensions Secretary Iain Duncan Smith', *BBC News*, 19 October 2010 (accessed at www.bbc.co.uk/news/uk-politics-11565723, 17 November 2014).

[10] 'How Iain Duncan Smith came to Easterhouse and left with a new vision for the Tory Party', *The Herald*, 23 March 2002; 'Conservatives: the party for the vulnerable', speech, March 2002 (accessed at www.totalpolitics.com/speech2003es/policy/poverty/34603/conservatives-the-party-for-the-vulnerable.thtml, 17 November 2014).

[11] CSJ, *Dynamic Benefits*, p. 4.   [12] *Ibid.*

income rose could see people lose 90p and sometimes more of each extra pound earned. In 2010 some 600,000 people potentially faced that situation. Well over two million faced marginal deduction rates, known as the taper, of more than 70p in the pound. As an extreme example, a single earner with two children on the national minimum wage could be less than £7 a week better off from working sixteen extra hours, before the travel costs of getting there. As the department's officials were later to put it, 'a system that produces this result cannot be right'.[13]

It was that situation that *Dynamic Benefits* aimed to correct by merging a string of benefits and using a single, lower, taper to withdraw benefit as income rose. That idea too, however, had its back story.

Ideas for finding a way to merge tax and benefits has a long history, stretching back to the 1960s and 1970s. But back in 2004, Kate Stanley, a researcher with the left-of-centre think tank IPPR floated the idea of a 'single working-age benefit' to radically simplify the system, an idea she then developed with Dr (now Professor) Roy Sainsbury of the social policy unit at the University of York. Sainsbury talked to Margaret Hodge, then a middle-ranking social security minister. In January 2006 a green paper briefly noted that 'there may be advantages in moving in the longer term towards a single system of benefits for all people of working age'. A benefits simplification unit was set up in the department.[14]

In late 2006, David Freud, a former City banker, was recruited by Tony Blair and John Hutton, the then Work and Pensions Secretary, to review its welfare-to-work programmes. His 2007 report did that. But it also devoted a chapter to a 'single system', outlining three very broad options. 'Whether the answer is a single benefit system may still be a matter for debate', he said, 'but that debate should certainly take place.'[15] Sainsbury had gone on to talk to Danny Alexander during the latter's time as Liberal Democrat work and pensions spokesman between 2007 and 2008, and to the Conservatives, while the Commons Work and Pensions Committee launched an inquiry into benefit simplification in 2007. The DWP aired the basic idea with notable enthusiasm in a 2008 white paper. It suggested that a start could be made with

---

[13] *21st Century Welfare* (Cm 7913, DWP, July 2010), p. 11.
[14] *A New Deal for Welfare: Empowering People to Work* (DWP, 2006), p. 92.
[15] David Freud, *Reducing Dependency, Increasing Opportunity: Options for the Future of Welfare to Work* (DWP, 2007), p. 100.

out-of-work benefits, but noted 'this would be a very significant reform and we will be undertaking further work to get both the structure of such a benefit and the journey towards it right'.[16]

Professor Sainsbury says: 'The idea of a single working age benefit had cross-party support from the early days. I thought it was an apolitical idea that was not rooted in any ideology at all. We just needed a simpler benefits system. I talked to all three parties about it and they were all on board.'[17]

What the idea still lacked was a full definition of what it would involve. Would it include both in- and out-of-work benefits? Would it take in child benefit and disability payments? And there was a further problem. It was instantly obvious that introducing a simpler system was either going to cost billions of pounds or there were going to be large numbers of losers. By 2009, there was none of the former available, and absolutely no desire to impose the latter as Labour's term of office drew to a close amid collapsing banks and a soaring deficit. The idea was reduced in a 2009 white paper to brief reference to it being a 'long-term ambition'.[18]

'The only people who took up the challenge [of actually defining a system] was Iain Duncan Smith in the Centre for Social Justice,' according to Lord Freud, who in February 2009 defected to the Conservatives, gaining a peerage and a place on the front bench.[19] There he worked first on the details of the Work Programme. From the autumn onwards, he concentrated on IDS's *Dynamic Benefits*, which the future Work and Pensions Secretary had launched in the September as 'a blueprint for reform' for an incoming Conservative government[20] – one which, as it turned out, he was going to get the chance to implement.

The welfare cuts begin

Well before any implementation, George Osborne, the Chancellor, had to produce his Emergency Budget. The result was a four-way tussle

---

[16] *Raising Expectations and Increasing Support: Reforming Welfare for the Future* (DWP, 2008).
[17] Interview with Roy Sainsbury, 27 June 2014.
[18] *Building Britain's Recovery: Achieving Full Employment* (DWP, December 2009).
[19] Freud interview in *Journal of Poverty and Social Justice*, 22:1 (2014), p. 38.
[20] 'Duncan Smith makes case for fewer benefits', *Financial Times*, 16 September 2009.

between DWP ministers, the Treasury, Number 10 and Nick Clegg, the Deputy Prime Minister and Liberal Democrat leader.

The DWP had long known that cuts were coming and had its own prepared list. The Treasury, as usual, had its own decidedly more draconian ideas, including much deeper cuts to housing benefit than eventually emerged. Clegg saw no sense in protecting winter fuel payments that went to the better off, and the Treasury had no sympathy for the idea. Number 10's prime concern was that Cameron's personal pledge to protect them and other benefits for the elderly would hold.

The Emergency Budget on 2 June produced, in the words of Robert Chote, director of the Institute for Fiscal Studies, the 'longest, deepest, sustained period of cuts to public services spending at least since World War II'.[21] Of the £99 billion of spending reductions by 2015/16, £11 billion were cuts to benefits and tax credits. Of the fifty policy decisions in the budget, twenty-three were welfare cuts.[22]

By far the biggest cut, though almost a silent one in terms of its public impact, was a switch from using the Retail Price Index to the Consumer Price Index as the basis for uprating benefits, tax credits and pensions, including public service pensions. There was a case that CPI was in fact a better measure of inflation. Indeed for many purposes RPI was soon to be retired as the government's standard inflation measure. But CPI tends to be lower. The switch was estimated to save almost £6 billion by 2014–15 and far more in the years to come. A small annual reduction in benefit uprating for millions of people would cumulatively become a huge one for the public purse.

Tax credits took a £3 billion hit from measures that included removing them from the better off and withdrawing them more quickly. The Child Trust Fund – Labour's attempt to build some capital for every child by age 18 – was killed off. Lone parents with children aged five and above were to be transferred from Income Support to Jobsee-ker's Allowance, requiring them actively to seek work. Those claiming Disability Living Allowance were to face medical assessments and be transferred to a new benefit, the Personal Independence Payment. Housing benefit expenditure was reduced by £1.7 billion by 2014/15.

[21] See www.ifs.org.uk/budgets/budgetjune2010/chote.pdf (accessed 17 November 2014).
[22] Budget 2010, pp. 40–1.

The element of that which drew the biggest headlines was to limit housing benefit for social housing tenants when they were judged to have more rooms than necessary – a £490 million a year saving by 2014/15 that the government described as the end of 'a spare room subsidy' but which its critics and the Labour Party promptly labelled a 'bedroom tax'. The Institute for Fiscal Studies judged the measures to be 'a mixed bag of reforms with no consistent objective beyond the desire to save money'.

Offsetting factors included implementation of the triple lock and an increase in child tax credits, which go to those on lower incomes – one element of the Chancellor's claim that 'we are all in this together'. It was partially paid for by a three-year freeze in the value of the universal child benefit.

These benefit cuts, however, were to prove only round one, not least because a way had to be found to pay for Iain Duncan Smith's big idea. Even *Dynamic Benefits,* which at the time involved two simpler benefits rather than one, had calculated that universal credit would cost an extra £3.6 billion a year while claiming that the single, lower taper would so strengthen work incentives that over time it would more than pay for itself.

The department got behind the programme, and did so enthusiastically. One of IDS's aides recalls the department's director of strategy greeting them with a copy of *Dynamic Benefits* in hand with the message that 'we believe we can do it, and that it will cost less than you think'. Another senior official says 'we took it away and came back with the view that it was deliverable, but that it was also the mother and father of all challenges'.[23]

They were faced, however, with a hostile Treasury and a highly sceptical chancellor, who were worried about both deliverability and cost. At the end of July an uneasy compromise saw DWP publish a green paper, *21st Century Welfare*, which canvassed five options for reform, although it was crystal clear that universal credit was the only one that Duncan Smith favoured.[24]

The battle for it produced the first of many tense encounters between the Work and Pensions Secretary and the Chancellor. Both the *Financial Times* and the *Mail on Sunday* reported in August a 'blazing,

---

[23] Unattributable interviews.   [24] *21st Century Welfare* (Cm 7913, DWP, July 2010).

shouting, grade-A row' between the two over something that Treasury officials regarded as 'unaffordable and impractical'.[25]

Duncan Smith, however, was determined. 'He was in that sense a very dangerous minister,' one senior DWP official says. 'He had no ambition for himself because he had been Tory leader and that had ended in tears. This was the only thing he wanted to do. And he would have walked away, if he had not been allowed to do it.'[26] Not least for that reason, Cameron backed him. Clegg and Alexander also supported the construction of universal credit – the Liberal Democrats having long advocated, not its detail, but some form of merger of the tax and benefits system. In the judgement of one senior Conservative minister it would have been 'touch and go' whether universal credit would have got through a purely Conservative government.[27]

The truth of the assessment that IDS was 'a very dangerous minister' was to come in 2012 when, with universal credit in deep trouble and the Treasury baying for more benefit cuts, IDS felt able to refuse Cameron's offer to move to be justice secretary.[28]

The resulting deal in 2010 was that DWP was given more than £2 billion over the next four years for implementation costs. But in return IDS had to agree to another £7 billion in benefit cuts so that the 'extra' benefit costs of universal credit were taken out of the system in advance. In addition the taper, the rate at which the benefit was to be withdrawn, was raised from IDS's aim of 55p in the £ to 65p, weakening the work incentive but making the scheme more affordable.[29]

The Comprehensive Spending Review in October 2010, which set out departmental spending in more detail, took that £7 billion out of welfare. The measures included a cap of £500 a week, or £26,000 a year, on the amount out-of-work benefits families could receive. The aim was 'to ensure that no family can receive more in welfare than

---

[25] 'Tough targets for benefit reforms', *Financial Times*, 16 August 2010; 'Iain Duncan Smith threatens to resign twice in row with George Osborne as way to win Cabinet backing for welfare reform', *Mail on Sunday*, 23 August 2010.

[26] Unattributable interview.   [27] Unattributable interview.

[28] D'Ancona, *In It Together*, pp. 292–4; 'Cabinet reshuffle – the best laid plans ...', *BBC News*, 4 September 2012 (accessed at www.bbc.co.uk/news/uk-politics-19473667, 17 November 2014).

[29] HM Treasury, *Spending Review 2010*, Box 2.6: 'Universal Credit: Welfare that works' (Cm 7597, DWP, November 2010).

median after tax earnings for working households'. There were further cuts to housing benefit and a further net saving of £2.3 billion by 2015/16 in tax credits. Bizarrely, in the name of 'localism' council tax benefit was cut by 10 per cent (though again pensioners were protected), devolved to councils, and taken out of universal credit – potentially replacing one means test for the benefit with hundreds of local ones and undermining the aim of a single, simple taper 'to ensure that work always pays'. DWP ministers regarded the decision as 'barmy'.[30] But in these early days of the coalition all departments were required to produce at least some measures of 'localism'. Like all departments, DWP faced a big cut in its administrative costs – 26 per cent.

Child benefit, one of the most fiercely guarded of the remaining universal benefits, was also cut. Gordon Brown, as Chancellor, had taken child benefit away from DWP to be run by HMRC. At the Conservative Party conference in October George Osborne – without reference to a furious IDS – had announced that it was to be withdrawn from higher-rate taxpayers. A clunky reform aimed at saving £2.5 billion, it left families where only one partner worked but earned £51,000 losing child benefit, while one where both earned up to £49,000, and thus had virtually double the income, kept it.

Other large savings came from higher pension contributions for 5 million public service workers and the announcement of a review of their schemes by Lord Hutton, the Labour former Work and Pensions Secretary. He took the task on because he felt Labour had ducked the issue in office. His recommendations, and subsequent decisions made by the Chancellor, were implemented after intermittent but repeated strike action across many of the public services. In essence the review equalized the pension age in these schemes upwards to 65 and replaced final salary pensions with ones based on average earnings. These changes, along with the higher contributions, significantly reduced the schemes' long-term costs, finally reflecting, albeit very partially as the pensions that remained in place were good ones, the cuts to final salary schemes that had devastated the private sector.[31]

The spending review also announced that the long-trailed rise in state pension age to 66 would now be brought forward from 2026 to 2020, with the increase to 67 due to be completed by 2028. In future,

[30] Unattributable interview.
[31] Independent Public Service Pensions Commission, *Final Report*, 10 March 2011.

regular reviews will use a formula aimed at holding the time spent on the state pension to one-third of an adult lifetime as life expectancy increases. Ten years' notice will in theory be given for future upward revisions, but the formula is likely to take the state pension age to 70 for today's youngest workers. The longer-term savings from all these changes began to give Steve Webb, the pensions minister, room for manoeuvre.

Pension reform

Webb's first act was to order up a review of automatic enrolment and NEST, the national pensions savings scheme. Webb had been sympathetic to the idea, but not its warmest advocate. And the Treasury had its worries. First, over the extra cost in tax relief as more people saved for a pension. And second, over whether even the initial 1 per cent employer contribution should be imposed when the economy was so fragile. The review made some minor adjustments, including to the band of earnings on which contributions would be paid.[32] Essentially, however, it declared the policy to be sound. It went ahead.

Webb's big ambition, however, was to simplify the state pension – to get to a single, decent, basic state pension in place of a highly complex two-tier one. He wanted, he used to say, the words 'single state pension' stamped on his gravestone.

In time, he got there. He was hampered by the Treasury's insistence that in no single year in the life of the government could he spend more beyond the triple lock – even if the change ultimately saved money. By January 2013 he was able to publish a white paper announcing that the new single-tier pension would come in from 2016, paid at a rate just above the means-tested pension credit, with new contributions to the state second pension ceasing.[33]

The last part of that decision potentially produced huge savings of some £5.5 billion a year, as employers from 2016 would no longer receive national insurance rebates for running pension schemes that were contracted out of a second-state pension that would no longer exist.

---

[32] *Making Automatic Enrolment Work* (Cm 7594, October 2010).

[33] *The Single Tier Pension: A Simple Foundation for Saving* (Cm 8528, DWP, January 2013) (accessed at www.gov.uk/government/uploads/system/uploads/attachment_-data/file/181229/single-tier-pension.pdf, 17 November 2014).

The vast bulk of such schemes, however, were by now in the public sector. If those savings were not handed back to public sector employers who include, for example, schools and hospitals, they would face a £4.7 billion jump in their pay bill. The coalition left the resolution of that headache to the next government. But on the DWP's figures, the long-term savings from the single pension would eventually be worth 0.5 per cent of GDP[34] – all of these savings making the single state pension acceptable to the Treasury, while leaving room for a future government to trim the costs further.[35]

This was a major reform. It would take decades fully to mature. But in essence it restored the principle behind the Beveridge basic state pension – that, at approaching 20 per cent of average earnings, it would provide a minimal standard of living but at the same time a platform on which private pension saving could be built. The coalition's decision in essence corrected the mistake made by the Conservatives back in 1981, and supported by Labour subsequently, of allowing the true value of the basic state pension to wither away. It completed the Turner Commission's vision of a decade earlier – a simpler state pension that adjusted to rising life expectancy, with automatic enrolment into private pension saving, backed by a fall-back state-sponsored scheme in NEST. This was no mean achievement. When the first results from auto-enrolment flowed in, far from the fears that up to 30 per cent would opt out, it appeared that 90 per cent were staying in.[36] The figures covered only a sample of the largest employers, the first group to introduce auto-enrolment. But by August 2014 4 million employees had been automatically enrolled.[37] Savings rates were still far too low to provide a decent pension – and would be even when the minimum contribution reached 8 per cent in 2017. But it was a significant start. The structure of pensions policy – though not the level of saving – was in a better place than it had been for decades. Webb also moved to cap the charges on

[34] *Ibid.*
[35] *The Long-term Cost and Spending Implications of the Single-Tier Pension* (Pensions Policy Institute, April 2014).
[36] 'Automatic enrolment opt-out rates', DWP, 2014 (accessed at www.gov.uk/government/uploads/system/uploads/attachment_data/file/227039/opt-out-research-large-employers-ad_hoc.pdf, 17 November 2014).
[37] '10,000 jumbo jets fly towards better retirement', DWP, 14 August 2014 (accessed at www.gov.uk/government/news/10000-jumbo-jets-fly-towards-better-retirement-with-automatic-enrolment, 17 November 2014).

private pensions and to allow new, more flexible collective designs for them – ones in which employers would promise to take on some of the risks of pension provision, but not all of them, as had been the case with final salary pensions.[38] The hope was that employers might repair, for the next generation of retirees, some of the damage from the spectacular decline in those defined benefit schemes.

Question marks remain about how long the 'triple lock' will last. Only the earnings link is in the legislation. And over time the better of earnings, prices and 2.5 per cent means state pensioners will do relatively better than the working population. The scale of these reforms, however, should not be underestimated.

Just when the ship appeared to be on calm seas, however, George Osborne in his 2014 Budget announced that in future no one would have to buy a lifetime income with the pot built up from a money purchase pension. Record low interest rates and rising life expectancy had dramatically cut the annual amounts people would receive from such annuities. Webb had been arguing that something needed to be done – 'in every interview I did extolling the virtues of automatic enrolment, journalists would say to me "ah but you have to buy a poxy annuity at the end of it"'.[39] Osborne went much further and much faster than even Webb expected. The arrival from 2016 of a single state pension meant the government had less need – though not no need – to worry about people falling back onto means-tested benefits if they blew their pension savings. 'If people do get a Lamborghini, and end up on the state pension, the state is much less concerned about that, and that is their choice,' Webb declared.[40] The decision threw the pensions industry into turmoil. Its long-term effects for good or ill remained the subject of furious debate as the 2015 election loomed. Would freedom to spend the money encourage saving, lead to people blowing their savings, intentionally or not, or indeed to them underspending in old age? Or, more likely, which mix of the three? It also raised a longer-term question. If pensions are to be pretty much like any other kind of saving, why would they still receive such generous tax relief?

[38] 'Pension Schemes Bill 2014 to 2015', DWP, 26 August 2014 (accessed at www.gov. uk/government/collections/pension-schemes-bill-2014-to-2015, 17 November 2014).

[39] Private interview.

[40] 'Pension pots "can be used to buy Lamborghinis", says Lib Dem minister', *The Independent*, 20 March 2014.

Battles over more cuts

If pensions policy, in the main, was going smoothly, welfare reform was not. By 2011, the biggest cuts to welfare had been announced. But the battle over how much further they should go rumbled on, and quite often round and round – the same ideas being trailed, vetoed and trailed again, only to be vetoed once more, or consigned to a possible Conservative manifesto commitment. There was some complex coalition politics in this. At times, IDS, under near-constant pressure from his own party for further welfare reductions to ease the spending pain elsewhere, appeared to support ideas such as limiting child benefit to the first two children in the certain knowledge that Clegg would veto them – as he did, along with the idea of removing housing benefit from those aged under 25.[41]

In November 2011 the Liberal Democrats went to war over whether benefits should be uprated fully for inflation in the coming year when it turned out to be unexpectedly high.[42] They won, and the 2012 Budget had little impact on welfare other than to confirm measures already announced. By 2013, however, it was clear that the deficit would not be eliminated in a parliament and that public spending cuts would extend way into the next one. What the media dubbed a 'National Union of Ministers' (after the National Union of Mineworkers) formed, led by the Conservatives Philip Hammond and Theresa May, the Defence and Home Secretaries. Half a per cent off the welfare budget would remove the need for further defence cuts, Hammond said, adding that 'there is a body of opinion within Cabinet that believes we have to look at the welfare budget again'.[43]

What followed was that the 2013 Budget announced that a whole range of benefits would increase by only 1 per cent for three

---

[41] 'Iain Duncan Smith targets families of more than two children for benefit cuts', *The Guardian*, 25 October 2012, and 'Nick Clegg's speech: Governing Britain from the centre ground', *Liberal Democrat Voice*, 17 December 2012 (accessed at www. libdemvoice.org/nick-cleggs-speech-governing-britain-from-the-centre-ground-building-a-stronger-economy-in-a-fairer-society-32221.html, 17 November 2014).

[42] 'Osborne looks to slash benefits bill', *Financial Times*, 2 November 2011.

[43] 'Slash benefit to save troops', *The Sun*, 2 March 2013 (accessed at www.thesun.co.uk/sol/homepage/news/politics/4820882/Defence-Secretary-demands-welfare-cuts-to-save-troop-numbers-sparking-Cabinet-spending-row.html#ixzz2MO48TwbD, 17 November 2014).

years from 2013/14, the same applying to child benefit for two years from 2014/15. That was justified by the fact that, cuts to entitlement aside, most benefit rates other than child benefit had broadly kept pace with inflation while real wages had been falling. Along with another trim to housing benefit, these measures produced further savings of £3.5 billion a year by 2016/17, producing total cuts to projected spending on the benefit bill over the parliament of some £20 billion a year.

The autumn statement of that year froze the amounts people could earn under universal credit before their benefit started to be withdrawn, again denting the work incentives it was meant to produce. The statement also sought to tie down the future. It announced a 'welfare cap' that would require future cuts – or an explanation of why they were not happening – if forecast spending was set to be exceeded on some twenty-four benefits, which covered just over half of total benefits expenditure.[44] Jobseeker's Allowance and state pensions were among the exclusions. The cap was in part a political trap. Would Labour vote for it? Labour did. But opinion was divided on whether this was a piece of gesture politics, a cap that would hold only as long as it suited, or whether in fact it was a 'potentially momentous punctuation mark' in the welfare state which, for the first time, 'sets borders to benefit land'.[45]

By 2014 it was too late in the parliament for radical new measures, but not for the post-election battleground to be set. In early 2014 Osborne warned of another £25 billion of public spending cuts to come after the election. Half of these, he said, should come from welfare, with benefits for the young rather than for pensioners the first target. Aides to IDS dubbed that 'unbalanced'. Clegg said it risked being 'a monumental mistake'. If the 2010 election had been largely silent on what was to happen to welfare, for 2015 it looked likely to be a big battleground, not least because Labour too would have to take a position on what to preserve and what to change.

[44] Guide to the benefit cap at 'The welfare cap' (House of Commons Library Standard Note SN06852' (accessed at www.parliament.uk/business/publications/research/briefing-papers/SN06852/the-welfare-cap, 17 November 2014).

[45] Matthew d'Ancona, 'Osborne has marked the borders of Benefit Land', *Daily Telegraph*, 22 March 2014; Gavin Kelly, 'Will the welfare cap stand the test of time?', Resolution Foundation blog, 25 March 2014 (accessed at www.resolutionfoundation.org/media/blog/will-welfare-cap-stand-test-time, 17 November 2014).

Delivery

Announcing radical changes to the benefit system is one thing. Delivering them quite another. The Cabinet Office and the Treasury run a Major Projects Authority, which regularly reviews large-scale departmental change programmes in an attempt to improve their success rate. DWP had no fewer than twelve projects with it. That looked like overload in a department that was going through a 26 per cent reduction in its running costs and which was reliant on external contracts for many services – contracts that the National Audit Office and others were repeatedly to point out had been far from always well negotiated.

The pension reforms went smoothly. Elsewhere, it was a sea of troubles. The transfer of people from Incapacity Benefit to the new Employment and Support Allowance, a programme the coalition inherited from Labour, proved a nightmare. The work capability assessment proved so harsh and inaccurate that huge numbers of those turned down won on appeal and the process was subject to repeated revision.[46] By June 2014 a backlog of 700,000 cases had built up. Atos, the contractor for the assessments, quit, saying its staff were being 'vilified' for carrying out government policy.

That in turn had an impact on the Work Programme. It was always debatable whether the coalition should have gone for the dislocation of scrapping all Labour's welfare-to-work schemes in favour of its modified approach. By July 2014, four years on from that decision, the National Audit Office judged the Work Programme, which ministers had argued would be transformational, to be performing 'at similar levels to previous programmes' for those on Jobseeker's Allowance. The NAO acknowledged that the potential for better results remained. But for the hardest-to-help, including those affected by the new Employment and Support Allowance, performance was well below expectation. Providers were spending less than half the originally expected amount on getting them back to work.[47]

[46] 'Simplifying the welfare system and making sure work pays', DWP, 16 April 2013 (accessed at www.gov.uk/government/policies/simplifying-the-welfare-system-and-making-sure-work-pays/supporting-pages/improving-the-work-capability-assessment, 17 November 2014).

[47] 'The Work Programme', National Audit Office (HC 266, Session 2014–15, 2 July 2014) (accessed at www.nao.org.uk/wp-content/uploads/2014/07/The-work-programme.pdf, 17 November 2014).

From 2013 the coalition introduced the new 'personal independence payment' to recognize the additional costs for working-age
adults of living with a disability. Introduced with no proper pilot, its
implementation also went awry. Again, huge delays resulted. A similar
backlog of 700,000 cases built up. The Commons Public Accounts
Committee said some of the most vulnerable people in society were
facing an 'inaccessible process'. The promised benefit savings were not
materializing.[48] Margaret Hodge, the Labour chair of the cross-party
committee, branded it 'a fiasco'.[49]

Most embarrassing, however, was universal credit, the department's and IDS's flagship reform. The initial assessment of officials that
it was 'the mother and father of all challenges' proved only too true. It
had been intended to roll it out at scale starting from 2013. However, a
long chapter of misjudgements, including an IT system that lacked the
necessary security, saw £40 million of software written off, a further
£90 million pounds' worth acknowledged to be of limited use, and
mounting delays, with the Treasury finally only approving continued
investment on a step-by-step basis. By the autumn of 2014, universal
credit was operating only for relatively small numbers of new cases in
limited parts of the country. Plans for it mainly to be claimed on-line
had gone into abeyance. Cross-party support for the idea behind it
remained high. But despite the overt confidence of ministers that all
would eventually be well, big questions remained over whether it would
ever live up to its promise.

Impact

The impact on individuals, and on groups in society, from these myriad
changes were many and varied. Many of the cuts and reforms were
still working their way through as the election loomed, although reporters had no difficulty finding tales of hardship and dislocation as they
started to bite. There was shock when a Birmingham woman committed

---

[48] Public Accounts Committee, *Personal Independence Payment* (HC 280, First report
of Session 2014–15).
[49] 'Margaret Hodge: Personal Independence Payment welfare scheme as a "fiasco"',
Daily Telegraph, 20 June 2014.

suicide, leaving a note blaming the bedroom tax.[50] She proved not to be the only case.[51]

But the housing benefit cuts appeared to be having some of the desired effects. Some private sector landlords were reducing rents, though not, initially, that many. More out-of-work people said they were looking for a job or longer hours to meet the shortfall between their rent and benefit payments. Six per cent of tenants – fewer than expected, and around the normal level of churn – moved in the first six months after the 'spare room subsidy' or 'bedroom tax' took effect in April 2013. The benefit cap had a similar effect. But rent arrears were mounting as a result of both measures, raising the prospect of later evictions. The DWP's own research had many people reporting that they were cutting back on essential as well as non-essential spending and getting into debt. The immediate impact was being eased by temporary cash provided to local authorities to spend at their discretion to ease in the changes, with the full long-term impact still uncertain.[52] IDS was able to claim in the summer of 2014 that with 46,000 households originally affected by the benefit cap, more than 7,000 no longer were because someone in the household had got a job.[53] How many would have done so without the cap was not known.

There was no doubt that the benefit system was getting tighter and tougher. The number of sanctions – withdrawal of benefit – rocketed. In 2013, after a more demanding requirement to seek work arrived in 2012, more than 900,000 sanctions were applied to those on Jobseeker's Allowance. This was more than double the 439,000 in Labour's last year in office. An additional 23,000 sanctions were applied to Employment and Support Allowance claimants.[54] That still left under 5 per cent of claimants having benefit withdrawn in an average month. Esther McVey, the work minister, said: 'The people

---

[50] 'Woman worried about bedroom tax killed herself, coroner finds', *The Guardian*, 12 August 2014.

[51] Commons Hansard, 5 September 2014, col. 580.

[52] *Evaluation of Removal of the Spare Room Subsidy* (Research Report No 882, DWP, July 2014); *The Impact of Recent Reforms to Local Housing Allowances* (Research Report No 874, DWP, July 2014); *Post-implementation Effects of the Benefit Cap* (DWP ad hoc research report no. 2, April 2014.

[53] DWP press release, 7 August 2014.

[54] *DWP Quarterly Statistical Summary*, First release, 13 August 2014 (accessed at www.gov.uk/government/uploads/system/uploads/attachment_data/file/344650/stats-summary-aug14.pdf, 17 November 2014).

who get sanctions are wilfully rejecting support [to get into a job] for no good reason.'[55]

However, an independent report commissioned by the government of sanctions in the welfare-to-work programmes showed that many claimants did not understand why their benefit had been stopped. The Department's 'legalistic' letters 'were hard to understand (even for those working in the area)', the review said. They were 'unclear as to why someone was being sanctioned'. Fewer than a quarter knew that hardship payments were available. A particularly vulnerable group struggled to understand the system and were thus sanctioned more often. Some seventeen recommendations for change were made and accepted.[56]

One apparent sign of strain was an explosion in food banks and the numbers using them – more than 900,000 people in 2013–14 according to the Trussell Trust, the charity that is their key sponsor. Lord Freud argued that the demand was 'supply led', as the trust worked hard towards its target of having a food bank in every town. The charity said the reasons for growing demand included 'rising food and fuel prices, static incomes, underemployment and changes to benefits'.[57] That diagnosis of multiple causes was broadly supported by a subsequent all-party parliamentary inquiry, which nonetheless reported that 'benefit-related problems was the single biggest reason given for food bank referrals by almost every food bank which presented evidence to us'.[58]

Anglican and Roman Catholic bishops accused the government of creating 'hardship and hunger'.[59] Vincent Nichols, Britain's most senior Roman Catholic cleric, dubbed the sanctions regime 'punitive', while arguing that 'the basic safety net that was there to guarantee that people would not be left in hunger or in destitution has actually been torn apart'.[60] Cameron responded, saying that was 'simply not true'. Welfare reform was a 'moral mission', with the number of workless

---

[55] 'Benefit sanctions soar under tougher regime', *The Guardian*, 6 November 2013.
[56] Independent review of the operation of Jobseeker's Allowance sanctions (DWP, July 2014).
[57] See www.trusselltrust.org (accessed 17 November 2014).
[58] *Feeding Britain: The Report of the All-Party Parliamentary Inquiry into Hunger in the United Kingdom* (December 2014)
[59] *Daily Mirror*, 19 February 2014.   [60] *Daily Telegraph*, 14 February 2014.

households steadily coming down, and a welfare system that supported people into work 'at the heart of our long term economic plan'.[61]

What was undeniable as the economy improved was that claims for JSA, the unemployment benefit, were falling and the numbers in employment were up – by more than a million from 2010. That happened as controversy over 'zero hours' contracts raged. But Mark Carney, the governor of the Bank of England, suggested the benefit changes may have played a part in the improving job numbers.[62]

At the highest levels of measurement, and at first sight counter-intuitively given the benefit cuts, income inequality did not rise over the first three years of the coalition. Indeed by comparison with the start of the global financial crisis in 2007–8, income inequality had in fact fallen by 2012/13 (the latest figures available). That happened chiefly because real earnings dropped sharply while – unlike in the great depression of the 1930s – many benefit rates had continued to increase by inflation. However, a number of the key benefit cuts did not take effect until April 2013. Some were only due for implementation in 2015 and 2016. As a result the Institute for Fiscal Studies judged in July 2014 that 'there is good reason to think that the falls in income inequality since 2007–08 are currently being reversed'. That might indeed happen 'swiftly' once real earnings growth resumes but the later benefit reductions take effect.[63] Furthermore, its modelling out to 2015 of the effect of the benefit and tax changes combined showed that despite the Chancellor's repeated claims that 'we are all in this together', the poorest 10 and 20 per cent had been hit appreciably harder than 'middle England'.[64] Even so, in percentage terms, the top 10 per cent had been hit hardest by these changes.

What the income figures showed most starkly, however, was the quite extraordinary degree of protection pensioners had enjoyed, both from the recession and from the coalition's spending cuts. The switch to CPI inflation, higher state pension ages, and the abolition of

---

[61] 'David Cameron: Why the Archbishop of Westminster is wrong about welfare', *Daily Telegraph*, 18 February 2014

[62] 'IDS doubts "bedroom tax" disability figures', *Daily Telegraph*, 13 August 2014.

[63] *Living Standards, Poverty and Inequality in the UK 2014* (Institute for Fiscal Studies, July 2014), pp. 34 and 55.

[64] David Phillips, 'Personal tax and welfare measures', Institute for Fiscal Studies (accessed at: www.ifs.org.uk/budgets/budget2014/personal_measures.pdf, 27 November 2014), Slide 11.

the second state pension would over time save money. But in the shorter term 'the triple lock', the indexation of many private pensions in payment and Cameron's refusal to cut other pensioner benefits saw average pensioner incomes grow consistently from 2007/8, 'in stark contrast', as the IFS noted, 'to the fortunes of young adults, who saw by far the largest falls in income'.[65]

The coalition effect

By 2015/16 – election year – total benefit expenditure was forecast to be taking a smaller share of national income than in 2010, with spending rising in real terms on pensioners and falling for children and working-age adults.[66] Conditionality for receipt of benefit had continued its onward march. In terms of serious structural reform, as opposed simply to saving revenue, there were two definites and two that are debatable. The definites were pensions and universal credit: one going well, the other much less so. More debatable were child benefit and the welfare cap. In the form of family allowances, child benefit had been a cornerstone of the 1948 welfare state, but had taken its first significant hit. The long-term effects of the welfare cap remained uncertain. But it held out the possibility of the budget for working-age benefits being squeezed steadily downwards.

Without the Liberal Democrats, it is highly unlikely that a Conservative government would have legislated for a single state pension – that was quite simply not on any Conservative agenda. It is more unlikely that it would have happened had Gordon Brown won the 2010 general election. Brown, throughout his time as chancellor, was a fierce advocate of means-tested pensions and acquiesced with ill-disguised resentment to the Turner settlement on which Webb built. Webb was a man on a mission. But it is far from certain that he would have got there without Iain Duncan Smith's whole-hearted support. IDS, for all his critics say of him, has a genuine interest in the *structural*

---

[65] IFS, *Living Standards, Poverty and Inequality in the UK 2014*, p. 34.

[66] Benefit expenditure and caseload tables 2014 (accessed at www.gov.uk/government/statistics/benefit-expenditure-and-caseload-tables-2014, 27 November 2014), Benefit summary table and Table 2b, expenditure by age group.

reform of social security to produce a system that works better, not just in one that costs less.

There was also a coalition effect on universal credit, though perhaps a less transparent one. Plainly it was IDS's big idea. His mission. But at crucial moments, not least around its troubled birth in the summer of 2010 and when implementation hit really big trouble in 2012, it could have died without the support of Clegg and Alexander in the face of Treasury officials' opposition and George Osborne's concerns – Alexander being particularly helpful in 2012.[67] The rapport between IDS and Webb was important: IDS trusting Webb on pensions; Webb becoming convinced of the long-term gains that universal credit would offer once – and if – it could be made to work. In all of this, the Quad was crucial. Every big social security decision went through it.

A Conservative-only government would certainly have tackled public sector pensions. However, Alexander, at the Treasury, was robust in support of the changes, fronting the case for them.

On the benefit cuts, the glib story which the Liberal Democrats would like told is that they mitigated the desires of slavering Conservatives, while supporting structural reform. The reality is more complex. For a start, the Liberal Democrat MPs and peers had to face, for the first time in decades, responsibility for decisions taken on welfare cuts rather than mere opposition to them. And these in turn had to be sold to a membership that is more social democrat than 'Orange Book' liberal. There were a few, relatively small, examples of peers in particular getting an announced proposal revised – for example over mobility payments. Clegg was able to claim he had vetoed some changes (see above). But the strain of all that was illustrated when Lib Dem ministers, including Danny Alexander, who as Chief Secretary to the Treasury had negotiated the 'spare room subsidy', voted for a private member's bill in mid-2014 to mitigate the 'bedroom tax'.

But IDS was also a territorial minister, not just a structural reformer. At times he furiously defended his budget,[68] seeking to protect those he saw as most vulnerable. At others he offered up to Conservative colleagues sacrifices that he knew the Liberal Democrats would not wear.

---

[67] Unattributable ministerial interviews.   [68] D'Ancona, *In It Together*, pp. 47, 91.

Furthermore, it is arguable that without universal credit, the welfare cuts might have just have been somewhat smaller. Some £7 billion of them were required to cut the benefit bill in advance so that the promise of no cash losers as the credit came in could be honoured – and the Liberal Democrats supported universal credit. Osborne, Clegg and IDS would have done something about the more fringe pensioner benefits such as winter fuel payments. It was Cameron who would not let them. 'It would be my tuition fees,' he told Clegg.[69] These are fine judgements, however. A test of their validity might lie in a Conservative victory in 2015, and on the evidence of what is then done, and in what way, to the budget for social security.

The future of working-age benefits – including perhaps the benefit cap and the impact of the welfare cap – will also be tested by the result of the Scottish referendum. The promise of more devolution all round may well see welfare policy start to diverge significantly across the UK for the first time since 1948 – as it has already for the management of health.

[69] *Ibid.*, p. 368.

13 THE COALITION AND FOREIGN AFFAIRS

MICHAEL CLARKE

Reviews and continuity

Foreign affairs and security matters were not uppermost in the minds of Conservative or Liberal Democrat leaders when the *Coalition Agreement for Stability and Reform* was drawn up in May 2010.[1] The foreign affairs that mattered most to the United Kingdom were no more unstable than usual and there was no obvious need to reform anything. The evolution towards a more coherent and strategic 'whole of government' approach to foreign, defence and security affairs was a matter of consensus throughout Whitehall and Westminster and the new government could look towards winding down military operations in Afghanistan along the same lines as those in Iraq had been. Some relationships with partners and allies were thought to need more attention and a review of how the UK was conducting its foreign affairs was the natural reaction of an incoming government.

An implicit commitment to a foreign policy review was complemented by an explicit commitment to a defence review that would also take place immediately after an election. The Conservatives had long been committed to building on the Labour Government's 1997 Strategic Defence Review with a long overdue Strategic Defence *and Security* Review (SDSR) that would explicitly put defence alongside internal

The author would like to thank Jean-André Prager for his assistance in preparing this chapter.

[1] *Coalition Agreement for Stability and Reform* (Cabinet Office, May 2010).

security, and all that implied, in a single framework that would not be run from the Ministry of Defence, but rather from the Cabinet Office, at the centre of government.[2] The only variation in the commitment to a review by the coalition partners was in the order of the words – the Conservatives' SDSR was rendered in the Liberal Democrat manifesto as the SSDR (for the sake of differentiation). Both parties were, in any case, building on the general direction of travel the Labour Government had been taking with its National Security Strategy of 2008 and the accompanying National Risk Register, alongside more sectoral policies such as cyber security or counter-terrorism.[3]

Insofar as there were important strategic considerations in the general sphere of foreign affairs, they concerned the need to maintain the UK's image as a significant international actor and partner in the face of inevitable public spending cuts that the economic crisis of 2010 presaged. To those who bitterly criticized public expenditure cuts in diplomatic and defence capabilities as somehow being 'un-strategic' – because they disagreed with them – the answer was that the national strategy of the coalition government, taking power in the midst of a manifest economic crisis, was to maintain the country's triple-A credit rating and stave off the most apocalyptic of the economic prospects for the UK. If that required immediate public expenditure cuts to steady the nerves of a barely rational international financial system, then that was judged to be the overriding national strategic priority.

No strategic shrinkage

Reassurance to the international community that the UK would not be crippled as an international actor by this painful necessity was an immediate priority. Thus it was that in William Hague's first speech as the coalition's Foreign Secretary in July 2010 the slogan that there would be 'no strategic shrinkage' in the UK's overseas engagements was picked out as the international headline the Government wanted to promote. The UK was part of a 'networked world' and its

---

[2] *Securing Britain in an Age of Uncertainty: The Strategic Defence and Security Review* (Cm 7948, October 2010).

[3] *The National Security Strategy of the United Kingdom: Security in an Interdependent World* (Cm 7291, March 2008); Cabinet Office, *National Risk Register* (2008); Cabinet Office, *Cyber Security Strategy of the United Kingdom* (June 2009); *Countering International Terrorism: The United Kingdom's Strategy* (Cm 6888, July 2006).

diplomatic partners would be expanded to include countries that had been relatively neglected by the previous government. More attention would be paid to the Gulf and to India, for example, and there would be a more explicit 'prosperity agenda' introduced into the UK's foreign affairs as an example of more 'enlightened self-interest'.[4] This was entirely consistent with the rhetoric in the Conservative election manifesto and was also implied, though never quite spelled out like that, in the Liberal Democrat manifesto. Insofar as there was a need to balance the partners' respective approaches to foreign affairs in the Coalition Agreement there was a natural symmetry between the commitment favoured by Liberal Democrats to lift international aid spending to the UN's target of 0.7 per cent of GDP and the more assertive promotion of 'our enlightened national interest' within an 'active foreign policy' enshrined in Conservative thinking. Mention was made of countries in Asia and peace processes in the Middle East that must be given greater priority in the future. In truth, it was not a hard balance to strike.[5]

Where rather more difficult deals had to be struck by the partners, they were postponed by simply making firm commitments – but not yet; and cast forward into a future parliament. The partners disagreed on the future role of the UK in the European Union, and while this was a matter of emphasis for the Liberal Democrats – to work within the EU to reform it and get more British influence into EU policy – it was a potential party-breaker for the Conservatives, many of whom saw it as an ever-present attack on UK sovereignty. The partners also disagreed on the renewal of the UK's nuclear deterrent, and while this was essentially a calculation of value for money and opportunity costs for the Conservatives, it was a potential party-breaker for the Liberal Democrats, many of whom took a stand on principle against the UK's nuclear deterrent and who had only been bought off in their own manifesto by a pledge to 'rule out the like-for-like

---

[4] 'Britain's foreign policy in a networked world', 1 July 2010 (accessed at www.gov.uk/government/speeches/britain-s-foreign-policy-in-a-networked-world–2, 27 November 2014). See also Michael Harvey, 'Perspectives on the UK's place in the world', *Chatham House Paper* 2011/01 (December 2011).

[5] HM Government, *The Coalition: Our Programme for Government: Freedom, Fairness and Responsibility* (London: Cabinet Office, May 2010), pp. 15, 20; Conservative Party, *Invitation to Join the Government of Britain: The Conservative Manifesto 2010* (London: Conservative Party, 2010), p. 109; Liberal Democrats, *Liberal Democrat Manifesto 2010* (London: Liberal Democrats, 2010), 'Your World'.

replacement of the Trident nuclear weapons system', while alternatives were investigated.[6]

So the Conservative partners agreed vaguely to play a leading role in the EU but committed to a national referendum in the event of any more transference of powers to the EU – a commitment the Prime Minister then made absolute for 2017 to keep his party together.[7] And the Liberal Democrat partners agreed vaguely to scrutinize the Trident replacement plan on a value for money basis while accepting that the current replacement plan would remain on the table until a final decision in 2016. The document that finally presented the review in July 2013 was a formal 'HM Government' document in which the first sentence asserted that 'This review is not a statement of government policy.'[8] The 'main gate decision' to procure a like-for-like replacement for the Trident nuclear deterrent – the full commitment of contracts with industry and the Atomic Weapons Establishment – was postponed for the next government. If UK policies on the EU and nuclear deterrence have little intrinsically to connect them, they nevertheless made for a symmetrical political deal when time was short and the constitutional imperative was great.

On security affairs the partners were committed to reviewing the counter-terrorism CONTEST strategy, first outlined in 2003 and based on the four alliterative policy streams; 'prevent', 'pursue', 'protect' and 'prepare'. The first of these, by common consent, was in need of review since it represents the most difficult set of tasks, attempting to turn 'vulnerable' Muslims away from violent radicalism and jihadism in response to their personal alienation from whatever combination of causes.[9] But there was no dissent from the general effectiveness and coherence of the CONTEST strategy as a whole and the increase in resources for the three principal security agencies that had occurred after the London bombings of 2005 had given them adequate, if not generous, funding to expand their operations appropriately. Security

---

[6] Liberal Democrats, *Manifesto 2010*, 'Your World'.

[7] In a speech on 23 January 2013, described as 'epochal' in *The Economist*, 26 January 2013.

[8] HM Government, *Trident Alternatives Review*, 16 July 2013.

[9] *Countering International Terrorism*, pp. 9–16; Charlie Edwards, 'The UK counterterror strategy: A return on investment', Royal United Services Institute Analysis, 10 April 2013.

chiefs anticipated some cuts to their lately enlarged budgets but not at levels that would put critical capabilities at risk.[10]

Cuts in the Home Office budget for policing would never be popular and there was recognition that this could be a political liability if it appeared to make the country more vulnerable to terrorist attacks. The UK's approach to countering terrorism, unlike that of the United States, was firmly based on criminal justice principles and not on the notion that it was engaged in a 'war on terror' – though its military operations in the Middle East and south Asia often seemed to make it complicit in such an approach. But intelligence-led policing must be seen in the forefront of counter-terrorism in the UK and certain constabularies – the Met, Greater Manchester, the West Midland, West Yorkshire and Thames Valley police forces – had been on the front line in foiling over fifty terrorist plots and incidents in or against the UK, wherein only two had been successful in over fifteen years.[11] Cutting policing budgets could be made to sound downright irresponsible in the context of counter-terrorism.

The coalition partners could at least rebut this charge with the shared commitment they both had before the 2010 election to continue the evolution (and the bureaucratic momentum) to create new machinery at the centre of government to deal with all security-related matters. A National Security Council would be established, headed by a National Security Adviser and a series of three Deputy NSAs with an appropriate central staff. It would be chaired on a weekly basis by the Prime Minister. In the same spirit of greater central coherence a new National Crime Agency was to be established, partly to replace the Serious Organised Crime Agency, but also to become responsible for counter-terrorist police coordination. In future, it was controversially argued, the inefficiencies and potential holes in the dragnet against terrorists would be addressed by a central agency rather than coordination between local police constabularies of different shapes and sizes

---

[10] Personal interviews. The three principal security agencies are the Security Service (MI5), the Secret Intelligence Service (MI6) and the Government Communications Headquarters (GCHQ).

[11] The successful incidents had been the July 2005 London bombings and the May 2013 murder of Gunner Lee Rigby. On the record of counter-terrorism in the UK see Michael Clarke, 'The fight against terrorism in the UK: are we winning?', in Douglas Alexander and Ian Kearns (eds.), *A Changing World: Future Challenges for British Foreign Policy* (London: Faber, 2013), p. 17.

as well as with intelligence agencies with their more specific security agendas. Any regrettable cuts in police budgets, it was argued, would not be relevant to the counter-terrorism strategy since the central organization of this was anyway being reorganized in a more efficient way. It was a neat enough argument but it left a swathe of cynical criticism in its wake, and not just from defenders of the devolved forty-three police forces of England and Wales. But in the end the Home Secretary backtracked and 'postponed' the counter-terrorism reorganization into the next parliament, leaving the issue unresolved.[12]

Inherited wars

In the wider security picture the coalition was inheriting politically divisive war-fighting operations: one ongoing in Afghanistan and the remains of another in Iraq. In different circumstances, both could have been highly problematical to the coalition. But in this case the timing was fortunate. As with all such expeditionary operations, major intervening powers choose a time to declare victory and leave. The UK had done this in Iraq, and by the spring of 2010 the majority of the fighting force had been withdrawn from the country for over a year and all remaining UK military personnel (mainly Royal Navy support staffs) were due to leave by May 2011.[13] In Afghanistan, the drawdown date of 'end-2014' had been announced by the United States and this gave the UK its own corresponding timetable that David Cameron was happy enough to accept. There would still be fighting to do in Afghanistan but now the accent was on transition and withdrawal rather than continued offensive operations.[14]

Fighting wars is intrinsically difficult from the opposition benches, having the power only to carp and criticize while the nation's young men and women put themselves in danger for what the government claims is a vital national interest. Naturally enough, therefore,

---

[12] Home Office Committee, *Counter-terrorism* (HC 231, 30 April 2013), paragraphs 136–41; 'Plans to strip Scotland Yard of terrorism role postponed', *Financial Times*, 10 October 2014.

[13] Hew Strachan (ed.), *British Generals in Blair's Wars* (Farnham: Ashgate, 2013), 'Conclusion' pp. 332, 342–4.

[14] Michael Clarke, 'Brothers in arms: The British–American alignment', in Adrian Johnson (ed.), *Wars in Peace: British Military Operations since 1991* (London: Royal United Services Institute, 2014), pp. 252–60.

Conservatives and Liberal Democrats before 2010 had concentrated on the service issues most affecting the troops in combat and at home. There had been commitments from both parties to enhance medical and welfare provision for the troops and to 'rebuild' the military covenant – though the troops had never themselves been very sure what this concept was. It had existed implicitly for some 400 years and was referred to somewhat elliptically in an Army document only in 2000.[15] There was little in it that could form the basis of policy but it helped get opposition parties off the hook of having to 'oppose' when the nation goes to others' wars.

The partners were on safer opposition ground in expressing their unspecified aspirations to address the perennial questions of Ministry of Defence spending and the costs of procuring military equipment. The perception of a £38 billion 'black hole' in the MoD's forward expenditure programme was a good issue on which to base a meaty political challenge that had obvious relevance in the midst of expensive foreign operations.[16] The MoD's budgetary practices would need to be reviewed, alongside its whole management structure – struggling, as it uniquely does, to be both a cost-conscious department of state as well as a strategic military headquarters that cannot afford to fail. Not just the MoD in Whitehall but the whole defence equipment and support organization based at Abbey Wood near Bristol – the 15,000 people responsible for £160 billion in defence equipment due to be procured over the next decade – should be rethought if defence was to get back into balance at a time when it was imperative an incoming government was seen to rein in public expenditure.

Even in the face of the inevitable public expenditure cuts to which the coalition government was committed no part of this foreign affairs agenda was strategically different from what had gone before. The issues most difficult inside each governing party had been put off without derailing anything the previous government already had in hand. There was continuity of policy in the counter-terrorism area and in ongoing military deployments and the usual promises of a fresh

---

[15] See Anthony Forster, 'The Military Covenant and British civil–military relations: letting the genie out of the bottle', *Armed Forces and Society*, 38:2 (2012), pp. 273–90.

[16] See Malcolm Chalmers, 'Looking into the Black Hole: Is the UK defence budget crisis really over?' Royal United Services Institute, Briefing Paper September 2011.

look and reviews of current organizations to do everything better, or at least more cost-effectively.

Foreign policy would be confident, more open to new partnerships and unapologetic about pursuing UK national interests, albeit in an enlightened form. The centrality of the transatlantic relationship to the UK was reaffirmed and hopes were high that as President Obama settled into his first term after eighteen months there would be a new approach to global leadership following the divisive neo-con interlude. The UK could line up confidently behind a new and internationally popular US leader. On the Arab–Israeli peace process, the problem of Iranian nuclear weapons proliferation, the relationship with Russia after the brief war with Georgia in 2008 and better understanding with China in the Pacific, there was real hope that the Obama Administration's investment in the concept of 'smart power' to review regional diplomatic relations would provide the UK with opportunities to exercise its diplomatic skills and help shape some key areas in the global environment to the benefit of UK interests.[17]

The 'no strategic shrinkage' slogan of July 2010 was therefore the epitome of a more general desire to convince the outside world, and ourselves, that the United Kingdom was on a business as usual track, no matter how unpalatable the economic medicine proved to be. In the event, the foreign and security capabilities of the country were more lightly pruned in the Comprehensive Spending Review of October 2010 than had been widely expected. Defence was cut by just 8.6 per cent in real terms after reductions in the order of 15 per cent had been anticipated, and in line with the overall level of total reductions in public expenditure. The Foreign and Commonwealth Office budget was reduced by 24 per cent but most of this was a cut in BBC World Services and only affected around 10 per cent of the FCO's

---

[17] Hillary Rodham Clinton, *Hard Choices* (New York: Simon and Schuster, 2014), pp. 33–4. Before the election Nick Clegg had argued that the 'special relationship' with the US was over, but he nuanced his view as Deputy Prime Minister in an interview on LBC Radio in January 2013 to argue that the relationship was still important to the UK for the benefits it could provide in EU diplomacy. See also William Hague's speech on 26 June 2013 that rejected any 'declinism' in western diplomacy (accessed at www.gov.uk/government/speeches/foreign-secretary-speech-on-rejecting-decline-and-renewing-western-diplomacy-in-the-21st-century, 18 November 2014).

core budget in real terms.[18] The international aid budget was due to be increased by some 37 per cent to meet the Coalition Agreement's (Liberal Democratic) commitment to set aid expenditure to 0.7 per cent of GDP by 2013.[19] The Security Services were also believed to have got off lightly. The Government's external affairs portfolio as a whole was one of the relative winners in the painful process of public expenditure cuts, suffering less than welfare delivered through local authorities, environment, business and most of the functions of the Home Office.[20]

Events and discontinuity

The gods of politics are seldom sympathetic to strategic reviews. The coalition government had completed its Comprehensive Spending Review in October 2010, a week after the Strategic Defence and Security Review was unveiled. By that time Foreign Secretary William Hague had made his series of keynote speeches around the generally upbeat themes for UK foreign policy, and work was under way to produce a revised version of the anti-terrorist CONTEST strategy in an atmosphere where the immediate terrorist threat had apparently diminished after the alarms of 2005 and 2006.[21]

The Middle East

On 17 December 2010 Mohamed Bouazizi in the town of Ben Arons south of Tunis immolated himself out of sheer frustration at the petty bureaucracy that prevented him working as a street fruit-seller. The Middle East had witnessed a great deal of conflict throughout the twentieth century but very little real strategic change since the Sykes–

---

[18] Foreign Affairs Committee, *FCO Performance and Finances* (HC 1618, 2012), para. 19.

[19] In official publications this is referred to as 0.7 per cent of GNI (Gross National Income), but GDP (Gross Domestic Product) is used here as a more common understanding of the commitment.

[20] HM Treasury, *Spending Review 2010* (Cm 7942, October 2010), p. 10. See also, Malcolm Chalmers, 'Looking into the black hole: Is the UK defence budget crisis really over?', Royal United Services Institute Briefing Paper, September 2011.

[21] It appeared as the third iteration of the document: *CONTEST: The United Kingdom's Strategy for Countering Terrorism* (Cm 8123, 11 July 2011).

Picot Agreement of 1916 established most of the modern boundaries from the Levant to the Gulf. Indeed, the Middle East was remarkable for having changed as little as it did in the face of so many, and so intractable, a series of conflicts. But Bouazizi's suicide now caught the imagination of the middle classes in Tunisia and thence via social media across the whole region, to set off a train of popular revolutions that rapidly brought down the autocrats in Tunisia, Egypt and Yemen, and sparked a Shia revolt in Bahrain that was put down only by Saudi Arabia's direct intervention. By spring 2011 there was outright civil war in Libya against the dictatorial Gaddafi regime and by autumn that year also in Syria, against the Assad family and the Alawites who controlled the state. By 2012 that civil war was turning deeply sectarian and was beginning to ignite a more general conflict between Shia and Sunni Muslims backed respectively by Iran and Saudi Arabia. Iraq was rapidly destabilized by this civil war for the heart of Middle East Islam and by June 2014 the spectre of real 'balkanization' across the Levant was evident in the rapid rise of the so-called Islamic State of Iraq and the Levant (ISIL), which acknowledged no existing international or domestic law, no national boundaries or jurisdictions – merely its own self-proclaimed 'caliphate'.[22] In just four years the Middle East had witnessed more major strategic change than in almost a century, from North Africa into the African Sahel region, from Syria across the Levant and within the Gulf as far as the southern peninsula of Arabia.

Amid this growing chaos Israel threatened loudly that it might unilaterally attack Iran during 2012 to damage its growing nuclear capacity if the US would not, repeating the threat in 2013 and again in 2014.[23] This followed a fluctuating but progressive tension dating back to 2008, when Iranian nuclear ambitions seemed to be approaching the point where they would be impossible ever to halt. The UK had tried quietly but unsuccessfully to get on better terms with Iran in 2003 during British operations in southern Iraq, making the most of the diplomatic presence it had in Tehran (unlike the US) after 1988. President Obama had tried to reach out to Iran in 2009 and press a

---

[22] See Gareth Stansfield, 'The unravelling of the post-First World War state system?', *International Affairs*, 89:2 (2013), pp. 259–82.

[23] 'Israeli PM Netanyahus "ready" to order strike on Iran', *BBC News*, 6 November 2012; 'Netanyahu threatens unilateral action against Iran', *Alakhbar*, 1 November 2013; 'Israel threatens to strike Iran's nuclear facilities in attempt to ratchet up international pressure on Tehran', *National Post*, 21 March 2014.

'reset button' on their relationship. This was publicly spurned by Tehran. By 2012 Israeli Prime Minister Netanyahu was arguing publicly that the Iranians had reached a point of no return in their weapons programme and that Western diplomacy and sanctions had clearly failed; only a bombing attack would now meet the challenge. Israel got some, but only some, traction for this argument in the international community.[24] More significant, the turmoil in the rest of the region became a threat to Iran's regional ambitions and certainly to its clients in the Assad regime in Syria, in Hezbollah in Lebanon and Hamas in Gaza. It stimulated the Sunni/Shia civil war in the heart of Middle East Islam and put Iran on the defensive as Saudi Arabia, Jordan and the Emirates, among others, formed a Sunni alliance – backed by Western powers – to combat ISIL and re-establish traditional Sunni dominance in the region over the forces of violent jihadist Sunnis and alienated Shias. The 'Arab Spring' appears to have had the net effect of making Iran even more determined to acquire nuclear technology in the face of a balance of power in the region that was moving against it.

The US pivot to Asia

In November 2011 President Obama made a series of visits within Asia and provoked a long debate about the United States 're-balancing' its attention from Europe and the Atlantic seaboard towards Asia and the Pacific. It was even, in many analyses, a 'pivot to Asia'.[25] Great uncertainty still surrounds this strategic re-orientation on the part of the UK's most important ally. Many US policymakers and analysts argue that the strategic shift is more apparent than real and the gods of politics have been correspondingly mischievous in pulling US attention back to the Middle East and Europe just as the President was claiming he intended to focus on Asia. Nevertheless, an eventual shift of US strategic attention towards Asia and the Pacific would seem to be inevitable as the twenty-first – 'Asian' – century unfolds. Whether or not President Obama is able to make good on his strategic instincts to re-orientate US policy, his behaviour in a series of leadership challenges during the first six years of his administration made clear that his attitude towards

---

[24] Shashank Joshi, *The Permanent Crisis: Iran's Nuclear Trajectory* (Whitehall paper 79, London: RUSI, 2012), pp. 29–50.

[25] Robert S. Ross, 'The problem with the pivot', *Foreign Affairs*, 91:6 (2012).

leadership among the Western allies would be different.[26] In short, after the coalition's reaffirmation of traditional transatlantic bonds in statements and speeches during the early years of the government, it found itself dealing with a somewhat different United States in both short- and long-term perspective.

New European crises

Not least among the new strategic challenges for the foreign and security policy of the coalition was the explicit return of great power intervention inside the European continent and the prospect of borders being changed unilaterally by force. The short war between Russia and Georgia in 2008 had marked a new waypoint in Russia's attempt to recover influence in the former Soviet territories. But it could partly be put down to Georgian miscalculation and unwise diplomacy on the part of NATO and the Western powers over the previous couple of years.[27] In November 2013 the situation changed dramatically with the mishandling of EU relations with Ukraine. President Putin's Russia stepped in crudely to displace a $13 billion deal with the EU and pull Ukraine's President Yanukovych decisively towards Moscow. A popular revolution in February 2014 removed Yanukovych and restored Ukraine's 2004 constitution. Amid the upheaval, Russian separatists in Crimea declared independence and Moscow annexed the territory while aiding more Russian separatists in the Donbas region of Ukraine. By March 2014 Ukraine was involved in a grumbling civil war that threatened to split it in two east of the Dnieper River. The reality was undeniable that Russia was involved in subversion and *de facto* intervention to bolster Russian separatists in the region.

On 18 March 2014 President Putin made a speech on the annexation of Crimea that took European security into territory it had not been in since the 1930s. He spoke of the 'outrageous historical injustice' in the events of 1991 when the Soviet Union collapsed amid the inability of Russia to do anything about it. He spoke of the need to

---

[26] See, for example, Charles Krauthammer, 'The Obama Doctrine: Leading from behind', *Washington Post*, 28 April 2011; Peter Beinart, 'Actually, Obama does have a strategy in the Middle East', *The Atlantic*, 29 August 2014.

[27] Nicolai N. Petro, 'The Russia–Georgia War: Causes and consequences', *Global Dialogue*, 11 (Winter/Spring 2009).

recognize historic links to the ethnic Russians now living in other states; the 'millions of people who went to bed in one country and awoke in different ones'.[28] The speech put Europe on notice that under Putin's leadership Russia would seek to recover the influence it felt was its due in former Soviet republics, while patterns of Russian behaviour over the Ukraine crisis indicated a return to military and economic subversion in foreign countries, underpinned by powerful media campaigns that played some of the West's own rhetoric – about self-determination, legality and the responsibility to protect – back to it in selective forms. The NATO summit in September 2014, hosted in the UK for the first time since the Soviet Union's collapse in 1991, marked the beginning of a perceptual shift in European security thinking. There would be no return to the Cold War; east and west Europe were already sufficiently transformed to make that impossible. But henceforth, as the summit declaration made clear, NATO would counter what it now explicitly referred to as 'hybrid warfare' and issued strong and very specific condemnations of Russian actions in Ukraine and elsewhere, committing itself to a series of military and economic enhancements to strengthen the armed force capacities of NATO countries and move the weight of its military preparedness in some areas right up to the borders of Russia.[29]

A coalition working through coalitions

The coalition had tried to be more overtly 'strategic' both in the process and outcomes of foreign and security policy. The creation of a National Security Council was intended to provide a powerful focus on strategic issues from the very centre of government. The personal commitment of David Cameron to maintain this arrangement was notable. There were relatively few occasions on which chairing the NSC was delegated. The NSC, rather than the Ministry of Defence, took the lead in running the Strategic Defence and Security Review, and the composition of the NSC gave new weight to the role of the intelligence agencies

---

[28] President of Russia, 'Address by the President of the Russian Federation', 18 March 2014 (accessed at http://eng.kremlin.ru/news/6889, 18 November 2014).

[29] 'NATO Summit 2014: Wales Summit Declaration', Prime Minister's Office, 5 September 2014 (accessed at www.gov.uk/government/publications/nato-summit-2014-wales-summit-declaration, 18 November 2014); see paragraph 13 on hybrid warfare, paragraphs 16–19 on Russian actions.

and the other government departments which should be involved in 'national strategy'.

This was generally regarded as an improvement on previous arrangements but it did not alter any of the hard realities the coalition faced in these years. Crisis after crisis dominated the NSC's agenda and insiders admitted that it was difficult to get ahead of the curve of immediate events. The NSC was more a better coordination mechanism than a 'strategic brain' at the heart of government. There was, at best, a 'thin patina of strategy' imposed over a series of cost-cutting exercises.[30]

The Foreign and Commonwealth Office was working hard to extend its diplomatic reach after cuts that left it with a core budget of less than £1.5 billion, but had very few people deployed in the zones that now mattered. It was under-represented in the Middle East as ISIL turned the region upside down in summer 2014, and under-skilled in Russian analysis as Mr Putin began to redraw the map of Europe.[31] Cuts had affected the traditional depth of analysis in the Foreign Office.[32] The UK was still a major power in the international aid sector, but it was difficult to mesh aid priorities to the crisis-driven needs in Afghanistan, Libya, Syria, Iraq, Somalia, Kenya and northern Nigeria, all of which absorbed the NSC's time.[33] The Armed Forces were being cut and trying to keep as many military capabilities alive as possible, with lower numbers, so that the forces would come back 'into balance' by 2020. Until then, they struggled to apply sufficient military weight to operations to be strategically decisive. There was no loss of military competence. In the air operations in Libya in 2011 or Iraq in 2014, for example, only the UK had the ability among European forces to attack the most difficult targets. But, however sophisticated it may be, if a certain weight of force cannot be applied, a military contribution could be useful but still not capable of making a strategic difference.[34] This

---

[30] Peter Hennessy, *Distilling the Frenzy: Writing the History of One's Own Times* (London: Biteback Publishing, 2012), p. 28.

[31] See, for example, a generic criticism by a former diplomat, Gerard Russell, 'Refocusing the Foreign Office', *Total Politics*, 15 March 2011.

[32] Hennessy, *Distilling the Frenzy*, p. 187.

[33] See Alexander Evans, 'Organizing for British national strategy', *International Affairs*, 90:3 (2014).

[34] See Malcolm Chalmers, 'Let debate commence: Key strategic questions for the 2015 SDSR', *RUSI Journal*, 34:1 (2014).

was increasingly the case as the Ministry of Defence struggled to trim itself down and reform its own processes.

Personalities in the coalition

Ultimately, the 'strategic brain' in any government comes down to that of the political leadership. An NSC can serve it but cannot substitute for it. Leadership personalities mattered. While in opposition George Osborne had been noted for hawkish views close to the US 'neocons', but as Chancellor he was regarded as sceptical about the efficacy of military power and alive to the spiralling costs of foreign commitments. The Libya, Mali and Iraq/Syria crises simply frightened him with their cost implications. He was said to be vocal in the NSC. His strong Euroscepticism added to his instinct that the UK was not currently in a position to be expansive, still less interventionist. He is believed to have argued against sanctions on Russia because of the economic damage it would do.[35] The UK, in his view, must make the most of its position as a good player in the globalization process through trade and knowledge-based investment.

Foreign Secretary William Hague was well respected abroad – a Foreign Secretary who exuded an old-school knowledge and gravitas in his personal dealings – but his FCO did not command a commensurate level of support within Whitehall, becoming cautious and ultra cost-conscious. He was instinctively pro-EU within a leadership that leaned increasingly towards Eurosceptic positions and he was increasingly overshadowed by the assertive role the Prime Minister played, as will always tend to be the case, in foreign crises as they occur.

David Cameron was naturally bullish in foreign affairs, though not obviously shrewd in a strategic sense. He was an international leader by default in the Libya operation. Not realizing that Obama would pull back from outright leadership after two weeks of operations, the UK and France had been assertive at the UN alongside their US ally in March 2011, but then found themselves unwittingly leading the whole thing during April when the US took a back seat. The Prime Minister had been pushing against the advice of his Chief of the Defence Staff, but he saw it through to the autumn when the Gaddafi

---

[35] Sue Cameron, 'David Cameron caught between a rock and a hard place', *Daily Telegraph*, 5 March 2014.

dictatorship was broken.[36] In 2012 he authorized assistance to French forces in Mali dealing with some of the chaos the Libya collapse had unleashed. In 2013 his instincts were again assertive in preparing an (aborted) bombing campaign against Syria, and yet again in 2014, much more cautiously this time, with an open-ended commitment to destroy ISIL in the Levant, however long that might take.

All these cases played to David Cameron's natural transatlantic instincts and away from placing any faith in the EU as vehicle for multilateral diplomacy. His instincts were not the same as those of William Hague and considerably different from those of Deputy Prime Minister Nick Clegg. Michael Gove, though Education minister and then Chief Whip, was a trusted confidant on world affairs and made frequent visits to the US, both privately and in his official capacity. Hugh Powell, though only a Deputy National Security Adviser, was one of an inner circle, effectively led by Number 10 Chief of Staff Ed Llewellyn, who had previously worked for Paddy Ashdown in Bosnia and now seemed to guide the Prime Minister in most foreign policy issues and certainly during crises. This group was described by observers as a close 'chumocracy' – not unusual for any Prime Minister, but one in which neither the FCO nor the Treasury was normally included.[37] If the Prime Minister was inclined to be a gambler, those close confidants around him were risk managers. But this did not amount to a strategic brain that the NSC was supposed to serve, and a prevailing pragmatism could not disguise a government that was 'coping and hoping' rather than shaping its future in foreign and defence policy.[38]

The coalition government could maintain its focus on any number of legitimate foreign affairs objectives – improving relations with China, establishing a meaningful partnership with India, promoting UK trade and investment, pursuing development in Africa and so on. But the essence of the coalition's foreign and security portfolio had changed dramatically by 2013. The strategic landscape had shifted in ways

---

[36] David Richards, *Taking Command* (London: Headline Books, 2014), pp. 314–16.

[37] Rachel Sylvester, 'Cameron's "dysfunctional chumocracy"', *The Times*, 15 January 2013.

[38] See, for example, a judgement on Cameron's EU approach, 'The Gambler', *The Economist*, 26 January 2013; or a view of Afghanistan by Michael Clarke, 'Helmand strategy: Britain reduced to a "cope and hope" strategy', *Daily Telegraph*, 2 April 2014.

certainly not anticipated in 2010. In reacting to such potentially tectonic movements the UK could only credibly work through international organizations and alliances. Bilateral relations were not irrelevant but the UK now found itself inhabiting a neighbourhood that was considerably less benign than had traditionally been assumed and that was the concern of the international community at many different levels. The domestic coalition would have to work through international coalitions.

The EU and the coalition

In this situation how much did the fact of a domestic coalition in government affect the conduct of foreign and security affairs? Against the generally accepted wisdom that party politics play a minor role in external affairs, did the coalition have to manage its internal dynamics any differently for the fact that it was a two-party coalition?

In some respects it did. The differences between the partners on the central question of the UK's relations with the European Union are dealt with in Chapter fourteen. In relation to foreign and defence policy, however, those differences illuminated some important divergence in expectations between the partners. In Liberal Democrat thinking, and certainly that of Nick Clegg, the EU should be the framework for a more united European approach to these big strategic questions, and one that could more appropriately integrate the political, economic, security and even military responses of its members. On many foreign questions, such as the Israeli–Palestinian conflict, energy security, sanctions against Iran, trade policy with China, etc., UK policy was, of necessity, EU policy. This increased the imperative to help reinvigorate the EU as a major actor in world politics. As Nick Clegg put it in November 2012, he wanted 'a strong UK, influential in Europe and so more influential in the world. Working with our allies on the issues that matter.' He criticized the Conservative approach of repatriating powers from Brussels as a recipe for growing isolation; instead, the UK should be 'strong, loud and present' in the 'new Europe'.[39]

[39] 'A vision for the UK in Europe: speech by the Deputy Prime Minister', Cabinet Office, 1 November 2012 (accessed at www.gov.uk/government/speeches/a-vision-for-the-uk-in-europe-speech-by-the-deputy-prime-minister, 18 November 2014). See also his speech, 'In Europe for the national interest', Cabinet Office, 8 October 2013 (accessed at www.gov.uk/government/speeches/deputy-prime-ministers-speech-on-britain-and-europe, 18 November 2014).

This was consistent enough with the government's overall line but not with a powerful and growing view within the Conservative Party and within the Prime Minister's inner circle that 'strong, loud and present' had become a series of euphemisms for submission to an EU that was incapable of reform and which diminished the UK's independent influence in the world. By contrast, the Prime Minister had long since nailed his EU colours to the mast of essential reform as the prerequisite to the UK's wholehearted participation. It was also his device for placating backbench Eurosceptics and putting off any in/out referendum on the EU until the next parliament. He had already said that EU reform was the key to unlocking growth in the EU.[40] In January 2013 he laid on the line at Bloomberg the fact that, 'For us, the European Union is a means to an end – prosperity, stability, the anchor of freedom and democracy both within Europe and beyond her shores – not an end in itself', before going on to outline the precise areas in which reform must take place. [41]

As events played out, both approaches could claim that their preferred vision of the EU as vehicle for more multilateral diplomacy was partly stymied by the other. But the more stark reality was that the financial crisis of 2008 created a deep introspection within the EU, over the future of the Euro, Germany's role, the economic viability of the southern members, the prospects – or the imperative – for greater fiscal union, all of which effectively diminished the EU's willingness and ability to be a prominent actor in global politics. The EU's aspirations to develop a greater defence identity were at a standstill by 2010 and its External Affairs Directorate was both overwhelmed by the volume of work and unable to play more than a semi-successful mediating role in the crises that now turned out to matter. There was some useful political success in the Balkans and in backing up the 'five plus one' approach to dealing with Iran, but the EU was hardly a leading player. There was no greater success for the EU than for any other actors in the Palestinian–Israeli conflict. It was effectively ignored in the failed attempts to build greater stability in the Maghreb and the Sahel after the fall of Gaddafi and had no significant diplomatic role to play in the deepening

---

[40] In the launch of the pamphlet, 'Let's choose growth', see: www.gov.uk/government/news/reform-the-key-to-unlocking-eu-growth–2 (accessed 18 November 2014).

[41] 'EU speech at Bloomberg', Cabinet Office, 23 January 2013 (accessed at www.gov.uk/government/speeches/eu-speech-at-bloomberg, 18 November 2014).

meltdown across the Levant. And where the EU took the lead in brokering a peace deal that might hold Ukraine together in February 2014, its efforts were in pieces within forty-eight hours. The EU's role in Ukraine since then has been more positive but nevertheless reactive, since the crisis has been played out through its own internal dynamics.

In these circumstances Liberal Democrat optimism that the UK could work more effectively through the EU seemed naive, and outright Conservative scepticism at the EU's diminished role in world affairs has seemed to create a self-fulfilling prophecy of UK exclusion on the margins of European diplomacy.

Crises and the coalition

The prospects of a unilateral Israeli attack on Iran, particularly in 2012 and 2013, left the partners in a deeply uncomfortable position with each other. An EU response would not take precedence in such a case over whatever reaction might come out of Washington. Multinational frameworks would not help them very much if Israel simply launched an attack, as it kept threatening to do. The US almost certainly would not condemn such an attack and it would therefore be unlikely that the Prime Minister would do so either. Liberal Democrat ministers and party officials struggled with a contingency plan that would respect liberal views in such a dangerous circumstance but would not split the coalition on a genuinely significant matter. In September 2012 the Liberal Democrat minister at Defence, Nick Harvey, was removed, leaving no Lib Dem representation in the MoD and creating speculation that this was due to tensions over the likely ministerial reactions to an attack on Iran.[42] At the Liberal Democrat party conference two weeks later it was still a lively, if discreet, issue.[43] It was fortunate for the coalition that the prospects of an Israeli attack on Iran remained hypothetical.

Completely real, however, was the latest Israeli incursion into Gaza during the crisis that began in June 2014 and the outrage that followed Palestinian casualties alongside Israeli evidence of continued

---

[42] 'Defence Minister: Clegg axed me because I won't support attack on Iran', *Daily Mail*, 15 September 2012.

[43] Geoffrey Payne, 'Will Israel attack Iran, and will this break the Coalition?', *Liberal Democrat Voice*, 28 September 2012.

rocket attacks. Amid widespread calls for official condemnation of what was perceived as yet again a disproportionate Israeli response to the problem, the government was silent. The former Chair of the Conservative Party, Baroness Warsi, resigned over the government's stance, citing her outrage that the Prime Minister could not bring himself to go even as far as the UN Secretary General had done. It was, she said, 'morally indefensible'.[44] Many, of all political persuasions, agreed with her, but it was a particularly awkward time for the Liberal Democrat leadership. Paddy Ashdown was outspoken and supported Warsi's decision. Nick Clegg had been pushing for a suspension of arms export licences to Israel – an almost entirely cosmetic measure in this context – and Vince Cable later admitted to party faithful that 'senior Lib Dems had been "making this case inside government"', but said they had '"not yet been able to get agreement"' [on export licenses] with Tory coalition partners'.[45] In the event nothing could be said in public until a fragile truce was in place. It was a bad time for the government as a whole, described privately by one Downing Street insider as 'the lowest point' he could recall since the coalition came to power.[46]

This may have felt like the most difficult time among senior partners in the coalition, but for the UK's partners and friends abroad, and for the sake of the international coalitions that were intrinsic to the UK's foreign and security affairs, the Syria vote of 2013 had already done a great deal of reputational damage. The blatant use of chemical weapons against Syrian civilians on 21 August 2013 provoked a sudden and difficult twist for the government in the regional civil war across the Middle East.[47] President Obama was prepared to take 'coercive' military action against the Assad regime but not to be drawn into the Syrian war itself. It was not clear how the US and its allies could somehow 'punish' the Assad regime through air attacks and yet not become part of the war; still less, what the next step might be if the punishment failed. It was a confused strategic position for both public and

---

[44] 'Baroness Warsi resigns over Gaza conflict saying she "can no longer support Government policy"', *The Independent*, 5 August 2014.

[45] 'Gaza: Clegg demands UK suspends arms export licences to Israel, Ashdown writes to Warsi to discuss next steps', *Liberal Democrat Voice*, 6 August 2014.

[46] Private conversation, 8 July 2014.

[47] 'More than 1400 killed in Syrian chemical weapons attack US says', *Washington Post*, 30 August 2013.

legislators on both sides of the Atlantic. Nevertheless, UK aircraft and all the associated services were in Cyprus and the eastern Mediterranean ready to be part of allied attacks on Syria within eight days of the chemical outrage.[48] With the shadow of 2003 hanging over it the government decided it had to go to Parliament, though whether for political cover or for constitutional authorization was never clear.

Having recalled Parliament for 29 August to debate the situation in Syria it was clear that military action would not be nodded through. The government backed off and promised that a second vote would anyway take place before any military action was authorized. The vote, therefore, was simply a decision to make another decision later. Even then, it was handled so badly by the government, though not by the whips, that the coalition was defeated by 13 votes, where 30 Conservatives and 9 Liberal Democrats voted against the government, along with 224 Labour members. For Labour, it was the first time since Suez in 1956 that the party had not voted with the government on a military deployment. For the Conservatives it ranked with comparable defeats only for Lord Palmerston, Lord Aberdeen and even Lord North, who had 'lost America'.

The Liberal Democrats had been the only party to vote against the 2003 war in Iraq and in the run-up to this vote Nick Clegg had tried to make a strong case that this was different, citing party support for successful humanitarian operations in Kosovo in 1999 and Sierra Leone in 2000.[49] In the end it was not the lack of a convincing humanitarian case that sank the government in the Commons; it was the lack of a strategic case, where parliamentarians simply did not believe in the efficacy of the proposed action and were not prepared to write a blank cheque for the effects of failure. Whether the parliamentary defeat was right or wrong the effect was stunning. Within seventy-two hours President Obama had backed off immediate attacks until he had consulted Congress, and it was immediately apparent that he could not guarantee its support. The military operation was aborted and a shaky diplomatic fix, thanks to Russia, was worked out with the

---

[48] 'Navy ready to launch first strike on Syria', *Daily Telegraph*, 25 August 2013; 'Syria crisis: Ministry of Defence confirms RAF Typhoon jets have been deployed to Cyprus', *The Independent*, 29 August 2013.

[49] Nick Clegg, e-mail to party members, 28 August 2013: www.markpack.org.uk/45141/this-is-not-iraq-nick-cleggs-email-to-party-members-on-syria (accessed 18 November 2014).

Assad regime. In effect, for good or bad, the Syria vote in Parliament had scuppered the US operation and damaged the UK's reputation around the world as a resolute power, a firm ally of the US and a country that was skilled in the political exercise of military leadership.[50]

It was, depending on one's view, the Labour Party or the thirty Conservative rebels who had made the crucial difference but with a defeat by thirteen, the nine Liberal Democrats could have won the vote for the government if most of them had followed their leader. It was difficult for either Cameron or Clegg to come out of this well and the episode became an example of the weakening of the coalition in relation to its respective parliamentary supporters as much as in relation to the two parties that constituted it.

Within a year the issue had come round again in an almost complete circle. In June 2014 ISIL's military gains in Syria and then Iraq became a manifest crisis of Middle East stability, and with beheading videos and explicit threats by ISIL spokesmen to create both individual and mass terror on the streets of Western capitals, the United States led an international coalition to 'degrade' and 'destroy' ISIL at source – which meant attacking it in Syria as well as Iraq.[51] For the first time since the end of the Cold War the UK was not in at the beginning of the effective declaration of war by the United States on a common enemy.[52] Parliament had first to be consulted. The UK's direct military contribution, by common consent, was limited compared to the relative scale of effort made in Iraq in 2003, Afghanistan in 2006 or even over Libya in 2011.[53] British political support for the US-led coalition

---

[50] See, for example, Ian Evans, 'Parliament rebukes Cameron on Syria: What damage did it do?', *Christian Science Monitor*, 30 August 2013; or Elizabeth Lee, 'Syria vote a humiliation for UK and a disturbing signal to dictators', *Henry Jackson Society, News Release*, 30 August 2013.

[51] 'Our objective is clear: We will degrade, and ultimately destroy, ISIL through a comprehensive and sustained counterterrorism strategy', The White House, 'Statement by the President on ISIL', 10 September 2014. For the later statement see Council on Foreign Relations, 'Statement by President Obama on ISIL', 23 September 2013.

[52] The United States had been operating an air campaign against ISIL forces in Iraq since June on the assumption that it was protecting US personnel on the ground in Iraq. UK forces had helped back these operations up in non-lethal ways. But on 23 September President Obama announced that the US would extend operations to Syria under different auspices and effectively declared outright war on ISIL.

[53] The UK committed six Tornado bombers to the operation in the first instance. This was a third of the number originally committed to the Libya operation of 2011.

would still be important, not least because of its relations with the five significant Arab members of it as well as the US. But this began as a curious piece of coalition politics for the UK: as a minor player behind France, Australia and the air forces of five Arab monarchies in a US-led operation. It began as an expression of limitation from a government that had been badly burned domestically and internationally the previous year and a military establishment with stretched resources as it tried to retrench itself around a better structure that would only be fully realized by 2020. Not least, it was a government just recovering from the shock two weeks previously of having almost lost the Scotland referendum, which would have dismembered the United Kingdom. As it was, the perception in Whitehall was that the very fact of the referendum and its close-call nature had already damaged the UK's reputation for leadership in the world and diminished its status as a significant player in global politics. Reputational damage limitation was required but this military operation did not emerge as an ideal vehicle to engineer it.

The ISIL challenge was a symptom of how different all the politics of the Middle East would be in the future. The government had little choice but to participate in the US-led coalition, even under less than favourable circumstances. But its ability to act as a transatlantic bridge, as both Cameron and Clegg for different reasons favoured, was not high. It could not realistically enhance consensus on the Middle East within the EU. It had more to offer in the NATO context, but NATO was more immediately and directly concerned with the shift in the European security equation.

The UK had made a significant effort during 2014 to re-engage more effectively with NATO after twenty years in which its various expeditionary operations had the effect of distracting it from European security concerns. During years when the political establishment in the UK was unenthusiastic about the EU as a global actor, it also took NATO somewhat for granted and stopped worrying about, or planning for, greater insecurity in Europe. But the Ukrainian crisis shocked the system and there was no discernible disagreement between the coalition partners that it was important to bolster NATO both as the political forum and the military alliance it always claimed to be. In truth, NATO was a shadow of the military alliance at readiness it had been during the Cold War and it was important to revive its practical effectiveness. The UK wanted to make significant efforts after the 2014 NATO summit to contribute to a new Readiness Action Plan and promote greater military readiness than NATO had enjoyed for many years.[54] Again, it was not a good time for the UK to act on these aspirations. The US, in its 'fierce minimalism', would engage decisively in the Middle East, where it felt itself to be directly threatened, but was more detached and less inclined to lead where more indirect interests were at stake, as in Europe.[55] The diminution of the UK's reputation as a consensus leader, either individually or often on behalf of the US, may turn out to be temporary. But 2015 is not a propitious moment for this government at the end of its term, or for a new government picking up the threads, to reverse a perception of limitation in foreign and security affairs; to reverse, in fact, exactly the trend towards 'strategic shrinkage' the government in 2010 said it would not allow.

Pragmatic or simply weak?

The coalition government came to power in an atmosphere of deep economic crisis. Its approach to foreign and security policy, however, was confident and based on a continuity of major trends that was understandable at the time. Nevertheless, it was hit by some tectonic shifts in world politics within three years that would have tested any government. On the basis of political culture and constitutional convention it would be expected that external relations would not generally provoke deep party-political divisions in a UK coalition. This is essentially true and partly ascribable to the sheer enormity of the new challenges the government faced. It was comparatively easy to do a foreign affairs deal in the first instance, since the big issues they disagreed on – the EU and Trident – were in any case best put off by the leaderships until the next parliament. There were difficult issues to manage along the way, particularly for the Liberal Democrats as junior partner, but in the face of Middle East and European crises, alongside a new attitude towards world politics within the Obama Administration, there was little leeway for the partners to disagree when so many issues were in flux and no one in government had many better ideas than to sit tight for the next part of the ride. Most governments deep into the

---

[54] See Louisa Book-Holland and Claire Mills, *NATO Wales Summit 2014: Outcomes*, House of Commons Library, SN06981, 12 September 2014.

[55] Beinart, 'Actually, Obama does have a strategy'.

second part of their parliamentary term move from the visionary to the pragmatic under the pressure of events. This does not always apply in foreign and security policy, however, since there are powerful incentives towards continuity.

But even in the face of the transformative events and crises described here, a perception of strategic decline attached itself to the coalition government. This is interpreted variously as a decline in the level of foreign ambition in the coalition government, of a preoccupation with austerity, of unwillingness to lead, or lack of weight when it tried to lead. *The Economist* described coalition foreign policy in 2014 as 'feeble'; *The Spectator* as 'dismal', for a variety of different reasons.[56] The 'liberal conservatism' of 2010 had become pessimistic about its ability to use military 'hard power' effectively and seemed unable to deploy the 'soft power' of its ideology and values to any compensating effect.[57] It is difficult to assess how much of this might be ascribed to the circumstances of the coalition itself. Certainly, both partners have compromised and neither partner has been able to articulate a full-blooded Conservative, or Liberal Democrat, vision of the UK's best foreign and security interests. But not much of either would have been likely to survive the winds that have blown through the UK's own neighbourhood since 2010.

[56] 'Running out of gas', *The Economist*, 21 June 2014; Alex Massie, 'Britain abandons foreign policy. And abandons debate about it too', *The Spectator*, 19 August 2014.
[57] See Oliver Daddow, 'Interpreting coalition foreign policy', European Consortium of Political Research Paper, March 2013 (accessed at http://ecpr.eu/Events/PaperDetails.aspx?PaperID=876&EventID=7, 18 November 2014).

14 EUROPE: THE COALITION'S POISONED CHALICE

JULIE SMITH

Introduction

'Europe' is an issue of domestic and international politics, with domestic ramifications and wider international implications. The UK's relationship with its partners and allies in the European Union (EU) has long been one of the most challenging issues in British politics, and one that the mainstream parties have sought to keep off the agenda. 'Europe' is also an area of major difference between the coalition parties. There is thus something of a dual coalition over European policy: that between the Conservatives and their Liberal Democrat colleagues, and that among Conservatives with increasingly divergent opinions on European matters. In an era of coalition government, policymakers have thus needed to work in three arenas: the internal Conservative, the coalition and the European. Yet, a policy area that might have been very controversial and sensitive appeared to be tackled effectively and constructively in the Coalition Agreement. And so matters would be tackled on a daily basis within government as Liberal Democrat and Conservative ministers and advisers developed positive and mutually respectful working relationships. Over the course of the Parliament the greatest tensions within the coalition over European issues were to be seen within the Conservative Party, rather than between the Conservatives and their Liberal Democrat colleagues. There was no clear sense of

The author is very grateful to those parliamentarians, special advisers and civil servants who consented to be interviewed, mostly off-the-record, for this chapter.

vision or leadership on European policy, which at times seemed to be driven by Eurosceptic Tory backbenchers rather than the party leadership. As this chapter will show, the coalition had some notable achievements within the EU but was unable to influence certain key policies at the EU level, notably failing to block the appointment of Jean-Claude Juncker as President of the European Commission in the summer of 2014. However, many of the positions adopted by the government were also supported by the Labour Party. Thus, the fact of a coalition government per se neither impeded nor enhanced the effective delivery of British European policy, although the personality and style of David Cameron and his internal party difficulties did have an impact.

Background: Britain's European Problem

For over half a century questions of the UK's relations with the European Union have divided the political class.[1] Traditionally the Conservatives were the more pro-European of the two main parties – it was, after all, Conservative Prime Minister Edward Heath who took Britain into the 'Common Market' in 1973. Yet in the decades that followed, opinion within the Conservative Party shifted from pragmatic pro-Europeanism to what by the time of the 2010 general election could be described as 'pragmatic Euroscepticism'. The official position was more or less critical of the EU but nonetheless believed that the UK's interests continued to be best served within the EU, ideally with some powers being repatriated. Yet this characterization belies the internal divisions over Europe that became increasingly clear during the coalition's five-year term of office, as some MPs and other party members espoused the view the Britain would be 'better off out'.[2] The Liberal Democrats had

[1] See, for example, Andrew Geddes, *Britain and the European Union* (London: Palgrave Macmillan, 2013); also Anne Deighton, 'European Union policy', in Anthony Seldon (ed.), *The Blair Effect: The Blair Government 1997–2001* (London: Little, Brown and Company, 2001), pp. 307–28.

[2] Euroscepticism has almost as many definitions as it has advocates. In 1998, Paul Taggart argued that a 'faction' of the Conservative Party was Eurosceptic. See Paul Taggart, 'A touchstone of dissent: Euroscepticism in contemporary Western European party systems', *European Journal of Political Research*, 33 (1998), pp. 363–88. By the time the party took office again in 2010, 'I am a Eurosceptic' had become something of a mantra among MPs, although their views ranged from a desire for immediate withdrawal to a general desire to remain in the EU, albeit a reformed one.

long been seen as *the* pro-European British party, a stance adopted under Jo Grimond in the 1960s and never abandoned. Despite, or perhaps because of, their differences over Europe, none of the mainstream parties were keen to go on the offensive on European issues – it was always a 'shield issue', on which they felt there was little to be won; much to be lost.[3] The rare exception was the Conservative Party in 2001, when William Hague as party leader used the general election as a campaign to save the pound. The party's disastrous showing in the election ensured that as Foreign Secretary for over four years in the coalition Hague would be reluctant to address European issues unless pressed, believing that there was little to be gained from playing the European card.[4] Similarly, Cameron hoped that his government would not be dominated by Europe.

Attempts by Labour and the Liberal Democrats finally to put the EU onto the agenda in the 2009 European Parliament (EP) elections were derailed by questions of MPs' expenses and a general sense of loss of trust in professional politicians.[5] This in turn benefited the anti-European United Kingdom Independence Party (UKIP), which came second in those elections, with 16 per cent of the popular vote and thirteen MEPs, against the Conservatives' 27 per cent and twenty-five seats. At the largest poll before the general election these results highlighted the electoral vulnerability of the Conservatives, who would have expected to top the polls still more comfortably, as they did in the county council elections held on the same day. The Liberal Democrats also saw their support collapse, dropping to fourth place, with 15 per cent of the vote compared to a very strong showing of 23 per cent in the local elections.[6] The EP election results raised questions about whether the Conservatives could win an outright victory at the general election and reinforced concern among many backbenchers and parliamentary candidates, who believed UKIP threatened their electoral prospects and thus became ever more vocal in their own Euroscepticism.

Changes at the European level had also ensured that 'Europe' had gradually acquired a central role in British politics. Ever since the

---

[3] Source: private information (interview with former Lib Dem adviser, 7 August 2014).

[4] As James Forsyth of the *Spectator* put it to me on 10 September 2014, 'The Hague view is that no good ever came out of Tories doing European things.'

[5] See Julie Smith, 'The United Kingdom', in Donatella Viola (ed.), *Routledge Handbook of European Elections* (London: Routledge, forthcoming).

[6] Results for the EP elections available at www.europarl.europa.eu, last accessed on 2 October 2014.

mid-1980s the EU has been involved in repeated treaty reforms, which have become increasingly controversial in the UK. In line with the traditional practice of parliamentary sovereignty, these treaties had all been ratified in Westminster, not by popular votes. Other countries, notably Ireland and Denmark, held referendums before ratifying treaties, an approach which began to look attractive in the UK. Following the 1992 Treaty on European Union (TEU or Maastricht Treaty), which the Danes initially voted against and hence were subsequently able to secure clarifications and revisions, demands for referendums began to grow. At the time of the Maastricht Treaty, maverick Tories were calling for a referendum. The creation of the Referendum Party founded by Sir James Goldsmith and the UK Independence Party established by Professor Alan Sked, coupled with growing Euroscepticism in the print media, caused the three main UK parties to reconsider the way they engaged in EU affairs.

By the mid-1990s all three were saying they would offer a referendum before taking the UK into the Euro. Labour Prime Minister Tony Blair then promised to hold a referendum on ratifying the Constitutional Treaty, agreed in 2003. That treaty collapsed thanks to 'no' votes in France and the Netherlands and so no referendum was held in the UK. Gordon Brown as the new Labour Prime Minister asserted that the subsequent Lisbon Treaty was sufficiently different from its aborted predecessor that ratification by referendum was not necessary. That other countries and the creator of the Constitutional Treaty, former President of France Valéry Giscard d'Estaing, took diametrically opposed views, asserting that the new Lisbon Treaty was virtually identical to the Constitutional Treaty, ensured that Brown's decision was at best contestable, at worst could be portrayed as a breach of faith.[7] The Conservatives thus argued that the new treaty should still be ratified by referendum, and David Cameron gave a 'cast-iron guarantee' that if the Treaty had not come into effect by the time his party took office he would hold a referendum.[8] Meanwhile, the Liberal Democrat leader, Nick Clegg, engaged in a degree of brinkmanship, suggesting that there should be a referendum not simply on approving the treaty but on the fundamental question of whether the UK should remain in

---

[7] See, for example, Toby Helm, 'Giscard: EU treaty is the constitution rewritten', *The Telegraph*, 29 October 2007.

[8] 'Timeline: Campaigns for a European Union referendum', *BBC News*, 31 March 2014 (accessed at www.bbc.co.uk/news/uk-politics-15390884, 19 September 2014).

the EU. Clegg's position was controversial within his own party, as many senior figures, notably members of the House of Lords who had been involved in the 1975 referendum, believed that this was a risky undertaking. Clegg's position prevailed, however, and was subsequently enshrined in the 2009 and 2014 EP and the 2010 general election manifestos, all of which deployed careful phrasing reiterating the party's commitment to an in/out referendum.

The referendum pledges, and the fact that none had ever resulted in a popular vote on European questions, led to growing frustration among Eurosceptic voters and the right-wing press. The sight of potential supporters drifting to UKIP focused the minds of the Tory MPs, candidates and the grass roots, who continued to press for a referendum on Lisbon, despite the fact that the Treaty had come into effect almost six months ahead of the 2010 general election, leaving the incoming Conservative Prime Minister and Foreign Secretary with a difficult task to keep their right wing onside.

The electoral dimension

By the time of the 2010 general election, Euroscepticism was the prevailing attitude within the Conservative family, while Labour retained the veneer of pro-Europeanism that it had acquired during the 'New Labour' period.[9] Brown personally had highlighted the UK's lack of engagement with the EU by failing to attend the signing of the Lisbon Treaty alongside the other twenty-six EU leaders. Citing pressing parliamentary business, Brown arrived to sign in splendid isolation. Nonetheless, Labour's ongoing commitment to the EU was clear in its manifesto, which focused more on challenging the Conservatives' position on Europe than on celebrating any specific successes of its own. Thus, Labour claimed that 'The contrast with the Tory view could not be starker: they are stuck in the past, spurning alliances in Europe and helpless to defend our interests or secure the global change we need.'[10] Yet, like the Lib Dems, Labour also sought 'a reformed Europe', which it

[9] See Deighton, 'European Union policy' and Julie Smith, 'A missed opportunity? New Labour's European policy 1997–2005', *International Affairs*, 81:4 (2005), pp. 703–21.
[10] Labour Party, *The Labour Party Manifesto 2010: A Future Fair for All* (London: Labour Party, 2010), p. 10:2.

felt could only be achieved by constructive engagement, which it argued the Conservatives could not deliver: 'In Europe they are not just isolated, but marginalized – in a tiny group of far-right parties that endorses extreme views and is stuck in climate-change denial. Elsewhere in the world their anti-European attitudes are seen as undermining British influence. They are helpless to shape change, or defend our interests.'[11]

Party politics aside, the language used by the three main parties in their manifestos was remarkably similar – there was little sign of any federal agenda from the Liberal Democrats, while the Conservatives' language was more constructive than the rhetoric of some of its parliamentary candidates, who favoured withdrawal from the EU.[12] Thus, the Conservatives asserted:

> We will work constructively with the EU but we will not hand over any more areas of power and we will never join the Euro.
>
> We will be positive members of the European Union but we are clear that there should be no further extension of the EU's power over the UK without the British people's consent. We will ensure by law no future government can hand over areas of power to the EU or join the Euro without a referendum of the British people. We will work to bring back key powers over legal rights, criminal justice and social and employment legislation to the UK.[13]

This approach, particularly the so-called 'referendum lock', would fundamentally shape the Europe section of the Coalition Agreement, although it would ultimately not go far enough for many on the right of the party.

The Liberal Democrats' support for the Union also appeared pragmatic and interest-based rather than ideological: 'Liberal Democrats believe that European co-operation is the best way for Britain to be strong, safe and influential in the future. We will ensure that Britain maximises its influence through a strong and positive commitment.'[14]

---

[11] *Ibid.*, p. 10:4.

[12] While the Party nationally has a manifesto, Tory candidates may additionally have a personal manifesto and some, including Mark Reckless, elected MP for Rochester and Strood in 2010, pledged to pull the UK out of the EU. (Source: Mark Reckless' speech to the UKIP Conference on 27 September 2014.)

[13] Conservative Party, *Invitation to Join the Government of Britain: The Conservative Manifesto 2010* (London: Conservative Party, 2010), p. 113.

[14] Liberal Democrats, *Liberal Democrat Manifesto 2010: Change that Works for you – Building a Fairer Britain* (London: Liberal Democrats, 2010), p. 66.

The party was anxious to show that it was not an uncritical supporter of the Union, asserting: 'But just because Europe is essential, that doesn't mean the European Union is perfect. We will continue to campaign for improved accountability, efficiency and effectiveness.'[15] Unlike the Tories they remained committed to eventual British membership of the Euro but felt 'Britain should only join when the economic conditions are right', which, at the height of a global financial and emerging Eurozone crisis, they were clearly not. In any case, such a move would happen only 'if that decision were supported by the people of Britain in a referendum'.[16] Labour took a very similar line, stating 'there will be no membership of the single currency without the consent of the British people in a referendum'.[17]

While all the parties advocated the idea of a referendum if ever Britain was on the verge of joining the Euro, only the Liberal Democrats advocated asking citizens' views on the more fundamental question of whether they wished to stay in the EU. The logic of their commitment, however, was in line with the thinking of many Conservative and UKIP supporters who favoured withdrawal from the EU: 'The European Union has evolved significantly since the last public vote on membership over thirty years ago', hence the need for a referendum.[18] The difference was that in the event of any such referendum Clegg's party would advocate remaining in the Union, UKIP would advocate leaving and Tories would be deeply divided on the matter.

The UK's relationship with the EU per se was not a major issue in the 2010 election but the related matters of immigration and free movement of people were. UKIP's poster campaign focused on immigration rather than EU membership, while both the Lib Dems and Labour found themselves in some difficulty over questions of immigration. The interplay of immigration and free movement alongside the Conservatives' pledge to cap immigration – a particularly tricky aspiration given the numbers of EU nationals exercising their rights of free movement – ensured that this key aspect of European politics was on the agenda but otherwise Europe was little discussed. This was about to change.

---

[15] *Ibid.*   [16] *Ibid.*, p. 67.   [17] Labour Party, *Manifesto 2010*, p. 10:4.
[18] Liberal Democrats, *Manifesto 2010*, p. 67.

The Coalition Agreement

A hung parliament and the determination of Nick Clegg to negotiate with the leader of the largest party, as he had consistently stated during the election, meant that the three main parties would need to address their respective European policies and decide whether they could be reconciled. The situation was complicated by the financial situation in Greece, which set the context in which all three parties and senior civil servants were anxious to get an agreement as swiftly as possible. The crisis also ensured that further, unpredicted European reforms would follow, which would put additional pressure on the Conservative–Lib Dem coalition.[19] Europe, along with defence and immigration, was one of David Cameron's red lines, and an area where Lib Dem negotiators thought coalition negotiations with the Conservatives might founder.[20] As Nick Clegg made clear to David Cameron, 'there are some key issues which will be very difficult for both sides to agree on, and which are really important to both parties – for example, Europe. We have to see if we can handle these "red lines".'[21] Cameron reaffirmed, 'our view is clearly that there should be no more passing of powers to the European Union in this parliament'.[22] Indeed, the Chairman of the House of Commons European Scrutiny Committee, Bill (now Sir William) Cash, wrote to Cameron to urge him not to enter a coalition with the Liberal Democrats in large part because of Europe. As Cash argued, 'To enter a coalition with a party that is diametrically opposed over Europe was bound to create an artificial government because the EU is *about* government and would guarantee that they would not be able to pursue a Conservative policy over the EU, namely the government at Westminster on which the 1972 Act is based.' The Lib Dems, he believed, would be a 'Trojan horse for Europe in Coalition'.[23] The European question was also picked up by Gordon Brown as he sought to create an alternative Lib–Lab coalition, telling Clegg, 'I want you to know that I attach

---

[19] In his personal account of the creation of the coalition, David Laws repeatedly remarks on the urgency to form a government that all the key players felt: David Laws, 22 *Days in May: The Birth of the Lib Dem–Conservative Coalition* (London: Biteback Publishing, 2010).

[20] *ibid.*, pp. 49–50.   [21] Quoted in *ibid.*, p. 52.   [22] *Ibid.*, p. 54.

[23] Interview, 10 September 2014.

importance to Europe, where I think we can find common ground ... it would be a pro-European government.'[24]

Undoubtedly a Liberal Democrat–Labour coalition would have found common ground on European matters rather more easily than the Lib Dems could achieve with the Conservatives. Both parties were part of the European mainstream, members of their respective EU-level political parties and, Brown's reluctance to join fellow leaders to sign the Lisbon Treaty notwithstanding, generally well plugged into European networks. Having pulled the Conservatives out of the main centre-right European People's Party (EPP) grouping in early 2009 to fulfil a pledge made during his party leadership campaign, Cameron was in a far more isolated position, unable to attend key meetings with fellow centre-right party leaders; a situation which was to prove detrimental to his ability to influence European affairs once he took office.[25] Factors other than Europe drove the final decision to enter a coalition, however, and the two negotiating teams needed to deal with the red lines rather than allow them to frustrate a deal. The fact that the economic conditions ensured there was no prospect of the UK joining the Euro meant that the potentially most sensitive question could be dealt with swiftly. Other aspects of European policy were less easy to resolve. As George Osborne noted, 'Europe is important for the Conservative Party. The wording on this is crucial. There must be no further EU integration. And there must be a referendum lock on any future transfers of power.'[26] Thus, the Coalition Agreement would contain a provision that in future powers could not pass from the UK (or, more precisely, from Parliament) to the EU without a referendum: 'We will amend the 1972 European Communities Act so that any proposed future treaty that transferred areas of power, or competences, would be subject to a "referendum lock".'[27] This commitment was taken word for word from the 2010 Conservative Party manifesto. However, for the Liberal Democrats too this device seemed acceptable, as it could be construed

---

[24] Laws, 22 *Days in May*, pp. 56, 60.

[25] In 1992 John Major negotiated a deal whereby the Conservatives sat alongside the EPP MEPs in a group in the European Parliament, but they never joined the EPP party, ensuring that they retained a good deal of flexibility – in particular not being required to sign up to the EPP manifesto.

[26] Laws, 22 *Days in May*, p. 184.

[27] HM Government, *The Coalition: Our Programme for Government* (London: Cabinet Office, 2010), p. 19.

as meeting their commitment to an in/out referendum at the time of major treaty change.

In line with the Conservative agenda, the Agreement stated that, 'We will ensure there is no further transfer of sovereignty or powers over the course of the next Parliament.'[28] Since there was no prospect of any treaty reform for several years, the Lisbon Treaty being seen as the definitive document for many years to come, this commitment raised little concern in May 2010, although this assumption was rapidly challenged by events in the Eurozone, sparking early tensions between the UK and its European partners. Also in line with the Conservative manifesto, the Agreement further stated: 'We will examine the balance of the EU's existing competences and will, in particular, work to limit the application of the Working Time Directive in the United Kingdom.'[29] There was no talk of 'repatriation', with the exception of the controversial Working Time Directive. A compromise was reached on Labour's legacy on matters of Justice and Home Affairs, where the UK had a right to 'opt in' – each case would be decided individually.[30] There was no mention of seeking to end or reform the EU's policies on free movement of people, which would become a major theme for the Conservatives during the coalition government.

Overall, the relatively detailed 'Europe' section of the Coalition Agreement reflected a constructive but pragmatic approach to the EU, a reluctance to cede further powers to the EU – no further loss of sovereignty could occur without popular agreement – and a refusal to countenance any preparation for joining the Euro. Even this last point was scarcely a loss for the Liberal Democrats, who recognized that the time was unlikely to be right for the UK to join for many years to come. Two key pieces of work would flow directly from the Agreement: the EU Act 2011 and the Balance of Competences Review. Both were the result of Conservative initiatives, reflecting that party's determination not to cede more powers to the EU and, ideally, to find ways of repatriating powers to the UK. These two items played out rather differently in practice, as the Liberal Democrats took their eye off the ball on the first, the Tories, arguably, on the second. Over the course of the coalition government, however, European policy would be driven more by external events and

---

[28] *Ibid.*, p. 19.   [29] *Ibid.*   [30] *Ibid.*

internal party divisions than by the Coalition Agreement or grand strategies from either coalition partner.

The coalition in practice

In contrast to other policy areas, where the Quad of Cameron, Clegg, Osborne and Alexander was crucial to decision-making, on European policy a triumvirate of Cameron, Osborne and Hague would dominate at the strategic level, even after Hague ceased to be Foreign Secretary. At times the strongly pro-European Danny Alexander would be tasked with brokering agreements with Oliver Letwin on European matters, and Cameron and Clegg would inevitably have to agree on major issues. All three senior Conservative ministers would call themselves 'Eurosceptic', but all believed that the UK was better off inside the EU, even though they wished for reform. While this pragmatic position over Europe assisted in working with the Liberal Democrats it ensured that at times the leadership was at odds with many of its backbenchers. Previously the 'poster-boy' of the Tory Eurosceptics, in 2014 William Hague would still say 'I am a rational Eurosceptic like most people in the country.' Yet he was no longer seen as sufficiently Eurosceptic by those on the right of the party. His position had remained broadly unchanged over the years; that of his party had shifted, particularly with the 2010 parliamentary intake.[31] When Philip Hammond replaced Hague towards the end of the five-year coalition, it seemed that Cameron had appointed someone whose views fitted more closely with the Eurosceptic right, but Hammond, like the triumvirate, held the line that Britain was better off in (a reformed) EU, refusing to be drawn by journalists to say he would ever support leaving the Union. One insider was clear: 'The new Foreign Secretary is a pragmatic Eurosceptic. He is not a "better-off-outer" in head or heart. His strong preference is for the UK to stay in the EU.'[32]

One of the remarkable things about the coalition's work on European policy was the positive nature of relations between the Conservatives and Liberal Democrats working together on a daily basis. While the parties' public positions differed, and diverged further during

---

[31] James Forsyth, personal communication, 10 September 2014.
[32] Private information (interview, 17 September 2014).

the course of the coalition, at least among those working on European matters within the confines of the Foreign and Commonwealth Office and the Cabinet Office, there was considerable mutual respect among politicians and advisers. Liberal Democrats welcomed the fact that as Foreign Secretary William Hague allowed them to attend all ministerial meetings – none were reserved just for Conservatives as was the case in some other departments. Tories privately welcomed the wealth of expertise and contacts on European affairs brought to the table by the Lib Dems' William Wallace. The constructive working relationship on day-to-day matters was assisted by the fact that David Cameron chose to appoint David Lidington to the post of Europe Minister, rather than Mark Francois, the more strongly Eurosceptic MP who had held the shadow post in opposition. This decision was clearly welcomed by the Liberal Democrats, but seems to have suited the Conservative leadership too. As one MP put it, 'Mark Francois was the Shadow Europe Minister but was seen as too Eurosceptic for Lib Dem colleagues and also probably for Number 10.'[33]

Despite the huge strategic importance of European affairs, much of the day-to-day work was left to relatively junior people: David Lidington was a minister below Cabinet rank, while Wallace was an unpaid government whip in the Lords. The fact that the European issue was one that no one really wanted to raise was compounded by the fact that Jeremy Browne, the Liberal Democrat minister in the FCO for the first two years of the coalition, saw his role as 'anything but Europe', while Hague was also keen to focus on restoring the status of the FCO more generally, focusing on areas that he felt had been neglected by the previous Government. 'Hague's position on Europe was to firm up the line on the EU but not to obsess about Europe. While he was leader, it was a very divisive issue and before 2010 Europe was not a priority for the electorate.'[34] It is notable, however, that the direction of foreign policy did not shift towards the US during the coalition, the old US–EU dichotomy in British politics perhaps fading as Cameron had no close links with Obama.

Hague did retain strategic oversight of the European question but was willing to delegate most European work to the Europe Minister, who was trusted by himself and Cameron, as well as being able to

[33] Private information (interview, 8 September 2014). [34] *Ibid.*

deal effectively with the Liberal Democrats. 'Number 10 was happy and I think the Lib Dems were also happy.'[35] Unlike the history of the previous government, where there was roughly one Europe minister for every year in office, Cameron kept Lidington in post throughout, alongside a key special adviser, Denzil Davidson, who remained in post when Hague left the FCO. Of course, European policy is not solely, or even primarily, about 'foreign' affairs, even if much of the policy work is handled by the FCO and the Europe Minister is based there rather than in the Cabinet Office. European policy could and should have been mainstreamed, but Lib Dem advisers in particular found it difficult to get special advisers in other Departments to engage effectively, particularly in the early years of the coalition. And if relations were positive within the FCO, the attitudes of backbenchers and ministers from other departments were not always so cordial. Nor could the coalition government always get its way in EU-level negotiations.

Towards a referendum

The government moved swiftly to introduce a bill that led to the EU Act 2011. Opening the second reading debate, Foreign Secretary William Hague asserted,

> Indeed, the crowning argument for the Bill was the behaviour of the last Government, who opposed a referendum on the EU constitution, then promised one, then refused to hold one on its substantially similar reincarnation as the Lisbon treaty. The Bill will prevent Governments from being so deceptive and double-dealing when it comes to giving voters a say.[36]

While Liberal Democrats had agreed to the Tory idea of a 'referendum lock', they would come to regret the format of the legislation that became the EU Act 2011. The prevailing private view was that the party had not paid sufficient attention to the drafting of the bill in the early stages, partly because they were understaffed and partly because the Lib Dems' man in the Foreign Office, Jeremy Browne, did not see Europe as his concern. By the time a core team of advisers and parliamentarians began to focus their attention on it, it was too late to craft it in a way

---

[35] *Ibid.*   [36] Commons Hansard, 7 December 2010, col. 191.

that suited Liberal Democrat interests.[37] The Tory side of the coalition had delivered their commitment to ensuring that no new powers could go to Brussels without a referendum. Yet here too there was disquiet, with several Eurosceptics, including Douglas Carswell, who would subsequently defect to UKIP, claiming that it did not really provide a 'lock' since no parliament can bind its successor.[38] Veteran Eurosceptic, or Euro-realist to use his own preferred term, Bill Cash was scathing about what he referred to as 'a mouse of a Bill' that would do little to protect parliamentary sovereignty: a line that was also taken by many other Tory backbenchers and some Labour MPs.[39]

Eventually the EU Act became law in November 2011 but Conservative MPs had already begun to call for a more tangible commitment to a referendum. Following an online petition calling for such a referendum, incidentally promoted by the *Daily Express*, whose editor Patrick O'Flynn subsequently became UKIP's Director of Communications and was elected to the European Parliament in May 2014, Tory MP David Nuttall secured a Backbench Debate on a motion:

> That this House calls upon the Government to introduce a Bill in the next session of Parliament to provide for the holding of a national referendum on whether the United Kingdom should
>
> (a) remain a member of the European Union on the current terms;
> (b) leave the European Union; or
> (c) re-negotiate the terms of its membership in order to create a new relationship based on trade and co-operation.[40]

The leaders of all three main parties were united in their opposition to this motion, imposing a three-line whip on their MPs to vote against. The time was not right, the Tory leadership argued. Nor was the question. The idea of a three-way referendum was felt to be inappropriate, just as coalition ministers would reject the idea of a three-option referendum on the future of Scotland. Tory backbenchers were furious and eighty-one rebelled against the Whip, including some like Adam Holloway, PPS to the Europe Minister David Lidington, who resigned government positions in order to do so. The majority of the rebels were Eurosceptics – as indeed were the vast majority of Tory contributors to

---

[37] This view came up in several interviews with Liberal Democrat insiders.
[38] Commons Hansard, 7 December 2010, col. 201.   [39] *Ibid.*, cols. 224; 205.
[40] Commons Hansard, 24 October 2011, col. 46.

384 / Julie Smith

the debate – and there were claims that some ministers privately shared their views. Some of the rebels were not Eurosceptics but were keen that citizens should have an early say, in the belief that this would secure a vote to stay in the EU. While the rebels were unsuccessful in the voting lobbies on that October day, they were able to help shape the agenda for subsequent UK negotiations within the EU, as Cameron's internal constraints were apparent to all his EU colleagues.

As backbenchers had argued, it seemed there was no prospect of treaty reform and thus no chance that the referendum lock enshrined in the EU Act would be triggered. Until, that is, member states began to consider seriously how to deal with the Eurozone crisis. As Tory MP Bernard Jenkin put it on the eve of a crucial EU summit in December 2011: 'The coalition agreement never envisaged confronting a major change to the EU treaties in this Parliament. The EU was meant to be off the agenda and, indeed, the leadership of the Conservative party deliberately downplayed the issue of Europe, both before the election and in the first part of this Parliament.'[41] The Eurozone crisis had shown that the institutional reforms enacted by Lisbon had not gone far enough to secure Eurozone stability, and further treaty reform was now being mooted. On 9 December, David Cameron attended a European Council meeting where treaty reform was discussed. Thanks to his decision to take the Tories out of the EPP in 2009, he had been absent from a vital dinner earlier in the week at which leaders had seemingly stitched up a deal. Trilateral discussions with German Chancellor Angela Merkel and French President Nicolas Sarkozy did not go well, as Cameron briefed his Deputy, Nick Clegg.[42] During the formal negotiations, Cameron produced a piece of paper indicating the UK's demands. He got nowhere, as fellow leaders were reluctant to consider items that had not been circulated in advance. Eventually, Cameron left the room, claiming that he had vetoed the treaty. The other states continued to negotiate, giving the distinct impression that Cameron had not vetoed anything at all: a veto would have stopped the treaty.

In fact, Cameron's actions did ensure that no *EU* treaty would be agreed. Rather an extra-EU international treaty was eventually adopted by twenty-five states (the Czechs like the UK remaining outside

[41] Hansard, 8 December 2011, col. 151WH.
[42] Private information. See also Matthew d'Ancona, *In It Together: The Inside Story of the Coalition Government* (London: Viking/Penguin Group, 2013), p. 247.

the new treaty). This had the twin merits from the PM's perspective of no moves to fiscal federalism and no trigger for a referendum, as powers were not shifting to the EU, a situation that also meant other member states were able to ratify the treaty rather more swiftly than if it had been an EU treaty. The Conservative Eurosceptics greeted the Prime Minister's actions with jubilation, claiming a British win in Europe, and one led by the PM.[43] For pro-Europeans it was seen as evidence that Cameron was both isolated in Europe and overly keen to throw red meat to the Eurosceptic backbenchers. In the words of pro-European Tory backbencher Mark Field,

> The invoking of a British 'veto' at last December's EU summit was billed as an aggressive demonstration of the UK's intention to retain its offshore/onshore model, protecting the City as its vital interest ... In reality, that veto was less about the future of the City and more a political gesture to a domestic audience aimed at keeping Eurosceptic wolves from the door ideally well beyond 2015.[44]

As we shall see, such attempts would soon fail, as Cameron moved ever further towards the referendum pledge his backbenchers sought – and potentially ever closer to 'Brexit'.

Meanwhile, relations between the coalition partners were sorely strained over the issue. Nick Clegg's first public reaction was entirely in line with his prior behaviour in coalition, namely to back up the PM and suggest that their positions were all but identical. Thus, he announced to the media on the Friday morning that the PM had kept him informed throughout and that he agreed with the PM's actions. Forty-eight hours later he appeared on the *Andrew Marr* programme expressing his anger at the outcome. Clegg's anger and disappointment were genuine, yet he had been kept abreast of what was going on throughout, to the extent that anyone not present in the room could have known completely what was happening.[45] A change in procedures under Lisbon meant that only one representative per member state was present instead of two, as had previously been the case. Thus neither Foreign Secretary nor DPM were

[43] Interview with Sir William Cash, 10 September 2014.
[44] Mark Field, 'The summit that lies ahead', *City A.M.*, 22 November 2012, reprinted in his *Between the Crashes: Reflections and Insights on UK Politics and Global Economics in the Aftermath of the Financial Crisis* (London: Biteback Publishing Ltd, 2013), p. 267.
[45] Both Conservative and Liberal Democrat sources confirmed this view of events.

there, although the former was at least in an adjacent room; the latter was down a telephone line. As a result of the debacle, an additional civil servant answerable to the DPM was added to the team sent to European Council meetings, the intention being to ensure that the Liberal Democrat side of the coalition could be fully informed of what was happening. There was much discussion at the time that the Foreign Office had also been outflanked, demonstrated by the decision to appoint Jon Cunliffe, a Treasury rather than an FCO man, as the UK Permanent Representative (or ambassador) to the EU. The FCO would surely have been able to handle negotiations better, given their long experience of bilateral and multilateral engagement within the EU. Yet, one FCO official put the matter in a very different perspective, attributing the outcome to personality rather than the strengths or weaknesses of those negotiating. 'On the decision to veto or not to veto in December 2011, Nick Clegg would have acted quite differently though even he recognized the risks for the UK of being sold a pup. Just wouldn't have played it in the same way.'[46]

Building alliances

Indeed, Cameron's leadership style, personality and relations with colleagues, whether within his own Conservative Party or within the EU, proved major factors in the UK's changing relations with the EU during the coalition government. Whereas Tony Blair had understood the need to work with colleagues from other EU member states, whether from the same party family or not, Cameron found it much harder to engage and did not cultivate the sort of alliances needed to secure what he wanted in the EU. To an extent this reflected the traditional Conservative view of bilateral relations – primarily with Germany – as an end in themselves rather than the means to an end, namely securing what they wanted in Europe. But for one prominent backbencher it reflected a deeper problem: 'David Cameron isn't really engaged – not in the EPP; not part of these alliances. Consider how European policy has developed over the year. There is a semi-detached approach to Europe. There was never a strategic sense of where the coalition was going.'[47]

[46] Private information (interview, 9 September 2014).
[47] Private information (interview, 2 July 2014).

Yet while critics viewed Cameron's behaviour over the fiscal compact as a sign of his 'petulance' and inability to build alliances, the truth was slightly different.[48] Over the years, Cameron established a solid working relationship with German Chancellor Angela Merkel.[49] Given his party's absence from the EPP, this was in itself no small achievement. On occasion Merkel seemed able to deliver for Cameron, notably on reducing the EU budget, which was greeted by British Conservatives as a very significant policy win; Cameron was hailed as the first Prime Minister to see a reduction in the British contribution to EU coffers since Margaret Thatcher, and the first to see a real-terms cut to the EU budget. Yet, again, the Labour opposition and Tory Right would claim victory on the matter of the reduced EU budget of which Cameron was so proud. Despite manifesto commitments to further reform of the EU budget, 'so that money is spent only on the things the EU really needs to do' as the Lib Dems put it,[50] there was no formal commitment to reducing the EU budget in the Coalition Agreement.

In 2012 Labour's Chris Leslie tabled an unsuccessful parliamentary amendment calling on the government to call for the 2013 EU budget and the multi-annual financial framework (MFF) for 2014–20 to be reduced in real terms.[51] The following year, an amendment put down by then Tory MP Mark Reckless similarly called for the MFF to be reduced in real terms. The combined forces of Tory rebels and the Labour parliamentary party ensured that the rebel amendment was passed. While technically this was not binding on the Prime Minister when he went to negotiate in Brussels, it would have been very difficult for him not to have fought for the position that represented the sovereign will of Parliament. The vote was a mixed blessing: both an excuse to explain to EU colleagues why certain outcomes would simply be unacceptable at home and, at the same time, a chore, as the government needed to devote time to persuading them that 'we were still worth talking to', as one insider put it. While party insiders saw this as a fantastic victory for Cameron, who had on this occasion been able

---

[48] Mark Field, 'The summit that lies ahead'.
[49] See Julie Smith, 'The view from London', *Europe's World*, June 2013; also d'Ancona, *In It Together*, pp. 254–5.
[50] Liberal Democrats, *Manifesto 2010*, p. 67.
[51] Commons Hansard, 12 July 2012, col. 523.

to work effectively with Merkel and the new French President, François Hollande, to secure the deal he wanted, the rebels also claimed victory.[52]

However, Cameron perhaps put too much faith in Merkel's ability to deliver. On some issues domestic politics constrained Merkel, as they did Cameron, albeit because of her coalition partners rather than difficulties within her own party.[53] This was clear in summer 2014 over the appointment of Jean-Claude Juncker as the Commission President. Juncker had been the candidate of the EPP in a new system of *Spitzenkandidaten* that arose from the Lisbon Treaty; the idea was to revitalize EP elections and create a link between the appointment of the Commission and Europe's citizens. None of the main British parties really bought into this change: the Tories were part of a sceptic grouping in the European Parliament that did not field a candidate; neither Labour nor the Liberal Democrats supported 'their' European parties' candidates either, with leaders reluctant to highlight the candidacies of, respectively, Martin Schultz or Guy Verhofstadt. Thus, when it came to the nominations, Cameron, Clegg and Miliband were as one in opposing the appointment of Juncker, who was deemed too federalist. Cameron believed he had Merkel's support to block Juncker and spent time working, rather publicly, with Merkel, as well as Mark Rutte, the Dutch Prime Minister, and their then Swedish counterpart Fredrik Reinfeldt. The German media and her Social Democrat coalition partners were deeply unhappy at the suggestion that Merkel would go against what they felt was the democratic will of the people and she ultimately backed Juncker. The UK was seen to be isolated and disengaged and Cameron was widely felt to have overplayed his hand. Had Cameron, the Conservatives or the UK more generally devoted more time to developing wider bilateral relations within the Union, such asymmetric dependence on Germany might have been less of an issue.

In fact, some members of the coalition did recognize the importance of working with their colleagues from other EU member states. None perhaps were as assiduous as Lib Dem Edward Davey, who established a 'like-minded group' of economic liberal states while a minister in the Department for Business, Innovation and Skills, before launching the Green Growth Group as Secretary of State for Energy

[52] Private information (interviews on 10 and 17 September 2014).
[53] Private information (interview, 17 September 2014).

and Climate Change, in initiatives very reminiscent of Blair's 'new bilateralism'.[54] Some Tory ministers also recognized the importance of cultivating bilateral relations, though usually for ad-hoc or single-issue purposes, with considerable efforts on British–French defence co-operation under both Liam Fox and Philip Hammond as successive Secretaries of State for Defence. The notable exception was David Lidington, who spent much time travelling to other European capitals and getting to know colleagues during an exceptionally long spell as Europe Minister. On becoming Foreign Secretary, Philip Hammond also decided that he should visit colleagues elsewhere in Europe, including the European Parliament, ahead of the proposed renegotiation to follow the 2015 election.[55] Such activities were obviously intended to prepare for the post-coalition Conservative government, should the polls fall the Conservatives' way, but certainly reflected a greater understanding of the workings of the EU and the need to cultivate than many were willing to give the government credit for.

Party management

If alliances were necessary at the European level, party cohesion was required at home and was something Cameron found very difficult to engender, thanks in part to the challenge of being in coalition. David Laws has commented of coalition, 'The prizes for Mr Cameron were obvious: government, not opposition; stability, not chaos; joint responsibility for tough decisions, not sole blame for the painful cuts to come; and an opportunity to change the entire perception of the Conservative Party and to reshape British politics.'[56] Yet, while these 'prizes' might have suited Cameron and his closest allies, they were not valued by many backbenchers, who felt he had ignored their views and railroaded them into coalition, which would have severe ramifications in terms of internal management of European policy. The coalition with the Lib Dems gave Cameron a sufficiently comfortable majority in the House of Commons to enable him to ignore those on the right of his party, at

---

[54] See Julie Smith and Mariana Tsatsas, *The New Bilateralism: The UK's Relations within the EU* (London: RIIA, 2002).
[55] Off-the-record interview, 10 September 2014.   [56] Laws, *22 Days in May*, p. 51.

least initially, and gave him cover to adopt more centrist policies than would have been acceptable in a single-party Conservative government.

This situation was in marked contrast to the Liberal Democrats, whose MPs enthusiastically endorsed moves to create the coalition. This was not simply a difference in fortunes, Lib Dems happy to secure a seat at the Cabinet table and ministerial cars as some critics would assert, though that may have been part of it. Rather, the fact that Lib Dem MPs had actually had a chance to discuss and vote on the creation of the coalition, alongside votes of the Lords parliamentary team and the party's Federal Executive, was part of an elaborate constitutional arrangement in the Lib Dems designed to ensure that their leaders could not go off and negotiate bilateral deals in the cavalier way that Cameron appeared to have done. While this might have seemed tiresome during those five days in May, the result was a Lib Dem parliamentary party that bought into the coalition and exercised considerable self-discipline throughout the coalition; the prospect of hitherto unexpected government jobs undoubtedly helped, as did the realization that an unwelcome second election in late 2010 was off the agenda. And on European issues, the Coalition Agreement did not cause too many concerns.

By contrast, the Tory backbenchers were frustrated by Cameron's failure to win the election outright, by their subsequent loss of job prospects as Lib Dems took plum jobs, and most profoundly the fact that they had not had a say. As one prominent Tory backbencher put it, 'We never even had a show of hands in the '22 [Committee]. We were bounced into this. I never bought into this unnecessary Coalition.'[57] On the European issue, the problems for the Conservative leadership were compounded by the fact that the Coalition Agreement's line on the EU was moderate and pragmatic, reflecting both Liberal Democrat influence and the views of the Conservative Party leadership (broadly, Cameron, Osborne and Hague), who believed that the UK should remain within the (reformed) EU – a position not universally shared by the parliamentary party, particularly many of the 2010 intake, who were deeply Eurosceptic and, as one veteran MP put it, 'hunted as a pack'.[58] The leitmotif of Tory selections ahead of the 2010 election had been opposition to the 1972 European Communities Act, which many claimed they wished to see repealed, in line with the views expressed by

[57] Private information (telephone conversation, 26 September 2014).
[58] Private information (interview, 8 September 2014).

most local Conservative Associations responsible for selecting parliamentary candidates: the Coalition Agreement simply did not reflect their views on Europe. All of these factors contributed to a willingness among backbenchers to vote as they saw fit on European matters, paying little heed to the views of Cameron or the party whips, with considerable results for British EU policy.

Without a coalition, it is likely that the Tories would have been divided but some of the factors that led to the rise of UKIP and heightened backbench Euroscepticism would not have arisen or would have been more muted. Egos would have been less crushed, there would have been more jobs 'for the boys' and more apparent flexibility for the PM. Defections may therefore have been staunched. When Mark Reckless defected to UKIP on the eve of the Conservatives' 2014 party conference, there was much discussion of Cameron's apparent disregard for his backbenchers. 'David Cameron only spends time with MPs because he has to, not because he likes us' was the view given by disaffected Tories to *Spectator* commentator Isabel Hardman.[59] One long-standing MP put it to the author that 'David Cameron's management of the parliamentary party was never good. He ruthlessly sacrificed some people over expenses and protected others. Then failed to get a majority and rushed through the Coalition without any discussion.' By 2014, some of those on the Eurosceptic right of the party had decided that they were not willing to accept the situation any longer and succumbed to the attractions of Nigel Farage and UKIP. The reaction of Tory whips, who allegedly threatened to impugn the 'personal integrity' of any other potential defectors, and Party Chairman Grant Shapps, who raged about Reckless's behaviour, did little to dispel the sense that backbenchers were not valued by the leadership.[60]

The leader who had seen 'Europe' as an issue of party management had failed to hold his party together on the issue. The more the sceptics tried to set the agenda, the more he appeared to bend to their way of thinking, moving from stated opposition to a referendum in October 2011 to a formal commitment to an in/out referendum by the time of his Bloomberg speech in January 2013. Hoping to take the issue off the agenda, Cameron argued that a referendum after renegotiation

---

[59] Speaking on the *PM* Programme, BBC Radio 4, 27 September 2014.

[60] Nicolas Watt and Rowena Mason, 'Tory whips issue threats to MPs tempted to join Nigel Farage and Ukip', *The Guardian*, 28 September 2014.

was the correct way forward. 2017 was chosen as the date for such a vote on the grounds that it was deemed to give the longest possible negotiating window within the EU – between the UK general election of May 2015 and the German elections of 2017. The hope was that this would assuage the sceptics; it failed. In 2012 Douglas Carswell brought forward a Private Member's Bill (PMB) seeking a referendum; by 2013, James Wharton's PMB had support from the Tory leadership, but was talked out in the House of Lords; a similar bill was introduced by Bob Neil in the final session of the parliament. These bills sought to make a referendum inevitable within a fixed timeframe, and fitted into the Conservatives' position at the 2014 European Parliament elections, at which they would argue that only the Conservatives could offer an in/out referendum because UKIP 'couldn't' and Labour and the Lib Dems 'wouldn't'. Yet voters did not seem persuaded by this any more than by Nick Clegg's attempts to brand the Lib Dems the party of 'in' in debates with UKIP leader Nigel Farage. The in/out debates starkly highlighted intra-coalition differences over Europe but assisted UKIP most of all. UKIP won nearly 30 per cent of the vote and twenty-four seats in the European Parliament, the Tory vote fell and the Lib Dems were nearly wiped out. For some Tory Eurosceptics such as Jacob Rees-Mogg, the answer was to get even closer to UKIP and re-unite the right, perhaps via electoral pacts.

Pro-European Damian Green urged Cameron not to try to position the Tories as UKIP-lite,[61] a strategy that Matthew d'Ancona also argued would be misguided, since pro-Europeans in the centre-ground would move away from the Tories.[62] Defections suggested that the sceptics did not really believe Cameron was moving their way, despite the referendum pledge, which was seen by some simply as a way to kick the issue into the long post-election grass. Cameron continued to stress his belief that the UK was better off in a reformed EU than outside. His approach was to advocate renegotiation and referendum, asserting, 'What I believe is that it is right for Britain to seek change and then to stay in a reformed EU.'[63] This was nonetheless spun

---

[61] Green speaking at a Conservative Party fringe meeting on 28 September 2014.

[62] Matthew d'Ancona, 'No great speech but he did land a blow on the PM', *Evening Standard*, 24 September 2014, p. 14.

[63] David Cameron on *The Andrew Marr Show*, BBC One, 28 September 2014.

by a *Daily Telegraph* headline-writer to imply 'I could campaign to leave the EU, warns David Cameron.'[64]

As time went by, the likelihood of the PM adopting such a line did indeed seem credible as he reacted to defections. He hoped, perhaps, to persuade the other twenty-seven EU member states that there was a credible threat that the UK would leave the Union if Cameron could not deliver the 'repatriation of powers' he sought, the most important of which related to the free movement of people. Thus, in his final pre-election Conference address Cameron boldly stated:

> But we know the bigger issue today is migration from within the EU. Immediate access to our welfare system. Paying benefits to families back home. Employment agencies signing people up from overseas and not recruiting here. Numbers that have increased faster than we in this country wanted ... at a level that was too much for our communities, for our labour markets. All of this has to change – and it will be at the very heart of my renegotiation strategy for Europe.
>
> Britain, I know you want this sorted so I will go to Brussels, I will not take no for an answer and when it comes to free movement – I will get what Britain needs. Anyone who thinks I can't or won't deliver this – judge me by my record. I'm the first Prime Minister to veto a Treaty ... the first Prime Minister to cut the European budget ... and yes I pulled us out of those European bail-out schemes as well. Around that table in Europe they know I say what I mean, and mean what I say. So we're going to go in as a country, get our powers back, fight for our national interest ... and yes – we'll put it to a referendum ... in or out – it will be your choice ... [65]

Yet if Cameron wanted to fight on his record as Prime Minister, he was very clear about one thing: it was his commitment as a Conservative leader, not a coalition prime minister, that he wanted people to remember. 'Let the message go out from this hall: it is only with a Conservative Government that you will get that choice.' Harking back to the Conservative mantra of the 2014 EP elections, he hoped to show that only with

---

[64] Peter Dominiczak and Christopher Hope, 'I could campaign to leave the EU, warns David Cameron', *Daily Telegraph*, 28 September 2014.

[65] http://press.conservatives.com/post/98882674910/david-cameron-speech-to-conservative-party (accessed 28 November 2014).

a Conservative government could the UK hope to secure the things he believed British people wanted: reform, renegotiation and referendum.

While this position had a certain innate logic to it, in practice, renegotiation was likely to be even harder than in the mid-1970s, when Wilson renegotiated the UK's terms of membership and then held a referendum on staying in. The problem for Cameron, quite apart from the reluctance of member states to grant the UK any concessions, was to persuade many in his own party that he could secure reforms on the scale that some were demanding. The Balance of Competences Review, a Tory 'win' in the Coalition Agreement, ultimately delivered relatively little for the Conservatives and certainly did not offer a blueprint for repatriating powers. Chastened by their experience negotiating the EU Act, the Liberal Democrats devoted a great deal of effort to securing terms of reference for the Balance of Competences Review that suited them. With the exception of Open Europe and the Taxpayers' Alliance, Eurosceptic groups failed to engage or submit evidence as they felt the review was not going to deliver what they had hoped for; evidence from business groups was predominantly in favour of the current balance. It was agreed that the nuanced reports should not provide for conclusions. Rather, it would be left for political parties to make such decisions. Cameron did outline his thoughts on a reform agenda in his Bloomberg speech in January 2013, including on free movement of people, but there could be no certainty at all that Cameron could deliver on his commitment: free movement of people is a fundamental part of the internal market of which the UK has been one of the keenest advocates. To remove this flank seemed inconceivable, as European Commissioners were quick to assert.

How far has the coalition achieved its aims?

Unlike the economy, on which the coalition parties claimed to have come together 'in the national interest' to solve the mess left by the previous Labour government, there was never a grand shared vision for European policy.[66] Indeed, it has been suggested that as Foreign Secretary William Hague told David Cameron that if it came down to a choice between the national interest and the Conservative interest he should opt for the

---

[66] *Programme for Government*, p. 19; the reference to the 'United Kingdom Sovereignty Bill' was ample indication of the divide between the two parties.

Conservative interest, as that was the British interest – not a position likely to have been endorsed by either the Liberal Democrats or the opposition.[67] Nor did either party have its own grand strategy. For the Conservative leadership, the aim was to 'manage' the issue within the party; to prevent the party from tearing itself apart. However, Cameron's record on this proved poor: feeding 'red meat' to the Eurosceptic dogs only appeared to make them hungrier for more. Thus, the party's position was dragged in an ever more sceptic direction, with Cameron repeatedly trying to block things in Brussels to appeal to his party faithful. His colleagues would go even further, with Chris Grayling as Justice Secretary questioning the UK's membership of the European Convention on Human Rights, not itself part of the EU, but a key indicator of the respect for human rights required of all EU member states. Yet trying to 'out-UKIP UKIP' was never likely to be a winning strategy, as the defection to UKIP of Tory MP Douglas Carswell in late August 2014 showed.

For the Liberal Democrats, the aim is to remain in a reformed EU, albeit without any strongly articulated areas where they envisaged reform. They could claim that the EU Act if triggered would permit the in/out referendum to which they were committed at the time of treaty reform. Since it was unlikely that the Act would be triggered during the lifetime of the coalition, it seemed a fairly safe bet, which was in turn one of the sources of frustration among Tory Eurosceptics – the unexpected Fiscal Compact treaty would have proved the exception, providing the perfect opportunity for a referendum that some sought and others feared. Cameron's attempts to veto the treaty, so widely praised by the sceptics in his own party, paradoxically precluded the very referendum they wanted. After all, a treaty outside the EU framework of which the UK was in any case not a signatory could scarcely trigger the referendum lock. Meanwhile the Lib Dems were able to claim that they had secured opt-ins to a wide range of crucial aspects of justice and home affairs, notably the European Arrest Warrant, which the anti-EU Conservatives opposed.

In August 2014, outgoing President of the European Council Herman van Rompuy asserted that his successor, Donald Tusk, would face three challenges: the stagnating European economy, the Ukraine crisis and 'Britain's place in Europe'.[68] While the coalition partners may

---

[67] Private information (off-the record interview, 7 August 2014).

[68] 'Italy's Mogherini and Poland's Tusk get top EU jobs', *BBC News*, 30 August 2014 (accessed at www.bbc.co.uk/news/world-europe-28989875, 28 November 2014).

have disagreed over European policy, neither party sought to leave office with the UK seen as a problem in Europe. Of course, this situation was not entirely new: in the mid-1990s other European states, frustrated by the negative approach of the Major government, made clear their intention to wait for the expected Labour victory before concluding the reforms that culminated in the Treaty of Amsterdam in May 1997. At that stage there was an assumption that 'New Labour' would be more constructive than the Conservatives had been; this assumption was initially vindicated under Blair, but a decade later the UK had again become semi-detached. Thus, the coalition was not taking the reins from a particularly pro-European, engaged Labour Party. This in many ways was symptomatic of the UK's overarching relations with the EU – unlike the majority of member states, there is little enthusiasm for integration in the EU and what support there is tends to be pragmatic and shallow. Moreover, there is significant convergence among party leaders, if not their members, whether over federalism, the choice of Commission President or the EU budget.

It is not clear, therefore, that the outcomes would necessarily have been so different under a Labour or Lib–Lab government. All three party leaders sought EU budgetary reform; all three opposed the nomination of Juncker as Commission President; all three broadly favour staying in a reformed EU. The language would have differed, so would actual and potential alliances. At the margins the outcomes would have differed, but on most issues there would have been scant difference in substance; there would have been differences in style. The one clear difference is over the decision to offer an 'in/out' referendum on membership of the Union, and the desire for prior renegotiation. Like Wilson in the 1970s, Cameron's pledge to hold a referendum was about party management rather than principle. It was about good party politics; whether his pledges were deliverable was another matter. Paradoxically, the Prime Minister who saw 'Europe' in terms of party management, as something to keep off the agenda if at all possible, had ultimately been dragged away from the centre-ground that he believed the coalition allowed him to occupy, pursuing ever more sceptic policies in the hope of holding his party together. The UK remained in Europe but its partners scarcely saw it as constructive or engaged; the prospect of a referendum and exit from the EU which neither coalition partner sought was rather closer in 2015 that when the coalition took office.

15 'WHAT THE COALITION DID FOR WOMEN': A NEW GENDER CONSENSUS, COALITION DIVISION AND GENDERED AUSTERITY

ROSIE CAMPBELL AND SARAH CHILDS

Introduction

One image – the all-male coalition frontbench of 2014/15 – and three little words – 'calm down dear' – will likely come to epitomize the 2010–15 Conservative/Liberal Democrat coalition's regard for women and gender equality.[1] The former embodies the maleness of the government; the latter symbolizes the masculinized nature of its politics.[2] Since its very inception, the coalition has been dogged by questions of women and gender equality. Two dominant tropes stand out. First, the coalition's austerity politics are accused of having a disproportionate and negative impact on women – as consumers, users and employees of the welfare state. Second, and linked, the coalition, and especially the Conservatives, are said to have struggled to attract the woman voter. That said, any serious account of what the coalition 'did for women' has to be more nuanced.[3] Since 2010, individual coalition policy

---

[1] 'Coalition all-male front bench an "own goal" for Tories, says deselected MP', *Daily Telegraph*, 6 February 2014; 'David Cameron's "calm down dear" outburst in the Commons exposes flaws', *The Guardian* online (accessed at www.theguardian.com/politics/wintour-and-watt/2011/apr/27/davidcameron-michael-winner, 19 November 2014); www.youtube.com/watch?v=VWKBSYqtu7M (accessed 19 November 2014).

[2] Only brief comment is made here regarding the descriptive representation of women in the coalition parliamentary parties. For a fuller account see R. Campbell and S. Childs, 'Conservative feminisation and the representation of women', in R. Hayton (ed.), Special issue of *British Politics*, forthcoming (2015).

[3] This chapter is not – and should not be read as – the 'final say' on whether the 2010–15 coalition was 'good' for women. Moreover, our analysis is limited to the legislative

developments and legislative interventions have, in many instances, opened up opportunities for women; offering women greater choice.[4] These include: greater flexibility in parental leave; the right to request flexible working, now available to all employees;[5] greater state support in the tax system for childcare; and various measures taken, domestically and internationally, to address women's health,[6] and violence against women (VAW). The commitment to protect NHS funding and overseas aid – the coalition made a firm commitment to retain the outgoing Labour government's pledge to allocate 0.7 per cent of GNI to development spending for example – had a significant gender dimension.[7] Collectively, these priorities and interventions arguably constitute evidence of a wider diffusion of liberal feminist values in British politics and society.

Such a development should not, in all respects, be that surprising given that the coalition followed the most feminist governments to-date, the New Labour years of 1997–2010.[8] By 2010 a cross-party

competencies of the Westminster Parliament, and does not consider the situation of women also affected by devolved legislative and policy interventions.–

[4] S. Childs and P. Webb *Sex, Gender and the Conservative Party* (Basingstoke: Palgrave, 2012). See Campbell and Childs, 'Conservative feminisation' for a discussion of neo-liberalism and feminism.

[5] For a summary of developments since the 2002 Employment Act, see Douglas Pyper, 'Flexible working' (House of Commons Library Standard Note SN01086, 3 June 2014). 'Flexible working applies to all employees with twenty-six weeks' continuous employment ... [the Act] removes the procedural requirements for employers' responses to the request' in favour of dealing 'with the application in a reasonable manner' and an obligation to notify employees of the decision within a three-month period, or 'such longer [period] as is agreed by the parties' (HofC 2014, 5). Note here, both an expansion of a right and a lessening of associated regulation.

[6] For example, in 2011 the then Secretary of State for International Development Austin Mitchell set out the UK's framework for improving reproductive, maternal and newborn health in the developing world, which was an overtly women-and-children-centred policy: 'Maternal health – an international cause worth fighting for', *The Guardian* online (accessed at www.theguardian.com/global-development/poverty-matters/2011/jan/18/maternal-health-uk-government-framework, 19 November 2014).

[7] See T. Heppell and S. Lightfoot, 'We will not balance the books on the backs of the poorest people in the world: understanding Conservative Party strategy on international aid', *Political Quarterly*, 83:1 (2012).

[8] S. Childs, *Women and British Party Politics* (London: Routledge, 2008); C. Annesley et al., *Women and New Labour* (Bristol: Policy Press, 2007). New Labour's feminization reflected both the presence of some 100 Labour women MPs and a Labour Party committed since at least the 1980s to a more feminist politics (J. Lovenduski, *Feminizing Politics* (Cambridge: Polity, 2005)). Critics will no doubt continue to debate the extent to which New Labour fulfilled its potential in this respect.

gendered marketplace in British politics was established: all the three main parties explicitly competed over a 'women's terrain'. Electoral offers were made to appeal, in particular, to the professional middle-aged mother,[9] and nodded to a 'cafe society' that seemingly characterized the (metropolitan parts of the) UK in the 2000s. Conservative developments very much reflect a politics of 'catch up' which characterized the modernization of the Conservative Party under David Cameron's leadership.[10] This involved an explicit feminization strategy from 2005 onwards, culminating in a serious policy review by the 'women's' parts of the party that, in turn, fed into the 2010 manifesto. Since 2010 the government's record also reflects the politics of coalition. The two parties were oftentimes in agreement regarding what constituted women's issues, but there were clear moments of disagreement over what was in the best interests of women. The substantive representation of women moreover refers to more than what a government does explicitly for women; it is also about the wider policies that bear directly and indirectly on women, gender roles and gender relations. Consequently serious acknowledgement has to be given to the overarching neo-liberal project characterized by the Coalition Agreement's prioritization of budget deficit reduction.[11] Theoretical comparison of feminism and neo-liberal economics suggests that such an economic settlement presupposes what many – particularly feminist economists and political scientists, social policy experts and feminist activists – would depict as an anti-feminist economic policy.[12]

The chapter opens by mapping the electoral offer made by the Conservative and Liberal Democrat parties at the last election, before examining the resultant Coalition Agreement. Two explicitly 'women's' policies are then considered in turn: forced marriages and childcare. The former examines the extent to which a concern with violence against women has become an issue over which there is much political consensus. That the coalition was keen to put such issues on the mainstream

[9] R. Campbell, 'What do we really know about women voters', *Political Quarterly*, 83:4 (2012).

[10] Childs and Webb, *Sex, Gender*.

[11] T. Quin, J. Barra and J. Bartle, 'The UK Coalition Agreement of 2010: who won', *JEPOP*, 21:2 (2011).

[12] V. Bryson and T. Heppell, 'Conservatism and feminism: the case of the British Conservative Party', *Journal of Political Ideologies*, 15:1 (2010); B. Campbell, *Iron Ladies* (London: Virago, 1987).

agenda – and to see high-profile politicians including William Hague (Foreign Secretary for much of the government), Theresa May (the Home Secretary) and the Prime Minister himself publicly make a stand on these – reflects a recognition that these are no longer feminist concerns on the margins of political debate. Childcare illustrates a second consensus: about women's necessary role in the paid employment market. But it also reveals distinctions between market-based and state solutions to childcare, and acknowledgement of a gendered reality in which childcare underpins the choices women can make about paid employment. Coalition divisions over childcare went public, and ultimately saw the Conservative side lose out to the Liberal Democrats. The chapter then moves on to assess the impact on women of the coalition's austerity politics. Here feminist analysis is unequivocal. Women have borne – and would always bear – the brunt of an economic strategy that cut public spending rather than raised taxes in order to bring the budget deficit down.[13] This conclusion raises, however, the question of whether women should be considered – as supporters of the strategy suggest – unfortunate 'collateral damage', or whether something more explicitly anti-women is going on. Related to this analysis is the introduction of marriage tax allowance, not least for what it says symbolically about a conception of conservative gender roles and relations it supports.

In order to explain the drivers of gendered coalition policies, we draw upon the insights of feminist researchers.[14] Feminist research has demonstrated that the sex of political actors matters and that institutions, including parties and parliaments, are gendered,[15] even as the relationship between the descriptive and substantive representation of women – the number of women in politics and 'acting for women' – is more complicated than some advocates of boosting the number of women in politics suggest.[16] The critical actors in Parliament and

[13] J. MacLeavy, 'A "new politics" of austerity, workfare and gender? The UK coalition govt's welfare reform proposals', *Cambridge Journal of Regions, Economy and Society*, 4 (2011); Fawcett Society, 'Women and the economy' (accessed at www.fawcettsociety.org.uk/our-work/campaigns/women-economy, 19 November 2014).

[14] Lovenduski, *Feminizing Politics*; V. Randall, 'Introduction', in R. Campbell and S. Childs (eds.), *Feminizing Politics after Joni Lovenduski* (Essex: ECPR Press, 2014).

[15] Lovenduski, *Feminizing Politics*; M. L. Krook and F. Mackay, *Gender, Politics and Institutions* (Basingstoke: Palgrave, 2012).

[16] S. Childs and M. L. Krook, 'Should feminists give up on critical mass? A contingent yes', *Politics and Gender*, 2:4 (2006).

government who act for women are largely but not exclusively feminist women.[17] Prior to 2010 these feminists were nearly always Labour women. Post-2010 there was potential for Conservative women MPs to seek to act for women in a liberally feminist fashion; these women have been shown to be more feminist and more economically wet than their male colleagues.[18] Accordingly, we examine the extent to which feminist political actors were present in the coalition and able to affect key policy decisions. In this both parties of the coalition had fewer women to hand than Labour had had during 1997–2010.[19]

What did the coalition 'do for women' 2010–15?

In their 2010 general election manifestos, all the main parties made pledges on women and development, women's health and education, and all addressed violence against women. Yet it was as mothers (and parents) that women were most frequently represented. Table 15.1 summarizes the 'key' women's policies in this respect. The Conservatives' electoral offering reflected a feminist analysis insofar as gender relations were recognized to be bifurcated, hierarchical and problematic – one indicator of the new gendered consensus in British politics we identified above. At the same time, these representations stood in tension with the policy goal of recognizing marriage in the tax system. This was a policy that notably did not come from the *women's* part of the party and reinforced, at least according to critics, the traditional single earner family, even if it did also cover those in civil partnerships.[20] Notably, none of the parties addressed the Fawcett Society's question of how the current economic situation and each of the parties' policies on tax and spending would affect women.[21]

---

[17] Childs, *Women and Party Politics*; C. Annesley and F. Gains, 'The core executive: Gender, power and change', *Political Studies*, 58:5 (2010).

[18] Childs and Webb, *Sex, Gender*.

[19] Rosie Campbell and Sarah Childs, '"Wags", "Wives" and "Mothers" … But what about women politicians?', in Andrew Geddes and Jonathon Tonge (eds.), *The UK Votes: The 2010 General Election* (Oxford: Oxford University Press, 2010); C. Annesley and F. Gains, 'Can Cameron capture women's votes? The gendered impediments to a Conservative majority in 2015', *Parliamentary Affairs* (2014), online advanced.

[20] Childs and Webb, *Sex, Gender*.   [21] Campbell and Childs, '"Wags"', p. 180.

Table 15.1 *Key women's policies in the 2010 Conservative and Liberal Democrat manifestos*

Pledge	Conservative	Liberal Democrat
Employment	• Equal pay audits compulsory for companies guilty of sex discrimination • Oblige job centres to ask employers if jobs could be advertised p/t or jobshare	• Equal pay audits compulsory for companies larger than 100 employees
Right to request flexible working	• First to all parents with children under 18, then public sector, and ultimately to all employees	• Also for grandparents
Maternity/paternity leave/pay	• Share maternity leave between the partners, if the mother goes back to work (at 14 weeks)	• Transfer whenever parents want • Aspiration of 18 months' paid leave
Families	• Recognize marriage and civil partnerships in the tax system • End couple penalty • Long-term funding for relationship support • Increased use of mediation	• Introduce a Default Contract Arrangement – dividing a child's time between their two parents in the event of a family breakdown, if there is no threat to the safety of the child • End govt payments into childcare trust funds
Childcare	• Free nursery care with a diverse range of providers	• Protect existing childcare support arrangements until the nation's finances can support a longer-term solution • Move towards 20 hours, from the age of 18 months
Sure Start	• Return to its original purpose: 'neediest' children • 4,200 Sure Start health visitors • Newly created early years support team	• Not mentioned

Table 15.1 (*cont.*)

Pledge	Conservative	Liberal Democrat
Violence against women	• Longer-term funding of rape crisis centres • More rape crisis centres • Concentration on reducing people trafficking	• Buses to stop 'mid-stop' • More diverse elected police authorities
Sexualization of children	• Help reverse the commercialization of childhood	• Regulate airbrushing
Pensions	• Bring forward the date at which the state pension age starts to rise to 66	• Citizen Pensions
Health	• Single-sex hospital accommodation • End closure of local maternity hospitals	• End of the closure of local maternity units

The progeny of coalition commitments 'for women' as announced in the Coalition Agreement was not always clear, in part because the language of the pledges became less specific than in the manifestos. Table 15.2 documents these pledges. Flexible working, shared parental leave and action on the gender pay gap were embraced, and complemented by commitments to promote gender equality on company boards. On sexual violence the funding of new rape crisis centres looked rather less secure than in the Conservative Party manifesto – with a shift in language from delivery to consideration.[22] Conservative priorities were identifiable in the pledges relating to Sure Start, maternity units and ending what that party termed the couples' penalty. Retention of recognition of marriage (and civil partnerships) in the tax system revealed the first coalition gendered policy difference. The Liberal Democrats were specifically allowed to abstain in any parliamentary vote, indicating that the Conservatives wanted very much to retain this policy as part of the Coalition Agreement.

---

[22] Later research would draw attention to local authority cuts that reduced funding for such services: S. Walby and J. Towers, 'Measuring the impact of cuts in public expenditure on the provision of services to prevent violence against women and girls', *Safe – The Domestic Abuse Quarterly*, 41 (2012).

Table 15.2 *Pledges for women in the coalition agreement*

	Pledge
Employment	• Promote equal pay and take a range of measures to end discrimination in the workplace • Maximize flexibility of 'employment/workplace laws' • Promote gender equality on boards of listed companies
Families	• Encourage shared parenting ... flexible parental leave • Extend right to request flexible working to all employees • Take Sure Start back to original purpose ... neediest families • 4,200 extra Sure Start health visitors • Marriage Tax Allowance
Childcare	• Take steps to stop commercialization and sexualization of childhood • Reduce spending on Child Trust Fund • Diverse range of childcare providers ... greater gender balance in early years workforce • Support provision of free nursery care for pre-school
Violence against women	• 15 new rape crisis centres; long-term funding • Recording hate crimes (inc. transgender) • Rape – extension of anonymity to defendants (N.B. Lib Dem policy) • Stop deportation of asylum seekers ... sexual orientation/ gender identification • Prioritize human trafficking
International development	• Tackle maternal and infant mortality

One gendered policy that garnered extensive critical media commentary, and which was ultimately overturned in the wake of a cross-party revolt by women MPs, was the pledge to grant rape defendants anonymity.[23] This was in neither of the parties' original manifestos. As has been written elsewhere, the advocacy of anonymity raised the question of whether 'the Coalition's fraternity [was] to be metaphorically

---

[23] The assumption that women are likely to lie over rape convictions is one argument that underpins the case for rape defendant anonymity – an argument feminists would take issue with. The issue is particularly problematic as this would be the only area of criminal law where the defendant would remain anonymous, suggesting that false rape allegations are more common than other false allegations of criminality, for which there is no evidence. Moreover, 'naming' the accused is regarded as key to encouraging other victims to come forward.

sealed on women's bodies'. Some in the media saw in the pledge the absence of women politicians from the coalition negotiation teams, and by implication the marginal role of May, who had yet to be appointed Home Secretary and Minister for Women.[24]

Violence against women as a key policy area for the coalition

Violence against women is no longer a policy concern at the margins of political debate in the UK.[25] What might once have been thought of as affecting only a few women, and of concern only to radical feminists bent on destroying the traditional family, VAW has become widely accepted as a legitimate political concern, internationally and domestically. New Labour, and the UK's first female Home Secretary Jacqui Smith, did much to highlight the issue in the 1990s and 2000s. Since 2010, coalition legislative interventions have included: making stalking a specific offence;[26] the enactment of the EU Commission's 2010 anti-trafficking directive, in the Protection of Freedoms Act 2012;[27] the development of a Modern Slavery Bill in 2014–15; and the introduction of an action plan regarding FGM (it was first made illegal in 1985).[28] A cross-government 'Violence against Women and Girls Strategy'[29] had four foci:

[24] Childs and Webb, *Sex, Gender*. Anne Begg in the debate on the Speaker's Conference in 2012 mentioned 'horrified female MPs from all political parties, who united to force the Government to back down. If only one or two MPs had objected, would the coalition have changed its mind? Probably not – but the critical mass of female MPs, speaking with a common voice, made the Government realise they had got things badly wrong' (Hansard, 12 January 2012, col. 403). Reinforcing the link between descriptive and substantive representation Sadiq Khan MP, speaking in Parliament in 2014 (Hansard, 27 February 2014, col. 509) stated: 'Had there been more women around the Cabinet table ... they would have said, "hold on a second".'

[25] A. Gill and T. Mitra-Kahn, 'Modernising the *other*: Assessing the ideological underpinnings of the policy discourse on forced marriage in the UK', *Policy and Politics*, 14:1 (2012).

[26] V. Bryson, 'As austerity measures begin to take full effect...', *LSE Blog*, 23 April 2012 (accessed at http://blogs.lse.ac.uk/politicsandpolicy/category/valerie-bryson, 19 November 2014).

[27] Hof C 2014, SN/HA/4324. See also CEDAW (Committee on the Elimination of Discrimination against Women) 2011, *CEDAW/C/GBR/7* (http://peacewomen.org/peacewomen_and_the_un/peacewomen-un-monitoring/committee-on-the-elimination-of-discrimination-against-women).

[28] CEDAW 2011, p. 55.

[29] The following draws on 'Domestic violence' (House of Commons Standard Note SN/HA/6337, 22 October 2014).

(1) prevention of violence, through challenging the attitudes and behaviours which foster violence, and intervening early where possible to prevent it;
(2) the provision of support, where violence does occur;
(3) working in partnership, to obtain the best outcome for victims and their families; and
(4) ensuring perpetrators are brought to justice, and taking action to reduce the risk to women and girls who are victims of these crimes.

A 2014 Action Plan listed what the coalition had achieved: a new official definition of domestic violence that included young people aged 16 and 17 and coercive or controlling behaviour; the rolling out of domestic violence protection orders (DVPOs), under which a perpetrator can be banned from returning to their home and having contact with the victim for up to twenty-eight days; the rolling out of a 'domestic violence disclosure scheme' under which an individual can check whether a partner has a violent past and the police will consider disclosing the information. In March 2014 May made a commitment to chair a national oversight group to monitor progress by police. Following a critical HM Inspectorate of the Constabulary report, all forces would have to have an action plan in place by September 2014.

The acceptance of VAW as part of mainstream government policy does not mean there is agreement regarding what constitutes women's interests in this area. Parties to the debate contest the nature of the problem and what should be done about it.[30] And it remains necessary to highlight the vocal criticisms relating to the government's financial commitment to various domestic VAW measures, with substantial concerns about funding cuts on the ground;[31] the lack of a ring-fencing of monies; and the relative financial prioritization given to other policy areas.[32] The Women's Budget Group (WBG) 2013 Spending Review, for example, contrasts the £8 million per year for specialist local support domestic violence services with the £200 million for 'troubled families' in 2014–15. Sylvia Walby's analysis identified a 31 per cent cut

[30] A comprehensive evaluation of individual VAW initiatives lies beyond the remit of this chapter.
[31] Bryson, 'Austerity measures'.
[32] Women's Budget Group, Spending Review 2013, p. 35.

to domestic violence and sexual abuse local authority provision between 2010/11 and 2011/12.[33]

Then there is the thorny question of whether VAW has come to represent a 'safe' women's issue for UK political parties. VAW initiatives may well reflect a feminist commitment to women's bodily integrity and human rights, but legislative initiatives in particular may very well cost very little in economic terms and have the additional potential to marry with wider and popular concerns about immigration, multiculturalism and 'British' values. Discussion of the coalition's approach to forced marriages illustrates this tension – a tension that also marked the New Labour years.[34] The Forced Marriages (Civil Protection Act) 2007 came into effect in 2008. The legislation had its origins in the campaigning work undertaken by the Labour MP, Ann Cryer,[35] a Home Office Working Group, a series of government consultations, and the Liberal Democrat Lord Lester's Private Member's Bill in 2006–7.[36]

> Forced marriage is when you face physical pressure to marry
> (e.g. threats, physical violence or sexual violence) or emotional and
> psychological pressure (e.g. if you're made to feel like you're
> bringing shame on your family).[37]

[33] Cited in 'Domestic violence' (House of Commons Standard Note), p. 8.

[34] This section draws extensively on 'Forced marriage' (House of Commons Standard Note SN/HA/1003, 16 September 2013). See Gill and Mitra-Kahn, 'Modernising the *other*' for a review of the policy under New Labour. They note a fluctuating and ambiguous approach: sometimes seeing the issue as VAW, other times as more a cultural issue, with immigration informing its approach. See Fauzia Shariff, 'Towards a transformative paradigm in the UK response to forced marriage', *Social Legal Studies*, 23 August 2012, who notes a shift from a concern with community exclusion to a construction of forced marriage as 'extracting' British citizens from abroad and a concern with British versus Asian values. Shariff was a secondee to the Forced Marriage Unit.

[35] S. Childs, *New Labour's Women MPs* (London: Routledge, 2004); Childs, *Women and Party Politics*; Gill and Mitra-Kahn, 'Modernising the *other*'.

[36] S. Jenkinson and D. Tapp, 'Forced marriage – culture or crime? Part 2', *Criminal Law and Justice Weekly*, 177:2 (2013), p. 24; Gill and Mitra-Kahn, 'Modernising the *other*', p. 110. See also G. Yurdakul and A. Korteweg, 'Gender equality and immigrant integration: Honor killing and forced marriage debates in the Netherlands, Germany, and Britain', *Women's Studies International Forum* 41 (2013).

[37] Forced Marriage Unit, www.gov.uk/stop-forced-marriage (accessed 4 December 2014). See also Jenkinson and Tapp, 'Forced Marriage' Part 1, *Criminal Law and Justice Weekly*, 177:1 (2013), pp. 4, 6.

New Labour's 2007 legislation offered civil remedies.[38] Victims and third parties could apply for a Forced Marriage Protection Order (FMPC).[39] The Forced Marriage Unit's (FMU) gave advice and support to between 1,500 and 1,700 victims per year in 2009–12. Over 80 per cent were female, and included, in 2012, 114 cases involving disability and 22 victims who identified as lesbian, gay, bisexual or transgender.[40]

The question of whether to criminalize forced marriage taken up by the coalition is, then, long-standing. Back in 2005 the FMU consulted on this, as did the Home Affairs Select Committee in 2008 and 2011. The latter's 2011 report favoured criminalization. The coalition consulted in 2011–12 too. A majority of respondents 'agreed that a new offence should be created', although the adequacy of the consultation has been queried.[41] In June 2012, Cameron confirmed that forced marriage would indeed become a criminal offence by 2014. Alongside the announcement of legislation, Cameron committed a £500,000 'fund to help schools and other agencies to spot early signs of a forced marriage, and a major summer campaign to raise awareness of the risk of forced marriage abroad'. The PM went on to host a summit on FGM and forced marriage later that summer.[42]

There were – and are – supporters and critics of criminalization.[43] Criminalization detractors argue that few victims will want to criminalize their families and that forced marriage will be driven underground.[44] Community 'exit' as a strategy is also said both to disregard

---

[38] CEDAW 2011, 46.   [39] See Jenkinson and Tapp, 'Forced Marriage', pp. 4, 6.

[40] 'Forced marriage' (SN/HA/1003), p. 5; Jenkinson and Tapp, 'Forced Marriage', pp. 8–9.

[41] 'Forced marriage has always been a crime in spirit', *The Guardian*, 9 June 2012.

[42] 'Forced marriage blights the lives of scores of learning disabled people', *The Guardian*, 1 August 2012.

[43] Gill notes the distinct interests of key actors: NGOs' interests lie with the victim and making sure any lasting damage is limited; the police are more concerned with preventing future cases. A. Gill, 'Criminalising forced marriage: Findings from an independent study', *Family Law Journal* (December 2011), p. 28. Jenkinson and Tapp, 'Forced Marriage', p. 14. See Shariff, 'Towards a transformative paradigm'. As Hester et al. make clear, as it concerns a 'hard to reach' group, it is difficult to determine the impact of changes in legislation: M. Hester, K. Chantler, G. Gangoli, J. Devgon, S. Sharma and A. Singleton, 'Forced marriage: the risk factors and the effect of raising the minimum age for a sponsor, and of leave to enter the UK as a spouse or fiancé(e)', www.bristol.ac.uk/media-library/sites/sps/migrated/documents/rk6612finalreport.pdf.

[44] Lady Warsi acknowledges this in *The Guardian*, 9 June 2012. See also Jenkinson and Tapp, 'Forced Marriage', p. 14.

victims' concern for subsequent familial reconciliation,[45] and to rely upon an assumption that British society is itself gender-equal.[46] Instead, a 'holistic' approach can be preferred,[47] one that emphasizes education and awareness-raising for victims, providers of support, and the police and criminal justice system, alongside more extensive provision of emergency and long-term accommodation, greater training, educational support, mediation and media and police campaigns.[48] This, according to critics of criminalization, was what was offered under the 2007 legislation – a focus on protection and prevention,[49] even if much more could have been done to have 'ensure[d] compliance'.[50] Some identify a greater role for community engagement.[51] In any case, there are further concerns about the burden of criminal proof; the length of time for criminal cases to be dealt with; and the harm that women might face as a consequence.[52]

In contrast, criminalization's supporters argue that such legislation symbolizes that forced marriage is wrong and will therefore act as a deterrent. Forced marriage here becomes more about the 'public interest' and does not rely on the victim initiating civil proceedings – a point some critics will admit.[53] There is also the potential 'therapeutic' effect for victims, who will realize that they have not done anything wrong.[54] The symbolic role played by criminalization has been emphasized by both Cameron and May:

> ... I want to send a clear and strong message: forced marriage is wrong, is illegal and will not be tolerated. (Cameron)

[45] Note that mediation is not unproblematic. Gill and Mitra-Kahn, 'Modernising the *other*', p. 110, cite the resignation of Southall Black Sisters from the New Labour working group over this. See also Shariff, 2012, especially p. 554.

[46] Gill, 'Criminalising forced marriage'; Gill and Mitra-Kahn, 'Modernising the *other*'.

[47] Gill, 'Criminalising forced marriage', p. 2; Demos cited in Jenkinson and Tapp, 'Forced Marriage', p. 14.

[48] Gill, 'Criminalising forced marriage', p. 25; Jenkinson and Tapp, 'Forced Marriage', p. 17. See also Hester et al, 'Forced marriage'.

[49] Yurdakul and Korteweg, 'Gender equality and immigrant integration', p. 212.

[50] Gill, 'Criminalising forced marriage', p. 6.

[51] See Shariff ('Towards a transformative paradigm', p. 550), who contends that qualitative research identifies 'more complex ways in which power relations are already being resisted and challenged internally'.

[52] Gill, 'Criminalising forced marriage', pp. 23–4.

[53] Gill, 'Criminalising forced marriage', p. 12.

[54] Gill, 'Criminalising forced marriage', p. 23.

> It is the right of every individual to make their own choices about their relationships and their future. Forced marriage is an appalling practice and by criminalizing it we are sending a strong message that it will not be tolerated. (May)[55]

In response to the coalition's announcement, an open letter signed by 138 activists calling criminalization a 'quick fix' was sent to the government.[56] In some critics' eyes there is a greater concern for symbolism than for the protection of victims of forced marriage in the coalition's criminalization strategy. In this way, the government is said to be perpetuating concerns with immigration, community cohesion, otherness and Britishness,[57] rather than perceiving forced marriage as part of the continuum of male violence that women universally face.[58] In this the coalition's decision to pursue criminalization would be considered a continuation of the later approach of New Labour.

Coalition division goes public over childcare

Childcare is where coalition divisions – as opposed to coalition distinctiveness over women's interests – went public. Ultimately it witnessed a Liberal Democrat veto of Conservative proposals to relax the ratios of childcarers to children. But before considering this conflict, it is worth noting that the coalition's focus on childcare reflected an agreement that access to childcare is something that governments of any political colour needed to attend to. This is because economic recovery and the consequent reduction in welfare spending requires the entry of women of working age into paid employment, even if, as critics on the right suggest, the coalition has been elusive in admitting this.[59] The *Daily*

---

[55] 'Forced marriage' (SN/HA/1003), p. 10. See also Shariff, 'Towards a transformative paradigm', p. 555.

[56] Yurdakul and Korteweg, 'Gender equality and immigrant integration', p. 212.

[57] Shariff, 'Towards a transformative paradigm'. See also Anne Phillips, 'It's my body and I'll do what I like with it: bodies as objects and property', *Political Theory*, 39:6 (2011), pp. 724–48.

[58] Gill, 'Criminalising forced marriage', pp. 15, 30; Gill and Mitra-Kahn, 'Modernising the *other*'. See also Yurdakul and Korteweg, 'Gender equality and immigrant integration'.

[59] James Kirkup, 'Childcare: ministers don't want mothers to stay at home – they want them to work. They should say so', *The Telegraph*, 19 March 2013. See also CEDAW 2011, 34.

Mail quoted Cameron denying that 'ministers were trying to force mothers back to work'; rather, he supported 'the choices mums make'.[60] One consequence of acknowledging the necessity for women's greater participation in paid employment is the problem of childcare. Caring for children, and indeed other dependents, is still something that women disproportionately do. One key approach, associated with the Liberal Democrats, is 'rolling out the entitlement to 15 hours a week pre-school education to all disadvantaged two year olds,[61] in addition to the 15 hours already available for children of 3 and 4 years of age',[62] although the funding of this has been via the 'early intervention grant', which is not ring-fenced.[63] Coalition policy on childcare was multi-faceted.

Sure Start

At the time of the general election the Conservative policy was clear: to return Sure Start to its original basis – namely the disadvantaged. This approach was designed to address the 'problem' of the 'bad' parent.[64] The Liberal Democrats made no mention of Sure Start in their manifesto.[65]

Working Tax Credit and Universal Credit

Coalition reforms reduced the amount of help to less well-off parents from 80 per cent to 70 per cent of childcare costs from 2011. Under the incoming Universal Credit, parents working fewer than 16 hours per week are intended to receive support for childcare costs,[66] a measure designed to encourage paid employment. In the 2013 Budget the coalition announced that parents in a couple or a lone parent earning the equivalent to the monthly income tax personal allowance could claim 85 per cent, rather than 70 per cent of childcare costs.[67]

---

[60] 'I WILL support stay-at-home mums: Cameron pledge hopes of marriage tax breaks', *Daily Mail*, 17 May 2013.

[61] By summer 2014 there were reports of waiting lists for disadvantaged 2-year-olds as middle-class nurseries turned their backs on these children ('Underprivileged two-year-olds being declined by "middle-class" nurseries', *The Observer*, 24 August 2014).

[62] Pyper, 'Flexible working', p. 2.   [63] *Ibid*, 4.

[64] S. De Benedictis, '"Feral" parents: Austerity parenting under neoliberalism', *Studies in the Maternal*, 4:2 (2012).

[65] Women's Budget Group, Report on Party Manifestos (2010).

[66] Pyper, 'Flexible working', p. 14.   [67] *Ibid*., p. 17.

Tax relief for childcare

The coalition inherited two forms of tax relief: First, nursery/play schemes. Here, employees who use this are not taxed on the value of the benefit. Second, if an employer subsidizes employees' costs via a voucher or contract with an approved childcarer, tax relief is given up to a set weekly limit.[68] The coalition agreed that the latter provision would be restricted in value so that higher-rate taxpayers would not benefit disproportionately. In March 2013 the coalition announced its new scheme – 'tax-free childcare' – for autumn 2015 onwards.[69] When both parents are aged 16 and over and in paid work, earning less than £150,000 per year (so not paying tax at the additional rate), and not in receipt of tax credits or Universal Credit, they would be eligible for 20 per cent of their yearly childcare costs up to £6,000 per year.[70] Initially it applies for children under 5, but ultimately will be for children under 12.[71] The policy received a mixed response from the public and policymakers. The IPPR considered it a 'regressive' policy that benefits higher-income families.[72] The WBG are critical of the language of 'tax-free' applied to this policy. They contend that it is used to bolster a wider 'anti-benefit rhetoric'. And then there are those who argue that such a policy does nothing to tackle the cost of childcare.

Child:Childcarer ratios

The coalition's – or rather the Conservative part of the coalition's – central policy innovation to reduce childcare costs was to relax the ratio of children to childcarer. Trumpeted by the minister Elizabeth Truss, this policy was highly contested both within government and beyond.[73] In doubting the plans, Clegg was said to be in agreement with education experts. By apparently 'dismantling' the policy, he won the support of Mumsnet founder Justine Roberts and the National Children's Bureau. Number 10 accused Clegg of 'shamelessly reneging on agreed childcare

---

[68] *Ibid.*, p. 10.   [69] House of Commons Research Paper 14/5, June 2014.

[70] Pyper, 'Flexible working', p. 11.

[71] For further details see House of Commons Research Paper 14/5, June 2014.

[72] *Ibid.*

[73] 'Liberal Democrats to make reducing childcare costs a key objective, says Nick Clegg',*The Independent*, 5 November 2012; 'Education experts share Nick Clegg's doubts on childcare reforms', *The Guardian*, 9 May 2013; 'Nick Clegg casts doubt on coalition's childcare reforms', *The Guardian* 9 May 2013; 'Nick Clegg hits out at coalition's child care plans', *The Telegraph*, 10 May 2013.

reforms' in an attempt to court women's votes and bolster his position as party leader.[74] The then Education Minister Michael Gove was said to be enraged.[75] Ultimately there was no 'cross-party agreement' and the reform was dropped at Report Stage.[76] Katherine Rake, ex-Chair of the Fawcett Society, then Chief Executive of the Family and Parenting Institute, had seen this coalition fault line coming from the outset.[77] The press in 2014 signalled further coalition differentiation, suggesting that the 2015 Liberal Democrat manifesto was set to include a commitment to free childcare for one-year-olds.[78]

Evaluating the coalition's overall childcare provisions, the WBG welcomed the decision of government to address the issue, provide more free childcare and subsidize the cost of childcare. However, as Table 15.3 highlights there is considerable criticism regarding the funding of childcare. There is criticism, too, of the distinctions that are drawn by coalition policy between working and non-working parents.[79] As Julie MacLeavy writes, 'unemployed single parents face heightened expectations to participate rather than withdraw from the paid labour market whilst performing care'. [80] This bias reflects the Conservative analysis of family breakdown and its links to economic dependence. According to this approach, when working-class children's parents work, working-class children would be in receipt of professional (read: better) childcare. The spectre of lone parenthood – and the inadequate mother – looms, although critics note that the dysfunctional parent also

---

[74] 'Coalition rift widens amid rows over EU and childcare', *The Guardian*, 9 May 2013; see also 'Clegg's "treacherous" U-turn on childcare condemned by MPs: Deputy PM publicly attacks plans to help cut costs for working families', *Daily Mail*, 9 May 2013.

[75] 'Clegg "sabotaged childcare plan to stop coup by Cable": Lib Dem leader reeling as Gove blows lid on party power battle', *Daily Mail*, 12 May 2013.

[76] Pyper, 'Flexible working', p. 23.

[77] 'Families are watching closely how the coalition's cuts and policies affect them', *The Guardian*, 22 June 2010.

[78] *The Independent*, 8 September 2013.

[79] See also A. McRobbie, 'Feminism, the family and the new "mediated" maternalism', *New Formations*, 80–1 (2012), pp. 119–37; Sara De Benedictis, '"Feral" Parents: Austerity parenting under neoliberalism', *Studies in the Maternal*, 4:2 (2012), www.mamsie.bbk.ac.uk.

[80] J. MacLeavy, 'A "new politics" of austerity, workfare and gender? The UK coalition government's welfare reform proposals', *Cambridge Journal of Regions, Economy and Society* (2011).

Table 15.3 *Evaluating coalition childcare policies*

Positive Measures	Critique	Preferred Policy
• Increases in childcare support • Tax-free childcare for under-12s worth 20% • 15 hours' free childcare for under-2s	• Sure Start no longer ring-fenced • Query emphasis on lone parents working • Critical of the reduction in childcare element in working tax credit • Subsidies unlikely to reduce costs; worsen quality • Marketplace is uncompetitive • Early years premium – is this a 'one off' expenditure? • Queries if parents with income of 300K need childcare assistance	• Childcare is an end in itself • Extend and increase free entitlement to childcare • Direct public provision of childcare by highly qualified and well-paid staff • Fund childcare at source • Increase spending on Sure Start • Abolish high income tax on child benefit for those families earning more than 50K

Sources: Women's Budget Group and MacLeavy, *Cambridge Journal of Regions, Economy and Society* (2011)

marked the New Labour years.[81] The WBG's prescriptions for childcare policy notably show a clear preference for the public provision of extensive childcare for children as a social good: in other words, the WBG seek a retreat from the market provision of childcare.

Coalition economic policy: Austerity is a feminist issue

The coalition's economic plan drew significant gendered opprobrium from the start. Yvette Cooper, then Labour's shadow Foreign Secretary and Minister for Women, drawing on Commons Library research, demonstrated that women would suffer most as a consequence of the coalition's Emergency Budget. This was a direct result of women's greater dependency upon the public sector and welfare state as both its employees and its beneficiaries. Such criticism, identifying the 'triple

---

[81] McRobbie 2012; De Benedictis, '"Feral" Parents'. Note the recognition of marriage in the tax system, which privileged marriage as the best form of family for the raising of children.

jeopardy', would continue apace:[82] 'austerity is a feminist issue' (following Susie Orbach). The logic of this criticism is illustrated in the following three quotations:[83]

> The government has made a gendered choice to focus on cuts to benefits rather than raising taxes.
>
> Wherever austerity has been implemented ... it has hurt women most and had a negative impact on gender equality, except in those few places that have tried to mitigate against adverse effects.
>
> A government committed to gender equality would try to use budgets as a way of offsetting the gender inequality that exists in markets, businesses, families and communities.

Greater emphasis on spending cuts relative to tax has increased over time, from 80:20 to 90:10. This reinforces Conservative preference within the coalition. Indeed, the 2010 manifestos identified a 'spending cuts: tax rise' ratio for the Liberal Democrats of 2.5:1 and for the Conservatives of 4:1.

Table 15.4 summarizes the WBG's assessment of the coalition's overall economic policy. Similar comments are articulated by the Fawcett Society, the UK's leading women's rights civil society group. The Table also identifies what the WBG considers is a gender-equitable economic strategy.

Having outlined the feminist critique of the 2010 coalition economic policy one is left with the question of assessing its approach. Here left/right politics come to the fore. For leftist feminists there is a nagging concern that individual coalition policies may be more explicitly masculinized than gender-blind. Did the government not realize that women are more likely to work in, benefit from and make use of the welfare state? Take an example: fuel and beer duty. These are budgetary measures that unequivocally benefit men more than women, both directly in terms of cost to individuals and families, but also

---

[82] Fawcett Society, 'Budget 2013 – Helping or hurting women?' (accessed at www.fawcettsociety.org.uk/wp-content/uploads/2013/03/Budget-2013-Helping-or-Hurting-women.pdf, 4 December 2014).

[83] Women's Budget Group, 'The impact on women of Autumn Financial Statement 2013' (www.wbg.org.uk/wp-content/uploads/2013/10/The-Impact-on-Women-of-Autumn-Financial-Statement-2013_final.pdf), pp. 7, 4; ' 'The impact on women of the coalition Spending Review 2010' (www.wbg.org.uk/RRB_Reports_4_1653541019.pdf), p. 1. See also Fawcett Society, 'Budget 2013'.

Table 15.4 *WBG's analysis of coalition economic policy (excluding childcare)*

Critique of coalition Budgets/Autumn Financial Statements	WBG approval of Budgets/AFS	WBG's 'Plan F'
• 80:20 and 90:10 spending cuts: tax raises	• Personal allowance: better-off taxpayers (men) gain more; women are 59% of those with no earnings	• Re-balance spending cuts/tax rises, in the latter's favour
• Cuts in additional rate of tax		• Halt cuts to public services
• Cuts in corporation tax	• Cap on unlimited tax relief for private pension/charitable donation	• Raise national minimum wage
• Help to buy – women less likely to benefit		• Repeal bedroom tax and benefits cap
• Bedroom tax is gendered	• Investment in rural enterprises led by women	• Raise taxes from wealthy and companies
• Private sector expansion likely to widen gender pay gap	• Extension of free school meals to all children in reception, yr 1 and 2; and to disadvantaged young people in further education and 6th form	• Introduce progressive personal and wealth taxes and reduce indirect taxation such as VAT
• Welfare cuts and cap: benefits = 20% of women's and 10% of men's income		• Re-establish universal child benefit
• Public sector pay freezes disproportionately affect women	• Up-rating of pensions	• Invest in social infrastructure: health, education, childcare, social housing, lifelong care
• Increase in VAT hits lone mothers/couples with children hardest	• Decision not to introduce regional pay in civil service, NHS or prison	• Increase training, pay, employment rights for paid care workers
• Tax give-aways – beer and petrol – benefit men; links between alcohol and VAW		• Increase public support for unpaid carers
• Bingo tax cuts benefit companies not women players		• Public and private sector employers to recognize duty of care re: high-quality care services
• Freeze in child benefit		• Reform UC so that women with employed partners gain from earning[a]
• Abolition of 'health in pregnancy' grant		
• Statutory maternity pay 'real cut'		• Invest in social housing
• Doubled notice period for women returning to work from maternity leave		• Do more to reduce gender pay gap
• Investment in infrastructure ignores social infrastructure		• Help-to-work schemes to recognize difficulties of women with

Table 15.4 (*cont.*)

Critique of coalition Budgets/Autumn Financial Statements	WBG approval of Budgets/AFS	WBG's 'Plan F'
• Bonfire of red tape • High-skilled apprenticeships favour men • Investment in STEM ignores women's under-representation therein • Increasing state pension age – women live longer but in worse health; women pensioners' poverty unlikely to be addressed by private pensions • Universal credit paid into one bank account per couple		children fulfilling mandated daily activities

^a UC is also a benefit that goes to the 'wallet' and not the purse (Bryson, 'Austerity measures').
Sources: Women's Budget Group (www.wbg.org.uk) reports: 2014 Budget; 2013, AFS; 2013 Budget; 2012 AFS; 2012 Budget; 2011 AFS; 2011 Budget; 2011 indirect Tax; 2010 Spending Review; 2010 Budget; 2010 party manifestos. See also Fawcett Society, 'The Impact of Austerity on Women' (2012); 'Budget 2013'.

indirectly in terms of the lost revenue that might have paid for the benefits and services that benefit women; the WBG are pointed:[84]

> Ironically, the cost of extending the fuel tax giveaway until August – 975 million – is exactly the amount the Chancellor saves in 2012–13 by not introducing the above-inflation increase in the child element of the Child Tax Credit.

Defenders of the coalition will likely deploy the aforementioned 'collateral damage' defence. Women may well as a group have been disproportionately and negatively impacted by the politics of austerity. But this was not intentional – the market does not discriminate on the basis of

---

[84] WBG (2013) commenting on AFS 2012, p. 5.

sex. It just so happens that women have higher rates of employment by the state, for example. Secondly, the coalition will argue that neo-liberal economics and not a Keynesian solution is the means to address the UK's financial crisis, from which women like men will ultimately benefit (see chapter six, this volume). In the public domain counter-criticism of the claim that austerity is a *feminist* issue has taken three forms. The first is to refute that feminism is by definition a leftist ideology. This is illustrated by Anushka Asthana, writing in *The Times* (27 July 2012), who presents a gendered reading of the neo-liberal economic defence just cited. The second is outlined by Catherine Bennett writing in *The Observer* (31 October 2010). She privileges a class analysis, asking, 'what is gained by identifying victims of the next round of economic punishment as overwhelmingly female, rather than overwhelmingly poor?' She goes on, 'even affluent female whingers about child benefit might shrink from describing this collective setback, as some protesters do, as part of an ideologically inspired campaign to re-domesticate women; a coalition remake of Rosie the Riveter'. The third response, arguably a broader critique, is articulated by Zoe Williams (*The Guardian*, 17 November 2011), who states that she does not 'believe the government hates women' but rather sees in the coalition approach a refutation of the 'underlying principle' that 'we will all, at points in our lives, be fiscally unproductive and it's the work of society to carry us'. Here is an appreciation of individuals' dependency as they go through the lifecycle and an appeal for governments to adequately provide for this.

Transferable tax allowance: Cameron's socially conservative 'Golden Hello'

The coalition introduced the transferable tax allowance (TTA), albeit belatedly for its advocates, in 2013. It would come into effect in 2015/16. The TTA allows:

> A spouse or civil partner who is not liable to income tax above the basic rate to transfer up to £1,000 of their personal allowance to their spouse or civil partner, provided that the recipient of the transfer is not liable to income tax above the basic rate.[85]

[85] www.gov.uk/government/uploads/system/uploads/attachment_data/file/264431/3._Transferable_tax_allowances_for_married_couples.pdf.

As noted above, the Liberal Democrats' parliamentary abstention, signed off in the Coalition Agreement, ensured that Cameron's pre-2005 commitment to marriage became part of the Government's legislative programme. This was despite Clegg publicly considering it a 'throwback to the Edwardian era'.[86] Caitlin Moran, one of the popular voices of UK feminism, was similarly unpersuaded, writing in *The Times*:

> if the intention of the coalition's £200 a year tax break is that it be spent solely and only on M&S lasagnes and huge trays of jam roly-poly in the interests of continued marital cohesion, then I can confidently declare that this is the most inspired Tory policy of the past two decades.[87]

If marriage recognition in the tax system was always Cameron's baby, its unwilling midwife in government was the Chancellor. No mention of the policy was made by George Osborne in either the 2010 or the 2011 budgets.[88] His difference of opinion with the Prime Minister was public knowledge.[89] According to Peter Oborne, writing before the 2010 general election, the Chancellor is 'an economic and social liberal' and 'doesn't believe it is the job of the State to meddle in people's private lives', whereas Cameron 'is determined to give incentives for marriage through fiscal means'. One *Daily Mail* headline read: 'Cameron ready to defy Osborne and Clegg to force policy through'.[90]

Recognizing marriage in the tax system was presented by Cameron as an inclusive policy – it would be available for those in civil partnerships as well as for heterosexual married couples. In this the Tories' claim to be the party of the (now inclusively defined) family was not felt by Cameron's team to be incompatible with liberal feminist views of gender roles and relations.[91] Feminist critics, long hostile to this policy,

---

[86] Toby Helm, Anushka Asthana and Polly Curtis, 'Tight election win could plunge UK into social chaos – Nick Clegg', *The Observer*, 11 April 2010.

[87] Caitlin Moran, *The Times*, 12 October 2013.   [88] Pyper, 'Flexible working'.

[89] Peter Oborne, *Daily Mail*, 1 Feb 2010; Andrew Rawnsley, *The Observer*, 8 April 2012.

[90] *Daily Mail*, 8 July 2014.

[91] Childs and Webb, *Sex, Gender*, p. 204. The purported 'radicalism' of this policy denoted by the inclusion of civil partnerships became ultimately redundant as gay marriage had already made it to the statute book, albeit not on the back of Conservative parliamentarians' votes: 'Gay marriage: more male Tories voted against bill than female colleagues', *The Guardian*, 6 February 2013; Philip Cowley, https://twitter.com/philipjcowley/status/299054633853263873 (accessed 20 November 2014). The policy was supported by the Centre for Social Justice ('It is time to back marriage',

queried its symbolic and substantive effects. The tax unquestionably undermines the principle of independent taxation – a pro-women policy introduced under Thatcher in 1990. It also favours in practice a 'male single earner model', reducing incentives for women to enter paid employment, and fails to make work pay.[92] By privileging one type of relationship it is also a socially conservative move and does not address the costs of children for those who are not married. Monetarily the 'recognition' is minimal, with only about one-third of married couples benefiting, and only 18 per cent of families with children receiving it, at a rate of £196 (for non-taxpayers and basic-rate taxpayers).[93] On the ground, 84 per cent of TTA beneficiaries would, however, be men.[94] In any case, TTA assumes that any monies are shared fairly within the families, even if the non-/lower earner would not benefit directly;[95] money would not be put into the hands of the non-earners, again mostly women.[96] In adopting TTA the Conservative part of the coalition risks re-contamination of the Tory party in the minds of those who regard marriage as either a 'lifestyle choice' independent of any moral value, or something that one aspires to but may not necessarily achieve.

The coalition appeal to women: Unpopular spending cuts and the question of winning or losing women's votes

The critique that the coalition and particularly Cameron and the Conservatives more generally were out of touch with women voters was a recurrent feature of the media coverage of the government's performance between 2010 and 2015. Opinion polls were repeatedly used as evidence that the coalition was increasingly unpopular with women voters. The survey evidence in fact demonstrates a great deal of vacillation in support for the coalition parties.

The Conservatives regained support among women voters in the 2010 election, but polls reported in the immediate aftermath suggested that women's hostility to cuts in public spending had eroded their

www.centreforsocialjustice.org.uk/UserStorage/pdf/Pdf_reports/Itistimetobackmarriage.pdf).
[92] WBG Spending Review 2010; WBG party manifesto; WBG marriage tax break.
[93] WBG Budget 2014; WBG (AFS) 2013, p. 9.   [94] WBG Budget 2014.
[95] WBG 2013, budget.   [96] WBG 2010 party manifesto.

support for the party.[97] This provoked a series of policy announcements targeted at women voters, although this left the overarching economic policy untouched. In early 2012 some opinion polls suggested that the coalition was regaining the support of women. Others showed Cameron and Clegg losing women's support. By January 2013 a sizeable gender gap between support for the Conservative and Labour parties appeared to have emerged, with an ICM poll for the *Guardian* showing a one-point lead for the Conservatives among men compared to a sixteen-point lead for Labour among women; the *Daily Mail* blamed the cut in child benefit and slow progress on expanding childcare provision for the gap.[98] However, even in February 2014, with just over a year to go before the 2015 election, there was no consensus as to whether the Conservative Party was haemorrhaging women's votes. The margin of error in opinion polls can often produce seemingly significant gaps between men and women that vacillate apparently at random over time.[99] YouGov's Anthony Wells used pooled opinion poll data to create an aggregate measure of men and women's party preferences and discovered almost no difference in support for the Conservative Party among men and women, with the Labour Party doing on average just 2 percentage points better among women than men.[100]

Examination of the British Election Study's (BES) panel, shows that there are only small sex differences in party support, as Figure 15.1 shows, with women averaging 3.52 and men 3.72 on the 0–10 Conservative Party scale (where 0 is strongly dislike and 10 is strongly like). The Liberal Democrats and the Labour Party prove marginally more popular among women than men.

Vote choice is importantly only one way of examining sex differences in support for the coalition. The public's attitudes towards cuts in public spending show clear evidence that women are more hostile to cuts in public spending *overall*, as Table 15.5 shows.

BES data on public attitudes towards *individual* spending cuts also reveal sex differences, as Table 15.6 shows.

[97] 'Revealed: Secret government plans to win back women', *The Guardian*, 13 September 2011; 'Leaked memo on support from women for the coalition government', *The Guardian*, 13 September 2011.

[98] 'Cameron lags 16% behind Miliband with female voters after cuts to child benefits and dithering on childcare reforms', *Mail Online*, 23 January 2013.

[99] Campbell, 'What do we really know about women voters'.

[100] See http://yougov.co.uk/news/2014/02/11/gender-gap (accessed 20 November 2014).

Table 15.5 *BES Panel Wave Feb/March 2014*

	Cuts to public spending				
	Not gone nearly far enough	Not gone far enough	About right	Gone too far	Gone much too far
Men	3.3%	13.0%	28.3%	32.6%	22.7%
Women	1.0%	7.5%	27.2%	42.8%	21.4%
Total	2.1%	10.2%	27.8%	37.8%	22.0%

Table 15.6 *Percentage of respondents describing proposed spending cut as fair BES CMS (Oct 2010–Jan 2012)*

Proposed spending cut	% proposed cut is fair		
	Men	Women	Sex Gap
Police	32	19	-13
NHS	25	13	-12
Pensions	24	15	-9
Armed forces	35	24	-9
Schools	27	19	-8
Universities	53	45	-8
Students	51	43	-8
Child benefit	57	51	-6
Housing benefit	68	66	-2
Social security benefit	66	65	-1
Unemployment benefit	65	65	0

N=14278

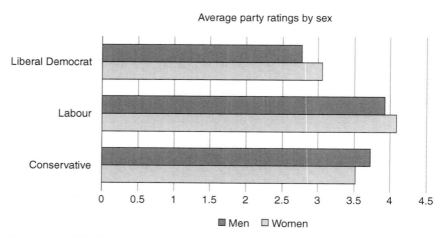

Figure 15.1 BES Panel Wave 1 Feb/March 2014

Women were, as Table 15.6 shows, less inclined to describe many of the proposed coalition spending cuts as fair, compared with men. The sex gap in perceived fairness of the cuts varies from 13 per cent more men than women believing cuts to police funding to be fair, to no difference in the perceived fairness of cuts to unemployment benefit. The largest sex gaps are evident in regard to the NHS, pensions, the armed forces, schools, universities and students. No real sex gap is evident in the perceived fairness of cuts to housing benefit, social security benefit or unemployment benefit (the three areas where there is most support for the cuts). On average women rated four out of the eleven proposed cuts as fair and men rated five, not a huge sex difference but one that could be electorally significant. The sex gap is, moreover, largest among Conservative Party identifiers: on average Conservative-identifying women thought one less proposed spending cut was fair than Conservative-identifying men. The sex difference was half a point among Labour identifiers. Again this suggests the possibility of an electoral effect.[101]

The determinants of coalition policy 'for women'

How might we best understand the drivers of the coalition effect on women and gender roles/relations? Reflecting on the early years of the coalition, it would be too simplistic to say that there was never any intention by the Conservative party to deliver on its liberal feminist pledges for women that had been made in their manifesto. Such a charge would be unfair to the many women and some men in the party who, often lacking sufficient resources, sought to ensure that the Conservatives adopted such gendered perspectives from the mid-2000s onwards. That is not to say that there are not some individuals around Cameron who have flown 'kites' for policies that directly challenge these policies.[102] Gender tension within the party is real. Either regulations help open up opportunities for women or they are 'red tape'. Or, as one critic put it: 'The reasons for shared parental leave must be purely

---

[101] Childs and Webb, *Sex, Gender*; Campbell and Childs, 'Conservative feminisation'.

[102] They have some friends in the press. See Louisa Peacock, writing in the *Telegraph*, query what she considers too extensive flexibility in parental leave (20 November 2013).

business focused.' Reform on the basis of gender equality has to be secondary.[103] In seeking to capture the determinants of change we see two key factors at work – the coalition's maleness and an apparent gender-blindness, working in conjunction with an overarching neo-liberalism that constrains the policy interventions that the coalition could offer to women.

The coalition's overwhelming maleness

This has been an ongoing story for both parties to the coalition individually, and for the coalition as a whole. The leaders' lieutenants were all male as the coalition was formed in the five days after the general election. The Quad (see chapter two) that drives the government is all male. And the lower numbers of women in both the Conservative and Liberal Democrat parliamentary parties, relative to the preceding Labour years, meant that there would be fewer women either in Cabinet or on the 'shoulder of the government',[104] holding them to account. In fact, there were no Liberal Democrat women in the Cabinet at all. Five major departments of government had no women over much of the period of the government.[105] Cameron's final reshuffle before the 2015 general election did see the number of Cabinet women rise to five – 24 per cent – with an additional three women attending Cabinet, a move that whilst not meeting his target did respond to critics of his 'chumocracy'.[106] Whilst there are arguments that Cameron had little choice but to have a majority male government given the percentage of new women MPs in his supply pool,[107] such a conclusion is arguable.

We furthermore surmised back in 2010 that Theresa May – the coalition's most senior woman MP and a Conservative with a clear

[103] Ibid..   [104] Childs, New Labour's Women MPs.
[105] Annesley and Gains, 'Can Cameron capture women's votes?'
[106] 'PM plays female card in reshuffle', Sunday Times, 13 July 2014. This compared with Labour's Shadow Cabinet, which was 40 per cent female (Campbell and Childs, 'Conservative feminisation').
[107] T. Heppell, 'Ministerial selection and the Cameron government: Female ministerial representation and the one-third objective', Representation, 48:2 (2012), pp. 209–19, at p. 214, writes that Cameron would need to add twenty female ministers from a pool of forty-four women ... a massively disproportionate number of female appointments, dismissing ministers at a far higher rate than the norm in British politics.

feminist agenda – would be too busy in Home Office to remain a critical actor for women, even though she was made Minister for Women and Equalities as well. The role of the Equalities Minister should have been critical; such a post has the potential to institutionalize the substantive representation of women within government.[108] Yet the junior equalities ministers have looked not to have the same authority and influence as May. Responses by Cameron included the appointment of a gender adviser to the Prime Minister – Laura Trott; a Vice-Chair for Women post was later re-established in the Conservative party. A parliamentary Conservative women's forum was also established. None of these have received much public attention. Revealingly, there have been calls from inside the Conservative Party for the greater use of 'Sam Cam in the election', revealing a woman-shaped hole in the coalition.[109] Indeed, it is frequently said that she is a big influence on him, although such claims are as yet unconfirmed. Similarly Cameron has a handful of key women in his team – Kate Fall (gatekeeper), Gabby Bertin (PM's link to business) and Liz Sugg (Head of Operations, oversees PM's visits and trips).[110] Whilst these women may well sit in on leader meetings they are not – as part of their job description – there to put women's issues and perspectives on the table, nor is there public evidence that they intervene in such a manner.

A failure to fully 'See Gender'

Coalition failure to fully appreciate the gendered impact of policymaking applies most obviously when the issue is not explicitly gendered. It occurs when gendered analysis is not integrated and institutionalized in the policymaking processes. One indicator of this failure is demonstrated by the aforementioned appointment of a gender adviser. It also

[108] In this we take issue with Zoe Williams' claim that 'female representation in parliament is the least of our worries; these looming inequalities will be solved by ideas, not by female apparatus', *The Guardian*, 17 November 2011.

[109] Annesley and Gains, 'Can Cameron capture women's votes?'; Campbell and Childs, '"Wags"'.

[110] See www.totalpolitics.com/print/444542/ladies-first.thtml; www.telegraph.co.uk/news/politics/9637991/Inside-David-Camerons-real-life-The-Thick-Of-It-team.html; www.thesundaytimes.co.uk/sto/comment/columns/adamboulton/article1277174.ece (all accessed 20 November 2014).

plays out in the criticism of the coalition's failure to provide high-quality Equality Impact Assessments (EIA) of its economic policy. The coalition's Emergency Budget in 2010 was challenged as unlawful by the Fawcett Society,[111] although the High Court ruling in December 2010 found against them. Note that it was a woman – May – who warned the government that in devising its emergency budget, a gender equality audit was necessary.[112]

The WBG's analysis of the coalition's budgetary EIAs is damning: they are either missing (absent), misplaced (not uploaded to websites), minimal (applied to some policies but not others) or misguided, suggestive of an approach that is at best 'perfunctory'. The WBG claim, moreover, that the Treasury says it is not possible to provide full gender analysis. WBG counter-charge that they and the Institute for Fiscal Studies have managed. An additional criticism of the coalition's approach is that it fails to consider the gender impact of measures that only impact on women, such as maternity allowance or paternity pay. Nor is there intersectional analysis. Illustrative examples of EIAs include:

- '4.1 million non-taxpaying/basic rate taxpayer married couples stand to gain an average of £196 *between them*' [from TTA] (emphasis added)
- [stamp duty changes] 'not expected to have an impact on any protected equality group'
- 'motorists who drive the same car and drive the same number of miles should broadly be affected by the same amount'

The coalition's commitment to equality assessments was further questioned by the review of the Public Sector Equality Duty.[113] The PSED requires public authorities to 'be proactive in eliminating gender discrimination and promoting equality of opportunity between women

---

[111] 'Fawcett Society loses court challenge to legality of budget', *The Guardian*, 6 December 2010. See House of Commons Library (2014) for an overview of the Public Sector Equality Duty (PSED) and EIA. It notes that EIAs are not required by law, although they are a way of facilitating and evidencing compliance with the PSED. The PSED is contained in part II, Chapter 1 of the Equality Act 2010. It came into force in April 2011 and 'unified the pre-existing equality duties into the single PSED, expanding upon them and adding six new protected characteristics' (HofC 2014, 5). See also CEDAW/C/GBR/7 (2011, 7, 9).

[112] 'Theresa May's letter to the Chancellor', *The Guardian*, 4 August 2010.

[113] M. A. Stephenson, 'Misrepresentation and omission – an analysis of the review of the Public Sector Equality Duty', *Political Quarterly*, 85:1 (2014).

and men'.[114] The 2012 review faced criticism.[115] The then Equalities Minister Maria Miller agreed that there should be a full evaluation in 2016. Notably, she closed her statement by emphasizing the importance of reducing 'red tape'.[116] Subsequently, Cameron told the CBI that government departments would no longer be required to carry out EIAs. He was 'calling time' on them. The Commons Library note that whilst the law does not require them, the 'courts place significant weight on the existence of some form of documentary evidence of compliance with PSED'.[117]

The coalition's commitment to spending cuts had additional consequences for the funding for, and indeed existence of, governmental institutions charged under previous governments with gender equality.[118] The 2010 Spending Review cut the budget of the Government Equalities Office by 38 per cent; reduced the staff and scaled back the work of the GEO and abolished the Women's National Council.[119] An Inter-Ministerial Group on Equalities, comprising twelve ministers and chaired by May, has again received little public profile.

Conclusion

The incoming coalition government in 2010 would inevitably address, at least symbolically, the 'women's terrain' that had become part of the political agenda over which all three main UK parties now compete. The feminization of the Labour party from the mid-1980s raised the bar for the representation of women in politics in the 1990s and 2000s, both in terms of women's presence in politics and in addressing women's issues and perspectives. Labour's impact was significant: the party's use of all-women shortlists, together with the prominence of feminist women within the party and government, ensured that gendered analysis strongly influenced the 1997–2010 legislative and policy outcomes.

[114] The Labour government had intended this to cover socio-economic disadvantage, but this was removed by May (*ibid.*, p. 76).
[115] O'Neill cited in Pyper, 'Flexible working', p. 18; Stephenson, 'Misrepresentation'.
[116] Pyper, 'Flexible working', p. 17.
[117] House of Commons Library, 2014 Human trafficking: UK Responses, SN/HA/4324, 21.
[118] Annesley and Gains, 'Can Cameron capture women's votes?'
[119] Annesley and Gains, 'Can Cameron capture women's votes?'; CEDAW, 2011.

This is not to say of course that the New Labour years were some kind of feminist nirvana, but they did very much set the agenda for subsequent inter-party competition. Accordingly, the legacy of New Labour would have influenced an incoming majority Conservative government as it did in practice the Conservative/Liberal Democratic coalition.

Since 2010 the coalition government has implemented a series of liberally feminist policy and legislative initiatives. These largely focused upon the less politically contentious women's issues that address women's health, international development and, discussed in a little more depth in this chapter, violence against women. This is not to say that critics are not vocal in questioning the sufficiency of these efforts, either in principle or in practice. Moreover, coalition consensus regarding aspects of the women's agenda did not always translate into coalition agreement on specific policies. In respect of childcare – another key area of coalition activity – we see division over what interventions would best facilitate the reconciliation of women's work and family commitments; a disagreement marked by left/right conceptions of the role of the state. This intra-coalition distinctiveness, together with the inability of the coalition to hide their differences, suggests that single-party Conservative government would have gone down a different road; with greater emphasis on deregulation, and private rather than state subsidy of childcare. If the kite-flying by the Liberal Democrats in 2014 is anything to go by, the 2015 Conservative and Liberal Democrat manifestos will almost certainly look divergent in this respect. Even so, the coalition's attention to childcare signalled another area of gender consensus regarding the role of women vis-à-vis the economy, and the necessity of childcare for women's enhanced participation therein.

In order to evaluate the representation of women, it is necessary to consider how the government imagines women's interests. How do they conceive of, and act in relation to, women and men, and gender relations? The Conservative Party's policy offer 'for women' in 2010 was one dimension of Cameron's wider pre-2010 modernizing agenda; significantly only recognition of marriage in the tax system directly appealed to a 1950s depiction of gender roles. Supporters would emphasize that even here this had been successfully modernized, with an 'inclusive' concept of the family. Efforts to address VAW and sex/gender-specific health issues are informed by feminist analysis, even as they may also coincide with more traditionally Conservative values.

Nevertheless, throughout the years 2010–15, feminist critics have strongly questioned the adequacy of the coalition's approach to women, and their relationships with the state. They frequently questioned the limited impact coalition austerity policies in particular could have on *transforming* gender relations. Over and above the analysis of specific coalition policies, many feminists situated their criticism of the coalition within a wider critique of neo-liberalism. From this perspective the claim that austerity is – by definition – a feminist issue renders the coalition's economic policy – by definition – anti-feminist. Cuts in public spending have had a deleterious effect on many women's position in the labour market relative to men's.[120] That said, coalition actors, of both parties, will no doubt continue to contest this interpretation of both what it did for women, and what is in the interests of women.

---

[120] Fawcett Society (2014), *The Changing Labour Market 2: Women, Low Pay and Gender Equality in the Emerging Recovery*.

16 THE COALITION AND CULTURE: 'BREAD, CIRCUSES AND BRITISHNESS'

RORY COONAN

Overview

'Whenever I hear the word "culture",' observed Hermann Göring, 'I reach for my revolver.'[1] Coalition ministers did not find it necessary to go armed when applying draconian cuts to public expenditure in the arts. Victims (including supernumerary quangos) made token protests or simply agreed. Those who had prospered at New Labour's feast could scarcely object to coalition famine. In anticipation of their demise, certain organizations craftily anticipated their own salvation (see *English Heritage* and *British Council*, below). Of all areas of public policy stitched together by the coalition, the development of the arts and cultural institutions appeared least contentious. It was most likely to evoke what Winston Churchill described as 'the broad harmony of thought' that linked Tory and Liberal philosophy.[2] However, the beginning was scarcely equitable. The Liberal Democrats' coalition voice in the conduct of cultural policy was mute since no elected Liberal

---

[1] The phrase, commonly attributed to Hermann Göring, 'Wenn ich Kultur höre ... entsichere ich meinen Browning!' ('Whenever I hear [the word] "culture" ... I remove the safety catch from my Browning [pistol]!'), is a line spoken by Thiemann, a character in Act 1, Scene 1 of *Schlageter*, a play by Hanns Johst.

[2] Churchill said: 'I find comfort in the broad harmony of thought which prevails between the modern Tory democracy and the doctrines of the famous Liberal leaders of the past.' He was speaking in 1951 in support of the Liberal general election candidate, Lady Violet Bonham-Carter, at Huddersfield Town Hall: quoted in P. Hennessy, *Having it so Good: Britain in the Fifties* (London: Penguin Books, 2007).

Democrats were appointed ministers in the Department of Culture, Media and Sport (DCMS). By the end of the coalition, total DCMS cultural spending reductions averaging 25 per cent, excluding the Olympic and Paralympic Games, at first condemned by the Left as reckless economy, had come to seem normal (see Table 16.1). The Labour Party, in its election manifesto for 2015, did not promise to reverse them.

State-funded theatres, museums and galleries restructured themselves to save costs. They contrived novel forms of sponsorship. Observing the age of hierarchies passing, they joined the new age of networks. This meant the unstoppable, global growth of social media. It meant that culture was everywhere, and always on; it knew no boundaries and was made outside academies of taste, beyond Britain's historic cultural institutions; it did not seek official approval because it did not need it.

The National Gallery bowed to the inevitable and permitted visitors to photograph paintings on display. Seeing was no longer believing; looking *became* photographing. The habit of copying challenged the concept of intangible creative value known as 'intellectual property'. A downloading generation had grown up, which appeared to care little for the idea. The tests of authentic and copy, original and fake, seemed so last century; yet these are categories of discernment upon which national museum collections and curatorial careers depend.[3]

A question for public policy was, how are living artists and creative producers to be paid, if their work is distributed and copied across the globe without recompense? The Berne copyright convention (to which the UK was a signatory) could not have anticipated the internet, yet the coalition government showed little appetite for reform. Its role in the creative, 'do-it-yourself' online culture of films, publishing, music and art was that of bystander. The Coalition Agreement (see below) did not include measures to punish illegal downloading of music and films. MPs were naturally reluctant to criminalize their own teenage offspring, on their own home computers.

The globalization of artistic production may help explain Conservative ministers' anxiety over 'British culture' and 'British values'. There was an undercurrent of loss of control in their pronouncements, although affirming 'British culture' over any other was potentially incendiary. It risked appearing both retrospective (a return to

---

[3] 'Authentic and copy, original and fake': Susan Sontag, *On Photography* (London: Penguin, new edition, 1979).

'traditional' values) and reactionary (excluding arrivals from other cultures and faiths).

Conservative 'Britishness' naturally included 'Englishness'; cultural complications presented by the province of Northern Ireland were simply baffling. The traditional dash of 'Scottishness' in the mix (a matter of historic ties and habits, including valiant regiments of the British army and royal summer residencies) survived the threatened amputation of Scotland from the United Kingdom in September 2014. The Scottish National Party cannily co-opted progressive, 'modern' Scottish culture to its ultimately unsuccessful bid for independence.

But 'Britishness' hardly amounted to a policy. It was more an attitude or a pose. It was about being rather than doing, about belief rather than evidence. It had nothing to do with cultural production, more to do with 'cultural identity'. There were no coalition spot-checks on the 'Britishness' of nativity plays at Christmas, or productions at the National Theatre. Instead, it implied a rebuke to the multi-culturalism of New Labour (a policy from which previous Conservative governments had not been immune). In so doing, it offered a veiled criticism of citizens whose 'Britishness' resided in their passports but (by implication) in little else.

The French, so this argument went, had not made this mistake; everyone in France was French first, from wherever they came. The imperative towards everyone being French first was reinforced by mass demonstrations which took place across France on 11 January 2015. These drew 4 million people onto the streets (according to *Le Monde*, 12 January 2015). They followed the murder of seventeen people by terrorists in Paris four days earlier. The victims included France's leading graphic artists and political satirists, 'les grands dessinateurs' ('masters of drawing') described by President Hollande in his TV address to the French people following the attacks.

Somehow, people in Britain had to acquire essential 'British culture' but it would be difficult and it would take time. Definitions were vague: Shakespeare was assumed, of course; when in opposition, a Conservative minister had offered Ealing comedies (films from the 1940s and 1950s) and the artist Tracy Emin (b. 1963) as cultural markers.

This was bold: in the casual way affected by a certain kind of floppy-haired, educated Conservative, 'Britishness' was ingrained in family DNA. For others, it oozed from the honey-coloured stone of medieval churches in Oxfordshire. Above all, it was not really to be discussed, let alone anatomized, an attitude summed up in Michael Gove's 2007 paradox: 'There is something rather un-British about seeking to define Britishness.' Anyway, was not the academic literature of 'cultural identity' dreary? It contains few jokes, and chapters written from a Conservative viewpoint are rare. It was best not to go there – at least in any detail.

Ultimately, the precise dangers of a decline in 'Britishness' were never spelled out. Would beer be served colder? Would the shadows on cricket grounds be shorter? Would old maids no longer bicycle to Holy Communion through morning mist?[4] In 2010, few were clear exactly what the problem about 'Britishness' was that needed solving, because whenever ministers heard the word 'culture', they understood different things. By 2015, we were certainly troubled by a single aspect, its Christian heritage. The Prime Minister had first affirmed this in December 2011:

> We are a Christian country. And we should not be afraid to say so.
> Let me be clear: I am not in any way saying that to have another faith – or no faith – is somehow wrong.[5]

To have 'another faith' is not wrong – but it is not really equivalent. Otherwise, why draw the distinction? In June 2014, the government announced that primary and secondary schools (20,000 establishments) should 'promote British values', including religious toleration. The context was urgent: the British way of life, including its values of plurality, tolerance and its Christian heritage, were under attack in far-away countries by people of whom we knew very much.[6]

In Iraq and Syria, to be a Christian could be a matter of life and death; some vicious actors there had British accents. The domestic political imperative, which gathered momentum from August 2014,

---

[4] 'Fifty years on from now, Britain will still be the country of long shadows on cricket grounds, warm beer, invincible green suburbs, dog lovers and pools fillers and, as George Orwell said, "Old maids bicycling to holy communion through the morning mist" and, if we get our way, Shakespeare will still be read even in school.' John Major (1993), quoting Orwell's 1941 essay 'The Lion and the Unicorn'.

[5] Prime Minister's King James Bible Speech, 16 December 2011 (accessed at www.gov.uk/government/news/prime-ministers-king-james-bible-speech, 20 November 2014).

[6] 'Consultation on promoting British values in school', 23 June 2014 (accessed at www.gov.uk/government/news/consultation-on-promoting-british-values-in-school, 20 November 2014).

was to enfold *everyone* in the embrace of 'British culture' and 'British values', lest more disaffected citizens escape to crueller shores, there to commit unspeakable crimes. Following the Charlie Hebdo murders in Paris in January 2015, British ministers attempted to pre-empt violent assaults at home while letting it be known through public officials in the security services that they were highly likely. Measures included a stern written exhortation to Muslim leaders to do more to oppose radicalization. The move incensed some Muslims, who felt that the separateness of Muslim culture from the mainstream was being reinforced. Cameron said: 'If some people have a problem with this, then I think they have a problem.'[7]

By this time, the Prime Minister must surely have realized that the profession of his personal faith (in April 2014, see below) conferred scant political dividend. Bishop David Walker, a turbulent Anglican priest in Manchester, said the government had a 'moral responsibility' to help people in Iraq. 'There has been too much silence, for too long, from too high up,' he said.[8] It was not clear how high up he meant to go.

Another cultural drama concerned the unstoppable and insatiable effects of disruptive technologies. Whether in services, in health care or the 'knowledge economy', ideas needing no permission for their invention poured forth. They included e-books and e-book readers; the global taxi-ordering application, Uber, the personal GP consultation platform Babylon, or Amazon, the über-retailer turning powerful publisher.

These inventions posed a significant threat to traditional British cultural habits, such as browsing in expensive bookshops, trying to get an appointment with a doctor and standing in the rain looking for a

---

[7] The trigger was a letter dated 11 January 2015 from Communities Secretary Eric Pickles MP and an unelected junior minister, Lord Ahmed of Wimbledon, to mosques in England and Wales. They said a great faith had been hijacked and that the heinous crimes in Paris were an affront to Islam: 'You have a precious opportunity and an important responsibility in explaining and demonstrating how faith in Islam can be part of British identity. There is a need to lay out more clearly … what being a British Muslim means today: proud of your faith and proud of your country. We know that acts of extremism are not representative of Islam but we need to show what is. British values are Muslim values.'

[8] Speech on the BBC, 17 August 2014 (accessed at www.bbc.co.uk/news/uk-28825723, 20 November 2014).

cab. From another point of view they threatened lazy monopolies that kept prices high for consumers, and whose convenience they placed last.

Predictable currents of the arts world flowed on, apparently unchecked by financial upheaval. Royal ceremonial persisted and official patronage continued. Judith Weir was appointed Master of the Queen's Music, the first woman to hold the post; Rona Fairhead, a business person, was appointed chair of the British Broadcasting Corporation, the first woman to hold that post.

Encouraged by a popular actress, the Chancellor of the Exchequer and the Mayor of London conjured money for the eccentric design of a new bridge, with trees growing on it, across the Thames in central London (provided others contributed to its construction and maintenance). For the *hoi polloi*, restoration money was promised by the government to the burghers of Southend, after the destruction of the town's pier by fire in summer 2014. It seemed that bread was still available for circuses.

By 2015 there were fewer public libraries in England (despite their unchanged statutory protection) but equally there was evidence of effort by communities to make books more widely available. Ministers' decisions to distribute Bibles in schools seemed like a good example, but their initial refusal to allow packages containing books to be sent to prisoners was a bad example (see *Britishness* and *Ministry of Justice*, below).

By the end of the coalition, international economic revival saw private affluence grow, even as public squalor (most apparent in underfunded health and social care in England) increased. For the arts in the metropolis, the picture was ambivalent. Visitor numbers to Tate galleries in 2013/14 dipped to 7 million from 7.8 million, as the 2012 London Olympics 'bounce' faded. (Tate Modern's ambitious expansion plans remained intact.) Conversely, audiences at the National Portrait Gallery in London grew from 1.8 million in 2010 to 2 million in 2013, aided by deft deployment of youthful royal patronage and inspired fundraising on the part of its director, Sandy Nairne.

As the economy grew modestly, wealthy patrons of the arts reached for their cheque books (for the rest, real wages remained stagnant). When a work by street artist Banksy went on sale at auction, art in public places turned into art in private hands. When the artist Tracy Emin's post-coital unmade bed sold for £2.2 million in 2014, art in private hands turned into art in public places. (It was bought by a

German Count, who lent it to Tate, which lent it to a gallery in Margate).[9] The good times were enjoyed chiefly in London, the world's cultural powerhouse. Attendances at London theatres in 2012–13 grew to 22 million, placing the capital ahead of New York.[10] There was no slack in the Thespian economy. It was rather the reverse, although dilapidated infrastructure was revealed when the ceiling of the 1901 Apollo Theatre in London collapsed.

For the rest of the country, the projected decline in English local authority funding presaged even deeper cuts. Unlike libraries (see *Libraries*, below), parochial arts and museums remained a non-statutory, discretionary function, with significant local autonomy. This was demonstrated in 2014 by the market sale of an Egyptian sculpture known as Sekhemka, from the Old Kingdom, Late Dynasty 5, circa 2400–2300 BC. It was in the collection of Northampton Museum. According to the auctioneers, the purpose of the statue (a figure clutching beer, bread and cake) was to nourish the departed in the afterlife. The Museum claimed a building extension would nourish its visitors in their earthly life.

Lord Northampton, whose ancestor brought the statue from Egypt in the nineteenth century, was a beneficiary of the sale, which raised £15.8 million. The Arts Council responded by stripping Northampton museums service of eligibility for future grants. As punishment for an egregious example of 'de-accessioning', it was no more than a slap on the wrist.

But in the grand scheme of things, this was an unfortunate blip. By the end, ministers could take comfort from a remarkable fact. Perhaps more by luck than judgement, no major national cultural institution, national collection or performing arts body was liquidated during the coalition, even as it enacted the most severe cuts in expenditure since public funding of the arts began in 1945. These were enforced strictly and with an erosion of the 'arm's length' principle governing the Arts Council's power to make decisions.[11] A notable

---

[9] 'Tracey Emin's bed returns to the Tate', *The Guardian*, 29 July 2014.

[10] 'Study puts London ahead of New York as centre for theatre', *Financial Times*, 30 July 2014.

[11] The 'arm's length' principle applied to detailed project decision-making on arts matters has operated since 1945. However, in a letter dated 3 July 2013 to the Arts Council, the then Secretary of State at DCMS, Maria Miller, said: 'Where Arts Council England has a major project ... it is not permissible to switch funding from that project [to other areas of capital expenditure] *without the permission of the*

episode was the Arts Council's dramatic cut of 29 per cent to English National Opera (equivalent to a £5 million reduction of its grant-in-aid). The Council offered ENO a one-off £7.6 million 'transition' grant, thereby robbing Peter to pay Peter, placing it in 'special measures'.

Conversely, the Chancellor of the Exchequer, George Osborne, proved generous to the arts in other ways: the artist Lucian Freud's (1922–2011) collection of paintings by Frank Auerbach (b. 1931), valued at £16 million, was accepted in lieu of inheritance tax. The pictures were shown at the Tate in London before being dispersed to museums across the country.

Attrition in public investment (planned) punctuated by munificence for one-off capital projects (unplanned) inevitably provoked suspicions of electoral pump-priming. In his Autumn Statement given on 3 December 2014 the Chancellor George Osborne, the MP for Tatton, a rural constituency south-west of Manchester, announced a £78m investment in The Factory, a new Manchester cultural centre. It had not been mentioned in the Coalition Agreement; the context was the government's support for a 'northern powerhouse', backed by local authorities, comprising science, technology and creativity. At the start of the 2015 general election campaign a Conservative MP, asserting his belief in the government's cultural policy, wrote: 'Shakespeare would certainly vote Tory if he were alive today.'[12]

While the policy of public astringency deprived administrators of titles and perquisites, it paved the way for national institutions to engage with phenomenal shifts in public consumption and taste on a

---

Department' [my italics]. See www.gov.uk/government/uploads/system/uploads/attachment_data/file/210517/arts-council-england-letter.pdf (accessed 20 November 2014). The political attraction of the arm's length principle was that ministers could avoid answering direct questions in Parliament on the latest Modernist outrage by simply declaring: 'This is of course a matter for the Arts Council.' The Marxist scholar Raymond Williams (a former Arts Council deputy chairman) observed: 'from an anatomical perspective, it is customary for the arm to direct the hand'.

[12] Nadhim Zahawi, MP for Stratford-Upon-Avon, 'Conservative Home', 15 December 2014 (accessed at www.conservativehome.com/thecolumnists/2014/12/nadhim-zahawi-mp-3.html, 3 January 2015): 'And to those who say culture and commerce don't mix, I say look at Shakespeare, a man who as a shareholder in the Globe made a tidy return from bums on seats, and who would certainly vote Tory if he were alive today.' The notion that William Shakespeare would today vote Conservative because he was in business almost defies satire. It is on a par, intellectually, with the belief that since the playwright knew a lot about birds, he would today be a shoo-in for President of the RSPB.

global scale. However, not all public institutions responded sure-footedly: the classical music channel BBC Radio 3, faced with static audience numbers, resorted to playing snatches of music backwards. This populist stunt, one of several aping commercial channels, suggested to discerning listeners that the station was moving in reverse. The apparent crisis of confidence was surprising in a period when the BBC's world-class Promenade Concerts grew in stature and public acclaim.[13] For individual artists, rather than the bodies that disseminated their works, the coalition's policies did little harm, since creativity is an impulse utterly indifferent to whether governments have lots of money or none. In the words of the poet W. H. Auden, it survived 'in the valley of its making / where executives would never want to tamper'.[14] But if no artists starved in the garrets of the coalition, few grew fat, either.

Policy – the manifestos and culture

Following the Victorian scholar Matthew Arnold, the ideal Conservative arts policy would be to promote sweetness and light by reference to the best that has been thought and said.[15] Unfortunately, from the Conservative viewpoint, this policy is undermined by popular disagreement about what constitutes 'the best'.

[13] BBC Radio 3 reached 1.9 million listeners per week while BBC Radio 4 reached 10.9 million per week, based on independent survey data. Radio 3's share of the listening audience in the coalition period averaged 1.2 per cent (a high point of 1.3 per cent was attained in 2013); the same data showed the commercial station Classic FM reached 5.1 million listeners per week. Possession of a digital audio device (DAB) in the home grew from 30 per cent in 2010 to almost 50 per cent by the end of the coalition. This increased fears of the demise of the frequency modulation transmission platform (FM) to which long-standing BBC listeners had become accustomed (RAJAR, based on UK individuals aged 15+, to the end of September 2014: www.rajar.co.uk).

[14] W. H. Auden, 'In Memory of W. B. Yeats' (1940).

[15] 'The best that has been thought and said' – Matthew Arnold, *Culture and Anarchy*, 1869. The context for the phrase is: 'The whole scope [of the essay] is to recommend culture as the great help out of our present difficulties; culture being a pursuit of our total perfection by means of getting to know, on all the matters which most concern us, the best which has been thought and said in the world, and, through this knowledge, turning a stream of fresh and free thought upon our stock notions and habits, which we now follow staunchly but mechanically, vainly imagining that there is a virtue in following them staunchly which makes up for the mischief of following them mechanically.'

Conservative voters may not have known much about the arts but they knew what they liked. 'Heritage', on the other hand (connected etymologically to 'inheritance', matters of property and money), was always a topic of lively interest.

There was a single cultural commitment in the 2010 Conservative manifesto: 'heritage and the arts will each see their original [National Lottery] allocations of 20 per cent of good cause money restored'. War on non-departmental public bodies ('quangos') was declared. They were to be abolished unless they performed 'a technical function or a function that requires political impartiality, or [which acts] independently to establish facts'.[16]

The Liberal Democrats could claim a duplicate policy in promising to save money by quangos, although limited to the extinction of merely 'wasteful' ones. The manifesto said:

> Liberal Democrats believe that the arts are a central part of civic
> and community life. They contribute to innovation, education,
> diversity, and social inclusion. The creative industries are one of the
> fastest growing sectors of the economy. Britain's culture and
> heritage play a vital role in attracting visitors to the UK and
> boosting the very important tourism industry. We will
> foster an environment in which all forms of creativity are able
> to flourish.

There were five Liberal Democrat manifesto cultural commitments. First, 'We will maintain free entry to national museums and galleries'; second, the Government Art Collection was earmarked 'for greater public use'; third, the promise of a 'creative enterprise fund'; fourth, the reform of live performance licensing; and fifth, reform of the National Lottery so that the operator's profits were taxed rather than punters' tickets.[17]

What survived of both manifestos in the 2010 Coalition Agreement, *Our Programme for Government*, was a modest number of commitments with a distinctly Conservative emphasis on using public money to lever philanthropic and corporate investment.

---

[16] The Conservative Party, *An Invitation to Join the Government of Britain: The Conservative Party Manifesto 2010* (London: Conservative Party, 2010).

[17] Liberal Democrats, *Liberal Democrat Manifesto 2010* (London: Liberal Democrats, 2010).

The notion of culture as a separate industry was played down. For some, this was a welcome shift of emphasis. By 2010, the phrase 'creative industries' had become hackneyed; services and industries of all kinds could claim that 'creativity' was central to their activities. (DCMS statistics regularly counted IT and software among them.) The term 'creatives' – historically familiar in advertising – was deployed (sometimes pejoratively) to describe personnel involved. The special place of 'art', not aspiring in all cases to be a commodity, and of 'artists', many of whom were reluctant to be co-opted into 'industry', had become submerged in this general category. Indeed, the economic return derived from the 'creative industries' had long been a political crutch in seeking public funds from the Treasury. This was by no means an exclusively Labour tactic: in the 1980s the then Arts Council of Great Britain had launched 'an urban renaissance' plan under Mrs Thatcher's government, which purported to show the economic return on investment in the arts. In 2010, when the public purse was empty, such arguments might be regarded as nugatory.

Nevertheless, the coalition continued to publish economic data on 'creative industries' while seeking to tighten definitions of creativity and improve measures of creative effort. Official figures published in *The Creative Industries Economic Estimates* (DCMS, January 2014) claimed that employment within the 'Creative Economy' grew by 143,000 (6 per cent) between 2011 and 2012.[18] This was a higher rate than for the UK economy as a whole (0.8 per cent) at that time.[19]

The Coalition Agreement cultural commitments were: to maintain the BBC's independence; to maintain free entry to national museums and galleries, and grant them greater freedoms; to 'examine the case' for changing the tax regime of the National Lottery, so as to benefit the distributors; to ban National Lottery distributors from lobbying and restrict the cost of their administration to 5 per cent of their income; to cut 'red tape' so as to encourage live music; to roll out fast broadband in towns and the countryside, helped by 'digital switchover' money set aside from TV licence fees.

[18] *The Creative Industries Economic Estimates*, 14 January 2014 (accessed at www.gov.uk/government/uploads/system/uploads/attachment_data/file/271008/Creative_Industries_Economic_Estimates_-_January_2014.pdf, 20 November 2014).

[19] Office for National Statistics, *Economic Review*, 8 January 2014 (accessed at www.ons.gov.uk/ons/dcp171766_348204.pdf, 20 November 2014).

Three of these – free entry, lottery reform and cutting music red tape – derived from the Liberal Democrats, although they received little credit for the measures. Nor did they appear to seek it: a feature of the coalition is that, wherever else broad harmony of thought existed, neither the Liberal Democrat leader Mr Clegg nor Mr Cameron revealed personal enthusiasm or joint affection for the arts. It is evident that cultural policy may have appeared thin, if the Conservatives had won an absolute majority and had formed a government on their own. The Liberal Democrats owed their manifesto arts emphasis more to Don Foster, MP for Bath, and less to a dour Scottish Highlander, the Chief Secretary to the Treasury, Danny Alexander, who with others presided over the Agreement.

If Labour had been returned once more and had expanded its many cultural bodies, a long overdue comparison of 'inputs' (taxpayers' money going in) and 'outputs' (the quality and durability of the arts produced) would finally have shown the lack of correlation between them. Labour's tide of 'boosterism' (using the arts as a 'feel-good' factor for the wider economy), swollen with public money, would surely have ebbed.

Olympic Festival

Although it soon became clear from coalition funding cuts (see below) that the arts in a much-reduced department were not intended (in Tony Blair's phrase) to be 'part of our core script', a script had conveniently been written in Zurich. The IOC (International Olympic Committee) contract for the 2012 London Olympic Games (in the zenith of its planning at the time of the Agreement) created a general feeling that if there was no bread, there could be circuses, provided these were free.[20] Investment in the Games had been committed years before under New

---

[20] 'Bread and circuses' – from Satire 10.77–81 of the Roman poet Juvenal (AD 100): *iam pridem, ex quo suffragia nulli / uendimus, effudit curas; nam qui dabat olim / imperium, fasces, legiones, omnia, nunc se / continet atque duas tantum res anxius optat, / panem et circenses.* ('Already long ago, from when we sold our vote to no man, the People have abdicated our duties; for the People who once upon a time handed out military command, high civil office, legions – everything, now restrains itself and anxiously hopes for just two things: bread and circuses.')

Labour, with Conservative agreement. The National Lottery had duly been raided for the purpose – again with Conservative consent.

The 2012 Olympics arts festival, inherited in 2010 by the incoming coalition government, was a compulsory appendage to athletics. The impresario Danny Boyle produced a kitsch entertainment for the opening ceremony, called 'Isles of Wonder'. While its sounds and sweet airs delighted billions on global television, its overtly left-wing political content baffled others. The industrial revolution, complete with revolving satanic mills, was celebrated as a Great British Invention (early capitalists were depicted as cuddly types). A dramatic paean to Britain's National Health Service, created in 1948 (now the third largest employer in the world), saw ranks of nurses dancing on antique iron bedsteads, while dressed in 'heritage' uniforms. Bliss was it then to be alive, the show suggested, but to be sick was very heaven. Historically, it was partial: fierce contemporary opposition of doctors' groups to the creation of the NHS went undramatized.[21] 'Isles of Wonder', drenched with sentiment, was dramatic art deployed as political 'boosterism'.

Conservatives in the coalition could roll their eyes at the content while salivating over the tremendous effect the event had on the United Kingdom's reputation for managerial competence. No props fell over on prime-time TV, as occurred at the 2014 Sochi Winter Olympics, organized by the President of Russia, Mr Putin. Despite wobbles over security guards and their replacement by soldiers (the Olympics were dubbed a 'Gucci assignment' in army slang), the Olympic circus passed off efficiently. Conservatives in the coalition compared the Games contentedly to the fiasco of the opening night of the Millennium Dome, on 31 December 1999. The difference was stark: with the Dome, Labour had inherited a Conservative project and failed; with the Olympics, Conservatives had inherited a Labour project and succeeded.

The 2012 Olympic arts festival sprinkled sports stardust among practising artists for whom elite competitions were (at least in the United Kingdom) regarded as a Bad Thing. One Olympic artistic legacy

[21] The role of some doctors historically in the creation of the NHS before 1947 is frequently submerged. Recording their opposition to his plans, Bevan said that the price he had to pay was to preserve their private practice privileges, so he 'stuffed their mouths with gold'. (He was speaking in 1955 or 1956 according to C. Webster, ed., *Aneurin Bevan on the National Health Service* (Oxford: University of Oxford, Wellcome Unit for the History of Medicine, 1991), pp. 218–22.)

Table 16.1 *Partial DCMS spending from 2010*

Sector	Area	Body	2010/11 £000s		2011/12 £000s		2012/13 £000s		2013/14 £000s		2014/15 £000s	2015/16 £000s	Reduction in Exchequer funding between 2010 and proposed 2015/16 spending
			Plans	Outturn	Plans	Outturn	Plans	Outturn	Plans	Provisional outturn	Plans	Plans	
Cultural	Museums & Galleries	Total		361,474		348,886		340,281	302,905	303,495	302,101	296,712	17.92% decrease
Cultural	Libraries	Total		113,298		109,079		110,952	95,703	95,494	93,743	93,381	17.58% decrease
Cultural	Arts	Arts Council England		437,523		392,877		424,549					–
Cultural	Museums & Galleries	Museums, Libraries and Archives Council (MLA) plus Renaissance in the regions		61,554		48,328		47,919					–
Cultural	Museums & Galleries	Pre 2012/13, Arts Council England and MLA plus Renaissance. From 2013/14 Total Arts Council England		499,077		441,205		472,468	464,283	458,696	445,094	368,777	26.11% decrease

was unavoidable: a tall sculptural 'helter-skelter' in the Olympic Park, sponsored by a steel and mining conglomerate and a lighting company. The ArcelorMittal Orbit was dubbed a 'collaboration' between sculptor Anish Kapoor and engineer Cecil Balmond. It described itself as 'a giant sculpture that swirls and swoops and delivers you to views of the familiar made unfamiliar, of the right way up inverted' (*sic*).[22]

The uncertain aesthetic consequences of the sculpture, which despite vaulting ambition remained subject ineffably to the laws of gravity, were equally baffling. They led to suspicions of other inversions, namely that the artist must have been in charge of engineering while the engineer dealt with art.

Department of Culture, Media and Sport (DCMS): Cuts in funding and keeping promises

In 2010 Jeremy Hunt, who had held the shadow culture brief along with Ed Vaizey, was first to enter the so-called 'Star Chamber', convened to determine departments' allocations. He apparently hoped the reward for keenness would be a penalty less severe than that certain to be inflicted by the Chancellor on spending ministers who hung back, waiting to see how the wind blew.

However, Hunt went away with a 50 per cent cut to the DCMS establishment (the department's own jobs and functions) and a slashed revenue budget. When passed on to its client organizations, this meant cuts averaging 22 per cent for national museums, galleries and centres of performing arts. (See Table 16.1.) For example, the outturn cost of Tate to DCMS in 2010/11 was £54.7 million. Tate Galleries' spending plan for 2015/16 was £31.4 million. The proportion of Tate's annual operating income from government grant-in-aid fell to 40 per cent, while the gallery generated a remarkable 60 per cent of its operating income from private and charitable sources.

DCMS, the department for 'creative industries', had to be creative about itself. An industrious permanent secretary, Jonathan Stephens, eviscerated the department humanely. Grand premises off Trafalgar Square were given up. A more diminished body (but still with

[22] The ArcelorMittal Orbit is a 114.5 metre sculpture and observation tower in the Queen Elizabeth Olympic Park in Stratford, London. See www.arcelormittalorbit.com for a description of the project and its history.

the broadcasting brief, guarantor of media coverage for ministers and with that, the possibility of glamour) set up shop in a corner of the Treasury.

The ensuing restructuring was dubbed inevitably 'the bonfire of the quangos'. Mr. Hunt's justification for the conflagration was 'openness, accountability and efficiency'; the argument for cuts in his department's grant-in-aid was 'the financial situation'. Pride was ruffled when twenty out of fifty-five public bodies and committees were proposed for abolition. The government got its way in most cases (the advisory committee on Historic Wrecks was perhaps an obvious target). Where for technical or legal reasons ministers could not achieve policy goals, they showed willingness to find creative solutions. Despite their savage accountancy, it seemed they might not, after all, be barbarians at the gate.

Some solutions (such as forming independent charities, as in the cases of NESTA, the Design Council and English Heritage) were encouraged by Ed Vaizey, who was promoted minister of state at DCMS in July 2014 (his responsibilities were shared with the Department for Business, Innovation and Skills). It was argued that organizations that form part of civil society, rather than subsisting as 'clients' of the state (where they were subject to occasional meddling by ministers) would stand a greater chance of survival. At first sight commendable, the process is not without risk (see *Heritage*, below).

Among the changes, the UK Film Council was abolished, having run through £160 million of National Lottery money on 900 films, including the successful *Bend it Like Beckham*. (Another investment was made in *Sex Lives of the Potato Men* but few saw them *in flagrante*.) The government deplored the Council's £3 million annual administration costs and abandoned a proposed £45 million investment in a new national film centre; lottery funds were still available for films.

The Museums, Libraries and Archives Council (MLA) and a library committee were abolished. The poet Andrew Motion – more lotion than potion – pledged as MLA chairman 'a smooth and orderly transition'. The MLA chief executive said helpfully: 'the country is bust'.[23] The MLA's functions were handed to the Arts Council.

The Commission for Architecture and the Built Environment (CABE), a flagship body of New Labour, was abolished, only to live on

---

[23] 'UK Film Council axed', *The Guardian*, 26 July 2010.

in a new guise. CABE had been conceived in 1997 out of the tatters of the Royal Fine Art Commission (once described as 'the best club in London' by its largely titled members). The Commission, and subsequently CABE, provided a valuable 'design review' function for local authorities and building developers who lacked confidence in architectural matters. The main political parties generally regarded it as a highlight of measures adopted by Chris Smith as New Labour's Secretary of State.

Next to be dislodged was the Design Council. This was an altogether more venerable body, which had been founded in 1944 as the Council of Industrial Design. Its first chairman was Hugh Dalton, President of the Board of Trade in the wartime government. It played an important role in the exhibition *Britain Can Make It* of 1946. Since then, the Council had helped boost British industry by introducing the public to the joys of consumerism through better product design. (No one appeared to notice the irony, that the coalition government was apparently repudiating a distinguished creation of the *last* coalition.)

But neither for the Design Council nor for CABE did withdrawal of funding mean extinction. Even though these bodies did not perform any technical function (and could therefore be ripe for abolition – see *Policy*, above), ministers nonetheless thought creatively. The Department for Business, Innovation and Skills, whose Secretary of State, Vince Cable, was a Liberal Democrat, continued to fund the Design Council, which became an independent charity. (Curiously, its Royal Charter assigned it responsibilities for the entire United Kingdom, even though coalition cultural funds were confined to south of the border with Scotland.) A much-reduced CABE operation was attached to this new charity. Transitional arrangements were put in place that would see their functions merge over time.

In the circumstances, it was the least worst outcome. It preserved the UK's pre-eminent reputation as 'thought leader' in design. For the first time in the UK, there existed a single body to promote architectural quality and the design of services to fit buildings; for the design of new products and examination of the needs of their users. If the 'new' Design Council succeeds, then it will count as a conspicuous coalition achievement.

A unique case was NESTA (the National Endowment for Science, Technology and the Arts), which had been conceived and developed independently in 1994 under a Conservative administration and created by Act of Parliament in 1997 with a £250 million endowment from the National Lottery.[24] Since then it had enjoyed cross-party political support for its work in promoting innovation, using income from its 'nest egg'. NESTA (dubbed 'the national trust for talent' by its creator) was unique among non-departmental public bodies in not having been established from 'public funds' (lottery funds are technically outside the 'control total' of public expenditure). That meant it would be difficult to abolish, except by legislation. Once again, a creative solution beckoned: on 1 April 2012 a new Nesta charity was created, safeguarding the original endowment. In 2014 it acquired the Cabinet Office behavioural insights team for an undisclosed sum.

Jeremy Hunt was succeeded briefly by Maria Miller as Secretary of State but she resigned in April 2014 over a matter of her expenses. The tourism minister, John Penrose, resigned and was not replaced. Sajid Javid became Secretary of State, the first Muslim to occupy the post.

The Olympic Lottery Commission was wound up in 2013. The coalition kept its promise to return National Lottery funds to distributors. The largest beneficiary was the Big Lottery Fund (BLF), to which £60 million was restored in 2014. The BLF, with annual income exceeding £0.7 billion, grew in importance as public funding declined. (It received a share of an unclaimed winning lottery ticket worth £64 million.) Chaired by a former Conservative MP, Peter Ainsworth, the BLF practised charitable virtues preached by the Conservative Party and its Leader before the 2010 general election, under the slogan 'Big Society'.

As for the remaining Coalition Agreement promises, HM Treasury, which has policy responsibility for Lottery Duty, examined the case for a move to Gross Profits Tax in 2010 and 2011. They concluded that the risk of a potential reduction in duty (and the returns to 'good causes') was too great to make any change. A note on lobbying and how it applied to lottery distributors was issued with the approval of ministers; distributors have a target to limit core administration costs to 5 per cent of their revenue.

A Live Music Act in 2012 amended the 2003 Licensing Act and removed 'red tape' as promised. The Act meant a licence was not needed for amplified live music performances, including audiences not

---

[24] For the conception and development of NESTA by Rory Coonan in 1994–7, see K. Oakley et al., 'The National Trust for Talent', *Journal of British Politics* (January 2014), an Arts and Humanities Research Council-funded study by Leeds University.

exceeding 200 persons, and in places of work and licensed premises. The legal exemption was extended to music with Morris dancing. This concession was calculated to please Liberal Democrat members of the coalition in the West Country, where traditional folk arts thrive.

'Superfast Britain' promised £1 billion investment in broadband and mobile infrastructure, to reach 95 per cent of homes and businesses by 2017. The programme included twenty-two 'super-connected' cities across the UK having high-speed public wireless connectivity, at a cost of £150 million. Sajid Javid, appointed Secretary of State in 2014, reflected criticism that the project was behind schedule by saying it was his top priority; the government claimed that 40,000 premises were gaining access to superfast broadband each week.

The promise of 'greater freedoms' to national museums and galleries was revealed in the 2013 spending round as a list of technical concessions. The Chancellor announced a four-year 'pilot' aimed principally at attracting more philanthropic donations. There was permission to spend previously generated revenues, removal of a 1 per cent pay award limit, the potential to borrow within a £40 million 'sector cap' and authority to invest non-grant income. However, these measures were scarcely calculated to set museums and galleries free of dependence on the state, in a period when the state's investment in them declined.

Cultural diplomacy: British Council and British Museum

If the coalition's marketing of 'Britishness' at home was ineffectual (see *Overview*, above), then 'soft power', through the work of the British Council abroad, survived external pressures. The British Museum, in a remarkable episode, demonstrated that bilateral cultural relations promoted by a single-minded museum director could resonate around the world.

The British Council is the principal instrument of UK 'soft power'. It received a Royal Charter in 1940 (making it, in common with the Design Council (see above), a creation of the last coalition government). Armed with Shakespeare, fortified by Jane Austen and bolstered by sculptor Henry Moore, the British Council had shown for decades that culture and education contribute to the UK's international standing and influence.

Just like English Heritage (below), the Council anticipated trouble before the coalition came to power. In 2010 it created a new 'Global Shared Services Centre' in Delhi, moving functions offshore in a manner redolent of private utilities but without the usual public opprobrium. The Council reduced its staff by 400. Grant-in-aid from the Foreign and Commonwealth Office fell from £185 million in 2010/11 to £157 million in 2014/15. This represents 20 per cent of the body's total income: the remainder derives from fees.

In 2013, the Foreign and Commonwealth Office (FCO) examined the British Council's operations, governance, performance and finances. The review concluded that the Council was a valuable asset to the UK as a promoter of the English language, UK education and culture, and that it made a significant contribution to the UK's international reputation.

But a question mark remained over whether some of its activities represented value for money. With 8,000 staff in more than 200 offices around the world, and present in over 100 countries, the British Council is in fact a successful examinations and English language factory. For example, in September 2014 the Council launched a 'Massive Online Open Course', which offered a six-week programme in English language and UK culture. More than 100,000 persons from 178 countries registered, making it the biggest English language class in the world. Since selling English makes money, it is not clear why UK taxpayers should be involved in an apparently massive market of willing buyers. The Council claimed 'modest surpluses' from selling English allowed cross-subsidy of its arts activities in far-flung places. This left unanswered the question, why are its surpluses merely modest? Mindful of competition issues, the FCO Review suggested exploring alternative models for the British Council's commercial activities.

However, the Review did not ask whether an extensive taxpayer-funded bureaucracy may no longer be required to achieve immeasurable 'soft power' goals, in an increasingly dangerous world. In 2011 the British Council office in Kabul, Afghanistan, was destroyed in a terrorist attack, causing the deaths of twelve persons.

The British Museum offered an alternative account of 'soft power' in an episode fraught with diplomatic dangers, political pitfalls and practical obstacles. In 2014 the Museum, which sees itself as a repository of moral, ethical and aesthetic values as much as of objects, lent a Parthenon marble to the State Hermitage Museum in

St Petersburg, Russia, to mark that institution's 250th anniversary. The event was planned in private and executed in secret. It was a *coup de théâtre* for the British Museum's director, Neil MacGregor. As a result, he assumed the informal role amongst museum executives of global purveyor-in-chief of Enlightenment values, a part once played by a predecessor as director of the National Gallery, Kenneth (Lord) Clark. But while Clark ran no risks for *Civilisation*, MacGregor took considerable risks for civilisation.[25]

The risks associated with the British Museum loan were that political instability arising from growing economic difficulties in Russia could mean that the marble (presented with others to Trustees of the British Museum by Parliament in 1816) was not returned; that the sculpture would break apart in transit or be otherwise damaged and that the claims of the Greek government, who dispute persistently Britain's title to objects removed from Greece by Lord Elgin, would be aroused inconveniently.[26]

Free access to national collections

The Coalition Agreement to maintain free access to museums and galleries in England – a Liberal Democrat policy – was put into effect. Scotland and Wales (whose national cultural policies, under

[25] The marble lent to the Hermitage by the British Museum was a sculpture of the river god Ilissos, a reclining male figure from the West pediment of the Parthenon dating from the fifth century BC. The Ilissos was a river outside Athens that provided cool walks for the citizens in summer. According to Plato, Socrates walked along the banks of the Ilissos with his young companion Phaedrus. They debated humanity's moral purpose and the nature of truth.

[26] The British Museum was well aware of the risks in lending the Marble, including its possible kidnapping. Evidence obtained by the author on 21 January 2015 from the Museum under the Freedom of Information Act included an internal note on the Marble headed 'Approval for the loan of objects to another institution', dated 13 October 2014. It says *inter alia*: 'The borrower will provide the a [sic] *letter of assurance from the [Russian] Deputy Minister of Culture confirming that the object will be protected from seizure during the period it is in the territory of the Russian Federation, and that the object will be returned to the British Museum immediately after the closing of the exhibition.*' The note also revealed that certain loan costs that might otherwise be borne by the Russians would be waived, as a *quid pro quo* for Russian loans to the UK. An insurance value was ascribed to the Marble but this was redacted under Section 31 (1) (a) of the Act, which deals with the prevention of crime.

Mrs. Thatcher, used to be decided by sub-committees of the Arts Council of Great Britain, sitting in London's Piccadilly) enjoyed devolved cultural powers, as did Northern Ireland. 'Free access' meant no charge at the door, even to foreigners. Tourists were delighted: tens of thousands of non-UK taxpayers thrilled at the prospect of using the British Museum, Victoria and Albert Museum and National Gallery (to name but a few) for nothing, a privilege scarcely enjoyed in their own countries.

Implicit in the coalition's commitment to retaining 'free access' was retention of the politically tri-partisan principle that knowledge should not be taxed. Its acme is zero-rating, for the purpose of VAT, of books, newspapers, magazines and periodicals. This is a concession granted by the European Union. Elsewhere in the EU, the VAT rate applied is 15 per cent. (In France, where they order things better, *l'exception culturelle* includes subsidies, tax-breaks and quotas for films, music and television; it is taken so seriously that in 2013 the French government threatened to scupper US–Europe trade talks unless these privileges were preserved.)[27]

However, the coalition's more restricted liberality had unintended consequences: not taxing the knowledge, for example, of the hordes of French schoolchildren descending daily on the Science Museum in London, meant that the deterioration of the Museum's fabric, to which they contributed so boisterously, went unfunded.

Nor was the underlying policy principle followed through consistently. The rapid growth, during the coalition period, of the digital economy produced an explosion of e-books and e-reader devices. Yet the price of acquiring *this* knowledge, by these means, was subject to VAT at the higher rate of 20 per cent. There was a further quirk: Scottish independence, which would have required renegotiation of EU membership, could have resulted in a book sold in Glasgow having VAT applied while over the border in Carlisle it had none.

[27] On 25 August 2014 Aurélie Filippetti, culture minister in President Hollande's Socialist government, claimed in her resignation letter to the President that 'unprecedented cuts in the culture ministry's budget, which is a symbol of the Left, have lasted two years'. In July, while confronting the worst economic crisis seen in France for decades, the President had devoted considerable personal time to sifting applicants for the directorship of the Comédie-Française. Leaving the appointment of regional theatre directors (still in the gift of the French state) to Mme Filippetti, he appointed Éric Ruf to the post. (*Le Monde*, 27 August 2014).

Libraries

The coalition did not set out to close libraries, any more than it banned books in prisons (see *Ministry of Justice,* below). It was, rather, an unintended consequence of severe reductions in central government funding of local authorities. Library services in England are a curious cultural anomaly. Unlike local museums or galleries, the law insists upon them. The coalition's significant reductions in central government grants to local councils left elected members with difficult choices. Some councils, seeing that their libraries made no money and were in some cases underused, saw them as soft targets for closure. The inevitable legal challenges did not, however, tend to favour local objectors. The courts in England were sympathetic to the balance councils had to strike between providing a reasonable library *service*, and the resources available to fund it. The number and distribution of library buildings was left to elected councillors and officers to decide.

Councils rationalized services, closing some libraries and opening others (sometimes in unexpected places, such as shops and community centres). To the chagrin of professional librarians, volunteers often staffed them. All the while (2010–13) Birmingham City Council completed the largest public library in Europe, a magnificent new building in Centenary Square. This project was all the more remarkable since it was undertaken in a period when Birmingham faced severe political difficulties in managing public services (notably children in care and education) and as it confronted a £1 billion reduction in government funding. The feeling of optimism in municipal life that the Library's opening had rekindled was, however, short-lived. In December 2014, soon after its grand public opening, the new Birmingham library cut its opening hours in half and reduced its staff by half. (The restored Birmingham Playhouse, an adjacent modern icon, was unaffected.)

The Ministry of Justice and books in prisons

The Ministry of Justice brought the absence of 'joined-up' cultural policy across the coalition government into focus. On 1 November 2013 the Lord Chancellor and Secretary of State for Justice, Chris Grayling, introduced a Prison Service Instruction (PSI 30/2013) which

amended an 'incentives and earned privileges' scheme (IEP) for convicted prisoners in England and Wales that had been in effect since
1995. (The Liberal Democrat minister in the justice department, Simon
Hughes, was appointed in December 2013).

Under the new policy, books were not included explicitly in
privileges. But Grayling banned simultaneously the sending of packages
by post to prisons. Since books come in packages, *ipso facto* books
could not be sent to prisoners. No variation was permitted, save in
relation to books for religious practice and for approved educational
purposes, and then at a governor's discretion.

The policy justification for 'privileges' was to improve behaviour and root out idleness. The justifications for banning small packages
were 'security' and 'volumetric control'.

The packages ban was interpreted as a ban on books. It caused
widespread protest, notably from English PEN, an Arts Council-funded
charity dedicated to removing barriers to literature, and from literary
types. In declining to meet them, Mr Grayling at first showed that the
pen is not always mightier than the sword.[28] In a letter to an objector,
the Poet Laureate Dame Carol Ann Duffy (whose post, given historically to unexceptionable versifying, the episode was to prove not inevitably somnolent), Mr Grayling said:

> Prisoners have full access to the same public library service in
> prisons as every other citizen, as well as the ability to order books
> from Amazon via the prison shop using their prison earnings or
> money sent in by relatives. There is a professionally run library
> service in every prison, and every prisoner has the right to order any
> available title and can have up to twelve books at any one time. If
> prisoners are reading a fraction of this total I would be delighted.[29]

[28] 'The Pen is mightier than the sword': From the play *Richelieu, or The Conspiracy*
(1839) by Edward Bulwer-Lytton.

[29] In an 'open' letter to Dame Carol Ann Duffy, Poet Laureate, dated 29 March 2014,
the Secretary of State complained of 'misinformation'. He invited her to meet prison
librarians and see how cleverly drugs and contraband were smuggled in. He said:
'Neither I nor any other Minister have made any policy changes specifically about the
availability of books in prisons. Despite some reports, we have not sought to include
them in a list of privilege items that have to be earned by offenders – to do so would be
wholly wrong. The only discussion about prison books that I have been involved in as
Secretary of State was to agree to make available the novel *50 Shades of Grey* in the
libraries in women's prisons because I judged that it might help encourage some
women offenders to read more, something I regard as highly desirable.'

In the same letter, Mr. Grayling said his sole service to literature as Justice Secretary had been to permit in women's prisons a notorious work of contemporary female pornography. He hoped to excite interest in reading and stimulate interest in books.

In the event, Mr Grayling protested too much. His policy adopted under PSI 30/2013 including books in IEP schemes was short-lived. A High Court Judge, Mr Justice Collins (Sir Andrew Collins), declared it unlawful in relation to books, following an action brought against the Secretary of State (Mr Grayling) and the prison governor. The claimant was a prisoner who was detained indefinitely for the protection of the public at Her Majesty's Prison Send, a place to which as a consequence of the policy no one could send a book. The prisoner had developed literary tastes whose need for books it was claimed the application of the policy frustrated. It was claimed that books were important for her rehabilitation; the prison's libraries (one is required under Prison Rules 1999 and under UN Standard Minimum Rules for the Treatment of Prisoners) were excellent and the staff did their best. However, in his written judgment of 5 December 2014 Sir Andrew acknowledged that, while there was no intention to prevent prisoners from having access to books, the issue was whether the ability to buy books under the IEP's modest weekly cash limits met all prisoners' requirements (from £4 'Basic' to £25.50 'Enhanced'), while access through the library imposed such severe restrictions that they amounted to an effective ban on reasonable possession of books by prisoners. He said the IEP 'seems to fail to recognize that it is deprivation of liberty that is the penalty imposed and that any further restrictions must be fully justified'. Noting that the access and content of some prison libraries 'leave much to be desired' he said: 'The ability to access what is needed from family and friends is most important', although volumetric limits on what could be stored could still apply. In a delightful passage summoning unbidden the vision of a prison cell attached to the Bodleian Library or some other highly agreeable literary establishment, he said:

> What in my view has not been taken into account is that for many there is a need to possess particular books to be treated as their own property. Some books are used as references, such as dictionaries ... others are regarded as those which need to be available to be reread or, such as for example a compendium of a particular

author's works, to be dipped into frequently. It is possession which can matter as much as access.[30]

Britishness, Bibles, and Christianity

An early adopter of 'Britishness' (see *Overview*, above) was Michael Gove, a Scot and former journalist who was Secretary of State for Education from 2010 to 2014. His public pronouncements on education frequently resembled those of the iconic winter robin, who defends his territory by singing fiercely from a high place. In a speech given on 5 October 2010, he bemoaned the 'tragic inequality' of 'countless children condemned to a prison house of ignorance' by misguided education policy 'ideologues', types he described as 'educational theorists'. Although none of these individuals was identified, perhaps for their own safety (the speech was given at the Conservative Party Conference), their crimes were serious. They included 'the trashing of our past' by 'a cursory run through Henry the Eighth and Hitler', the pursuit of 'pseudo-subjects' and 'denying children the opportunity to hear our island story'.

Discrediting abstract 'theory' by comparing it with the accumulated wisdom of 'practice' was of course a tried and tested Conservative approach. It was also calculated to appeal across the political divide (politicians are parents too). Michael Gove's 'island story' of the United Kingdom was strikingly different from Danny Boyle's 'Isles of wonder', a celebration of welfare state monuments (see *Olympic Festival*, above). Rather, it was a story of swinging swords and mighty pens:

> The great tradition of our literature – Dryden, Pope, Swift, Byron, Keats, Shelley, Austen, Dickens and Hardy – should be at the heart of school life. Our literature is the best in the world. It is every child's birthright and we should be proud to teach it in every school.[31]

---

[30] Case No: CO/2081/2014 heard on 29 October 2014 at the Royal Courts of Justice, Strand, London (Queen's Bench Division) before the Honourable Mr Justice Collins. The Claimant was The Queen (on the application of Barbara Gordon-Jones); the Defendants were The Secretary of State for Justice and the Governor of HM Prison Send.

[31] Michael Gove, Speech to Conservative Party Conference, 5 October 2010.

Leaving aside the fact that Jonathan Swift was Irish, Michael Gove's proposed application of 'Britishness' to the national curriculum proved divisive. Moreover, by volunteering personal information in the same speech, he showed that every child's birth is not always simple (he said he was adopted at birth) and that 'birthright' may depend more on individual circumstances than on cultural privileges conferred (he said his adoptive parents scrimped and saved for his education).

Michael Gove returned to his theme in May 2012 when he announced that copies of the King James Bible, published by Oxford University Press, would be sent to all primary and secondary schools. Hedge funds, private equity firms and an ennobled motor trade entre-preneur contributed to the £370,000 initiative. In an accompanying letter Mr Gove said: 'I believe it is important that all pupils – of all faiths or none – should appreciate this icon and its impact on our language and democracy.' The fact that it is the work of a committee was not dwelt upon. That much of its poetry has passed into common speech did not persuade all head teachers. Some promised churlishly to keep it on a high shelf.

No one could doubt the need for the population to speak and write English better. An OECD (Organisation for Economic Co-operation and Development) survey carried out in October 2013, based on interviews with 166,000 persons in twenty-four countries, placed England and the province of Northern Ireland in a dismal twenty-second place.[32] If British citizens could not write a job application or read a timetable, then exposure to the plangent cadences of the Bible in English would be of little use.

In this light, the 'Bible in schools' appeared a merely superficial gesture but Mr Gove did no more than follow the Prime Minister. In December 2011, on the Bible's 400th anniversary, David Cameron said:

> The King James Bible has bequeathed a body of language that permeates every aspect of our culture and heritage. Just as our language and culture is steeped in the Bible, so too is our politics.[33]

---

[32] OECD Skills Outlook 2013, Revised Version (November 2013) (accessed at http://skills.oecd.org/documents/OECD_Skills_Outlook_2013.pdf, 20 November 2014).

[33] Prime Minister's King James Bible Speech, 16 December 2011 (accessed at www.gov.uk/government/news/prime-ministers-king-james-bible-speech, 20 November 2014).

The government's attempt to align texts from the Bible to the conduct of democratic politics – barely nascent in seventeenth-century England – appeared crude. Anyone watching the weekly affray at Prime Minister's Questions would struggle to see its connection with the Bible, while terms of imprisonment served by members of both Houses of Parliament during the coalition were a reminder that sinners sat on Westminster's red and green benches too.

In July 2014 Michael Gove, who had disputed with the Home Secretary and lost, suffered under the yoke of his transgressions and was sacked. Lamentation (notably among the teaching unions) was restrained. However, he discovered swiftly that Mr Cameron's house has many mansions, and was appointed Conservative Chief Whip.

In April 2014 David Cameron returned to his 2011 religious affirmation (see *Overview*, above) by declaring in a *Church Times* Easter message that he presided over a Christian country with a rich Christian cultural history. Using the word 'evangelical' once and 'evangelism' twice, he praised the role of faith in helping people to have a moral code, adding: 'Of course, faith is neither necessary nor sufficient for morality.' Anyway, Christian values 'are shared by people of every faith and none'.[34]

Mr Cameron said he was a 'classic' member of the Church of England. This meant that he was 'not that regular in attendance' and was 'a bit vague on some of the more difficult parts of the faith'. Drawing on his family's efforts to preserve his local church in Oxfordshire, he praised the Anglican Church for its fine record of community work and 'for giving great counsel'. Inevitably, there was a political component: he announced £20 million of public funds 'for repairing our great cathedrals' (including Roman Catholic cathedrals) and an £8 million 'Near Neighbours' programme, which will help support local projects.

From August 2014 this heartfelt endorsement by the Prime Minister of his personal faith was overtaken by events. The cruel murders in Syria of British, American and Japanese hostages by a terrorist apparently with a London accent made action politically imperative. The British public was made aware of thousands of fighters across Syria and Iraq who held 'British culture' generally and Christianity in particular in contempt.

---

[34] David Cameron, 'My faith in the Church of England', *Church Times*, 16 April 2014.

Perverting the Christian motto ('I am my brother's keeper'), they practised another ('Be my brother, or I'll kill you'). A part of the government's response was to redouble efforts to co-opt British Muslims in a community effort to prevent young persons from going abroad to wage war.

British values and British culture no longer seemed reducible to a 'lifestyle' choice from a 'classic' menu of preferences, highlights, episodes and memorable works. They might have to be fought for.

English Heritage

An episode in the 'bonfire of quangos' deserves greater scrutiny. In 2010 English Heritage was custodian of a vast public estate of historic buildings, structures and sites, including Stonehenge. It cared for collections and archives of incomparable quality and importance. Its jewels included the *Survey of London*, envy of scholars worldwide. It employed archaeologists, planners and conservation experts. It gave advice on ancient monuments. It helped place structures on a protected list, on grounds of their architectural or historic importance.

However, New Labour had neglected it. While bodies that exercised fascination for the 'creative industries' had seen their funding grow, English Heritage appeared dowdy. Tweed suits did not mix with open-necked shirts; it was not 'cutting edge'. By the time of the coalition, accrued 'efficiency savings' of £7 million were reported in its accounts. It was in danger of becoming another ancient monument.

In 2010 English Heritage hatched a plan to save itself. It would capitalize on growing public interest in English heritage and divide itself into two. The plan was not mentioned in the Coalition Agreement but trailed by ministers in 2012. Although conducted behind closed doors (public consultation followed after) it had their support in principle. As a prelude, the organization made 370 posts redundant, including 9 directors and more than 100 experts. It closed down sites over winter; church repair grants went to the heritage branch of the lottery; the National Trust for Places of Historic Interest or Natural Beauty received no more money.

One new body was for planning and conservation, called 'Historic England' and the other a charity called 'English Heritage'. This will conserve and manage in a more business-like way the sites and buildings open to the public described as 'The National Heritage Collection'.

The Treasury offered a 'dowry' or one-off payment of £83 million, to smooth the passage of the new arrangements, which have eight years to prove themselves. In the Autumn Statement 2014, the Chancellor sprang a surprise: a long-awaited 3 km road tunnel under Stonehenge, a World Heritage site, would go ahead, at a cost in excess of £1 billion.

However, there was a sting attached to the overall English Heritage deal: public grants to the charity would decline from 2015/16 and cease altogether in 2022/23. The expectation is that by then, it will be self-sufficient. In his foreword to *The English Heritage New Model* consultation document (2013), Ed Vaizey said confidently: 'By the end of the eight years, the management of the National Heritage Collection will be completely self-financing.'[35]

However, this bold plan, coming a century after the 1913 Ancient Monuments Act, carried risks. Growth in income (to meet and subsequently to surpass declining public investment) was predicated on growth in visitor numbers and ability to raise funds from other sources. While the public's appetite for days out in 'ruined abbeys' (shorthand for the Heritage Collection, to distinguish it from National Trust 'roofed houses') is strong, it cannot be guaranteed. Changes in mortgage rates from historically low levels will affect families' disposable income (heritage experiences are discretionary). There is the risk of rival destinations being created, quite apart from the existing competition posed by Historic Royal Palaces and the National Trust, both major players in the 'visitor attractions' market. On top of these, shifts in public taste are unpredictable.

The coalition's radical arrangements for English Heritage, which appear to have attracted little Liberal Democrat interest, are a gamble. If they pay off, then future generations will praise them as far-sighted. If not, then inalienable cultural riches and chattels from English history will revert to the government of the day.

The Home Office and visas for artists

The coalition's attitude to and sympathy for the arts was put to the test in immigration policy. The context was the Conservative pledge in

---

[35] English Heritage New Model: Consultation, December 2013 (accessed at www.gov. uk/government/uploads/system/uploads/attachment_data/file/263943/1291-B_English_ Heritage_Accessible__1_.pdf, 20 November 2014).

2010 for net annual migration (broadly, the difference between those leaving and arriving) to be fewer than 100,000 persons by the time of the May 2015 election. By August 2014 the figure was 243,000; the goal (which Liberal Democrats claimed was not formally part of the Coalition Agreement) appeared unattainable.[36] It was little surprise that every sector that gave rise to movement to the UK, however marginal, should come under scrutiny. However, the application of a strict 'points-based' system meant that some artists were refused visas when they applied, while others were deported when they arrived.

On 2 February 2012 Damian Green, a Home Office minister, admitted in a speech delivered at Policy Exchange that this had been 'a sore point'. He announced a new 'Exceptional Talent' Tier 1 visa entry route (later extended to include persons of 'Exceptional Promise') for 'top of the range professionals, senior executives, technical specialists, entrepreneurs and exceptional artistic and scientific talent'. The policy required the Arts Council and the Royal Society, amongst other 'sectoral bodies', to become migration regulators, by certifying individual talent. Praying in aid 'the FA Premier League' (see *Sport*, below), Mr Green regarded the assessment of artistic and sporting talents as interchangeable:

> The principle of engagement in the migration system by sectoral
> bodies is important. Already the regulation of migration by
> sportspeople is delegated to a large extent to the sports governing
> bodies, which exercise it in a responsible manner. [For example,]
> the Arts Council has endorsed applications from one of today's
> leading pianists, and from an expert on visual effects considered to
> be a pioneer in the field, whose works include many of the recent
> James Bond films.[37]

There was more to come. On 29 February 2012, Theresa May, the Home Secretary, announced a new 'Permitted Paid Engagement' scheme. It allowed artists to visit the UK for short periods to engage in paid work, without placing bureaucratic burdens on host arts

---

[36] ONS, *Migration Statistics Quarterly Report, August 2014* (accessed at www.ons.gov. uk/ons/rel/migration1/migration-statistics-quarterly-report/august-2014/index.html, 20 November 2014).

[37] Damian Green, Speech on Immigration, 2 February 2012 (accessed at www.gov.uk/ government/speeches/damian-greens-speech-on-making-immigration-work-for-britain, 20 November 2014).

organizations. She said this new route had also been created 'in response to feedback that sponsorship requirements in the [points-based system] can be unduly onerous and inflexible'. Guidance issued in March 2014 to Immigration officials encouraged them to show sensitivity:

> To qualify, applicants must be able to demonstrate this is their full time profession. In assessing this you must consider factors such as standing, reputation, earnings (recognizing that some artists may earn lower salaries in certain countries) and existing work commitments outside the UK. Arts professionals can include fields across the performing and creative arts, for example musicians, visual artists, writers, circus practitioners, film makers, dancers, choreographers, or photographers where this is being done for an artistic rather than commercial purpose (such as media work or studio portraits).[38]

The coalition's response to criticism of its apparently inflexible, target-driven immigration rules rebutted the Home Office's flinty reputation. The co-option of arm's length bodies into the day-to-day application of immigration policies did not ignite the wrath of Liberal Democrats in the coalition or of the Labour Party.

Sport

The London 2012 Olympic and Paralympic Games represented the *ne plus ultra* of circuses. Britain did better than expected, winning sixty-five medals, of which twenty-nine were gold. Later, in the football World Cup of 2014, England was ejected early in the competition. To some, this did not seem to matter: the country's international prowess evidently lay in *organizing* sports, not winning them. In summer 2014, with a convincing test series win over India, England's cricket team showed what could be achieved on the field of play.

The government invested £10 million in the *Grand Départ de Yorkshire* (and from Cambridge) for the 2014 Tour de France. Apart from undertaking to support England's bid to host the 2018 football World Cup, the Coalition Agreement promised to work with the Mayor of London, Boris Johnson, to run the Olympic and Paralympic Games in London in 2012, and make plans 'to deliver a genuine and lasting legacy'.

---

[38] Guidance: Special visitor, permitted paid engagement: VAT30.3.4, 2 May 2014.

Other commitments were made to use cash in dormant betting accounts to improve local sports clubs; to help football fans form co-operatives to own their clubs, by encouraging reform of the game's governance; to support Olympic-style competitive sport events in schools and to 'seek to protect' school playing fields.

After the Games were over, a public park was created; the athletes' village had been designed presciently as flats, and these were sold. Other land sales (which will eventually benefit national lottery distributors) were deferred due to the depressed state of the property market. Some stadia were reduced in size to more manageable proportions; there was controversy over which football club should occupy the Olympic stadium itself.

The intended Olympic sporting legacy, the 'bounce', that was supposed to invigorate grass-roots sport, remained elusive. Vast amounts of public money had been thrown at the Games and would be strewn in the path of greater public participation afterwards. (The Olympics' projected cost was £9.3 billion; by 2014 the outturn cost showed a saving of £0.5 billion). But enthusiasm for sports by audiences did not necessarily translate into their own athletic efforts. (Perhaps this was an inflated expectation: after all, we do not require audiences of *Hamlet* to take up acting.)

Frustrated by the apparent lack of dividend, the coalition tinkered with sports administration. It expanded lottery funding for participation, committed £300 million to sports in primary schools over two years and £1 billion for 'grass root sports' over four years. Ministers claimed 'merging UK Sport and Sport England will create a more effective structure to deliver *elite* sports success and a wider sports legacy from the 2012 games'.

The ideology of 'participation' (sport for all, regardless of ability) ran up against the Olympian ideology of elitism (medals for the few). The contradiction was of course insoluble. The finals of 'School Games' set up in 2011 were held at the Olympic Park in 2012, in Glasgow in 2013 and in Manchester in 2014.

There was another winner of the Olympic and Paralympic Games. It was the apparent shift in public awareness of disability. Coincidentally, this translated into greater public awareness of disabilities resulting from war. The Invictus games, held in 2014 (supported by the Princes Harry and William, the Ministry of Defence and Jaguar Land Rover, subsidiary of an Indian motor manufacturer), drew attention to elite abilities of British service personnel who had sustained serious injuries in Afghanistan and elsewhere. Every ticket was sold but sceptics remained: an opinion poll by the disability charity Scope, taken amongst disabled people on the anniversary of the Paralympics in 2013, concluded that over 80 per cent thought that attitudes towards them had failed to improve; around 22 per cent felt they had deteriorated.[39] Conversely, a poll conducted by the government in early 2014 said that 70 per cent of British people as a whole thought attitudes to disability had improved since the Paralympics.[40] There is evident disparity between the opinions of disabled persons (some of whom think things have not improved) and the views of wider society (some of whose members think they have).

Certain elite sportsmen lay beyond the coalition's reach. The English Premier League stands in relation to football as does California's economy in relation to the GDP of medium-sized European countries. Its scale dwarfs everything around it; it sucks up talent from across the world; the rewards for its top players are beyond the dreams of avarice. Revenues for its twenty clubs in the 2014–15 football season were estimated at £3 billion. Unwholesome effects of the admixture of money and sport were seen in the controversy that raged around the decision by FIFA to stage the 2022 World Cup in Qatar, a very small, very hot and very wealthy country. The sports minister, Helen Grant, said it was 'essential that major sporting events are awarded in an open, fair and transparent manner'.[41] Premier League TV rights fetched £5.1 billion in February 2015, a 70 per cent increase.

Women's sports and athletics blossomed. England won the Women's World Cup in Rugby 2014, a victory that seemed to show that women's sports could finally insist on equal treatment. The lawful opt-outs available to private clubs in the UK told another story. The 2013 Open Golf Championship was played at Muirfield, a Scottish course where women cannot be members on grounds of their sex. Royal Troon, defending its own exclusive policy, said 'we share our facilities with an active Ladies Golf Club'. In September 2014 the 2,400 all-male members of the Royal and Ancient Golf Club of St Andrews, in Fife,

---

[39] 'Paralympics legacy in balance as attitudes fail to improve', 29 August 2013 (accessed at www.scope.org.uk/About-Us/Media/Press-releases/August-2013/Paralympics-legacy-in-balance-as-attitudes-fail-to, 20 November 2014).

[40] 'Paralympic data from the ONS Opinions and Lifestyle Survey', July 2014 (accessed at www.gov.uk/government/uploads/system/uploads/attachment_data/file/326220/opinions-survey-ad-hoc-paralympic-statistics-release-july-2014.pdf, 20 November 2014).

[41] Helen Grant interview with Sky News, 1 June 2014.

where the rules of golf were established, voted to amend ancient rules and admit women.

The Football Association (FA) launched a Women's Super League; the Prime Minister chaired a summit in February 2012 on tackling discrimination in football. The FA launched an anti-discrimination action plan and set up an Inclusion Advisory Board.

One 'genuine and lasting legacy' of the 2012 Games was not in the IOC script. This was the legacy delivered to the Mayor of London, Boris Johnson. Mr Johnson was a Caesar who wielded the pen of Cicero. He was a pillar of the Tories and a column in the *Telegraph*. He had promoted the London Games and transmitted 'Olympo-mania' to the world. In 2014 he was adopted as a Conservative parliamentary candidate. He aimed to bring Oxbridge to the London borough of Uxbridge. But the move portended an Olympic contest in the circus maximus of British politics once the coalition came to an end, should David Cameron lose the general election or fail to form a government. Mr Johnson declared he could be an MP at the same time as being Mayor. For many, it was just another example of his piling Pelion on Ossa ...[42]

---

[42] Pelion on Ossa: to make matters worse, by aggravating a situation or compounding a difficulty. When the giants Otus and Ephialtes wanted to storm Olympus, they piled Mount Pelion on top of Mount Ossa.

Part III

The coalition and political culture

Morten Morland for The Times / News Syndication

17 THE COALITION AND THE CONSERVATIVES

PHILIP NORTON

The effect on the Conservative Party of being in a coalition government from May 2010 onwards was profound. It challenged the essence of the party's approach to government. It did so in two respects.

First, the party was used to being in government – it was the 'in' party in British politics throughout the twentieth century – and to being in office as a single-party government. British Conservatism has a rich pedigree,[1] but parties, as Robert Blake observed, rarely philosophize when in office.[2] The party has seen itself as a practical party of government, attuned to British interests, and able to act in those interests. Power has been a necessary condition for pursuing those interests. 'Of all the features of the Conservative Power', wrote Richard Rose, 'the intense concern with winning elections and holding office is the most notable.'[3] The party had some experience of coalition, or national government, but this was almost wholly in conditions where it could have governed alone.[4] It was not dependent on its coalition partners to deliver a majority.

---

[1] See Kieron O'Hara, *Conservatism* (London: Reaktion Books, 2011); Philip Norton, 'Philosophy: The principles of Conservatism', in P. Norton (ed.), *The Conservative Party* (Hemel Hempstead: Prentice Hall/Harvester Wheatsheaf, 1996), pp. 68–82.

[2] Robert Blake, 'A changed climate', in Lord Blake and J. Patten (eds.), *The Conservative Opportunity* (London: Macmillan, 1976), p. 1.

[3] Richard Rose, *Politics in England* (London: Faber, 1965), p. 143.

[4] Philip Norton, 'The politics of coalition', in N. Allen and J. Bartle (eds.), *Britain at the Polls 2010* (London: Sage, 2011), p. 242.

Second, the party is hierarchical and the emphasis historically has been on the role of the leader. Ultimate authority has been vested in the leader, with other bodies serving in an advisory capacity.[5] The leader has been the fount of all policy. The leader selects the members of the Conservative front bench and those who will lead the party organization. When in office, the leader has exercised all the prerogatives of the monarch's first minister. As Lawrence Lowell laconically observed at the start of the twentieth century, 'When appointed, the leader leads and the party follows.'[6] Though the relationship has not been as Hobbesian as these comments may suggest,[7] leaders have nonetheless been able to rely for much of the time on the loyalty of MPs and party activists. The party has a reputation for being prepared to axe unsuccessful leaders, but until the time comes for execution has proved loyal. The key point is that the party looks to the leader to lead – that is, to make decisions and to be decisive in leading government. The leader may draw on others, but ultimately is responsible for the actions of his or her ministry.

The conditions in which the party entered coalition in 2010 – the consequence of an indecisive election outcome – and the experience of it were unprecedented and, by deviating from the norms of Conservative politics, created a dilemma for the party. For Andrew Gamble, Conservative politics is the art of balancing the politics of support (mobilizing electoral support) with the politics of power, not just exercising power but preserving particular interests.[8] Now the politics of support (Liberal Democrat votes in the two Houses) was intertwined with the politics of power. The party was hungry for power, especially after thirteen years in the wilderness, but it was used to exercising it on its own terms. Being in power had meant that its interests were protected, not challenged. Now there was a choice. 'For the Conservative Party, it was faced with an unenviable clash in which holding power entailed making sacrifices which in terms of principle may

---

[5] Philip Norton and Arthur Aughey, *Conservatives and Conservatism* (London: Martin Robertson, 1982), pp. 240–67; Philip Norton, 'The party leader', in Norton (ed.), *The Conservative Party*, pp. 142–56.

[6] A. Lawrence Lowell, *The Government of England*, Vol. 1 (New York: Macmillan, 1908), p. 457.

[7] See Norton, 'The party leader', pp. 142–4.

[8] Andrew Gamble, *The Conservative Nation* (London: Routledge & Kegan Paul, 1974).

constitute a step too far.'[9] The choice lay ultimately with the leader. Having made the choice, he then had not only to carry his own party with him, but to do so in conditions where his powers as Prime Minister were constrained.

Coalition formation

The coalition was the result of agreement between party leaders. David Cameron was able to use his power as party leader to bring it about, but in creating it he also assumed responsibility for it. He took the initiative in offering negotiations with the Liberal Democrats for the formation of a coalition. He consulted some leading figures in the party before doing so,[10] but the decision was his.

The Liberal Democrat leaders were ready to engage in such discussions, favouring a full coalition, but expecting the outcome to be a 'confidence and supply' agreement.[11] Cameron made a 'big, open and comprehensive offer' and negotiations got under way. How far Cameron and his fellow negotiators were prepared to go in the discussions was influenced by the perception that talks between the Liberal Democrats and Labour were serious – Cameron expected a Lab–Lib Dem pact to emerge[12] – and by ambiguity as to what Labour was offering the Liberal Democrats in respect of electoral reform.[13] Cameron came to believe that Labour was offering the introduction of the Alternative Vote without a referendum on the subject. The fact that there was ambiguity as to what had been offered subsequently contributed to criticism of Cameron by critics in the party, believing that he had been outmanoeuvred by the Liberal Democrat leader, Nick Clegg.

---

[9] Philip Norton, 'Speaking for the people: A conservative narrative of democracy', *Policy Studies*, 33:2 (2012), p. 130.

[10] Adam Boulton and Joey Jones, *Hung Together: The Cameron–Clegg Coalition* (London: Simon & Schuster, 2012), pp. 129–30; see also Matthew d'Ancona, *In It Together* (London: Viking, 2013), pp. 14–17.

[11] David Laws, 22 *Days in May* (London: Biteback Publishing, 2010), pp. 17–21.

[12] Boulton and Jones, *Hung Together*, p. 235.

[13] Rob Wilson, 5 *Days to Power* (London: Biteback Publishing, 2010), p. 206; France Elliott and James Hanning, *Cameron: Practically a Conservative* (London: Fourth Estate, 2012), pp. 399–401.

The motivation for the two parties coming together in coalition was not ideological. Liberal Democrat parliamentarians would have preferred a 'progressive coalition' with Labour. Clegg conceded to Gordon Brown 'There isn't really a policy issue between us.'[14] Rather, the reasons were instrumental and personal. There were various options available in terms of government formation, but the only realistic one in terms of generating a minimum winning coalition was a Con–Lib Dem deal. Additionally, the body chemistry in the two sets of negotiations reflected a wider animosity between Labour (or at least some Labour politicians) and the Liberal Democrats and a closer relationship between the Conservatives and the Liberal Democrats.[15] It was the relationship at the very top that was crucial to the successful outcome of the talks.[16] Cameron and Clegg formed a partnership that formed the glue of the coalition.

The glue at the top may have been firm but it was less so further down the party hierarchy. Although Clegg achieved the support of his party, Cameron did not require the formal endorsement of his. During the negotiations, he called a meeting of Conservative MPs to keep them abreast of developments. The position of the leader was well put by Boulton and Jones:

> The Tories were now back in government and the party's 'secret weapon of loyalty' was likely to kick in, even though, or even precisely because, it had been sorely tested in the years since the fall of Thatcher. Conservative party democracy was in any case comparatively rudimentary and tribal and no single parliamentary meeting could derail a coalition deal.[17]

The meeting of MPs was not for the purpose of endorsing a deal as such, but rather to acquiesce in the proposal for a referendum on AV. Cameron made clear that the alternative may be a Lab–Lib Dem coalition with AV imposed anyway.[18] No vote was taken, but the absence of widespread opposition was taken as endorsement of the leadership's

---

[14] Andrew Adonis, *5 Days in May* (London: Biteback Publishing, 2013), p. 119. Though see Ben Yong, 'Formation of the Coalition', in Robert Hazell and Ben Yong (eds.), *The Politics of Coalition* (Oxford: Hart Publishing, 2012), p. 32.

[15] Janan Ganesh, *George Osborne: The Austerity Chancellor* (London: Biteback Publishing, 2012), pp. 246–8.

[16] Norton, 'The politics of coalition', p. 255.

[17] Boulton and Jones, *Hung Together*, p. 247.   [18] Wilson, *5 Days*, p. 219.

position. However, as one MP recorded, 'There was an undercurrent in the meeting that a minority Conservative government would be a preferable outcome to a coalition with the Liberal Democrats, so that the concession was unnecessary.'[19] It was also a meeting of MPs summoned by the leader. It was not a meeting of the 1922 Committee, the body comprising Conservative Private Members.[20] It was also confined to MPs. No Tory peers were invited. (Indeed, the peers were specifically told that it was a meeting only for MPs.) The parliamentary party in each of the two Houses was thus not a party to the deal, but instead expected loyally to support the leadership that was.

The negotiators agreed an interim Coalition Agreement;[21] this was followed by a fuller programme for government, which formed the basis of government policy.[22] The Conservatives achieved their principal goal in terms of measures to tackle the deficit. The Liberal Democrats were amenable to their approach to tackling the nation's economic problems – indeed, the state of the public finances made it difficult for the party to decline the invitation to be in government.[23] For Conservatives, demonstrating competence in handling the nation's finances has been core to their success.[24] Having the Liberal Democrats with them not only delivered a parliamentary majority, but also gave them legitimacy, providing cover for difficult decisions.[25]

However, there was a price to pay from a Conservative perspective. Quantitatively, as one study concluded, 75 per cent of the Liberal Democrat manifesto found its way into the agreement, against 60 per cent of the Conservative manifesto.[26] More important was the

---

[19] Wilson, 5 Days, p. 221.

[20] Philip Norton, The Voice of the Backbenchers: The 1922 Committee: The First 90 Years, 1923–2013 (London: Conservative History Group, 2013).

[21] Coalition Agreement for Stability and Reform (Cabinet Office, May 2010).

[22] HM Government, The Coalition: Our Programme for Government (London: Cabinet Office, 2010).

[23] Norton, 'The politics of coalition', pp. 253–4; Yong, 'Formation of the coalition', p. 33.

[24] See Philip Norton, 'The Conservative Party: "In office but not in power"', in A. King (ed.), New Labour Triumphs: Britain at the Polls (Chatham, NJ: Chatham House, 1998), p. 77.

[25] Timothy Heppell, The Tories (London: Bloomsbury, 2014), p. 154. See also Simon Lee, 'We are all in this together: The coalitionagenda for British modernisation', in S. Lee and M. Beech (eds.), The Cameron–Clegg Coalition: Coalition Politics in an Age of Austerity (Basingstoke: Palgrave Macmillan, 2011), pp. 3–23.

[26] Jasper Gerard, The Clegg Coup (London: Gibson Square, 2011), p. 157.

qualitative cost, primarily in terms of constitutional change. As Ruth Fox noted of the Coalition Agreement, 'Overall, the Conservatives got the better of the deal in the economic arena, and the Liberal Democrats the political and constitutional reform agenda.'[27] Under the heading 'Political reform', the agreement – as already discussed in chapter two – committed the coalition to introducing fixed-term parliaments, a predominantly elected second chamber, and a referendum on AV for parliamentary elections, 'as well as for the creation of fewer and more equal sized constituencies'.[28]

The compromises and concessions on constitutional issues provided the most obvious basis for tensions within the party. Here there was a clear ideological divide. The Liberal Democrats adhere to a liberal view of the constitution, seeing it as a constraining mechanism and wishing to disperse power through a radical series of constitutional reforms.[29] The Conservatives are principally wedded to the traditional, or Westminster, approach, emphasizing the accountability and flexibility at the heart of the political system and wishing to preserve those attributes.[30] The two are almost at opposite ends of the spectrum.[31] In essence, the Liberal Democrats take the view that the constitution is beyond repair; the Conservative view is that it is fundamentally sound. However, in the Coalition Agreement, the former view prevailed: 'The Government believes that our political system is broken.'[32] This statement essentially encapsulates the basis for dissent within Tory ranks. Cameron was more easily persuaded of the merits of change than many of his supporters.

The party's commitment to 'political reform' thus provided the principal, but not the exclusive, basis for conflict within the party. This was especially the case in the first, long session (2010–12). The failure of the government to deliver on all the commitments led to tensions

[27] Ruth Fox, 'Five days in May: A new political order emerges', in A. Geddes and J. Tonge (eds.), *Britain Votes 2010* (Oxford: Oxford University Press, 2010), p. 34.
[28] *Programme for Government*, pp. 26–7.
[29] Philip Norton, *The Constitution in Flux* (London: Martin Robertson, 1982), pp. 275–9.
[30] Norton, *The Constitution in Flux*, pp. 279–87; see also Norton, 'Speaking for the people', pp. 121–32.
[31] See Philip Norton, *The British Polity*, 5th edn (New York: Longman, 2011), p. 438.
[32] *Programme for Government*, p. 26.

between coalition partners. The first year was one of comity between the two; the period after May 2011 was one of conflict.

A shaky start

The first session of a parliament is normally seen as a honeymoon period for an incoming Conservative government, the Prime Minister enjoying unchallenged authority and the party's MPs loyally voting for the flagship Bills promised in the party manifesto. The creation of a coalition government meant that neither condition applied.

David Cameron could call on the party to support him, because he was the leader, but he did not command the clout that would be expected of a new Conservative Prime Minister. He was limited by the fact that it was a Conservative-led government, but not a Conservative government. This had a number of consequences, both for Cameron as Prime Minister and as leader of the Conservative Party.

As Prime Minister, his patronage powers were restricted. The allocation of posts to Liberal Democrats limited the number of posts to be filled by Conservatives. This constricted the prospects of promotion for Conservative MPs as well as leaving some that had served on the frontbench in Opposition without preferment. Also, crucially, he could not announce government policies unless they had the support of the Liberal Democrats. Nick Clegg had an effective veto. Policies were either blocked or left to be pursued as party policies, which might not enjoy majority support in the House. What policies were pursued were justified on grounds of being in the Coalition Agreement, not the Conservative party's election manifesto.

There were two other constraints. Cameron had agreed to the Liberal Democrats' policy of fixed-term parliaments. (Indeed, according to Matthew d'Ancona, he and George Osborne were as much the instigators of the policy as the Liberal Democrats.[33]) The Fixed-term Parliaments Act 2011 not only limited his capacity to select an election date to favour the Conservatives, but also had the effect of limiting his capacity to threaten an election through making a vote one of confidence. He thus gave up an important tool of party control. Also, to the

---

[33] D'Ancona, *In It Together*, pp. 15–16.

annoyance of Tory MPs, Cameron was not able to enforce collective ministerial responsibility on Liberal Democrat members of the government. When in 2013 Nick Clegg instructed Liberal Democrat ministers to vote against the orders implementing constituency boundary changes, there was nothing the Prime Minister could do about it. The convention was not suspended (something for which there was a precedent), nor, as provided for in the *Coalition Agreement for Stability and Reform*, 'explicitly set aside' – it was simply ignored.

As party leader, his position was notably constrained compared to his predecessors. The fact that he was not able to satiate fully the Tory appetite for power affected the politics of hierarchy. He lacked the kudos that attaches to a Conservative leader who has led his party to victory in the polls. The election had seen a major increase in Tory ranks, the consequence of winning seats, but also of the departure of many of the parliamentary old guard in the wake of the expenses scandal. New MPs comprised almost half – 48 per cent – of the parliamentary party. This would normally be expected to deliver a body of backbenchers highly supportive of the leadership. However, many new MPs were as likely to ascribe their election success to their own efforts as to those of the party leader. As Fraser Nelson observed, most believed they were elected despite Cameron, not because of him: '"I could have doubled my majority if he wasn't so wishy-washy", moaned one of the higher-profile new candidates to me last week. It is a fairly typical complaint.'[34]

There was also some wariness in the relationship between the premier and his backbenchers by virtue of his background and his perceived 'wishy-washy' beliefs. These were reinforced rather than dispelled as his premiership proceeded. Cameron was not only an Old Etonian, but also was perceived as surrounding himself with Old Etonians, either as ministers or advisers. His reliance on the old school was noted not only by commentators, but also by backbench MPs. David Davis, who had contested the leadership against Cameron in 2005, wrote in May 2013: 'please, please, no more Old Etonian advisers'.[35] It was a view given public expression by other MPs, including – from different wings of the party – Dr Sarah Wollaston and Nadine Dorries.

---

[34] Fraser Nelson, 'To keep your seat, stick to your principles', *The Times*, 14 May 2010.

[35] David Davis, 'Tories must start listening to ordinary voters, not their old school chums', *Daily Telegraph*, 3 May 2013.

However, being an Old Etonian may have a much deeper relevance. As the headmaster of Eton, Tony Little, recorded, it is a school 'dedicated to a certain idea of public service, and always has been'.[36] This could be seen as propelling pupils to a life of public service, but the emphasis was on service rather than holding a particular set of beliefs. Cameron seemed to fit the mould. There was no clear set of ideological beliefs. He was on the back benches for too short a period of time to carve out a reputation and voting pattern as someone from a particular strand of Conservative thought. When asked after making a particular statement if he thought it was his Clause IV moment, he replied: 'I don't believe in these "Clause IV moments". Leading a party is about trying to make the right judgement all of the time, trying to take your party in the right direction all of the time, making it fit for power, giving it the right ethos.'[37]

As party leader after 2005, Cameron had set out to give the party a fresh image. He sought to move the party in a new direction, stressing what it was for (such as the family, childcare, environmental protection and the NHS) rather than what it was against.[38] He also gave a series of speeches on social responsibility,[39] which, in office, became the concept of the 'Big Society'.[40] However, the particular themes or policies did not come together into a coherent or enduring whole. It lacked, as Robin Harris put it, 'a directing idea'.[41] David Marquand claimed that Cameron was essentially a Whig, embodying the themes of 'responsive evolution, gradual progress and flexible statecraft' and saw his task as one of accommodating his party to the cultural, social and political shifts of the past twenty years.[42] It was a view endorsed by

[36] Jason Cowley, 'Eton eternal', *New Statesman*, 10 May 2013, p. 25.

[37] Peter Snowdon, *Back from the Brink* (London: Harper Press, 2010), p. 358.

[38] Philip Norton, 'David Cameron and Tory success: Architect or by-stander?', in S. Lee and M. Beech, *The Conservatives under David Cameron* (Basingstoke: Palgrave Macmillan, 2009), pp. 38–40; Tim Bale, *The Conservative Party: From Thatcher to Cameron* (Cambridge: Polity, 2010), pp. 381–2; Richard Hayton, *Reconstructing Conservatism? The Conservative Party in Opposition, 1997–2010* (Manchester: Manchester University Press, 2012), pp. 142–3.

[39] Snowdon, *Back from the Brink*, p. 258.

[40] See Jesse Norman, *The Big Society* (Buckingham: University of Buckingham Press, 2010) for an articulation of the concept.

[41] Robin Harris, *The Conservatives: A History* (London: Bantam Press, 2011), p. 516.

[42] David Marquand, 'In search of electoral El Dorado', *New Statesman*, 1 March 2010, p. 24.

Cameron's Oxford tutor, Vernon Bogdanor: 'He is a Conservative in the Macmillan, not the Thatcher mould – pragmatic and socially concerned, but not committed to any fixed blueprints.'[43]

Margaret Thatcher generated an eponymous philosophy. John Major did not. However, both were Tories in their approach to the constitution and to institutions that formed the Westminster model of government. Cameron, like his predecessors, was certainly a unionist – he fought hard in 2014 to keep Scotland in the Union – but he was less wedded to other established structures. He was also less steeped in practice and conventions of government. Like Tony Blair, he had never held ministerial office and rather shared his approach to institutions. He was prepared to contemplate institutional change in a way that would cause conflict with some of his supporters, but it was a willingness that enabled him to negotiate the Coalition Agreement.

Backbench doubts about Cameron's leadership were to be compounded almost immediately by what may be seen as an unforced error: an attempt by Cameron to influence the outcome of the election of the chairman of the 1922 Committee. Graham Brady, MP for Altrincham and Sale West, was the leading candidate for the vacant post, Sir Michael Spicer having retired at the election after nine years in the chair. Brady was a former frontbencher who had resigned in 2007 over the party's stance on grammar schools. (Brady was a strong supporter; Cameron's failure to favour an expansion of grammar schools was attributed to insensitivity born of the fact he had gone to Eton.) Cameron called a meeting of all Conservative MPs on 20 May 2010 and got them to agree that ministers could be full voting members of the 1922.[44] However, 118 MPs opposed the move and they were not slow in expressing their anger at the outcome. One, Bill Cash, threatened legal action.[45] It was not in the gift of a meeting of MPs summoned by the PM to change the rules of the 1922 Committee. 'The decision proved to be pyrrhic. Such was the backlash, Cameron had to back down and abandon the attempt.'[46] Ministers were permitted to attend as observers, but that had been agreed by the 1922 at the end of the previous parliament. The 1922 elected Brady as chairman, beating Richard

[43] Vernon Bogdanor, 'No more Mr Nasty Guy', *New Statesman,* 1 March 2010, p. 44.
[44] Norton, *Voice of the Backbenchers,* p. 39.
[45] Bill Cash, 'Composition controversy', *The House,* 17 May 2013, p. 11.
[46] Elliott and Hanning, *Cameron,* p. 418; see also d'Ancona, *In It Together,* p. 244.

Ottaway (the candidate presumed to be preferred by Number 10) by 126 votes to 85.

The Prime Minister thus began the parliament facing a chairman of the 1922 Committee whose election he was perceived as seeking to prevent and who led a body which was now in a distinctive, and powerful, position, given that – as in the period of coalition from 1940 to 1945 – it could claim to be *the* body within Parliament representing the integrity of the party.[47]

The start of the parliament thus bore no relationship to that which usually existed between a new Conservative Prime Minister and his or her party. The same applied to the rest of the parliament. The challenge for Cameron was to hold together both the coalition and his own party. In seeking to do so, we can identify essentially three stages: delivery, reaction and regrouping. There were also clashes with some party members on issues unrelated to the politics of coalition.

Delivery

On some measures relating to domestic issues, most notably tuition fees and welfare, the Liberal Democrats made considerable sacrifices. For Conservatives, the sacrifices were primarily on constitutional issues. Opposition from some Tory MPs meant that the party witnessed unprecedented dissent in the first session,[48] with the most persistent dissent taking place on the Parliamentary Voting Systems and Constituencies Bill. Tory MPs were reluctant to concede a referendum, but accepted that it was part of the deal to deliver more equal constituency electorates. The deal was, in essence, embodied in the Bill.

As Philip Cowley has shown in chapter five, what dissent did occur was notable more for its persistence than its effect. Although, in the first ten months of coalition, a quarter of Conservative MPs voted against the government on one or more occasions, the number in each division was not large, and nowhere near enough to threaten the

[47] Norton, *Voice of the Backbenchers*, pp. 13–15, 67–9.

[48] See chapter five, this volume, and Philip Cowley and Mark Stuart, 'A coalition with wobbly wings: Backbench dissent in the House of Commons', *Political Insight*, 3 (2012), pp. 8–11; Philip Norton, 'Coalition cohesion', in T. Heppell and D. Seawright (eds.), *Cameron and the Conservatives* (London: Palgrave Macmillan, 2012).

government's majority. The party remained a party of tendencies rather than factions, so the nature of dissent differed from issue to issue.[49] Tory MPs were predominantly Eurosceptic, but there was no ideological strand enjoying majority support in the party.[50] The only time the government's majority slumped (from 82 to 21) – on tuition fees – was a result primarily of Liberal Democrat cross-voting.

Tory MPs who were critics of the government were able in any event to pursue other avenues to express their disagreement. The 1922 Committee provided a valuable arena for Members to express their exasperation within the confines of the party.[51] Some were elected as officers or members of the 1922 executive. Some used other channels within the House. Two were elected to membership of the newly formed Backbench Business Committee, which allocated debates in backbench time.[52] The Committee variously chose topics that government may have preferred not to be debated, such as the war in Afghanistan, prisoner voting rights and a referendum on continued membership of the European Union.

The 1922 Committee also established five policy groups to help feed in ideas for the party manifesto for the next election.[53] The chairman of each was elected, giving the occupant a useful platform for public comment. Other MPs, not necessarily critics of the leadership, also took the opportunity to envisage a future Conservative government, publishing manifestos for that eventuality. The title of one, by a group of newly elected MPs, encapsulated the approach: *After the Coalition: A Conservative Agenda for Britain*.[54] Another, while avowing support

---

[49] Philip Norton, *Conservative Dissidents* (London: Temple Smith, 1978), p. 244; Anthony Seldon, 'David Cameron could be scuppered by his own party', *Evening Standard*, 14 April 2014. See Philip Cowley and Mark Stuart, *The Four Year Itch* (Nottingham: University of Nottingham/Revolts.co.uk, 2014) for the differing dissenting lobbies.

[50] See Timothy Heppell, 'Cameron and Liberal Conservatism: Attitudes within the parliamentary Conservative Party and Conservative ministers', *The British Journal of Politics and International Relations*, 15:3 (2013), pp. 340–61.

[51] Norton, *Voice of the Backbenchers*, p. 188.

[52] Philip Norton, *Parliament in British Politics*, 2nd edn (Basingstoke: Palgrave Macmillan, 2013), pp. 32–3.

[53] Norton, *Voice of the Backbenchers*, p. 56; Ben Yong, 'The coalition in Parliament', in Hazell and Yong, *Politics of Coalition*, pp. 111–13.

[54] Kwasi Kwarteng et al., *After the Coalition: A Conservative Agenda for Britain* (London: Biteback Publishing, 2011).

for the coalition, noted that the government was constrained in being able to create a long-term vision for Britain. It sought to fill the gap.[55] The approach reflected the ingrained Conservative view of power. The reference was to the government, but the focus was the future of Conservatism.

Despite backbench disquiet, the coalition government got its business. For the Prime Minister, there was also some evidence of the parliamentary party rallying to his support. Backbench critics on the executive of the 1922 Committee were displaced in 2012, with loyalist members of the 2010 intake organizing and winning a virtual clean sweep of their own slate of candidates.[56] In the House, Philip Hollobone and Peter Bone, two leading members of the awkward squad, were voted off the Backbench Business Committee.[57] Critics of the government within Conservative ranks were vocal, but not necessarily effective.

By 2012, the coalition could claim to be holding together, tackling the deficit – a key motivation for its existence – and delivering on constitutional and domestic measures embodied in the Coalition Agreement.[58] The Conservatives had supported passage of the Fixed-term Parliaments Act and the Parliamentary Voting Systems and Constituencies Act, and had seen the publication and referral to a joint committee of a draft House of Lords Reform Bill. None of these measures as such would have emerged under a Conservative Government, but they were seen as the price to pay for being in government and for implementing measures to tackle the nation's economic problems.

Cameron, in short, had engaged in the Conservative statecraft for which his background qualified him. 'The very fact of being in coalition has ... helped Cameron strengthen his claim to be an essentially pragmatic politician and buttressed the discourse of national interest used to justify the cuts.'[59] The party had achieved its major

55 David Davis, 'Introduction', in D. Davis, B. Binley and J. Baron (eds.), *The Future of Conservatism Revisited* (London: ConservativeHome, 2011), p. 3.

56 Norton, *Voice of the Backbenchers*, p. 52.

57 Unlike other select committees, the membership is elected each session and not for a parliament.

58 See Robert Hazell, 'Case study I: Constitutional reform', in Hazell and Yong, *The Politics of Coalition*, pp. 156–9.

59 Richard Hayton, 'Conservative Party statecraft and the politics of coalition', *Parliamentary Affairs*, 67:1 (2014), p. 19.

goals in the economic sphere, support for an austerity programme undermining support for its coalition partner rather than destroying its own electoral base. However, what this narrative masks is an underlying disquiet on the Conservative benches and a desire for a more robust stance by the Prime Minister. This was seen in response to the AV referendum campaign but then built up from 2012 onwards.

Reaction

Tory MPs and peers had voted for an AV referendum in return for reform of constituency boundaries and because they were free to campaign for a 'no' vote in the referendum campaign. Both had essentially been embodied in the Coalition Agreement. However, fear of losing the referendum led to tensions within the party.

Cameron had not planned to take a leading role in the referendum campaign. Pressure from MPs changed his mind. The 'No' campaign was poorly resourced and looked like losing. Early in 2011, the party co-chairman, Baroness Warsi, was given a hard time at a meeting of the 1922 Committee about the party's commitment of resources. The whips picked up the mood among backbenchers. The 1922 executive pressed the Prime Minister to take a lead in the campaign. 'Defeat in the referendum would make a scratchy mood positively poisonous. The fractious Tory tribe would become openly seditious.'[60] Cameron decided he had to play a leading role and did so, strengthening his relationship with his backbenchers, but annoying his Liberal Democrat allies. A coming together of PM and Tory MPs was at the expense of the relationship of the coalition partners. However, the relationship was to prove more strained as a result of the government's failure to achieve an elected second chamber.

As already discussed in chapter two, the government in May 2011, as part of a white paper on Lords reform, published a draft House of Lords Reform Bill, providing for 80 per cent of members of the second chamber to be elected. The Bill was sent to a joint committee set up for the purposes of pre-legislative scrutiny. It reported in March 2012 and recommended that the proposal be subject to a referendum.[61]

---

[60] D'Ancona, *In It Together*, p. 80.
[61] Joint Committee on the Draft House of Lords Reform Bill, *Draft House of Lords Reform Bill: Report* (HL 284-I, HC 1313-I, Session 2010–12), pp. 92–6.

Almost half the members of the committee, including a majority of the Tory members, published an alternative report opposing election.[62] The government introduced the Bill three months later. Conservative MPs opposed to it formed a body known as 'The Sensibles', led by Jesse Norman, the MP for Hereford and South Herefordshire. They ran a military-style operation, with weekly meetings and members appointed as whips to sound out the opinion of other members. Packs of briefing notes were prepared for supporters. It was a more rigorous campaign than that run by Conservative whips in support of the Bill.

During the two-day debate on Second Reading, members of the group ensured they were present in some numbers throughout and were prominent in voicing their opposition.[63] When the House divided, more than 100 Tory MPs rebelled: 91 voted against the Bill and a further 19 abstained from voting. The Opposition voted for the Bill, but made clear that it would not support a programme motion to limit debate on the Bill. As the motion was also opposed by the Tory opponents of the Bill, the government lacked a majority to carry the motion and it was not moved. This opened the prospect for endless debate on the Bill, similar to that experienced during an earlier attempt in 1968–9 to reform the Lords.[64] The government bowed to the inevitable and Nick Clegg on 6 August announced the government would not be proceeding with the Bill.

Regrouping

Many Tories were frustrated that they were voting through, or being asked to vote through, measures favoured by the Liberal Democrats, but not being able to vote through measures they wanted. Two were, in effect, hived off to commissions of inquiry: the proposals to introduce a British Bill of Rights and to provide for 'English votes on English laws' as a response to the West Lothian question. As we have seen

[62] *House of Lords Reform: An Alternative Way Forward* (London: Campaign for an Effective Second Chamber, 2012).

[63] See Commons Hansard, 9–10 July 2012, cols. 24–132, 188–274.

[64] Janet Morgan, *The House of Lords and the Labour Government 1964–1970* (Oxford: Clarendon Press, 1975), pp. 208–22.

(chapter two), both commissions produced reports – the former in 2012[65] and the latter in 2013[66] – but no legislation resulted.

However, the two reforms blocked by the Liberal Democrats that caused especial resentment were those on constituency boundaries and an in/out referendum on membership of the European Union. Cameron was as exasperated as his backbenchers by the first, but found himself having to shift his position on the second.

The outcome of the House of Lords Reform Bill delighted many Tory MPs, but enraged Liberal Democrats. They retaliated by voting in January 2013 against the orders to give effect to the boundary changes to provide for more equal constituency boundaries. An amendment to delay the changes until after the next election was carried in the Lords by 300 votes to 231, and then upheld in the Commons by 334 votes to 292. This confirmed in the minds of many Tory MPs that the Liberal Democrats were unreliable and that there was little point in maintaining the coalition. They felt they had delivered on their part of the deal – an AV referendum in return for boundary reform – and now the Liberal Democrats were linking Lords reform with boundary changes. Lords reform in their view was a free-standing issue; some also took the view that the Coalition Agreement had, in any event, been delivered, in that the commitment was to establish a committee to bring forward a Bill. This legalistic view of the wording was ascribed to George Osborne, but it was not one that carried much sway with Liberal Democrats. There was mutual resentment on the part of coalition partners. Lords reform was second only to electoral reform for Liberal Democrats in terms of their constitutional agenda. For Conservatives, achieving more equal electoral boundaries was core to their strategy for winning the next election.[67]

Cameron had delighted his own party in 2011 when he had exercised his veto at the European summit on a treaty amendment on fiscal rules in the Eurozone, but had then bowed to Liberal Democrat pressure to allow the European Court of Justice to enforce rules on

[65] Commission on a Bill of Rights, *A UK Bill of Rights? The Choice Before Us*, Vol. 1 (London: Ministry of Justice, 2012).

[66] McKay Commission, *Report of the Commission on the Consequences of Devolution for the House of Commons* (London: Commission on the Consequences of Devolution for the House of Commons, 2013).

[67] See Heppell, *The Tories*, p. 153.

excessive debt procedure in the Eurozone.[68] The Liberal Democrats also blocked the introduction of a Bill to provide for a referendum on continued membership of the European Union. Conservative Eurosceptics were annoyed that there had been no referendum on the Lisbon Treaty and wanted an in/out referendum. Initial pressure for such a Bill was resisted by the party leadership. When David Nuttall, the MP for Bury North, achieved a backbench debate on holding a referendum, the party leadership imposed a three-line whip. 'Number Ten made it clear that the vote was not an issue of conscience but of party loyalty, and that each rebel vote would be interpreted unambiguously as a gross discourtesy.'[69] Despite a somewhat heavy-handed whipping operation, 81 Tory MPs still voted for Nuttall's motion. After the vote, the rebels 'filled the bars, embraced one another and toasted what they considered a moral victory. The coalition had picked a fight with the Conservative Party, and had been given a bloody nose.'[70]

Cameron's reaction exemplifies a change of stance in the latter half of the Parliament. He had crafted a coalition and helped keep the coalition partners on board in order to tackle the deficit. Now, his parliamentary party was restive and he needed to secure his base in the party. 'In general, Cameron and his colleagues are felt to have shown too much concern for their coalition partners and too little for their own side.'[71] Some Tory MPs were reported to have written to the Chairman of the 1922 calling for a vote of confidence in the leader. At one point, the number was put at fourteen (way short of the forty-six necessary to trigger a vote),[72] but there was no independent verification of the number. The only one known to have written, Andrew Bridgen, withdrew his letter in April 2014.

Some MPs – and ministers – were already looking ahead to the next election and beyond. The opinion polls were not disastrous for the party, but neither did they deliver confidence as to the outcome of the election. Some ministers were not unhappy to utilize the EU debate as a means of promoting their own standing within the party. Some

---

[68] Eunice Goes, 'The coalition and Europe: A tale of reckless drivers, steady navigators and imperfect roadmaps', *Parliamentary Affairs*, 67:1 (2014), pp. 53–4.

[69] D'Ancona, *In It Together*, p. 243.   [70] *Ibid.*, p. 245.

[71] Harris, *The Conservatives*, p. 522.

[72] Steerpike, 'Exclusive: Fourteen Tory MPs stab David Cameron so far', *Spectator* Blogs, 2012 (accessed at http://blogs.spectator.co.uk/steerpike/2012/09/exclusive-fourteen-tory-mps-stab-david-cameron-so-far, 21 November 2014).

backbenchers were already thinking of the leadership succession and making a case for their preferred candidates. The names of Chancellor George Osborne, Home Secretary Theresa May and Education Secretary, and later to be Chief Whip, Michael Gove were variously mentioned. So too was that of London mayor, Boris Johnson, widely seen as positioning himself for a return to front-line parliamentary politics, a fact confirmed in 2014 when he sought and gained a parliamentary candidature. Osborne was adept at recommending his supporters for preferment in ministerial reshuffles. In 2014, he was also reported to be taking a more relaxed view about the UK leaving the EU.[73] However, the only person more or less overtly promoting his own merits as a future leader was a backbencher. Adam Afriyie, MP for Windsor since 2005, a wealthy businessman and former frontbencher, mounted an active campaign, though he was ultimately to miscalculate his strategy on an EU referendum.

Cameron's strategy to rally his backbenchers can be seen most notably on the issue of an EU referendum, but also in a wider, more intense, campaign. He moved to make the case for negotiating reform within the EU and then putting the renegotiated terms to the people in a referendum. This stance cheered backbenchers – 'As he took his seat for the first PMQs after his dramatic intervention, he was cheered to the rafters by his fellow Tories waving their order papers'[74] – but many pressed for legislation to provide for a referendum in the next Parliament. In May 2013, two Tory backbenchers moved an amendment to the Queen's Speech regretting the absence of any mention of a referendum bill. Though defeated, by 277 votes to 130, a total of 114 Tory MPs voted for it.

The scale of the support for the amendment spurred Cameron to take more tangible action. Downing Street produced a draft Bill, providing that a referendum must be held before 31 December 2017. When James Wharton, the youngest Tory MP, came top in the ballot for Private Members' Bills, he decided to introduce it. A Conservative, but not a government, three-line whip was imposed in support of the measure. The Prime Minister hosted a barbecue at Number 10 for MPs and peers. He later met senior Tory peers to discuss tactics in the Lords.

---

[73] Sam Coates, 'Osborne ponders British exit as dismay with Europe grows', *The Times*, 1 September 2014.

[74] D'Ancona, *In It Together*, p. 257.

Although the Bill cleared the Commons – neither Labour nor the Liberal Democrats supported it, but neither voted against it – it was brought down in the Lords on 31 January 2014, when Labour and Liberal Democrat peers voted to adjourn debate on the last day available for its committee stage.[75] During its passage, Adam Afriyie effectively killed his leadership bid by moving an amendment to hold the referendum in 2014. It annoyed fellow backbenchers, who considered it a major distraction, and it was lost by 249 votes to 14.

Cameron's holding of meetings at Number 10 with supporters was utilized on other occasions as a means of building consensus. The approach demonstrated an awareness of the need to strengthen his party base, but it was not something he took to naturally. Statecraft was one thing, but party management was another. Cameron's stance on issues was in the mould of Harold Macmillan, but some MPs felt that his way of handling his supporters was more in the style of Ted Heath.[76] He lacked the natural charm of John Major and the intensity of Margaret Thatcher. His appearances before the 1922 Committee were well received, his talks generally given without notes, but noted for being the sort that might have been given to any party gathering.[77] There remained the appearance of being somewhat aloof, still surrounded by a coterie of trusted, and like-minded, advisers.

This perception of 'cosy cliques' contributed in part in August 2014 to the defection to UKIP of Clacton MP Douglas Carswell, 'a maverick intellectual and virulent Eurosceptic',[78] who claimed the Prime Minister's stance on Europe was not sincere. He was followed a month later by Rochester and Strood MP Mark Reckless. Both resigned their seats in order to trigger by-elections, which they subsequently won. Their defections served to highlight Tory divisions – primarily on Europe, but more generally the Prime Minister's seemingly reactive stance in response to events. 'The suspicion', wrote Janan Ganesh, 'is that he is not a man you can set your watch by.'[79]

---

[75] Lords Hansard, 31 January 2014, cols. 1545–7.

[76] See Norton, *Conservative Dissidents*, ch. 9.

[77] Norton, *Voice of the Backbenchers*, p. 31.

[78] Sam Coates and Laura Pitel, 'Cameron braced for more UKIP defections', *The Times*, 29 August 2014.

[79] Janan Ganesh, 'Cameron plays his part with polish but no passion', *Financial Times*, 2 September 2014.

Cameron's detachment – his tendency to determine policy without reference to his MPs – also led to a major defeat in the Commons as well as to the closest challenge to his premiership. The former was in the field of foreign policy and the latter his attempt to keep Scotland as part of the United Kingdom.

The conflict in Syria led him to favour the use of a military response to the Assad regime's use of chemical weapons against insurgents. Parliament was recalled on 29 August 2013 to debate the use of force. The whips failed to grasp the scale of backbench opposition until it was too late. The Opposition, initially expected to support the government, switched to oppose the government's motion. The House failed to carry an Opposition amendment, but some thirty Tories (and nine Liberal Democrats) joined with Labour to defeat the government motion by 285 votes to 272. Cameron immediately accepted the outcome. 'It is very clear tonight that, while the House has not passed a motion, the British Parliament, reflecting the views of the British people, does not want to see British military action. I get that, and the Government will act accordingly.'[80]

According to the BBC's political editor, the defeat meant that 'the prime minister has now lost control of his own foreign and defence policy, and as a result he will cut a diminished figure on the international stage'.[81] It also had a knock-on effect in the summer of 2014 in response to advances, and slaughter, in Iraq by Islamic militants calling themselves the Islamic State (IS). Cameron appeared reluctant to act for fear of repeating what happened over Syria. The government reiterated that there would be 'no British boots on the ground' and only moved in support of air strikes once the whips were clear that a majority could be mobilized in favour of such action.

Closer to home, Cameron had conceded to pressure from the Scottish National Party executive in Scotland that there should be a referendum in 2014 on Scotland becoming an independent nation. He initially avoided playing a central role in the campaign, recognizing that his presence north of the border was not necessarily an asset to the campaign. He left it to the 'No' campaign to ensure that its initial 20-point lead in the opinion polls was translated into a majority in the

---

[80] Commons Hansard, 29 August 2013, cols. 1555–6.
[81] 'Syria crisis: Cameron loses Commons vote on Syria action', *BBC News*, 30 August 2013 (accessed at www.bbc.co.uk/news/uk-politics-23892783, 21 November 2014).

referendum. When the polls narrowed shortly before the referendum – one showing a lead for the 'yes' campaign – the prospect of Scotland leaving the union not only galvanized Cameron, but also panicked many in the parliamentary party. The week before the referendum, Cameron – along with Labour leader Ed Miliband and Deputy PM Nick Clegg – dispensed with attending Prime Minister's Question Time in order to go to Scotland to make impassioned pleas for the Scots to vote 'no'.

The prospect of Scotland voting for independence led some Tory MPs to signal that a 'yes' vote would lead to a challenge to Cameron's leadership. A number of commentators speculated that there would be the numbers sufficient to trigger a vote of confidence which, even if he survived it, would leave him badly wounded. Some suggested that being the Prime Minister who 'lost' Scotland would in itself be sufficient to prompt Cameron's resignation. Jonathan Foreman imagined what the resignation letter would look like, essentially encapsulating the criticisms levelled at Cameron: being outsmarted by Salmond and not taking advice.[82] In the event, the 'no' campaign triumphed and it was Scottish First Minister, Alex Salmond, who resigned rather than Cameron. Cameron moved immediately to shore up support among backbenchers, and outflank UKIP, by announcing his support for 'English votes for English laws', a 'move of political brilliance' according to Peter Oborne.[83] He was also protected by the fact that, had he been under pressure to go, there was still no clear successor. However, resentment swelled at the fact that he had conceded more powers to Scotland if it voted no. Criticism of the way he had handled the issue came from former ministers as diverse as Owen Paterson and Ken Clarke.[84] As Isabel Hardman reported, 'there is a groundswell of irritation in Westminster that this has been decided without any proper debate or scrutiny'.[85]

---

[82] Jonathan Foreman, 'David Cameron's draft resignation letter in the event of a Yes vote', *Spectator Coffee House*, 17 September 2014.

[83] Peter Oborne, 'Only unity can shape change this profound', *The Daily Telegraph*, 20 September 2014.

[84] Tim Shipman, 'Top Tories lash PM over Scotland deal', *The Sunday Times*, 21 September 2014.

[85] Isabel Hardman, 'David Cameron's final plea to Scottish voters', *Spectator Coffee House*, 15 September 2014.

Attempts by Cameron to shore up his base within the party after 2012 were thus variously blown off course. There was an awareness of what needed to be done, but no sustained strategy for achieving it by Number 10. Cameron was nonetheless protected by the nature of Conservative politics. MPs expressed their dissatisfaction, either by voice or vote – Carswell and Reckless were exceptional in choosing exit – but were limited by the absence of any clear consensus behind a successor as leader, by the disparate nature of groupings within the party, and by the fact that they were geared to power. Cameron was going to lead the party into the 2015 election and electors do not reward a divided party. Backbenchers may not approve of what the leader was doing, but he was the leader. He maintained the support of the party not out of personal loyalty, but by virtue of the fact that the party was determined not to see a Labour government in 2015.

There remained nonetheless a sense of detachment from supporters. Furthermore, it was not confined to the parliamentary party. As Robin Harris put it, 'The leadership's failure to take the party seriously in Parliament has been matched by lack of regard for the constituency stalwarts.'[86]

Within the family

Cameron had a reputation for being somewhat aloof from the party that had elected him. In the view of a former Deputy Chairman of the party, there had been 'a steady erosion of engagement within our party'.[87] Cameron's adoption in opposition of an A-list of candidates, identifying candidates favoured by the leadership, had not always been well received by constituency parties, historically protective of their autonomy in candidate selection. Some activists also resented his pursuit in government of legislation to permit same-sex marriage.

Legislation for same-sex marriage had not been included in the Coalition Agreement and some party members felt it had come out of the blue. Although surveys consistently showed public support for the measure, including among Tory supporters, some long-standing activists

---

[86] Harris, *The Conservatives*, p. 523.
[87] Don Porter, 'Engaging with success', in Davis, Binley and Baron, *The Future of Conservatism Revisited*, p. 353.

vehemently opposed it. A number resigned their party membership;[88] some past and present constituency officers were photographed on the steps of Number 10 delivering a protest letter against it. On a free vote, Tory MPs divided against the Bill by 136 votes to 126. It was carried (by 400 votes to 175) because of support from other parties. Tory peers proved more supportive: 80 supported the Bill and 66 opposed it. Although the Bill was passed, and Cameron received praise for his steadfast support for it, even some supporters thought he may have made a tactical error by not letting it proceed as a Private Member's Bill.

The dispute came at a time when the party was losing members and having to contend with a challenge from UKIP supporters. Cameron relied on the traditional politics of deference, but recognized the need to bolster his support with party activists. There were attempts to engage more with the grass roots. This was exemplified in the leader's speech at the 2013 party conference, which was geared as much to those sitting in front of the Prime Minister as to the cameras. As the *Guardian* reported:

> No greenery, no 'big society' and certainly no injunction against 'banging on about Europe'. There was a time when David Cameron sought out the ire as much as the adulation of his tribe, but he sought to persuade the thin ranks of the Conservative faithful in Manchester that he was one of their own.[89]

In 2014, following local election losses and the success of UKIP candidates, the leadership addressed issues, not least immigration, designed to shore up support among traditional supporters. This was followed at the party conference, Cameron promising tax cuts under a future Conservative government as well as a British Bill of Rights. The signals were that a future Conservative government would address issues that under the coalition would not get past the Liberal Democrats.

The task, though, was an uphill one. Though party funding remained relatively healthy (Electoral Commission data showed almost £16 million in donations in 2013, and almost £14 million in 2012), much came from wealthy donors rather than grass-roots activists.[90]

---

[88] See Christopher Hope, 'Conservative party members quit Cabinet ministers' seats in protest over government policies', *Daily Telegraph*, 17 August 2014.

[89] *The Guardian*, editorial, 2 October 2013.

[90] See Jane Merrick, 'Hedge fund chiefs donate £1.3m to Tory party in just 12 weeks', *The Independent*, 16 February 2014.

Party membership continued to decline. In 2013, the party claimed to have 134,000 members, compared with 253,000 in 2005. Some ascribed the decline to Cameron's detachment. 'Douglas Carswell, the Conservative MP, has previously warned that the party is "haemorrhaging" members because of David Cameron and his "remote clique" at Westminster.'[91] Carswell's defection to UKIP was seen by some as exemplifying Cameron's detachment from his own party's grass roots. 'The pattern of the leader's action', wrote Charles Moore, 'conveys a message to party workers they are the problem.'[92]

Though decline in party memberships is a long-term development and not confined to the UK, the party leader carries the can for a failure to reverse its electoral fortunes and membership. Whatever the complex of causes responsible for decline, party activists were prone to ascribe it to the absence of a clear message, certainly a clear Conservative message, to electors.

Changes for the future

For the Conservative Party, the parliament represented the best of times and the worst of times. The party was in government, rather than in the political wilderness, but the price was the abandonment or failure of some cherished policies and the acceptance of others that appeared in the election manifesto of the Liberal Democrats.

For Conservatives of the Cameron mould, for whom the economy was the most important issue facing the nation, the coalition was necessary and essentially achieved its purpose. Measures that were thought probably impossible to achieve under a minority government were implemented. Though the Tories had difficulty breaking through in the opinion polls, and party membership continued to fall, they did not suffer the dramatic collapse of support witnessed by their coalition partners. 'In general, the Tories as a party have probably benefited from coalition, whereas the Liberals have not.'[93] For Conservatives who were

[91] Peter Dominiczak, 'Conservative Party membership has halved since David Cameron and "clique" came to power', Daily Telegraph, 18 September 2013.
[92] Charles Moore, 'Douglas Carswell can see where politics is going – he's a true moderniser', Daily Telegraph, 29 August 2014.
[93] Harris, The Conservatives, p. 524.

more attached to the integrity of the nation's enduring constitutional relations, it was not necessary and created the potential, one that was realized, for permanent change to the constitutional fabric of the state.

The principal effect of coalition on the Conservative Party is on the position of the leader. The approach to power remains part of the party's DNA. However, the leader in future will be constrained, both by statutory changes (fixed-term Parliaments) and by the party. Tory MPs have proved willing to express themselves independent of the leadership. Though, as we have seen, independence has had little effect in votes, other than on Syria – the most important government defeat on military involvement since the mid-nineteenth century – the impact is in terms of the culture of the parliamentary party. This is perhaps demonstrated most vividly by the fact that Cameron conceded that the parliamentary party would in the event of another hung Parliament have a veto over any coalition. The leader no longer enjoyed the freedom exercised in 2010.

The coalition was justified by both parties in terms of the need to tackle the nation's economic problems. However, what that misses is that it was born also of fear that a 'confidence and supply' arrangement with the Liberal Democrats, the Liberal Democrats being independent of government but voting to keep it in office, might prove unstable. According to Ganesh, 'the Conservatives knew that a "confidence and supply" arrangement would break down before long. A second election might then be lost in the autumn or the new year to an invigorated Labour Party.'[94] Cameron and his team did not want to exist by putting together majorities on an ad hoc basis: 'better to try for a stable coalition that might last five years than to form a minority government that would probably collapse after a few months'.[95] The nation got a coalition in large part because the Tory leadership's quest for power took precedence over the 'true faith' favoured by the wider party.[96] Many backbenchers were not necessarily persuaded that the two were mutually exclusive.

---

[94] Janan Ganesh, *George Osborne: The Austerity Chancellor* (London: Biteback, 2012), p. 245.
[95] D'Ancona, *In It Together*, p. 15.   [96] *Ibid.*, p. 15.

18 THE COALITION AND THE LIBERAL DEMOCRATS

MIKE FINN

> The Liberal Democrats now face a slow and painful death at the hands of the voters.
>
> MARK STUART, POLITICAL SCIENTIST (2011)[1]

> The one thing I'm not prepared to do is be the last leader of the Lib Dems.
>
> NICK CLEGG MP, DEPUTY PRIME MINISTER (2012)[2]

> The ultimate failure of attempts to use the party's policy process as a way of controlling the decisions of the party within government has strongly reinforced [the] feeling of disillusion.
>
> DAVID HOWARTH, LIBERAL DEMOCRAT MP FOR CAMBRIDGE, 2005–10 (2014)[3]

First phase: Power and (un)popularity, 2010

On 12 May 2010, Nick Clegg did what his predecessors Paddy Ashdown and Charles Kennedy had failed to do, and led his party into

[1] Mark Stuart, 'The formation of the coalition', in Simon Lee and Matt Beech (eds.), *The Cameron–Clegg Government: Coalition Politics in an Age of Austerity* (Basingstoke: Palgrave, 2011), p. 53.

[2] Cited in Matthew d'Ancona, *In It Together: The Inside Story of the Coalition Government* (London: Penguin, 2014), p. 288.

[3] David Howarth, 'The Liberal Democrats and the functions of policy', *Journal of Liberal History*, 83 (2014), p. 31.

power following a general election.[4] With the title of Deputy Prime Minister and accompanied by four other Liberal Democrat Cabinet ministers, Clegg might have been forgiven for feeling a measure of satisfaction at ensuring the first ministerial offices for politicians in the liberal tradition since the Second World War. The Liberal Democrats had, at last, achieved what had been much vaunted since their formation – the credibility of power. Here was their chance, finally, to 'break the mould of British politics'.[5]

For some scholars, such as Emma Sanderson-Nash (a former Liberal Democrat party staffer), this was the result of the 'modernization' of the party, the increased 'professionalization' of the Liberal Democrats which had been the hallmark of Clegg's tenure as party leader.[6] The professionalization of the party meant that it had been in a position to seize the opportunity of a hung parliament to forge an effective coalition agreement and enter into government.[7] An alternative reading might be that having emphatically lost the election, the Liberal Democrats nonetheless found themselves in a fortuitous position due to the inability of either of the two main parties to win it. For a second consecutive general election, Liberal Democrat performance had been, to say the least, disappointing – at least to those whose attention span only registered the formal campaign itself. 'Cleggmania', the phenomenal popularity of Clegg personally following his unequivocal success in the first prime ministerial debate on 15 April, momentarily – according to some polls at least – appeared to propel the Liberal Democrats into second place and sparked the possibility that genuine damage might be wrought to the entrenchment of Britain's two-party system.[8] When the results of the real poll on 6 May were declared, with the Liberal

---

[4] It would be unfair to include his immediate predecessor, Sir Menzies Campbell, in this list, as he did not face a general election.

[5] Tony Little and Robert Maclennan, 'Breaking the mould', *Journal of Liberal Democrat History* 25 (1999–2000), p. 40.

[6] Tim Bale and Emma Sanderson-Nash, 'A leap of faith and a leap in the dark: The impact of coalition on the Conservatives and Liberal Democrats', in Lee and Beech (eds.), *The Cameron–Clegg Government*, pp. 246–7; Elizabeth Evans and Emma Sanderson-Nash, 'From sandals to suits: Professionalisation, coalition and the Liberal Democrats', *British Journal of Politics and International Relations*, 13 (2011), pp. 459–73.

[7] Evans and Sanderson-Nash, 'Sandals to suits', p. 459.

[8] Julian Glover and Hélène Mulholland, 'Nick Clegg now in contention as potential PM, *Guardian*/ICM poll shows', *The Guardian*, 16 April 2010.

Democrats losing five seats on the previous General Election, and six seats net when including the 2006 by-election win in Dunfermline and West Fife, the performance looked, at best, underwhelming.[9]

The Cleggmania bounce however masked the fact that through the course of the 2005 Parliament the Liberal Democrats had flitted between crisis and obscurity. Poll ratings had often been low, reaching a nadir of 13 per cent during the scandal-hit leadership election which followed Charles Kennedy's resignation.[10] Even in late 2009, Liberal Democrat support had only stabilized at around 18 per cent.[11] As late as April 2010, polling was reporting that two-thirds of voters didn't know who Clegg was.[12] The significance of subsequent Cleggmania lay undoubtedly in novelty, but notwithstanding (in Clegg's words) the 'disappointing night for the Liberal Democrats' on 6 May, it was still a minor victory of sorts that the party had managed to hold fifty-seven seats after all.[13] Expectations had been raised by the debates, but the longer-term decline of the party's support between 2005 and 2010 had been arrested by Clegg's performance and the party's campaign. In fact, despite the depths to which Liberal Democrat popularity had sunk in those years, 2010 saw the party record its highest vote share since the pre-merger days of the SDP–Liberal Alliance in 1983, with nearly a million more votes than in 2005.[14] Despite the disappointment, it had not been a campaign which 'did not matter'.[15]

In no small measure, this had frustrated David Cameron's attempts to form a majority Conservative government; though he had made inroads into Liberal Democrat territory (gaining nine seats net from them), this was nothing like enough to reverse the Liberal

---

[9] David Denver, 'The results: How Britain voted', in Andrew Geddes and Jonathan Tonge (eds.), *Britain Votes 2010* (Oxford: Oxford University Press, 2010), p. 11.

[10] 'Labour retake the lead as Lib Dems collapse', UK Polling Report, 26 January 2006 (accessed at http://ukpollingreport.co.uk/blog/archives/130, 3 October 2014).

[11] 'YouGov daily poll: 40/29/18', UK Polling Report, 29 September 2009 (accessed at http://ukpollingreport.co.uk/blog/archives/2286, 3 October 2014).

[12] Allegra Stratton, 'Nick Clegg spearheads election strategy of "northern offence, southern defence"', *The Guardian*, 7 April 2010.

[13] Laura Roberts, 'Quotes of the Night', *Daily Telegraph*, 7 May 2010.

[14] Dennis Kavanagh and Philip Cowley, *The British General Election of 2010* (Basingstoke: Palgrave, 2010), p. 351.

[15] David Cutts, Edward Fieldhouse and Andrew Russell, 'The campaign that changed everything and still did not matter? The Liberal Democrat campaign and performance', in Geddes and Tonge (eds.), *Britain Votes 2010*, pp. 109–24.

Democrat gains made from the Conservatives in 1997, 2001 and 2005.[16] The Liberal Democrats might have unequivocally lost; but the manner of their losing helped ensure the Tories lost too. Though reduced in numbers, Clegg's party's resilience had played a role in delivering the hung parliament which presented an opportunity to gain power. Despondent as Clegg was on the morning of 7 May, defeat did not mean destruction, either for his ambitions or those of much of his parliamentary party.

Following the conclusion of the coalition negotiations (discussed in chapter one, this volume), and during the legitimization of the coalition by the Liberal Democrats' 'triple-lock' mechanism (including a special conference of party members held on 16 May), Clegg entered his first Cabinet meeting on 13 May believing that he had been able to secure a good deal for his party, both in terms of ministerial representation and policy commitments. Critically, he had extracted a commitment to a binding referendum on electoral reform, the success of which was vital to the party's chances following any popular backlash against a deal with the Tories. His team had also – according to one estimate – managed to get three-quarters of the Liberal Democrat manifesto into the final *Programme for Government*, which would be published on 20 May.[17]

Power, however, brought with it unprecedented levels of scrutiny. David Laws, the chief secretary to the Treasury and arguably the leading thinker in the party, had met with approbation from both the conservative press and the Conservative Party on taking office.[18] In part this was due to his enthusiasm for cuts and fiscal retrenchment – a deeply held view he shared with the Chancellor, George Osborne. He lasted just seventeen days in post before he was compelled to resign following a story in the *Daily Telegraph* regarding irregularities in his expenses.[19] It was the first of a series of scandals which would bedevil

[16] House of Commons Library RP 10/36, *General Election 2010: Preliminary Analysis* (London: HMSO, 2010).

[17] Ben Yong, 'Formation of the coalition', in Robert Hazell and Ben Yong, *The Politics of Coalition: How the Conservative–Liberal Democrat Government Works* (Oxford: Hart, 2012), p. 37.

[18] Jasper Gerard, *The Clegg Coup: Britain's First Coalition Government since Lloyd George* (London: Gibson Square, 2011), p. 173.

[19] David Laws, 22 *Days in May* (London: Biteback, 2010), pp. 258–61.

senior Liberal Democrat figures during their tenure in coalition.[20] The Laws resignation was not critically damaging in terms of public opinion – the resignation was relatively swift and it took place in the coalition's 'honeymoon' period – but it signified the greater attention now being paid by the media to Liberal Democrat politicians, and may have weakened Clegg in terms of intra-government relations. Though Laws' replacement, Danny Alexander, was Clegg's 'closest political friend', and subsequently emerged as a competent Chief Secretary to the Treasury, the removal of Laws robbed Clegg of a significant ally until his return as a junior minister with cross-departmental responsibilities in September 2012.[21]

Liberal Democrat strategy in government focused on establishing the credibility of the party as a party of government (and thus entrenching three-party politics), establishing the credibility of coalition as a form of government (and thus reinforcing the first aim) and attempting to maintain a distinct identity from the Conservatives. This last was initially at least the lowest priority. In the short run, the party leadership had to deal with the immediate concerns of power, namely how Clegg and his Liberal Democrat Cabinet colleagues were to function in the context of a coalition government. For Clegg the question was acute, as the role of Deputy Prime Minister in his case was more than an honorific; if events did not bear out the 'dual premiership' the Rose Garden press conference might have implied, it was nonetheless true that Clegg was from the off involved in all government issues and was consulted at all points, including regular bilaterals with the Prime Minister.[22] The evolution of the Quad – Cameron, Osborne, Clegg and

---

[20] Chris Huhne, the Energy Secretary was forced to resign over allegations of perverting the course of justice in early 2012; he was convicted and imprisoned for 62 days in 2013. Lord Rennard, the party's former chief executive, was accused of sexual harassment in a TV news report in early 2013; an internal party investigation declared the witnesses 'broadly credible' but refrained from further action as the evidence did not meet the burden of proof. Rennard's suspension was ultimately lifted but several prominent figures in the party quit in protest. Mike Hancock, MP for Portsmouth South, was suspended from the party in 2013 following a civil suit alleging sexual misconduct; his research assistant had previously been questioned as a suspected Russian spy. Hancock eventually settled the civil suit out of court and issued an apology.

[21] Chris Bowers, *Nick Clegg: The Biography* (London: Biteback, 2011), p. 90.

[22] Robert Hazell, 'How the coalition works at the centre', in Hazell and Yong, *Politics of Coalition*, pp. 51–2, 57.

Alexander – as a driving force within government on fiscal policy in particular was but the most recognized example of a quickly entrenched relationship amongst the party elites and an investment by both parties in making it work.[23]

Clegg in particular sought to 'own everything' that the coalition was responsible for; the problem with this, however, was that as a junior partner it left the Liberal Democrats little opportunity (even when they deserved it) to gain the credit for policy successes, such as their flagship policy of raising the income tax threshold to £10,000.[24] Rightly or wrongly, the government's successes were attributed to the Conservatives and its failures in large part to the Liberal Democrats. Owning everything, when the junior partner in government, could be seen as owning nothing. Had Clegg opted instead to take a major government department for himself and sought to carve out a distinctly Liberal agenda (at, for example, the Home Office) this would have given him both a power base and a policy record of his own which he would have been able to stand on at the next General Election.[25] It was also true that Liberal Democrat Cabinet ministers were in departments – Energy and Climate Change, Scotland, and Business, Innovation and Skills – which denied them the opportunity to establish a coherent party agenda within government.[26]

Entering into government cut the party leadership off from the party as a whole, both in the country and in Parliament.[27] Whilst a disproportionate number of Liberal Democrats found themselves in some form of ministerial office (given the need for the party to have a minister at as many departments as possible), those left behind on the backbenches and even party staff felt themselves to be shut out.[28] In Hazell and Yong's study, stress is laid on the pressures of government – that the Liberal Democrats 'prepared well for a hung parliament' but

---

[23] *Ibid.*   [24] Bowers, *Nick Clegg*, pp. 266–8.

[25] A point made by numerous others. For example, Yong, 'Formation of the coalition', p. 43.

[26] Partly because of policy U-turns at Energy and BIS and partly because of the marginalization of the Scotland Office post-devolution as a Cabinet department, notwithstanding the independence referendum of 2014.

[27] Ben Yong, 'The coalition in Parliament', in Hazell and Yong, *Politics of Coalition*, p. 104.

[28] Ben Yong, 'The political parties', in Hazell and Yong, *Politics of Coalition*, p. 125.

'not ... for government'.[29] Often isolated in government departments, Liberal Democrats were forced to contend with power without the formidable independent resources the Conservatives could command. On taking office, the removal of state subventions received by the third party on the basis of its role in opposition saw an effective £2 million hit in the party's budget.[30] The party, already in a parlous financial state, saw its policy unit shut down and its staff dismissed.[31] Ministers became overburdened, overly reliant on civil servants, and simply without time to relate to their wider party.[32] Nowhere was this more true than in the case of the party leader, whose appearances at the weekly meetings of the parliamentary party became perfunctory, with Clegg often late.[33] Clegg was also confrontational in approach to his party – both in public at conferences and behind closed doors in parliamentary party meetings, attacking Ming Campbell over his views on the tuition fees policy.[34] Clegg spent less time at party conferences, and when he did he was minded to remind his audiences that 'his way was the only way'.[35] One commentator from the magazine *Liberator* commented in 2013 that Clegg had reached the point where he could 'no longer disguise his contempt for his own party'.[36]

Aside from Clegg's views of his own members, relations with the parliamentary party required new structures as the party became increasingly unhappy about the lack of differentiation from the Conservatives, and a series of party committees were established to provide distinctive Liberal Democrat perspectives on policy issues, in effect a shadow front bench for a party already in government.[37] Though channels were opened to parliamentarians, their effectiveness was limited.[38] The leadership was increasingly isolated not just from the electorate and the party in the country but the party in Westminster, something the Prime Minister for his part also stood accused of in relation to the Conservatives.[39] In the early stages of coalition, much

[29] Yong, 'Formation of the coalition', p. 28.
[30] Yong, 'The coalition in Parliament', p. 102.   [31] *Ibid.*   [32] *Ibid*, p. 104.
[33] *Ibid.*   [34] Gerard, *Clegg Coup*, p. 165.
[35] Simon Tittley, 'A coup against Clegg?', *Liberator's Blog*, 26 June 2013 (accessed at http://liberator-magazine.blogspot.co.uk/2013/06/a-coup-against-clegg.html, 3 October 2014).
[36] *Ibid.*   [37] Yong, 'The coalition in Parliament', pp. 104–6.   [38] *Ibid.*
[39] See chapter seventeen, this volume.

was made of the shared social backgrounds and real chemistry between Prime Minister and Deputy Prime Minister. Increasing isolation from the parties they led was something else they had in common.

The emerging distance between Liberal Democrats in government and the parliamentary party manifested itself in a breakdown in party discipline, most notably over the tuition fees vote in December 2010. Tuition fees was the biggest and most notorious policy U-turn of the Liberal Democrats' tenure in office, and ultimately saw the party split three ways on the parliamentary vote.[40] It was characterized as a 'betrayal', but it was not the first policy shift which had caused the party significant discomfort.[41] The party had made great play of its opposition to a 'Tory VAT bombshell' in the weeks preceding the election; the first Liberal Democrat crisis of faith took place in late June and July when their MPs voted to support the Emergency Budget which raised VAT to 20 per cent from January 2011.[42] Discipline, in this case, was largely maintained; only two Liberal Democrat MPs rebelled in the July vote despite threats from others.[43] The autumn – and the first substantial parliamentary session since the election – heralded the real rupture between Clegg and his party. The Coalition Agreements had attempted to square the circle between the Liberal Democrats' stated opposition to university tuition fees and the probability of forthcoming proposals for government to raise them – and they had failed.[44] Both the interim agreement and the *Programme for Government* referred the question of tuition fees to the outcome of the review headed by Lord Browne which had been established by the previous Labour government and which was due to report in the autumn.[45] As the interim agreement put it:

[40] Peter Waller and Ben Yong, 'Case studies II: Tuition fees, NHS reform, and nuclear policy', in Hazell and Yong, *Politics of Coalition*, p. 176.

[41] Mehdi Hasan, 'Down and dirty with the Lib Dems', *New Statesman*, 8 July 2010.

[42] *Ibid.*

[43] Stephen Tall, 'When is a rebellion not a rebellion?', *Liberal Democrat Voice*, 15 July 2010 (accessed at http://www.libdemvoice.org/when-is-a-rebellion-not-a-rebellion-20307.html, 2 October 2014).

[44] The agreements provided for the possibility of abstention on the part of Liberal Democrat MPs, which would satisfy neither supporters of party policy nor those supporting the leadership in the quest for credibility.

[45] HM Government, *The Coalition: Our Programme for Government* (London: Cabinet Office, 2010), pp. 31–2.

> If the response of the Government to Lord Browne's report is one
> that Liberal Democrats cannot accept, then arrangements will be
> made to enable Liberal Democrat MPs to abstain in any vote.[46]

The introduction of tuition fees was part of drastic reform to British
higher education in the wake of the first Blair landslide in 1997.[47]
Between 1962 and 1998, higher education in Britain had, in effect, been
'free' at the point of delivery.[48] Students' fees were paid by government
and students received a maintenance grant. Though not a consequence
of the Robbins Report,[49] this settlement became emblematic of the
'Robbins era' and the 'Robbins principle' – that higher education should
be 'available for all those who are qualified by ability and attainment to
pursue [it] and who wish to do so'.[50]

The party was firmly committed to the restoration of that settlement. Though Clegg, as well as other leading figures within the party, was
extremely sceptical of the viability of such a return to the *status quo ante*
given the huge increases in student numbers since the 1960s, it remained
party policy, despite Clegg's attempts to convince his party to withdraw
from the commitment.[51] It was in this context that the leadership took
what would retrospectively be seen as a highly unwise decision to embrace
the sacred cow of free higher education. Most notably Clegg – and other
Liberal Democrat MPs and candidates – signed the National Union of
Students' (NUS) pledge to vote against increases in tuition fees in the next
parliament.[52] In addition, the very first image in the Liberal Democrat
General Election broadcast (entitled *Say Goodbye to Broken Promises*),
was a shot of a Labour pledge, stating 'no student tuition fees'.[53]

There was an electoral logic to it – the party traditionally
commanded strong support from students, and in Oxford West

[46] 'Conservative–Liberal Democrat coalition negotiations: Agreements reached',
11 May 2010 (accessed at www.conservatives.com/~/media/Files/Downloadable%
20Files/agreement.ashx?dl=true, 8 September 2014), p. 5.

[47] Andrew McGettigan, *The Great University Gamble: Money, Markets and the Future
of Higher Education* (London: Pluto Press, 2013).

[48] See Malcolm Tight, *The Development of Higher Education in the United Kingdom
since 1945* (London: Open University Press, 2009).

[49] Committee on Higher Education, *Report of the Committee* [Robbins Report], (Cm
2154, London: HMSO, 1963).

[50] *Ibid.*, p. 8.   [51] See chapter one, this volume.

[52] Waller and Yong, 'Case studies II', p. 173.

[53] Liberal Democrat General Election Broadcast, 13 April 2010 (accessed at www.
youtube.com/watch?v=jTLR8R9JXz4, 16 September 2014).

incumbent MP Evan Harris was in trouble, whilst in Norwich South Simon Wright aspired to take the seat from Labour with the help of the University of East Anglia's students. Whilst Clegg and his allies had sincerely felt the party's commitment to scrap tuition fees to be unaffordable (and as late as the party's 2009 pre-manifesto attempted to downgrade it to an 'aspiration'), the apparent volte-face of 2010 through the pledge signing and the emphasis on 'broken promises' in campaign media made subsequent attempts by the leadership to distance themselves from the policy more than a little disingenuous.[54] As Katherine Dommett notes, tuition fees was one of a number of issues where the party's pre-election rhetoric established an 'expectations gap' between what the party promised and what it was willing (rather than *able*) to deliver.[55] The final *coup de grâce* on the issue of tuition fees was delivered in November 2010 when a *Guardian* report revealed that the party's coalition planning team had in March earmarked tuition fees as a policy which could be dropped in coalition – weeks before the party's politicians signed a pledge promising not to raise them.[56]

Sticking with the commitment in public (if not in private) then was good electoral politics, which helped to deliver Simon Wright's candidacy in Norwich South even if it failed to save Evan Harris in Oxford West and Abingdon. It was calculated, and it was effective. It was, after all, ruthlessly professional. The pledge was broken not because the party had suddenly realized they could not deliver the policy in coalition, but because their leaders – and their Leader in particular – were not invested in it. As Nick Robinson commented:

> Because the leadership were arguing for a policy the leadership didn't believe in and had tried to change, they probably thought the public already knew they had no intention of doing it and didn't really believe in it. But the public didn't know that.[57]

---

54 Patrick Wintour and Hélène Mulholland, 'Nick Clegg apologises for tuition fess pledge', *The Guardian*, 20 September 2012.

55 Katherine Dommett, 'A miserable little compromise? Exploring Liberal Democrat fortunes in the UK coalition', *Political Quarterly*, 84:2 (2013), p. 220.

56 Nicholas Watt, 'Revealed: Lib Dems planned before election to abandon tuition fees pledge', *The Guardian*, 12 November 2010.

57 Cited in Brian Walker, 'The coalition and the media', in Hazell and Yong, *Politics of Coalition*, p. 143.

Deploying the pledge in the campaign cycle also represented a funda-mental misunderstanding of the place of free higher education in Liberal Democrat voters' hierarchy of priorities. What the leadership saw essentially as an outdated sectional issue which could be used to mobil-ize a target group in marginal seats was, in fact, a key differentiator for the party with voters as a whole.[58] The implications of tuition fees ranged beyond simply one policy in one area for one voter constituency, but went to the core of the Liberal Democrats' definition of difference from the two main parties. As David Howarth has noted:

> Those who wanted to maintain the party's position on fees during the crucial period of 2008–10 did so because of what it represented: that the Liberal Democrats were a party that valued education for its own sake ... For their part, the opponents of the fees policy might have thought of themselves as hard-headedly sacrificing students to secure more resources for primary schools ... but their real difference with the supporters of the fees policy was that they treated it as a technical matter, not one that defined the party or themselves.[59]

Though the outcome of the Browne Review was unknown at the time of the Coalition Agreement, it was difficult to foresee a scenario which did not increase the burden on the student and decrease that on the tax-payer, particularly in the broader context of fiscal austerity. Thus, when Browne reported on 12 October 2010, the stage was set for a political crisis within the party. Browne's key recommendations did include the transfer of a greater proportion of the financial burden onto students in the form of uncapping student tuition fees, which since 2004 had stood at a maximum of £3,000 per annum. In practice, the government resolved on allowing universities to charge up to £9,000, with the attendant proviso that those charging in excess of £6,000 were required to demonstrate a clear, schematic plan for widening participation for students from non-traditional backgrounds.[60]

The riots began on 10 November. A national demonstration held in Westminster under the auspices of the NUS and the University and College Union (UCU) attracted over 50,000 people from around

---

[58] Howarth, 'Liberal Democrats and the functions of policy', 31.   [59] Ibid.
[60] Cable later claimed this as a success for Liberal Democrat ministers in government (Bowers, Nick Clegg, p. 260).

the UK, before several hundred besieged Conservative Party headquarters on Millbank, eventually breaking in and engaging in acts of criminal damage. One protester, 18-year-old sixth form student Edward Woollard, was ultimately jailed for two years and eight months for throwing a fire extinguisher from the roof of the building.[61] Further demonstrations were held on 24 November, which occasioned 32 arrests,[62] 30 November, which resulted in 153 arrests,[63] and 9 December, this last timed to coincide with the vote in the House of Commons which would see the Browne recommendations translated into legislative action.[64] During the 9 December protests a car transporting the Prince of Wales and the Duchess of Cornwall was attacked, and Charlie Gilmour, the son of Pink Floyd guitarist David Gilmour, was arrested for swinging from the Cenotaph. He was subsequently jailed for sixteen months, of which he served four.[65]

Notwithstanding the attack on Conservative Party headquarters, student anger was focused on the Liberal Democrats, who had advocated free higher education, pledged to vote against fee rises, and who now seemed certain to renege on their promises. Matters were made worse by the fact that the Department to which Browne reported – Business, Innovation and Skills (BIS) – was headed by a Liberal Democrat minister, in the form of Vince Cable, who would have to propose the parliamentary motion (which he did, in fact, agree with). It became clear as the vote drew near that the situation was close to untenable for Liberal Democrat politicians. D'Ancona claims that

> Clegg was starting to look tired and to mutter about the
> workload ... 'What should we do?' he asked his Tory colleagues.
> Osborne replied, 'I wouldn't sign up to it. I think it's fair – but
> you're going to have real problems.' But Clegg's question had been

[61] Charlotte Gill, 'Teenage student protestor who hurled a fire extinguisher during the tuition fees riots is jailed for 2 years and 8 months', *Daily Mail*, 12 January 2011.

[62] Sean Coughlan, 'Students stage day of protests over tuition fee rises', *BBC News*, 24 November 2010 (accessed at www.bbc.co.uk/news/education-11829102, 3 October 2014).

[63] Sean Coughlan, 'Student tuition fee protest ends with 153 arrests', *BBC News*, 1 December 2010 (accessed at www.bbc.co.uk/news/education-11877034, 3 October 2014).

[64] Frances Booth, 'Cribsheet, 09.12.10: Tuition fees protest and vote', *The Guardian*, 9 December 2010.

[65] 'Charlie Gilmour released from prison after four months', *The Guardian*, 15 November 2011.

rhetorical. 'I respect your candour,' he told the Chancellor, 'but we have to do this.'[66]

Abstention – the escape route offered to the party's MPs – was not viable, and certainly not for its ministers. A whipped vote thus ensued which saw twenty-one Liberal Democrat MPs rebel, unsurprisingly including new Norwich South MP Simon Wright.[67]

The scale of the damage the tuition fees saga did both to Clegg personally and the Liberal Democrat brand in general is difficult to overestimate. Dommett notes a collapse in the party's 'trust' rating which followed, and which it could not recover.[68] The tuition fees commitment was not the only 'USP' policy ('Unique Selling Point') to be derailed by the compromises of coalition, but it was by far the most iconic. Nuclear energy – which the party had, in the words of the interim agreement, 'long opposed' – was another.[69] This time it was Chris Huhne, as Energy Secretary, who introduced a new generation of nuclear power stations in direct repudiation of his own words of only months earlier. By the end of 2010, the party appeared to have divested themselves of the core recognizable policies they championed, and were widely characterized in the media as duplicitous.[70]

So far, so harsh. But fair? Not entirely. The problem the party faced internally which gave birth to the difficulties they would face in coalition was a major disjuncture, present before 2005 but which grew thereafter, between party elites, the wider membership and the electorate. Nick Clegg could quite reasonably (and sincerely) claim the Coalition Agreements as – taken together – a 'good deal' based on the priorities enunciated in the manifesto. In none of those four principal areas – fairer taxation, economic policy, schools and political reform – did any of the 'USP' policies amount to central planks of the document.[71] The USP policies were from an earlier age; the leadership's commitment to them, as shown with the internal debates over fees,

---

[66] D'Ancona, *In It Together*, p. 63.

[67] 'Tuition fees: How Liberal Democrat MPs voted', *BBC News*, 9 December 2010 (accessed at www.bbc.co.uk/news/uk-politics-11964669, 3 October 2014).

[68] Dommett, 'A miserable little compromise', p. 220.

[69] 'Conservative–Liberal Democrat coalition negotiations: Agreements reached', p. 7.

[70] See chapter twenty, this volume.

[71] Liberal Democrats, *Liberal Democrat Manifesto 2010: Change That Works for You* (London: Liberal Democrats, 2010).

was lukewarm in some cases. The problem was that the public – and sections of the party – felt they had been hoodwinked. A key plank of the professionalization thesis offered by Sanderson-Nash and echoed by other commentators, not least the party leader himself, is the apparent 'modernization' of internal party structures and processes.[72] In practice, this meant attempting to reduce the power of conference as the sovereign policymaking body within the party, and attempting to marginalize or reform the Federal Policy Committee and other party bodies which might challenge the leadership's authority in the policy arena. The pre-manifesto of 2009 (*A Fresh Start for Britain*) had been a way of short-circuiting conference by forcing it to a 'take it or leave it' vote on a document which relegated to 'aspirations' many of the key USP policies, notably tuition fees.[73] The legacy of coalition was merely to exacerbate the power of the leadership as bully-pulpit, making policy *de facto* without reference to party structures.[74]

December 2010 was a bad month for the party not merely due to student unrest, but also due to a sting carried out by the *Daily Telegraph* which embarrassed senior figures such as Paul Burstow, Vince Cable and Michael Moore. The *modus operandi* was for *Telegraph* reporters to attend the MPs' constituency surgeries purporting to be constituents and then elicit unguarded statements about sensitive issues which would secretly be recorded. Most significant were Cable's hyperbolic claims that he could bring down the government and that he was at war with Rupert Murdoch. With the ongoing dispute over the media mogul's bid for outright control of BSkyB in Cable's in-tray, this led to a reallocation of responsibilities within Cabinet, but Cable survived the crisis.[75]

Phase two: Searching for definition, 2011–2013

The Liberal Democrats entered 2011 in desperate need of a political 'win' which would legitimate the 'Clegg coup' (in Jasper Gerard's words) of coalition.[76] Constitutional reform, part of Clegg's personal brief as Deputy Prime Minister, was the supposed answer. The referendum on the

---

[72] Evans and Sanderson-Nash, 'Sandals to suits'.   [73] See chapter one, this volume.
[74] Howarth, 'Liberal Democrats and the functions of policy', p. 29.
[75] D'Ancona, *In It Together*, p. 70.   [76] Gerard, *Clegg Coup*.

Alternative Vote was scheduled for May, and was part of a package of measures which the Deputy Prime Minister claimed amounted to the 'biggest shake-up of our democracy since 1832'.[77] Alternative Vote – which Clegg had famously condemned as a 'miserable little compromise' – was not the party's favoured choice of electoral system, which remained Single Transferable Vote, a complex form of proportional representation.[78] As ever, principle remained entangled with politics: STV was the bulwark of the Liberal Democrats' appeal for 'fair votes'. STV by definition offered proportionality – seats allocated in the legislature according to the share of the vote received by the relevant party. PR was not unknown to UK elections; the list system was introduced for European elections in 1999, and STV itself was in use in Northern Ireland for both Northern Irish Assembly elections and the European Parliament, in addition to Scottish local authority elections.[79] It had even been used for Westminster elections in the university constituencies before their abolition in 1950.[80]

It was, however, a bridge too far for coalition and was never seriously considered. It was only following a degree of sleight of hand over what was on offer to the Liberal Democrats from the Labour Party that the Conservatives were won over to the prospect of a binding referendum on electoral reform at all.[81] In this context, it was AV – Clegg's 'miserable little compromise' – which was settled upon. The campaign for AV, run under the banner of Yes to Fairer Votes, was mired in this from the start. 'Fairer votes' was to 'fair votes' what 'safer sex' was to 'safe sex' after the 1980s: put simply, a bit of a let-down. AV did not solve the problem of a lack of proportionality in the electoral system, and in fact targeted a fundamentally different issue – the lack of majority support for an MP in a given constituency.

---

[77] Cited in Mike Finn and Anthony Seldon, 'Constitutional reform since 1997: The historians' view', in Matt Qvortrup (ed.), *The British Constitution: Continuity and Change* (Oxford: Hart, 2013), p. 18.

[78] Andrew Grice, 'I want to push this all the way declares Clegg', *The Independent*, 22 April 2010.

[79] 'Voting systems in the UK', *parliament.uk* (accessed at www.parliament.uk/about/how/elections-and-voting/voting-systems, accessed at 3 October 2014).

[80] Millicent B. Rex, 'The university constituencies in the recent British election', *Journal of Politics*, 8:2 (1946), pp. 201–11.

[81] Rob Wilson, *5 Days to Power: The Journey to Coalition Britain* (London: Biteback, 2010), pp. 218–20.

AV was clearly a system that might benefit the Liberal Democrats electorally, but not one in line with their values and philosophical stance on electoral reform. Yes to Fairer Votes suffered from a lack of clear political leadership, partly because of the toxicity associated with the party who most stood to benefit. The party's poll ratings on the day before the launch were a mere 10 per cent and set to fall still lower.[82] Labour leader Ed Miliband – who personally supported the change, though his party was divided – refused to share a platform with Nick Clegg.[83] D'Ancona recounts that Clegg believed he had an understanding with Cameron that the Conservative Party would stand above the referendum, with Cameron himself in the background.[84] When the Conservatives launched an all-out attack on the proposal in the spring with Cameron in the forefront, Clegg's political naivety was brought into the open.[85]

The vote on 5 May saw the proposal defeated by 67.9 per cent to 32.1.[86] It was a devastating blow for Clegg and the party as a whole. The results of the local elections held on the same day made it a double-whammy; the *Guardian* described the losses as the party's 'worst electoral drubbing in nearly 30 years'.[87] The party had lost over seven hundred councillors, setting a trend which would continue in subsequent local elections.[88] In addition, the party's 2011 returns to the Electoral Commission showed a collapse in membership numbers, with more than 16,000 choosing to quit the party in the first year of coalition – reducing it in size from 65,000 to 49,000.[89] A pattern was set. The numbers would fall still further to 43,000 in 2013; the party had lost over a third of its membership in the first three years of government.[90] However, it was electoral reform – the main strategic *raison d'être* for coalition from

---

[82] YouGov, *Voting Intention*, 1 April 2011 (accessed at http://d25d2506sfb94s.cloudfront.net/today_uk_import/yg-archives-pol-sun-results-310311.pdf, 3 October 2014).

[83] Bowers, *Nick Clegg*, p. 294.   [84] D'Ancona, *In It Together*, pp. 80–5.   [85] *Ibid.*

[86] John Curtice, 'Politicians, voters and democracy: The 2011 UK referendum on the Alternative Vote', *Electoral Studies*, 32 (2013), p. 220.

[87] Hélène Mulholland, 'Lib Dems suffer worst losses in a generation', *The Guardian*, 6 May 2011.

[88] 'Vote 2011: Nick Clegg quit calls after council losses', *BBC News*, 7 May 2011 (accessed at www.bbc.co.uk/news/uk-politics-13303885, 3 October 2014).

[89] Richard Keen, 'Membership of UK political parties' (Parliamentary Standard Note SN/SG/5125, 2014), p. 6.

[90] George Eaton, 'Lib Dem money woes grow as party membership hits new low', *New Statesman*, 25 July 2013.

a Liberal Democrat perspective – which was of the most immediate impact on the party's sense of direction. The central plank of the 'political reform' agenda they had subscribed to, changing the electoral system for Westminster, had been rejected. The second – to complete the unfinished business of Lords reform – followed suit in 2012.[91] Again, principle and politics were entwined. For the Liberal Democrats, it was a *sine qua non* that legislators should be elected; after all, it had been Liberals who took on the Lords in the first place in the battle over the 'People's Budget' after 1909, leading to two general elections in 1910 and the passage of the first Parliament Act in 1911.[92] To say Lords reform was a long-standing Liberal Democrat commitment was thus a claim in no danger of overstatement.

In addition, introducing an element of proportional representation for the upper house might conceivably salvage Liberal Democrat electoral fortunes. It would help to offset any damage done to the party's representation in the Commons in 2015. Clegg's initial proposals for Lords reform were published in the form of a draft Bill and white paper on 17 May 2011, less than a fortnight after the AV defeat and the local election massacre, in an attempt to regain some momentum.[93] The publication of the draft Bill began a saga which would continue into the late summer of 2012. The tone of the foreword was unequivocal:

> In a modern democracy it is important that those who make the laws of the land should be elected by those to whom those laws apply. The House of Lords performs its work well but lacks sufficient democratic authority.[94]

However, the caveats soon crept in. The discussions on the proposed reforms had been mired in difficulty and even by the stage of the draft Bill, full agreement was not possible (as the foreword subsequently acknowledged).[95] The full proposals outlined in the draft Bill were for a partly elected house of 300 Lords, with 240 elected and a residual 60 subject to an appointments process.[96] Members of the new house

---

[91] D'Ancona, *In It Together*, p. 288.

[92] Kenneth O. Morgan, '"Rare and refreshing fruit": Lloyd George's People's Budget', *Public Policy Research*, 16:1 (2009), pp. 28–33.

[93] House of Lords Library, *Library Note: House of Lords Reform Draft Bill* (2011).

[94] HM Government, *House of Lords Reform Draft Bill* (London: HMSO, 2011), p. 5.

[95] *Ibid.*   [96] *Ibid.*, p.7.

would have 'a single non-renewable membership term of three normal election cycles – in practice (given 5 year fixed term Parliaments) that is likely to be 15 years.'[97] Elections in the Commons and Lords were to be held simultaneously, save for the possibility of an early Commons election. Crucially, Clegg ensured the Liberal Democrats' favoured electoral system – STV – was proposed as the electoral system of choice.[98]

Though Cameron's signature was alongside Clegg's at the bottom of the draft bill's foreword, it was clear that this was Clegg's agenda and in many respects the last stand for the Liberal Democrat project of constitutional reform. The Fixed-term Parliaments Bill, which finally became law in September 2011, was nothing like as contentious and was as desirable to the Conservatives (for locking the Liberal Democrats into coalition) as it was to their junior partner.[99] Lords reform was an area where the Liberal Democrats might be able to make some headway on their philosophical obsessions, attain clear differentiation, and score a political victory into the bargain.

Predictably, it was a disaster. The cross-party committee had been unable to achieve agreement before the Bill was put forward for pre-legislative scrutiny and the media, and prominent commentators, were no more kind. During the early stages of debate in the Lords, Lord Tebbit – a conduit for rebellious Tory peers to express themselves to the press – condemned the legislation as a 'dog's dinner'.[100] A Labour peer described the Bill as 'ill-considered legislation', whilst another argued (though not in so many words) that it should be 'kicked into the long grass once again'.[101] *The Guardian* reported that 'the deputy prime minister faced Tory and Labour hostility bordering on contempt in both houses of parliament' and made explicit the link between the defeat of AV and the sudden appearance of the Lords reform Bill.[102]

---

[97] *Ibid.*   [98] *Ibid.*, p. 8.

[99] For the 'traditional' Liberal Democrat position on fixed-term parliaments, see Simon Hughes, 'Democracy: Towards a new constitutional settlement', in Julian Astle, David Laws, Paul Marshall and Alasdair Murray (eds.), *Britain after Blair: A Liberal Agenda* (London: Profile, 2006), p. 272.

[100] Norman Tebbit, 'Nick Clegg's draft House of Lords Reform Bill is an absolute dog's dinner', *Daily Telegraph*, 17 June 2011.

[101] *Ibid.*

[102] Patrick Wintour and Nicholas Watt, 'House of Lords reform: Peers and MPs scorn Nick Clegg's plans', *The Guardian*, 17 May 2011.

Arguably, Clegg had left it too late to be bold; by the 2012–13 parliamentary session, when the Bill was expected to make progress towards the status of law, Cameron had his own problems and supporting his Deputy Prime Minister was not the first thing on his mind. The 'omnishambles' budget of 2012 had put Cameron – and his Chancellor – on the back foot with a range of enemies, not least their own increasingly volatile backbenchers.[103] Expending precious political time and energy arguing for a proposal Cameron was manifestly uninterested in to save the blushes of his junior coalition partner was hardly a serious consideration. The Bill made little progress during the session and when a tactical alliance between the Labour Party and Tory rebels was set fair to scupper it, Clegg bowed to the inevitable in August 2012 and pulled the plug.[104] The Bill was withdrawn from consideration, but not without a spectacular parting shot from Clegg:

> An elected House of Lords was part of the Coalition Agreement: a fundamental part of the contract that keeps the coalition parties working together in the national interest . . . the Conservative party is not honouring the commitment to Lords reform and, as a result, part of our contract has now been broken . . . I cannot permit a situation where Conservative rebels can pick and choose the parts of the contract they like, while Liberal Democrat MPs are bound to the entire agreement . . . So I have told the Prime Minister that when, in due course, parliament votes on boundary changes for the 2015 election I will be instructing my party to oppose them.[105]

Clegg faced a real dilemma: a political defeat of this magnitude, on top of all the previous defeats and this time inflicted directly by members of his own coalition, could not pass unchallenged. However whilst this surely merited a response, the character of the response was highly questionable – as were the moral premises Clegg cited to justify it. What was in fact simply tit-for-tat was dressed up as a point of principle, and it was not in fact true that a commitment to an elected House of Lords was part of the Coalition Agreement, which was Clegg's contention. The best the two parties had been able to manage was one mention in the *Programme for Government* of the establishment of 'a committee to

---

[103] Andrew Gamble, 'Austerity as statecraft', *Parliamentary Affairs* (2014).
[104] D'Ancona, *In It Together*, p. 288.
[105] 'House of Lords reform: Nick Clegg's statement in full', *BBC News*, 6 August 2012 (accessed at www.bbc.co.uk/news/uk-politics-19146853, 23 November 2014).

bring forward proposals for a wholly or mainly elected upper chamber on the basis of proportional representation'.[106] The agreements did not commit the coalition to implementing any such proposals.

Clegg's retaliation was the nuclear option – given current electoral boundaries, the Conservatives were (and now remain) at an unfair disadvantage vis-à-vis the Labour Party, with more votes required to elect a Conservative MP than a Labour one. Removing this anomaly had been part of the agreement to bring forth legislation for the Alternative Vote referendum. Clegg's attempt to link Lords reform with constituency boundaries was therefore nakedly political and not obviously related to the issue presently under discussion. It was also not clear that the Conservatives had, in fact, reneged on a key plank of the Coalition Agreements. Clegg's decision to retaliate was based not simply on the impact of the Lords reform defeat but the cumulative defeats and humiliations the party had faced over the previous two years.

Unfortunately, drawing battle-lines over Lords reform, and sending Liberal Democrat MPs into the opposite division lobby to Conservatives on constituency boundaries, did not resonate with the wider public. Clegg was widely described as 'petulant', and it was ironic that a party which had spent decades campaigning for 'fair votes' was now happy to entrench inequality in the voting system simply as a desperate political tactic. Another significant proposal of the 'political reform' agenda, the recall of MPs accused of wrongdoing, foundered on the question of what such wrongdoing might be. A draft Bill had been published in 2011 but legislative action took place in fits and starts until September 2014, by which point it was increasingly unlikely the latest iteration would ever see the statute book.[107] Even were it to do so, it only made provision for recall – the triggering of an election to recall a named MP – if the MP was convicted of an offence or suspended from the House for more than twenty-one days (later amended to ten sitting days), effectively leaving the power to recall in the hands of Parliament itself.[108] It was years late, was effectively neutered by the restrictions within it, and did not assuage either the public or those in Parliament (such as Conservative backbencher Douglas Carswell, who in August 2014 defected to the UK Independence Party, or Zac Goldsmith, who

---

[106] *Programme for Government*, p. 27.
[107] *Recall of MPs Bill*, House of Commons Bill 94 [2014–2015].   [108] *Ibid.*, p. 1.

introduced his own Bill[109]) who sought more direct accountability of politicians to their constituents. Finally, the shared commitment of both the Liberal Democrats and the Conservatives to a bill of rights mean-while translated itself into a Liberal Democrat commitment to preserve the Human Rights Act and a Tory one to repeal it.[110] Despite the establishment of another, fractious cross-party committee, no progress was made before 2015. The 'biggest shake-up' of the constitution 'since 1832' amounted to almost nothing.[111]

The civil liberties agenda – once intimately related to consti-tutional reform in Liberal Democrat thinking – was also in disarray. Despite the repeal of identity cards (which had already been signifi-cantly scaled back before Labour left office and which Labour had been prepared to scrap in coalition negotiations with the Liberal Demo-crats[112]), the party found itself increasingly erring in favour of security over liberty during its tenure in office. Despite clear success in vetoing the mooted 'snoopers' charter' – the Data and Communications Bill that gave legal cover to the security services to do what Edward Snowden later revealed they were doing anyway[113] – discontent culminated internally in a major dispute over the leadership's support for the Justice and Security Bill during 2012–13. Led by Jo Shaw, a party activist and prospective parliamentary candidate (PPC), accompanied by other prominent figures including Dinah Rose QC and Philippe Sands QC, a grass-roots campaign – Lib Dems Against Secret Courts – sought to force the leadership to withdraw its backing for the provisions of the Bill which implemented 'closed material procedures' – so-called 'secret courts' – where defendants would not know the nature of the evidence against themselves.[114] The campaign won two floor votes on motions opposed to the proposal decisively at successive party conferences, but the will of conference was simply ignored by the parliamentary party. Shaw, Sands and Rose all resigned – Shaw at the end of her conference

[109] *Recall of Elected Representatives Bill*, House of Commons Bill 88 [2014–2015].

[110] Robert Hazell, 'Case study I: Constitutional reform', in Hazell and Yong, *Politics of Coalition*, pp. 167–9.

[111] Finn and Seldon, 'Constitutional reform', p. 18.

[112] Andrew Adonis, *5 Days in May* (London: Biteback, 2012), p. 49.

[113] Luke Harding, *The Snowden Files: The Inside Story of the World's Most Wanted Man* (London: Guardian Books, 2014).

[114] The campaign website is available at www.libdemsagainstsecretcourts.org.uk (accessed 3 October 2014).

speech – at the Spring Conference in 2013 following their success in the second vote.[115] The result was in effect the same as had been the case with conference votes on NHS reform, a case where (as Howarth pithily notes) the leadership simply 'carried on regardless'.[116]

Phase three: Endgame, 2014–2015

As pressure grew within the party to differentiate itself from the Conservatives, Clegg's conference speeches and public statements began to focus on Tory policies the Liberal Democrats had blocked. This defined the party's contribution to coalition in negative terms. As Clegg put it in his 2013 conference speech, 'sometimes compromise and agreement isn't possible, and you just have to say no'.[117] This marked a clear acceleration of the party's plans for differentiation, which were originally scheduled to begin only in 2015. By the midway point of the coalition, there was a clear sense that this might be too late. When in May 2014 serial rebel Lord Oakeshott attempted to launch a coup on behalf of his ally Vince Cable, its abject failure reflected both Oakeshott's lack of real influence in the parliamentary party and a sense of fatalism.[118] It was not clear that Cable, who had sponsored the tuition fees U-turn, would (notwithstanding Oakeshott's private polling) prove a winning leader, nor had any other credible candidate emerged. Tim Farron, often heralded as a tribune of the left in the party, had been elected as Party President in 2010 ostensibly to hold Liberal Democrats in government to account, but despite his increased profile in the media it was not clear that Farron was either credible or prepared to advance an alternative. That there was in the end no challenge to Clegg in the period between 2010 and 2015 reflects the effective emasculation of the parliamentary party and a lack of real alternatives, rather than a seal of approval on the road the leadership took.

[115] Patrick Wintour, 'Lib Dems quit over leadership's "betrayal" on secret courts', *The Guardian*, 10 March 2013.

[116] Howarth, 'Liberal Democrats and the functions of policy', p. 21.

[117] Nicholas Watt, 'Nick Clegg boasts of blocking 16 Tory policies in "tooth and nail" fight', *The Guardian*, 18 September 2013.

[118] Oliver Wright and Nigel Morris, 'Botched coup against Nick Clegg: Vince Cable ally Lord Oakeshott accused of "serious disloyalty"', *The Independent*, 27 May 2014.

By spring 2014, Clegg was definitively in the risk business; as Labour considered 'core vote plus' as a possible electoral strategy, the Liberal Democrat leadership was concerned purely about survival. Europe – traditionally seen as a weakness for the party with the electorate – thus became an opportunity. As the most pro-European mainstream party in British politics, the Liberal Democrats had failed in government to articulate a coherent or convincing case for continued membership of the European Union. With the Prime Minister effectively held hostage by his right, this was a nettle that Clegg grasped in the build-up to the European elections in 2014 by agreeing to face the UKIP leader Nigel Farage in televised debates.[119] Clegg's apparent defeat in the debates reflected a number of truths – the distance travelled since he himself had been an insurgent 'outsider' like Farage, and consequently the damage done to the pro-European case by his apparent assimilation into the 'political class'.[120] Attacking Europe became another way of attacking Westminster; Liberal Democrat participation in coalition and the consequent betrayal of their 'values' had rendered this an open goal for Farage which the UKIP leader proved unable to miss.

Clegg's intention in participating in the debates was to remind Liberal Democrat voters concerned about UKIP why they had voted for the party in the past, but the effect was another humiliation; by this stage (and in truth far earlier) the leadership had long lost control of the party's narrative in the public sphere. Attempts to regain the initiative at the last autumn conference before the election – by turning fire on the Conservatives' record on welfare – drew charges of hypocrisy, as in most cases the Liberal Democrats had voted for the measures themselves.[121] By the time of the significant events of the early stages of the 2014–15 session, with Cameron taking on the role of war leader and gaining parliamentary approval for intervention in Iraq, the Liberal Democrats in coalition had completed a transition from a public perception of treachery in 2010–11 to one of irrelevance, as they stagnated

[119] Peter Dominiczak, 'Nigel Farage agrees to EU debate with Nick Clegg', *Daily Telegraph*, 21 February 2014.
[120] Patrick Wintour, Nicholas Watt and Rowena Mason, 'Farage v Clegg: Ukip leader triumphs in second televised debate', *The Guardian*, 3 April 2014.
[121] Jane Merrick, 'Lib Dem conference: Labour gets personal with new slogan "You Can't Trust Nick Clegg"', *Independent on Sunday*, 5 October 2014.

in the polls eight to twelve percentage points behind UKIP, fighting with the Greens for fourth place.[122]

The emergence of UKIP represented an existential challenge to the values of political liberalism in Britain, though perhaps not to the Liberal Democrats themselves. Though much attention has focused on the impact of UKIP on the right, and increasingly focus is shifting to UKIP's relationship to former Labour voters, the Liberal Democrat 'connection' is worth discussing.[123] In part, the Liberal Democrats created political space for UKIP with their entry into government, depriving the electorate of a centre-left protest party and replacing it with one of the right. However, though there is some evidence of transfer of votes from the Liberal Democrats to UKIP, the most significant role the Liberal Democrats can be said to have played in the rise of UKIP is less to do with the direct movement of votes and more to do with the damage the 'values party' has done to the credibility both of their issues and of the political system generally through their participation in government.

UKIP's rise, demonstrated unequivocally following the debates by that party's clear victory in the European elections, nonetheless presented a perverse opportunity for the Liberal Democrats. Although they themselves had been annihilated in the 2014 European Parliament elections, reduced to just one MEP, the growing presence of a 'UKIP constituency' across the country, and in particular in Liberal Democrat–Conservative marginals, meant the Liberal Democrats might just hang on to more seats in the Commons in the 2015 general election than they had bargained for.[124] This had been a purported lesson of the Eastleigh by-election success which had followed Chris Huhne's conviction.[125] Polling released by Lord Ashcroft during the final Conservative Party conference showed that Conservative votes lost to UKIP in marginals where the Liberal Democrats were incumbents might be enough to see some Liberal Democrat MPs – just – home, notably in Cheadle,

---

[122] 'YouGov Tory lead and Survation Heywood and Middleton Poll', *UK Polling Report*, 2 October 2014 (accessed at http://ukpollingreport.co.uk/blog/archives/9016, 3 October 2014).

[123] Robert Ford and Matthew Goodwin, *Revolt on the Right: Explaining Support for the Radical Right in Britain* (London: Routledge, 2014).

[124] Oliver Wright, 'With Ukip stealing vital Tory votes, Lib Dems reassess 2015 election strategy to target marginal seats', *Independent on Sunday*, 10 March 2013.

[125] *Ibid.*

Eastbourne and St Ives.[126] Ironically, whilst the Liberal Democrats had created rhetorical space for UKIP, and whilst UKIP posed a direct threat to their issues, a UKIP surge might yet ensure greater residual Liberal Democrat Westminster representation than might otherwise have proved possible.

Conclusions

The role of the Liberal Democrats within coalition and the impact of the coalition on the Liberal Democrats is necessarily a dialectical relationship. The impact of coalition on the Liberal Democrats has been profound, most notably in quantitative terms. By 2015, there were simply far fewer of them – in terms of voters, party members, councillors, members of the European Parliament and members of devolved assemblies. The dramatic fall in Liberal Democrat support in every area outside the green benches of the House of Commons, a consistent pattern through the life of the parliament, represented the sword of Damocles scheduled to finally fall on the party's MPs (thanks to the Fixed-term Parliaments Act) on 7 May 2015. By 2015, the Liberal Democrats had only one MEP. In Scotland, where they had been in coalition government as recently as 2007 and which was a significant party stronghold at Westminster level, they were reduced to five MSPs. In large areas of the country, they had almost ceased to exist as a political force. In Liverpool, where the Liberal Democrats had run the council for twelve years from the late 1990s, the party was annihilated. In 2003, they had 63 councillors to Labour's 31; Liverpool, with its successful European Capital of Culture bid and subsequent year in the sun in 2008, was one of the party's flagship achievements in local government, a Labour parliamentary heartland turned uniformly yellow at local level and regularly mentioned in party leaders' speeches. By 2015, only three Liberal Democrat councillors remained to face election, awaiting the inevitable. Perhaps most critically, the collapse in Liberal Democrat support leaves open the real possibility that they

---

[126] Lord Ashcroft, *General Election 2015 Constituency Polling Report: Wider Liberal Democrat Battleground September 2014* (accessed at http://lordashcroftpolls/wp-content/uploads/2014/09/LORD-ASHCROFT-POLLS-Wider-Lib-Dem-battleground-September 2014.pdf, 29 September 2014).

will not have a single female member of the House of Commons following the 2015 General Election.[127]

The party did not reap the benefit of 'credibility' which the leadership felt they might gain through participation in coalition. Surveys recorded that voters felt the Liberal Democrats were the least competent of the three main parliamentary parties,[128] and policy defeat after policy defeat left the party articulating a negative message that they had been able to 'restrain' the Conservatives. Many of their former supporters felt their very presence in coalition had 'enabled' the Conservatives in the first place, and were thus unconvinced. In the party's defence, health reform would have gone much further had it not been for Liberal Democrat opposition,[129] notably in the House of Lords, and the Gove revolution in schools, though real, was still influenced by Liberal Democrat choices on free school meals and, substantively, the introduction of the pupil premium.[130] Nonetheless, the party struggled in the 'credit-claiming' aspect of coalition;[131] real policy 'wins' such as the raising of the tax threshold were overshadowed by purported 'betrayals' such as the VAT rise.

In terms of post-coalition prospects, a return to traditional Liberal Democrat community campaigning is, in the short run, the best option to salvage parliamentary representation for a cause which at national level is – for the moment – seriously tarnished. As Craig Johnson has recently noted, the Liberal Democrats have long placed faith (sometimes wrongly) in the strength of local parties and local organization in the election of their MPs.[132] However, where the Liberal Democrats retain local strength and an infrastructure to campaign,

---

[127] Mark Pack, *Liberal Democrat Newswire* 52, 29 September 2014.

[128] YouGov, *Voting Intention and National Issues*, 23 July 2014 (accessed at http://d25d2506sfb94s.cloudfront.net/cumulus_uploads/document/7tva44wn7w/YG-Archives-Pol-Sun-results-230712.pdf, 7 October, 2014).

[129] Waller and Yong, 'Case studies II', pp. 176–84.

[130] Although even the pupil premium came under attack from one of its creators, former Director of Policy Richard Grayson, who argued that the original pupil premium concept had been intended to introduce extra money into the system, not replace money which had been cut elsewhere: Richard Grayson, 'Why I am not renewing my Liberal Democrat membership', *Compass Online*, 7 July 2013.

[131] Isabel Hardman, 'The Lib Dems must start to claim credit for the coalition's economic successes', *Spectator Coffee House*, 3 June 2014.

[132] Craig Johnson, 'The importance of local parties and incumbency to the electoral prospects of the Liberal Democrats', *Politics*, 34:3 (2014), pp. 201–12.

their community politics focus and incumbency bounce may be enough to hold on to more seats than might otherwise be considered feasible.

To pose a complex series of counterfactuals, had the Liberal Democrats come to an agreement with Labour rather than the Conservatives in 2010 they would still have suffered amongst their right-leaning supporters, but assuming Russell and Fieldhouse's profiles of Liberal Democrat voters are accurate,[133] this would have been less severe than the impact of coalition with the Conservatives. If the Liberal Democrats had decided to agree a confidence-and-supply arrangement – where they would support the Conservatives on votes of confidence and financial bills only – then they might have been damned by the electorate for eschewing the opportunity of power. Had the Liberal Democrats simply stayed out, and allowed the Conservatives to govern in a minority, a second election would likely have taken place in the near future which the party simply could not fight due to financial exhaustion. In any case, Conservative minority government combined with a loss of seats for the Liberal Democrats might have provided the opportunity for a challenge to Clegg's leadership. Thus future historians must bear in mind that Nick Clegg and his team – whatever the legacy of the 2010–15 coalition government – faced an unpalatable series of choices in 2010. As with most political decisions, there was no unequivocally 'right' answer. The biggest problem Clegg faced, at least in part of his own making, was that the coalition of minorities which the Liberal Democrats represented was close to breaking point in 2010 and was arguably 'tested to destruction' in office.[134] In Grayson's words, under Clegg the party had become 'a party of the centre-left led by the centre-right'.[135] Such a coalition – both in the electorate and within the party membership – could not survive the exigencies of office with an unambiguously centre-right senior partner. This was above and beyond the historical truth that Liberal–Conservative coalitions in UK politics traditionally ended badly for the Liberals.

Strategic and tactical mistakes were made on arrival in office: the attempt to turn the Deputy Prime Minister's role into something

---

[133] See chapter one, this volume.
[134] Mike Finn, 'Tested to destruction? Ideology and the Liberal Democrats in office' (*forthcoming*) and Mike Finn, 'The coalition and the Liberal Democrats: The radical centre in action?', paper presented at the Political Studies Association 'Rebels and radicals' conference, April 2014.
[135] Grayson, 'Why I am not renewing my Liberal Democrat membership'.

approaching a co-premiership – notwithstanding Clegg's real and undoubted influence in government – was a vainglorious one. It would have been better had the party staked out clear terrain in government so it could distinguish itself from the beginning, especially in terms of departmental politics. The kind of coalition envisaged by Clegg was not the kind of coalition that could be sold to the public at large. The quest to prove that 'coalition works' above all else and the subordination of Liberal Democrat identity to that purpose was fatal to a party that David Howarth has accurately characterized as a party of values, not interest. Howarth's assessment correlates with Russell and Fieldhouse's view that there is no true 'core vote' for the Liberal Democrats, merely those attracted by their values.[136] Those values, represented by the 'USP' policies of free higher education, anti-nuclear energy and nuclear weapons, pro-civil liberties, were all called into question on entry into office.

The Liberal Democrats did play a significant role in government. Notably, Danny Alexander, as chief secretary to the Treasury, helped design and deliver austerity. They did see policies such as the raising of the tax threshold and the pupil premium enacted. And historically, the Liberal Party and its successors have proved difficult to extinguish completely. Nick Clegg's fear is unfounded – he will not be the last leader of the Liberal Democrats; the array of leadership candidates touting for business for a prospective post-election contest during the 2014 autumn conference paid adequate testament to that.[137] However, it is a fair assessment that the Liberal Democrats' effect on the coalition (other than in facilitating its existence) was undeniably less profound than the coalition's devastating effect on the Liberal Democrats.

---

[136] Howarth, 'Liberal Democrats and the functions of policy'.
[137] Ned Simons, 'The Lib Dem leadership race isn't even subtle anymore', *Huffington Post UK*, 7 October 2014.

19 THE COALITION AND THE LABOUR PARTY

GUY LODGE AND ILLIAS THOMS

Introduction

Ed Miliband believed that the global financial crash provided an opportunity for a 'progressive moment' in British politics, to rival the generational shifts that took place in 1906, 1945 and 1979. The crisis and the deep recession it precipitated, he argued, undermined the core economic orthodoxy of the last thirty years that self-regulated market economies can be relied upon to deliver prosperity for the nation as a whole. His solution was a more 'responsible capitalism'[1] – a rewiring of Britain's political economy with growth directed at boosting the living standards of the majority, not lining the pockets of a privileged elite. It was a highly ambitious agenda, both economically and politically, but one which, he believed, chimed with the times of twenty-first-century Britain.

Whether or not it actually did is open to debate. What is beyond doubt, however, is that during five years of opposition to a largely unpopular coalition government, Ed Miliband struggled to convince the British electorate that the Labour Party was the appropriate agent to bring about this far-reaching change. The double-digit lead Labour had over the Conservatives started to melt away in the final stages of the

[1] 'Responsible capitalism' expressed in numerous speeches including Ed Miliband's speech at Google's Big Tent event on 22 May 2013 (accessed at www.theguardian.com/commentisfree/2013/may/22/google-corporate-responsibility-ed-miliband-speech, 4 December 2014).

parliament, with most experts anticipating a very tight race and the almost guarantee of another hung parliament.[2] Partly, this is because Labour did not do enough to persuade sufficient numbers of voters it was ready to govern again – in particular, the party was not trusted to run the economy.[3] Moreover, Labour misjudged the public mood: anger over the financial crisis did not manifest itself in support for the conventional centre-left party but was instead channelled into rising support for populist parties – UKIP in England and the SNP in Scotland – who capitalized on the widespread sense of disaffection with the political mainstream at large. Consequently, it is far more likely that the government elected in 2015 will look and feel more like the fragile and ultimately politically weak Wilson/Callaghan governments of the 1970s, with the real prospect of Labour or the Conservatives ruling as a minority government,[4] than the transformational premierships of Attlee and Thatcher. As the 2015 election approached it became clear that whilst Labour could win, they could not do so convincingly; if victory was to come, it would do so with the party crawling over the finishing line, aided and abetted by the distortions of the first-past-the-post electoral system and the haemorrhaging of the Tory vote to UKIP.[5] If British politics is to be refashioned, as it surely must, it may well fall not to David Cameron or Ed Miliband, the politicians of the interlude, but to the next generation.

The story of Labour under the Coalition is one of anaemic recovery from its catastrophic electoral position in 2010, when it secured just 29 per cent of the vote, its second worst result since 1918. While its revival over the course of the parliament enabled it to compete for power in 2015, in the end, this arguably had less to do with the efforts of the Labour leadership and more to do with the political circumstances of the time. Most obviously, Labour's improvement on

---

[2] John Curtice, 'World in motion: How globalisation is reshaping the party system', *Juncture*, 12:3 (2014), pp. 201–14.

[3] Tom Clark, 'Voters trust Cameron-Osborne most with the economy, poll finds', *The Guardian*, 6 October 2014.

[4] The Wilson/Callaghan governments had to cope first as a minority government, then surviving with a wafer-thin majority which was subsequently lost, prompting Callaghan to organize a pact with the Liberals. See Anatole Kaletsky, 'Why Britain's days as a haven of political, economic stability are numbered', *Reuters*, 21 November 2014 (accessed at http://blogs.reuters.com/anatole-kaletsky/2014/11/21/britain-may-turn-into-europes-most-politically-unpredictable-country, 5 December 2014).

[5] See chapter twenty-one, this volume.

its 2010 result was based almost entirely on the transfer to Labour of disaffected former Liberal Democrat voters who felt betrayed by the party's decision to enter into a coalition with the Conservatives.[6] True, these left-leaning voters felt sufficiently reassured by Miliband's efforts to jettison the more divisive elements of the New Labour years to convert to the Labour cause; Miliband had made a direct appeal to former Liberal Democrats during his leadership election bid.[7] And more significantly, without the degree of party unity achieved by Miliband during these years, a relatively impressive accomplishment for a party with a history of endemic factionalism, Labour would not have been taken seriously as a credible alternative party of government. Nevertheless, the basic fact remains that a significant number of these former Liberal Democrat voters became Labour almost by default (a clear sign of a coalition *effect*). Labour's failure to extend its electoral appeal beyond a precarious alliance of this group and its heartlands (what critics dubbed 'the 35 per cent strategy') is striking: indeed, once the Liberal Democrat 'bonus' is discounted it is possible that Labour's core vote across the parliament may have fallen below the nadir of 2010 (a clear sign of both UKIP's incursion into Labour's traditional blue-collar base and the profound naivety of not trying to reach out to other parts of the electorate).[8] As its poll lead across the parliament shrivelled, so the lofty rhetoric of building 'One Nation Labour' was quietly dropped from the party's narrative.[9]

This chapter explores the different factors that help explain why Labour's progress during 2010–15 was so limited. Inevitably it focuses on the leadership of Ed Miliband, the central figure in the story. Tellingly for the son of an academic, it is a story where actions needed to speak louder than words. In broad terms Miliband realized from early on the path that Labour would need to tread if it was to renew itself, but for a

---

[6] The Liberal Democrats received 23 per cent of the vote in the 2010 general election. Lord Ashcroft said that the Lib Dems would lose 71 per cent of their 2010 voters, and of those 71 per cent, 29 per cent would vote Labour or Green (http://lordashcroftpolls.com/2013/03/what-are-the-liberal-democrats-for, accessed 4 December 2014).

[7] Ed Miliband, 'Dear Lib Dem voter', *The Guardian*, 23 August 2010.

[8] 'The Lib Dems have lost 7 in 10 of their voters. Where have they gone?', *New Statesman*, 3 November 2014.

[9] 'One nation' was mentioned forty-six times in Miliband's Manchester conference speech of 2012, but only 6 times in his 2013 Brighton speech (www.psa.ac.uk/insight-plus/blog/ed-miliband's-conference-speech-should-be-understood-part-narrative-reorientation, accessed 4 December 2014).

variety of reasons he failed to put in place the measures needed to revitalize the Labour cause. In short, Miliband began to articulate a credible post-crash reform agenda for social democracy, but he failed to convert this into a political *project* around which he could mobilize the country.

Inheritance and context

Historical assessments of Labour under Miliband have to start with an appreciation of the state of the party he inherited and the prevailing political and economic circumstances at the time. The picture is, unsurprisingly, quite mixed.

In electoral terms the scale and nature of Labour's defeat in the 2010 general election undoubtedly put them firmly on the back foot. The 29 per cent share of the vote not only marked fatigue with the Labour Party, but also completed the reversal of the inroads into 'middle England' it had first made during New Labour's landslide in 1997.[10] Between 1997 and 2010 Labour lost nearly five million votes, with its share of the vote declining across three successive general elections (2001, 2005 and 2010).[11] Labour found itself pinned back into its heartlands in the north of England, Scotland and Wales. Another fortress was inner London, but across the rest of the south of England, Labour was all but annihilated (it held 12 seats out of a possible 210).[12] The Labour vote was reduced to its core; however, there were worrying signs that its support among its base was fragile too. IPSOS Mori noted a big swing to the Conservatives from Labour among poorer voters (so-called C2DEs).[13] Perhaps the biggest challenge facing Labour was the toll the election took on its reputation. In their authoritative study, Kavanagh and Cowley show how the 2010 election revealed that many voters believed that Labour were more interested in helping immigrants and those on welfare benefits than 'hard-working families'.[14] This was all a far cry from Tony Blair's desire that Labour become the party of the aspirational classes.

[10] In 1997 Labour won 418 seats and 43.2 per cent of the vote. In 2010 it was reduced to 258 seats on 29 per cent of the vote.

[11] Dennis Kavanagh and Philip Cowley, *The British General Election of 2010* (London: Palgrave, 2010), p. 340.

[12] http://news.bbc.co.uk/1/shared/election2010/results/.

[13] Kavanagh and Cowley, *British General Election of 2010*, p. 340.   [14] *Ibid.*, p. 341.

Miliband's inheritance was also tarnished by the reputation of the much-derided Brown government, which suffered the humiliation of being in power when the economy went into freefall. Despite his immense contribution to saving the banking system during the 2008–9 global financial crisis, Brown could not escape the blame for the major recession that followed in its wake, especially given his hubristic claim to have ended 'boom and bust'.[15] As output collapsed and Britain's deficit soared, Brown's reluctance, in particular, to talk about how public spending could be brought under control did his and Labour's reputation irreparable damage.[16] Late in the day Alistair Darling set out a plan to halve the deficit across the parliament, but by then it was too late to reverse the collapse in public confidence. Labour was once again confronted by the blunt political truth that it is much easier to lose reputations for economic competence than to gain them.[17] The situation was made all the more perilous in the first few months of the coalition, as the Conservatives and Liberal Democrats mounted a coordinated and devastating attack on Labour's economic record. While the Labour Party was busy inwardly focusing on choosing its new leader, through an epic four-month-long campaign, the coalition partners were able to travel around the country tirelessly repeating the mantra that they were a government formed in the 'national interest' to fix 'the economic mess the Labour Party left us in'.[18] The failure of the Labour Party to respond adequately to these highly effective assaults left them exposed on an issue that would help define the next five years of British political life.

Three factors were regularly identified in the post-election analysis for why Labour took such a drubbing: the unpopularity of Gordon Brown; being blamed for crashing the economy; and perceived failures to address immigration, which was becoming an increasingly salient issue in British politics, and one on which Labour looked out

---

[15] Gordon Brown, Pre-Budget Report, 9 November 1999: 'Under this Government, Britain will not return to the boom and bust of the past.'

[16] Anthony Seldon and Guy Lodge, *Brown at 10* (London: Biteback, 2010): see introduction and epilogue.

[17] Previous examples of Labour's economic credentials being damaged include devaluation in 1967 and the 'winter of discontent' from 1978.

[18] This phrase was frequently quoted by figures within the government, including the Prime Minister.

of touch (epitomized during the campaign by Gordon Brown calling Mrs Duffy a bigot).[19] More generally there was the basic fact that after thirteen long years in power, the country had become bored and disillusioned with Labour. The many achievements of the 1997–2010 era had faded from view: instead the lingering memories of the Labour government were of unedifying factionalism and the bitter civil war waged between the Blairites and Brownites, economic catastrophe and the long shadow cast by Iraq. Early on, the most significant challenge Ed Miliband faced was to get his party listened to again, which was particularly difficult given that all eyes were focused firmly on the novelty of Britain's first peacetime coalition since the 1930s.

History suggests that it takes time for a party recently rejected from office to get a hearing from the public. This perhaps explains why so few parties return to office after one term out of power: only once since 1945 has a party achieved this feat, Harold Wilson in February 1974, and then only as a minority government.[20] We have to go back ninety years, to 1924 and the fall of the first Labour government, and thus fairly exceptional circumstances, to find the last time a party – Stanley Baldwin's Conservatives – returned to office with a majority after one stint in opposition.[21] The path back to power can be especially challenging for parties that experience a long spell in government: this was the case for the Conservatives following the Thatcher/Major years, where the party lost three consecutive elections. Wilson's one-term interregnum came on the back of just six years in Downing Street (1964–70); Ed Miliband, by contrast, was attempting to catapult Labour

---

[19] See Kavanagh and Cowley, *The British General Election of 2010*; Dominic Wring, Roger Mortimore and Simon Atkinson (eds.), *Political Communication in Britain: The Leader Debates, the Campaign and the Media in the 2010 General Election* (London: Palgrave Macmillan, 2011). See also G. Evans and K. Chzen, 'Explaining voters' defection from Labour over the 2005–10 electoral cycle: Leadership, economics and the rising importance of immigration', *Political Studies*, 61(Suppl. S1) (2013), who argue that immigration best explains why people were reluctant to vote Labour.

[20] Wilson held another election in October 1974, when he managed to secure a wafer-thin majority of three seats. See Ben Pimlott, *Harold Wilson* (London: HarperCollins, 1992).

[21] Looked at from the point of view of the governing party, then, the corresponding explanation for why they tend to win a second term (of some sort) is the advantage of incumbency. Only Heath failed to secure a second term in the post-war period.

back to power following more than a decade in office and to do so on the back of Labour's abysmal electoral performance.

The very fact that Labour was even able to challenge for power might seem impressive when judged against these historic parallels. Yet in other important respects the contemporary political and economic conditions in 2010–15 favoured the left. The deepest recession since the 1930s created an opportunity for Labour to be the party of choice for the large swathes of the country caught in the trap of falling living standards and rising economic insecurity. In electoral terms, as noted above, Labour benefited almost immediately from the transfer of a large number of Liberal Democrat voters who felt betrayed by their party's decision to enter into a coalition with the Conservatives (especially after the party did its infamous U-turn on university tuition fees).[22] The psephologist John Curtice estimates that this boosted Labour's poll rating by around seven points, which almost wholly accounts for the advance Labour made from 2010.[23]

Nor did Labour have to compete against a formidable Tory opponent. Indeed for much of the parliament the Tory party looked as if it was ungovernable, characterized as it was by splits and defections. Miliband's critics would lament his failure to land more blows against such a dysfunctional governing party. In stark contrast Labour remained relatively united. Whatever else might be said about Ed Miliband's leadership, history will record that he bucked Labour's pathological tendency for civil war. The famously fissiparous party split badly on falling from power in 1931, 1951 and 1979, leaving it stranded on the opposition benches for nine, thirteen and eighteen years respectively. Of course there were divisions on strategic direction – most significantly over the direction of economic policy, with Ed Balls reluctant to embrace the Miliband agenda (discussed below) – and on big policy decisions and tactics (examples of the former include the decision over whether to back an in-or-out referendum on Europe and examples of the latter included whether or not to come out so strongly against the Murdoch press after the Hackgate affair), but on the whole the party pointed in the same direction. There were no significant ideological differences to rival the battles of the 1980s. Nor were there the factional and personal splits that so disfigured the Blair–Brown years.

---

[22] See chapter 18, this volume.   [23] Curtice, 'World in motion'.

Critics would, however, argue that party unity came at the expense of strategic political positioning, especially on the deficit.

The prevailing economic and political conditions, in other words, provided an opportunity for Labour's revival. Against this favourable background, even the claim of achieving party unity, can be questioned. It would take skill not to be able to unite the left in the face of falling living standards and George Osborne's austerity programme. Besides, Miliband did not have to contend with the pressures that Neil Kinnock faced in the 1980s – with Militant on his left flank, and the SDP assault coming from the right. And of course Miliband benefited from the disunity on the right, marked by the surge in support for UKIP.

However, while the UKIP threat initially appeared of greatest immediate significance to the Conservatives (no less than seven in ten of 2010 Tory voters who defected went to UKIP), as the parliament progressed it became clearer that UKIP also posed a serious threat to the Labour Party. UKIP's hard line on immigration and its message of a Westminster elite out of touch with the country as a whole resonated with traditional Labour voters; the cultural politics of the contemporary British working class erupted during the Rochester and Strood by-election, when then Shadow Attorney General Emily Thornberry was sacked by Miliband for tweeting a picture apparently mocking a home bedecked with English flags.[24] Miliband's overreaction to Thornberry's tweet highlighted the extent to which the success of UKIP against Labour had rattled the leader's cage, notably with Farage's party nearly capturing Heywood and Middleton near Manchester in another by-election despite having few resources available to campaign. UKIP also made significant council gains in Labour constituencies, most notably in Rotherham, and began to target Labour seats as well as Tory ones. The longer-term danger to Labour from UKIP – mobilizing those voters in hitherto safe seats who felt 'left behind' by the politics of Blairism and 'triangulation' – represented a significant challenge to the party's electoral interests.

Less conspicuously, Labour also began to lose votes to the Greens, an anti-austerity party who styled themselves as the authentic voice on the left, and who benefited from Labour's increasingly tough

---

[24] Rowena Mason, 'Emily Thornberry resigns from shadow cabinet over Rochester tweet', *The Guardian*, 20 November 2014.

rhetoric on immigration in 2014.[25] In a very tight race, the lift in the Green vote, if sustained, could hurt Labour. However, a far more fundamental challenge to Labour's electoral prospects emerged in Scotland.

Despite the victory for unionism in the Scottish independence referendum in September 2014, the campaign revealed the depths of Labour's problems north of the border, particularly among its working-class base. Organizationally the party was in disarray, but more profoundly it didn't appear to have a vision for Scotland in a devolved union. It was heavily divided over extending powers for Holyrood, whereas public opinion overwhelmingly backed the case for a stronger Scottish Parliament. Many in Labour's ranks resented the idea of giving the nationalists a 'consolation prize', and moreover feared that further powers would open up the Pandora's box of the West Lothian question, and the possibility of restricting the voting rights of Labour's Scottish contingency at Westminster. The net result was that Labour appeared to be putting party interest ahead of national interest – never a sensible move.[26] Into the mix went the charge by the SNP that Labour were part of a Westminster elite for whom Scotland was only an afterthought. Not long after the referendum, Labour's polling in Scotland went into free-fall: an Ipsos MORI poll put the SNP on 52 per cent with the Labour party only on 23 per cent, its lowest level since 2007, and a lead that would hand the nationalists the majority of Scotland's 59 seats.[27] The prospects of an electoral earthquake in Scotland provoked the resignation of its leader, Johann Lamont. As Labour nosedived, the SNP's membership tripled to more than 80,000.[28] The key result of this new electoral geography in Scotland was that the SNP's inroads into Labour territory in Scotland had much the same effect as UKIP's inroads into

---

[25] Green Party membership grew throughout the 2010–15 parliament, and by a staggering 45 per cent in 2014 alone (http://greenparty.org.uk/news/2014/10/03/green-surge-membership-of-the-green-party-up-45-in-2014-alone, accessed 4 December 2014).

[26] Labour produced the weakest package of additional powers among the unionist parties in the run-up to the referendum. In the end, a more substantial offer was made through the Smith Commission and in February 2015, Jim Murphy and Gordon Brown promised even greater powers, particularly over welfare in Scotland.

[27] Ipsos MORI, 'SNP open up significant lead ahead of general election vote', 30 October 2014 (accessed at www.ipsos-mori.com/researchpublications/researcharchive/3469/SNP-open-up-significant-lead-ahead-of-General-Election-vote.aspx, 4 December 2014).

[28] 'Labour faces losing up to 20 seats in Scotland as SNP support surges', *The Guardian*, 3 November 2014.

Conservative territory in England, rendering majority rule for both major parties of British politics much harder to achieve.

Miliband faced the prospect of a General Election in 2015 under attack from nationalists in England and Scotland, both of whom were making populist overtures to his core voters. These difficulties were not confined to the UK – all mainstream parties across Europe faced similar pressures from populist movements. Nonetheless, and notwithstanding Miliband's ephemeral success with the 'cost of living crisis', Labour seemed unable to form a strategy over how best to respond to incursions into its vote.

Miliband vs Miliband

There may have been five candidates for the Labour leadership contest but it was always going to be a battle between the two Miliband brothers.[29] David, the elder and more experienced (he was Foreign Secretary in the Brown premiership and had co-authored the 1997 party manifesto), was the clear favourite. The chink in his armour was that he was perceived to be the Blairite candidate, which made him vulnerable in the union section of the electoral college.[30] Ed exploited this by putting clear red water between himself and the divisive parts of the New Labour legacy, hence his vocal opposition to tuition fees and the Iraq war.[31] By distancing himself from Labour's past he hoped to project himself as the candidate for the future. Indeed his aides argue that Ed's main motivation for standing against his brother, with all the family tension this doubtlessly generated, was because of his clear belief that he was best placed to oversee a period of substantial revisionism which he believed was necessary for the party to rebuild itself. His campaign speeches were peppered with arguments about how New Labour's hands-off approach to economic management had failed to deliver adequate economic security for those on middle and low incomes; and how its ambivalence about runaway inequality at the top was no longer in step with public opinion. Announcing his candidacy he spoke about how 'globalisation is not simply an untameable

---

[29] The other candidates were Ed Balls, Andy Burnham and Diane Abbott.
[30] The Labour electoral college compris: MPs and MEPs; party members; and affiliated members (including union members).
[31] Patrick Wintour, 'Ed Miliband's team confident their man will win Labour's race on second votes', *The Guardian*, 5 September 2010.

force of nature to which we must adapt or die', a clear departure from New Labour's accommodation of market forces.[32]

The party faithful were also told 'Ed speaks human', which was very deliberately intended to contrast his supposed down-to-earth demeanour with his brother's aloofness;[33] ultimately this was to become an unwise hostage to fortune as 'speaking human' did not prove to be a strength of the younger brother, who would repeatedly struggle to connect with ordinary voters.

The result went down to the wire. Ed Miliband was behind right until the final round of reallocations when Ed Balls' voters' second preferences were reallocated, pushing him up to 50.65 per cent.[34] As is well known, Ed Miliband triumphed over his brother on the back of second preference votes and by securing the overwhelming support of trade union members. In politics a win is a win, but nonetheless the nature of Ed Miliband's victory had important implications for his leadership across the parliament. Most obviously Miliband failed to secure the support of his colleagues in the Parliamentary Labour Party (PLP), raising questions about his legitimacy. He was the first choice of only 32 per cent of MPs, thus bucking a trend whereby all previous party leaders have been the preferred choice of the parliamentary party.[35] The truth is that large swathes of the PLP were never reconciled to his leadership, and many felt that the party had chosen the wrong Miliband. Grumblings about Miliband's leadership ability would be a constant feature of his reign, becoming most vocal during the so-called 'Bonfire plot' in the autumn of 2014 when on the back of a dismal conference speech and a spate of poor polls, especially in Scotland where support for Labour collapsed after the referendum, and a near-death experience in the Heywood and Middleton by-election, it was rumoured that twenty Labour frontbenchers were actively considering

---

[32] http://labourlist.org/2010/05/ed-miliband-announces-his-intention-to-stand-for-lead-ership-full-speech (accessed 4 December 2014).

[33] Medhi Hassan, 'Medhi hassan on Ed Miliband's race for the Labour leadership: Ed speaks human', *New Statesman*, 26 August 2010.

[34] http://archive.labour.org.uk/votes-by-round (accessed 4 December 2014). Labour used the Alternative Vote system (AV), whereby the candidate with the lowest number of votes is eliminated and their voters' second preferences are reallocated until one candidate has more than 50 per cent of the vote.

[35] Peter Kellner, 'How Ed Miliband won' (accessed at https://yougov.co.uk/news/2011/05/16/how-ed-miliband-won, 4 December 2014).

Table 19.1 *Labour Party leadership election results, fourth round, 2010*

4th Round	MPs and MEPs	%	Labour Party Members	%	Affiliated Members	%	Total
David Miliband	140	17.812	66,814	18.135	80,266	13.400	49.35
Ed Miliband	122	15.522	55,992	15.198	119,405	19.934	50.65
Total	262	33.333	122,806	33.333	199,671	33.333	100

Source: http://archive.labour.org.uk/votes-by-round

moving against him.[36] It came to nothing, not least because Alan Johnson – 'the postman-across-the-water' – turned down the offer of a coronation.[37] The plot was a typical Labour shambles. As with the revolts against Gordon Brown, all it served to do was illuminate the fact that the PLP had lost faith in their hapless leader.[38]

Next he had to cope with the charge that he was in hock to the unions, given that they had played such a big part in his victory (he had 20 per cent support among trade union members, which dwarfed the lead David had in other parts of the electoral college; see Table 19.1). This was a favourite line of attack from the right-wing press, who pilloried him as 'Red Ed' from day one, but it resonated only with a minority of the public. Far more damage was inflicted on him because the public believed that he had 'stabbed his brother in the back', which is perhaps what he was best known for among the electorate. Whereas his aides believed his decision to stand against and defeat David was evidence of his steeliness and inner strength, the public did not hold this view. Nevertheless, Ed Miliband's unquestionably difficult decision to run against his brother highlights the fact that he felt that he had something genuinely different to add to the debate and believed in a new project of transformational politics that argued that the status quo simply wasn't working. Despite the lack of clarity at this stage, it seemed Miliband had grand ambitions for a new type of progressive Labour politics.

[36] Jason Goves, 'Bonfire Night plot to oust Ed: Labour in crisis as MPs hold secret meeting and demand "Axe leader or we'll lose the election"', *The Daily Mail*, 6 November 2014.

[37] 'Postman across the water' is a quotation from Andrew Rawnsley, 'Labour angst about their leader risks echoing the Tories' jeers', *The Observer*, 9 November 2014.

[38] Jason Goves, 'Bonfire Night plot'.

What is Milibandism? Responsible capitalism and the return of political economy

> As we emerge from the global economic crisis, we face a choice: we can return to business as usual or we can challenge old thinking to build a new economy.
>
> *(Ed Miliband conference speech 2010)*[39]

The weakest criticism levelled at Ed Miliband is that his leadership lacked a clear sense of purpose; that he was a cork adrift in a hostile sea. On the contrary, Miliband deserves credit for advancing a personal agenda for reforming contemporary capitalism, although it was undoubtedly embryonic. These ideas did manage to have some traction with a public coping with the fallout from the most significant economic crash since the depression of the 1930s, but crucially not enough.[40] There was such a thing as Milibandism, even if it was often poorly articulated and communicated. There were also flashes of brilliance, such as his proposal to freeze energy prices, when his agenda cut through to make the political weather, which can't be said of all leaders of the opposition.[41]

Miliband's central insight was that the financial crash had exposed the limitations of the traditional Croslandite model of social democracy, and the cruder version pioneered during the Blair and Brown years, which depended – overly depended – on tax-funded redistribution to deliver social justice.[42] Not only did the 2008–9 crash, and new fiscal reality that followed in its wake, blow apart the centre-left's traditional statecraft, which was premised on building political coalitions on the back of sustained public spending, Miliband argued that trying to ameliorate the iniquities of advanced market economies through downstream transfers alone leaves unaddressed the root causes of inequality. Hence his relentless focus on 'the cost of living crisis' and the need to repair the severed link between growth and prosperity,

---

[39] *BBC News*, 28 September 2010 (accessed at www.bbc.co.uk/news/uk-politics-11426411, 4 December 2014).

[40] Numerous books have been published on the 2008 financial crisis, including Andrew Ross Sorkin's *Too Big to Fail* (London: Viking, 2009).

[41] Ed Miliband, Party conference speech, 24 November 2013.

[42] There was of course much more to Crosland's revisionist account of social democracy than this caricature allows for. See Anthony Crosland, *The Future of Socialism* (London: Jonathan Cape, 1956).

which had started to unravel long before the crash, manifesting itself in a decade-long fall in real wages, especially for those in the bottom half of the income distribution, but which was masked by tax credits and rising personal debt.[43]

The immediate triggers of the 2008–9 crash were deregulation of the financial sector and an asset bubble. But for Miliband the more important observation was that these events revealed deep-rooted structural weaknesses inherent in British capitalism, which could only be addressed by a dose of radicalism. In addition to the broken link between growth and wages these included the long tail of pedestrian, low-skill and low-productivity sectors of the economy, in which millions of workers are employed on low wages, with no prospect of career advancement.[44] Then there was Britain's excessive dependence on the financial sector – representing 10 per cent of gross value added at its peak in 2009.[45] In short, Miliband argued, the British growth model was not only highly volatile, and prone to regular crises, but also generated worrying levels of inequality and stagnating living standards for the vast majority.

Miliband's response was what he termed a more 'responsible capitalism'.[46] To be more resilient and stable, he argued, the British economy needed to be rebalanced, with growth and tax revenues flowing from a broader range of sectors and firms. Central to his thinking was the need to sweep away vested interests and break down concentrations of power – by substituting rent-seeking with greater competition. Stewart Wood – one of his closest aides – talked of the need for a 'supply side revolution from the left' to strengthen the skills of workers and give them a bigger stake in their jobs. All this, he believed, would create not just a more productive economy but a fairer one too.

---

[43] Ed Miliband, Speech on the cost of living crisis, Battersea, 5 November 2013 (see www.newstatesman.com/politics/2013/11/ed-milibands-speech-cost-living-crisis-full-text, accessed 4 December 2014).

[44] Gavin Kelly and Nick Pearce, 'After the coalition: What's left?', *IPPR*, 26 September 2012 (accessed at www.ippr.org/juncture/after-the-coalition-whats-left, 4 December 2014).

[45] Lucinda Maer and Nida Broughton, 'Financial services: contribution to the UK economy', SN/EP/06193 (accessed at www.parliament.uk/briefing-papers/sn06193.pdf, 4 December 2014).

[46] Ed Miliband, 'What responsible capitalism is all about', *The Guardian*, 22 May 2013.

In policy terms this meant tackling oligopolistic practices in key economic sectors – hence his commitments to freeze energy prices and cap the market share of the five big banks. He backed a state investment bank to provide for 'patient' capital.[47] He sought to curb the predatory practices of firms with his attack on payday lenders and the use of zero-hours contracts. Miliband backed the roll-out of apprenticeships and vocational training – as well as models of employee ownership. He recognized that fiscal constraints inhibited the ability to boost low-to-middle income families through transfers (i.e. tax credits) and thus shifted the burden onto raising employment income. These were the origins of the push for raising the minimum wage and incentivizing firms to introduce the living wage. Miliband also emphasized the need to increase the employment rate of women and older workers to help raise household incomes.

Of course there were critics who questioned the logic of this approach. Many Blairites remained unconvinced that it was possible to win from the left; indeed Tony Blair was quoted as saying as much in December 2014 (and in fact Team Miliband agonized about this themselves). Predictably, voices on the left were uneasy with any retreat from the traditional politics of redistribution. Others provided more considered criticism. Lane Kenworthy, for instance, suggested the 'predistribution' school was guilty of wishful thinking: the best institutional force to counteract low wages is the trade unions, yet unionization rates, despite stabilizing recently, have fallen drastically over the last thirty years.[48] In the absence of the unions being revived, where would the pressure for boosting living standards come from?[49] Nor did Miliband adequately explain how the growing numbers of self-employed workers fitted into his schema; and he paid only lip service to the role of small businesses.

Doubtless achieving such a transformation is a formidable challenge: the cultural and institutional shift required to move British capitalism down a path of high wages and high productivity and investment are considerable. Indeed some so-called 'Varieties of Capitalism'

---

[47] Ed Miliband, Speech to the British Chambers of Commerce, 14 March 2013.
[48] James Achur, 'Trade union membership 2010', Department for Business, Innovation and Skills, 2011.
[49] Lane Kenworthy, 'What's wrong with predistribution', 20 September 2013 (accessed at www.ippr.org/juncture/whats-wrong-with-predistribution, 4 December 2014).

Table 19.2 *YouGov poll: 'Who would you trust more to run the economy?'*

	Cameron and Osborne	Miliband and Balls	Not sure
2014			
January 9–10	40	29	31
2013			
July 25–6	39	26	35
June 27–8	36	26	38
February 24–5	35	29	37
2012			
December 6–7	37	26	37
July 26–7	34	31	35
April 26–7	36	28	35
2011			
March 24–5	39	30	31

Source: YouGov, 2014.

scholars say it is almost impossible to change radically the basic political economy of a country.[50] Miliband believed that such a view was unduly defeatist. Perhaps so; yet regardless of the merits of his thinking, the political truth is that Miliband failed to convert this agenda into a project. There were various reasons why this proved to be the case. Three stand out: the failure to improve Labour's reputation for economic competence proved a major obstacle; then there were questions about Ed Miliband's standing as a potential Prime Minister; finally, the populist backlash against the established parties that had recast the political landscape in this period meant Labour were never considered the party of insurgency capable of delivering change.

The question of economic competence

It is difficult to see how Labour felt they could be considered the party to deliver far-reaching economic change, when so few people trusted them to run the economy. The Tory lead on economic competence proved unassailable throughout the parliament (see Table 19.2), despite George Osborne conspicuously failing to meet his goal of eliminating

---

[50] Peter A. Hall and David Soskice, *Varieties of Capitalism* (Oxford: Oxford University Press 2001).

the deficit.[51] Even at the height of the government's economic problems – with GDP figures seeming to show that the country had tipped back into recession[52] and Osborne's infamous 'omnishambles' Budget of 2012 – the public still trusted the pair of Cameron and Osborne with the economy more than they trusted Miliband and Balls; a powerful example of just how dire the levels of trust in the Labour Party's economic competence were after the debacle of 2008–9.

The Labour Party simply did not do enough to try to address deep-seated concerns amongst the electorate, who regarded cuts as undesirable but necessary, that they could again be trusted with the stewardship of the nation's finances. Few truly believed that the party had internalized the need for fiscal constraint, which the leadership signed up to. This was most graphically illustrated in the last autumn party conference before the 2015 General Election, when Miliband 'forgot' to mention the deficit in his leader's speech – a spectacular Freudian slip.[53] It was an astonishing omission, which inevitably drew ridicule from the coalition parties. George Osborne put it bluntly via the social media site Twitter: 'Ed Miliband didn't mention the deficit once. Extraordinary. If you can't fix the economy you can't fund the NHS.'[54]

For all the talk of fiscal toughness, it was almost impossible to point to a specific piece of public spending a Labour government would cut. At one point in early 2012, Jim Murphy, then Shadow Defence Secretary, said Labour would accept £5 billion of cuts to the defence budget. He was then sacked in the next reshuffle. Ed Balls strongly resisted the idea of signing Labour up to specific cuts, believing that the party could never beat the Tories in such an auction. Doubtless there were some risks, but the obvious downside to this approach is that it looked like Labour was incapable of making tough decisions.[55] Miliband and Balls failed to learn the critical lesson from the Brown

[51] See www.theguardian.com/money/2014/sep/23/osborne-deficit-reduction-target-uk-borrowing-rise (accessed 4 December 2014).

[52] 'Economy tracker: GDP', BBC News, 30 September 2014 (accessed at www.bbc.co.uk/news/10613201, 4 December 2014).

[53] Patrick Wintour, 'Ed Miliband admits he forgot key section of Labour conference speech', The Guardian, 24 September 2014.

[54] George Osborne on Twitter: https://twitter.com/George_Osborne/status/514426118875910144.

[55] Jim Murphy, interview with Nicholas Watt, The Guardian, 5 January 2012.

premiership: until the party was considered credible on paying down Britain's debts, it would not get a hearing for its wider plans for economic renewal.[56]

The bitter irony for Labour is that Miliband's espousal of what he wonkishly called 'predistribution' did in fact provide a direct response to the question that loomed large: what is social democracy for when there is no money to spend? The predistribution approach explicitly rejects the idea that incomes and life chances can best be improved through increasing government transfers, by emphasizing alternative policies to boost living standards, including: tackling Britain's chronically under-skilled jobs market through apprenticeships, increasing the employment rate via better access to childcare, enhancing incomes through stronger profit sharing and a higher minimum wage. This would also require a more active industrial policy, as well as fundamental structural reform to the economy to enhance competition (in, for instance, the banking and energy sectors) to give the consumer a better deal. Had he combined his vision of delivering a more responsible capitalism with a more convincing approach to public spending he might have broadened the appeal of his party (particularly to centrist voters). Contrary to the views of some on the left this would not have meant 'surrendering' to Tory austerity – it was possible to reconcile the case for measured and fairer deficit reduction, underpinned by some illustrative examples of 'Labour cuts', with the need to avoid choking demand in the economy.[57]

Historians will ponder why it was that Miliband – who grasped the intellectual case – nevertheless failed to reposition his party on such a fundamental issue of public trust. One possible explanation is that Miliband chose the path of least resistance and decided to place party unity ahead of making tough decisions on public spending. Avoiding the fate of previous party civil wars was his gift to Labour, but it came at a price. No doubt a clearer position on spending would have put the party under pressure, but firm oversight from the beginning might have

---

[56] See Seldon and Lodge, *Brown at 10*, for a discussion of the Brown premiership.

[57] There were signs of an important shift in Labour's position after Osborne's 2014 Autumn Statement, when Miliband and Balls effectively set out a commitment to both deficit reduction and economic reform, making clear how Labour's proposals for managing the nation's finances were distinct from the excessive austerity of the Tory approach. This was precisely the sort of policy formulation Labour needed to be advocating earlier. The question is whether this position was achieved with sufficient time to convince a sceptical public ahead of the election.

worked; after all, the PLP voted for David Miliband, who had made clear the need for fiscal constraint. In the absence of such decisions the party drifted into its comfort zone.

Bad luck also played its part. Alan Johnson's resignation as Shadow Chancellor over his wife's affair paved the way for Ed Ball's promotion to this most critical of Shadow Cabinet posts. This proved to be highly problematic for Labour, not only because no one better embodied the tax-and-spend caricature of the Brown years, but because Balls had little interest in prosecuting Miliband's more radical economic reform agenda. An intellectual fault line opened up on the left during this period between those like Miliband who argued that the British economy was structurally weak and in need of radical surgery and those, like Balls, who believed that the fundamentals were sound enough and that, after a dose of Keynesian expansion, Labour should return to the *status quo ante*. Balls has had to endure much criticism in recent years, over his character and his approach to politics, but perhaps his real failing was exposed during this period of opposition, namely his profound lack of imagination.

Politically Balls' positioning also inflicted serious damage: betting the house on austerity leading to a double-dip recession left Labour vulnerable once the recovery got under way, not to mention denying them the opportunity to address early on its reputational weakness on the deficit. Economically, Balls was right that Osborne's austerity extinguished the growing economy he inherited, and no doubt it played its role in delaying the return to growth. But unfortunately for Balls the electorate did not think in terms of counterfactuals. As the economy picked up, Labour sought to reframe the public debate around the cost of living crisis; however, addressing living standards took Labour around the question of deficit reduction, not through it.

Miliband's basic instincts on the economy were right. But to reconcile the case for radical economic reform while embracing a realistic approach to the fiscal context demanded a new approach to the role of the state. If New Labour was seen as 'too hands-off with the market, too hands-on with the state', the party had to try to align its economic reform agenda with a new approach on social policy. Yet Miliband was always more at ease reforming markets than he was the state, the latter representing a lacuna in his thinking. Despite the efforts of Blue Labour figures like Jon Cruddas and Maurice Glasman, Miliband remained wedded to a traditional account of the state, which forced Labour into defensive positions on public service and welfare reform.[58] A paradox Miliband didn't appear to want to grasp was that while the financial crash undermined core nostrums of New Right thinking, it was not matched by growing support for a more active state. His campaign to tackle concentrations of power was very rarely directed at vested interests in the state, which questioned its authenticity. (However, as we shall see later over the Falkirk crisis, he did prove willing to take on interests in the Labour Party itself, which won him rare plaudits from the Blairites.)

Miliband as a leader – potential Prime Minister?

Rebuilding Labour's reputation for economic competence would have lent much-needed credibility to his endeavours to reshape British capitalism. But on its own it was insufficient. While the Labour message was sometimes popular, the messenger never was. Freezing energy prices, a mansion tax, curbing the power of landlords, defending British companies from hostile takeovers all struck a chord with voters The problem, whether fair or not, was that the country never warmed to Miliband. His personal ratings were dire, worse than those of Hague and Kinnock and only just better than Michael Foot (see Figure 19.1).[59] 'Red Ed' was the charge levelled at him by the right-wing press, but in the public's mind it was more a case of Odd-Ed.[60] When voters closed their eyes they just couldn't imagine him standing outside 10 Downing Street or representing Britain on the world stage. Despite his best efforts to set the agenda, which he did successfully on several occasions, on the cost of living, on News International, on predatory capitalism,[61] he continuously struggled to look 'prime ministerial', even to Labour supporters. The best politicians have a presence, which eluded him.

---

[58] See www.nextleft.org/2011/07/so-what-is-blue-labour.html (accessed 4 December 2014).

[59] Ipsos MORI, Political Monitor, November 2014.

[60] Simon Walters and Glen Owen, 'Oh brother! Red Ed Miliband beats his sibling David to be Labour's new leader', *Daily Mail*, 26 September 2010 and Toby Young, 'Ed Miliband's seven weirdest moments', *Daily Telegraph*, 7 November 2014.

[61] His 'predators and producers' 2011 Party Conference speech was widely derided at the time but the basic themes endured and proved influential.

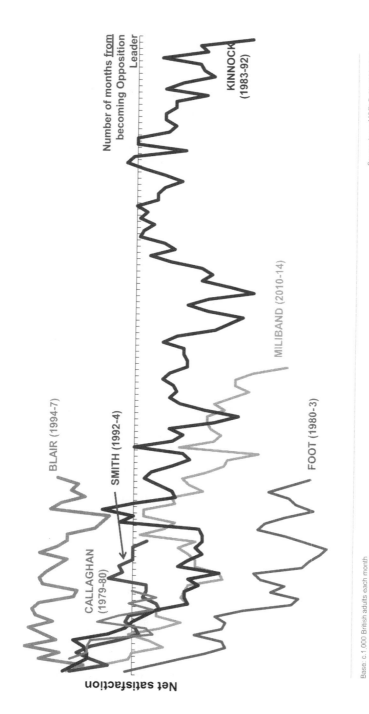

Net satisfaction

Number of months from becoming Opposition Leader

BLAIR (1994-7)

SMITH (1992-4)

CALLAGHAN (1979-80)

KINNOCK (1983-92)

MILIBAND (2010-14)

FOOT (1980-3)

Base: c.1,000 British adults each month

Ipsos MORI

Source: Ipsos MORI Political Monitor

Note: Data collected prior to September 2008 were collected via face-to-face methodology; data collected from September 2008 were via telephone

Figure 19.1 'How satisfied or dissatisfied are you with the way … is doing his job as leader of the … Party?'
Source: IpsosMORI Political Monitor.

Figure 19.2 President Barack Obama drops by National Security Advisor Susan E. Rice's meeting with Opposition Leader Ed Miliband of the United Kingdom, in the National Security Advisor's West Wing Office of the White House, July 21, 2014. (Official White House Photo by Pete Souza)

Labour candidates and activists would return from the doorstep bamboozled by what to do about the 'Ed Miliband problem'. The double whammy of Alan Johnson's forced resignation was that as Miliband's deputy, as he would have become in all but name, Johnson would not only have helped on the economic side, but he would have helped to compensate for Miliband's lack of personal appeal.

Miliband faced questions about his leadership skills and prime ministerial attributes from the moment he became party leader. The combination of a slightly awkward demeanour, demonstrated in pictures of him with Barack Obama, the President of the United States, in July 2014 (see Figure 19.2), his infamous encounter with a bacon sandwich, an unusual voice and a self-acknowledged resemblance to the character Wallace, from *Wallace and Gromit*, all contributed to Miliband's struggles in appearing prime ministerial.[62] Whether fair

---

[62] Adam Withnall, 'Ed Miliband fails to look normal while eating bacon sandwich ahead of campaign tour', *The Independent*, 21 May 2014; Joe Murphy, 'Ed Miliband: I look like Wallace and don't look good eating bacon sandwiches ... but I can lead', *London Evening Standard*, 25 July 2014.

or not, it is undeniable that these presentational issues contributed to Miliband's inability to lead David Cameron on polls about leadership and suitability for the role of Prime Minister.[63] It is striking that despite the fact that his closet aides were all aware of his image problems from day one, Miliband and his team inexcusably did almost nothing to try and address them.

Labour would counter that they were subjected to relentless attacks from the right-wing media, who were intent, especially after Leveson, to play the man instead of the ball – going for Miliband personally, as they had with Kinnock when he was leader. Interestingly the only time the public appeared to get behind Miliband came on the back of the *Daily Mail*'s attack on his father, Ralph Miliband, in September 2013, when they ran an article entitled 'The man who hated Britain'.[64] The article was widely criticized and Miliband responded vigorously, with a strongly worded criticism of *Mail* editor, Paul Dacre.[65] The dispute with the *Mail* clearly stirred Miliband's blood and presented him to the public in a passionate and sympathetic manner, something that was all too rare during the 2010–15 parliament. Miliband's calls for Rupert Murdoch's empire to be dismantled in an interview with the *Observer* in 2011 demonstrated another example of bravery and prime ministerial leadership.[66]

On issues where he felt intellectually self-confident, such as on economic reform, he would be bold and decisive. In other instances, however, Miliband would prevaricate and dither. He had a number of blind spots on major areas of policy: on welfare, on public service reform, on Scotland and the union, and on foreign policy. The result was that these were largely neglected areas of his leadership. In some cases, on welfare for instance, he felt his own instincts were out of sync with the country so he shied away from it. It didn't help that he only really looked and sounded like a compelling leader when he could speak authentically. In other cases, notably education, he simply failed to form a strong view. There was also a tendency to try to shoehorn everything

[63] In a YouGov/*The Sun* poll from 23–4 September 2014, when asked the question, 'Which of these would make the best prime minster?', 37% said David Cameron, 21% Ed Miliband, 4% Nick Clegg and 37% didn't know.

[64] Geoffrey Levy, 'The man who hated Britain', *Daily Mail*, 28 September 2013.

[65] Ed Miliband, 'Why my father loved Britain', *MailOnline*, 1 October 2013.

[66] Toby Helm, Jamie Doward and Daniel Boffey, 'Rupert Murdoch's empire must be dismantled – Ed Miliband', *The Guardian*, 16 July 2011.

into his account of the crisis of capitalism, which meant he sometimes misjudged his response. He never properly grasped, for instance, the role of nationalism and identity in the referendum debate in Scotland. For him it was all about living standards.

Indecision was often the product of him acting more like an adviser than a leader. Intellectually brilliant, he could deconstruct issues in forensic detail, interrogating proposals from every policy and political angle. The downside was the tendency to go round in circles, with decision-making regularly a tortuous affair. As Jonathan Freedland put it:

> As an analyst, Miliband is persuasive. But this is the trouble. The job he is applying for is not to describe the country's problems but to fix them. And it's in that latter regard that he does not quite convince. Miliband doesn't want to be Britain's senior tutor but its Prime Minister. With just eight months to go, he doesn't yet look the part.[67]

Miliband as a radical

Not only was Miliband considered to lack the gravitas necessary to be Prime Minister, he never made a convincing radical either. Miliband saw himself as a Thatcher on the left, tackling orthodox thinking, but as far as the public were concerned he was considered an insider, not an insurgent. Amidst the rowdiness of UKIP and SNP populists, Miliband was cast as part of the political establishment. Ultimately leaders need followers and Miliband attracted very few to his cause. The so-called 'left behind', those who have lost out from globalization and a constituency Miliband targeted, headed not to Labour but to Farage's 'people's army'. As John Curtice argues, UKIP and the SNP, who challenged the hegemony of the Westminster parties in the 2010–15 period, can be seen at least in part to represent a response to the challenges posed by globalization.[68] UKIP supporters are most pessimistic about Britain's future economic prospects, while support for the Yes vote in the Scottish referendum was highest amongst the working class who are 'the losers from our current economic arrangements'.[69]

---

[67] Jonathan Freedland, 'Ed Miliband: Coherent and together – but still not yet looking the part', *The Guardian*, 23 September 2014.

[68] Curtice, 'World in motion'. [69] *Ibid*.

While Miliband was right to understand that the *status quo ante* was not an option after the events of 2008–9 – he realized this argument better than and ahead of any other European social democrat leader – he nevertheless failed to factor into his calculations that the financial crash did not result in an automatic swing to the left. Instead its real impact was to heighten disaffection with the 'political class': Miliband was, unfortunately for him, a fully paid-up member of it. In fairness Cameron and Clegg were also completely wrong-footed by rising populism and could not muster an effective response. The coalition should in theory have provided Labour with an intrinsic advantage, becoming the first port of call for voters disaffected with the government. Other than in the early phases of the parliament, however, Labour failed to capitalize on these circumstances.

Miliband could be inspirational, but not for long enough to matter. Political momentum he generated would soon dissipate – with his critics lambasting him for presiding over endless relaunches. Too often he had a tin ear for popular opinion – on immigration, on welfare, on the contempt for politics, and on the nascent politics of English nationhood. He was right to believe that the post-2008/9 world provided an opportunity for progressive politics; but there was nothing inevitable about this. It was not 1945, when Attlee, a less charismatic leader than Miliband, was swept into power on the back of organized labour and the idealism generated under wartime conditions (and a determination, as Peter Hennessy has powerfully shown, not to return to the laissez-faire Toryism of the 1930s).[70] It was more akin to the 1906–14 era, where the opportunity for political change was much narrower, due in part to the ferocious opposition of vested interests, but also the absence of a clearly defined electoral coalition that could be mobilized behind reform. These are similar conditions to those that prevail today. Back then it took bold and decisive leadership of the Edwardian radicals like David Lloyd George to make the best of the hand they were dealt. Alas, Ed Miliband was no Lloyd George. Still there were things that could have been done better. Basic errors were made: the party failed to reach out to the business community to try to build support behind its responsible capitalism agenda. Miliband was far better at bashing the predators than he was at wooing the wealth creators. Nor was it ever really clear what

[70] Peter Hennessy, *Never Again: Britain, 1945–1951* (London: Penguin, 2nd edition, 2006).

Labour's offer to middle England amounted to, fuelling suspicion that the party was pursuing a core vote strategy.

Syria vote and Middle Eastern foreign policy

Foreign policy has long been an area where politicians can emphasize their prime ministerial credentials. And yet, Miliband often shied away from foreign affairs, another example of a policy blind spot. He backed intervention in Libya but it was over Syria that his actions proved most significant, leading in the summer of 2013 to the first time a government had been defeated on foreign policy since 1792, which William Hague described as the 'worst moment' of his career as Foreign Secretary.[71] It marked a new low point for relations between Number 10 and the opposition.[72]

The breakdown between Number 10 and Ed Miliband's office was due to the perceived lack of clarity from Ed Miliband and his team. Miliband was accused of 'buggering around' and 'playing politics' as he had changing his position repeatedly in a manner that was 'not credible or serious'.[73] The criticism from the government was clear: Miliband had behaved irresponsibly, with a lack of clarity, and with too much concern for the internal party politics of a Labour Party that was still dealing with the hangover of the 2003 Iraq war. But is this fair? The government believed that they had the Labour Party's support on the evening of Wednesday 28 August, having adapted their position to accommodate talks with the Labour leadership and were therefore shocked when Miliband's office informed Number 10 that they would not enjoy the Labour Party's support. Douglas Alexander claims that the Labour team were in constant communication with Number 10 and that the failure to come to an agreement therefore lay with the government. Alexander argued, not unreasonably, that the Prime Minister had

---

[71] BBC Radio 4, 'The Syria Vote: One Day in August', 10 November 2014.

[72] 'Syria crisis: Cameron loses Commons vote on Syria action', *BBC News*, 30 August 2013 (accessed at http://www.bbc.co.uk/news/uk-politics-23892783, 4 December 2014).

[73] Toby Helm, 'No 10 launches bitter assault on Ed Miliband over Syria vote', www.theguardian.com/politics/2013/aug/31/syria-commons-vote-cameron-miliband (accessed 4 December 2014).

given undertakings to President Obama that he could deliver the House of Commons on an accelerated timetable and was therefore attempting to 'shoehorn a timetable for legitimacy of the British parliament into a timetable for credibility of the American president'.[74] It is difficult to tell where the failure for consensus lies but it is hard to deny the opportunity to defeat the government was very politically enticing for Miliband. His unwillingness to engage in military action in Syria came to the fore again in 2014 when it was said that the British air strikes against Islamic State (ISIS) were confined purely to Iraq, unlike the American strikes, due to the leader of the opposition's unwillingness to back action in Syria.[75]

After the defeat of the government over Syria in 2013 and the refusal to support the Labour amendment, the Prime Minister declared that, 'It is very clear tonight that while the House has not passed a motion, ... the British parliament, reflecting the views of the British people, does not want to see British military action.'[76] Miliband gratefully took this cue by stating that, 'Military intervention is now off the agenda for Britain.'[77] Discerning Miliband's thinking on military intervention is difficult, but it seems to be one of extreme caution. He was prepared to intervene in Iraq in 2014 only after six tests had been passed. These were that military intervention had to: have a just cause; be a last resort; be legal; have a reasonable prospect of success; have regional support; and be proportionate. These six criteria were laid out in Miliband's speech to the Commons on 26 September 2014.[78] These criteria represent a significant clarification of Miliband's position on intervention in the Middle East since the 2013 Syria vote and whilst he appears to have indeed been inconsistent and unclear in 2013, the speech on air strikes in Iraq in 2014 added detail to his foreign policy and also credibility to his position as a potential Prime Minister-in-waiting.

---

[74] Douglas Alexander, speaking on BBC Radio 4, 'The Syria Vote: One Day in August', 10 November 2014.

[75] Tim Ross, 'Ed Miliband under pressure to back air strikes in Syria', 5 October 2014 (accessed at www.telegraph.co.uk/news/worldnews/islamic-state/11141395/Ed-Miliband-under-pressure-to-back-air-strikes-in-Syria.html, 4 December 2014).

[76] George Eaton, 'Syria: Ed Miliband has had a lucky escape', *New Statesman*, 30 August 2013 (accessed at www.newstatesman.com/politics/2013/08/syria-ed-miliband-has-had-lucky-escape, 4 December 2014).

[77] *Ibid.*   [78] Ed Miliband's speech to the House of Commons, 26 September 2014.

Miliband therefore did make an effort to clarify his foreign policy over the duration of the parliament. This was perhaps motivated by an understanding that it was a weak point in not only his political framework but also his efforts to appear more like a potential Prime Minister. However, as with his attacks on Murdoch and Dacre, Miliband's approach to foreign policy over the entire parliament was one of periods of success and periods of indecision.

Falkirk and party reform

"You can't touch me, I'm an MP!"
(Eric Joyce, when being arrested on 12 March 2012)[79]

One area in which Miliband was able to take the initiative, and win rare plaudits from the right of his party, was in the realm of party reform. Eric Joyce's resignation from the Labour Party in March 2012 following a fracas in the House of Commons Strangers' Bar proved to be a source of major embarrassment for the party.[80] Arrested on 22 February 2012, Eric Joyce later admitted four charges of assault, was fined £3,000 by Westminster Magistrates' Court, ordered to pay £1,400 to his victims, given a weekend curfew and twelve-month community order, and the final insult, banned from entering any pubs for three months.[81] Whilst the situation appeared to be taken directly from an episode of the hit BBC show *The Thick of It*, with its combination of farce, embarrassment and profanity, the long shadow cast over the Labour Party was to be over the selection of the new candidate for Joyce's constituency of Falkirk. It would also turn the spotlight once again towards the hot topic of the Labour Party's relationship with the unions and allow Ed Miliband to grasp

[79] www.telegraph.co.uk/news/uknews/crime/9135107/You-cant-touch-me-Im-an-MP-said-Eric-Joyce.html (accessed 4 December 2014).

[80] Hélène Mulholland and Andrew Sparrow, 'Eric Joyce gives up Labour membership after bar brawl', *The Guardian*, 12 March 2012.

[81] 'Eric Joyce fined £3,000 for assault in House of Commons bar ', *The Guardian*, 9 March 2012.

this nettle with proposals for reforming the financial link between unions and the party.[82]

Soon after Joyce's resignation, Stephen Deans – at the time, a local shop steward in Falkirk – was elected chairman of the Falkirk West Constituency Labour Party (CLP), which covered about 70 per cent of the Falkirk parliamentary constituency.[83] It was subsequently alleged that he started to recruit Unite members into Falkirk West CLP and pay their membership fees, which, at the time, was in line not only with Unite policy but also with Labour Party rules. These members would then be able to vote in the PPC selection process. Alongside this unfolding narrative in Falkirk, Karie Murphy, the former Chair of the Scottish Labour Party and close friend of Unite's Len McCluskey, announced her intention to be Labour's candidate in Falkirk. Into this mélange, the now independent Joyce began to blog about how the CLP was being flooded with new Unite members who would be able to vote in the PPC selection.

The complaints of Lorraine Kane that she and her family had been signed up to the Labour Party without their agreement triggered an investigation into malpractice that was to rumble on for months and by June 2013 ended up involving Labour Party headquarters, when they implemented 'special measures' and took direct control of candidate selection in Falkirk. The selection of the candidate in Falkirk had come to signify the wider issue of candidate selection and the Labour Party's relationship with trade unions, particularly for the right-wing press, who seized upon it with gusto.

A Labour Party spokesman said:

> After an internal inquiry into the Falkirk constituency we have found there is sufficient evidence to raise concern about the legitimacy of members qualifying to participate in the selection of a Westminster candidate.[84]

It was in this climate that Ed Miliband made his speech on trade union funding on 9 July 2013 in which he said, 'Every time something like

---

[82] 'Ed Miliband union funding speech', 9 July 2013 (accessed at www.politics.co.uk/comment-analysis/2013/07/09/ed-miliband-union-funding-speech-in-full, 4 December 2014).

[83] Erik Joyce, 'Unite in Falkirk: amateur and irresponsible', *The Guardian*, 5 July 2013.

[84] 'Labour Party acts on Falkirk selection row', *BBC News* (accessed at www.bbc.co.uk/news/uk-scotland-scotland-politics-23055830, 4 December 2014).

Falkirk happens, it confirms people's worst suspicions.'[85] Despite calling for a change in the way that trade unionists are often automatically affiliated with the Labour Party, it would be a mistake to claim that Miliband's speech sought to dilute the relationship between the unions and the Labour Party. As ever, Ed Miliband was walking the tightrope of courting union support – the 'Red Ed' albatross still hanging around his neck – and reforming the party in the mould of Tony Blair. In the speech, Miliband argued that removing automatic affiliation fees would serve to strengthen, not weaken, the bond between Labour and the unions.

Miliband argued that:

> In the twenty-first century, it just doesn't make sense for anyone to be affiliated to a political party unless they have chosen to do so. Men and women in Trade Unions should be able to make a more active, individual choice on whether they become part of our Party. That would be better for these individuals and better for our Party.[86]

The proposals managed to gain support from unlikely bedfellows – Tony Blair and Unite general secretary Len McCluskey. Blair praised Miliband's leadership and said he wished he had made the move himself, whilst McCluskey added, 'It's not often I agree with Tony Blair but I think he is spot on.'[87] It appears that Miliband's speech achieved its purpose of galvanizing support across the Labour Party for reform. It achieved this through its appeal to the importance of the unions and their members as well as to the need for reform.

The speech did not, however, mark an end to the controversy surrounding Falkirk. On 3 November, Stephen Deans stood down as Labour chair in Falkirk West, despite having been cleared of being involved in vote-rigging earlier in the year. This was in a climate in which the *Sunday Times* claimed it had seen thousands of emails to and from Deans that proved the extent of the electoral corruption. The *Sunday Times* was also claiming that Miliband had been forced to abandon the inquiry, set up by the National Executive Committee (NEC), due to intense pressure from Unite on witnesses to withdraw

---

[85] 'Ed Miliband union funding speech', 9 July 2013.   [86] *Ibid.*

[87] Patrick Wintour, 'Ed Miliband's union-levy proposals gain support from Blair and McCluskey', *The Guardian*, 9 July 2013.

their evidence.[88] Tom Watson, who had already resigned from his position as Labour Party campaign coordinator on 4 July 2013 due to the mounting pressure over Falkirk, was implicated by Gregor Poynton, a former Labour Party election strategy manager, of being involved in 'all the shenanigans'. It marked the first time Watson had been accused publicly by another party figure of wrongdoing over the Falkirk selection. Poynton also claimed that the party leadership 'knew what was going on' in Falkirk.[89] What all this showed was that Miliband had been right to call for a renegotiation of the relationship between the party and the unions, but also served to show just how toxic that relationship could be, especially given Miliband's abiding personal need for union support for his leadership.

On 16 July, only four days after Miliband's speech at the St Bride's Foundation, the Labour national executive agreed the terms of reference for the inquiry into how the party could refashion its relationship with the trade unions. Lord Collins of Highbury, the former Labour general secretary, was asked to head the review. This review appeared in February 2014, entitled 'Building a One Nation Labour Party: The Collins Review into Labour Party Reform'. It argued for a transitional period of five years, after which affiliation fees should only be accepted on behalf of levy payers who have consented to the payment of those fees. It mirrored Miliband's speech in calling for closer relations with trade unionists by arguing that levy-paying trade unionists should be able to be attached to a CLP and vote in leadership elections. It also argued that the Electoral College for leadership elections should be abolished and that multiple voting in leadership elections should be ended. The ironies of these suggestions coming from an Ed Miliband-initiated report was not be lost on anyone reading the proposals. The Collins review failed to provide any sort of timetable or deadline for when the leadership election should be reformed. Finally, the review called for the NEC to have the power to ensure that the selection of the London mayoral candidate be completed by a closed primary and that the NEC set an appropriate level of spending limits for internal party selections.

---

[88] David Leppard, 'Revealed: Ed Miliband's dossier on union plot', *The Sunday Times*, 3 November 2013.

[89] Glen Owen, 'Tom Watson "was behind union vote rigging scandal": Explosive accusation by Labour candidate for Falkirk seat', *Mail on Sunday*, 2 November 2013.

The review was clearly born out of Ed Miliband's desires to reform the party, which in turn were motivated by the debacle over Falkirk. The Falkirk crisis has since become a byword for what many on the right see as the Labour Party's broken relationship with the trade unions and for many on the left as Miliband's betrayal of the union movement. In this light, the aims of the Collins review were admirable but the lack of concrete proposals, in terms of delegating future decisions to the NEC, and the lack of a timetable for many of the proposals led to scepticism.

Conclusion

It is true that unpopular leaders can sometimes win elections. Attlee defeated Churchill in 1945, Callaghan fell victim to the widely disliked Thatcher in 1979. It's also true that parties can win when they are less trusted on the economy, as Wilson proved in October 1974. Peter Kellner points out, however, that historically, no party has won when they are behind on both.[90] However, due to a fracturing of the electorate, and the rupture in particular on the right with the emergence of UKIP as a major political source, and Cameron's failure to achieve constituency boundary changes, it is possible for Labour in 2015 to defy history and win.

Lacking a decisive mandate for his agenda, he will, if Labour wins, face the prospect of governing in deeply uncertain times. Labour could scrape a majority or perhaps most likely end up the largest party in another hung parliament. The option of a strong and stable coalition might not be there for the taking this time. It is far from clear that Labour would prefer a coalition over some sort of confidence and supply arrangement, and besides, the Liberal Democrats may fail to secure enough seats to be kingmaker. The haemorrhaging of Labour support in Scotland might mean Labour needs the backing of its tartan nemesis the SNP to form a government. Such an arrangement would likely see Labour trying to govern without a majority of seats in England, which could provoke a constitutional storm over the English

[90] Peter Kellner, *The Guardian*, 14 April 2014.

Question. Moreover, the spending cuts Miliband would have to enact in the next parliament will test the unity of the country and that of the Labour Party itself. As leader of the opposition he did not prepare his party for what lies around the corner, and the ground could open up beneath him. It will be an immense test of his leadership. He has the ability to rise to the challenge, and has proved on different occasions that he has the resilience and inner strength not to be underestimated. He will desperately want to avoid the fate of the Hollande presidency in France, which in the face of economic reality had to mount a humiliating U-turn on austerity, splitting the PS (Parti Socialiste) and leaving him with the lowest poll ratings in the history of the Fifth Republic.[91]

If he loses in 2015, what then? Conventional wisdom suggests his career will be over. Recent precedent suggests he would resign the leadership of his party. He would still be just 45, with much left to contribute. As one of the few figures in the Labour Party who truly understood that the post-2008/9 world called for a serious change in the structure of capitalist society he would be ideally placed to continue to lead the debate on this topic. During 2010–15 no key text emerged to define Miliband's responsible capitalism agenda. There was no equivalent of Crosland's iconoclastic *The Future of Socialism*. It would be fitting if it fell to Miliband to write it. As with Crosland, it is possible that Miliband's most important contribution to the left will come from his thinking.

[91] See http://uk.reuters.com/article/2014/09/04/uk-france-politics-poll-idUKKBN0GZ 24020140904 (accessed 4 December 2014).

20 THE COALITION AND THE MEDIA

PETER PRESTON

The Coalition Agreement offered few aspirations for media reform, just like the Conservative and Liberal Democrat election manifestos that preceded it. A mere forty-two words in its founding document vaguely promise to set up TV stations in co-operation with local newspapers and to let the dogs of the National Audit Office loose on the BBC in order to strengthen the corporation's 'independence'.[1] Apart from a standard genuflection to the wonders of high-speed broadband, the agenda ends there. No vision thing; no stretching menu for change. David Cameron and Nick Clegg pledged very little in this area, and fulfilled their modest ambitions. Which, of course, does not mean that what the media said and did during the years of combined government wasn't important – indeed, at times, an obsession that consumed politicians and editors alike. Passions rise when the spotlight shines.

Normally, political journalism – in print, in broadcasting, in the lobbies of Parliament – operates to a settled, almost stately routine. Parties prepare manifestos, polls are watched, pundits and editorial writers deliver their verdicts. Then a government is elected and the game begins. Who's up? Who's down? Comment develops a sharper edge as the years roll away. Allegiances, mostly already clear, become fervent. And then it happens all over again. More Blair, more Thatcher, more Whoever or Whatever, more clichés portraying despair or joy. The circle of political life turns. Except in 2010, when coalition altered the

[1] HM Government, *The Coalition: Our Programme for Government* (London: Cabinet Office, 2010), p. 14.

whole context, nature and point of the story – and, oddly, the media seemed to find it more difficult to cope with than the politicians themselves.

Three potent factors changed the nature of media coverage and relationships after May 2010. One was the simple arithmetic of the general election itself, decided against a background of global economic crisis.[2] Another was the need to discover a narrative that could survive in such constrained circumstances. And then, running in parallel, there was rippling crisis within the media village itself as phone hacking scandals and Lord Justice Leveson's inquiry pushed newspapers onto the defensive,[3] and the legacy of sex-abuse scandals past slithered back to haunt the BBC[4] – all of this set against a background of technical churn and growing uncertainty.

But first, that election result. In a sense, the press lined up much as expected ahead of polling day. *The Times* and the *Sun*, once reliable Conservative supporters, had moved to back Blair rather than John Major in 1997 and stayed with him to the end. Now they, and of course Mr Rupert Murdoch, swung behind David Cameron and the Tories. The two *Mails* and Richard Desmond's *Express* and *Star* were Conservative voters, too; as, axiomatically, were the *Daily* and *Sunday Telegraph*. The arguments deployed struck familiar notes. 'Large sections of the UK are starting to resemble parts of the Third World', said the *Mail on Sunday*'s editorial.[5] 'It is not "racist" to fear the effect on British workers.' Worse, Gordon Brown's alternative economic remedy, 'to continue flooding the economy with taxpayers' money, would be a disaster'. Britain, dangerously close to the 'basket case' economies of Greece and Portugal, could once again experience 'the humiliation of an IMF bailout'.

The floating voters of Fleet Street were *The Guardian*, *The Observer* and the two *Independents*. All had manifest difficulty in reaching a conclusion. *The Guardian*, in particular, had supported Labour with greater or lesser conviction since the 1950s; yet in the

---

[2] For a full breakdown of the results, see Dennis Kavanagh and Philip Cowley, *The British General Election of 2010* (Basingstoke: Palgrave, 2010).

[3] Lord Justice Leveson, *An Inquiry into the Culture, Practices and Ethics of the Press: Report* (London: The Stationery Office, 2012).

[4] The subject of the Dame Janet Smith review (www.damejanetsmithreview.com, accessed 3 October 2014).

[5] 'Who can you trust to clear up this mess?', *Mail on Sunday*, 1 May 2010.

summer of 2009 it openly lost patience with Prime Minister Brown and called on him to quit.[6] How could it now advocate five more years of Brown sitting in Downing Street? But, equally, how could it move to the Conservatives (a step unknown since the paper was the *Manchester Guardian*)? Nick Clegg's widely praised TV debate performances offered a handy third way. 'The Liberal Democrats were green before the other parties and remain so. Their commitment to education is bred in the bone. So is their comfort with a European project that, for all its flaws, remains central to this country's destiny.'[7] Add in the brave Liberal Democrat stand on Iraq, their fine record on press freedom, and the 'revelatory' election campaign they had fought – and opportunity knocked. 'A newspaper that is proudly rooted in the liberal as well as the labour tradition – and whose advocacy of constitutional reform stretches back to the decades of 1831–32 – cannot ignore such a record. If not now, when? The answer is clear and proud. Now.' For the first time in modern electoral history, the Liberals had at least one newspaper group's clear endorsement and a seemingly continuing promise of support for what was advocated.

In practice, however, melding opinion poll predictions with principle, the *Guardian* group's fundamental hope was that a Labour–Lib Dem coalition would emerge led by anybody but a vanquished Brown, thus seeing every circle of editorial conference difficulty squared. *The Independent*, in more opaque terms, seemed to agree. There was scope for tactical voting here. What nobody envisaged with any relish or belief was the prospect of a Conservative–Lib Dem coalition. 'The more I look at the prospect of a Con–Lib coalition, the more I think it's not sustainable for long,' wrote one of *The Guardian*'s leading political columnists, Jackie Ashley.[8] 'The pressures of hostile Liberal grassroots and the differences between the parties would bust it up ... A bored and irritated electorate would then properly punish the Lib Dems.' In short, a coalition on these lines wasn't a runner: until, in five hectic days of post-election negotiation, it scrambled to its feet and breasted the tape in ways beyond pundit imagining.

---

[6] 'Gordon Brown: Labour's dilemma', *The Guardian*, 3 June 2009.
[7] 'The liberal moment has come', *The Guardian*, 30 April 2010.
[8] Jackie Ashley, 'A Conservative–Lib Dem coalition is most likely, but it's not sustainable', *The Guardian*, 25 April 2010.

556 / Peter Preston

It is important to understand what the arithmetic of the vote (and so the inchoate will of the electorate) decreed: 306 Tories, 258 Labour, 57 Liberal Democrats, 28 others.[9] Perhaps, in theory, Gordon Brown, nursing a loss of ninety-one seats, could have cobbled together a rickety alliance with the Liberal Democrats, the Nationalists, the Greens, the Northern Irish. But this was never practical politics – especially against a background of economic turmoil. Brown himself was unsentimentally dismissed even by his own party. A Conservative–Lib Dem liaison, hammered out fast in quite exhaustive detail, was the only obvious possibility. Crucially, and wholly unexpectedly, it was also accompanied by joint acceptance of fixed-term parliaments. Barring wholly unlikely contingencies, the next election would be on 7 May 2015.

That meant two important things. The coalition parties were trussed together, sharing power in carefully prescribed ways. They were committed. Backbench MPs could – and did – revolt on issues as they arose. There were 59 rebellions in the first 110 parliamentary votes called by the new government.[10] Europe, in particular, was often a grotesque embarrassment to the whips. A hard core of Conservative backbenchers barely listened to their pleas. But it didn't matter fundamentally. The coalition could not and did not disintegrate. There was no early rush to the country based on a few rosy polling results; nor an abandonment of hope and morale in the dog days of 2012. Simply, the whole game was played to different rules – rules that profoundly altered the mindset of the printed press's political classes. For story after story was now deprived of its potential headline conclusion. Rebellions didn't threaten apocalypse because they merely registered dissent; they did not often change policy, nor seem to foretell government collapse. There could be no prime ministerial threat to resign and go to the country because, even under extreme pressure, neither coalition participant was brave or foolhardy enough to seize the initiative – or to contemplate the lugubrious rules for premature divorce. Westminster presented its normal menu of work and manipulation. But it was no longer the big

[9] Kavanagh and Cowley, *British General Election of 2010*, p. 351. Kavanagh and Cowley's figure of 307 Conservatives includes the Speaker, John Bercow.
[10] Philip Cowley and Mark Stuart, 'A coalition with wobbly wings: Backbench dissent since May 2010', Revolts.co.uk (2010) (accessed at www.revolts.co.uk/Wobbly%20Wings.pdf, 3 October 2014).

picture. It could not hold the administration to ultimate account – because the Coalition Agreement on fixed terms, as it passed into law, represented a fundamental injunction to plod right on till the end of the road.

From partners to victims

Of course there was plenty to write about. For one thing, the novelty of coalition government, allied to evident public opinion poll backing, produced gentle but cautious approval in the Conservative press. As the first hundred days ticked away, there seemed far more amity than prophesied – even on the stringencies of economic cuts. 'Many Lib Dems had been on an intellectual journey over the last five or more years to which insufficient attention (including by the media) had been paid,' wrote Jonathan Freedland in *The Guardian*.[11] 'The likes of Clegg and Laws and the sainted Cable share more common ground with the Tories on fiscal policy than had been understood.' He could have added that this media inattention was also related to a lobby lifetime of zealously following the two big parties, their movers and shakers, leaving coverage of the Liberal Democrats far down the food chain. Until Nick Clegg's TV debate performance, they were deemed peripheral, not worth cultivating or buying a drink for. But when the moment arrived that correspondents needed an inside track, they themselves were simply left outside. Their entire coverage model needed drastic updating.

That was far easier said than done. Unexpected harmony at the top of government, partnership smilingly sealed in Number 10's garden, seemed a story with a distinct sell-by date. News (basically the unexpected rather than the predictable) might find the spectacle of opposing parties working together novel enough for a while, but the attractions of crisis and threat remained as habitually potent as ever. There had to be an underlying narrative carrying forward month after month. Somebody, in the nicest possible way, had to suffer.

It couldn't be David Cameron and George Osborne at this relatively early point in the cycle: Osborne faced an all-consuming

---

[11] Jonathan Freedland, '100 days of the coalition government', *The Guardian*, 18 August 2010.

economic crisis; Ed Miliband and the Labour Party could be left to suffer later: therefore the weakest link in the chain had to be Nick Clegg. Within a few weeks of coalition formation, indeed, Liberal Democrat strength in the opinion polls had slithered to 17 per cent (YouGov for the *Sun*) and showed every sign of heading further south over the years. Conservative papers, accustomed through history to attacking the Liberal Democrat enemy, had no compunction about exploiting that weakness. The underlying assumption was still that the coalition couldn't last for long – and certainly not for a full term, whatever pledges had been forthcoming. Belabouring the Lib Dems was therefore loyal Conservatism, not betrayal: which swiftly became a theme to be exploited over the years, the second great story to keep political correspondents in business. Story One was a tale of Conservative grit in the grip of an economic hurricane, a saga of sacrifice and resolution without predictable ending before May 2015. Story Two, with echoes of the old *Spitting Image* puppet combination of a dynamic, determined David Owen and small, squeaky David Steel, was the tortured end of the ephemeral condition dubbed 'Cleggmania'. Inevitably, little in the new politics of coalition developed smoothly. The old curse of Harold Macmillan – 'events, dear boy' – remained as formidable as ever.

The first rotten repercussions of agreement between the two parties involved the Liberal Democrats abandoning their somewhat grandiose pledge to abolish university tuition fees. That pledge – drafted by the National Union of Students, no less – left no wiggle room. 'I pledge to vote against any increase in fees in the next parliament and to pressure the government to introduce a fairer alternative.'[12] It was a florid campaign with loads of media picture opportunities, and all fifty-seven Liberal Democrat MPs had supported it. Therefore papers and TV stations up and down Britain could provide footage of Clegg and Co. waving big cardboard pledge cards for the camera. But, of course, the promise itself had been fudged in the Coalition Agreement, pending Lord Browne's ongoing review of university funding – and the publication of that review in October left the Liberal Democrats with nowhere to hide. Browne wanted to remove the cap on funding. An agonized coalition response made it £9,000. The NUS took to the streets in demonstrations that spilled over into violence. A Channel

---

[12] See chapters one and eighteen, this volume.

Four/OpinionPanel poll showed that among students, 42 per cent of whom had voted Lib Dem in May, support had shrivelled to 11 per cent as the new cap was passed in the House. 'In most governments with a highly contentious programme, there is a hate figure who arouses great anger in sections of the populace,' wrote Andrew Rawnsley in *The Observer*.[13] 'Before the election, many of us expected that position to be filled by George Osborne, who seemed a natural for the role . . . But it is instead the Lib Dem leader, the erstwhile "Nice Nick", who has become the lightning rod for discontent.'

From his first half-year in office on, then, Mr Clegg was a prime target for almost all of the press and a growing chorus of public opinion. Look back from the aftermath of the disastrous May 2014 local and European elections and you can find supposed public contempt for conventional (non-UKIP) politics laid early at his door. 'He is a metropolitan, condescending, untrustworthy Europhile, detached from the concerns of ordinary people,' wrote Stephen Glover for the *Daily Mail*.[14] 'Most egregious was his support for the tripling of university fees, although he had campaigned passionately in favour of abolishing them. Such perfidy will not be forgotten by the voters.' Nor political commentators, for that matter. John Rentoul in the *Independent on Sunday* was playing the same tune. 'It turns out that voters notice and care when a party and its leader makes a solemn pledge which they underline with personal declarations and big signatures on placards, and then break it. It is good and democratic and right that there should be a heavy price to pay.'[15]

Pausing over the fees debacle, though, illuminates media deficiencies just as clearly as Liberal Democrat foolishness in allying themselves so heedlessly to a student campaign. Mr Clegg apologized profusely in 2012. He shouldn't have made a promise he couldn't keep. But promises shelved or scrapped are a necessity as separate manifestos turn to coalition agreements. The university fees pledge was different only in the histrionic way it had been presented. Even commentators such as Martin Kettle of the *Guardian*, who would have been far more

[13] Andrew Rawnsley, 'Nick Clegg's unexpectedly quick journey from idol to hate figure', *The Observer*, 4 December 2010.

[14] Stephen Glover, 'Just deserts for the most dishonest politician in Britain: How Nick Clegg led his party toward electoral Armageddon', *Daily Mail*, 24 May 2014.

[15] John Rentoul, 'Nick Clegg's paradox: The policies are fine, he's not', *Independent on Sunday*, 27 July 2014.

content with a Labour or Lib–Lab victory, wrote that Clegg had 'no realistic alternative' to an alliance with the Conservatives; that – amid the gathering economic panic – there had to be stability, not a hung parliament ducking and weaving towards a second election.[16] But newspapers and broadcasters are not time-shift travellers. Once the crisis began to fade, so too did sympathetic understanding of coalition dynamics. And, because policies that can be simply explained are the crucial platform for democratic success, the tangles of 'then' and 'now', the seeming imperatives for co-operation in May 2010 were easily brushed aside as months passed.

(It's instructive to draw a parallel here with the numerous promises of a referendum on Europe, sometimes merely a block on an unwelcome treaty change, sometimes a definitive choice of 'in' or 'out' after a renegotiation of terms never fully specified, offered in various permutations by all three major parties at points of the debate in contexts swiftly forgotten. The message to the public became one of a referendum pledged but never redeemed, a further betrayal in UKIP's pantheon of betrayal because no broadcast interview could ever take the fifteen minutes or so necessary to sort one promise from another. But time for such contextual explanation can seemingly never be forthcoming in a modern media setting. The twenty-four-hour news cycle that weighed down Tony Blair and which Alastair Campbell so often complained about was as nothing to the onrush of tweets and blogs which developed during the coalition years. Perhaps they didn't change the basic shape of things overall: but they filled every waking minute of governance, lent an edge of bitterness to every debate, seemed to deliver damning verdicts on demand. No wonder political spin doctors shrugged bemusedly and hurried on to the next sound bite.)

Public amity, private bile

Coalitions, of their nature, are inherently complex. They spell compromise in a lost two-party world where one policy, or its opposite, can be easily encapsulated. They disturb tribal loyalties and, in the case of newspapers, a relationship with readers that is difficult to

---

[16] Martin Kettle, 'The coalition honeymoon is over, but the marriage has plenty left', *Guardian*, 24 June 2010.

disentangle – for readers pay the money that keep newspapers in business. Both John Smith and Tony Blair used to refer to *The Guardian* as the 'house journal' their activists read; the *Daily Telegraph* over decades has been thought of in a parallel Tory role. Veering off course for either of them is a bold, potentially costly step. Adjusting direction in any fundamental way must invite activist anger; and though a great majority of readers are not, in fact, activists, the weight of bitter or sneering emails and letters proclaiming a sell-out can prove unnerving for journalists and editors alike.

The positioning of newspapers as the coalition developed was full of difficulties, then. Editors were anxious to paint a simple picture, one their core audience could understand and react to. But there could be no early election (the simplest story of the lot); and praise or blame, too, had to be mixed and matched between coalition partners. Worse, though Prime Minister and Deputy Prime Minister could sing from the same hymn sheet in public, their supporters – and individual support staffs – had no such imperatives in private. The public script might talk constantly about amity and co-operation; the two private scripts shunned such solidarity. They were claims to particular credit for particular initiatives, not a general paean to coalition. And the first great test of open, agreed policy difference between the partners – over voting reform – starkly showed the difficulties and the imbalances of power. Once Macmillan's fearful tide of events turned, little seemed to go right.

The winter of 2010–11 was cruel for the coalition, and crueller still for the Liberal Democrats. Nick Clegg might have won a referendum on electoral reform and even on the principle of the AV, the alternative vote, a year earlier. Changing the voting system was one of the most cherished Lib Dem causes. But could it arrive wearing a blue rosette? 'Here at last is the historic chance to heal the pointless rift between two near-identical progressive parties, divided only by history, tradition and a rotten voting system,' wrote Polly Toynbee as coalition-building commenced.[17] 'Clegg would badly misread the mood of this country if he opted for the Conservatives now – despite their "final" AV offer.' So there was disillusion and suspicion from the beginning: and by the time the promised referendum came around, in the spring of 2011,

---

[17] Polly Toynbee, 'Lab–Lib – The only legitimate coalition', *Guardian*, 10 May 2010.

events had moved on. Cleggmania was dead and buried. AV itself wasn't the chosen system for reformers anyway, merely a stepping stone towards something more radical. Worse, Conservative acquiescence was chilly going on icy cold. '"We have been inundated with queries from sitting MPs asking how their seats will be affected",' a spokesman for the Electoral Reform Society told Andrew Gilligan of the *Sunday Telegraph*.[18] 'Badly for the Tories, could be the answer: the party would have won about twenty-five fewer seats if this election had been held under AV, and the system was rejected by the 1998 Jenkins commission because ... it was "unacceptably unfair" to the Conservatives.' All this, moreover, within the great box of stability enforced by fixed-term Parliaments. AV was a stinging Lib Dem disappointment waiting to happen – and a sitting target for the Conservative press.

Referendum defeat 'revealed beyond doubt just how small, isolated and unrepresentative our liberal elite is', the *Mail on Sunday* concluded exultantly.[19] 'The tiny number of electoral divisions that voted in favour of this fatuous change were all either university cities or suburbs crammed with radical academics and students – or gentrified quarters of the capital, famously thick with pretentious pseudo-intellec-tuals.' See, yet again, a developing message. The Liberal Democrats – thin on the ground, thinner at representing heartland Great Britain – were untrustworthy and out of touch. Anything that went wrong for the coalition was surely their fault. Anything that went right added to David Cameron's lustre. Inevitably, the Liberal Democrats hit back. Andrew Lansley's NHS reforms hadn't been spelled out in manifesto or agreement. The press didn't like them. The Liberal Democrats didn't either. A 'Number Ten source' told *The Times* that 'Lansley should be taken out and shot.'[20] Instead he was shovelled aside, as Leader of the House. But more damagingly and lastingly, Mr Cameron's plans to redraw the electoral map, reducing the number of constituencies by 10 per cent (and Labour prospects of victory by rather more than that) then fell for lack of Lib Dem support as the *Daily Mail* fumed. Another betrayal? In principle perhaps, but not in agreement detail. Tit-for-tat

[18] Andrew Gilligan, 'The public seems happy with the "breakneck coalition"', *Daily Telegraph*, 31 July 2010.

[19] 'Proof Britain's kept its solid good sense', *Mail on Sunday*, 8 May 2011.

[20] Juliette Jowit, Patrick Wintour and Hélène Mulholland, 'David Cameron backs Andrew Lansley over NHS reform Bill', *The Guardian*, 8 February 2012.

warfare, Tory backbenchers egged on by a Tory press, had given David Cameron an unwanted extra electoral mountain to climb.

Moreover, it seemed that it wasn't just Lib Dem policies you couldn't trust. The coalition partners themselves, we were told, had proved personally dishonest time and again. David Laws, Chief Secretary to the Treasury and one of the main negotiators of the Coalition Agreement, lasted only seventeen days in office before the *Daily Telegraph*, arch-crusader against MPs' expenses fiddles, managed to drive him onto the back benches for a while.[21] Vince Cable, Business Secretary and thus the minister responsible for handling Rupert Murdoch's controversial bid to buy back all of BSkyB, told a couple of *Telegraph* women reporters (posing as simple constituents) that he was 'at war' with Mr Murdoch and would never approve the deal.[22] Chris Huhne, the Energy Secretary, was caught in the toils of an extramarital affair by the Sunday tabloids in an almost Strindbergian saga that bizarrely saw both him and his bitterly estranged wife sent to prison for perjury.[23]

Of course the press always seeks to ferret out and expose bad behaviour in government. By some lights, the biggest fishes landed in coalition time were Conservatives not Liberal Democrats: Liam Fox, the Defence Secretary and leading right-winger in the government, pursued (mostly by *The Guardian*) in a complex story of when and why a friend and unofficial adviser accompanied him on ministerial visits;[24] Andrew Mitchell, the Chief Whip, who had to resign after an altercation in Downing Street featuring policemen, false witness and the *Sun*;[25] Maria Miller, the hapless Culture Secretary, swept away by more expense muddles.[26] But Liberal Democrats – stumbling over cash claims, gullible about reporters fishing for a tale and lying when suspicion encircled them – offered constant vulnerability. In part this was naivety. Nobody in the previous parliament had sought to put individual Lib

[21] David Laws, 22 *Days in May: The Birth of the Lib Dem–Conservative Coalition* (London: Biteback, 2010), pp. 258–61.

[22] Robert Winnett, 'Vince Cable: I have declared war on Rupert Murdoch', *Daily Telegraph*, 21 December 2010.

[23] Peter Walker, 'Chris Huhne and Vicky Pryce each jailed for eight months', *The Guardian*, 11 March 2013.

[24] Allegra Stratton, 'Liam Fox resigns', *The Guardian*, 14 October 2011.

[25] 'Police apologise to Andrew Mitchell for plebgate affair', *Daily Telegraph*, 20 January 2014.

[26] 'Maria Miller resigns as culture secretary over expenses row', *The Guardian*, 9 April 2014.

Dem frailties under the microscope. They were simply not important enough to warrant such scrutiny. But when Liberal Democrats moved into Cabinet posts, all that naturally changed. Now they were there to be examined and perhaps exposed. Now high office, and their reputation for teeth-grinding piety, exacted its natural toll.

At which point, the coverage of politics and politicians by the media turned acrid – and cut both ways. Chris Huhne made the change himself in a *Guardian* column written after his release.

> My endgame began when Neville Thurlbeck, the chief reporter of the now defunct *News of the World*, heard gossip that I was having an affair. Rather than cheap-skating on the proposed investigation by hacking my phone, the *News of the World* put me under extensive surveillance by a retired policeman ... Why was News International prepared to invest so much to tail an opposition Liberal Democrat back in 2009? Maybe it was coincidence, but that summer I was the only frontbencher who, with Nick Clegg's brave backing, called for the Metropolitan Police to reopen the voicemail hacking inquiry into Rupert Murdoch's empire.[27]

Such linkage – alleging that the treatment meted out to politicians by the press was directly connected to political pressure on journalists over phone hacking – wasn't greatly welcomed or believed. Huhne briefly became a figure of Fleet Street derision. But the long saga of Lord Justice Leveson's report into press regulation, and into politicians' relations with journalists, made that connection far more soberly. Leveson was no side-show for the coalition – or indeed for all politicians. To the contrary, it was a constant descant throughout this parliament.

New hacks, old scandals

For proper understanding, the phone-hacking saga needs history and a context. In the years around the millennium it became quite usual for many Fleet Street papers secretly to hire the services of private detectives – professionals paid to trace car numbers, discover private telephone numbers and other tasks that weren't immediately suited to

[27] Chris Huhne, 'People despise politicians, but whose fault is that?', *The Guardian*, 8 September 2013.

conventional investigative reporting. A new Data Protection Act allowed such activities when a public interest could be cited. Inevitably, perhaps, on at least some papers, that interest spilled over to cover less elevated services – and a cluster of detective agencies offered to monitor and transcribe messages left on mobile phones in a general, trawling exercise. It was a growth industry. The Information Commissioner became alarmed and, with Hampshire Police, prompted Operation Motorman, an inquiry and prosecution designed to bring one errant private eye to book.[28] But when that case was finally, and expensively, brought, it subsided into confusion. The public weren't much exercised by intrusions into privacy which only came to assume more menacing proportions when a mundane royal gossip paragraph in the *News of the World* prompted another police investigation and, this time, the jailing of a journalist – Clive Goodman, the royal editor – and Glen Mulcaire, his hacker of choice. Andy Coulson, the paper's editor, professed personal innocence, but stood down as an act of supposed contrition.[29]

The Information Commissioner, however, was concerned by these data protection breaches. He went to the Press Complaints Commission, which issued warning guidelines to newspapers. An early trickle of victims – not just the young princes at the Palace, but Gordon Taylor, the football union leader, and Max Clifford, the celebrity fixer – began to grow into a flood. The *Guardian* investigative reporter, Nick Davies, was on the case. So were lawyers scenting a potential revenue stream. Gordon Taylor initiated a suit for damages against the *News of the World*. The paper's lawyers wanted confidentiality, and paid £725,000 to help secure it. But the story leaked and gradually, after 2008, *The Guardian* began to assemble a much broader and more alarming account of a newspaper spun out of control: one, moreover, that couldn't be relied on to tell the truth about itself.

David Cameron, in opposition, was looking for a spin doctor in the Alastair Campbell mould. Andy Coulson was out of a job; he was offered this one.[30] The links between Wapping and the Conservative

---

[28] Leveson Inquiry, 'Operation Motorman/Associated Newspapers Ltd', 10 July 2012 (accessed at www.levesoninquiry.org.uk/wp-content/uploads/2011/11/Operation-Motorman-and-ANL-10-July-2012.pdf, 3 October 2014).

[29] Nick Davies, *Hack Attack: How the Truth Caught up with Rupert Murdoch* (London: Chatto and Windus, 2014).

[30] Francis Elliott and James Hanning, *Cameron: Practically a Conservative* (London: Fourth Estate, 2012), pp. 326–9.

Party couldn't have been more manifest – nor more personally dangerous to Mr Cameron's reputation, in *The Guardian*'s opinion. The
paper's deputy editor wrote privately to Cameron advising him not to
appoint Coulson as his Downing Street spokesman after the election,
but to no avail.[31] When, in March 2011, Nick Davies produced the
incendiary (and, in the event, slightly misleading) story that the *News of
the World* had hacked into the phone of the murdered teenager, Milly
Dowler, giving her distraught parents hope that she was still alive, the
whole affair suddenly became politically explosive. Andy Coulson, still
protesting his innocence, left Number 10. A 'humiliated' Rupert Murdoch closed down Britain's biggest-selling Sunday paper. Scotland
Yard, notably dilatory in the earlier stages of this scandal, moved into
overdrive (if not overkill). David Cameron, needing to do something,
called for Lord Justice Leveson and instituted a full inquiry – initially
into the general behaviour of the press (since hacking itself was under
continuing police inquiry) plus relationships between police, politicians
and press.

Here, then, was an infernal tangle of strands and motives, much
complicated by the fact of coalition (and thus inability to take a firm
stand on an issue far beyond that initial agreement). Both Tony Blair
and Gordon Brown had been devout worshippers at the Temple of
Rupert: Prime Minister Blair was godfather to one of Murdoch's children by his third wife, Prime Minister Brown had invited the new
mistress of Wapping, Rebekah Brooks, for a family weekend at
Chequers. Labour, historically, was not best placed to wash its hands
at the temple door. But its new leader, Ed Miliband, wanted an issue
that would help him define a fresh start. Here it was, especially as a
weakened Rupert and deeply troubled younger son, James, struggled to
extricate their reputations from a swamp. And the Liberal Democrats,
of course, owed nothing to the Murdoch press, which had never given
them the time of day. So a combination of Labour, the Liberal Democrats, and a small, yapping pack of Cameron-haters on the PM's own
backbenches, made the whole inquiry – not to mention the police
investigation – a fraught experience for top politicians and press
barons alike.

---

[31] Nick Davies, 'Andy Coulson: Questions remain for David Cameron and others', *The
Guardian*, 25 June 2014.

There was some relief for Number 10 as the inquiry wound on. Sir Brian Leveson shrewdly declined, either in person or in his report, to ruffle their feathers overmuch. Nevertheless, in terms of currying press support by any of the normal means – from tea and biscuits in Number 10 down – the Conservatives were hugely constrained. They could promise little and realistically expect to deliver even less. There was scant chance, for instance, of waving through Rupert Murdoch's hopes for re-purchasing all of BSkyB, for 'Murdoch' had become a toxic name. What they did have, though, was at least the prospect of influence when it came to delivering Leveson's conclusions on a revised, more draconian structure of press regulation. Nick Clegg could raise 'serious questions on basic corporate governance in the Murdoch empire' permitting illegal invasions of privacy on an industrial scale. Ed Miliband could openly ask whether Murdoch was a 'fit and proper' owner of BSkyB.[32] The Conservatives could not jump to meet the public mood too obviously; they had to play a more convoluted game. So the business of 'implementing the full Leveson' (as the pressure group *Hacked Off* demanded) slowly became a mystery buried in a miasma. On the one hand, the tabloid press didn't like it because they feared that statutory intervention, however light touch, would further limit their chances of telling the celebrity human interest tales they believed shifted most copies. They perceived themselves trapped in a shrinking industry already. This was one last squeeze to be avoided. Perhaps backstairs lobbying wasn't a potent factor in these circumstances. The clout of the Murdochs had shrivelled. But newspapers, if they lined up together, could still give politicians – especially in a divided government – pause.

Thus the prospect of a regulator monitored by Ofcom (i.e. by a state-sanctified quango) was amended after vigorous press opposition. Downing Street came up with an alternative: regulation by royal charter. That seemed at first sight to provide proper independence, until the details of agreement (a non-agreement, because it included representatives of *Hacked Off* but not of the publishers over chocolate biscuits late one night in Ed Miliband's office) came under acerbic analysis. The will of Parliament was clear. The Privy Council had its charter. Nobody on the press side of the table, however, wished to go forward with it. There was no stable parliamentary majority that could bring pressure

[32] Daniel Boffey and Toby Helm, 'Ed Miliband will urge MPs to halt Murdoch's BskyB takeover', *The Observer*, 9 July 2011.

to bear. Coalitions of any sort, when asked to address complex issues of principle, couldn't exert the necessary authority: and compromise, equally, could be resisted (in this case by the press).[33]

Gradually, at least until beyond the next election, the whole chapter of threats and arguments ran into the sands. The court that had spent eight months trying Coulson and Brooks saw a jury find Coulson guilty (along with five other ex-*News of the World* employees) but stop far short of convicting Brooks.[34] Chains of possible pursuit to Rupert Murdoch in New York were duly severed. Most of the press got on with doing its own Independent Press Standards Organisation thing and left the charter side of the equation drifting in limbo.[35] There was political agreement, after a fashion, between all front benches at Westminster. But there was no concerted will to enforce such agreement. Fleet Street's accounts of the Brooks/Coulson verdict on the morning told their own story. *The Guardian*, crusader against hacking, headlined Coulson's guilt; *The Times*, the most acceptable face of Murdoch, led with Brooks' acquittal; and perhaps the most powerful paper of the lot, the *Daily Mail*, turned all its guns on David Cameron – for hiring the wrong spin doctor and then for setting up Leveson. Too many agendas ... especially in a coalition sinking further into the swamps of European angst over the appointment of a new Brussels commission president.

The longer the accords of May 2010 went on, the thinner and more fractious their observance became. The closer a new general election loomed, the greater the press excitement (elections mean change and business as usual). But there was no settled agenda to any of this, no easy predictability. Whom would the *Mail* and the *Sun* support if not David Cameron? Nigel Farage and his surging UKIP offered easy allure. But that, for any big newspaper group seeking influence in future, wasn't a realistic option. The confusions of coalition were taking their toll. A complex balance of power and promises invites a web of commentary and allegiance in return. And that clearly goes for the broadcasters as well.

---

[33] Elizabeth Rigby, 'Press and politicians still miles apart on UK regulation', *Financial Times*, 24 June 2014.

[34] Lisa O'Carroll, 'Andy Coulson jailed for 18 months for conspiracy to hack phones', *The Guardian*, 4 July 2014.

[35] Lisa O'Carroll, 'Press industry pushes ahead with new regulator despite political deadlock', *The Guardian*, 8 July 2013.

The ghost of Savile, a haunted BBC

Broadcasting in Britain is more than the BBC of course; but still, at its heart, in the way that it covers news, and particularly political news, it is the BBC. The corporation's Political Editor is the most authoritative source of reference on Westminster and Whitehall's passing parade. Whilst the BBC's political discussion programmes are watched by relatively few – *Newsnight* has an average audience of 600,000, substantially less than *Guardian* readership alone; the *Daily Politics* may attract no more than 15,000 viewers, far fewer than many local papers – they nevertheless help set agendas. Politicians and corporation are bound together off-screen in an often sickly, sometimes poisonous embrace. What the public hears on air is only a sliver of the contacts and pressures behind the scenes. Governments, in a particular crisis, can secure the removal of BBC chairmen and director-generals. They can tear up existing structures for governance and impose fresh ones. And they can clearly, on their record, make sure that the top authority at the corporation is exercised by someone politically acceptable to them. This is a zone of suppressed conflict for journalism.

No one, as the coalition took office in the midst of economic crisis, could see such conflict fading away. There were obvious weaknesses which politicians could exploit. When Mr Cameron set his own salary as a reasonable benchmark for public service, it was less than an eighth of the money going to the then Director-General. Pay-offs to departing BBC executives reaching more than £1 million were a chewed bone of constant contention. And then, in the late autumn of 2011, the ghost of Jimmy Savile returned, igniting a malevolent crisis of its own.

Savile, an eccentric disc jockey and perfect, gentle knight of charitable deeds so far as the British public was concerned, died on 29 October. A BBC tribute to one of its oldest stars aired on 11 November. But by then, a *Newsnight* team, long suspicious of Savile's activities with vulnerable children and women, on corporation territory or off, had begun to put together an investigation that showed him to have been an energetic, ruthlessly exploitative paedophile. Somehow, though, this embryo programme was scrapped by *Newsnight*'s editor. Had he been nobbled higher up the chain? Where did a brand new Director-General, George Entwistle, stand in this swirl of events? ITV showed a documentary that trod much the same path as *Newsnight*'s blocked investigation. Entwistle, ruthlessly questioned on the *Today* programme, performed feebly – and resigned. The whole system of BBC governance under the BBC Trust system (and chairman Lord Patten, once chairman of the Conservative Party) came under bitter criticism. Lord Hall, a one-time BBC Head of News, was brought back at short notice from the Royal Opera House to serve as Director-General on Patten's say-so, with obvious Downing Street approval. Then Patten himself retired early, pleading ill health. Who would succeed him was essentially a Number 10 decision. The Cabinet Secretary was the most formidable member of the initial selection committee – and the question of Trust survival also rested with Number 10. The future of the corporation, and its role as Britain's most important news provider, was in play long before the grant of the next royal charter in 2017.

Note the disparity here between the lines of command and theoretical control which link politicians and the press and politicians and broadcasters. Politicians courted the press, and got into dire trouble as a result. David Cameron, like Brown and Blair before him, laid out the Downing Street welcome mat for Rupert Murdoch. Rebekah Brooks was a weekend chum on the Oxfordshire cocktail circuit. Andy Coulson was appointed Number 10 press secretary with a diary full of contacts. The whole process involved flattery, favours and fawning on every side. It was not direct. There are no simple levers to be pulled. But broadcasting – in particular, relations with the BBC – was and remains very different. Here power flows straight from the Prime Minister. He selects the governing Trust chairman himself, after a few manoeuvres including a hand-picked panel of experts (including his own Cabinet Secretary). He set the frozen licence fee level in direct negotiations with Mark Thompson, the former Director-General. He can appoint a top BBC producer, Craig Oliver, as his press secretary without anyone raising an eyebrow. He can also sign up a former head of BBC corporate strategy, turn her into a peer and make her leader of the House of Lords if he so wishes. And he can treat his Culture Secretary, Maria Miller, as little more than a post box when the going gets rough.

The BBC, in so many ways, answers to him – either by straightforward or by second-phase appointments. Of course that doesn't mean that every news bulletin responds at the click of his fingers. The BBC, in its staff antipathy to political manipulation, still retains a battered independence. Andy Coulson, in Downing Street action, was a notably more effective – and respected – spin doctor than Oliver. But there is absolutely no doubt where the lines of control, and of eventual retribution, run. The corporation can be brave; but not too brave. There is always the next licence settlement, and the next royal charter renewal, just down the track. And see, yet again, how the swift agreements of coalition left all of this influence – over both broadcasters and the press – in Conservative hands. The Deputy Prime Minister had no hot line to Broadcasting House. He chose no appointments committees, approved no selections, was allowed no ministers in the higher reaches of the DCMS. He had no friends in Oxfordshire, no Chequers (only a part share in Chevening), no ready access to press barons, few favours of his own to bestow. Even his weekly phone-ins on LBC soon faded from public consciousness. The terms of media trade, as they became manifest, were wholly one-sided. Indeed, at moments of high risk such as the July 2014 reshuffle, it was almost as though the Liberal Democrats had ceased to exist. This was a Conservative shake-up engineered by a Conservative Prime Minister, no partners seemingly involved.

Change, and no change

What lessons can be drawn over these five years, either for possible new coalitions thrown up in the immediate future or for the prospects of other coalitions further down the track as party allegiances grow even fainter and more notional? The most obvious and immediate, perhaps, is that Britain's media, in their understanding of electoral reform and the whole structure of governance, are as yet wholly unsuited to the give-and-take of coalition chronicling. The weaker party can be bullied unashamedly. The stronger party can often seem to govern alone. Electoral reform that might, over time, re-balance power and expectation is a passion that soon fades once it leaves Westminster's corridors. The reality of power in a two-party system can endure many sacrifices and disappointments before it is truly relinquished. And with that goes the reality of media power as well.

There was barely a moment, once the early sheen had worn off, where the Liberal Democrats were portrayed as more than an irritating irrelevance – or their leader as a politician of stature. Fair comment? When this coalition government camped on front pages, as it did for the days of the July 2014 reshuffle, it was as though the junior partners had

ceased to exist. By far the biggest headlines were reserved for Michael
Gove, and his grumpy transition from Education Secretary to Chief
Whip. 'Teachers gleeful at Gove sacking', reported *The Times*.[36] 'Sack
your most dynamic minister? Pathetic,' replied that same paper's Philip
Collins.[37] Gove, a *Times* journalist before he turned to politics full-time,
was storm centre for Downing Street, which busily pointed out that
junior ministers keen on the Gove reforms had been put in place to keep
revolution rolling. But none of this acknowledged the continuing influence of Gove's most effective and long-running deputy, David Laws,
minister of state for schools and – four years before – the most dedicated,
engaged broker of coalition on the Liberal Democrat side. It was as
though he had vanished from sight. No policy and no influence attached
to him because, after May 2015, he and his party were assumed to be
doomed. Fixed terms played both ways. They offered certainty in the
beginning and a very different sort of certainty at the end. Number 10
had no need to worry about the shifts of public opinion early on, because
public opinion brought no immediate demands to bear. But, as the
months ticked away, perceptions and media scrutiny turned full circle.

There was, for instance, no real debate about why Michael
Gove had been demoted. *The Times*, with natural concern for an old
newsroom retainer, soon revealed the 'greatest threat' to the Education
Secretary's career prospects: Lynton Crosby, the Australian campaign
adviser hired by David Cameron.

> A senior figure in the Conservatives' new party headquarters said
> that Crosby, while admiring Mr Gove's intellectual abilities as a
> 'think tank on legs', was dismayed by the flow of controversy from
> his department. In all the focus groups and surveys, Gove achieved
> the unwanted double of being recognized and disliked by the
> public. One YouGov poll found that 55 percent of the public
> thought he was doing badly at the job. The picture that emerged of
> polling in marginal seats was said to be even starker, especially in
> areas with high numbers of public sector workers.[38]

In one sense, as all papers picked up the same briefing, there seemed no
more open tribute to media power – and no more profoundly bleak

---

[36] Greg Hurst, 'Teachers gleeful at Gove sacking', *The Times*, 16 July 2014.
[37] Philip Collins, 'Sack your most dynamic minister? Pathetic', *The Times*, 18 July 2014.
[38] Francis Elliot and Greg Hurst, 'Three assassins who finished off Cameron's friend
Michael Gove', *The Times*, 16 July 2014.

comment on political feebleness. Michael Gove was out of departmental office because the electorate, especially teachers, didn't like him. Therefore, with only ten months to go to an election, he had to be shuffled out of the headlines. It wasn't a matter of whether his reforms were good or bad. (Philip Collins, with his 'Pathetic' verdict, was actually a Labour speechwriter in earlier days.) It was a question of reading the numbers and ditching people the public didn't like – just as, because the same polls suggested a lack of key women in Cabinet office, so 'middle-aged, tired, white men' must collect their cards. The *Daily Mail*, mounting its own 'cat walk' across two whole pages, showed David Cameron's new female choices striding out, one with a slit skirt, one with a formidably tight dress. What the voter apparently wanted, the voter would jolly well get.

And here you can sense more than the normal operation of electoral politics, a twist in the whole concept of coalition operation. Of course the Liberal Democrats were victims, but the whole media context for coalition in a fixed-term parliament had changed. Tony Blair took Labour to the polls after four years as a matter almost of routine. He couldn't abide being fenced in by the calendar. He hugged his room to manoeuvre close. There was thus a building of excitement in the press lobby, a feeling of momentous events to come as new initiatives, new sweeties, were showered on the electorate. The aim, always, was to demonstrate that those who ruled us today had the fire to do so tomorrow. But no such momentum operated in fixed-term Westminster. The 'government', that is the coalition, had little of the original agreement left to implement. The cupboard of promises was notably bare. Neither partner was campaigning for a renewal of their power on current terms. Many Conservatives could not abide the thought of a further liaison with the Liberal Democrats, and vice versa. Some Liberal Democrats (in the old *Guardian–Independent* camp) still favoured an alliance with Labour; some, mostly Liberal Party survivors in what was already a coalition with the Social Democrats, predicted only extinction along that route. There was, then, no chance of the government we have battling to become the government we should re-elect. On the contrary, partnership on anything but a day-to-day level was redundant. Conservative aspirations, such as pulling out of the European Convention on Human Rights, could only be promises, bitterly opposed by their Liberal Democrat coalition allies (to the fury of the *Daily Mail, Telegraph* et al.).

In which case the reshuffle of July 2014 became clearly more than a freshening of the Tory team; rather, it was a statement of ideological intent delivered in human terms. Dominic Grieve, the Attorney-General who had always seen legal problems in quitting the Human Rights Convention, was surprised – he confessed to Andrew Marr – to find himself peremptorily removed. Ken Clarke, last of the true European defenders in Cabinet, was definitively retired. The Euro-sceptics got what they were asking for; UKIP had its pounds of flesh. But Gove, too, was shifted away from the front line and a young mum put in his place. David Cameron might not be able to move coalition policy. He could, though, move the outward, visible, and personal pawns around the board to show where he wanted to go and how astutely he read the polls presented to him each week. There was nothing else to do.

Credit for the successes of past years was difficult to claim and harder to apportion. Liberal Democrats could recall the national emergency of 2010 and burnish their own part in recovery. But too much praise couldn't be heaped on Chancellor Osborne, who was now a *de facto* enemy. The emergency had (allegedly) passed, therefore Nick Clegg, Danny Alexander and Co. deserved gratitude. But gratitude was no mandate for a renewal of this coalition – a renewal that couldn't be guaranteed or even straightforwardly voted for after the failure to implement electoral reform. Success, in any case, meant that a minority government would be sorely tempted – or, in the case of the Conservatives, mandated – to govern alone pending a further election.

Never again, except by accident?

In sum, at one level, five years of profound change seemed to signal very little change. There was nil nostalgia for the Blair and Brown era. No editors, even of Labour-supporting papers, bothered to construct scenarios of what might have transpired if Gordon Brown had triumphed in 2010 and sailed on without boom or bust. (Not so much promising media what-if territory as a wasteland). The coming election outcome itself, amid all the predictable wrangling over TV debates, seemed more impenetrably uncertain than in 2010. The leader writers of Fleet Street were poised to repeat themselves: the *Mail*, *Telegraph* and *Sun* lining up behind the Conservatives, the *Mirror* and now the *Guardian* able to back Labour with greater or lesser intensity, the *FT* sure to manifest a certain distaste over Labour's business policies, the *Independent* ready to echo its masthead name and embrace no party in particular and only the *Express* flirting with UKIP.

There were major differences to register, of course. Rupert Murdoch was unwelcome now, even via the back entrance to Downing Street. His power to intimidate politicians had waned with humiliation. Who needed to buy back all of BSkyB? He could make huge profits in the satellite-strewn skies over Europe after his empire had been carved in two, its press presence a much diminished beast. The prospect of a majority Conservative government forgetting all about Leveson and royal charters, thus lending a fat slice of self-interest to the outcome, was motive enough to keep the Tory press faithful in any case – and no help whatsoever to Labour or Liberal Democrats. The incidence of a new BBC royal charter, with all its opportunities to soften Broadcasting House resistance, brought a damp blanket of apprehension to Broadcasting House. Meanwhile, party loyalties, and thus voter loyalties, weakened by the year. Nigel Farage and Boris Johnson rose because, in media eyes, they were not conventional politicians dishing out the same careful formulas. They sounded different. Boris's past sexual adventures didn't matter any more to the electorate than Farage's breezy attitude to MEP expenses – a topic of repeated *Times* attack – or his ditching of the entire UKIP 2010 manifesto with a laugh and shrug.[39] They couldn't be 'exposed' because, uncaring, even chortling, they seemed happy to expose themselves.

Some things had changed, of course; some things were changing. There was a sense, in journalism as in politics, of assumptions flaking under pressure. But it was wrong to see incremental movements as upheaval – especially as digital revolution. Between 2010 and 2014, on Ofcom's reckoning, the major TV news bulletins had lost three or so points of their viewing audience while news on mobile apps had bounded forward from 32 per cent to 41 per cent. The young especially were sitting in front of a TV set much less. But the BBC Online was still the most favoured source of digital news, providing a steady diet of fairness, balance and muted opinions.

---

[39] Rowena Mason, 'Nigel Farage disowns Ukip's entire 2010 election manifesto', *The Guardian*, 24 January 2014.

Perhaps, at the margins, the thought of future coalitions seemed less frightening, more normal in the process. It did not, however, become a settled perception. The media game, which theoretically aimed to lead public opinion, was still way behind as newspaper print circulations dipped year after year by between 5 and 10 per cent. Some of that decline, to be sure, was due to the march of instant digital verdicts: Michael Gove's departure was a major Twitter event; criticisms of Alex Salmond's debate performances in Scotland's referendum flooded cyberspace. Internet outrage was the flavour of moment after moment in a world that often appeared to be dominated by trolls, pouring out their bile and disappointments in ways that seemed to spread outrage as a contagion into print, too. Yet the old terms of media trade had not vanished completely. This was a very slow revolution, if revolution at all; in ends, if not means. The daily YouGov poll findings, dutifully carried on the *Spectator* website, reported Labour's lead eerily static for year after year. The earth was not moving beneath politics.

Against all expectation, moreover, the parties of potential government had clung together remarkably efficiently through the storm. The story of coalition-building and policy implementation might not have been as exciting as political correspondents wished, but it nevertheless represented solid achievement. The politicians could move where the pundits and the voters would not. Embarrassing wobbles such as the premature leaking of George Osborne's 2012 Budget (by Liberal Democrat chatter) were never repeated.[40] Personal relationships inside many departments were often notably good. In practical, human terms there was much to celebrate. Politicians could work together. There were new ways of running things. But, alas, that wasn't 'the story'. And next time round – in when-and-if land – there'll be even fewer editors celebrating as their hopes of a clear overall majority for their chosen ones fade.

---

[40] Asa Bennett, 'The 2012 Budget – as revealed in leaks to the press days beforehand', *Huffington Post UK*, 20 March 2012.

21 THE COALITION, ELECTIONS AND REFERENDUMS

JOHN CURTICE

Party stances

The Liberal Democrats have long exhibited a particular interest in constitutional and electoral reform. For many years the party has wanted to get rid of an electoral system for the House of Commons that does it no favours. Ever since the late nineteenth century it has expressed a belief in 'home rule' and thus in separately elected devolved institutions. Meanwhile, it was a Liberal government that at the beginning of the twentieth century first limited the power of the Lords and envisaged its ultimate replacement by an elected body.

In contrast, the Conservative Party has often looked like the party of the constitutional status quo. It has consistently been sceptical of the case for electoral reform, has opposed Lords reform and was the last mainstream party to embrace devolution. Elections and referendums in their many potential and varied guises might thus be thought to constitute a potential sticking point in any attempt to fashion a coalition between the two parties. However, the May 2010 election occurred against a backdrop that meant that even a party whose instinct has often been to defend Britain's organic, uncodified constitution was in fact proposing significant change to the electoral process, as well as the more extensive use of referendums.

There were a number of reasons for this development. By no means the least was a crisis of confidence at Westminster. Politicians had already been worrying for a decade or more about apparently falling levels of trust, both in them as a group and in the political system that they ran, an erosion that many felt was reflected in declining levels of turnout at election time.[1] But then in the year before the 2010 election a scandal erupted about the expenses paid to MPs. The *Daily Telegraph* obtained and published details of the claims made by MPs between 2004 and 2008, details that the Commons authorities had fought hard in the courts to avoid being made public under the provisions of the Freedom of Information Act. The public were outraged at hearing of a system that was apparently exploited by MPs to help them buy a second home as well as fund the cost of seemingly inessential items such as a duck house and the maintenance of a croquet lawn. As the man supposedly in charge of the administration of the Commons, the Speaker, Michael Martin, was forced to fall on his sword and resign. But the scandal also stimulated all the parties to respond to the public's anger by considering proposals for reducing the cost of politics and making MPs more accountable to voters for their alleged sins.

Meanwhile, what had once been regarded as an instrument incompatible with British parliamentary democracy, the referendum, had come to be a regular feature of the nation's life during the previous thirteen years of Labour government. Within six months of coming to power Labour had held referendums to secure public consent for the establishment of devolved institutions in Scotland and Wales. That was followed – with varying degrees of success – by referendums to restore city-wide government (including a Mayor) in London, directly elected executive Mayors in some English and Welsh local authorities, and a regional assembly in the north of England. Meanwhile Northern Ireland held a referendum on its constitutional future, the second since the outbreak of the Troubles in the late 1960s, in this case to endorse the Good Friday Agreement that it was hoped would bring the province's civil strife to an end. In short, it had almost become the norm that major constitutional reform should be preceded by a vote at the ballot box – a principle that could also be easily to thought to apply to Britain's relationship to Europe, which, after all, had been the subject of the UK's first and hitherto only state-wide referendum back in 1975.

---

[1] C. Pattie and R. Johnston, 'A low turnout landslide: Abstention at the British general election of 1997', *Political Studies*, 49 (2001), pp. 286–305; J. Curtice, 'Bridging the Gulf? Britain's democracy after the 2010 election', in A. Park, E. Clery, J. Curtice, M. Phillips and D. Utting (eds.), *British Social Attitudes: The 28th Report* (London: Sage, 2011), pp. 1–20.

Consequently the 2010 Conservative manifesto contained many a proposal for electoral change.[2] In the wake of the MPs' expenses scandal it proposed that the number of MPs be cut by 10 per cent, while just before the election it had experimented with selecting its candidates via postal ballots of all voters in a constituency. It also proposed that errant MPs should potentially be subject to 'recall', that is, be forced to fight a by-election should enough voters demand one. At the same time, the party wanted to see a substantial shake-up of the rules for creating parliamentary constituencies in the first place, aware as it was of a 'bias' in the current system that ensured that in 2010 the party was unable to secure an overall majority despite being seven points ahead of Labour in terms of votes.[3] In addition the party wanted to give the public a greater voice in policing by introducing elected police commissioners, one for each police force in England and Wales outside of London, a proposal that would create an entirely new electoral process.

Meanwhile, the Conservative manifesto was littered with proposals for referendums. The party proposed to bind itself and future governments to holding a referendum in the event of any proposal that significant further powers be transferred to the European Union. Closer to home, the party also wanted to require local councils to hold a referendum should they wish to increase their council tax by more than what the central government was recommending, while voters themselves would be able to force a local council to hold a referendum on a subject of local concern if 5 per cent of them were to petition that such a ballot be held. At the same time, the party said that it 'would not stand in the way' of holding a referendum on granting the National Assembly for Wales full legislative powers, a ballot for which the previous Labour government had already legislated and which the Welsh Assembly Government now wanted to hold. The Conservatives even championed the directly elected Mayors that Labour had originally introduced,[4] proposing that referendums on introducing the post be held in the twelve largest provincial English cities.

[2] The Conservative Party, *An Invitation to Join the Government of Britain: The Conservative Party Manifesto 2010* (London: Conservative Party, 2010)

[3] J. Curtice, 'So what went wrong with the electoral system? The 2010 Election result and the debate about electoral reform', *Parliamentary Affairs*, 63 (2010), pp. 623–38

[4] J. Curtice, B. Seyd and K. Thomson, 'Do mayoral elections work? Evidence from London', *Political Studies*, 56 (2008), pp. 653–78

As we might anticipate from their long-standing interest in reform, many if not quite all of these proposals also appeared in the Liberal Democrats' manifesto.[5] Indeed, despite the party's long-standing pro-European stance, this even included holding a referendum on the principle of Britain's membership of the European Union should there be a proposal for a transfer of powers to Brussels. True, the party did also have a few ideas of its own. It wanted an even deeper cut in the number of MPs – to just 500. The voting age, it argued, should be reduced to 16. It anticipated introducing elections to (English and Welsh) police authorities rather than the election of a single commissioner, and the creation of elected local health boards (in England) too. It also proposed taking away the almost unfettered right of a Prime Minister to call an election at a time of his or her choosing and switch instead to a system whereby parliaments would normally be of a fixed length. But in truth for the most part the two parties did not seem that far apart when it came to elections and referendums.

Indeed that was even the case when it came to the contentious issue of Lords reform. This had become unfinished business after the previous Labour government had successfully legislated in 1999 for the removal of most of the upper chamber's hereditary members, but had failed to implement any alternative, thereby accidentally turning the Lords into a chamber of lifetime appointees whose democratic credentials were arguably just as open to challenge as those of the former hereditary members. But not only did the Liberal Democrats, as we would anticipate, propose that the Lords become a body whose members should be elected via a system of proportional representation, but the Conservatives too had at least a guarded reference to Lords reform, stating that they would 'work to build a consensus for a mainly elected Second Chamber' – though critics might note that securing such a consensus had hitherto proven elusive.

However, that still left one potentially serious difference between the two prospective coalition partners – changing the electoral system for the House of Commons. The Liberal Democrats were committed to their traditional position that the Commons (and indeed local councils) be elected by proportional representation (preferably the Single Transferable Vote), a switch that the party anticipated would transform

[5] Liberal Democrats, *Liberal Democrat Manifesto 2010* (London: Liberal Democrats, 2010)

its electoral prospects and might be regarded as the most valuable prize it could secure from being part of a coalition government for the first time since 1945. In contrast, this was one area where the Conservatives retained their traditional stance in favour of the constitutional status quo. Much rested in the negotiations between the two parties on whether and how the two positions on this issue could possibly be reconciled.

The Programme for Government

In the event a compromise was found – in the form of yet another referendum, arguably a classic example of that institution's potential role as a means of resolving policy differences. However, rather than a vote on the introduction of proportional representation, the coalition's Programme for Government stated that it would be one on a much less radical change, to the so-called Alternative Vote.[6] This system retains the principle of single-member constituencies to which many Conservatives were wedded, but enables voters to place the candidates in their constituency in order of preference rather than simply placing an 'X' against the name of the candidate that they most prefer. In the event that no candidate secures at least half (plus one) of the votes cast, those given to the least popular candidates are redistributed in accordance with the second and subsequent preferences expressed by those candidates' voters until one candidate does reach that threshold.[7] Given that third-placed Conservative and Labour voters would be more likely to give their second preferences to the Liberal Democrats than to their opponents, the system offered the Liberal Democrats at least some prospect of wining more seats, while there would still be quite a high likelihood that one party (and thus the Conservatives) could secure an overall majority.[8]

Otherwise, so far as electoral issues and the referendum are concerned, the coalition's Programme for Government was largely a collation of the heavily overlapping ideas contained in the two parties' individual manifestos. Thus, apart from the proposals that appeared in

[6] HM Government, *The Coalition: Our Programme for Government* (London: Cabinet Office, 2010)

[7] A. Renwick, *A Citizen's Guide to Electoral Reform* (London: Biteback, 2011).

[8] J. Curtice, 'Politicians, voters and democracy: The 2011 UK referendum on the Alternative Vote', *Electoral Studies*, 32 (2013), pp. 215–23.

both documents for referendums on Welsh devolution and on any future transfer of powers to the European Union, the programme incorporated the Conservative proposal for referendums on allegedly excessive council tax increases and on introducing directly elected Mayors together with the Liberal Democrat idea that voters themselves should be able to initiate referendums on issues of local concern. Meanwhile the Liberal Democrats secured the introduction of fixed-term parliaments, thereby gaining insurance against the risk that the Conservatives would seek to go to the country early in the hope of winning an overall majority, while the Conservatives secured a commitment to reform of the system of drawing up Commons constituencies, a move they hoped would improve their chances of winning an overall majority when the next election did eventually come around. At the same time the programme included the idea of giving voters the power to recall an MP (an idea backed by both parties), the establishment of a committee to develop proposals for an elected House of Lords (an apparent compromise between the two parties' positions on the subject), and reducing the number of MPs by fifty (rather less than had been proposed by both parties when in opposition). Reform of the governance of the police appeared in the form of the Tory proposal that a single commissioner should be elected in each police area, albeit one who was clearly accountable to the local police authority. There was also one commitment that did not appear in either manifesto (even though the Tories had experimented with the idea) – to fund 200 all-postal primary elections in constituencies where parties were selecting candidates for the 2015 election, while, on the other hand, the Liberal Democrat proposals for elected health authorities and votes at 16 were dropped.

So, contrary to what we might have anticipated would be the case, the entry of the Liberal Democrats into government for the first time since 1945 did not on its own force reform of electoral processes onto the policy agenda. Many of the proposals for changing or creating elections or introducing referendums were ones that the two parties shared in common. To that extent, much of the coalition's agenda might well still have been pursued even if the Conservatives had been in government alone. The one exception was that a step was taken towards a possible change to the electoral system used in elections to the House of Commons, but even then the proposition was for a possible change that fell quite a way short of the Liberal Democrats' ambition for electoral reform.

Indeed, much of the agenda to which the coalition was committed was also shared with the Labour party, and thus might well have been pursued anyway.[9] Ironically, it was Labour's manifesto that had originally proposed that there should be a referendum on introducing the Alternative Vote. Labour also backed an elected Lords using a system of proportional representation, albeit it envisaged that all rather than just most of its members would be elected and only after a referendum had been held to endorse the principle. The power to recall errant MPs, a referendum on primary legislative powers for the National Assembly for Wales, and referendums for a new set of directly elected Mayors also appeared in Labour's manifesto. The only significant proposal in Labour's programme to which the coalition was not committed was holding a free vote on lowering the voting age to 16 – though some of what the coalition wanted to do, most notably reform of the system of drawing constituency boundaries, was not necessarily to Labour's taste.

Implementation

Against that backdrop of substantial prior agreement between the two coalition parties and of an opposition that apparently shared much of the same agenda, it might be expected that the coalition would have largely been successful in making significant changes to the electoral process. Nothing, however, proved to be further from the truth.

The electoral process

Very few of the changes in the electoral process that were envisaged in the coalition's Programme for Government were implemented. Although the referendum on introducing the Alternative Vote (AV) was duly held within twelve months of the coalition's formation, voters rejected the proposal in May 2011 by 68 to 32 per cent. The system, about which there had previously been very little public discussion and thus about which the level of public knowledge was low, had few friends. The Conservatives campaigned strongly against the idea (as the Coalition

[9] Labour Party, *The Labour Party Manifesto 2010* (London: Labour Party, 2010)

Agreement permitted them to do), Labour proved to be divided on the subject, while by the time the referendum was held the Liberal Democrats were unpopular advocates after having undertaken a U-turn the previous autumn on the issue of university tuition fees (see chapter eighteen, this volume). Indeed, that incident provided the opponents of reform with a particularly powerful example of how manifesto promises could be disregarded if, as a result of the reform, more coalitions were necessary in future. Meanwhile, those who were campaigning for a Yes vote struggled to make the case for a change that fell far short of the proportional representation most of them really wanted. They tried to tap into the anti-politics mood created by the MPs' expenses scandal by suggesting that the requirement to win over 50 per cent of the vote would make MPs more accountable to their constituents, but this argument proved difficult to pursue given that in all probability in most seats the winner would be exactly the same. In any event, the No side also found a way of tapping into that mood, by suggesting that the more complex counting procedure required under AV would increase the costs of running elections. The No camp also raised questions over whether, thanks to the process of transferring votes, it was fair for some people's votes to be counted 'twice'. Against such a backdrop it was not surprising that those who bothered to vote (just 42 per cent of the electorate) were not persuaded of the merits of the proposed change. Consequently the Liberal Democrats failed to extract from their first taste of power any change at all in the Commons electoral system that treated its relatively geographically evenly spread vote so harshly.

Still, although the AV referendum was lost, the party anticipated that it would still have the compensation of seeing an elected Lords put in place, with its members being elected to boot by a system of proportional representation under which the party would flourish. Indeed, shortly after the AV referendum, the government published a draft Bill that envisaged the establishment of a 300-member chamber, 80 per cent of whose members would be elected by the Liberal Democrats' most preferred electoral system, the Single Transferable Vote, a system much like the Alternative Vote except that, crucially, more than one person is elected in each constituency.[10] Elections would take place at the same time as general elections, but with just one-third of the

[10] Renwick, *Citizen's Guide to Electoral Reform*.

House being elected at any one time and with members serving a non-renewable term of fifteen years. This proposal was then examined by a joint committee of peers and MPs under the chairmanship of the former Labour minister, Lord Richard.[11] Although far from unanimous in its view, the committee backed most of the government's ideas so far as the proposed electoral process was concerned, although it was felt that voters should be able simply to back a party (and thus that party's candidates in the order in which they were listed by the party) if they did not wish to go to the trouble of ordering the candidates for themselves. The committee also reckoned the house should have 450 members (plus a dozen bishops) rather than 300.

A Bill was duly introduced into the House of Commons in the summer of 2012. The one significant departure from what had been previously proposed in respect of its electoral arrangements was that, instead of being elected by the Single Transferable Vote, members were to be elected using a flexible regional party list system under which voters could either endorse a party's list as ordered by that party or express a preference for a particular candidate. Votes of the latter type would boost the chances of a candidate being elected if he or she received a personal vote from at least 5 per cent of their party's voters. The Liberal Democrats had evidently given ground on the details if not the principle of proportional representation.

But the Bill fell victim to parliamentary manoeuvring by those who felt it went too far (not least because of a fear that an elected Lords might feel better able to challenge the Commons) and those who reckoned it did not go far enough (by, for example, still retaining some appointed members). No less than ninety-one Conservative MPs voted against the Bill's second reading in July 2013. Meanwhile, although Labour voted for the second reading, it was unwilling to vote for the motion that would timetable subsequent debate, claiming that the Bill needed more detailed scrutiny than the motion would allow. Reluctant to allow the issue to clog up the parliamentary timetable (as a constitutional Bill its committee stage would take place on the floor of the Commons rather than in committee), the coalition subsequently withdrew the Bill – and the attempt to establish an elected Lords bit the dust.

---

[11] Lord Richard (chairman), *Draft House of Lords Reform Bill: Report*, HL 284 (London: The Stationery Office, 2012).

That in turn ensured that another coalition reform ran into the buffers too. The legislation required to change the way in which parliamentary constituency boundaries were redrawn and to reduce the number of MPs to 600 had secured its passage in the first year of the coalition's life – as part of the Act that had also paved the way for the referendum on AV. The Act had rewritten the rules such that the size of constituencies would now be more equal (no seat could have an electorate that was more than 5 per cent above or below the national average) and for the first time ensured that (the Northern and Western Isles apart) the number of MPs in Scotland, Wales and Northern Ireland would be proportionate to their share of the UK electorate. The measure had been as close to the hearts of Conservatives as the Alternative Vote had been to the Liberal Democrats' because it would reduce (though not necessarily eliminate) the difference of 3,733 voters between the average electorate in a Conservative-held constituency in 2010 and that in a Labour one, a difference that helped make it markedly more difficult for the Conservatives than for Labour to win an overall majority.[12]

However, by 2012, by which time the boundary commissions that were responsible for drawing up the constituencies had unveiled their initial proposals, it had become apparent that the Liberal Democrats could be the biggest losers from the reforms. Estimates of what would have happened in the 2010 election if the commissions' initial proposals had been in place at that election suggested the Liberal Democrats would suffer proportionately the biggest loss.[13] Many of their constituencies represent relatively isolated concentrations of support for the party and thus any very substantial redrawing of boundaries of the kind demanded by the review inevitably created a risk that those concentrations would be diluted. In any event, by this stage the party had come to appreciate that it was in significant electoral trouble and thus many of its MPs might well be heavily reliant in 2015 on their local personal popularity in order to secure re-election. That popularity would be worth a lot less if an MP were to have to fight a heavily redrawn constituency, many of whose voters that MP would not have previously represented.

---

[12] Curtice, 'So what went wrong with the electoral system?'

[13] P. Kellner, 'Lib Dems face big challenges ahead', YouGov, 18 June 2012 (accessed at yougov.co.uk/news/2012/06/18/clegg-and-lib-dems-face-big-challenges, 24 November 2014).

Initially, the boundary review had been presented as a quid pro quo for the referendum on the Alternative Vote (and indeed, as already noted, the two pieces of legislation were part of the same Act). But not least of the reasons why AV had been lost were the campaigning efforts of the Conservative Party, and when it had become apparent before the second reading of the Lords Reform Bill that a proportionately elected Lords was now also at risk thanks to Tory backbench opposition, the Liberal Democrat leader, Nick Clegg, warned that his party would retaliate by voting against the boundary commissions' detailed proposals when they came before the Commons. Given that Labour would also vote against proposals that would heavily disadvantage them, the Liberal Democrats would thus likely secure their defeat. In the event, just a few months later, the Liberal Democrats and Labour were able to add a clause to a Bill on electoral registration that was currently going through Parliament, the effect of which was to suspend the redrawing of the boundaries until 2018, that is, safely after the next election.

Meanwhile, not only did the electorate scupper the proposed reform of the Commons electoral system, they also largely turned down the opportunity to elect their own Mayor. Such elections would be held – as was the case where directly elected Mayors were already in place – under a variant of the Alternative Vote, known as the Supplementary Vote, under which voters express just a first and a second preference. In May 2012 referendums on whether to introduce such a system were held in the eleven largest provincial cities in England that did not currently have a directly elected Mayor – a twelfth city, Liverpool, avoided having a referendum when the city council voted to create one without consulting the city's voters. But in only one case, Bristol, did a majority back the idea. Thus, rather than being the most common form of local government in England's large cities, as the coalition had intended, outside of London directly elected Mayors continue to be found in only a patchwork quilt of just a dozen local authorities.

Still, not every proposed electoral change came to naught. One wholly new set of local elected offices was created and introduced systematically across England and Wales (outside of London). These were the new police and crime commissioners, one in each of forty-one local police forces, who in exercising responsibility for the strategic direction of their local force were now to replace police authorities rather than, as implied in the Programme for Government, be answerable to them. However, the experience of holding such elections was a far from happy one. Initially, the first elections, held using the same Supplementary Vote system used in elections for directly elected Mayors, were to have been held on 3 May 2012, when local elections were due to take place in much of England and Wales and thus voters were due to go to the polls anyway. But delays in the legislative process meant that the first round was postponed until mid-November 2012, when no other regular elections were timetabled to take place. Meanwhile, the contest was poorly advertised (the government refused to give candidates access to the freepost facilities granted to parliamentary candidates) and was for a post whose role and function few voters understood. As a result, just 15 per cent participated, by far the lowest turnout ever in any major ballot in the UK. As an exercise in using elections to promote greater accountability the innovation can only be judged a failure. It is thus little surprise that not only are Labour committed to getting rid of the post, but the Liberal Democrats have now also decided that the policy was a mistake. The long-term future of the innovation is thus highly uncertain.

In addition, one major change to the parliamentary electoral process did make it to the statute book. This was the proposal that parliaments should normally be elected for a fixed term, that is, once every five years, rather than be capable of being dissolved by the monarch at the behest of the Prime Minister at more or less any time during its maximum life span of five years. Under the provisions of the Fixed-term Parliaments Act, the only circumstances under which an early election can be held are (a) if the government loses a vote of confidence in the House of Commons and no new government secures a vote of confidence within fourteen days, or (b) if two-thirds of MPs vote in favour of holding an election (a higher threshold than the one of 55 per cent envisaged in the Programme for Government). The legislation puts the House of Commons on much the same footing as the devolved institutions in Scotland and Wales, except that their terms are fixed at four years rather than five. One consequence of this discrepancy is that devolved elections and a UK general election can sometimes be timetabled for the same day, as indeed would be the case in 2015. The Act in fact postpones the 2015 Scottish and Welsh elections until 2016, but that still leaves a likely clash in 2020. Subsequently the Welsh and Northern Irish assemblies have been put permanently on a five-year cycle, while the Scottish Parliament is likely to follow suit. Prime Ministers have, of course, often opted to go to the country after four years rather than five if they thought they had a good chance of being re-elected. So in fixing the length of Parliaments at five years, the Act ensures that Britain will go to the polls less often than previously. As it happens, however, there was never a time during the 2010–15 parliament when it looked as though it might be advantageous for the Conservatives to hold an early election, and thus the change may well have had little or no impact on the timing of the May 2015 election.

Meanwhile, one final piece of electoral legislation – provision for the recall of MPs – only progressed towards the statute book in the final months of the parliament, even though it was the measure that was most obviously stimulated by the 2009 MPs' expenses scandal. Initially the government moved quite quickly on this issue, publishing a draft Bill in December 2011. But then the impetus for passing legislation that would potentially make MPs vulnerable to electoral sanction appeared to be lost. However, following further scandals involving MPs, two of which led to resignation (and in one case imprisonment), the coalition eventually committed itself in its final Queen's Speech to introducing a measure. The legislation provides that an MP can be forced to resign and face a by-election if he or she has been sent to prison for a year or less (MPs who are imprisoned for more than a year already automatically lose their seats), or if convicted of submitting false expenses, or if, after having broken the rules of the House, their membership of the Commons has been suspended for a fortnight or more. Such a by-election would only be held if 10 per cent of the registered electorate in the relevant constituency petitioned for one. In short, the legislation would only apply in relatively limited circumstances and will require considerable organizational effort to trigger; it certainly does not create any opportunity for voters to recall an MP simply because they disapprove of his or her performance.

Referendums

But if the coalition's path to electoral change was strewn with many a failure, it had a rather better strike rate when it came to referendums. Almost all of the referendums that the coalition anticipated holding were legislated for, while in many cases a ballot has actually been held.

We have already noted that the referendum on the introduction of the Alternative Vote was held in 2011 – it was only the second ever state-wide referendum to be held in the UK – together with referendums on directly elected mayors the following year. In addition, the proposed referendum on granting full legislative powers to the National Assembly for Wales in its areas of competence, the necessary primary legislation for which had been passed by the previous Labour government, was held in March 2011. The proposal passed quite easily – by 63 to 37 per cent. However, the turnout was relatively low, just 36 per cent. Seemingly many voters wondered why a referendum was necessary given that by that stage the Commons could already grant the Assembly the power to pass specific pieces of primary legislation, and thus all that appeared to be at stake was whether that power should simply become more general and permanent.[14]

Two other provisions for referendums that were envisaged in the Programme for Government also reached the statute book, though neither has as yet been used. First, the law now requires that a referendum be held if a UK government proposes to agree to a treaty or other change that would involve the transfer of significant power or an area of competence from the UK to the European Union. Second, a local authority is now required to hold a ballot if it wishes to increase its council tax by more than the Secretary of State considers desirable. In both cases the referendum was evidently regarded as a mechanism that would make it more difficult for those in power in future to pursue a policy that the coalition considered undesirable.

But some of the most significant developments with respect to referendums were ones that were not envisaged by the Programme for Government at all. In May 2011 the Scottish National Party (SNP) succeeded in winning an overall majority in the devolved Scottish Parliament. Included in its manifesto was a commitment to hold a referendum on whether Scotland should become independent. Although the UK Government was to go on to argue that the Scottish Parliament lacked the legal authority to hold such a referendum (a position that the Scottish Government disputed), the Prime Minister immediately indicated that he accepted that the SNP had won the moral authority to hold such a ballot. In January 2012 the UK government published a consultation paper which proposed that the UK Parliament should give the legal authority to the Scottish Parliament to hold a referendum,

---

[14] R. Wyn Jones and R. Scully, *Wales Votes Yes: Devolution and the 2011 Welsh Referendum* (Cardiff: University of Wales Press, 2012).

[15] Scotland Office, *Scotland's Constitutional Future*, CM 8203 (London: The Stationery Office, 2012).

subject to certain conditions.[15] The most important of these were, first, that any referendum would have to be held by the end of 2014 and, second, that the referendum could only ask a single question, that is, whether people supported or opposed independence. That latter stipulation was designed to make it impossible for the Scottish Government to ask a second question on whether the Scottish Parliament should be given more powers short of independence, an idea with which it had previously toyed but which the UK Government felt would obscure the central issue and would represent a potential 'consolation' prize for the SNP. Doubts were also expressed about whether it would be possible to devise a process that would give an unambiguous indication of which of three possible options (independence, more devolution and the status quo) the public liked best.

After both much public debate and some weeks of negotiation between the two governments, in October 2012, the Prime Minister and Scotland's First Minister, Alex Salmond, signed what came to be known as the Edinburgh Agreement. The two governments agreed that a single-question referendum on independence should be held by the Scottish Government before the end of 2014. Crucially both governments agreed to respect the outcome, and that thus if Scotland did vote in favour of independence – by whatever margin – negotiations would take place on the terms and conditions under which independence would come about. This was clearly not only the most important referendum to be held during the lifetime of the coalition, but also the most important since the first state-wide referendum on the UK's membership of the then Common Market in 1975.[16]

In agreeing to the referendum the coalition was taking a gamble. Given that the opinion polls all indicated that only a minority of people north of the border wanted to leave the UK, it anticipated that the result would finally remove the 'threat' that Scotland might opt to leave the union, a threat that had arguably been hanging over the UK ever since the SNP first became a significant electoral force in the early 1970s. In practice the outcome proved to be not as decisive as the UK government had hoped. Although Scotland voted on 18 September 2014 to remain part of the union, the result – No 55 per cent, Yes 45 per cent – was narrower than had originally been anticipated, thereby

---

[16] D. Butler and U. Kitzinger, *The 1975 Referendum* (Basingstoke: Macmillan, 1976).

failing to dispel the possibility that Scotland might eventually opt to leave the Union. Meanwhile, even though the possibility of more devolution had been excluded from the ballot paper, during the course of the referendum campaign all of the three main parties arguing in favour of a No vote (the two coalition parties plus the opposition Labour Party) published proposals for more devolution. Moreover, following a narrowing of the No side's lead during the final phases of the campaign, the three party leaders committed themselves to developing on an accelerated timetable an agreed set of proposals for more devolution that would then be implemented by the next UK government irrespective of the outcome of the 2015 general election.

The Scottish referendum was also of interest for two other reasons. First, the turnout, 85 per cent, was extraordinarily high. Indeed it represented the highest turnout in a Scotland-wide ballot since the advent of the mass franchise at the end of the First World War. Such a high level of public engagement suggested that despite the lower levels of turnout at recent elections (including not least in the Police and Crime Commissioner elections), voters can still be persuaded to go to the polls if they feel the choice being put before them really matters. Second, in line with SNP policy (though not, it should be said, as a result of any encouragement from the coalition), those aged 16 and 17 were permitted to vote. Advocates of reducing the voting age to 16 can be expected to cite the experience of the referendum, with its record high turnout, as evidence in favour of their point of view.

If the unexpected electoral success of the SNP occasioned one referendum, the unprecedented success of another, the United Kingdom Independence Party (UKIP), brought about the promise of another. UKIP's signature policy is to hold a referendum on Britain's membership of the European Union, with a view to then campaigning for Britain's withdrawal. Following an increase in UKIP support during the course of the previous year, in January 2013 the Prime Minister announced that a future majority Conservative government would attempt to renegotiate Britain's terms of membership of the European Union and then hold a referendum on whether it should remain a member. This, however, was decidedly not a coalition policy; the Liberal Democrats were unwilling to go beyond the legislation for a referendum on the transfer of more powers to the EU that had already been put in place. So far as making any legislative progress on the issue was concerned, the Conservatives had to resort to encouraging two backbench MPs to put forward private members' bills for an in/out referendum, but these inevitably were talked out by their opponents. In this instance being in coalition clearly limited the Conservatives' freedom of manoeuvre.

Meanwhile, one proposal for a referendum that was included in the Programme for Government did not make it to the statute book. When it was first introduced, the legislation that made provision for referendums on directly elected Mayors, the 2011 Localism Act, also envisaged that if 5 per cent of local voters petitioned for one, a local authority could be required to hold a referendum on any issue of local concern. The measure was quietly dropped when it came up against opposition in the House of Lords (not least from Liberal Democrat peers) on the grounds of costs, ineffectiveness and apparent potential for abuse.

Evaluation

In one respect the coalition can be said to have helped change one of the norms of British constitutional practice. No longer can it said that the United Kingdom is simply a representative democracy in which those who are elected to office are charged with the responsibility of making policy decisions on voters' behalf. Instead, on occasion at least, it is now accepted that decisions should be put to the electorate itself. This is most commonly the case in respect of constitutional issues, such as Europe, the electoral system or devolution, where it might be argued that issues of legitimacy (that is, who the public thinks should have the right to make decisions) are at stake and thus are best resolved by securing a clear expression of public assent. However, the coalition's as yet unused legislation for council tax referendums indicates that we should not assume that the practice will necessarily continue to be confined to constitutional issues.

Not that we can say that the responsibility for this development can simply be laid at the door of the coalition. As we noted at the beginning of this chapter, numerous referendums on both devolution and directly elected Mayors had also been held by the previous Labour government. But in continuing and extending this practice to Europe and the electoral system the coalition effectively ensured that, rather than being the unusual practice of a particular government, it could now be regarded as a norm. As a result, we perhaps should not be surprised if in future there prove to be calls for a referendum before any proposal to reform the House of Lords that does manage to pass through Parliament is in fact implemented. It would, after all, represent a significant constitutional reform.

Equally, we cannot say that the increased use of referendums has simply been occasioned by a belief in the principle that major constitutional reforms ought to be endorsed by a public vote. Rather, referendums have been seized upon as a way of securing political advantage and/or managing internal dissent. In the case of the coalition, the latter consideration was clearly central to the decision to hold a referendum on the Alternative Vote – putting the issue in the electorate's hands was a way of resolving a serious difference of opinion between the two coalition partners. Meanwhile, the idea of a referendum on Scottish independence was accepted by the coalition in the belief that it represented an opportunity to inflict a defeat on the SNP. Equally, as we noted earlier, the coalition's legislation on referendums on Europe and on council tax increases had the attraction of making it more difficult to pursue a particular policy in future.

However, if the coalition has proven to be instrumental and effective in promoting the use of referendums, its attempts at changing electoral processes have done little more than leave behind a wreckage of unfinished business. That so little was achieved has much to do with tensions within and between the coalition partners. The Conservatives scuppered the Liberal Democrats' hopes of electoral reform, while a section of the party at least then also ensured that there was no chance of introducing an elected House of Lords. The Liberal Democrats responded by ending the Conservatives' hopes of reforming the way in which parliamentary constituencies are drawn. The story might be regarded as a classic illustration of how partisan differences can result in coalition governments getting very little done (Hazell and Yong, 2012).[17]

But the story does not end there. As a result of having achieved so little between them, both coalition partners will face the electorate in 2015 with their electoral prospects looking weaker than would otherwise have been the case. The Liberal Democrats' chances of winning

---

[17] R. Hazell and B. Yong, *The Politics of Coalition: How the Conservative–Liberal Democrat Government Works* (Oxford: Hart Publishing, 2012).

seats have been diminished by the failure to introduce the Alternative Vote, while the Conservatives' task of winning an overall majority has been made markedly more difficult by the failure to redraw parliamentary boundaries. Meanwhile, with the benefit of hindsight it might be argued that the Conservatives made a mistake in opposing the introduction of the Alternative Vote in the first place. The party certainly did not anticipate the rise in UKIP's fortunes, a rise that has been achieved disproportionately at the expense of the Conservatives. Under first-past-the-post, UKIP's rise threatens the Conservatives with a loss of seats to Labour that might not have looked so serious if the party were in a position to appeal to UKIP supporters to give it a second preference. It is also ironic that at the very same time that the party was so energetically rejecting AV for Commons elections, it was promoting the use of a very similar system, the Supplementary Vote, in elections for directly elected Mayors and for the ill-fated introduction of elected Police and Crime Commissioners.

In any event, these failures have certainly left a legacy of unfinished business for the next government. The redrawing of constituency boundaries and the reduction in the number of MPs has simply been postponed until 2018, and at the moment at least, both would now be implemented in advance of the 2020 election. The next government will have to decide whether this is indeed what should happen, a prospect that is unlikely to be palatable to Labour, while any attempt to reduce the number of MPs leaves all of them worrying about the implications for their careers. Yet given that in 2015 the constituency boundaries will reflect a population geography that by then (in England) will be nearly fifteen years old, it seems inescapable that the boundaries will have to be redrawn under some set or other of rules during the next parliament.

Meanwhile, of course, the House of Lords continues to be an unreformed, appointed body. This position is clearly at variance with public opinion. According to the 2011 British Social Attitudes survey, as many as 72 per cent believe that at least half of the members of the upper house should be elected.[18] It seems inevitable that further attempts at reform will be made – though whether they will be

---

[18] J. Curtice and B. Seyd, 'Constitutional reform: a recipe for restoring faith in our democracy', in A. Park, R. Clery, J. Curtice, M. Phillips and D. Utting (eds.), *British Social Attitudes: The 29th Report* (2012) (accessed at http:/bsa-29.natcen.ac.uk, 24 November 2014).

successful is another matter. Many an MP is wary of being faced with an elected body that might feel better able to challenge the judgement of the Commons, while many a Lord is reluctant to vote for an early retirement.

That leaves us with the one substantial legacy of the coalition so far as the electoral process is concerned – the introduction of fixed-term parliaments. Its impact has yet to be seen. It certainly reduces the power of Prime Ministers. They are no longer able to use the threat of an early election to quell attempts by the opposition and/or backbenchers to inflict a parliamentary defeat on the government – and these days backbenchers are much more inclined to be rebellious.[19] Equally, they will no longer be able to dangle before their party the prospect of calling an election at an electorally propitious time (and thereby keep the opposition in uncertainty). Minority governments, in particular, will have to try and carry on rather than look to call an early election that might give them a majority. Indeed, if future parliaments do indeed prove to be ones in which no one party has an overall majority, Britain may even have to get used to the sight of power passing from one government to another without an election being called. What the electorate would make of such a development can only be guessed at.

Conclusion

Elections are the primary preoccupation of politicians and political parties. Any attempt to change what elections take place and under what rules they are contested rapidly arouses considerations of personal and partisan interest. Politicians and parties will always be inclined to find reasons to oppose changes that they think might adversely affect the continuity of their careers or chances of office, an inclination from which even government backbenchers are not necessarily immune.

So changing the electoral rules can prove difficult for even the strongest of majority governments. It thus should not perhaps come as a surprise that a coalition government whose component parties have

[19] P. Cowley and M. Stuart, 'This parliament remains on course to be the most rebellious since 1945', *Conservative Home*, 14 May 2013 (accessed at www.conservative-home.com/platform/2013/05/philip-cowley-and-mark-stuart-for-1000am-tuesday.html, 24 November 2014).

what they regard as very different electoral interests should have hit so many difficulties in its efforts to change those rules. Reform of the Commons electoral system was, after all, the most difficult issue for the two parties to resolve in forming the coalition in the first place, and thus it always seemed to be particularly capable of driving a wedge between them.

In contrast, holding a referendum can be a way of avoiding difficult decisions. That was certainly true, so far as the coalition was concerned, of the referendum on the Alternative Vote. Parties unable to resolve their differences can hope that their side of the argument prevails in the court of public opinion. Equally, the politician who is convinced that the public is on their side can look to referendums to wrong-foot their opponents, be they local councillors who dislike the idea of an elected Mayor or who would like to increase the council tax, or a devolved administration that would like their part of the UK to become an independent state. Instituting change in this area thus perhaps always looked like the brighter prospect – and it is certainly one where the coalition has clearly left its mark.

Part IV

Conclusion

Morten Morland for The Times / News Syndication

22 CONCLUSION: THE NET COALITION EFFECT

MIKE FINN

Britain's first peacetime coalition government since the 1930s came into being due to perceived political necessity, but, as this volume has shown, this did not prevent it setting high ambitions for itself nor did it impinge on its ability to generate 'effects' – in legislative terms, economic terms, in terms of the machinery of government, or in terms of its impact on political culture and society as a whole. If Cameron will go down in history as a significant premier, so too will the administration he led.[1]

The ambitions, however, might be the 'catch' in terms of any verdict on the coalition's place in history. Both in terms of vision and operational considerations the coalition on formation enunciated grandiose ideas of what it might achieve. In terms of vision, the coalition's two leaders espoused the virtues of 'a new politics'; in the Coalition Agreement's *Programme for Government* they were clear that the unexpected union of the two parties might yield possibilities and opportunities greater than those available to a single party governing alone. This was, on the face of it, a bold claim – the equivalent of claiming that the coalition was, in Panglossian vein, the best of all possible worlds, better even than a government simply Conservative or simply Liberal Democrat in character. It also had a ring of truth; both Cameron and Clegg were undoubtedly happier working with each other than with the right and left of their parties respectively. Part of

[1] See Anthony Seldon, 'Introduction', this volume.

the measure of the coalition's effect must be to assess whether the voters were convinced that this 'new politics' was meaningful and, in fact, desirable.

Beyond the nebulous, the specifics – which animated the original coalition documentation – were clear: eradicating the structural deficit within the life of the parliament, establishing firm control of public finances and restoring the economy to growth. They were fundamentally economic in focus; not unreasonably so given the undeniable crisis in the economy and the public finances which the coalition inherited from their predecessors. Though the blame game would continue (and still does), the reality was that the crash of 2008 was a global event, more or less accentuated in the UK by the centrality of financial services within the economy and then by government policy and spending (and probably in that order). As Johnson and Chandler have shown, the government was successful in at least some of its ambitions here – critically restoring the economy to growth – but not without failure in some significant areas. Double-dip recession was an unwanted perceived 'reality' (although later figures implied the UK had just missed it) before growth returned, and by pre-crash standards growth remained anaemic. The coalition oversaw an expansion in jobs and employment, but were criticized for the extent to which underemployment – the scourge of the British labour market in the late nineteenth and early twentieth century – returned to the fore through the mechanisms of zero hours and fixed-term contracts. At least for a time, the Opposition was able to make headway through rebranding the economic situation as a 'cost of living crisis', highlighting the problems employed households were facing in terms of rising energy bills, the impact of inflation, and the reality of wage freezes – especially in the public sector. The economy recovered, but it did so slowly, and not all felt the benefit of it. More worryingly, the government's pledge to eliminate the structural deficit was downplayed and then largely forgotten (at least by the governing parties), replaced by an emphasis on a 'long-term economic plan' which the Conservatives argued they would need a majority in 2015 to see through. By October 2014 it became clear that government borrowing was rising at an alarming rate. The ambitions of 'austerity' had not delivered on their promises.

Nonetheless the government's cuts in public spending were profound by the standards of previous administrations and had significant impact on both departments in Whitehall and the public at large.

Though it seemed that the public accepted a measure of retrenchment given the international financial crisis, it was not clear that they accepted the full implications of the cuts, and the coalition's continued commitment to their programme led to charges of ideologically motivated state shrinkage by post-Thatcherite Conservatives and Orange Book Liberals, especially when juxtaposed with Iain Duncan Smith's crusade to cut the welfare bill at DWP. This was a charge that resonated, especially when funding cuts to local government hit public services amongst local communities. The 'Big Society', it was alleged, was no more than a rhetorical smokescreen for privatization and cutbacks. The departure of Hilton – though an oft-derided figure by commentators – robbed the government and Cameron personally of the one figure who might have been able to translate such policies into a meaningful agenda.

Beyond public finances and economic growth, the coalition had committed itself to protecting the NHS in an uncertain financial climate, fostering the aforementioned 'Big Society' (or 'localism', depending on your ideological bent), a significant constitutional reform package and safeguarding Britain's commitment to international development. NHS reorganization – not announced in the coalition documentation but revealed (as Glennerster reminds us) via a white paper in the Commons in summer 2010 – was by the final year of the coalition's life regarded as a disaster by all, save perhaps Andrew Lansley. Having argued against top-down reorganizations before the 2010 General Election, Cameron found himself arguing about the semantics of reorganization from above or below, when in fact he had never committed himself to Lansley's plans (and neither had Nick Clegg). Lansley, in effect, went rogue – as Glennerster, Waller and Yong have all shown.[2] This had spectacular consequences for the coalition at a crucial time in its life, especially on the much-vaunted metric of public trust in the parties' management of public services. Yet it would be wrong not to acknowledge the 'effect' of the coalition on the NHS. The Health and Social Care Act set in train a series of processes that developed market

---

[2] Glennerster, this volume, chapter eleven; Peter Waller and Ben Yong, 'Case studies II: Tuition fees, NHS reform and nuclear policy', in Robert Hazell and Ben Yong (eds.), *The Politics of Coalition: How the Conservative-Liberal Democrat Government Works* (Oxford: Hart, 2012).

mechanisms in health beyond anything Labour had anticipated when they had attempted to do the same. The NHS was a different beast in many respects in 2015 than it had been in 2010 – no mean feat. Here, there was a real 'effect', but it was in truth less a coalition effect than a Lansley one.

The Big Society, partly due to Hilton's departure but also due to Cameron's tendency to be overwhelmed by operational concerns and to devolve strategy to Osborne (part of the reason Hilton left in the first place), failed emphatically as a unifying ideal. Even at the end of the coalition's life few in government or the public could clearly articulate what it had been supposed to mean, and fewer still cared. It was yesterday's politics. The commitment to international development (notably the 0.7 per cent of GDP) was maintained, and Britain continued to show leadership in this area, especially in response to the 2014 Ebola outbreak in West Africa.[3] Constitutional reform, however, was a damp squib; Lords reform failed due to coalition politics (which was the principal reason for its demise, notwithstanding Labour opportunism), the British Bill of Rights – which both parties had promised, but by which both meant very different things – came to naught, the referendum on the alternative vote was lost – not least because of the powerful late intervention of the Prime Minister. The balance sheet of constitutional reform paled by comparison to the early Blair years, and fixed-term parliaments, a long-term Liberal Democrat commitment, were only enacted due to the political expediency of 'locking in' the junior partner to the coalition government.

As with health, the coalition created space for a strong minister to create a distinctive legacy in education – though the Liberal Democrats had precious little say in it, save tokens such as free school meals and the nomenclature of the pupil premium (though it had been a Liberal Democrat policy, it was not enacted in the fashion that made it distinctively Liberal Democrat). Michael Gove was probably the most successful minister in terms of carrying forward his personal agenda – whilst Lansley's reforms were at least moderated by Number 10 and Clegg working in concert,[4] there was no brake on Gove until

---

[3] Martin Bagot, 'Ebola crisis: More British soldiers to fight killer virus in Africa following Afghanistan pullout', *Daily Mirror*, 30 October 2014.
[4] Waller and Yong, 'Case studies II'.

his dismissal in mid-2014.[5] An idiosyncratic, self-consciously intellectual minister, he was (and remains) a man of fierce certainties – and it was this which allowed him to drive through an agenda which fundamentally remade the English education system at school level by 2015. Though his critics seldom give him credit for this, Gove believed that what he was doing – emphasizing standards in examinations, revising mechanisms of teacher training, rewriting curricula – would act in a progressive way, enabling social mobility by facing up to the 'real' issues in British education. This commitment was admirable, but it was not matched by a willingness to listen to others or to base policy on evidence, other than (as Tim Hands has noted[6]) his own personal experience.[7] The Gove legacy in education is profound, and probably lasting, but it was not a 'coalition' effect – it was a solo project in the vein of Anthony Crosland, very different in character.

By its mid-point, the coalition honeymoon was definitively over – and eyes began to turn to 2015 as the two parties sought to differentiate themselves and avoid the possibility of a second unwanted marriage. Anti-politics – which had superseded apathy as the principal concern of those worried about British democracy – took solid form with the rise of the UK Independence Party, which in turn drove the coalition's agenda.[8] Cameron, reactive as a party leader and with no real feel for his right wing (as Norton has shown), was compelled to throw bones to his Eurosceptic right but in doing so failed to grasp the potency of the UKIP challenge, as did Ed Miliband. UKIP wasn't just about Europe, it was about politics as a whole and the sense that an elite establishment was divorced from the country at large. This was a perception highlighted by the 2009 expenses scandal and exacerbated

---

[5] See Mike Finn, 'Introduction – The Gove ascendancy: Michael Gove as Secretary of State for Education' and Jonathan Simons, 'The Gove legacy and the politics of education beyond 2015', in Mike Finn (ed.), *The Gove Legacy: Education in Britain after the Coalition* (London: Palgrave, 2015).

[6] Tim Hands, 'The Gove legacy in independent schools: The making and unmaking of a Supreme Goviet', in Mike Finn (ed.), *The Gove Legacy: Education in Britain after the coalition* (London: Palgrave, 2015).

[7] Gove's unwillingness to listen was memorably characterized in Anthony Horowitz's recollections of a meeting with the Education Secretary, published in *The Spectator*: Anthony Horowitz, 'I always defended Michael Gove. Then I met him', *The Spectator*, 15 March 2014.

[8] Robert Ford and Matthew Goodwin, *Revolt on the Right: Explaining Support for the Radical Right in Britain* (London: Routledge, 2014).

by the differential impacts of recession and austerity, not to mention the longer-term decline of party alignment and the perceived abandonment of those in 'safe' seats in the eternal quest for 'swing' voters. It was ironic that the rejection of AV also ensured the continuation of such intrinsic inequities in the electoral system.

The coalition's net effect was profound, but not always in the ways it intended. It did not achieve its economic targets, though the government was brave in staying the course on austerity and eventually confounded the IMF. It did not achieve much at all on constitutional reform, and its huge impacts on the NHS and the education system were divisive by their nature (and at least in the first case, increasingly disowned). In foreign policy, the relationship with Europe deteriorated significantly, but less through calculation and more due to domestic dynamics, whilst the Prime Minister advocated an interventionist stance in theatres such as Iraq and Libya but could not carry the House (or the country) over Syria in 2013. Parliament was significantly more rebellious (as Cowley has shown) but the coalition did not turn out to be the weak, vacillating entity many had expected and in truth functioned as a more or less effective legislative machine. This had its price. Some of the most devastating coalition effects were on the parties themselves, raising the possibility of a split on the right for the Conservatives and total annihilation for the Liberal Democrats. After five years, England still did not love coalitions – however effective – and voters as a whole blamed their parties of choice for whatever ills they felt them to be responsible. So much, so familiar, but for the Conservatives and Liberal Democrats – with the genuine emergence of four-party politics – the consequences, the real 'net' coalition effect, were far more significant than usual.

A final point about the standard of measurement for any 'coalition effect'. Much has been made of measuring the coalition's performance 'against' the Coalition Agreement. While there is some merit in this approach, as with the traditional approach of measuring the single party against its manifesto, there is a sense in which the coalition has been held to a higher standard than a single-party government, with U-turns and derogations eliciting a violent response from one or other coalition partner and the media. This is perhaps a lesson for future coalitions in the UK. What might be more meaningful is a stock-take on the extent to which the coalition's effect was based on a coherent agenda. In this respect, it is clear that the 'net' coalition effect was principally on the economy and the public finances, where the parties set themselves ambitious targets and failed to meet some of them. In terms of the semantics of the Coalition Agreement, they achieved uniform stability, but only patchwork reform (albeit profound in certain areas). The unintended net coalition effect was the creation of four-party politics at Westminster, a legacy with unknown yet potentially far-reaching implications for Britain at home, and abroad.

INDEX

Abu Qatada 23
academies *see* education
Academies Act (2010) 3
Adams, Abi 184
Adonis, Andrew (Lord Adonis) 43, 49,
    210–11, 219–20, 222, 242
Afghanistan, British involvement in 20–2,
    350–1, 358–9
Afriyie, Adam 484–5
*After the Coalition: A Conservative
    Agenda for Britain* 478
aid expenditure 353
Ainsworth, Peter 447
airports expansion 215, 219–21, 227
Alexander, Danny 6, 15, 38, 48, 51, 55,
    99, 119–20, 128, 177–8, 215, 294,
    325–7, 343, 380, 440–1, 495–6
all-postal primaries 140
Allan, Sir Alex 116
Apollo Theatre 435–6
Appointments Commission
    74–5
Arab Spring 14, 24,
    353–5
Armitt, Sir John 212
arts *see* culture
Arts Council 335, 440, 451
Ashcroft, Michael A. 37
Ashdown, Paddy 38, 492
Ashley, Jackie 555
Assets of Community Value 236

Asthana, Anushka 418
Atomic Weapons Establishment 348
Audit Commission 232, 251–2
austerity measures 6, 160, 169–70, 230–2,
    255, 319, 397, 418, 602, 606, 17
AV (Alternative Vote) referendum 98–9,
    104–5, 480, 482, 506–8, 511,
    561–2, 581, 583–4, 586–7,
    589–90, 594–5, 597
AV (Alternative Vote) system 6, 15–16,
    24–5, 53, 62, 67–9, 71, 90, 137,
    140–1

Backbench Business Committee 142, 154,
    478
backbench dissent/pressure 22–3, 146–54,
    476–9
backbench 1922 Committee 476–80,
    483
Balance of Competencies Review 379–80,
    394
Balls, Ed 4, 173–4, 215, 219–20, 17
Bank of England 186–8
    Financial Policy Committee 191–2
    financial regulation 191–2
    interest base rate 171, 187, 193
    monetary policy 188
    quantitative easing policy 186–7
    and the Treasury 186–8
Banking Reform Act (2013) 191–2
banking regulation reform 47–8, 191–2

Banksy 435–6
Barnett Formula 106, 231–2
BBC
  independence 440–1
  news and political coverage 569
  political/prime ministerial influence over
    569–71
  royal charter 575
  salaries and pay-offs 569
  and Savile 569–70
  World Service 352–3
Beckett, Margaret 201–2
bedroom tax 94, 247, 249, 328–9, 339,
    343
Belfast Agreement 110
benefits see welfare
Bennett, Catherine 418
Bercow, John 136, 143
Berne Copyright Convention 431
Bernstein, Sir Howard 224
Bertin, Gabby 11, 425
BES (British Election Study) 421–3
Better Care Fund 245–6
Better Together campaign 20, 91–4,
    106–7
Big Bang Localism 44
Big Society 3, 13, 44, 233–4, 475–6,
    602–4
Bill of Rights commissioners 78–80
Blair, Tony
  and Afghanistan 20–1
  EU alliances 386
  EU referendum 373
  and infrastructure 210
  memoirs 2
  and NHS 312
  as PM 27, 113–14, 130
  and Rupert Murdoch 566–7
  Scottish referendum 105
  trade union affiliations 549
  Welsh referendum 105
Blanchard, Oliver 6, 170–1
BLF (Big Lottery Fund) 447
Bloody Sunday report 19–20
Bogdanor, Vernon 66, 475–6
Boles, Nicholas 44
books in prison 452
boom and bust 166
Border Agency 251

Bouazizi, Mohammed 353–4
Boulton, Adam 470
Boundary Commissions see constituency
    boundary reform
boundary reform see constituency
    boundary reform
Boyle, Danny 442
Brady, Graham 476–7
Breakdown Britain 325
Breakthrough Britain 325
Bridgen, Andrew 483–4
British Bill of Rights 78, 481,
    604
British Council 448
Britishness 431–3, 448, 455–8
broadband network 215–16, 226
Brooks, Rebekah 566, 568, 570
Brown, Gordon
  and Bank of England 186
  as Chancellor 26, 130, 165–6
  and Clegg 15, 49
  economic policy 554
  end of premiership 556
  and EU 373, 377
  and expenses scandal 141–2
  on Lisbon Treaty 373–6
  and pensions 342–3
  press criticism of 554–5
  as Prime Minister 10, 62–3, 113–14,
    373
  resignation as PM 42–3
  on Scottish devolution 88, 108
  on Scottish independence 83–4,
    92–3
  and transport 210
Browne, Jeremy 381–2
Browne, John (Lord Browne) 133, 152
Browne Review 53–4, 502–4
BSkyB 567, 575
Budget (2008) 161
Budget (2009) 180–1
Budget (2010) 3, 161, 167–8, 328–9, 426
Budget (2012) 3–4, 181, 335, 510, 576
Budget (2013) 17, 162–3, 184–5, 187–9,
    335–6
Budget (2014) 162–3, 174–6, 334
Budget Red Books 178
Burstow, Paul 116–17, 505
business rate retention 239

CABE (Commission for Architecture and
the Built Environment) 445–6
Cabinet committees 120, 124
Cabinet continuity 11–12
Cabinet government revival 130
Cabinet Manual 62–3
Cable, Vince 46, 54, 120, 126, 170–1,
189–91, 364, 446, 503–5, 513,
563
Calman Commission 81, 108
Cameron, David
advisers to 11
and Afghanistan 20–1
age on becoming PM 14–15
and Assad regime 6
and Blair 35–6, 41
and Christianity 433–4, 455–8
and Clegg's veto power 473
Commons defeat 149
Conservative feminization strategy
398–9
constitutional reform 93
early stages in Coalition 473–7
economic policy 13–14
economy as priority 188
English Question 105
and EU 362, 380, 396, 482–3
EU alliances 386–9
EU budget cuts 387, 393
EU fiscal rules veto 482–3
foreign policy 14, 20–1, 27, 359–60
future judgement of 25–7
as government manager 12, 14
and Health and Social Care Act (2012)
297–8
historic significance of term in office 1–2
and HM the Queen 14
and House of Lords 15–16, 23, 74–5,
154–6
on immigration 393
impulsiveness 14–15
infrastructure speech 213
leadership challenge to 483–4
and Libya 20–1
and Merkel 10, 20, 384, 387–8
and Miliband 16–17
and Murdoch 570
NHS reform 18–19, 39–40
and 1922 Committee 476–80, 483

on Northern Ireland public sector
dependence 94–5
and Obama 3–4, 10
Old Etonian connections 474–5
over-promotion of female MPs 148–9
Parliament problems 22–3
and party candidates 488
at party conference (2012) 5
as party leader 32–3, 35–6
as party manager 13
party policy reform 32–3
peerages created by 74–5, 154–6
policy groups 39
and Policy Unit 12–13
pre-Coalition negotiations 469–73
press criticism 21–2
as Prime Minister 1–27, 32–3, 42–3
prime ministerial patronage powers
473
prime ministerial style 10–17
Queen's Speech (2013) 153
relationship with Clegg 6, 15, 47–8, 57
relationship with Osborne 25–6
reshuffles 11–12, 571, 574
and Salmond 82, 107–8
Scottish campaigning by 107–9, 487
on Scottish independence 91, 107–8,
486–7
senior staff 10–11
as sexist 11
and Syria 365–7, 486, 606
and tax cuts 178
and Tory vision/ideals 13–14
and UKIP 14, 16–17, 25, 605–6
as unionist 476
welfare protection 318–19.
see also coalition government;
Conservatives
Cameron, Ivan 39–40
Cameron, Samantha 11
Campbell, Menzies 33, 38
capital projects 214
Carbon Emission Reduction Target 204
carbon floor price 206
Carbon Reduction Commitments 204
Care Act (2014) 313
Care Quality Commission 308–9
Carmichael, Alistair 99
Carney, Mark 187–8, 341

Carswell, Douglas 7, 25, 27, 383, 392,
      395, 485, 488–90, 511–12
Carter, Neil 41
Cash, Sir William 377, 383, 476–7
central government employment 241–2
centralist localism 254
Centre for Cities 244
Centre for Social Justice 324–5, 327
CfD (contract for difference) 197–9
Channel Tunnel 210–11
child benefit 331, 335
child poverty 319–20
child tax credits 319–20, 417
Child Trust Fund 328–9
childcare 399–400, 403–5, 410–14, 402
   carer/child ratios 412–13
   policies summary 410–14
   tax relief 412
Chote, Robert 165, 328
Christian heritage 433–4
city regions 243–4
civil liberties reform 47, 228–9, 512–13
civil service
   appointment of Permanent Secretaries
      133–4
   changes to 117–25, 131–5
   and coalition government 117–25,
      131–5
   role of 117–18
Civil Service Compensation Scheme 114
Clacton by-election 7, 25, 27, 485
Clark, Greg 195–6, 242–3
Clarke, Kenneth 12, 120, 574
Clegg coup 441–4
Clegg, Nick
   on AV 53
   and Brown 15, 49
   childcare 412–13
   city regions 243
   as Deputy PM 15–16, 55, 64, 122–3,
      492–3, 496, 518–19, 571
   education policy 41–2
   and EU 361, 380, 385–6
   Farage debate 514
   foreign policy 360, 364
   and Health and Social Care Act (2012)
      297–8
   House of Lords reform 508–11, see also
      House of Lords reform

hung parliament strategy 116–17
influence on BBC/media 571
leadership bid 38
leadership challenge to 513, 518
media attacks on 557–60
office location 122–3
and Orange Book 37–8
relationship with Cameron 6, 15, 47–8,
      57
Scottish campaigning by 107–9, 487
and Syria 365–7
on tuition fees 558–9
urban policy 242–3
veto power 473
and welfare 177–8, 343
see also coalition government; Liberal
      Democrats
Cleggmania 58, 493–4, 558, 562
Clifford, Max 565
Climate Change Act (2008) 195, 205–6
Climate Change Agreements 204
climate change leadership 206
Climate Change Levy 205
Clinical Commissioning Groups 304
CMA (Competition and Markets
      Authority) 207
co-operatives 43–4
The Coalition: Our Programme for
      Government 31–58, 62–3, 67, 69,
      72–6, 87–8, 121, 136–7, 147,
      229–30, 377–80, 387, 391, 403–5,
      439, 495, 510, 581–97, 601,
      606–7
Coalition Agreement see The Coalition:
      Our Programme for Government
Coalition Agreement for Stability and
      Reform 50, 55, 59–60, 63–4,
      118–19, 121–2, 345
Coalition Committee 63–4
coalition government
   achievements 17–21
   adverse factors during 21–4
   advisers 122–4
   as asymmetrical 129–31
   and BBC 569–71
   and the British constitution 59–86
   common policies 45–6
   and Conservatives 467–91
   constitutional implications 84–5

coalition government (cont.)
and culture 430
decline of Liberal Democrats 571–4
differing government philosophies
59–60
discussions on 115–17
early harmony 557
and the economy 159–93, 490–1
election campaigning 128–9
and elections 577–97
and energy policy 194–208
and Europe 370–96. see also EU
and the executive 113–35
failures 17–21
and foreign affairs 345–69, see also
foreign policy
formal arrangements for 118–19
formation 42–56
future arrangements 129–30
gender issues 397–429, see also gender
issues
and health 290–316
and home affairs/local government
228–56
and infrastructure 209–27
inter-party splits 146–54
and collective responsibility 152–4
and Labour 520–52
and Liberal Democrats 492–519
Liberal Democrats' caution over 115
and long-term care 290–316
and the media 553–76
ministerial appointments/portfolios
15–16, 55–6, 119, 315–16
in Northern Ireland 87–112
and Parliament 136–56
party stances 577–81
previous experience in 117
prime ministerial power 129
and referendums see referendums
relationships between parties 125–9
reshuffle (2014) 571, 574
in Scotland 87–112
transactional period 127–8
triple-lock mechanism 495
in Wales 87–112
and welfare 317–44
women in 148–9, 424–5, 573
women voters 420

coalition government phases 2–8
phase one (May 2010–March 2012) 2–3
phase two (March 2012–March 2013)
3–5
phase three (February 2013–April
2014) 6–7
phase four (April 2014–May 2015) 7–8
coalition options 2
collective responsibility 84, 121, 152–4
College of Policing 250–1, see also
policing
Collins, Philip 572–3
Collins, Ray 550–1
Collins Review 550–1
combined authorities 249
community budgeting 245–6
community planning 234–7
Comprehensive Spending Review (2010)
330–1, 352–3
Conservatives
backbench problems 146–54, 389–91
Coalition Agreement 42–56, see also
Coalition Agreement; coalition
government
and coalition government 467–91
coalition government and election
campaigning 128–9
and constitutional reform 577
domestic policies 228–9
early stages in coalition 473–7
and electoral reform see electoral reform
energy policy 195–7
EU position 75, 371–2, 375–6
Euroscepticism 374–6
feminization strategy 398–9
fiscal policy 173–4
government experience 467
government philosophy 59–60
health plans 292–5
House of Lords reform see House of
Lords
ideological divide with Liberal
Democrats 228–9, 472
immigration 376, 379
leader's role 468–9, 491
leadership challenge to Cameron 483–4
leadership changes 32–8
and Lib Dem policies 228–9, 472

Liberal Democrat voter similarities
36–8
manifesto 42–56, 75, 122, 154, 291,
294, 322–4, 335, 345–6, 375–6,
378–9, 438–41, 553, 579
ministerial portfolios in coalition
15–16, 55–6
1922 Committee 476–80, 483
parliamentary problems 146–54
party cohesion 389–94
party conference (2014) 172–3, 178
party funding 489–90
party image 40–1
party logo 40–1
policies in coalition 15–16
policy groups 39
policy reform 32–3, 38–42
pre-coalition negotiations 469–73
pre-election plans 114–17
reshuffle (2014) 571, 574
standing in Scotland 101, 107–8
standing in Wales 101
the Sensibles 481
and UKIP see UKIP
unionist position 99–101
Vote Blue, Go Green slogan 40–1
women's policies in manifesto 402
see also Cameron, David; Liberal
Democrats
constituency boundary reform 61, 67–71,
473–4, 480, 482, 586–7, 595
Constitutional Implications of Coalition
Government 84
constitutional reform 47, 85, 604
Constitutional Reform and Government
Bill (2010) 67–8, 76–7
Constitutional Treaty 373–4
CONTEST strategy 348–9, 353
Convery, Alan 100
Cooper, Andrew 5, 123–4
Cooper, Yvette 414–15
copyright 431
core vote plus 514
Coulson, Andy 10–11, 16–17, 123–4,
565–6, 568, 570
council budgets 240–2
council cuts 253–4
council employment 241–2
council funding 237–40

council tax see tax
counter-terrorism policy 348–52
Cowley, Philip 477
Crafts, Nicholas 186
Creative Industries Economic Estimates
440
Crosby, Lynton 7–8, 10–11, 16–17,
123–4, 572
cross-cutting 55–6
Crossrail 210, 215–16, 218–19, 221–2,
227
Cryer, Ann 407
CTB (council tax benefit) 248, see also tax
culture 430
art galleries 435, 450–1
artists' visas 459–61
arts world 435
BBC independence 440–1
books in prison 452
Britishness 431–3
Christian heritage 433–4
as creative industry 440
DCMS spending 443
disruptive technologies 434–5
free access policy 450–1
heritage 439
libraries 435, 445, 452
local authority funding 436
and manifestos 438–41
museums 445, 450–1
spending on 431
sport 461
state-funded 431
urban renaissance plan 440
Cunliffe, Jon 386

Daily Express 574–5
Daily Mail 554, 559, 563, 568, 573–5
Daily Politics 569
Daily Telegraph 554, 561–3, 573–5,
578
Dalton, Hugh 446
d'Ancona, Matthew 32, 120, 126–7, 392,
506–7
Darling, Alistair 211
on Scottish independence 92, 106–8
tax rises 179–81
Data and Communications Bill 512–13
Data Protection Act 565

Davey, Ed 119, 197–8, 203–5, 207, 388–9
Davidson, Denzil 382
Davidson, Ruth 101
Davies Commission 227
Davies, Howard 220
Davies, Nick 565–6
Davis, David 32, 474
DCC (Data and Communications Company) 205
DCLG (Department for Communities and Local Government) 245–6, 253–4
DCMS (Department of Culture, Media and Sport) 431, 440, 444–8
Deans, Stephen 548–50
DECC 200–1, 204–5, 207–8
defence cuts 352–3, 358–9
defence review 345–6
defence strategic shrinking policy 346–50, 352–3
deficit reduction 52, 128, 160, 164–82
Deighton, Paul, Lord 212, 224
Delivery Unit 113–14
departmental boundaries 119
Design Council 445–6
Desmond, Richard 554
devolved powers 88–9, 228–32, 234–7, 243–4
Dilnot, Andrew 312–14
Disability Living Allowance 328–9
Dommett, Katherine 102–3, 501, 504
Dorrell, Steven 302
Dorries, Nadine 11, 474
double-dip recession 602
Dowden, Oliver 11
Dowler, Milly 565–6
Downing Street Policy Unit 123
Draghi, Mario 162
Duffy, Carol Ann 453
Duncan Smith, Iain 19, 177–8, 322, 324–5, 327, 329–31, 335, 342–4, 602–3
DUP (Democratic Unionist Party) 89
DVPOs (domestic violence protection orders) 405–6
Dynamic Benefits 324–5, 329

Eagle, Angela 11
economic undertaking 304
economy, under the coalition 161–4
Edinburgh Agreement 82, 90–1, 93, 101, 591
education
  Bibles in schools 456–7
  and Britishness 455–8
  Browne Report 53–4
  and coalition government 604–5
  grammar schools 41–2
  higher education funding 15–16, 41–2, 53–4, 62–3, 126, 152, 499–504, 558–9
  Michael Gove see Gove, Michael
  policy 41–2
  pupil premium 127
  reform 18–19
  spending 175–6
  spending cuts protection 175, 230–1
  student finance see higher education funding
  student riots 502–3
  tuition fees see higher education funding
EIA (Equality Impact Assessments) 426
Electoral Commission 69
electoral reform 6, 15–16, 24–5, 53, 61–2, 67–70, 577, 582–9, 594, 596–7
  see also House of Commons; House of Lords
Electoral Registration and Administration Bill (2013) 70–1, 151, 153
electric vehicle charging 215–16
electricity prices 206–7, 439
Elliott, Francis 40–1
Emin, Tracy 432, 435–6
employment 163–4, 176–7, 193, 241–2, 602
Employment and Support Allowance 322–3, 339–40
EMR (Energy Market Reform) 195
Energy Act (2013) 201–2
energy bills 203–4, 206–7
Engel, Natascha 141
English Heritage 445, 458–9
English National Opera 436–7

English PEN 453
English Premier League 463
English Question 105
Entwistle, George 569
environment 47–8
EPP (European People's Party) 378, 384–6
equity loan scheme 184–5
EU
  budget cuts 387, 393
  budget rebate 20
  Cameron's alliances 386–9
  climate change 194–5
  coalition achievements in 394–6
  coalition decision makers 380–2
  coalition parties' cohesion 389–94
  Conservative/Liberal Democrat
    co-operation over 380–1
  Conservative/Liberal Democrat
    differences over 377–80, 385–6
  External Affiars Directorate 362–3
  free movement of people policy 379
  human rights constraints 23–4, 573
  Large Combustion Plant Directive
    200–1
  MEP expenses 575
  and Middle East 362–3
  referendum 6–7, 23, 27, 62, 77, 90,
    141, 149, 382–6, 396, 482–5, 580
  referendum lock 382–4
  relationship with 61, 368, 370–96
  Renewables Directive 195
  and sovereignty 75–7
  Tory backbench rebellion 383–4
  transfer of powers to 582
  and UK foreign policy 361–3
  UK parties approach to 395–6
EU Commission anti-trafficking directive
  405–6
EUETS (EU Emissions Trading Scheme)
  205
European Arrest Warrant 395
European Communities Act (1972) 61–2,
  378–9, 390
European Convention on Human Rights
  78, 573–4
European Court of Human Rights 78–80
European Court of Justice 482–3
European Parliament election (2009) 372
European Parliament election (2014) 393

European Union see EU
European Union Act (2011) 76–7,
  379–80, 382–6, 394–5
European Union Treaty (1992) 373–4
Eurozone crisis 17, 20, 170
expenses scandals 4, 495–6

Falkirk crisis 547–51
Fall, Kate 10–11, 123–4, 425
Family and Parenting Institute 412–13
Farage, Nigel 391–2, 514, 568, 575
Farron, Tim 513
Fawcett Society 401, 412–13, 426
feminist research 400–1, see also gender
  issues
Field, Mark 385
Fieldhouse, Ed 36, 54, 518–19
Financial Conduct Authority 191–2
financial crisis (2008) 2, 159, 602
Financial Policy Committee (Bank of
  England) 26, 191–2
financial regulation 191–2
financial sector reform 45–6, 191–2
Financial Services Authority 26, 191–2
Financial Times 169–70, 574–5
Finkelstein, Danny 35–6
fiscal consolidation 169–74, 193
Fiscal Responsibility Act (2010) 171–2
fiscal targets 171–2
fiscal tightening 167
FiTs (Feed-in-Tariffs) 197–9, 202–3
five days to power 42–3, 48–9
Fixed Term Parliaments Act (2011)
  15–16, 23, 54, 64–7, 130–1, 135,
  140–1, 473–4, 479, 509, 516, 562,
  582, 588–9, 596, 604
Flexible New Deal 319–20
food banks 340
forced marriage see gender issues
Forced Marriage Protection Order
  (FMPC) 408
Forced Marriage Unit (FMU) 408
Forced Marriages (Civil Protection
  Act)(2007) 407–10
Foreign and Commonwealth Office, cuts
  358–9
foreign policy 345–6, 352–3
  changes in 360–1
  and China 352

foreign policy (cont.)
and crises 363–8
effectiveness of 369
and the EU 361–3
leadership personalities 359–61
and Middle East 352–5, 358–60,
363–7
and NATO 363–7
and Obama government 352, 355–6
and Russia 352, 356–9
Foreman, Jonathan 487
fossil fuels 203–5, 439
Foster, Don 440–1
four-party politics 606–7
Fox, Liam 11–12, 563
Fox, Ruth 472
Francis Report 302
Francis, Robert 291–2
François, Mark 381
Fraser, Murdo 101
Freedland, Jonathan 557
A Fresh Start for Britain 41–2, 504–5
Freud, David (Lord Freud) 324–5, 327, 340
Freud, Lucian 437
The Future Forum 297–8

Galloway, George 101
Gamble, Andrew 468–9
Ganesh, Janan 485, 491
gas energy policy 439
gas power stations 200–1
gas supply 200–1
GDP 161–2, 173
Geidt, Sir Christopher 116
gender issues 397–429
austerity 397, 418
BES (British Election Study) 421–3
childcare see childcare
Coalition Agreement pledges 403–5
coalition legislation 405–6
coalition policy determinants 423–4
coalition and women voters 420
Conservative feminization strategy
398–9
domestic violence protection 405–6
employment 403–5, 402
families 403–5, 402
FGM (female genital mutilation)
405–6

flexible working 402
forced marriages 399–400, 407–10
criminalization, 410–12
health 402
Labour all women shortlists 138
male/female balance in coalition
424–5
manifesto promises 402
maternity units 403–5
maternity/paternity leave 402
pensions 402
perceived failings by coalition
425–7
policy/legislation and women 397–8
rape crisis centres 403–5
rape defendants' anonymity 404–5
sexual violence 403–5
sexualization of children 402
Sure Start 403–5, 411, 402
tax and marriage 401, 403–5
transferable tax allowance 418–20
violence against women (VAW)
403–10, 402
WBG analysis of coalition economic
policy 415–17
women in coalition government
148–9, 424–5, 573
women voters 397, 420
general election (2010) 32–3, 42–3, 96,
137–40, 166, 493–4, 549, 556–7
general election (2015) 24–5, 27, 65, 68,
87–8, 129–30, 192, 520–1
single-party government implications
130
general election results (Scotland and
Wales 1979-2010) 97
Gerard, Jasper 505
Gill, Ameet 11
Gilligan, Andrew 562
Gilmour, Charlie 503
Global Shared Services Centre
449
Glover, Stephen 559
Goldsmith, Sir James 25,
373–4
Goldsmith, Zac 511–12
Good Friday Agreement 104–5
Goodman, Clive 565
Gould, Philip 35–6

Gove, Michael 3, 8, 11–12, 18–20, 125, 360, 412–13, 433, 455–8, 483, 572–4, 576, 604–5
Government Art Collection 439
government philosophies 59–60
Government of Wales Act (2006) 104
grammar schools 41–2
Grayling, Chris 19, 79–80, 120, 324, 395, 452
Greater Manchester city region 243–4
Greece, financial crisis 377
Green, Damian 392, 460
Green Deal 204–5
Green Growth Group 388–9
green parties 196–7
Grieve, Dominic 574
growth policies 188–92
growth restoration 185–91, 193
Growth Review 190–1
Guardian 554–5, 557, 559, 561, 563–8, 574–5

Hacked Off group 567–8
Haddon, Catherine 116
Hague, William
    and Europe 380–3, 394
    as Foreign Secretary 11–12, 346–7, 353, 359
    gender issues 400
    as party leader 34–5
Hall, Tony (Lord Hall) 569–70
Hammond, Philip 107, 177–8, 216, 221, 335, 380, 388–9
Hands, Tim 605
Hanning, James 40–1
Hardman, Isabel 391
Harris, Evan 501
Harris, Robin 475–6, 488
Harrison, Rupert 11
Harvey, Nick 363
Hay, Colin 57
Hazell, Robert 130, 497
health
    coalition party manifestos 291
    elected health authorities 582
    GP access 308
    Health and Well Being Board 245, 298
    hospital waiting times 307–8

Joint Wellbeing Boards 296, 310
long-term care 311–14
    funding 311–14
    resources 314
    mental health 308–10, 316
NHS
    budget protection 305–7
    changes in England 291–2, 300
    and demographic changes 300–1, 310–11
    efficiency improvement programme 305
    as European model 303–4
    international comparisons with 310–11
    reform 18–19, 39–40, 53, 126, 192–3, 245, 562–3, 603–4, 606
    scandals 302
    spending 175–6
    spending cuts protection 175, 230–1, 603–4
    under Labour 290–1
Primary Care Trusts 294–6
quality of care 308–9
Strategic Health Authorities 291, 295–6
Health and Social Care Act (2012) 292–5, 603–4
    changes to 297–9
    and mental health 309–10
    opposition to 297–9
    seen as end of the NHS 303
    seen as misdirected 300–2
    views on 300–5
    white paper (2010) 296
Heath, Edward 371
Heathrow Airport 215, 219–21
Help to Buy Scheme 17, 184–5
Heseltine, Michael, Lord 190–1, 210–12, 242
Hewitt, Patricia 201–2
Heywood, Sir Jeremy 3–5, 12–13, 113–14, 116, 123–4, 130–1, 133–4
Higgins, Sir David 223–4
Higgins Report 223–4
higher education funding 15–16, 41–2, 53–4, 62–3, 126, 152, 499–504, 558–9
Highways Agency 218, 225, 227
Hill, Lord 14

Hilton, Steve 2–3, 7–8, 19, 26, 44, 122–4, 602–4
HMRC 180
Hodge, Margaret 143, 239–40, 252, 325, 338
Hollande, François 388
Holloway, Adam 383–4
Holtham Commission 106
Home Affairs Committee 120
Home Office reform 19
hourly wages 183
House of Commons
    backbench dissent 146–54
    constituency boundary reform 61, 67–71, 473–4, 480, 482, 586–7
    electoral reform see electoral reform
    MPs' accountability 511–12, 582
    MPs and constuency work 140
    MPs' diversity 138–40
    MPs' expenses scandal 114, 136–7, 141–2, 578, 584
    MPs' numbers 579–80, 595
    MPs' recall/wrongdoing 140–1, 511–12, 579, 582–3, 589
    new MPs in 2010 137–40
    PMQs (Prime Minister's Questions) 145
    political class 139–40
    reform 140–3, 580–1
    select committees 141–3
    Speaker 143
    Syria recall 365–7.
    see also coalition government; Fixed-term Parliaments Act
House of Lords Act (1999) 71–2
House of Lords discipline 23
House of Lords reform 15–16, 47–8, 61–2, 71–5, 127, 150–1, 154–6, 508–11, 580, 582–5, 593–6, 604
House of Lords Reform Act (2014) 155
House of Lords Reform Bill (2012) 73, 150–1, 479–82
household benefits cap 248
household incomes 193
housing benefit 339
housing market 184–5
housing policy 246–7
Howard, Michael 33
Howarth, David 502, 513, 519
HRA (Housing Revenue Account) 246–7

HS1 (High Speed One) 210–11
HS2 (High Speed Two) 211–12, 214–16, 218–20, 222–4, 227
HS3 (High Speed Three) 211–12
Hughes, Simon 51
Huhne, Chris 38, 50, 54, 116–17, 119, 196–9, 203–5, 504, 563–4
human rights 23, 77–80, 127, 228–9, 573
Human Rights Act (1998) 23, 78–80, 512
Hunt, Jeremy 18–19, 226, 299, 302, 444–5, 447
Hutton, John 201–2, 325
hybrid warfare 357

IDS see Duncan Smith, Iain
IMF 189
immigration
    artists' visas 459–61
    Cameron on 393
    EU free movement of people policy 379
    immigration cap 54–5
    party views on 376
Immigration Bill (2014) 153
income inequality 341
Independent 554–5
Independent Commission on Banking 191–2
Independent Police Complaints Commission 250–1
Independent Press Standards Organisation 568
Independent on Sunday 554–5, 559
Industrial Emissions Directive 200–1
industrial policy 190–1
inflation, and low-income households 184
inflation target 187–8
infrastructure
    in 2010 210–11
    2010–15 211–14
    assessment of success 219
    and coalition government policy 209–27
    digital 226
Infrastructure Bill (2014) 211–12, 218
Infrastructure Planning Commission 212, 224
Infrastructure UK 225

Institute for Fiscal Studies 341
Institute for Government 122
intellectual property 431
international development
        604
Invictus games 462
Iraq, British involvement in 350–1,
        358–9
Irish relations 19–20
IS (Islamic State) 366–7, 424–5, 486

Javid, Sajid 447–8
Jenkins, Simon 44, 93
Jobseeker's Allowance 337, 339–41
Johnson, Boris 5, 215, 219–21, 244, 254,
        483, 575
Johnson, Craig 517
Joint Committee on House of Lords
        Reform 72
Joint Wellbeing Boards see health
Jones, Alexandra 244
Jones, Joey 470
A Journey 2
Joyce, Eric 547–8
Jubilee Line extension 210–11
Juncker, Jean-Claude 371, 388, 396
Justice reforms 19
Justice and Security Bill 512–13

Kane, Lorraine 548
Kellner, Peter 551
Kennedy, Charles 33, 38, 492,
        494
Kerslake, Sir Bob 133–4, 239–40
Kettle, Martin 559
King, Mervyn 187–8
King's Fund Commission 314
Kirby, Paul 123–4

Labour
    all-women shortlists 138
    benefits reform 325–6
    Better Together campaign 20,
        91–4
    and coalition government 520–52
    core vote plus 514
    dominance in Scotland (Westminster)
        95–6
    dominance in Wales 87, 95–6
    economic competence 535–9
    energy policy 194–6
    EU position 372, 374–6
    Falkirk crisis 547–51
    feminization of 427–8
    fiscal policy 173–4
    and general election (2010)
        521–2
    and general election (2015) 520–1
    immigration 376
    and leadership election (2010) 529–32
    manifesto 375–6
    NHS 290–1
    party conference (2013) 184, 206
    party conference (2014) 7
    regional governance 233
    shared Coalition agenda 583
    and trade unions 547–51
    and UKIP 522
    unionist position 99–101
    welfare policy 319–21
    and YouGov poll
        see also Miliband, Ed
Lamb, Norman 297, 313
Lansley, Andrew 4, 12–13, 18–19, 53,
        292–5, 299, 562–3, 603–4
Large Combustion Plant Directive 200–1
Laws, David 33, 35, 37–8, 49, 55–6,
        116–17, 119, 389, 495–6, 563,
        572
Lawson, Nigel 165–6
Layfield Report 237
LCM (Levy Control Mechanism) 197–8
leadership changes 32–8
LEPs (Local Enterprise Partnerships) 212,
        242–3
Leslie, Chris 387
Lester, Anthony (Lord Lester) 407
Letwin, Oliver 3, 10–11, 48, 51, 116–17,
        213, 294, 380
Leveson, Sir Brian 567
Leveson Inquiry 4, 564, 567, 575
Lewis, Brandon 254
Lewis, Sir Leigh 78–9
LGA (Local Government assocoation) 252
liberal conservatism 34
Liberal Democrats
    1st phase (2010) in coalition
        government 492–505

Liberal Democrats (cont.)
  2nd phase (2011-13) in coalition
    government 505–13
  3rd phase (2014-15) in coalition
    government 513–16
  AV referendum 506–8, see also AV
    (alternative vote)
  caution over coalition 115
  civil liberties reform 228–9, 512–13
  Clegg/Farage debate 514
  coalition agreement 42–56
  and coalition government 492–519
  coalition government and election
    campaigning 128–9
  and Conservative policies 228–9
  Conservatives voter similarities 36–8
  and constituency boundary changes
    586–7
  constitutional reform 577
  decline of 571–4
  distancing phase in coalition 126–7
  domestic policies 228–9
  early phase in coalition 126
  effects of coalition on 102–3
  electoral losses 507, 516–17
  electoral reform see electoral reform
  energy policy 196–9
  EU position 75–6, 371–2, 375–6, 395
  Federal Policy Committee 504–5
  fiscal policy 173–4
  government philosophy 59–60
  as green party 196–7
  House of Lords reform see House of
    Lords
  human rights 228–9
  ideological divide with Conservatives
    472
  immigration 376
  Labour negotiations 49
  leadership changes 32–8
  leadership isolation from party/
    backbenchers 497–500
  manifesto 42–56, 75–6, 114–17, 154,
    178–82, 291, 311, 322–4, 345–6,
    375–6, 438–41, 495, 553
  membership losses 507
  ministerial portfolios in coalition
    15–16, 55–6
  opinion polls 557–8

Orange Book 37–8, 294, 343, 602–3
party conference (2013) 513
party credibility in government 496–7,
  517
party image 41–2
policies in coalition 15–16, 126–7
policy reform 41–2
policy unit closure 498
pre-coalition negotiations 469–73
pre-election plans 114–17
press statements by 505
and regional devolution 228–9
reshuffle (2014) 571, 574
standing in Scotland 102
standing in Wales 102
unionist position 99–101
USP policies 504–5
vote abstention 504
women's policies in manifesto 402
see also Clegg, Nick
LIBOR interest rate 191–2
LibsDems4Cameron 33
Libya 20–1, see also foreign policy
Lidington, David 381–4, 388–9
Life Peerages Act (1958) 71–2
Lisbon Treaty 76, 373–6, 378–9, 382–4,
  483
Little, Tony 475
Live Music Act (2012) 447–8
living standards 182–5
Llewellyn, Ed 10–11, 123–4, 360
Lobban, Iain 20–1
Local Audit Bill 252
local authority funding 231
  council budgets 240–2
local government funding 237–40
Local Government Resource Review 238
Local Sustainable Transport Fund 225
localism 47–8
Localism Act (2011) 234–7, 254, 593
London
  investment in 3104
  local government in 254
London Finance Commission 244
Lowell, Lawrence 468

Maastricht Treaty see Treaty on European
  Union (1992)
McAnulla, Stuart 33

McCluskey, Len 548–9
McGuinness, Martin 109–10
MacKenzie, Polly 51, 122
McLeavy, Julie 413
McLoughlin, Patrick 211, 220
McVey, Esther 339
Mail on Sunday 554, 562
Major, John 210–11
Major Projects Authority 132–4, 225, 337
Manchester Guardian 554–5
Mandelson, Peter (Lord Mandelson) 109–10
manifestos *see* individual parties
Manning, Sir David 113–14
Manzoni, John 134
Marquand, David 475–6
Marshall, Paul 37–8
Martin, Chris 12–13
Martin, Michael 136, 143–5, 578
Massive Online Open Course 449
Maude, Francis 19–20, 133–4
May, Theresa 11–12, 19, 79–80, 120,
    250–1, 324, 335, 400, 404–5, 424,
    460–1, 483
mayoral elections 587, 593–4
mayoral government model 249
media
    and coalition government
        553–76
    Data Protection Act 565
    digital revolution 575
    Leveson Inquiry 4, 564
    Milly Dowler case 565–6
    and Ofcom 567–8
    phone hacking 564–8
    press allegiances 554–5
Merkel, Angela 10, 20, 25, 384,
    387–8
Metrolink (Manchester) 224
Mid Staffordshire Foundation Trust
    291–2, 302
Middle East *see* foreign policy
Milburn, Alan 298
Miliband, David 16–17,
    529–32
Miliband, Ed
    and 2010 leadership election
        529–32
    at 2014 party conference 7

and Cameron 16–17
economic competence 535–9
energy policy 194–6, 206–7
and Heathrow Airport 219–20
Labour Party reform 522–9
Middle East policy 545–7
as party leader 16–17, 520–1, 523–9,
    551–2, 543
personal image 539–43
as potential PM 4, 6–7, 539–43, 551–2
as radical 543
Scottish campaigning by 107–9, 487
and Syria vote 545–7
and trade unions 548–51
and UKIP 605–6.
see also Labour
military covenant 351
Millennium Dome 442
Miller, Maria 14, 426–7, 447, 563, 570–1
ministerial appointments/portfolios
    15–16, 55–6, 119, 315–16
Ministerial Code 118
ministerial twinning 55–6
Ministry of Defence spending 351
Ministry of Justice, and prison books 452
minority party leverage 86
Mirror 574–5
Mitchell, Andrew 55, 123–4, 563
MLA (Museums, Libraries and Archives
    Council) 445
Modern Slavery Bill (2014-15) 405–6
Monetary Policy Committee 186
Montgomerie, Tim 325
Moody's credit ratings 6, 170–1, 346
Moore, Charles 489–90
Moore, Michael 99, 505
Moran, Caitlin 419
Morgan, Nicky
mortgages 184–5
Motion, Andrew 445
MPs (Members of Parliament) *see* House
    of Commons
Mulcaire, Glen 565
Mumsnet 412–13
Murdoch, Rupert 554, 563–8, 575
Murphy, Jim 92
Murphy, Karie 548
Murrin, Kris 123–4
Muslim radicalism/jihadism 348–9

mutuals 43–4
My Scotland, Our Britain: A Future Worth Sharing 93

National Audit Office 239–40, 251, 337
National Children's Bureau 412–13
National Crime Agency 349–50
National Economic Council 113–14
National Gallery 431
national income 174
National Infrastructure Plan 189–90, 225
National Insurance 179
National Lottery 440–1, 447, 462
National Portrait Gallery 435
National Security Adviser 349–50
National Trust for Places of Historic Interest or Natural Beauty 458
National Union of Students 500
NATO
  and coalition policy 367–8
  summit (2014) 357
neighbourhood planning 234–7
Neil, Bob 392
Nelson, Fraser 474
NESTA (National Endowment for Science, Technology and the Arts) 445–7
Netanyahu, Benjamin 355
Network Rail finance 213, 218, 227
New Deal 319–20
New Homes Bonus 239
New Statesman on austerity 169–70
News International phone hacking 4, *see also* Murdoch
News of the World 564–6, 568
Newsnight 569–70
NHS *see* health
Nichols, Cardinal Vincent 340–1
Nicholson, David 305
1922 Committee 476–80, 483
No Stone Unturned: In Pursuit of Growth 190–1, 242
Norman, Jesse 481

Northampton, Lord 436
Northern Ireland
  austerity measures 255
  AV (Alternative Vote) referendum result 98–9
  coalition government in 87–112
  devolved powers to 87–9, 104–5, 255, 578
  dysfunctional politics 94–5
  General Election (2010) result 96
  health care 300, 315
  local government funding 231–2
  long-term care 315
  political legitimacy 89–90
  political symbolism 91
  power-sharing 94–5, 109–10
  public sector dependence 94–5
  Secretary of State post 99
  unionism in 103
NSC (National Security Council) 20–1, 120–1, 349–50, 357–8
nuclear defence/deterrent 62–3, 347–8, 368
nuclear energy 15–16, 53–4, 62–3, 152, 196, 201–3
NUS (National Union of Students) 500
Nuttall, David 383, 482–3

Oakeshott, Matthew (Lord Oakeshott) 513
Oates, Jonny 122
Obama, Barack 3–4, 352, 354–6, 364–5
OBR (Office for Budget Responsibility) 162–5, 170–1, 177, 180–1
O'Brien, Neil 252
Observer 554–5
O'Casey, Eimear 55–6
O'Donnell, Sir Gus (Lord O'Donnell) 178, 2, 116, 133–4
O'Flynn, Patrick 383
Oliver, Craig 10–11, 123–4, 570–1
Olympic arts festival 441–4
Olympic Delivery Authority 212
Olympic Games 4, 212, 221, 461–3
Olympic Lottery Commission 447
One Wales coalition 103
ONS (Office for National Statistics) 6, 162–3

Operation Motorman 565
Orange Book 37–8, 294, 343,
        602–3
Osborne, George
    and the arts 437
    at London Olympics 4
    austerity measures 6, 17
    as Chancellor 2–3, 11–12, 25–6, 128,
        167–8
    on coalition 15
    as dominant figure 6–7
    energy policy 197–8
    and EU 378
    fiscal strategy 167–8
    foreign policy 359
    and Laws 35
    Plan A 17, 192
    as potential party leader 483
    pre-coalition planning 116–17
    relationship with Alexander 6
    relationship with Cameron
        25–6
    on Scottish independence 93
    spending review 230–2
    and tax rises 178
    visits Obama in Washington 3–4.
    see also Budgets
O'Shaughnessy, James 3, 51, 123–4
Ottaway, Richard 476–7
Overman, Henry 240
overseas aid spending 175–6
Owen, David 297, 299

Pack, Mark 44
Paine, Thomas 85–6
Paisley, Ian 109–10
Parliament Act (1911) 71–2
Parliamentary Commission on Banking
        Standards 191–2
parliamentary reform see House of
        Commons; House of Lords
Parliamentary Voting System and
        Constituency Act (2011) 140–1,
        479
Parliamentary Voting System and
        Constituency Bill (2010) 477
ParliOut 144
party manifestos 42–56, see also
        individual parties

party relations 125–9
party whips 147
Passport Office 251
Patten, Chris (Lord Patten) 569
PCCs (police and crime commissioners)
        249–51, 587–8
Penrose, John 447
pensions
    as gender issue 402
    manifestos 322
    money purchase pension 334
    pension cap 322–3
    pension contributions 331
    pension protection 192–3, 318–19,
        341–2
    pension tax relief 179
    pensioner benefits 177–8
    public sector 343
    state pension age 322, 332
    state pension reform 332–4, 337, 342–3
    triple lock 323, 334, 341–2
    under Labour 320–1
    Work and Pensions reform 19
Personal Independence Payment 328–9,
        338
phases of coalition government see
        coalition government phases
Phillips, Anne 139
phone hacking 564–8
Pickles, Eric 19, 232, 234, 245–6, 249,
        251–4
Plaid Cymru 101, 103, 105
Planning Inspectorate 224
Pletsch, Lena 122
PMQs (Prime Minister's Questions) 145
policing
    College of Policing 250–1
    and counter-terrorism/security 349–50
    elected police and crime commissioners
        249–51, 587–8
    reform 249–51, 582
    in Scotland 255–6
Policy Exchange 44, 252
policy publications 49–51
political class 139–40
Political and Constitutional Reform
        Committee 74–5, 130–1
political journalism 553–4
political legitimacy 95–104

politics of presence 139
poll tax 228
popular sovereignty 61
postal elections 582
Powell, Hugh 360
Powell, Jonathan 123–4
power decentralization 115
Poynton, Gregor 549–50
pre-election plans 114–17
Preamble to the Parliament Act (1911)
    71–2
Press Complaints Commission 565
Primary Care Trusts *see* health
prime ministerial power 129
prison books 452
prisoner voting 78–9, 141
private financing 213
private sector recruitment 133
productivity 193
programme for government 60–4
proportional voting system 61
prudential borrowing rules 246
PSED (Public Sector Equality Duty) 426–7
Public Accounts Committee 239–40, 252
public expenditure 230–2
public health 245
public sector net borrowing 168
public sector reform 19–20, 114–17
public sector salaries 114
public sector spending cuts 174–8, 602–3
    extended beyond 2015 election 178
    protected areas 175
public–private wage differential 176–7
pupil premium 127
Putin, Vladimir 24, 356–9, 442
PVSC (Parliamentary Voting System and
    Constituencies Act)(2011) 68, 70

Quad group 55, 63–4, 125, 496
quantitative easing policy 186–7
Queen's Speech (2010) 159
Queen's Speech (2013) 153, 484–5
Queen's Speech (2014) 211–12

Rake, Katherine 412–13
rape defendants' anonymity 404–5
Rawnsley, Andrew 559
RCEP (Royal Commission on
    Environmental Pollution) 194–5

Rebuilding the House 141
recall of MPs 140–1, 511–12, 579, 582–3,
    589
Recall of MPs Bill (2011) 140–1
Reckless, Mark 27, 387, 391, 485, 488
referendum lock 382–4
Referendum Party 25, 373–4
referendum promotion 85–6
referendums 589–93, *see also* AV; EU;
    mayors; Scotland; Wales
Regional Development Agencies 190–1
regional governance 233, 242
Regional Growth Fund 190, 242, 244
regional policy 229
regional spatial strategies 233
Reinfeldt, Fredrik 388
renewable energy 197–9
Renewables Obligation 197–9
Rentoul, John 559
ResPublica 244
Richard, Ivor (Lord Richard) 585
Richards, David 14–15, 20–1
Riddell, Peter 116
Riley, Jon 165
Robbins Report 499
Roberts, Justine 412–13
Robertson, George 92
Robinson, Nick 501
Rochester and Strood by-election 485
ROCs (Renewable Obligation Certificates)
    197–9
Rogers, Richard 242
Rogers, Sir Robert 146
Rose, Dinah 512–13
Rose, Richard 467
Russell, Andrew 36, 54, 518–19
Rutte, Mark 388
Rycroft, Philip 117

Sainsbury, Roy 325–7
St Andrews Agreement 110
Salmond, Alex 16–17, 82–3, 93, 107–8,
    487, 576, 591
same-sex marriage 488–9
Sanderson-Nash, Emma 493, 504–5
Sands, Philippe 512–13
Sarkozy, Nicolas 384
Savile crisis 569–70
Say Goodbye to Broken Promises 500

schools *see* education
Schultz, Martin 388
Scotland
  austerity measures 255
  AV (Alternative Vote) referendum result
    98–9
  coalition government 87–112
  Conservative unionist position on
    99–101
  council tax support scheme 248
  devolved powers to 87–9, 110–11, 255,
    578
  Edinburgh Agreement 82, 90–1, 93,
    101, 591
  fire service 256
  general election results 96–7
  health care 300, 315
  independence referendum 14, 16–17,
    20, 81–4, 90, 104–5, 585, 594
    campaign 91–4
    currency union 107
    and EU membership 110
    result 92
  Labour dominance (Westminster) 95–6
  Labour unionist position on 100
  Liberal Democrat unionist position on
    100
  local government funding 231–2
  long term care 315
  police service 255–6
  political legitimacy 89–90
  public health measures 315
  Secretary of State post 99
  SNP dominance (Scottish Parliament)
    87
Scotland Act (1998) 82
Scotland Act (2012) 81, 90–1, 108–9
Scotland's Future white paper 82–3
Scottish Independence Bill (2014)
  82–3
Scottish Independence Referendum Act
  (2013) 82
Scottish National Party *see* SNP
Scottish Parliament 61
  election results (2011) 98–9
Scottishness 432
Scully, Roger 90, 105
SDP–Liberal Alliance 494
Secretary of State posts 99

security policy 348–50
Security Services expenditure 353
Sekhemka sculpture 436
Select Committee on the Constitution
  76–7, 84–6
the Sensibles 481
Serious Organised Crime Agency 349–50
Sewel Convention 81
sex offenders' register 78–9
shale gas 439
Shapps, Grant 391
Shaw, Jo 512–13
Silva, Rohan 11, 123–4
Sked, Alan 373–4
smart meters 205
Smith, Chris 445–6
Smith, Jacqui 405
Snowden, Edward 512–13
Snowdon, Peter 39
SNP
  dominance of 87, 101
  election win (2011) 20, 81, 590.
  see also Scotland
Sochi Winter Olympics 442
Social Care Act (2012) 292–5
social enterprises 43–4
social security *see* welfare
sovereignty, and EU 75–7
spare room subsidy *see* bedroom tax
Speaker of the House of Commons
    see House of Commons
Spectator 576
spending reviews 230–2,
    427
Spicer, Sir Michael 476–7
Spitting Image 558
Stanley, Kate 325
Star Chamber 444
Statutory Appointments Commission
  72–3
Stephens, Jonathan 444
Stevens, Simon 316
Stewart, Rory 142
Strategic Defence Review 345–6
Strategic Defence and Security Review
  345–6, 357–8
Strategic Health Authorities *see* health
strategic shrinking policy 346–50, 352–3
Strategy Unit 113–14

Strathclyde Commission Report 99
student fees *see* education
student riots 502–3
STV (Single Transferable Vote) 61, 67,
    580–1, 584–5
Sugg, Liz 11
Sun 554, 558, 563, 568, 574–5
Sunday Telegraph 554, 562
Sunday Times 169–70
Superfast Britain 448
Supplementary Vote 587, 595
Sykes–Picot Agreement (1916) 353
Syria, military action in 151
Syria rebellion 151

Tate galleries 435, 437, 444
tax
    bedroom tax 94, 247, 249, 328–9, 339,
        343
    and benefits 325
    child tax credits 319–20, 417
    childcare tax relief 412
    corporation tax 179, 182, 190
    council tax 184, 248, 314, 331, 582
    council tax referendums 593
    CTB (council tax benefit) 248
    fuel duty 179–80, 182, 184
    granny tax 181
    green taxes 184
    Gross Profits Tax 447
    higher income bands 179–82, 184
    inherited tax increases from Labour 179
    mansion tax 181
    and marriage 62–3, 152, 401, 403–5,
        418–20, 426
    pasty tax 181
    pension tax relief 179, 193
    personal allowance 179, 182, 184,
        193
    stamp duty 179
    tax changes 178–82
    tax credit cap 323
    tax credit removal 328–9
    tax thresholds 54, 126
    transferable tax allowance (TTA) 418–20
    VAT 179, 181, 499
    working tax credit 411
Taylor, Gordon 565
Tebbit, Norman (Lord Tebbit) 509

TEU *see* Treaty on European Union
    (1992)
Thames super-sewer 227
Thameslink 221
Thatcher, Margaret 13, 27, 40–1, 57,
    210–11, 228
Thompson, Mark 570–1
Thurlbeck, Neville 564
The Times 554, 562–3, 568, 572
Timmins, Nicholas 292–5, 297
total managed expenditure 230–1
Toynbee, Polly 561
trade union funding 548–51
Transitions: Lessons Learned 116
transport funding 217–18, 222–4
transport policy 215–19
Transport Secretaries 211
Travers, Tony 314
Treasury, and Bank of England 186–8
Trident nuclear defence 62–3, 347–8, 368
Triple-A credit rating 6, 170–1, 346
Trott, Laura 425
Troubled Families Initiative 245–6
Truss, Elizabeth 412–13
tuition fees *see* education
Turner Commission 320–1, 333, 342–3
Tusk, Donald 395
21st Century Wefare 329

UK Film Council 445
UKIP
    Cameron and 14, 16–17, 25
    Clacton by-election 7, 25, 27, 485
    and Conservatives 391, 487
    debates 392
    defections from Conservatives 7, 25, 27,
        485, 488–90, 511–12
    on EU membership 376, 592–3
    European Parliament Election 372
    Farage/Clegg debate 514
    on HS2 214
    immigration 376
    and Labour 522
    manifesto 575
    and the media 568
    rise of 374, 489–90, 515–16, 595, 605–6
    Rochester and Strood by-election 485
The Unfinished Revolution 35–6
United Kingdom Sovereignty Bill 55, 61–2

Universal Credit 19, 324–7, 338, 343, 411
university tuition fees *see* education

Vaizey, Ed 444–5, 458
Van Rompuy, Herman 395
Verhofstadt, Guy 388
Vickers Committee 26, 191–2
Vickers, Sir John 191–2
Violence against Women and Girls
    Strategy 405–6, *see also* gender
    issues
Vote Blue, Go Green slogan 40–1
voting *see* electoral reform
voting age 580, 583

wages 193
Walby, Sylvia 406–7
Wales
  austerity measures 255
  AV (Alternative Vote) referendum result
    98–9
  coalition government 87–112
  Conservative unionist position 99–101
  council tax support scheme 248
  devolved powers to 87–9, 91, 255,
    578–9, 582
  general election (2010) result 96
  general election results (1979-2010) 97
  health care 300, 315
  Labour dominance 95–6
  local government funding
    231–2
  long-term care 315
  political legitimacy 89–90
  referendum 578–9, 583, 589–90
  Secretary of State post 99
  Welsh Assembly 61–2, 80–1, 83–4,
    578–9
  Welsh Assembly election results (2011)
    98–9
Wallace, Jim 117
Wallace, William 381
war game discussion 116
Warsi, Sayeeda (Baroness Warsi) 364, 480
Watson, Tom 549–50
WBG (Women's Budget Group) 406–7,
    415–17, 426
Webb, Steve 42, 323, 333–4, 342–3
Weir, Judith 435

welfare
  bedroom tax 94, 247, 249, 328–9, 339
  and coalition 317–44
  cuts 327–32, 335–6, 343, 602–3
  housing benefit 339
  and inflation 335–6
  manifestos 322–4
  protection 318–19
  reform 19, 94, 247–9, 337–42
  Retail/Consumer Price Index switch 328
  sanctions 322–3, 330–1, 335–6, 339–42
  social security spending 177–8
  and tax 325
  under Labour 319–21, 323, 325–6
  Universal Credit 19, 324–7
  use of term 317–18
  welfare/benefits caps 330–1, 342
  Work and Pensions reform 19. *see also*
    Budgets
Wells, Anthony 421
Welsh Referendum (2011) 90, 104–5
Werritty, Adam 11–12
West Lothian question 106, 481
Wharton, James 392, 484
Williams, Shirley 297, 299
Williams, Zoe 418
Wilson, Rob 116–17
*With Respect to Old Age: A Report by the
    Royal Commission on Long Term
    Care* 312
Wollaston, Sarah 142, 474
women and the Coalition *see* gender issues
women's sport 463–4
Woollard, Edward 503
work capability assessment 337
Work and Pensions reform 19
Work Programme 322–3, 337
working tax credit *see* tax
Working Time Directive 378–9
Wright Committee 141–3
Wright Reforms 22
Wright, Simon 501, 504
Wright, Tony 141–2
Wyn Jones, Richard 90, 105

Yanukovych, Viktor 356
Yes campaign 94, 106–7
Yes to Fairer Votes 506–7
Yong, Ben 52, 56, 497